Mastering
AutoCAD® Civil 3D® 2008

Dana Probert, E.I.T.

James Wedding, P.E.

with Mark Scacco, P.E., and Jason Hickey

Wiley Publishing, Inc.

Acquisitions Editor: Willem Knibbe

Development Editor: Kari Gulbrandsen

Technical Editor: Ryan Wunderlich

Production Editor: Elizabeth Campbell

Copy Editor: Liz Welch

Production Manager: Tim Tate

Vice President and Executive Group Publisher: Richard Swadley

Vice President and Executive Publisher: Joseph B. Wikert

Vice President and Publisher: Neil Edde

Media Project Supervisor: Laura Atkinson

Media Development Specialist: Kit Malone

Media Quality Control: Angie Denny

Book Designer and Compositor: Happenstance Type-O-Rama

Proofreader: Jen Fu

Indexer: Jack Lewis, JJ Indexing

Anniversary Logo Design: Richard Pacifico

Cover Designer: Ryan Sneed

Dear Reader,

Thank you for choosing *Mastering AutoCAD Civil 3D 2008*. This book is part of a family of premium quality Sybex books, all written by outstanding authors who combine practical experience with a gift for teaching.

Sybex was founded in 1976. More than thirty years later, we're still committed to producing consistently exceptional books. With each of our titles we're working hard to set a new standard for the industry. From the paper we print on, to the authors we work with, our goal is to bring you the best books available.

I hope you see all that reflected in these pages. I'd be very interested to hear your comments and get your feedback on how we're doing. Feel free to let me know what you think about this or any other Sybex book by sending me an email at nedde@wiley.com. Or, if you think you've found a technical error in this book, please visit http://sybex.custhelp.com. Customer feedback is critical to our efforts at Sybex.

Best regards,

Neil Edde
Vice President and Publisher
Sybex, an Imprint of Wiley

For our families, friends, and clients

Acknowledgments

This book is a team effort, with more authors than on are the front cover. We all have people to thank and acknowledge. Thank you to our clients and peers, specifically Carter & Burgess, Conklin Associates, George Butler Associates, and Jones & Boyd. Their generous sharing of data, time, and energy made many of the exercises and lessons in this book possible. We learn as much from our clients as we ever teach them.

Thank you to the team at Wiley: Willem Knibbe, Peter Gaughan, Kari Gulbrandsen, and Ryan Wundelich. This team of editors turned engineers into authors, a daunting task on the best of days. Combining tight deadlines and this rookie authoring crew, they've completed a yeoman's job in delivering this book to your hands.

Thank you to our friends in Manchester, New Hampshire. Autodesk has some truly great people working there, delivering the best product they can to users worldwide. Getting out the 2008 release of Civil 3D, all the while answering questions from this team of authors and reviewers, they answered our inquiries with patience and thoroughness. Special thanks to Glen Albert, Peter Funk, Chakri Gavini, Dan Philbrick, Scott Kent, Chris Putnam, Rob Todd, PLS, and Nick Zeeben. These people help make the great product we've built this book around.

—The Authors

Words can't say thank you enough to my wife Melinda and my girls, Carson and Parker. They've put up with more than they deserve over the past few months. Thanks, Mom and Dad, for things beyond measure. Thank you to Mary McFarland for teaching a future engineer to use a dash correctly. I owe Greg Boyd, P.E., a thank-you for letting me do what I love and being a great mentor for life and the engineering business. Finally, thanks to my partners at Engineered Efficiency, my fellow authors here and at civil3d.com, all the clients, 'deskers, and newsgroup folks I've met over the past few years. Your enthusiasm for what we're all doing is what makes this job fun. And thank you, Willem, for talking me off the ledge over the past few months as we prepared this book.

—James Wedding, P.E.

My participation in this project would not be possible without the constant help and support from my husband Alastair and my parents. I'd also like to thank Beth Uczynski, Joe Rupp, Mark Scacco, and Jason Hickey for always being there with ideas and encouragement. I would never know what it really takes to use Civil 3D in practice without Shelly Lambert, Kathy Walla, and Todd Bichsel, who gave me the chance to work with them on many live projects over the past two years. And finally, special thanks to James Wedding for inviting me to his authoring team at civil3d.com and beyond.

—Dana Probert, E.I.T.

After being in consulting for as long as I have, the list of those who have either directly or indirectly helped make this book possible is incredibly long. Suffice to say that the entire Civil 3D community as a whole has contributed by allowing me to work with them to dig into the application and understand the nuances that make it work in everyday use. That said, I would be remiss if I failed to thank a few people by name, including my wife Danielle, my two business partners, Marc Meyers and James Wedding, our coauthor and all-star Dana Probert, and our publishers and editors at Wiley.

—*Mark Scacco, P.E.*

I'd like to thank my beautiful wife, Teresa, and our daughter, Elizabeth, for their support as I was writing this book. Without their patience when "Daddy" was grouchy, I'd have never gotten this done. I'd also like to thank the sales team at ALACAD for providing the motivation that I needed to do this job. Last, but definitely not least, my heartfelt thanks goes out to the team of Engineered Efficiency for allowing me to be a part of the team and website. It's great to work with a great group of people and love what you do!

—*Jason Hickey*

About the Authors

This book was written as a team effort from day one. Dana, Mark, Jason and I have covered the country and parts of the world training and teaching Civil 3D. Here's a bit more about each of us.

Dana Probert, E.I.T., received her BSCE from Georgia Tech in 1998. Since then she has worked for consulting engineers in the United States and Canada, doing a variety of civil projects such as large planned residential communities, small subdivisions, commercial site design, stormwater management, road design, sanitary sewer networks, stream restoration projects, and municipal GIS. For most of this work, she has used AutoCAD-based products, including Land Desktop, Civil Design, Raster Design, Autodesk Map, and Civil 3D. Dana began instructing Civil 3D users in October 2004, and since then has used Civil 3D herself for subdivision layout design, road design, grading, stormwater management, and utility projects.

In addition to her own design work, Dana has been working closely as a team member with several firms on their Civil 3D pilot projects and implementation plans, and taught many Civil 3D training classes. Oh, and she also built the best 52-baseline corridor known to man.

James Wedding, P.E., spent nearly a decade in the Dallas/Fort Worth land development industry before partnering with Engineered Efficiency in February 2006. A graduate of Texas Tech with a BSCE in 1997, he worked as a design engineer focused on private development. His design experience includes small commercial to multiphase single-family and master planned communities. James has served as president of the Preston Trail Chapter of the Texas Society of Professional Engineers, and was selected their Young Engineer of the Year in 2003.

One of the earliest gunslingers for the Civil 3D product, James has worked extensively with the Autodesk product team to shape and guide the software's development. James is a highly rated repeat presenter at Autodesk University and a presenter on the Friday Civil 3D webcasts.

Mark Scacco, P.E., has been a consultant in the land development and construction industry for over a decade and has experience in all phases of development, from conceptual preliminary design through final platting and construction. He has designed projects ranging from small, one-acre sites to 500-acre, multiphase subdivisions and is still currently active as a civil designer. Mark received his BSCE from Purdue University and is a registered Professional Engineer in Illinois. He is a member of the American Society of Civil Engineers, the National Society of Professional Engineers, and the Geospatial Information & Technology Association.

Mark has authored several training manuals, frequently writes articles for industry magazines, and is a regular presenter at training seminars. Mark is a member of the Autodesk Civil 3D Gunslingers, authored the Civil 3D Implementation Certified Expert training material, and has trained dozens of the top resellers. He is an Autodesk Certified Instructor and has provided training and consulting across the United States and internationally in Korea and Japan.

Jason Hickey has 13 years of experience using Autodesk software for civil design. He started off his career surveying, and has progressed through the ranks of the industry since. With extensive experience in surveying, civil design, CAD management, and network administration, he fully grasps the concept of "field to finish." Jason is a noted AUGI CAD Camp instructor and has trained companies both large and small in Civil 3D and, along with Mark, James, and Dana, maintains www.civil3d.com.

Contents at a Glance

Contents

Introduction

Civil 3D was introduced in 2004 as a trial product. Designed to give the then Land Development desktop user a glimpse of the civil engineering software future, it was a sea change for AutoCAD-based design packages. While there was need for a dynamic design package, many seasoned LDT users wondered how they'd ever make the transition.

Over the past few years, Civil 3D has evolved from the wobbly baby introduced on those first trial discs to a mature platform used worldwide to handle the most complex engineering designs. With this change, many engineers still struggle with how to make the transition. The civil engineering industry as a whole is an old dog learning new tricks.

We hope this book will help you make the transition easier. As the user base grows and users get past the absolute basics, more materials are needed, offering a multitude of learning opportunities. Designed to help you get past the steepest part of the learning curve and teach you some guru-level tricks along the way, *Mastering AutoCAD Civil 3D 2008* should be a good addition to any Civil 3D user's bookshelf.

Who Should Read This Book

The *Mastering* book series is designed with specific users in mind. In the case of *Mastering AutoCAD Civil 3D 2008*, we expect you'll have some knowledge of AutoCAD in general, and some basic engineering knowledge as well. We expect this book should appeal to a large number of Civil 3D users, but we envision a few primary users:

- ◆ Beginning users looking to make the move into using Civil 3D. These people understand AutoCAD and some basics of engineering, but are looking to learn Civil 3D on their own, broadening their skillset to make themselves more valuable in their firm and in the market.

- ◆ Experienced Land Desktop users looking to transition to Civil 3D. These users understand design practice, and need to learn how to do the familiar tasks in Civil 3D. They'll be able to jump to specific chapters and learn how to accomplish the task at hand.

- ◆ Civil 3D users looking for a desktop reference. With the digitization of the official help files, many users still long for a book they can flip open and keep beside them as they work. These people should be able to jump as needed to the task at hand for further information about a confusing dialog or troublesome design issue.

- ◆ Classroom instructors looking for better materials. This book was written with real data from real design firms. We've worked hard to make many of the examples match the real-world problems we have run into as engineers. This book also goes into greater depth than many basic texts, allowing short classes to teach the basics, leaving material for self-discovery, while longer classes can cover the full material presented.

The Civil 3D learning curve is steep. We consider this book a great resource for learning, but we have also included a list of other resources in Appendix B. These resources are accurate as we're writing this, but as with everything on the Internet, things can and do change. Every user should spend time on the blogs, websites, and other materials listed there. The user base of Civil 3D grows with every release, and the community knowledge is invaluable. The biggest benefit of using these resources is their freshness. The blogs and discussion groups around Civil 3D don't have to wait for a new edition of their book to update the information available!

This book can be used front to back as a self-taught or instructor-based instruction manual. Each chapter has a number of exercises and most (but not all) build on the previous exercise. You can also skip to almost any exercise in any chapter and jump right in. We've created a large number of drawing files on the accompanying disc to make picking and choosing your exercises a simpler task.

What You Will Learn

This book isn't a replacement for training. There are too many design options and parameters to make any book a good replacement for training from a professional. This book will teach you to use the tools available, exploring a large number of the options available, and leave you with an idea of how to use each tool. At the end of the book, you should be able to look at any design task you run across, consider a number of ways to approach it, and have some idea of how to accomplish the task. To use one of our common analogies, reading this book is like walking around your local home improvement warehouse. You see a lot of tools, and use some of them, but that doesn't mean you're ready to build a house.

What You Need

Before you begin learning Civil 3D, you should make sure your hardware is up to snuff. Visit the Autodesk website and review graphic requirements, memory requirements, and so on. One of the most frustrating things that can happen is to be ready to learn, only to be stymied by hardware-related crashes. Civil 3D is a hardware-intensive program, testing the limits of every computer that it is run on.

We also really recommend using a dual-monitor setup. The number of dialogs, palettes, and so on make Civil 3D a real estate hog. By having the extra space to spread out, you'll be able to see more of your design along with the feedback provided by the program itself.

Finally, some of the exercises are based on functionality that is only available in Civil 3D 2008 Service Pack 1. Please be sure to update your installation before attempting the exercises.

The *Mastering* Series

The *Mastering* series from Sybex provides outstanding instruction for readers with intermediate and advanced skills, in the form of top-notch training and development for those already working in their field, and clear, serious education for those aspiring to become pros. Every *Mastering* book features:

◆ The Sybex "by professionals for professionals" commitment. *Mastering* authors are themselves practitioners, with plenty of credentials in their areas of specialty.

◆ A practical perspective for a reader who already knows the basics—someone who needs solutions, not a primer.

◆ Real World Scenarios, ranging from case studies to interviews, that show how the tool, technique, or knowledge presented is applied in actual practice.

◆ Skill-based instruction, with chapters organized around real tasks rather than abstract concepts or subjects.

◆ Self-review test "Master It" problems and questions, so you can be certain you're equipped to do the job right.

What Is Covered in This Book

Chapter 1: Getting Dirty: The Basics of Civil 3D will introduce you to the interface and many of the common dialogs in Civil 3D. This chapter will look at the Toolbox and some underused Inquiry tools as well.

Chapter 2: Took Long Enough: Lines and Curves will examine various tools for creating linework. These tools include new best-fit tools that will let you interpolate a line or curve between known points.

Chapter 3: Lay of the Land: Survey looks at the Surveying Toolspace and the unique toolset it contains for handling field surveying and fieldbook data handling. We also look at various surface and surveying relationships.

Chapter 4: X Marks the Spot: Points introduces Civil 3D points and the various methods of creating them. We also spend some time discussing the control of Civil 3D points with description keys and groups.

Chapter 5: The Ground Up: Surfaces in Civil 3D introduces the various methods of creating surfaces, using free and low-cost data to perform preliminary surface creation. Then we look at the various surface edits and analysis methods.

Chapter 6: Don't Fence Me In: Parcels describes the best practices for keeping your parcel topology tight and labeling neat. It examines the various editing methods for achieving the desired results for the most complicated plats.

Chapter 7: Laying a Path: Alignments introduces the basic Civil 3D horizontal control element. This chapter also examines using layout tools that maintain the relationships between the tangents, curves, and spiral elements that create alignments.

Chapter 8: Cut to the Chase: Profiles looks at the sampling and creation methods for the vertical control element. We also examine the editing and element level control.

Chapter 9: Slice and Dice: Profile Views examines all the various creation methods for building up profile views to reflect the required format for your design and plans. We also check out the new wizards used for creating split profile views.

Chapter 10: Templates Plus: Assemblies and Subassemblies looks at the building blocks of Civil 3D cross-sectional design. We look at the available tool catalogs and at building up full design sections for use in any design environment.

Chapter 11: Easy Does It: Basic Corridors introduces the basics of corridors, building full designs from horizontal, vertical, and cross-sectional design elements. We look at the various components to understand them better before moving to a more complex design set.

Chapter 12: The Road Ahead: Advanced Corridors looks at using corridors in unusual situations. We'll look at building surfaces, intersections, and some other areas of corridor use that make them powerful in any design situation.

Chapter 13: Stacking Up: Cross Sections looks at a portion of the program that was revamped for 2008. Working with the new wizards and tools, we'll show you how to make your sections to order.

Chapter 14: The Tool Chest: Parts List and Part Builder gets into the building blocks of the pipe Network tools. We'll look at modifying an existing part to add new sizes, then building up parts lists for various design situations.

Chapter 15: Running Downhill: Pipe Networks works with the creation tools for creating pipe networks. We look at both plan and profile views to get your plans looking like they should.

Chapter 16: Working the Land: Grading examines both feature lines and grading objects. We look at creating feature lines to describe critical areas, then using grading objects to describe mass grading. We also explore using the basic tools to calculate some simple volumes.

Chapter 17: Sharing the Model: Data Shortcuts looks at the Data Shortcut mechanism for sharing data between Civil 3D users. We also look at updating and modifying the XML files that are behind the scenes.

Chapter 18: Behind the Scenes: Autodesk Data Management Server walks you through installing and managing your own server for using Autodesk Vault as your project-management system. We also look at creating vaults and users for your design teams.

Chapter 19: Teamwork: Vault Client walks you through bringing data into the ADMS created in Chapter 18, creating references between drawings and the update mechanism. We also look at the new security features that allow team management in ways that weren't possible in 2007.

Chapter 20: Out the Door: Plan Production introduces this brand-new feature for 2008. We walk through the basics of creating view frame groups and creating sheets, then look at some of the styles, templates, and editing techniques involved.

Chapter 21: Playing Nice with Others: LDT and LandXML looks at getting data back and forth with other software users. We look at importing data from your existing LDT projects to Civil 3D. We also examine the format of LandXML files to help you understand better what you can expect when you receive or send one out for sharing.

Chapter 22: Get the Picture: Visualization completes the book by taking all of the design elements and making presentation graphics from the design already modeled. We look at using the various rendering methods built into AutoCAD as well as some of the Civil 3D–specific tools.

Appendix A gathers together all the Master It problems from the chapters and provides a solution for each.

Appendix B offers a collection of other resources that we think are invaluable in learning and working with Civil 3D on a daily basis.

How to Contact the Authors

We welcome feedback from you about this book or about books you'd like to see from us in the future. You can reach us by writing to Mastering@eng-eff.com. For more information about our work, please visit our website at www.eng-eff.com.

Sybex strives to keep you supplied with the latest tools and information you need for your work. Please check their website at www.sybex.com, where we'll post additional content and updates that supplement this book if the need arises. Enter **Civil 3D** in the Search box (or type the book's ISBN—**9780470167403**) and click Go to get to the book's update page.

Thanks for purchasing *Mastering AutoCAD Civil 3D 2008*. We appreciate it, and look forward to exploring Civil 3D with you!

—*James Wedding, P.E.*

Chapter 1

Getting Dirty: The Basics of Civil 3D

Just as with any piece of software, understanding Civil 3D's controls and operation is critical to its mastery. With a dizzying array of options and settings, getting Civil 3D to just look and feel comfortable can take some effort. A whole new host of dialogs and tool palettes are critical to driving Civil 3D and getting feedback about your design. In this chapter, we'll explore the makeup of Civil 3D as a CAD program, the unique components that make up the Civil 3D interface, and how you can create a working environment that matches the way you design.

By the end of this chapter, you will be able to:

◆ Find any Civil 3D object with just a few clicks

◆ Modify the drawing scale and default object layers

◆ Modify the display of Civil 3D tooltips

◆ Add a new tool to the Toolbox

◆ Create a basic label style

◆ Create a new object style

Windows on the Model

If you're familiar with AutoCAD, opening up Civil 3D won't bring any major surprises—until you look a little further. Civil 3D is a design package for the civil engineer, so special tools are needed.

The most obvious change to the interface is the addition of two new palette sets that you won't find in any other Autodesk product: Toolspace and Panorama. These two palette sets offer Civil 3D users a way to interact with their data and watch their design change unlike anything previously offered. Both of these palette sets can be docked and resized like typical AutoCAD palettes and toolbars, making their use on screen as flexible as you like. Most users find that they are constantly referring to information displayed in these palette sets, so Toolspace and Panorama remain open nearly all the time. Figure 1.1 shows both of these palette sets displayed in a typical environment.

FIGURE 1.1
Civil 3D 2008 in a typical environment

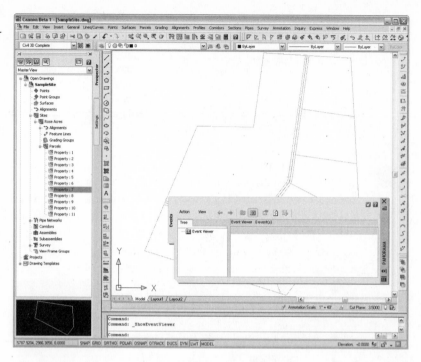

CONFUSED YET?

Bothered by the naming convention yet? After discussion with the Civil 3D team in Manchester, New Hampshire, we think we have it right. Toolspace and Panorama are palette sets, acting as containers for the palettes they contain. Examples of palettes are Event Viewer, Settings, Elevation Editor, and so on. We will use the terms tools, tabs, and palettes pretty much interchangeably throughout the text because we find that's how they are referred to in the wild. Apologies in advance for any confusion—we've been using program for five years and still had to get an official ruling from Autodesk!

Toolspace

Toolspace is one of the unique Civil 3D palette sets. Toolspace can have as many as four tabs to manage user data:

- Prospector
- Settings
- Survey
- Toolbox

Using a Microsoft Windows Explorer-like interface within each, these tabs drive a large portion of the user control and data management of Civil 3D.

PROSPECTOR

Prospector is the main window into the Civil 3D object model. This palette or tab is where you "go mining" for data and also shows points, alignments, parcels, corridors, and other objects as one concise, expandable list. In addition, in a project environment this window is where you will control access to your project data, create references to shared project data, and observe the check-in/check-out status of a drawing. Finally, you can also use Prospector to create a new drawing from the templates defined in the Drawing Templates branch in your AutoCAD Options dialog. Prospector has the following branches:

- Open Drawings
- Projects
- Drawing Templates

MASTER AND ACTIVE DRAWING VIEWS

If you can't see the Projects or Drawing Templates branch in Figure 1.1, look at the top of the Prospector pane. There is a dropdown menu for operating in Active Drawing Only or Master View mode. Selecting Active Drawing Only only displays open drawings. The Master View mode, however, displays the Projects and Drawing Templates branches, as well as the branches of any other drawings you might have open.

In addition to the branches, Prospector has a series of icons across the top that toggle various settings on and off:

 Project State Toggle   Turns on and off the display of project item state icons in the Prospector palette—very important when you're working with a team of designers so that you know when others have made changes to project-related data. Leave this one on!

 Drawing State Toggle   Turns on and off the display of the drawing item state icons in the Drawings collection. This is how you know that an object is in use, has been modified, or has dependent objects—profiles that depend on alignments. This same button on the Settings tab of Toolspace will turn on the icons that indicate a style is in use or has dependencies that keep it from being deleted. Another one to usually leave on.

 Modifier Toggle   Turns on and off the display of the drawing item modifier icons at the individual object level. For example, these icons will inform you when a surface is out of date or when a corridor needs to be rebuilt. This information is important when working with project data that has been referenced to your current drawing.

 Item Preview Toggle   Turns on and off the display of the Toolspace item preview within Prospector. These previews can be helpful when you're navigating drawings in projects (you can select one to check out) or when you're attempting to locate a parcel on the basis of its visual shape. In general, however, this one can be turned off—it's purely a user preference.

 Panorama Display Toggle   Turns on and off the display of the Panorama window (which we'll talk about in a bit). To be honest, there does not seem to be a point to this button, but it's here nonetheless.

 Help   This should be obvious, but it's amazing how many people overlook it.

HAVE YOU LOOKED IN THE HELP FILE? LATELY?

In the past, the included Help files were notoriously bad. Since Civil 3D's creation, the team in Manchester, New Hampshire, has worked hard to make the Help files in Civil 3D top notch and user friendly. The Help files should be your first line of support!

Open Drawings

This branch of Prospector contains the drawings currently open in Civil 3D. Each drawing is then subdivided into groups by major object type, such as points, point groups, surfaces, and so on. These object groups then allow you to view all the objects in the collection. Some of these groups are empty until objects are created. You can learn details about an individual object by expanding the tree and selecting an object. See Figure 1.2 for a typical parcel object's display in Prospector.

Within each drawing, the breakdown is similar. If a collection isn't empty, there will be a plus sign next to it, as there is next to the second Alignments collection in Figure 1.2. Selecting any of these top-level collection names displays a list of members in the preview area. Right-clicking on the collection name allows you to select various commands that apply to all the members of that collection. For example, right-clicking on the Point Groups collection brings up the menu shown in Figure 1.3.

FIGURE 1.2
A parcel shown in the preview area of Prospector

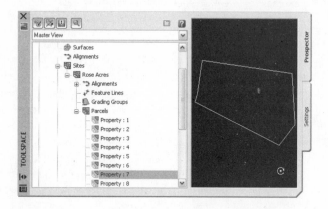

FIGURE 1.3
Context-sensitive menus in Prospector

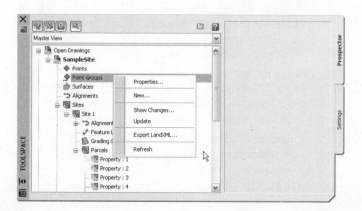

In addition, right-clicking on the individual object in the list view offers two more commands unique to Civil 3D: Zoom To Object and Pan To Object. By using these commands, you can find any parcel, point, cross section, or other Civil 3D object in your drawing nearly instantly.

Many longtime users of AutoCAD have resisted right-clicking menus for their daily tasks. In other AutoCAD products that might be possible, but in Civil 3D you'll miss half the commands! We will focus on the specific options and commands for each object type when we talk about the objects in particular.

Projects

The Projects branch of Prospector is the starting point for real team collaboration. This branch allows you to sign in and out of Vault, review what projects are available, manage the projects you sort through for information, check out drawings for editing, and review the status of drawings, as well as that of individual project-based objects. We'll spend much more time talking about the Project branch in Chapters 19 and 20.

Drawing Templates

The Drawing Templates branch is added more as a convenience than anything else. Creating new drawings can still be done via the standard File ➢ New option, but by using the Drawing Templates branch, you can do the same thing without ever leaving Prospector. The Drawing Templates branch searches the file path specified in your AutoCAD Options dialog and displays a list of all the .dwt files it finds. You can customize this path to point to a server or other folder, but by default it's a local user settings path. Right-clicking on the name of a template presents you with the options shown in Figure 1.4.

FIGURE 1.4
Creating a new drawing from within the Drawing Templates branch of Prospector

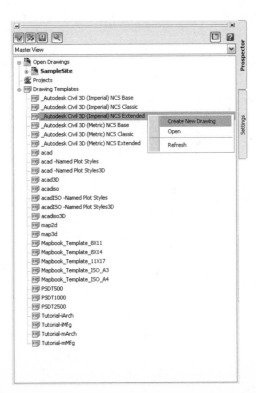

Civil 3D is built on both AutoCAD and Map, so Civil 3D 2008 comes with a variety of templates. However, most users will want to select one of the top few, which start with _Autodesk Civil 3D and then have some descriptive text. These templates have been built on the basis of customer feedback to provide Civil 3D with a varying collection of object styles. These templates give you a good starting point for creating your own personal template file.

SETTINGS

The Settings tab of Toolspace is the proverbial rabbit hole. Here you will adjust how the drawing relates to the real world, how Civil 3D objects look, and how the Civil 3D commands work. You control styles, labels, and command settings for each component of Civil 3D here. We'll start by looking at the top level of drawing settings and a few command settings to get you familiar, and then we'll cover the specifics for each object's styles and settings in their respective chapters.

CONSISTENCY OF FEEDBACK

Just as in Prospector, the button on the top row toggles the display of the various drawing item state icons that tell you if a style or label is in use. There's also a dropdown menu for a few different views of the Settings window.

Drawing Settings

Starting at the drawing level, Civil 3D has a number of settings that must be understood before the program can be used efficiently. Civil 3D understands that the end goal of most users is to prepare construction documents on paper. To that end, most labeling and display settings are displayed in inches for imperial users and millimeters for metric users instead of nominal units like many other AutoCAD objects. Since much of this is based on an assumed working scale, let's look at how to change that setting, along with some other drawing options.

1. Open the file SampleSite.dwg from the installed sample files.

2. Switch to the Settings tab.

3. Right-click on the filename and select Edit Drawing Settings to display the dialog shown in Figure 1.5.

Each tab in this dialog controls a different aspect of the drawing. Most of the time, you will pick up the Object Layers, Abbreviations, and Ambient Settings from a companywide template. But the drawing scale and coordinate information change for every job, so the Units And Zone and the Transformation tabs are visited frequently.

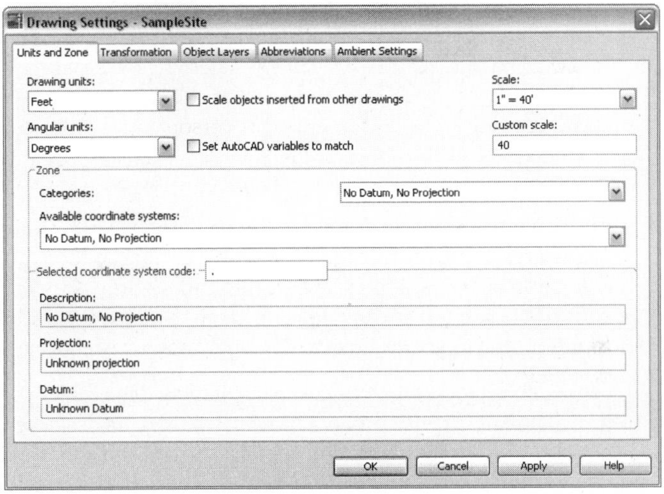

FIGURE 1.5
Drawing Settings
dialog

Units And Zone Tab

The Units And Zone tab lets you specify metric or imperial units, as well as control the assumed plotting scale of the drawing. The drawing units typically come from a template, but the options for scaling blocks and setting AutoCAD variables depend on your working environment. Many engineers continue to work in an arbitrary coordinate system using the settings as shown earlier, but using a real coordinate system is easy! For example, setting up a drawing for the Dallas, Texas, area, you'd follow this procedure:

1. Select USA Texas from the Categories dropdown menu on the Units And Zone tab.

2. Select NAD83 Texas State Planes, North Central Zone, US Foot from the Available Coordinate Systems dropdown menu.

There are literally hundreds, if not thousands, of available coordinate systems. These are established by international agreement and because Civil 3D is a worldwide product, almost any recognized surveying coordinate system can be found in the options here. Once your coordinate system has been established, you can change it on the Transformation tab if desired.

Transformation Tab

With a base coordinate system selected, you can now do any further refinement you'd like using the Transformation tab. The coordinate systems on the Units And Zone tab can be refined to meet local ordinances, tie in with historical data, or account for minor changes in methodology. These changes can include the following:

Apply Sea Level Scale Factor, which that takes into account the mean elevation of the site and the spheroid radius that is currently being applied as a function of the selected zone ellipsoid.

Grid Scale Factor, which is based on a 1:1 value, a user-defined uniform scale factor, a reference point scaling, or a prismoidal transformation in which every point in the grid is adjusted by a unique amount.

Reference Point, which can be used to set a singular point in the drawing field via pick or via point number, local northing and easting, or grid northing and easting values.

Rotation Point, which can be used to set the reference point for rotation via the same methods as the Reference Point.

Specify Grid Rotation Angle—you enter an amount or set a line to North by picking an angle or deflection in the drawing. This same method can be used to set the azimuth if desired.

Most engineering firms are working on a defined coordinate system or an arbitrary system with none of these changes necessary. Given that, this tab will be your only method of achieving the necessary transformation for certain surveying and Geographic Information System (GIS)-based tasks.

Object Layers Tab

Setting object layers to your company standard is a major part of creating the feel you're after when using Civil 3D in your office. The nearly 50 objects described here make up the entirety of the Civil 3D modeling components and the objects you and other users will be dealing with every day.

The layers listed in this dialog by default reflect a modified National CAD Standard (NCS) setup. This layering standard is built into many places in Civil 3D's templates and is becoming more widely adopted in the land development industry. In addition to being fairly comprehensive and well known among engineering firms, the NCS has the benefit of being the roadmap for the future in terms of out-of-the-box content from Autodesk. Adopting this standard means you'll have fewer things to change with every release of the software. Nevertheless, every user still needs know how to modify these defaults.

One common issue with the shipping templates is that the templates assume that road design is the primary use of alignments. Use the following procedure to change the Alignment setting to the NCS for laying out a sanitary sewer:

1. Click on the Layer column in the Alignment row, as shown in Figure 1.6.

2. In the Layer Selection dialog list, select C-SSWR-CNTR and click OK.

FIGURE 1.6
Changing the Layer setting for the Alignment object

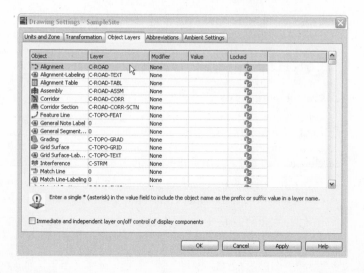

ONE OBJECT AT A TIME

Note that this has only changed the Alignment object itself. If you wanted to change the standard of all the objects, you would need to adjust the Alignment Labeling, Alignment Table, Profile, Profile View, Profile View Labeling, and so on. To do this, it's a good idea to right-click in the grid view and select Copy All. You can then paste the contents of this matrix into Microsoft Excel for easy formatting and reviewing.

One common question that surrounds the Object Layers tab is the checkbox on the lower left, Immediate And Independent Layer On/Off Control Of Display Components. What the heck does that mean? Relax—it's not as complicated as it sounds.

Many objects in Civil 3D are built from underlying components. Take an alignment, for example. It's built from tangents, curves, spirals, extension lines, and so on. Each of these components can be assigned its own layer—in other words, the lines could be assigned to the LINES layer, curves to the CURVES layer, and so on. When this checkbox is turned on, the *component's* layer will exert some control. In the example given, if the alignment is assigned to the ALIGN layer and the box is on, freezing the LINES layer will make the line components of that alignment disappear. Turn off this control, and the LINES layer status will not have any effect on the visibility of the alignment line components.

Finally, it's important to note that this layer control determines the object's parent layer *at creation*. Civil 3D objects are like any other object in that once they are made, they can be moved to other layers. Also, changing this setting will not change any objects already in place in the drawing.

Abbreviations Tab

Users can go for years and never notice the Abbreviations tab. The options on this tab allow you to set the short forms that Civil 3D uses when labeling items as part of its automated routines. The prebuilt settings are based on user feedback, and many of them are the same as the settings from Land Desktop, the last-generation civil engineering product from Autodesk.

To change an abbreviation, it's as simple as clicking in the Value field and typing in a new one. Notice that the Alignment Geometry Point Entity Data section has a larger set of values and some formulas attached. These are more representative of other label styles, and we will visit the label editor a little later in this chapter.

THERE'S ALWAYS MORE TO LEARN

It really can be years. Until December 2006, James was still advising users to add a "t." to their labels to get "Rt." or "Lt." in the final label. He'd forgotten that the abbreviations being used were being set here! By changing the Left and Right abbreviation from "L" and "R" to "Lt." and "Rt.," respectively, that step in the label setup can be skipped. Sometimes there are just too many options to remember them all!

Ambient Settings Tab

The Ambient Settings tab can be quite daunting at first. These settings control much of the math, labeling, and display features, as well as the user interaction of Civil 3D. However, being familiar with the way this tab works will help you further down the line, as almost every other setting dialog in the program works just like the one shown in Figure 1.6.

There are a couple of ways to approach this tab:

◆ Top to bottom—Expand one branch, handle the settings in that branch, then close it and move to the next.

◆ Print and conquer—Expand all the branches using the Expand All Categories button found on the lower right 🔽. Once you have them expanded, right-click in the middle, and select Copy To Clipboard and paste to Excel for review, like we did with the Object Layers tab.

SHARING THE WORKLOAD

The second approach makes it easy to distribute multiple copies to surveyors, land planners, engineers, and so on and let them fill in the changes. Then, creating a template for each group is a matter of making their changes. If you're asking end users who aren't familiar with the product to make these changes, it's easy to miss one. Going line by line is pretty well foolproof.

After deciding how to approach these settings, get to work. These settings are either dropdown menus or text boxes in the case of numeric entries. Many of these are self-explanatory and common to land development design. The General branch of the Ambient Settings tab is new to Civil 3D, so let's look at its settings in more detail (see Figure 1.7).

FIGURE 1.7
The Ambient Settings tab with the General branch expanded

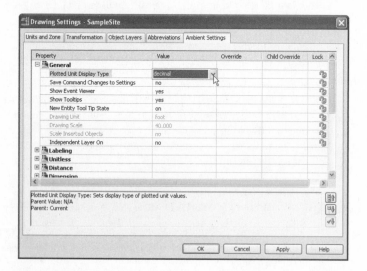

Plotted Unit Display Type Remember, Civil 3D knows you want to plot at the end of the day. In this case, it's asking you how you would like your plotted units measured. For example, would you like that bit of text to be 0.25″ tall or ¼″ high? Most engineers are comfortable with the Leroy method of text heights (L80, L100, L140, and so on), so the decimal option is the default.

Save Command Changes To Settings This setting is incredibly powerful but a secret to almost everyone. By setting this to YES, your changes to commands will be remembered from use to use. This means that if you make changes to a command during use, the next time you call that Civil 3D command, you won't have to make the same changes. Since it's frustrating to do work over because you forgot to change one out of the five things that needed changing, this setting is invaluable.

Show Event Viewer   Event Viewer is Civil 3D's main feedback mechanism, especially when things go wrong. It can get annoying, however, and takes up valuable screen real estate (especially if you're stuck with one monitor!), so many people turn it off. At the end of the day, we have to recommend leaving it on and simply pushing Event Viewer to the side if needed.

Show Tooltips   One of the cool features that people remark on when they first use Civil 3D is the small pop-up that displays relevant design information when the cursor is paused on the screen. This includes things like Station-Offset information, Surface Elevation, Section information, and so on. Once a drawing has numerous bits of information, this can be overwhelming, so Civil 3D offers the option to turn these tooltips off universally with this setting. A better approach is to control the tooltips at the object type by editing the individual feature settings. You can also control the tooltips by pulling up the properties for any individual object and looking at the Information tab.

New Entity Tool Tip State   The same tooltips that we just discussed can be controlled on an individual object level. For instance, you might want tooltip feedback on your proposed surface but not on the existing surface. This setting controls whether the tooltip is turned on at the object level for new Civil 3D objects.

Drawing Unit, Drawing Scale, and Scale Inserted Objects   These settings were specified on the Units And Zone tab but are displayed here for reference and so that you can lock them if desired.

Independent Layer On   This is the same control that was set on the Object Layers tab.

The settings that are applied here can also be applied at the object levels. For example, you might want elevation to generally be shown to two decimal places, but when looking at surface elevations you might want just one. The Override and Child Override columns will give you feedback about these types of changes. See Figure 1.8.

FIGURE 1.8
Child Override indicator in the Elevation values

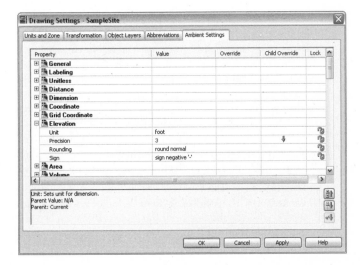

The Override column shows if the current setting is overriding something higher up. Since we are at the Drawing Settings level, these are all clear. However, the Child Override column has a down arrow symbol, indicating that one of the objects in the drawing has overridden this setting. After a little investigation through the objects, we find the override is in the Edit Feature Settings of the Profile View, shown in Figure 1.9.

Notice that in this dialog, the box is checked in the Override column! This indicates that we're overriding the settings from earlier, and it's a good alert that things have changed from the general Drawing Settings to this Object Level setting.

But what if we don't want to allow those changes? In each settings dialog, there's one more column we haven't discussed: the Lock column. At any level, you can lock a setting, graying it out for any lower levels. This can be handy for keeping users from changing settings at the lower level that perhaps should be changed at a drawing level, such as sign or rounding methods.

FIGURE 1.9
Profile Elevation Settings and the Override indicator

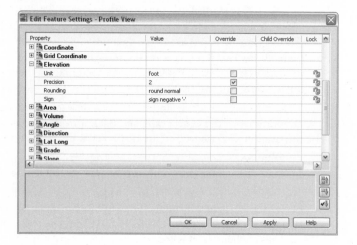

Object Settings

If you have clicked the expand button next to the drawing name, you'll see the full array of objects that Civil 3D uses to build its design model. Each of these has some special features unique to the object being described, but there are some common features as well. Additionally, there's a General collection for settings and styles that are applied to various objects across the entire product. Let's look at those now.

The General collection serves as the catchall for the styles that apply to multiple objects and to the settings that apply to *no* objects. For instance, the Civil 3D General Note object doesn't really belong with the Surface or Pipe collections. It can be used to relate information about those objects, but since it can also relate to something like "Don't Dig Here!" it falls into the general category. The General collection has three components (or branches), and we'll look at each.

Multipurpose Styles These styles are used in many objects to control the display of component objects. The Marker Styles and Link Styles collections are typically used in cross-section views, whereas the Feature Line Styles collection is used in grading and other commands. Figure 1.10 shows the full collection of Multipurpose Styles and some of the Marker Styles that ship with the product.

FIGURE 1.10

General Multipur-
pose Styles and some
Marker Styles

Label Styles   The Label Styles collection was a new addition with the 2007 release of the product and a much-requested change at that. These labels allow Civil 3D users to place general text notes or label single entities outside the parcel network while still taking advantage of the Civil 3D flexibility and scaling properties. With the various Label Styles shown in Figure 1.11, you can get some idea of the usage.

Since building label styles is a critical part of producing plans with Civil 3D, we will look at how to build a new basic label and some of the common components that appear in every label style throughout the product in a later section of this chapter.

Commands   Every branch in the Settings tree contains a Commands folder. Expanding this folder as shown in Figure 1.12, you will find the long, unspaced commands that refer to the parent object.

SURVEY

The Survey palette is displayed optionally and controls the use of the survey, equipment, and figure prefix databases. Survey is an essential part of land development projects, but because of the complex nature of this tab, we will devote a whole chapter to it. See Chapter 3 for a full exploration of the Survey palette.

FIGURE 1.11

Line styles

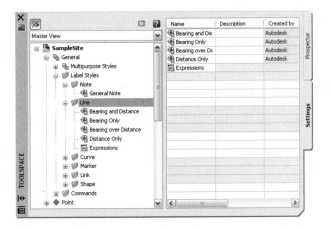

FIGURE 1.12
Surface command settings in Toolspace

TOOLBOX

The Toolbox was added in Civil 3D 2007 as a launching point for add-ons and reporting functions. You access and add it to Toolspace by selecting General ➤ Toolbox. Toolbox out of the box contains reports created by Autodesk, but the functionality can be expanded to include your own macros or reports. The buttons on the top of the Toolbox shown in Figure 1.13 allow you to customize the report settings and add new content.

FIGURE 1.13
Toolbox palette with the Edit Toolbox Content button circled

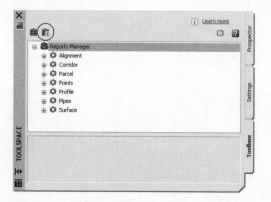

Real World Scenario

A TOOLBOX BUILT JUST FOR YOU

The Toolbox content and the Report Settings can be edited by selecting the desired tool, right-clicking, and then executing. Don't limit yourself to the default reports that ship in the Toolbox, though. Many firms find that adding their in-house customizations to the Toolbox gives them better results and is more easily managed at a central level than by customizing via the AutoCAD common user interface (CUI) and workspace functionality.

Let's add one of the sample Civil 3D Visual Basic Application (VBA) macros to a new Toolbox:

1. Click the Edit Toolbox Content button shown in Figure 1.13 to open the Toolbox Editor in Panorama.

2. Click the button shown here to add a new root category.

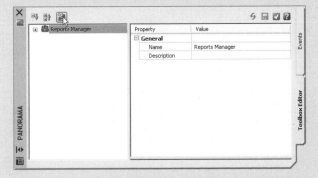

3. Click on the Root Category1 toolbox that appears. The name will appear in the preview area, where you can edit it. Change the name to **Sample Files**, and press ⏎.

4. Right-click on the Sample Files toolbox, and select New Category as shown here.

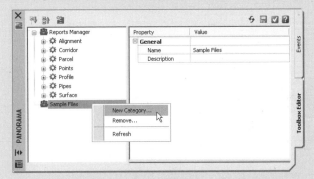

5. Expand the Sample Files toolbox to view the new category, and then click on the name to edit it in the preview area. Change the name to **VBA**, and press ⏎.

6. Right-click on the VBA category and select New Tool.

7. Expand the VBA category to view the new tool, and then click on the name to edit it in the preview area. Change its name to **Pipe Export**.

8. Change the Description to **Runs Autodesk's sample Pipe Export VBA Macro**.

9. Working down through the properties in the preview area, select VBA in the dropdown menu in the Execute Type field.

10. Click in the Execute File field and then click the More button 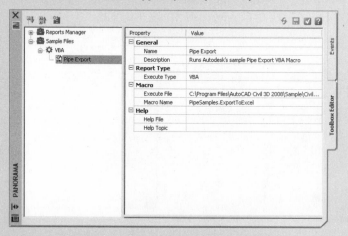 to browse.

11. Browse to C:\Program Files\Autocad Civil 3D 2008\Sample\Civil 3D API\VBA\Pipe\ and select the file Pipe Sample Application.dvb.

12. Click Open.

13. Click in the Macro Name text field, and type **PipeSamples.ExportToExcel** as shown here.

The text PipeSamples.ExportToExcel was determined by using the AutoCAD VBAMAN command to load up the same .dvb file, clicking the Macros button in that dialog and copying the text from the Macro Name text field. The portion of the text that comes after the .dvb file extension in that text box is the macro name as required by the Toolbox Editor.

14. Click the green checkbox in the upper right to dismiss the editor.

You've now added that sample VBA macro to your Toolbox. By adding commonly used macros and custom reports to your Toolbox, you can keep them handy without modifying the rest of your Civil 3D interface or programming buttons. It's just one more way to create an interface and toolset for the way you work.

Panorama

The Panorama window is Civil 3D's feedback and tabular editing mechanism. Designed to be a common interface for a number of different Civil 3D-related tasks, it can be used to provide information about the creation of profile views, to allow the editing of pipe or structure information, or the running of basic volume analysis between two surfaces. Panorama typically isn't displayed when Civil 3D is launched. Select General ➤ Utilities ➤ Event Viewer to display the Event Viewer, one of many Panorama uses. We'll explore and use Panorama more as we get into specific objects or tasks.

RUNNING OUT OF SCREEN REAL ESTATE?

It's a good idea to turn on Panorama using this technique, then drag it to the side so that you'll always see any new information. While it is possible to turn it off, it's not recommended—you won't know when Civil 3D is trying to tell you something! Place it on your second monitor (by now, you see why you do need to have a second monitor, don't you?), and you'll always be up to date with your Civil 3D model.

And in case you missed it, we were using Panorama when we added the sample VBA macro in the previous exercise.

It's All About Style

Before we get into the program itself, it's important that we cover one bit of vocabulary and how it relates to Civil 3D: style. To put it simply, styles control the display properties of Civil 3D objects and labels. Styles control everything from the color of your point markers to the interval of your surface contours and from your profile view grid spacing to the text height in the Station-Offset label of your road alignment. Styles truly are where the power in Civil 3D lies. Label styles and object styles are the two major categories.

The difficult thing about styles is that it's hard to talk about them without being specific. We'll spend a fair amount of time in later chapters talking about the specifics of the styles for each object and some time in this chapter looking at the common aspects of style manipulation, but they might remain a mystery until you really get your hands dirty in later chapters.

Label Styles

To get started, we can look at the styles in the Spot Elevation branch by expanding the Surface branch and then the Label Styles branch on the Settings tab, as shown in Figure 1.14.

There are two basic label styles in the Spot Elevation branch. Let's create a new one and explore the options for making labels. Remember, almost all of these options will be present in other, object-specific label styles.

FIGURE 1.14
Spot Elevation
label styles

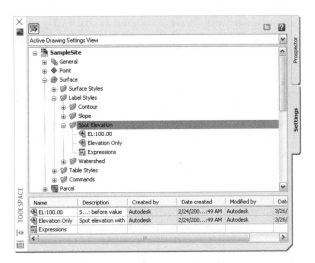

First, right-click the Spot Elevation folder and select New in the pop-up menu to open the Label Style Composer, as shown in Figure 1.15.

On the Information tab, change the name to something appropriate. In this case, we'll use **JW-EG**.

FIGURE 1.15

Label Style Composer

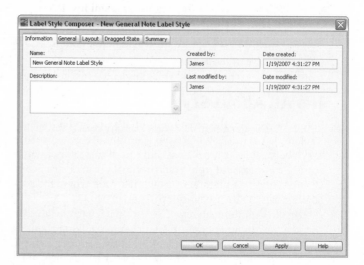

WHO BUILT THAT STYLE?

It's a good idea to always put something in the style name to indicate it wasn't one in the box. Putting your initials or firm at the beginning of the style is one way to make it easy to differentiate your styles from the prebuilt ones. Here, JW stands for James Wedding (EG stands for Existing Ground).

Next, switch to the General tab. Change the layer to **C-TOPO-TEXT** by clicking the layer cell and then the More button to the right of that cell. There are a fair number of options here, so let's look at them further:

Text Style is the default style for the text components that will be created on the Layout tab. It's a good practice to just use a zero-height text style with the appropriate font since you'll set the plotted heights in the style anyway.

Layer is the layer that the *components* of a label get inserted on, not the layer the label *itself* gets inserted on. Think of labels as nested blocks. The label (the block) gets inserted on the layer on the basis of the object layers we looked at earlier. The components of the label get inserted on the layer that is set here. This means a change to the specified layer can control or change the appearance of the components if desired.

Orientation Reference sets an object to act as the up direction in terms of readability. Civil 3D understands viewpoint rotation and offers the option to rotate or flip labels to keep them plan readable. Most users will want to set this to View to maintain the most plan-readable labels with the smallest amount of editing later.

Forced Insertion makes more sense in other objects and will be explored further. This feature essentially allows you to dictate the insertion point of a label on the basis of the object being labeled.

Plan Readable text maintains the up direction in spite of view rotation. This tends to be the "Ooooh, nice" feature that sets users to smiling. Rotating a hundred labels is a tedious, thankless task, and this handles it with one click.

Readability Bias is the angle at which readability kicks in. This angle is measured from the zero degree of the X axis that is common to AutoCAD angle measurements. When a piece of text goes past the readable bias angle, the text spins to maintain vertical orientation, as shown in Figure 1.16. Note how the label on the far left has rotated to accommodate the rotation past 110 degrees, the default bias angle.

Flip Anchors With Text determines how the text flips. Most users find that setting this to False gives the best results, but sometimes flipping an anchor point will position text as needed. We'll talk more about anchor points on the Layout tab.

Switch to the Layout tab. Again, there's a whole lot going on here, so we'll work through the options, and then make changes. As shown in Figure 1.17, each component of the label has a whole host of options.

FIGURE 1.16
Examples of plan-readable text

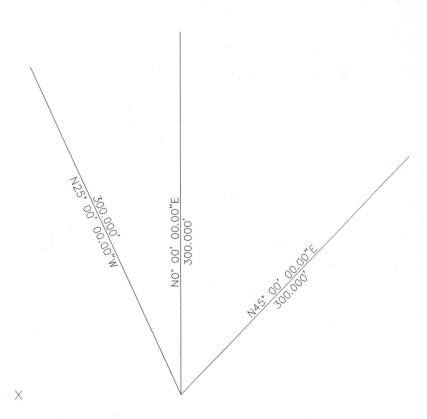

FIGURE 1.17

Options for the label components

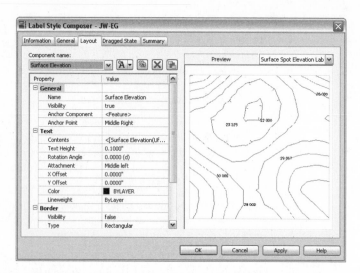

To the right-hand side is a preview of the label you are creating or editing. This view can be panned or zoomed as needed to give you a better feel for the label style's appearance as you make changes.

A Full Three-Dimensional Label Preview?

This preview defaults to a 3D orbit control. Don't ask us why; we honestly are as confused as you are. Inevitably, you will rotate the view out of a plan-top view, making the plan harder to understand. When this happens, right-click and select Preset Views ➤ Top to reorient yourself.

Labels are made of individual components. A component can be text, a block, or a line, and the top row of buttons controls the selection, creation, and deletion of these components:

The Component dropdown menu activates which component is being modified in the options below. These components are listed in the order in which they were created.

The Create Text Component button allows for the creation of new components. These components can be Text, Lines, Blocks, Reference Text, or Ticks. Some options are not available for every label style.

The Copy Component button does just that. It copies the component currently selected in the Component dropdown menu.

The Delete Component button deletes components. Elements that act as the basis for other components cannot be deleted.

The Component Draw Order button allows the components to be shuffled up and down within the label. This feature is especially important when using masks or borders as part of the label.

Let's work our way down the component properties and adjust them as needed for our label:

Name is self-explanatory. It is the name used in the Component dropdown menu and when selecting other components. When building complicated labels, a little name description goes a long way.

Visibility set to true means that this component will show on screen. Invisible components can be invaluable when creating complicated labels, as you'll see in later chapters.

Anchor Component and **Anchor Point** are straightforward, but many users have issues when first using these options. Every component of the label has an anchor component, anchor point, and attachment. The Anchor Component is how you tell Civil 3D where you want to hang the label component. This component is bounded by a box, with nine anchor points, as shown in Figure 1.18. In this illustration, the nine possible anchor points are represented with X's and the nine possible attachments with O's.

FIGURE 1.18
Anchor and attachment points

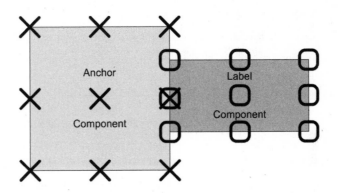

The middle portion of the dialog changes depending on the type of component, but the concepts are similar. In the case shown here, the middle portion is the Text property. Under Text, the first option is Contents, which determines the actual content of the text.

1. Click the Contents Value cell, then click the ellipsis button that appears to the right to open the Text Component Editor.

2. Click in the preview window of the Text Component Editor. This is a simple text editor, and you can type anything you'd like in a label here. Additionally, you can insert object information from Civil 3D objects as we'll do now.

3. Highlight and delete the text that is in the preview window.

4. On the left-hand side, select Surface Elevation from the dropdown list in the Properties text box.

5. Change the precision to one decimal place by clicking in the column next to precision and selecting 0.1, as shown in Figure 1.19.

6. Click the blue arrow circled in Figure 1.19 to insert your label text and elevation code into the preview area.

7. Click OK to exit this dialog, and you'll be back at the Label Style Composer.

FIGURE 1.19
Setting label precision

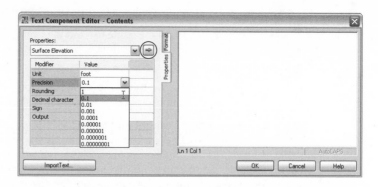

HOW MANY DIALOGS IS THAT?

You can now see why many Civil 3D instructors refer to label creation as heading down the rabbit hole. We're a couple of dialogs deep in just making the simplest of label styles, with one static text component. It's easy to get confused, but don't worry—it becomes second nature! The Text Component Editor is another common dialog that appears in every label style creation exercise.

Let's look at the rest of the options, even though we won't be making any changes:

Text Height determines the plotted height of the label. Remember, Civil 3D knows you're going to print and will attempt to give you inches or millimeters.

Rotation Angle, **X Offset**, and **Y Offset** give you the ability to refine the placement of this component by rotating or displacing the text in an X or Y direction.

Attachment determines which of the nine points on the label components bounding box will be attached to the anchor point. See Figure 1.19 for an illustration.

Color and **Lineweight** allow you to hard-code a color if desired. We suggest you leave these values set to ByLayer unless you have a good reason to change them.

The final piece of the component puzzle is a Border option. These options are as follows:

Visibility is an obvious one, turning the border on and off for this component. One thing to remember is that component borders shrink to the individual component, so if you are using multiple components in a label, they all have their own borders.

Type allows you to select a rectangle, a rounded rectangle (slot), or a circle border.

Background Mask allows the user to determine whether linework and text behind this component is masked. This can be handy for construction notes in place of the usual wipeout tools.

Gap determines the offset from the component bounding box to the outer points on the border. Setting this to $\frac{1}{4}$ or $\frac{1}{2}$ the text size usually creates a visually pleasing border.

Linetype and **Lineweight** allow the usual control of the border lines.

After working through all of the options for the default label placement, you need to work through the options that come into play when a label is dragged. Switch to the Dragged State tab. When a label is dragged in Civil 3D, it typically will create a leader and text will rearrange. The settings that control these two actions are on this tab. Unique options are explained here:

Arrow Head Style and **Size** control the tip of the leader. One thing to note is that Arrow Head Size also controls the tail size leading to the text object.

Type controls the leader type. Options are Straight Leader and Spline Leader. At the time of this writing, the AutoCAD multiple leader object cannot be used.

Display controls whether components rearrange their placement to a stacked set of components (Stacked Text) or maintain their arrangement as originally composed (As Composed). Most users expect this to be set to As Composed for the most predictable behavior.

Switch to the Summary tab and click the Expand All button circled in Figure 1.20. Working down the Summary tab, you can review all of the options that have been selected for an individual label, as well as look for overrides, just like we did on the Settings tab. Click OK to exit the dialog; your new style will appear on the Settings tab.

The purpose of this exercise wasn't to build a Surface Spot Elevation label style; it was to familiarize you with the common elements of creating a label: the Label Style Composer and the Text Component Editor. We'll cover more complex label styles and the creation of more common labels in later chapters.

FIGURE 1.20
Summary tab with the Expand All button circled

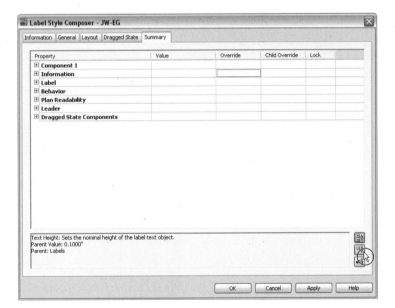

Object Styles

Beyond the styles used to label objects, Civil 3D also depends on styles to control the display of the native objects, including points, surface, alignments, and so on. Just as in label styles, certain components of the object styles are common to almost all of the objects, so let's create a new alignment style to introduce these common elements.

1. Expand the Alignment branch on the Settings tab, and then right-click on the Alignment Styles folder. Select New, as shown in Figure 1.21.

2. Type a new name for your style on the Information tab and enter a description if desired.

3. Switch to the Display tab. While the other two tabs are unique for alignment objects, the Display tab is part of every Civil 3D object style.

4. Turn off the Arrow component by clicking the lightbulb in the column next to it.

5. Near the top of the dialog, change the View Direction setting in the dropdown menu to 3D and notice the change.

6. Click OK to dismiss the dialog. Your new alignment style will appear under the Alignment Styles branch in the Settings tab.

Objects can have distinctly different appearances when being viewed in a plan view versus a 3D view. For example, surfaces are often represented by contours in plan view, but triangular faces or a grid in 3D.

Object styles are a major component of efficient Civil 3D object modeling. Objects appear differently in varying plans. Having a full set of object styles to handle all of these use cases will make plan production as painless as possible.

A good way to start creating object styles is to pull out a set of existing plans that represent your firm's standards accurately. Pick an object, such as alignments or surfaces, and then begin working your way through the plan set, creating a new object style for all of the various use cases in your plan set. Once you complete one object, pick another, and repeat the exercise.

FIGURE 1.21
Creating a new
alignment style
via Prospector

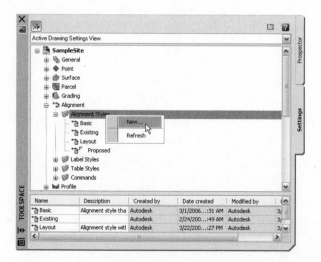

The Underlying Engine

Civil 3D is part of a larger product family from Autodesk. During its earliest creation, various features and functions from other products were recognized as important to the civil engineering community. These include the obvious things like the entire suite of AutoCAD drafting, design, modeling, and rendering tools and then to some more esoteric options like Map's GIS capabilities. An early decision was made to build Civil 3D on top of the AutoCAD Map product, which in turn is built on top of AutoCAD.

This underlying engine provides a whole host of options and powerful tools for the Civil 3D user. AutoCAD and Map add features with every release that change the fundamental makeup of how Civil 3D works. With the introduction of workspaces in 2006, users can now set up Civil 3D to display various tools and palettes depending on the task at hand. Creating a workspace can be thought of as having a quick-fix bag of tools ready for the job at hand: preliminary design calls for one set of tools, and final plan production calls for another.

Workspaces are part of a larger feature set called the custom user interface, typically referred to as CUI in the help documentation and online. Creating workspaces is relatively simple, especially as we'll be focusing on the display and control of toolbars and not creating new ones.

Table 1.1 shows the default workspaces and their menus that ship with Civil 3D 2008. As you can see, there are a fair number prebuilt for major design tasks. This is a marked improvement from 2007, when only one basic Civil 3D workspace was included in the product.

The Workspaces toolbar is on by default, but if it is not visible, you can access it by right-clicking in any gray area around the drawing window and selecting ACAD ➢ Workspaces to display the toolbar.

TABLE 1.1:   Workspace and Menu Reference Table

MENU	CIVIL 3D COMPLETE	DESIGN	ANNOTATION AND DRAFTING	SURVEYING AND TOPOGRAPHICAL	VISUALIZATION AND RENDERING
File		×	×	×	×
Edit	×	×	×	×	×
View		×	×	×	×
Insert	×	×	×	×	×
General		×	×	×	×
Lines/Curves	×	×		×	
Points		×		×	
Surfaces	×	×		×	
Parcels		×		×	
Grading	×	×			
Alignments	×	×		×	

TABLE 1.1: Workspace and Menu Reference Table *(CONTINUED)*

MENU	CIVIL 3D COMPLETE	DESIGN	ANNOTATION AND DRAFTING	SURVEYING AND TOPOGRAPHICAL	VISUALIZATION AND RENDERING
Profiles	×	×			
Corridors	×	×			
Sections		×			
Pipes		×			
Survey				×	
Annotation	×		×		
Inquiry		×	×	×	
Express		×	×	×	×
Window	×	×	×	×	×
Help		×	×	×	×

As you can see from the table, each of these workspaces was designed with user roles in mind. By using these as templates for your own workspaces, you can make Civil 3D work the way you do.

The Bottom Line

Find any Civil 3D object with just a few clicks. By using Prospector to view object data collections, you can minimize the panning and zooming that are part of working in a CAD program. When common subdivisions can have hundreds of parcels or a complex corridor can have dozens of alignments, jumping to the desired one nearly instantly shaves time off everyday tasks.

Master It Open `SampleSite.dwg` from the sample data set and find the parcel Property : 9 without using any AutoCAD commands.

Modify the drawing scale and default object layers. Civil 3D understands the end goal of most drawings is to create hard-copy construction documents. By setting a drawing scale and then setting many sizes in terms of plotted inches or millimeters, Civil 3D removes much of the mental gymnastics that other programs require when sizing text and symbology. By setting object layers at a drawing scale, Civil 3D makes uniformity of drawing files easier than ever to accomplish.

Master It Change `SampleSite.dwg` from a 40-scale drawing to a 200-scale drawing.

Modify the display of Civil 3D tooltips. The interactive display of object tooltips makes it easy to keep your focus on the drawing instead of an inquiry or report tools. When too many objects fill up a drawing however, it can be information overload, so Civil 3D gives you granular control over the heads-up display tooltips.

Master It Within the same Sample Site drawing, turn off the tooltips for the Alignment-(2) alignment.

Add a new tool to the Toolbox. The Toolbox provides a convenient way to access macros and reports. Many third-party developers are exploiting this convenient interface as an easier way to add functionality without disturbing users' workspaces.

> **Master It** Add the Import From Excel macro from `C:\Program Files\Autocad Civil 3D 2008\Sample\Civil 3D API\VBA\Pipe\` and select `Pipe Sample Application.dvb`.

Create a basic label style. Label styles determine the appearance of Civil 3D annotation. The creation of label styles will constitute a major part of the effort in making the transition to Civil 3D as a primary platform for plan production. Your skills will grow with the job requirements if you start with basic labels and then make more complicated labels as needed.

> **Master It** Create a copy of the Elevation Only Point label style, name it **Elevation With Border**, and add a border to the text component.

Create a new object style. Object styles in Civil 3D allow the user to quit managing display through layer modification and move to a more streamlined style-based control. Creating enough object styles to meet the demands of plan production work will be the other major task in preparing to move to Civil 3D.

> **Master It** Create a new Surface style named **Contours_Grid** and set it to show contours in plan views but a grid display in any 3D view.

Chapter 2

Lines and Curves

Engineers and surveyors are constantly creating lines and curves. Whether the task at hand involves re-creating and checking existing geometry from deeds or record plats, or designing a new land plan, it is important to have tools to assist in the accurate creation of this linework.

The lines and curves tools in Civil 3D, along with the complementary tools on the Transparent Commands and Inquiry toolbars, provide robust methods for creating and checking lines and curves. This linework can then be used as is, or as a foundation for creating sound parcels, alignments, and other Civil 3D object geometry.

It is important to note that the creation Civil 3D objects such as parcels and alignments from this foundation geometry is necessary for robust reporting and labeling, such as legal descriptions, segment tables, and more detailed design and analysis.

By the end of this chapter, you will be able to:

- Create a series of lines by bearing and distance
- Use the Inquiry commands to confirm that lines are drawn correctly
- Create a curve tangent to the end of a line
- Create a best-fit line for a series of Civil 3D points
- Label lines and curves

Label Lines and Curves

There are many ways to draw lines in an AutoCAD-based environment. The tools found under the Lines/Curve menu create lines that are no more intelligent than the regular AutoCAD Line command. How the Civil 3D lines differ from the regular Line command is not in the resulting entity, but in the process of creating them. In other words, Civil 3D will want us to provide directions to these line commands in survey terminology rather than in generic Cartesian parameters (see Figure 2.1).

Note that you can switch between any of the line commands without exiting the command. For example, if your first location was a point object, use Line By Point Object, and then without leaving the command, go back up to the Lines/Curves menu and choose any Line or Curve command to continue creating your linework. You can also press the Esc key once, while in a Lines/Curve menu command, to resume the regular Line command.

FIGURE 2.1

Line creation tools

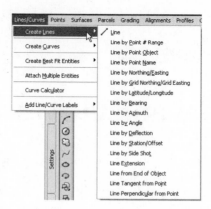

Coordinate Line Commands

The next few commands help you create a line using Civil 3D points and/or coordinate inputs. Each command requires you to specify a Civil 3D point, a location in space, or a typed coordinate input. These line tools are useful when you have Civil 3D points in your drawing that will serve as a foundation for linework, such as the edge of pavement shots, wetlands lines, or any other points that you'd like to connect with a line.

LINE COMMAND

The Lines/Curves ➢ Create Lines ➢ Line command is the standard AutoCAD Line command. It is exactly equivalent to typing **line** in the command line or clicking the Line tool on the Draw toolbar.

LINE BY POINT # RANGE COMMAND

The Line By Point # Range command prompts you for a point number. You can type in an individual point number, press ↵, and then type in another point number. A line will be drawn connecting those two points. You can also type in a range of points, such as **640-644**. Civil 3D will draw a line that connects those lines in numerical order—from 640 to 641, and so on (see Figure 2.2). This order would not give you the desired linework for edge of asphalt, for example.

Alternatively, you can enter a list of points such as **640, 643, 644** (Figure 2.3). Civil 3D will draw a line that connects the point numbers in the order of input. This is useful when your points were taken in a zigzag pattern.

LINE BY POINT OBJECT COMMAND

The Line By Point Object command prompts you to select a point object. To select a point object, locate the desired start point and click on any part of the point. This tool is similar to using the regular Line command and a Node osnap.

LINE BY POINT NAME COMMAND

The Line By Point Name command prompts you for a point name. A point name is a field in Point properties, not unlike the point number or description. The difference between a point name and a point description is that a point name must be unique.

To use this command, simply enter the names of the points you wish to connect with linework.

FIGURE 2.2

A line created using
640-644 as input

FIGURE 2.3

A line created using
640, 643, 644 as input

LINE BY NORTHING/EASTING AND LINE BY GRID NORTHING/EASTING COMMANDS

The Line By Northing/Easting and Line By Grid Northing/Easting commands allow you to input northing (y) and easting (x) coordinates as endpoints for your linework. The Line By Grid Northing/Easting command requires that the drawing have an assigned coordinate system.

LINE BY LATITUDE/LONGITUDE COMMAND

The Line By Latitude/Longitude command prompts you for geographic coordinates to use as endpoints for your linework. This command also requires that the drawing have an assigned coordinate system. For example, if your drawing has been assigned Delaware State Plane NAD83 US Feet and you execute this command, your Latitude/Longitude inputs will be translated into the appropriate location in your state plane drawing.

Direction-Based Line Commands

The next few commands help you specify the direction of a line. Each one of these commands requires you to choose a start point for your line before you can specify the line direction. You can specify your start point by physically choosing a location, using an osnap or one of the point-related line commands discussed earlier.

LINE BY BEARING COMMAND

The Line By Bearing command will likely be one of your most frequently used line commands.

This command prompts you for a start point, followed by prompts to input the Quadrant, Bearing, and Distance values. You can enter values in the command line for each input, or you can graphically choose inputs by picking on screen. The glyphs at each stage of input guide you in any graphical selections. After creating one line, you can continue drawing lines by bearing or switch to any other method without leaving the command simply by going back up to the Lines/ Curves menu and choosing another line tool (see Figure 2.4).

FIGURE 2.4
The command line and tooltips prompt you for (a) a quadrant, (b) a bearing, and (c) a distance.

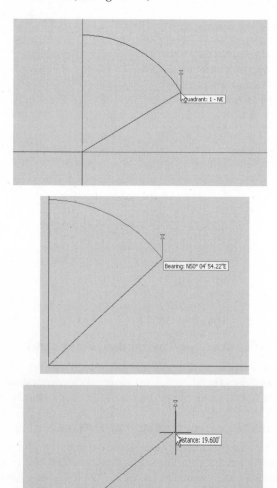

Line By Azimuth Command

The Line By Azimuth command prompts you for a start point, followed by a north azimuth and a distance (Figure 2.5).

Line By Angle Command

The Line By Angle command prompts you for a turned angle and a distance (Figure 2.6).

Line By Deflection Command

By definition, a deflection angle is the angle turned from the extension of a line from the backsight extending through an instrument. Although this is not the most frequently used tool in surveying in this day of data collectors and GPSs, there are still occasions where you may need to create this type of line. When you use the Line By Deflection command, the command line and tooltips prompt you for a deflection angle followed by a distance (Figure 2.7).

FIGURE 2.5
The command line and tooltip for the Line By Azimuth command first prompt for a north azimuth.

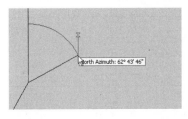

FIGURE 2.6
The command line and tooltip for the Line By Angle command first prompt for a turned angle.

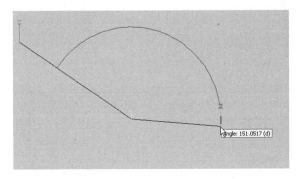

FIGURE 2.7
The command line and tooltips for the Line By Deflection command first prompt for a deflection angle.

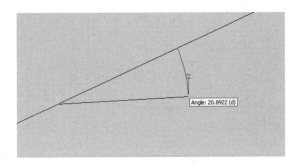

LINE BY STATION/OFFSET COMMAND

To use the Line By Station/Offset command, you must have an alignment in your drawing. The line created from this command allows you to start and/or end a line on the basis of a station and offset from an alignment.

You will be prompted to choose the alignment and then input a station and offset value. The line will *begin* at the station and offset value. On the basis of the tooltips, you might expect the line to be drawn from the alignment station at offset zero and out to the alignment station at the input offset. This is not the case.

When prompted for the station, you will be given a tooltip that tracks your position along the alignment (Figure 2.8). You can graphically choose a station location by picking in the drawing (including using your osnaps to assist you in locking down the station of a specific feature). Alternatively, you can enter a station value in the command line.

Once the station has been selected, you will be given a tooltip that is locked on that particular station and tracks your offset from the alignment (Figure 2.9). You can graphically choose an offset by picking in the drawing, or you can type an offset value in the command line.

FIGURE 2.8
The Line By Station/ Offset command provides a tooltip to track stationing along the alignment.

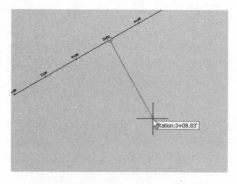

FIGURE 2.9
The Line By Station/ Offset command gives a tooltip to track the offset from the alignment.

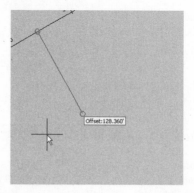

LINE BY SIDE SHOT COMMAND

The Line By Side Shot command allows you to occupy one point, designate a backsight, and draw a line that has endpoints relative to that point. The occupied point represents the setup of your surveying station, whereas the second point represents your surveying backsight. This tool may be most useful when creating stakeout information or re-creating data from field notes. If you know where your crew set up and you have their sideshot angle measurements but you do not have electronic information to download, this tool can help. To specify locations relative to your occupied point, you can specify the angle, bearing, deflection, or azimuth in the command line or simply pick locations in your drawing.

While active in the command, you can toggle between angle, bearing, deflection, and azimuth by following the command-line prompts.

When using the Line By Side Shot command, you will be given a setup glyph at your occupied point, a backsight glyph, and a tooltip to track the angle, bearing, deflection, or azimuth of the side shot (Figure 2.10). You can toggle between these options by following the command-line prompts.

LINE EXTENSION COMMAND

The Line Extension command is very similar to the AutoCAD Lengthen command. This command allows you to add length to a line or specify a desired total length of line.

You will first be prompted to choose a line. The command line will then prompt you to "Specify distance to change or [Total]." This distance is added to the existing length of the line. The command draws the line appropriately and also provides a short summary report on that line. The summary report in Figure 2.11 indicates that the beginning line length was 100 feet and that an additional distance of 50 feet was specified with the Line Extension command.

FIGURE 2.10

The tooltip for the Line By Side Shot command tracks the angle, bearing, deflection, or azimuth of the side shot.

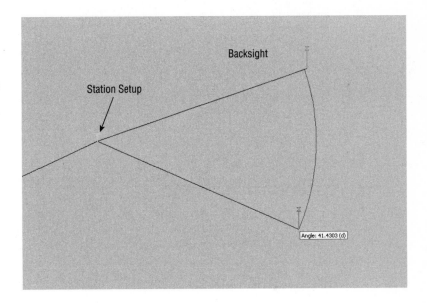

FIGURE 2.11

The Line Extension command provides a summary of the changes to the line.

```
Select line object:
Specify distance to change, or [Total]: 50
--------------------------------------------------------------------------------
                             LINE DATA
--------------------------------------------------------------------------------
Begin . . . . .  North: 6935078.5251'      East: 2450248.0169'
End . . . . . .  North: 6935199.4098'      East: 2450336.8251'
                 Distance: 150.000'      Course: N36° 18' 11"E
```

If, instead, you specify a total distance on the command line, then the length of the line will be changed to the distance you specify. The summary report shown in Figure 2.12 indicates that the beginning on the line was the same as that in Figure 2.11 but with a total length of only 100 feet.

LINE FROM END OF OBJECT COMMAND

The Line From End Of Object command allows you to draw a line tangent to the end of a line or arc of your choosing. Most commonly, you'd use this tool when re-creating deeds or other survey work where you have to specify a line that continues a tangent from an arc (see Figure 2.13).

FIGURE 2.12

The summary report on a line where the command specified a total distance

```
LINEEXTENSION
Select line object:
Specify distance to change, or [Total]: t
Specify total distance, or [Change]: 100
--------------------------------------------------------------------------------
                                  LINE DATA
--------------------------------------------------------------------------------
Begin . . . . .  North: 6935078.5251'       East: 2450248.0169'
End . . . . . .  North: 6935159.1149'       East: 2450307.2223'
                 Distance: 100.000'          Course: N36° 18' 11"E
```

FIGURE 2.13

The Line From End Of Object command can add a tangent line to the end of the arc.

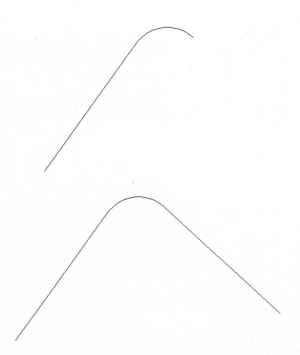

LINE TANGENT FROM POINT COMMAND

The Line Tangent From Point command is similar to the Line From End Of Object command, but Line Tangent From Point allows you to choose a point of tangency that is not the endpoint of the line or arc (Figure 2.14).

FIGURE 2.14

The Line Tangent From Point command can place a line tangent to the midpoint of an arc (or line).

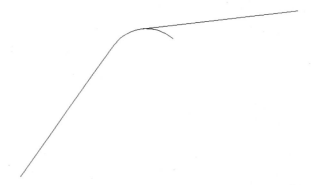

LINE PERPENDICULAR FROM POINT COMMAND

Using the Line Perpendicular From Point command, you can specify that you would like a line drawn perpendicular to any point of your choosing. In this example (Figure 2.15), a line is drawn perpendicular to the endpoint of the arc.

FIGURE 2.15

A perpendicular line is drawn from the endpoint of an arc, using the Line Perpendicular From Point command.

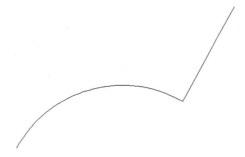

Curves

Curves are an important part of surveying and engineering geometry. In truth, curves are no different from AutoCAD arcs. What makes the curve commands unique from the basic AutoCAD commands is not the resulting arc entity but the inputs used to draw that arc. In other words, Civil 3D wants us to provide directions to these line commands in survey terminology rather than generic Cartesian parameters.

Please refer to the Civil 3D Users Guide PDF (located under the Help menu), Chapter 17, "Lines and Curves," page 518, for a figure showing all the different curve parameters used by AutoCAD Civil 3D 2008. Figure 2.16 shows the menu options.

FIGURE 2.16

Create Curves commands

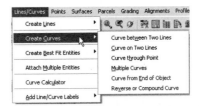

Standard Curves

When re-creating legal descriptions for roads, easements, and properties, we often encounter a variety of curves. Though standard AutoCAD arcs could draw these arcs, the AutoCAD arc inputs are designed to be generic to all industries. The following curve commands have been designed to provide an interface that more closely matches surveying and engineering language.

CURVE BETWEEN TWO LINES COMMAND

The Curve Between Two Lines command is very much like the standard AutoCAD Fillet command except that you are not just limited to a radius parameter. The command draws a curve that is tangent to two lines of your choosing. This command also trims or extends the original tangents so that their endpoints coincide with the curve endpoints. In other words, the lines are trimmed or extended to the resulting PC and PT of the curve. You might find this command most useful when creating foundation geometry for road alignments, parcel boundary curves, and other similar situations.

The command prompts you to choose the first tangent and then the second tangent. The command line gives the following prompt:

```
Select entry [Tangent/External/Degree/Chord/~CA
Length/Mid-Ordinate/miN-dist/Radius]<Radius>:
```

Pressing ↵ at this prompt allows you to input your desired radius. Pressing T changes the input parameter to tangent, pressing C changed the input parameter to chord, and so on.

As with the Fillet command, your inputs must be geometrically possible. For example, your two lines must allow for a curve of your specifications to be drawn while remaining tangent to both. Figure 2.17 shows two lines with a 25´ radius curve drawn between them. Note that the tangents have been trimmed so that their endpoints coincide with the endpoints of the curve. If either line had been too short to meet the endpoint of the curve, then that line would have been extended.

FIGURE 2.17
Two lines before (a) and after (b) using the Curve Between Two Lines command

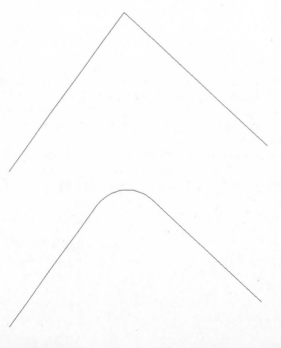

CURVE ON TWO LINES COMMAND

The Curve On Two Lines command is identical to the Curve Between Two Lines command except that the Curve On Two Lines command leaves the chosen tangents intact. In other words, the lines are not trimmed or extended to the resulting PC and PT of the curve.

Figure 2.18, for example, shows two lines with a 25′ radius curve drawn on them. The tangents have not been trimmed, and instead remain exactly like they were drawn before the Curve On Two Lines command was executed.

FIGURE 2.18
The original lines will stay exactly the same after executing the Curve On Two Lines command.

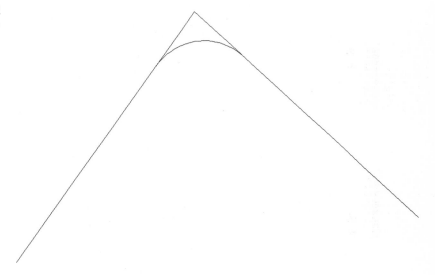

CURVE THROUGH POINT COMMAND

The Curve Through Point command lets you two choose two tangents for your curve followed by a pass-through point. This tool is most useful when you do not know the radius, length, or other curve parameters but you have two tangents and a target location. It is not necessary that the pass-through location be a true point object; it can be any location of your choosing.

This command also trims or extends the original tangents so that their endpoints coincide with the curve endpoints. In other words, the lines are trimmed or extended to the resulting PC and PT of the curve.

Figure 2.19, for example, shows two lines and a desired pass-through point. Using the Curve Through Point command allows you to draw a curve that is tangent to both lines and that passes through the desired point. In this case, however, the tangents have been trimmed to the PC and PT of the curve.

FIGURE 2.19
(a) Two lines with a
desired pass-through
point. (b) The Curve
Through Point com-
mand draws a curve
that is tangent to both
lines and passes
through a chosen
point.

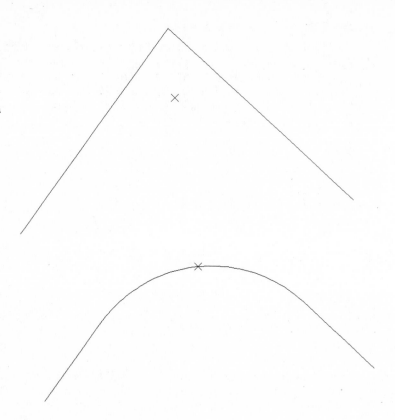

MULTIPLE CURVES COMMAND

The Multiple Curves command allows you to create several curves that are connected. The resulting curves have an effect similar to an alignment spiral section.

The command prompts you for the two tangents. Then the command line prompts as follows:

```
Enter Number of Curves:
```

The command allows for up to 10 curves between tangents:

```
Enter Floating Curve #:
```

One of your curves must have a flexible length that will be determined on the basis of the lengths,
radii, and geometric constraints of the other curves. Curves are counted clockwise, so enter the
number of your flexible curves:

```
Enter curve 1 Radius:
Enter curve 1 Length:
```

Enter the length and radii for all of your curves. The floating curve number will prompt you for a
radius but not a length.

Like all other curve commands, the specified geometry must be possible. If the command cannot find a solution on the basis of your length and radius inputs, it will return no solution (see
Figure 2.20).

FIGURE 2.20
Two curves were specified with the #2 curve designated as the floating curve.

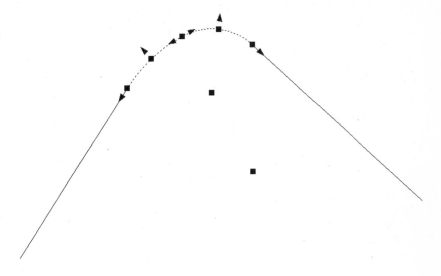

CURVE FROM END OF OBJECT COMMAND

The Curve From End Of Object command enables you to draw a curve tangent to the end of your chosen line or arc.

The command prompts you to choose an object to serve as the beginning of your curve. You can then specify a radius and an additional parameter (such as delta, length, and so on) for the curve or the endpoint of the resulting curve chord (see Figure 2.21).

FIGURE 2.21
A curve, with a 25´ radius and a 30´ length, drawn from the end of a line

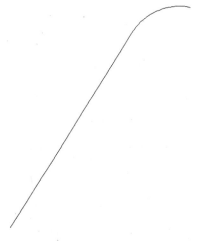

REVERSE OR COMPOUND CURVES COMMAND

The Reverse Or Compound Curves command allows you to add additional curves to the end of an existing curve. Reverse curves are drawn in the opposite direction from the original curve to form an S shape. In contrast, compound curves are drawn in the same direction as the original curve (see Figure 2.22). You'll find this tool most useful when re-creating a legal description of a road alignment that contains reverse or compound curves.

FIGURE 2.22
(a) A tangent and curve before adding a reverse or compound curve. (b) A compound curve drawn from the end of the original curve. (c) A reverse curve drawn from the end of the original curve.

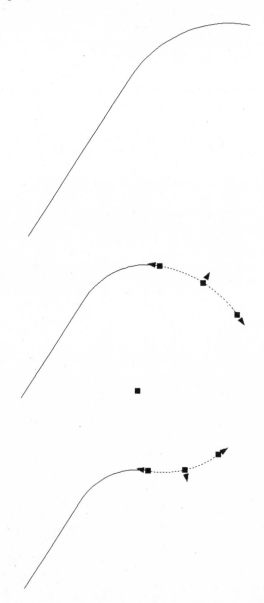

Best Fit Entities

Although we do our best to make surveying and engineering exact sciences, there comes a time when we need tools like the Best Fit Entities commands.

Roads in many parts of the world have no defined alignment. They may have been old carriage roads or cart paths from hundreds of years ago that evolved into automobile roads. Surveyors and engineers are often called to help establish official alignments, vertical alignments, and right-of-way lines for such roads on the basis of a best fit of surveyed centerline data.

Other examples for using Best Fit Entities include property lines of agreement, road rehabilitation projects, and other cases where existing survey information must be approximated into "real" engineering geometry (see Figure 2.23).

CREATE LINE COMMAND

The Create Line command under the Create Best Fit Entities option takes a series of Civil 3D points, AutoCAD points, or entities or drawing locations and draws a single best-fit line segment from this information. In Figure 2.24, for example, the Create Line By Best Fit command draws a best-fit line through a series of points that are not quite collinear. Note that the best-fit line will change as more points are picked.

Once you have selected your points, a Panorama window (Figure 2.25) appears showing you information about each point you chose.

FIGURE 2.23
The Create Best Fit Entities menu options

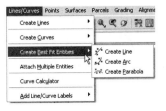

FIGURE 2.24
A preview line drawn through points that are not quite collinear

FIGURE 2.25
The Panorama window allows you to optimize your best fit.

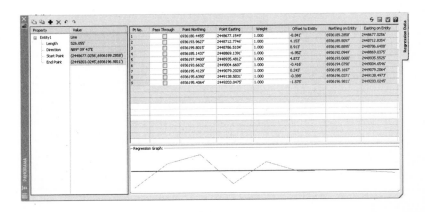

This interface allows you to optimize your best fit by adding more points, checking the Pass Through column to force one of your points on the line, or adjusting the value under the Weight column, as shown in Figure 2.26.

CREATE ARC COMMAND

The Create Arc command under the Create Best Fit Entities option works identically to the Create Line command under this option, except the resulting entity is a single-arc segment as opposed to a single-line segment (see Figure 2.27).

CREATE PARABOLA COMMAND

The Create Parabola command under the Create Best Fit Entities option works in a similar way to the line and arc commands we've described. This command will be most useful when you have TIN sampled or surveyed road information and you would like to replicate true vertical curves for your design information.

After selecting this command, the Parabola By Best Fit dialog appears (see Figure 2.28).

You can select inputs from entities (such as lines, arcs, polylines, or profile objects) or by picking on screen. The command then draws a best-fit parabola on the basis of this information. In Figure 2.29, our shots were represented by AutoCAD points, so we selected the By Clicking On The Screen option and used the Node osnap to pick each point.

Once you have selected your points, a Panorama window appears showing information about each point you chose. Also note the information in the right-hand pane regarding K-value, curve length, grades, and so forth.

FIGURE 2.26
The resulting best-fit line through a series of points that are not collinear

FIGURE 2.27
The Create Arc command under the Create Best Fit Entities option

FIGURE 2.28
The Parabola By Best Fit dialog

In this interface (Figure 2.30), you can optimize your K-value, length, and other values by adding more points, checking the Pass Through column to force one of your points on the line, or adjusting the value under the Weight column.

FIGURE 2.29
The best-fit preview line changes as more points are picked.

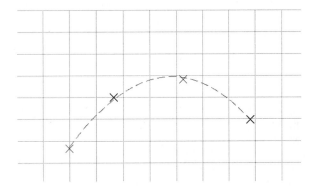

FIGURE 2.30
The Panorama window allows you to make adjustments to your best-fit parabola.

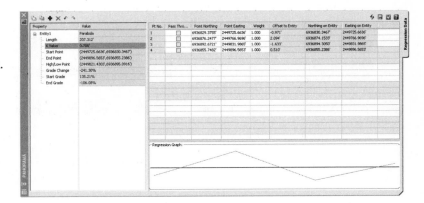

Attach Multiple Entities

The Attach Multiple Entities command combines the Line From End Of Object and Curve From End Of Object commands. This command will be most useful for reconstructing deeds or road alignments from legal descriptions when each entity is tangent to the previous entity. Using this command saves you time because you do not have to constantly switch between the Line From End Of Object and Curve From End Of Object commands (see Figure 2.31).

FIGURE 2.31
The Attach Multiple Entities command draws a series of lines and arcs so that each segment is tangent to the previous one.

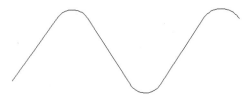

The Curve Calculator

There are times when you do not have enough information to draw a curve properly. Though many of the curve creation tools we discussed will assist you in calculating the curve parameters, you may find an occasion where the deed you are working with is simply incomplete.

The Curve Calculator will assist you in calculating a full collection of curve parameters on the basis of your known values and constraints. The units used in the Curve Calculator match the units assigned in your Drawing settings.

The Curve Calculator can remain open on your screen while you are working through commands. You can send any value in the Calculator to the command line by pushing the button next to that value (see Figure 2.32).

The button at the top left of the Curve Calculator will inherit the arc properties from an existing arc in the drawing, and a dropdown list box in the Degree Of Curve Definition selection field allows you to choose whether to calculate parameters for an arc or a chord definition.

A dropdown list box in the Fixed Property selection field also gives you the choice of fixing your radius or delta value (Figure 2.33) when calculating the values for an arc or a chord, respectively. Whichever parameter is chosen as the fixed value will be held constant as additional parameters are calculated.

As we explained, any value in the Curve Calculator can be sent to the command line using the button next to that value (Figure 2.34). This would be most useful while you are active in a curve command and would like to use a certain parameter value to complete the command.

FIGURE 2.32

The Curve Calculator

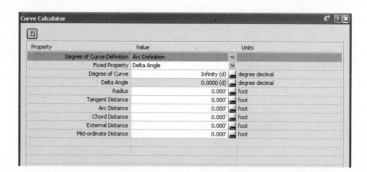

FIGURE 2.33

A dropdown gives you the choice of fixing your radius or delta value.

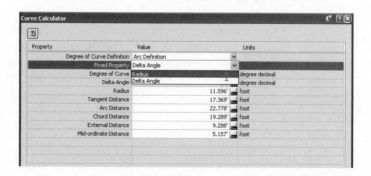

FIGURE 2.34
Click the button next
to any value to send
it to the command line.

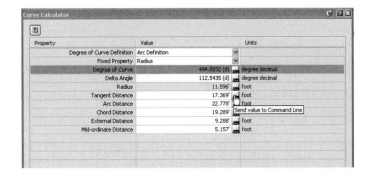

Line and Curve Labels

While most robust labeling of site geometry is handled using Parcel or Alignment labels, there are limited line and curve annotation tools in Civil 3D (see Figure 2.35).

You can add the general line and curve labels by using the menu options shown in Figure 2.36.

FIGURE 2.35
A typical curve label
and line label

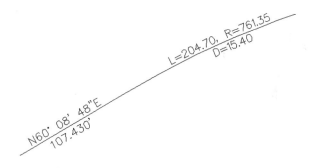

FIGURE 2.36
Add Line/Curve
Labels

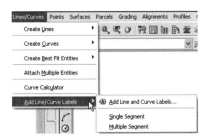

WHAT IF YOU NEED TAG LABELS OR A SEGMENT TABLE?

Before using the general line and curve labels, be sure that you will not need to create tags or a segment table for your entities. General line labels do not include segment tags or table capabilities. If you need to create tags and/or tables, please see Chapter 6 on parcels and Chapter 7 on alignments.

The line and curve labels are composed much the same way as other Civil 3D labels, with marked similarities to Parcel and Alignment Segment labels (see Figure 2.37).

The text style, layer, orientation, and readability are some of the settings on the General tab of the Label Style Composer (Figure 2.38).

The Layout tab of the Label Style Composer for line labels allows for text, line, block, direction arrow, and reference text (Figure 2.39). Note that settings and options in the Layout tab are identical to other Civil 3D labels, such as anchor components, text size, and so on.

Many properties of lines can be labeled including length, direction, and the starting and ending coordinates (Figure 2.40). If you are labeling a polyline, you can create a label with an overall length. If you are labeling a closed polyline, you can label with an overall area.

The Layout tab for a curve label is similar to that of a line label, with one exception: curves cannot have a direction arrow (see Figure 2.41).

As with lines, many properties of a curve can be labeled, including length, radius, coordinates, and more.

FIGURE 2.37

The general line and curve labels provided by _AutoCAD Civil 3D (Imperial) NCS Extended.dwt

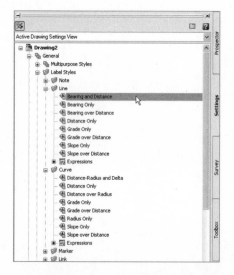

FIGURE 2.38

The General tab of the Label Style Composer for line labels

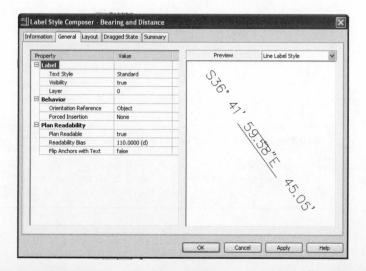

FIGURE 2.39
The Layout tab of the
Label Style Composer
for line labels

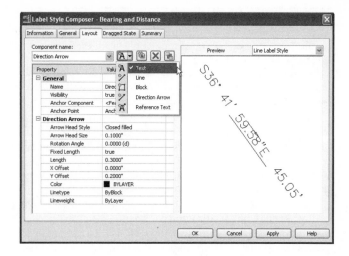

FIGURE 2.40
The Text Compo-
nent Editor for
line label text

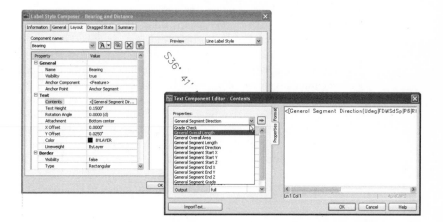

FIGURE 2.41
The Layout tab of the
Label Style Composer
for a curve label

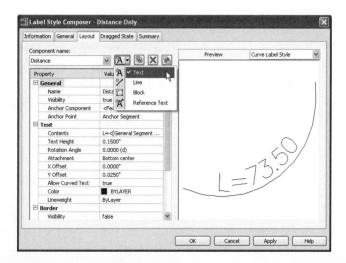

Transparent Commands

In many cases, the "line" entries under the Lines and Curves menu are simply the standard AutoCAD Line command combined with the appropriate transparent command.

A transparent command behaves somewhat similarly to an osnap command. You cannot simply click the endpoint button and expect anything to happen—you must be active inside another command, such as a line, arc, or circle command.

The same principle works for transparent commands. Once active in the Line command (or any AutoCAD or Civil 3D drawing command), you can choose the Bearing Distance transparent command and complete your drawing task using a bearing and distance.

As stated earlier, the transparent commands can be used within any AutoCAD or Civil 3D drawing command, much like an osnap. For example, you can be actively drawing an alignment and use the Northing/Easting transparent command to "snap" to a particular coordinate, then press Esc once and continue drawing your alignment as normal.

While active in a transparent command, you can press Esc once to leave the transparent mode but stay active in your current command. You can then choose another transparent command if you'd like. For example, you can start a line using the Endpoint osnap, activate the Angle Distance transparent command, draw a line-by-angle distance, and then press Esc, which takes you out of angle distance mode but keeps you in the Line command. You can then draw a few more segments using the Point Object transparent command, press Esc, and then finish your line with a Perpendicular osnap.

The transparent commands can be activated using keyboard shortcuts (see Chapter 35 of the Civil 3D Users Guide PDF for more information) or by using the Transparent Commands toolbar. Be sure you include the Transparent Commands toolbar (Figure 2.42) in all of your Civil 3D and survey-oriented workspaces.

The six profile-related transparent commands will be covered in Chapter 8.

FIGURE 2.42
The Transparent
Commands toolbar

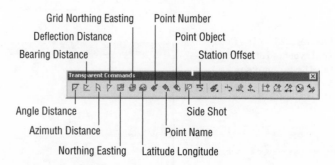

Standard Transparent Commands

The transparent commands shown in Table 2.1 behave identically to their like-named counterparts from the Lines/Curves menu (discussed earlier in this chapter). The difference is that these transparent commands can be called up in any appropriate AutoCAD or Civil 3D draw command, such as a line, polyline, alignment, parcel segment, or pipe creation command.

TABLE 2.1:   The transparent commands

Tool Icon	Menu Command
	Angle Distance
	Bearing Distance
	Azimuth Distance
	Deflection Distance
	Northing Easting
	Grid Northing Easting
	Latitude Longitude
	Point Number
	Point Name
	Point Object
	Side Shot
	Station Offset

Matching Transparent Commands

We often have construction or other geometry in our drawing that we would like to match with new lines, arcs, circles, alignments, parcel segments, or other entities.

While actively drawing an object that has a radius parameter, such as a circle, arc, alignment curve, or similar object, you can choose the Match Radius transparent command 🟢, then select an object in your drawing that has your desired radius. Civil 3D will draw the resulting entity with a radius identical to that of the object you chose during the command. You will save time using this tool because you don't have to first list the radius of the original object, then manually type in that radius when prompted by your circle, arc, or alignment tool.

The Match Length transparent command 🔧 works identically to the Match Radius transparent command except that it matches the length parameter of your chosen object.

Inquiry Commands

A large part of a surveyor's work involves querying lines and curves for their length, direction, and other parameters. The Inquiry Commands toolbar (Figure 2.43) provides a robust set of tools for navigating the coordinate geometry in the drawing.

The Inquiry Commands toolbar is in the Civil toolbar collection and makes a valuable addition to your Civil 3D and survey-related workspaces.

FIGURE 2.43

The Inquiry tool

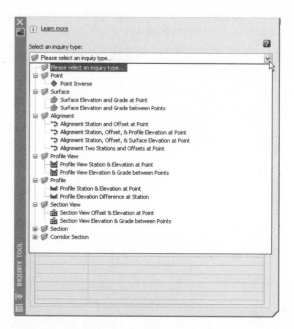

The Inquiry tool (see Figure 2.44) provides a diverse collection of commands that assist you in studying Civil 3D objects. Since the focus of this chapter is linework as opposed to Civil 3D objects, we won't have a detailed discussion about this tool right now.

For more information on any of the following inquiry commands, see Chapter 36 of the Civil 3D Users Guide PDF.

The Line and Arc Information tool provides a short report about the line or arc of your choosing (see Figure 2.45). This tool also works on parcel segments and alignment segments. Alternatively, you can type **P** for points at the command line to get information about the apparent line that would connect two points on screen.

The Angle Information Inquiry tool allows you to pick two lines (or a series of points on the screen). It provides information about the acute and obtuse angles between those two lines. Again, this also works for alignment segments and parcel segments.

The Continuous Distance tool provides a sum of distances between several points on your screen, or one base point and several points.

FIGURE 2.44

The Inquiry Commands toolbar

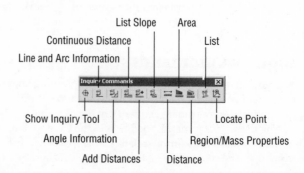

The Add Distances tool ▣ is similar to the Continuous Distance command, except the points on your screen do not have to be continuous.

The List Slope tool ▣ provides a short command-line report (like the one in Figure 2.46) that lists the elevations and slope of an entity (or two points) that you choose, such as a line or feature line.

The Distance tool ▣ is the standard AutoCAD Distance command that you may already be familiar with. This command measures the distance between two points on your screen.

The Area tool ▣ is the standard AutoCAD Area command. This tool allows you to calculate the area and perimeter of several points on your screen.

The Region/Mass Properties tool ▣ allows you to learn about the properties of a region or solid. Since it is rare that you will create such an object while working with survey-type data, you may not use this too frequently.

The List tool ▣ is the standard AutoCAD List command. This tool provides an AutoCAD text window report of the entity type and some properties.

The Locate Point tool ▣ is identical to the standard AutoCAD ID command. This tool provides a short command-line report of the X, Y and Z coordinates of any location you select on your screen. You might most commonly use this tool for studying part of a surface to identify its Z elevation.

FIGURE 2.45
The results of a line inquiry and an arc inquiry

```
Select object or [Points]:
-----------------------------------------------------------------
                         LINE DATA
-----------------------------------------------------------------
Begin . . . . .   X: 2449247.950'       Y: 6935520.120'
End . . . . . .   X: 2449743.105'       Y: 6935520.120'
                  Distance: 495.155'        Course: N90° 00' 00"E

Select object or [Points]:
-----------------------------------------------------------------
                         ARC DATA
-----------------------------------------------------------------
Begin . . . . .   X: 2449247.950'       Y: 6935520.120'
Radial Point. .   X: 2449247.950'       Y: 6935495.120'
End . . . . . .   X: 2449223.048'       Y: 6935497.327'
PI . . . . . .    X: 2449225.068'       Y: 6935520.120'
    Tangent: 22.882'      Chord: 33.759'      Course: S47° 31' 57"W
Arc Length: 37.060'      Radius: 25.000'       Delta: 84.9350 (d)
```

FIGURE 2.46
The List Slope command-line report

```
Select object or [Points]:
First elev: 5.000', Second elev: 10.000', Elev diff: 5.000'
Grade: 2.37%, Slope: 42.28:1, Horiz dist: 211.389'

Select object or [Points]:
```

Drawing Settings

As we have worked through this chapter, there have been several places where your Drawing settings have come into play. Let's take a look at a few of the locations where settings such as the coordinate system, precision, and units should be established.

You access the Drawing Settings dialog by right-clicking on the drawing name on the Settings tab of Toolspace.

Drawing Settings: Units And Zone

In this chapter, we've noted several tools that require you to assign a coordinate system to your drawing. The coordinate system, among other settings, is assigned on the Units And Zone tab of the Drawing Settings dialog (see Figure 2.47).

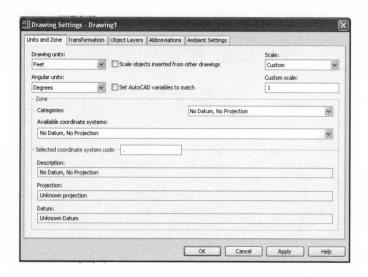

Drawing Settings: Ambient Settings

The Ambient Settings establish the default settings for all commands in Civil 3D. These settings can be overridden at the individual command settings level.

For example, perhaps your default precision for distance is three decimal places, but for Alignment Layout you would like to track eight decimal places. You can make that change under the Alignment Commands tree on the Settings tab of Toolspace (see Figure 2.48).

Although many of the ambient settings apply to the creation of coordinate geometry, there are two categories that frequently need adjusting (see Figure 2.49).

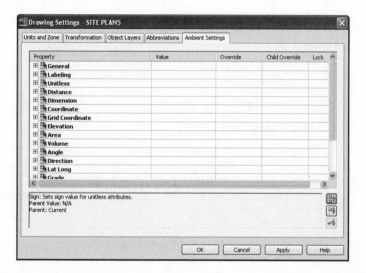

FIGURE 2.49
The Ambient Settings
for Direction

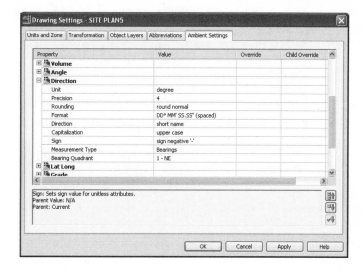

FIGURE 2.49
The Ambient Settings
for Direction

DRAWING PRECISION VS. LABEL PRECISION

Label styles can be created to annotate your objects using different precision, units, or specifications than those set in the ambient or command settings dialog. Establish settings to reflect how you would like to input and track your data, not necessarily how you would like to label your data.

The Ambient Settings for Direction offer the following choices:

◆ Unit: Degree, Radian, Grad

◆ Precision: 0 through 8 decimal places

◆ Rounding: Round Normal, Round Up, Truncate

◆ Format: Decimal, two types of DDMMSS, and Decimal DMS

◆ Direction: Short Name (spaced or unspaced), Long Name (spaced or unspaced)

◆ Capitalization

◆ Sign

◆ Measurement Type: Bearings, North Azimuth, South Azimuth

◆ Bearing Quadrant

From this list, it becomes clear where these settings would apply to the tools discussed in this chapter. When using the Bearing Distance transparent command, for example, these settings control how you input your quadrant, your bearing, and the number of decimal places in your distance.

Explore the other categories, such as Angle, Lat Long, and Coordinate, and customize the settings to how you work.

At the bottom of the Ambient Settings tab, there is a category called Transparent Commands (see Figure 2.50):

Prompt For 3D Points   Controls whether you are asked to provide a Z elevation after X and Y have been located.

Prompt Y Before X   Specifies your preference for Y and X.

Prompt For Easting Then Northing   Specifies your preference for Northing and Easting.

Prompt For Longitude Then Latitude   Specifies your preference for Longitude, then Latitude.

FIGURE 2.50

The Transparent
Commands area
of the Ambient
Settings tab

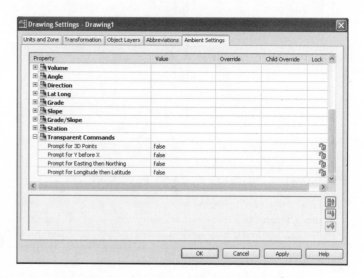

Real World Scenario

RE-CREATING A DEED USING COORDINATE GEOMETRY TOOLS

This exercise will help you apply some of the tools learned in this chapter to reconstruct a typical property deed.

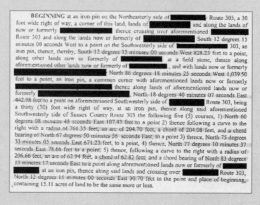

For this exercise, we will use information adapted from a property deed. You can see the original legal description in the accompanying illustration. For ease of reading and clarity, we've summarized the description here:

```
From Point of Beginning
Lines:
South 12 degrees 15 minutes 00 seconds West 828.23 feet to a point
North 86 degrees 18 minutes 25 seconds West 1039.50 feet to a point
North 18 degrees 40 minutes 07 seconds East 442.98 feet to a point
North 60 degrees 08 minutes 48 seconds East 107.43 feet to a point
Curve to the RIGHT:
Radius 761.35 feet
Arc length 204.70
Chord Length 204.08 feet
Chord Bearing North 67 degrees 50 minutes 56 seconds East to a point
Lines:
North 75 degrees 33 minutes 05 seconds East 671.23 feet to a point
North 77 degrees 10 minutes 37 seconds East 78.66 feet to a point
Curve to the RIGHT:
Radius 937.094
Arc length 62.94 feet
Chord Length 62.82
Chord Bearing North 79 degrees 52 seconds 29 minutes East
Returning to Point of Beginning
The resulting enclosure should be: 15.11 acres (more or less)
```

1. Open the Deed Create Start.dwg file.

2. Before beginning the exercise, locate the ambient settings for this drawing, and note that the Direction option is currently set to DD.MMSSSS (decimal DMS). If you are more comfortable with another input format, feel free to change this setting. Explore the other settings and make similar adjustments as necessary.

3. Pick a beginning point anywhere in the drawing and execute either the Lines/Curves ➤ Create Lines ➤ Line By Bearing/Distance or the regular AutoCAD Line command and the Bearing Distance transparent command. Create the first four line courses.

4. When you arrive at the first curve, it might be helpful to use the Curve Calculator to confirm all the curve values.

5. Place the first curve. There are several ways you could approach creating the curve. Since we have been given radius and length, we can use the Curve From End Of Object command. Alternatively, since there is chord bearing and distance as well, we could draw the chord as a line and come back to place a curve between the two endpoints. The Curve From End Of Object command, where you specify radius and then the length, is our first choice in this situation.

6. Resume the Line By Bearing/Distance or Line with the Bearing Distance transparent command and create the next two courses.

7. Create the final curve.

8. Note any errors in closure. This deed has a closing error of 4.56~. Typically, rounding errors, especially with the different curve parameters, can cause an error in closure. Perhaps reworking the deed holding a different curve parameter would improve your results. Consult your office survey expert in how this would be handled in house, and refer to Chapter 3 for more information about traverse adjustment and similar tools.

9. Use Lines/Curves ➢ Add Line/Curve Labels ➢ Multiple Segments to add labels to each line and curve that you just drew.

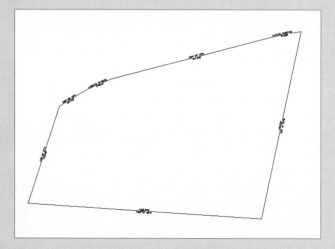

10. Use the Line and Arc information Inquiry tool on the Inquiry Commands toolbar to list the first line of the deed. Note that though the command-line report lists Course (direction) in a format that matches the ambient settings, the line label shows the course as S12°15′00″. Civil 3D labels can be customized to annotate the raw drawing information in many different ways.

11. Once you are satisfied with the line and curve geometry, you can save this drawing and come back to it in Chapter 6 for further study and subdivision.

12. A completed drawing (Deed Create Finished.dwg) is in the data folder for Chapter 2 on this book's CD for you to check your work.

The Bottom Line

Create a series of lines by bearing and distance. By far the most commonly used command when re-creating a deed is Line By Bearing and Distance.

Master It Open the Mastering Lines and Curves.dwg file. Start from the Civil 3D point labeled START and use any appropriate tool to create lines with the following bearings and distances (note that the Direction input format for this drawing has been set to DD.MMSSSS):

N 57°06′56.75″ E; 135.441′

S 41°57′03.67″ E; 118.754′

S 27°44′41.63″ W; 112.426′

N 50°55′57.00″ W; 181.333′

Use the Inquiry commands to confirm that lines are drawn correctly.

Master It   Continue working in your drawing. Use any appropriate Inquiry command to confirm that each line has been drawn correctly.

Create a curve tangent to the end of a line.   It is rare that a property stands alone. Often, there are adjacent properties, easements, or alignments that must be created from their legal descriptions.

Master It   Create a curve tangent to the end of the first line drawn in the first exercise that meets the following specifications:

Radius: 200.00′; Arc Length: 66.580′

Create a best-fit line for a series of Civil 3D points.   Surveyed point data is rarely perfect. When creating drawing linework, it is often necessary to create a best-fit line to make up for irregular shots.

Master It   Locate the Edge of Pavement (EOP) points in the drawing. Use the Line By Best Fit command to create a line using these points.

Label lines and curves.   Though converting linework to parcels or alignments offers you the most robust labeling and analysis options, basic line and curve labeling tools are available when conversion is not appropriate.

Master It   Add line and curve labels to each entity created in the exercises. Choose a label that will specify the bearing and distance for your lines and length, radius, and delta of your curve.

Chapter 3

Lay of the Land: Survey

All civil-engineering projects start with a survey. Base maps provide engineers with data, which normally contain existing conditions. These maps can be used to develop an engineering-design model. Civil 3D 2008 provides an integrated solution that surveyors can use to create base maps that will reside in the same native format that the engineers will use, thus reducing potential (and costly) errors that result from translating data from one design software to another. In this chapter, you will learn tools and techniques that will link your survey equipment directly into the software, automate your drafting procedures from fieldwork, and provide a secure and independent database for storing and manipulating your survey data.

In this chapter, you will learn to

◆ Properly collect field data and import it into AutoCAD Civil 3D 2008

◆ Set up styles that will correctly display your linework

◆ Create and edit fieldbook files

◆ Manipulate your survey data

Understanding the Concepts

Before you start working with the survey portion of Civil 3D, you first need to understand some basic concepts. When the majority of people think about surveying in any software, they generally think about going out into the field with a survey instrument and some form of data collection and returning to the office with a group of points—text entities with unique identifiers, northings, eastings, elevations, and some sort of descriptors. That point file, whether it be in ASCII format, text format, CSV format, or otherwise, is imported into a survey program that displays those points in some way, allowing drafters to essentially play a game of "connect the dots" to create a base plan. However, with the survey crew and the office staff working together, much of the "connect-the-dots" game can be played in the field. For example, in Figure 3.1, parking stripes, curb and gutter, asphalt, and concrete features have been connected correctly in the field with figures. This is important to surveyors because it has the potential to reduce liability—always an important topic of conversation with surveyors. Since the field crew is on site and have actually witnessed existing conditions, they are in a better position to create the linework than a drafter who may have never seen the site.

Aside from having to get the survey field crew and the office staff working in harmony, there are a few other things that you need to know. The first thing to know is that the survey functionality in Civil 3D doesn't use the old Point, Northing, Easting, Zed, Description (PNEZD) text file, but uses the RAW data from your data collector to process an Autodesk Fieldbook (FBK) file. Granted, the option to use the PNEZD file is still there if you want dumb points. But if you use an FBK file for your surveys, you have much more than just points on a screen—you actually have a record of how those points were collected. You will have the information needed to be able to edit this file if needed. Instead of calculating new coordinates for a bad point, you will actually be able to navigate to the setup from which that point was collected and edit the rod height, instrument height, vertical angle, horizontal angle, or any other information that can be input directly into a data collector. This information is imported, stored, and manipulated in the survey database. The survey database is simply a Microsoft Access–formatted database file with all the information required to create the survey network, as shown in Figure 3.2.

FIGURE 3.1
A portion of an as-built survey created with Civil 3D

Observation : Table

Id	Point	Data0	Data1	Data2	Mask	ObservationTyp	CorrectionPress	EquipmentNam	EquipmentEdm	EquipmentCarrierWaveCo	EquipmentFreq	EquipmentCent	EquipmentTarg	EquipmentPoint
38	111	570099.037092	316093.630042	226.545648	28	56	-1E+20	5605	3.04800609601	105.45	287.96	0.00152400305	0.00152400305	1.2120342E-05
40	112	570126.374702	316314.731962	231.3727656	28	56	-1E+20	5605	3.04800609601	105.45	287.96	0.00152400305	0.00152400305	1.2120342E-05
42	113	570152.962613	316566.222442	236.6772	28	56	-1E+20	5605	3.04800609601	105.45	287.96	0.00152400305	0.00152400305	1.2120342E-05
44	114	570144.764712	316605.203009	236.934756	28	56	-1E+20	5605	3.04800609601	105.45	287.96	0.00152400305	0.00152400305	1.2120342E-05
47	1000	570190.870894	316060.050835	227.8596408	28	56	-1E+20	5605	3.04800609601	105.45	287.96	0.00152400305	0.00152400305	1.2120342E-05
49	1001	570178.128425	316061.247175	227.1787176	28	56	-1E+20	5605	3.04800609601	105.45	287.96	0.00152400305	0.00152400305	1.2120342E-05
51	1002	570175.723553	316061.459926	227.0738664	28	56	-1E+20	5605	3.04800609601	105.45	287.96	0.00152400305	0.00152400305	1.2120342E-05
53	1003	570173.054419	316061.777832	226.9370112	28	56	-1E+20	5605	3.04800609601	105.45	287.96	0.00152400305	0.00152400305	1.2120342E-05
55	1004	570169.395906	316062.214001	226.74834	28	56	-1E+20	5605	3.04800609601	105.45	287.96	0.00152400305	0.00152400305	1.2120342E-05
57	1005	570164.726064	316062.996118	226.5371136	28	56	-1E+20	5605	3.04800609601	105.45	287.96	0.00152400305	0.00152400305	1.2120342E-05
59	1006	570160.718249	316064.05225	226.3935528	28	56	-1E+20	5605	3.04800609601	105.45	287.96	0.00152400305	0.00152400305	1.2120342E-05
61	1007	570157.892143	316065.073634	226.1686104	28	56	-1E+20	5605	3.04800609601	105.45	287.96	0.00152400305	0.00152400305	1.2120342E-05
63	1008	570151.597414	316066.923466	226.3271064	28	56	-1E+20	5605	3.04800609601	105.45	287.96	0.00152400305	0.00152400305	1.2120342E-05
65	1009	570150.900946	316064.938303	226.6047792	28	56	-1E+20	5605	3.04800609601	105.45	287.96	0.00152400305	0.00152400305	1.2120342E-05
67	1010	570146.244211	316068.34932	226.3222296	28	56	-1E+20	5605	3.04800609601	105.45	287.96	0.00152400305	0.00152400305	1.2120342E-05
69	1011	570145.380713	316068.070123	226.3258872	28	56	-1E+20	5605	3.04800609601	105.45	287.96	0.00152400305	0.00152400305	1.2120342E-05
71	1012	570145.039032	316067.375484	226.3319832	28	56	-1E+20	5605	3.04800609601	105.45	287.96	0.00152400305	0.00152400305	1.2120342E-05
73	1013	570144.606826	316063.322558	226.2749866	28	56	-1E+20	5605	3.04800609601	105.45	287.96	0.00152400305	0.00152400305	1.2120342E-05
75	1014	570128.608509	316064.180570	226.35972	28	56	-1E+20	5605	3.04800609601	105.45	287.96	0.00152400305	0.00152400305	1.2120342E-05
77	1015	570114.33348	316066.285214	226.041204	28	56	-1E+20	5605	3.04800609601	105.45	287.96	0.00152400305	0.00152400305	1.2120342E-05
79	1016	570114.751666	316066.424813	225.8616768	28	56	-1E+20	5605	3.04800609601	105.45	287.96	0.00152400305	0.00152400305	1.2120342E-05
81	1017	570114.803786	316070.531993	226.1548944	28	56	-1E+20	5605	3.04800609601	105.45	287.96	0.00152400305	0.00152400305	1.2120342E-05
83	1018	570114.632514	316071.239434	226.164648	28	56	-1E+20	5605	3.04800609601	105.45	287.96	0.00152400305	0.00152400305	1.2120342E-05

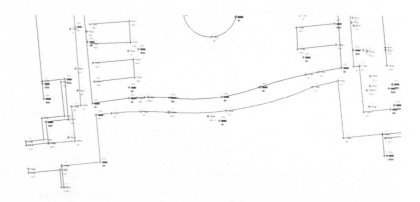

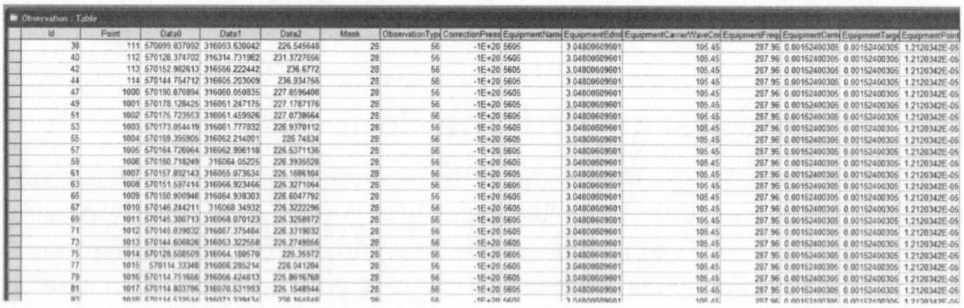

FIGURE 3.2
A sample of the data stored in a typical survey database

IF IT'S JUST A DATABASE....

You may be tempted to think that Microsoft Access would give you an easy way to externally edit this database file. However, we advise you to *not* edit this information unless you are using the Civil 3D editing functions. These database records are not exactly named with intuitive and user-friendly names, and units may not be quite what you would expect. If you choose to edit this information in an external database program, you are doing so at your own risk!

Since this survey database file is located external to the drawing, it can be used in multiple drawings simultaneously, even if those drawings have different coordinate systems. The coordinate system information is set in the survey database settings and will automatically translate to any coordinate system set up in the drawing settings. This external database requires you to treat the survey database a bit differently than you would other aspects of Civil 3D. For example, many settings will reside in the survey database settings and not in the drawing template as is common for other Civil 3D settings. Other settings will reside in the Survey User Settings dialog, as shown in Figure 3.3.

The settings in this dialog control many of the default choices for creating survey objects, much like Command settings do on the Settings tab of Civil 3D. Let's take a look at some in this exercise:

1. Create a new drawing from the NCS Extended Imperial template file.

2. On the Survey tab in Toolspace, click the Edit Survey Settings icon in the upper-left corner, as shown in Figure 3.4. If the Survey tab is not available, choose Survey ➢ Open Survey Toolspace.

3. The Survey User Settings dialog opens. Look through the options and settings and observe all the defaults that can be chosen.

4. Click Cancel to dismiss the dialog without saving any changes.

Now that we've looked at the settings, let's get into the databases behind the scenes.

FIGURE 3.3
Survey User
Settings dialog

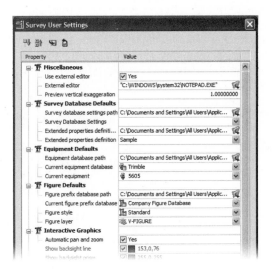

FIGURE 3.4
The Survey tab
in Toolspace

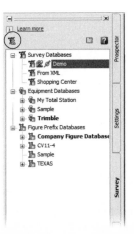

Databases Everywhere!

The Survey tab of Toolspace contains three different types of databases. The first is the survey database, where your survey networks are created and stored. This database contains the survey data that you can import into the program from the field. The equipment database is where you create replicas of your existing survey equipment for use when performing traverse analyses. The last type of database is the figure prefix database, in which you enter your figure prefixes for use when you import a fieldbook with linework into the program. First, we'll spend time looking at the last two types of databases because we'll end up creating and working with a survey database.

The Equipment Database

The equipment database is where you set up the different types of survey equipment that you are using in the field. This will allow you to apply the proper correction factors to your traverse analyses when it comes time to balance your traverse. Civil 3D comes with a sample piece of equipment for you to inspect to see what information you will need when it comes time to create your equipment. The equipment Properties dialog (see Figure 3.5) provides all the default settings for the sample equipment in the equipment database. Expand the Equipment Databases ➤ Sample branches, right-click on Sample, and select Properties to access this dialog in Toolspace. You will want to create your own equipment entries and enter the specifications for your particular total station. If you are unsure of the settings to enter, refer to the user documentation that you received when you purchased your total station.

FIGURE 3.5
The Equipment
Properties dialog

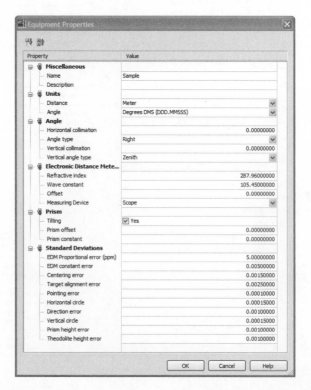

The Figure Prefix Database

Figures are created by codes entered into the data collector during field collection. Figures can have line segments, curve segments, elevations, and linetypes or colors assigned to them. For example, your field crew may locate a water line in the field and have it come in as line segments colored blue with a waterline linetype. Or they could locate the back of a curb and display it with a solid line and a concrete style. They could set the back of this curb to come in as a breakline for surface creation. Figure 3.6 shows the Figure Prefixes Editor in Panorama.

We'll need to have some styles ready to go when we create our figures, so let's build a few now.

1. Create a new drawing from the `NCS Extended Imperial` template file.

2. In Toolspace, click the Settings tab.

3. Expand the Survey branch.

4. Right-click on Figure Styles and click New. The Figure Style dialog opens.

5. On the Information tab, enter **CL** (for Centerline) in the Name text box. This is the name of the new style you are creating.

6. Switch to the Display tab, and make sure that Figure Lines is the only Component Type that is visible. Turn off any other ones that are visible.

7. Set the Layer for the Figure Lines component to V-FIGURE by clicking in the Layer cell. The Layer Selection dialog appears, with the available layers on a dropdown list. Since V-FIGURE is not part of the template, you will have to create it. Click New to open the Create Layer dialog. Enter **V-FIGURE** as the name of your new layer. Layer settings will be unimportant for this layer, since the properties will be assigned by the style. Click OK to dismiss the Create Layer dialog, and click OK again to dismiss the Layer Selection dialog.

8. Set the Color for the Figure Lines component to Red and the Linetype to CENTER2.

9. Now create figure styles having the following names: PROP, CONC, WATER, CATV, GAS, BREAK, BLDG, and OHP. Apply different colors and linetypes to each figure style as desired. Save the drawing—you will use it in the next exercise.

10. Click OK to dismiss the Figure Style dialog.

FIGURE 3.6
The Figure Prefixes
Editor in Panorama

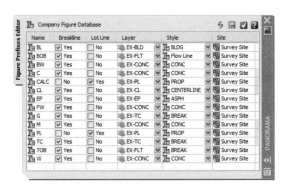

FIGURE SETTINGS

The following six settings can be specified for each figure prefix:

Name   This specifies the name of the figure prefix. The figure prefix is used when you import a fieldbook into a survey database network.

Breakline   This specifies whether the figure should be used as a breakline during surface creation. These figures will have elevation data, allowing them to be selected manually in the breakline section of the surface definition.

Lot Line   This specifies whether the figure should behave as a parcel segment. When toggled on, these figures are used to create parcels when inserted into a drawing and can be labeled as parcel segments.

Layer   This specifies the layer that the figure will reside on when inserted into the drawing. If the layer already exists in the drawing, the figure will be placed on that layer. If the layer does not exist in the drawing, the layer will be created and the figure placed on the newly created layer.

Style   This specifies the style to be used for each figure. The style contains the linetype and color of the figure. If the style exists in the current drawing, the figure will be inserted using that style. If the style does not exist in the drawing, the style will be created with the standard settings and the figure will be placed in the drawing according to the settings specified with the newly created style.

Site   This specifies which site the figures should reside on when inserted into the drawing. As with previous settings, if the site exists in the drawing, the figure will be inserted into that site. If the site does not exist in the drawing, a site will be created with that name and the figure will be inserted into the newly created site. Since a figure can create parcels and surface breaklines, this functionality can be used to place those objects on the correct site.

Now let's look at these settings in a practical exercise. We will use the styles created in the previous exercise:

1. Create a new drawing from the `NCS Extended Imperial template` file (all survey functionality requires that a drawing be open and active to use or edit any of the survey features).

2. In the Survey tab of Toolspace, right-click on Figure Prefix Databases and select New. The New Figure Prefix Database dialog opens.

3. Enter **Mastering Civil 3D** in the Name text box, and click OK to dismiss the dialog. Mastering Civil 3D will now be listed under the Figure Prefix Databases branch in the Survey tab on Toolspace.

4. Right-click on the newly created Mastering Civil 3D figure prefix database and select Edit. The Figure Prefixes Editor in Panorama will appear.

5. Right-click on the grid in the Figure Prefixes Editor and select New.

6. Double-click on the SAMPLE name and rename the figure prefix **EP** (for Edge of Pavement).

7. Check the No box in the Breakline column to change it to Yes so the figure will be treated as a breakline. Leave the box in the Lot Line column unchecked, so the figure will not be treated as a parcel segment.

8. Under the Layer column, select V-FIGURE.

9. Under the Style column, select EP.

10. Under the Site column, leave the name of the site set to Survey Site.

11. Complete the Figure Prefixes table with the values shown in Table 3.1.

12. Click the green check mark in the upper-right corner to dismiss Panorama. You will receive a message that you have made changes but not applied them. Click Yes to apply the changes.

We've completed setting up the figure prefix database, now it's time to look at actually getting some data.

TABLE 3.1: Figure Settings

NAME	BREAKLINE	LOT LINE	LAYER	STYLE	SITE
PROP	No	Yes	V-FIGURE	PROP	PROPERTY
WALK	Yes	No	V-FIGURE	CONC	SURVEY SITE
CL	Yes	No	V-FIGURE	CL	SURVEY SITE
WATER	No	No	V-FIGURE	WATER	SURVEY SITE
CATV	No	No	V-FIGURE	CATV	SURVEY SITE
GAS	No	No	V-FIGURE	GAS	SURVEY SITE
BOC	Yes	No	V-FIGURE	CONC	SURVEY SITE
GUT	Yes	No	V-FIGURE	BREAK	SURVEY SITE
BLDG	No	No	V-FIGURE	BLDG	SURVEY SITE
OHP	No	No	V-FIGURE	OHP	SURVEY SITE

The Survey Database

Once you have all the front-end settings configured, you are ready to create your survey database. This database is stored in your working folder, which can be set by your network administrator or CAD manager if you are a Vault user, or it can simply be set to C:\Civil 3D Projects. When a survey database is created, it creates a folder with that database name in your working folder. Inside that folder, you will find one folder for each network in your database: a survey.sdb file, a survey.sdx file, and a survey.bak file. The SDB file is the Microsoft Access database format file that was mentioned earlier.

Let's create a survey database and explore the database options before we look at the components of the database:

1. Create a new drawing from the NCS Extended Imperial template file.

2. On the Survey tab of Toolspace, right-click on Survey Databases and click New Local Survey Database. The New Local Survey Database dialog opens.

3. Enter **Settings** in the text box. The Settings survey database will be created under the Survey Databases branch in the Survey tab of Toolspace.

4. Right-click on your newly created survey database and select Edit Survey Database Settings. The Survey Database Settings dialog opens.

5. Browse through the various settings.

6. Click Cancel to dismiss the Survey Database Settings dialog.

SURVEY DATABASE COMPONENTS

Once you create a survey database and open it in the Survey tab of Toolspace, you will find that it contains six components:

Networks   A survey network is a collection of connected data that is collected in the field. The network consists of setups (or stations), control points, non-control points, known directions, observations, setups, and traverses. This data is typically imported through an FBK file that is converted from raw data from the data collector, although it can also be imported through a LandXML file. A network must be created in a survey database before any data can be imported. A survey database can have multiple networks. For example, you can use different networks for different phases of a project. If working within the same coordinate zone, some users have used one survey database with many networks for every survey that they perform. This is possible because individual networks can be inserted into the drawing simply by dragging and dropping the network from the Survey tab in Toolspace into the drawing. You can hover your mouse over any Survey Network component in the drawing to see information about that component and the survey network. You can also right-click any component of the network and browse to the observation entry for that component.

Network Groups   Network groups are collections of various survey networks within a survey database. These groups can be created to facilitate inserting multiple networks into a drawing at once simply by dragging and dropping.

Figures   As discussed earlier, figures are linework created by codes and commands entered into the raw data file during data collection. These figures typically come from the descriptor of a point. A typical way of creating figures is illustrated in the following entry from an FBK file:

```
BEG EC
NE SS 3202 10040.90000 10899.21000 793.75000 "EC"
CONT EC
C3
NE SS 3203 10056.53000 10899.45000 793.47000 "EC"
NE SS 3204 10058.52000 10897.42000 793.53000 "EC"
NE SS 3205 10055.94000 10895.19000 793.61500 "EC"
CONT EC
C3
NE SS 3206 10040.43000 10895.11000 793.61500 "EC"
NE SS 3207 10038.18000 10896.59000 793.58000 "EC"
NE SS 3208 10040.47000 10899.34000 793.50500 "EC"
END
```

This FBK entry is going to create a figure named EC, which comes from the point description. This particular figure will have one line segment, and then a compound curve will be created from two three-point curves. The BEG EC, CONT EC, C3, and END commands tell the program how to draw the figure. Figures can be 2D or 3D (that is, they can be used simply for horizontal geometry or as breaklines for vertical geometry), can be used as parcel segments, and can be displayed in any of the same ways that a regular polyline can. The behavior of these figures is controlled by the Figure Prefix Library, which matches point descriptors with figure styles and displays them appropriately. Figures can be added to a drawing by dragging and dropping them into the drawing from the Survey tab in Toolspace.

Figure Groups   Similar to network groups, figure groups are collections of individual figures. These groups can be created to facilitate quick insertion of multiple figures into a drawing.

Survey Points   One of the most basic components of a survey database, points are the basis for each and every survey. Survey points look just like regular Civil 3D point objects and can be controlled just as easily. However, one major difference is that a survey point cannot be edited within a drawing. Survey points are locked by the survey database, and the only way of editing is to edit the observation that collected the data for the point. This provides the surveyor with the confidence that points will not be accidentally erased or edited. Like figures, survey points can be inserted into a drawing by either dragging and dropping from the Survey tab of Toolspace or by right-clicking on Surveying Points and selecting the Points ➤ Insert Into Drawing option.

Survey Point Groups   Just like network groups and figure groups, survey point groups are collections of points that can be easily inserted into a drawing. When these survey point groups are inserted into the drawing, a Civil 3D point group is created with the same name as the survey point group. This point group can be used to control the visibility or display properties of each point in the group.

WHY ARE POINTS SO HARD TO EDIT?

The fact that points cannot be easily edited in the survey database has been a major source of contention from some Civil 3D users. This is by design—a surveyor typically does not want to just manually edit points, but to find the shot that created the incorrect point and edit that observation. A user can now unlock points in a drawing by expanding the Survey Database, right-clicking on Survey Points, and selecting the Points ➤ Unlock In Drawing option. Extreme care should be taken here, because the points are no longer connected to the survey database and are now part of the drawing. Any updates to the survey database will not be reflected in the points, which could cause disparate data between the database and the drawing. Use this command at your own risk!

THE SURVEY DATABASE SETTINGS

Each survey database has numerous settings that control the database (see Figure 3.7). These settings are explained next:

Units   This is where you set your coordinate zone. It is the master coordinate zone for the database. If you insert any information in the database into a drawing with a different coordinate zone set, the program will translate that data to the drawing coordinate zone. Your coordinate zone units will lock the distance units in the Units branch. You can also set the angle, direction, temperature, and pressure units under this branch.

FIGURE 3.7
The Survey Database
Settings dialog

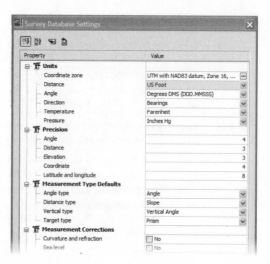

Precision   This is where the precision information of angles, distance, elevation, coordinate, and latitude and longitude is defined and stored.

Measurement Type Defaults   This is where you define the defaults for measurement types, such as angle type, distance type, vertical type, and target types.

Measurement Corrections   This is used to define the methods (if any) for correcting measurements. Some data collectors allow you to make measurement corrections as you collect the data, so that needs to be verified, because double correction applications could lead to incorrect data.

Traverse Analysis Defaults   This is where you choose how you perform traverse analyses and define the required precision and tolerances for each. There are four types of 2D-traverse analyses: Compass Rule, Transit Rule, Crandall Rule, and Least Squares Analysis. You can find more information and definitions of these analyses in the Civil 3D Help file.

There are also three types of 3D-traverse analyses: Length Weighted Distribution, Equal Distribution, and Least Squares Analysis. More information and definitions of these analyses can also be found in the Civil 3D Help file. It should be noted that a 3D Least Squares Analysis can only be performed if the 2D Least Squares Analysis is also selected.

Least Squares Analysis Defaults   This is where you set the defaults for a least squares analysis. You only need to change settings here if least squares is the method you will use for your horizontal and/or vertical adjustments.

Survey Command Window   This is the interface for manual survey tasks and for running survey batch files. This is where the default settings are defined for the Survey Command window interface.

Error Tolerance   This is where tolerances are set for the survey database. If you perform an observation more than one time and the tolerances set within are not met, an error will appear in the Survey Command window and ask you what action you want to take.

Extended Properties   This defines settings for adding extended properties to a survey LandXML file. This is useful for certain types of surveys, including Federal Aviation Administration (FAA)-certified surveys.

Working with Fieldbooks

Once you have a survey database created, you have to create a network within that database to enable you to import survey data. As mentioned earlier, individual survey databases can be created for each survey job that you do, or you can create one overall database per coordinate zone and create individual networks for each survey job. Once you create a network, you can import either an FBK file or a survey LandXML file. This data can then be used to bring survey figures and survey points into a drawing or can be analyzed and adjusted. Figure 3.8 illustrates a typical network, with control points, directions, setups, and a traverse. This network also includes figures and survey points that have been derived from the network data.

CONTROL POINTS

Control points are typically points in your data that have a high confidence factor. Figure 3.9 illustrates the data related to a typical control point shown in the Preview pane of Toolspace.

FIGURE 3.8
A typical survey
database network
and its data

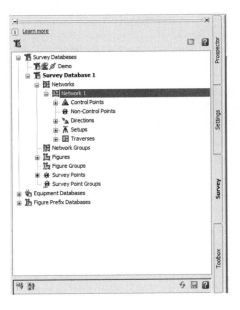

FIGURE 3.9
Control point data as
shown in the Preview
pane of Toolspace

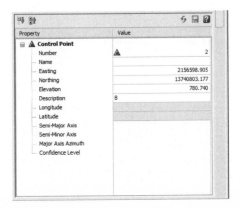

NON-CONTROL POINTS

Non-control points are also stored in the survey database. Manually created points (hand-entered) or GPS-collected points, such as those located by real-time kinematic (RTK) GPS, are the only types of points that can be non-control points.

DIRECTIONS

Directions from one point to another have to be manually entered into the data collector for it to show up in the survey network. The direction can be as simple as a compass shot between two initial traverse points that serves as a rough basis of bearings for a survey job. In the past, changing this direction was the easiest way to rotate a survey network but only worked if provided in the raw data. An example of a direction is shown in Figure 3.10.

SETUPS

The setup is typically where the meat of the data is found, especially when working with conventional survey equipment. Every setup, as well as the points (sideshots) located from that setup, can be found. Setups will contain two components: the station (or occupy point) and the backsight. Setups, as well as the observations located from the setup, can be edited. The interface for editing setups is shown in Figure 3.11. Angles and instrument heights can also be changed in this dialog.

FIGURE 3.10
The direction from point 2 to point 1 is 79°29′00″

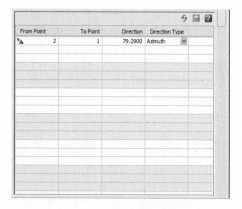

FIGURE 3.11
Setups and observations can be changed in the Setups Editor of Panorama.

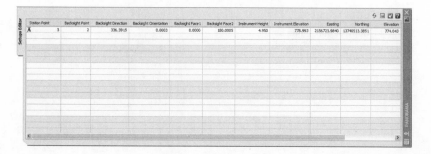

TRAVERSES

The Traverses section is where new traverses are created or existing ones are edited. These traverses can come from your data collector, or they can be manually entered from field notes via the Traverse Editor, as shown in Figure 3.12. You can view or edit each setup in the Traverse Editor, as well as the traverse stations located from that setup.

FIGURE 3.12

The Traverse Editor in Panorama

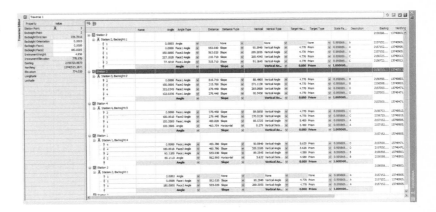

1. Create a new drawing from the NCS Extended Imperial template file.

2. Navigate to the Survey tab of Toolspace.

3. Right-click on Survey Databases and select New Local Survey Database. The New Local Survey Database dialog opens.

4. Enter **Shopping Center** as the name of the folder that your new database will be in.

5. Click OK to dismiss the dialog. The Shopping Center survey database is created as a branch under the Survey Databases branch.

6. Expand the Shopping Center survey database, right-click on Networks, and select New. The New Network dialog opens.

7. Expand the Network branch in the dialog if needed. Name your new network **As-Built**.

8. Click OK. The As-Built network is now listed as a branch under the Networks branch in Prospector.

9. Right-click on the As-Built network and select Import Field Book.

10. Navigate to C:\Mastering Civil 3D 2008\CH 3 and select shopping_center.fbk, then click OK. The Import Field Book dialog opens.

11. Make sure your settings for importing the fieldbook file match the settings in Figure 3.13. The important settings are Show Interactive Graphics, which will allow you to see the network as it is being created, and Insert Figure Objects. We do not want to import the network points at this time.

FIGURE 3.13
The Import Field
Book dialog

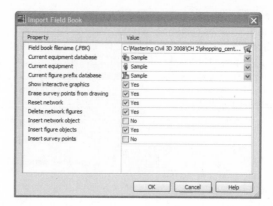

12. Click OK to dismiss the dialog and watch your network as it is created. It may take a few minutes to import the entire network, but once it's imported, you should see figure objects in the drawing. Look at the network data within the survey database. All points in the network are listed as Non-Control Points because the entire job was located using RTK GPS.

13. Save the drawing as Shopping Center.dwg to C:\Mastering Civil 3D 2008\CH3 and close it.

Once you have defined a traverse, you can adjust it by right-clicking on its name and selecting Traverse Analysis. You can adjust the traverse either horizontally or vertically, using a variety of methods and required precision. The traverse analysis can be written to text files to be stored, and the entire network can be adjusted on the basis of the new values of the traverse.

1. Create a new drawing from the NCS Extended Imperial template file.

2. Navigate to the Survey tab of Toolspace.

3. Right-click on Survey Databases and select New Local Survey Database. The New Local Survey Database dialog opens.

4. Enter **Traverse** as the name of the folder that your new database will be in.

5. Click OK to dismiss the dialog. The Traverse survey database is created as a branch under the Survey Databases branch.

6. Expand the Traverse branch, right-click on Networks, and select New. The New Network dialog opens.

7. Expand the Network branch in the dialog if needed. Name your new network **Traverse Practice**.

8. Click OK. The Traverse Practice network is now listed as a branch under the Networks branch of the Transverse survey database in Prospector.

9. Right-click on the Traverse Practice network and select Import Field Book.

10. Navigate to C:\Mastering Civil 3D 2008\CH 3, select the traverse.fbk file, and click OK. The Import Field Book dialog opens.

11. Make sure your settings match the settings in Figure 3.14. You will be inserting the points into the drawing this time.

12. Click OK.

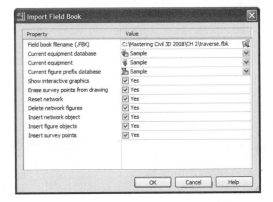

FIGURE 3.14

The Import Field Book dialog

Inspect the data contained within the network. You have one control point—point 2, which was manually entered into the data collector. There is one direction, an azimuth from point 2 to point 1, and four setups. Each setup combines to form a closed polygonal shape that defines the traverse. Notice that there is no traverse definition. You will be creating that traverse definition next for analysis:

1. Right-click on Traverses under the Traverse Practice network and select New to open the New Traverse dialog.

2. Name the new traverse **Traverse 1.**

3. Enter **2** as the value for the Initial Station and **1** for the Initial Backsight.

4. The traverse will now pick up the rest of the stations in the traverse and enter them into the next box

5. Enter **2** as the value for the Final Foresight (the closing point for the traverse). Click OK.

6. Expand the Traverse branch and right-click on Traverse 1. Select Traverse Analysis.

7. In the Traverse Analysis dialog, select Yes for the Do Traverse Analysis and Do Angle Balance.

8. Select Least Squares for the Horizontal and Vertical Adjustment Method.

9. Select 30,000 for the Horizontal And Vertical Closure Limit 1:X.

10. Make sure the option Update Survey Database is set to Yes.

11. Click OK.

The analysis is performed, and three text files are displayed on your screen that show the results of the adjustment. Note that if you look back at your survey network, all points are now control points, as the analysis has upgraded all the points to control point status.

Figure 3.15 shows the results of the analysis and adjustment. Here, you can see the Elevation Error, Error North, Error East, Absolute Error, Error Direction, Perimeter (of the traverse), Number Of Sides, and Area (of the traverse). We also can see that our new Precision is 1:147401.562, which is well within the tolerances set in step 10.

Figure 3.16 displays the results of the vertical analysis, displayed automatically upon completion of the analysis. You can see the individual points and their initial elevation, along with the adjusted elevations. In this example, the elevations required no adjustment, as evidenced by the delta values of 0.0000.

The third text file is shown in three separate portions. The first portion is shown in Figure 3.17. This portion of the file displays the various observations along with their initial measurements, standard deviations, adjusted values, and residuals. You can view other statistical data at the beginning of the file.

FIGURE 3.15

Traverse analysis results

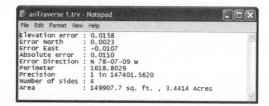

FIGURE 3.16

Vertical analysis results

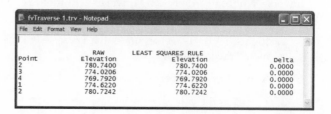

FIGURE 3.17

Statistical and observation data

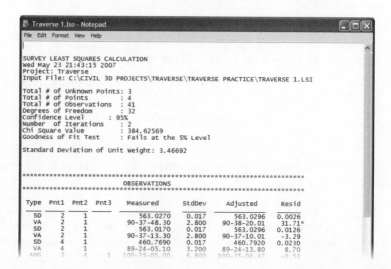

Figure 3.18 shows the second portion of this text file and displays the adjusted coordinates, the standard deviation of the adjusted coordinates, and information related to error ellipses displayed in the drawing. If the deviations are too high for your acceptable tolerances, you will need to redo the work or edit the fieldbook.

Figure 3.19 displays the final portion of this text file—the Blunder Detection and Analysis. Civil 3D will look for and analyze data in the network that is obviously wrong and choose to keep it or throw it out of the analysis if it doesn't meet your criteria. If a blunder (or bad shot) is detected, the program will not fix it. You will have to edit the data manually, whether by going out in the field and collecting the correct data or by editing the FBK file.

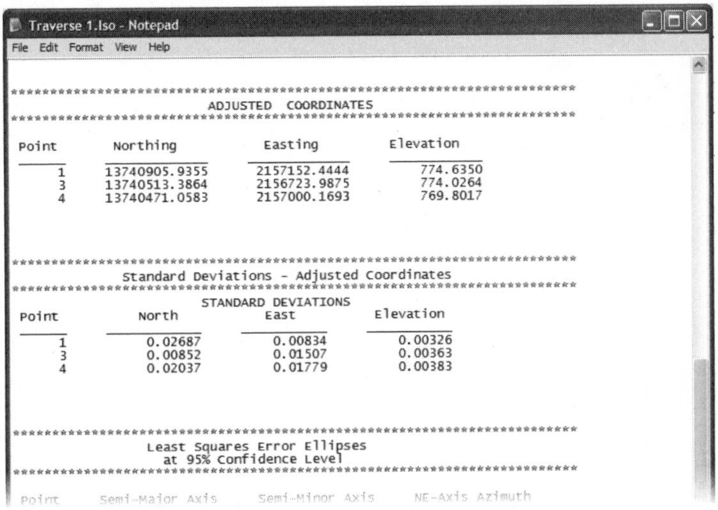

Traverse 1.lso - Notepad

File Edit Format View Help

ADJUSTED COORDINATES

Point	Northing	Easting	Elevation
1	13740905.9355	2157152.4444	774.6350
3	13740513.3864	2156723.9875	774.0264
4	13740471.0583	2157000.1693	769.8017

Standard Deviations - Adjusted Coordinates

Point	STANDARD DEVIATIONS North	East	Elevation
1	0.02687	0.00834	0.00326
3	0.00852	0.01507	0.00363
4	0.02037	0.01779	0.00383

Least Squares Error Ellipses
at 95% Confidence Level

Point Semi-Major Axis Semi-Minor Axis NE-Axis Azimuth

FIGURE 3.18
Adjusted coordinate information

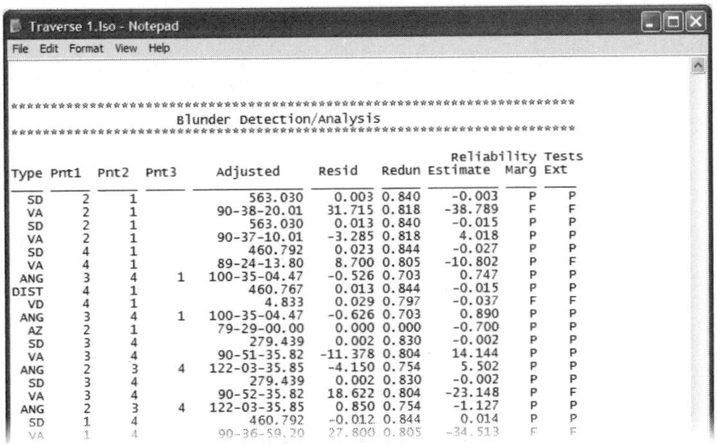

Traverse 1.lso - Notepad

File Edit Format View Help

Blunder Detection/Analysis

Type	Pnt1	Pnt2	Pnt3	Adjusted	Resid	Redun	Reliability Estimate	Tests Marg	Ext
SD	2	1		563.030	0.003	0.840	-0.003	P	P
VA	2	1		90-38-20.01	31.715	0.818	-38.789	F	F
SD	2	1		563.030	0.013	0.840	-0.015	P	P
VA	2	1		90-37-10.01	-3.285	0.818	4.018	P	P
SD	4	1		460.792	0.023	0.844	-0.027	P	P
VA	4	1		89-24-13.80	8.700	0.805	-10.802	P	F
ANG	3	4	1	100-35-04.47	-0.526	0.703	0.747	P	P
DIST	4	1		460.767	0.013	0.844	-0.015	P	P
VD	4	1		4.833	0.029	0.797	-0.037	F	F
ANG	3	4	1	100-35-04.47	-0.626	0.703	0.890	P	P
AZ	2	1		79-29-00.00	0.000	0.000	-0.700	P	P
SD	3	4		279.439	0.002	0.830	-0.002	P	P
VA	3	4		90-51-35.82	-11.378	0.804	14.144	P	P
ANG	2	3	4	122-03-35.85	-4.150	0.754	5.502	P	P
SD	3	4		279.439	0.002	0.830	-0.002	P	P
VA	3	4		90-52-35.82	18.622	0.804	-23.148	P	F
ANG	2	3	4	122-03-35.85	0.850	0.754	-1.127	P	P
SD	1	4		460.792	-0.012	0.844	0.014	P	P
VA	1	4		90-36-59.20	27.800	0.805	-34.513	F	F

FIGURE 3.19
Blunder analysis

One more method of creating traverses is to create a traverse from figures. Originally introduced to Civil 3D 2008 as a program extension, this command allows a user to connect points with a polyline, create a figure from that polyline, and then define a traverse from the newly created figure.

1. Open the `Traverse Analysis.dwg` file.

2. This drawing shows four points, numbered 1 through 4.

3. Select the Line tool to draw a polyline from point 2 to point 3 to point 4 to point 1, and then point 2. It is best to use the Point Number transparent command when creating this polyline. To do this, first select the Line tool, then click the Point Number transparent command and enter the point number. Press ↵, and enter the next point number. Continue until your closed polyline is complete, and press Esc to exit from the transparent command.

4. Choose Survey ➤ Create Figure From Object.

5. Pick the polyline connecting the points. The Create Figure From Object dialog opens.

6. Name the figure **TRAV** and be sure the Associate Survey Points To Vertices property is set to Yes; then click OK to dismiss the dialog.

7. Expand the Traverses ➤ Figures branches. You will see one figure named TRAV. Drag and drop it into the current drawing.

8. Choose Survey ➤ Define Traverse Stations From Figure.

9. In the following dialog, set the Survey Network to Traverse From Figure, and then click Next.

10. At the bottom of the dialog, select New Traverse.

11. In the next dialog, select the TRAV figure and click Next.

12. Your Initial Station should already be filled in as Station 2. The stations should be entered into the gray area as 3,4,1,2. Enter **1** as the Initial Backsight and **2** as the Final Foresight.

13. Save the drawing and close it.

ADDITIONAL SURVEY FUNCTIONALITY WITH FREE ADD-ONS

Two commands mentioned in this chapter are not found in a typical Civil 3D 2008 installation: Translate Survey Network and Define Traverse Stations From Figures. These commands are a part of the Survey extension from Autodesk. Not predicted to be available in a service pack, this is a freely downloadable add-on for Civil 3D 2008. You can download the file from http://civilcommunity.autodesk.com/content/utilities/view/5891. Please note that you must be registered with the Civil Community site to be able to download content, but registration is free. Comprehensive instructions for installation are included with the downloaded file. This extension must be installed prior to attempting the following exercises.

Other Methods of Manipulating Survey Data

Often, it is necessary to edit the entire survey network at one time. For example, rotating a network to a known bearing or azimuth from an assumed one happens quite frequently. However, unless directions are defined in the fieldbook file, changing that rotation is difficult. Previously, you would have to calculate several coordinates to make a rotation and/or translation. However, a Survey menu command allows you to translate a survey network with the 2008 release (again, initially released as a program extension).

 Real World Scenario

Manipulating the Network

Translating a survey network can move a network from an assumed coordinate system to a known coordinate system, it can rotate a network, and it can adjust a network from assumed elevations to a known datum.

1. Create a new drawing from the NCS Extended Imperial template file.

2. In the Survey tab of Toolspace, right-click and select New Local Survey Database. The New Local Survey Database dialog opens. Enter **Translate** in the text box. This is the name of the folder for the new database.

3. Click OK, and the Translate database will now be listed under the Survey Databases branch on the Survey tab.

4. Select Networks under the new Translate branch. Right-click and select New to open the New Network dialog. Enter **Translate** as the name of this new network. Click OK to dismiss the dialog.

5. Right-click on Translate network, and select Import Fieldbook File.

6. Navigate to the traverse.fbk file, and click OK. The Import Field Book dialog opens.

7. Update the Point Groups collection in Prospector so that the points show up in the drawing if needed.

8. Draw an orthogonal polyline to the north from point 3. It can be any length.

9. Choose Survey ➢ Translate Survey Network. For the purposes of this exercise, we are going to leave the points on their same coordinate system, but change the bearing from point 3 to point 2 to due north. Elevations will remain unchanged.

10. In the first window of the Translate Survey Network dialog, select Translate Network and click Next.

11. In the next window, type **3** for the Base Point Number (this is the number we will be rotating the points around). Click Next.

12. In the next window, click the Pick In Drawing button in the lower-left corner to specify the new angle.

13. Using osnaps, pick point 3 and then point 2 for your Reference Angle.

14. Next, pick point 3 and then somewhere along the orthogonal polyline for the second point to define the new angle. The new angle should be just over 23 degrees. Click Next.

15. In the next window, click the Pick In Drawing button on the lower left to pick point 3 as the Destination Point. This will essentially negate any translation features and only provide you with a rotation.

16. Leave the Elevation Change box empty. If you were raising or lowering the elevations of the network, this box is where you would enter the change value.

17. Click Finish.

18. Go back to the drawing and inspect your points. Point 2 should now be due north of point 3.

19. Close the drawing without saving. Even though you did not save the drawing, the changes were made directly to the database.

Other Survey Features

Two other components of the survey functionality included with Civil 3D 2008 is the Astronomic Direction Calculator and the Geodetic Calculator. The Astronomic Direction Calculator, shown in Figure 3.20, is used to calculate sun shots or star shots.

The Geodetic Calculator is used to calculate and display the latitude and longitude of a selected point, as well as their local and grid coordinates. It can also be used to calculate unknown points. If you know the grid coordinates, the local coordinates, or the latitude and longitude of a point, you can enter it into the Geodetic Calculator and create a point at that location. Note that the Geodetic Calculator only works if a coordinate system is assigned to the drawing in the Drawing Settings dialog. In addition, any transformation settings specified in this dialog will be reflected in the Geodetic Calculator, shown in Figure 3.21.

FIGURE 3.20

The Astronomic Direction Calculator

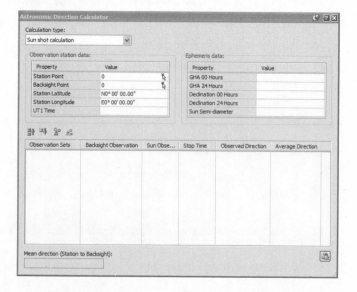

FIGURE 3.21

The Geodetic Calculator

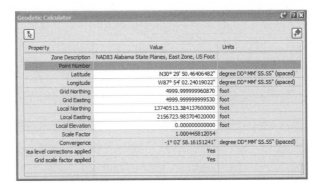

Property	Value	Units
Zone Description	NAD83 Alabama State Planes, East Zone, US Foot	
Point Number		
Latitude	N30° 29' 50.46406482"	degree DD° MM' SS.SS" (spaced)
Longitude	W87° 54' 02.24019022"	degree DD° MM' SS.SS" (spaced)
Grid Northing	4999.999999960870	foot
Grid Easting	4999.999999999530	foot
Local Northing	13740513.384137600000	foot
Local Easting	2156723.983704020000	foot
Local Elevation	0.000000000000	foot
Scale Factor	1.000445812054	
Convergence	-1° 02' 58.16151241"	degree DD° MM' SS.SS" (spaced)
iea level corrections applied	Yes	
Grid scale factor applied	Yes	

Data Collection with Civil 3D 2008

There are definitely many different types of data collectors on the market. Some of those data collectors interface directly with Civil 3D, including the Trimble and Leica data collectors. This is because both Trimble and Leica make their own add-ins for Civil 3D that allow them to communicate directly with Civil 3D and convert their raw data into a FBK file for use with Civil 3D. Carlson Software (www.carlsonsw.com) makes Carlson Connect, an add-in for Civil 3D that allows not only direct connections with Carlson data collectors and import/export functions for Carlson point objects, but also adds in functionality for many other data collector brands as well. For users who cannot find a suitable solution within the three free downloads, a program called Stringer Connect is available from CADApps in Australia.

The Bottom Line

Properly collect field data and import it into AutoCAD Civil 3D 2008.   You learned best practices for collecting data, how the data is translated into a useable format for the survey database, and how to import that data into a survey database. You learned what commands draw linework in a raw data file, and how to include those commands into your data collection techniques so that the linework is created correctly when the fieldbook is imported into the program.

Master It   In this exercise, you will create a new drawing and a new survey database and import the Shopping_Center.fbk file into the drawing.

Set up styles that will correctly display your linework.   You learned how to set up styles for figures. You also learned that figures can be set as breaklines for surface creation and lot lines and that they can go on their own layer and be displayed in many different ways.

Master It   In this exercise, you will use the Mastering1.dwg file and survey database from the previous exercise and create figure styles and a figure prefix database for the various figures in the database.

Create and edit fieldbook files.   You learned how to create fieldbook files using various data collection techniques and how to modify the various data in the files to achieve a very accurate survey database.

Master It   In this exercise, you will create a new drawing and survey database. Import the traverse.fbk file and rotate the entire network so that a line running from point number 3 to point number 4 is running due east. Then, export that FBK file to a new file and import the new file into a new network to verify the changes.

Manipulate your survey data. You learned how to use the traverse analysis and adjustments to create data with a higher precision.

Master It In this exercise, you will use the survey database and network from the previous exercises in this chapter. You will analyze and adjust the traverse using the following criteria:

◆ Use the Compass Rule for Horizontal Adjustment.

◆ Use the Length Weighted Distribution Method for Vertical Adjustment.

◆ Use a Horizontal Closure Limit of 1:25,000.

◆ Use a Vertical Closure Limit of 1:25,000.

Chapter 4

X Marks the Spot: Points

The foundation of any civil engineering project is the simple point. Most commonly, we think of points as identifying the location of existing features, such as trees and property corners; topography, such as ground shots; or stakeout information, such as road geometry points. However, points can be used for much more. This chapter will focus on both traditional point uses and introduce ideas to apply the dynamic power of point editing, labeling, and grouping to other applications.

By the end of this chapter, you will be able to:

◆ Import points from a text file using description key matching

◆ Create a point group

◆ Export points to LandXML and ASCII format

◆ Create a point table

Anatomy of a Point

Civil 3D points are intelligent objects that represent x, y, and z locations in space. Each point has a unique number and, optionally, a unique name that can be used for additional identification and labeling.

In previous releases of Civil 3D, points were not really individual objects. The point group was considered the object, and a point was considered a component of the point group. In Civil 3D 2008, the point (see Figure 4.1) behaves as an individual object that can be moved, rotated, and manipulated with far greater ease than in previous releases. Point properties can be viewed and changed in the AutoCAD Properties palette, as shown in Figure 4.2.

FIGURE 4.1
A typical point object showing a marker, point number, elevation, and description

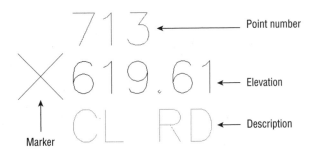

713 ◄——— Point number

619.61 ◄— Elevation

Marker

CL RD ◄— Description

FIGURE 4.2
The AutoCAD
Properties
palette

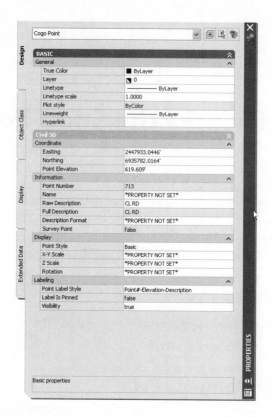

Creating Basic Points

Points can be created in many ways, using the flyout menus under Points or the Create Points dialog. Points can also be imported from text files or external databases or converted from AutoCAD, Land Desktop, or Softdesk point objects.

Point Settings

Before you begin creating points, it is important to investigate which settings may make the task easier. Individual point objects are placed on an object layer that controls their visibility, which can be managed in both the Command settings and the Create Points dialog. You can also establish default style, default label style, and default elevations, names, and descriptions in your Civil 3D template, which will make it easy to follow your company standard when creating points.

DEFAULT LAYER

For most Civil 3D objects, the object layer is established in the Drawing settings. In the case of points, the default object layer is set in the Command settings for point creation and can be overridden in the Create Points dialog (see Figure 4.3).

FIGURE 4.3
The Point object layer should be set before creating points.

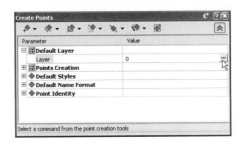

PROMPT FOR ELEVATIONS, NAMES, AND DESCRIPTIONS

When creating points in your drawing, you have the option of being prompted for elevations, names, and descriptions (see Figure 4.4). In many cases, you will want to leave these options set to Manual. The command line will ask you to assign an elevation, name, and description for every point you create.

If you are creating a whole batch of points that have the same description or elevation, you can change the Prompt toggle from Manual to Automatic and then provide the description and elevation in the default cells. For example, if you are setting a series of trees at an elevation of 10′, you can establish settings as in Figure 4.5.

Be sure to change these settings back to Manual before importing points from external sources that provide a Z elevation. If not, all imported points will be assigned the default elevation regardless of the Z provided by the imported file.

FIGURE 4.4
The Elevation, Name and Description settings can be changed from Manual to Automatic.

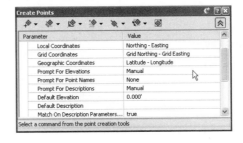

FIGURE 4.5
Default settings for placing tree points at an elevation of 10′

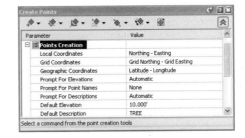

Importing Points from a Text File

One of the most common means of creating points in your drawing is to import an external text file. This file may be the result of surveyed information or an export from another program (see Figure 4.6).

The import process supports these point file formats: TXT, PRN, CSV, XYZ, AUF, NEZ, and PNT. The following are the most common formats for imported point lists:

◆ Autodesk Uploadable File

◆ External Project Point Database

◆ ENZ, space delimited or comma delimited

◆ NEZ, space delimited or comma delimited

◆ PENZ, space delimited or comma delimited

◆ PENZD, space delimited or comma delimited

◆ PNE, space delimited or comma delimited

◆ PNEZ, space delimited or comma delimited

◆ PNEZD, space delimited or comma delimited

An elevation adjustment, a coordinate system transformation, or a coordinate data expansion can also be performed on import.

FIGURE 4.6
(a) The Import Points tool in the Create Points dialog. (b) Creating a point group for the newly imported points.

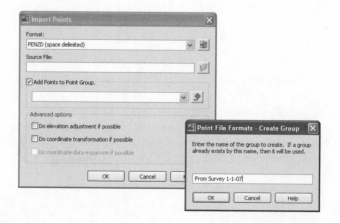

An elevation adjustment can be performed if the point file contains additional columns for thickness, Z+, or Z-. These columns can be added as part of a custom format. See the Civil 3D 2008 Users Guide section "Using Point File Format Properties to Perform Calculations" for more details.

A coordinate system transformation can be performed if a coordinate system has been assigned to both your drawing (under the Drawing settings) and as part of a custom point format. In this case, the program can also do a coordinate data expansion, which calculates the latitude and longitude for each point.

IMPORTING A TEXT FILE OF POINTS

In this exercise, you will learn how to import a `.txt` file of points into Civil 3D:

1. Open the `Import Points.dwg` file.

2. Open the Import Points dialog by selecting Points ≻ Import/Export Points ≻ Import Points or by selecting Points ≻ Create Points and clicking Import Points.

3. Change the Format to PENZD Space Delimited.

4. Click the file folder button to the right of the Source File field and navigate out to locate the `PENZD space.txt` file.

5. Leave all other boxes unchecked.

6. Click OK. You may have to zoom extents to see the imported points.

7. The completed exercise can be seen in the `Import Points Finished.dwg` file.

Converting Points from Land Desktop, Softdesk, and Other Sources

Civil 3D contains several tools for migrating legacy point objects to the current version. The best results are often obtained from an external point list, such as a text file, LandXML, or external database. However, if you come across a drawing that contains the original Land Desktop, Softdesk, AutoCAD, or other types of point objects, there are tools and techniques to convert those objects into Civil 3D points.

A Land Desktop point database (the `Points.mdb` file found in the COGO folder in a Land Desktop project) can be directly imported into Civil 3D in the same interface in which you'd import a text file.

Land Desktop point objects, which appear as AECC_POINTs in the AutoCAD Properties palette, can also be converted to Civil 3D points (see Figure 4.7). Upon conversion, this tool gives you the opportunity to assign styles, create a point group, and more.

Occasionally you will receive AutoCAD point objects drawn at elevation from aerial topography information or other sources. It is also not uncommon to receive Softdesk point blocks from outside surveyors. Both of these can be converted to Civil 3D points under the Points ≻ Utilities submenu or on the Create Points dialog (see Figure 4.8).

FIGURE 4.7
The Convert Land
Desktop Points option
(a) opens the Convert
Autodesk Land Desk-
top Points dialog (b).

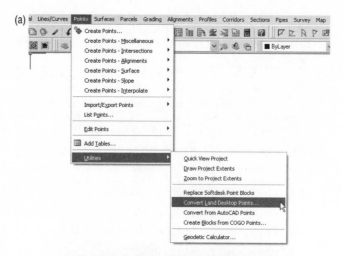

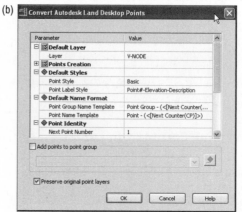

FIGURE 4.8
Use the Create Points
dialog to convert
AutoCAD point enti-
ties or Softdesk point
blocks.

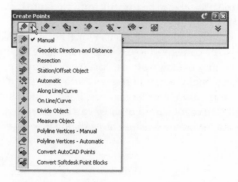

USING THE AUTOCAD ATTRIBUTE EXTRACTION TO CONVERT OUTSIDE PROGRAM POINT BLOCKS

Occasionally, you may receive a drawing that contains point blocks from a third-party program. These point blocks may look similar to Softdesk point blocks, but you cannot convert them directly to Civil 3D points using Civil 3D tools.

The best way to handle this would be to ask the source of the drawing (the outside surveyor, for example) to provide a text file or LandXML file of their points database. However, often this is not possible.

Since these objects are essentially AutoCAD blocks with special attributes, we can use the Data Extraction tools from AutoCAD to harvest their attributes and make a text file. We can then import this text file back into Civil 3D to create Civil 3D points. The points should store number, description, and elevation information in their attributes. As AutoCAD objects, they also understand their x and y position. These properties can all be extracted and reimported using the following procedure:

1. Use the Data Extraction tool under your Tools menu or type **EATTEXT** in the command line to launch the Data Extraction wizard.

2. Select the radio button to create a new data extraction, and click Next. The Save Extraction As dialog will appear, prompting you to name and save this extraction. Give the extraction a meaningful name and save it in the appropriate folder. Click Next.

3. Confirm that the drawings to be scanned for attributed blocks are on the list:

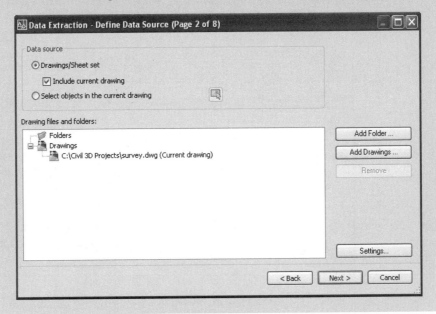

4. In the Select Objects screen of the Data Extraction dialog, select the Display Blocks Only radio button and check Display Blocks With Attributes Only; this will include our point blocks and a few others. Eliminate the other types of attributed blocks by unchecking their boxes. (If you are unsure which block is your survey point block, exit the wizard and investigate one of your point blocks. Depending on what software package they came from, they might have a different name and different attributes.) Click Next.

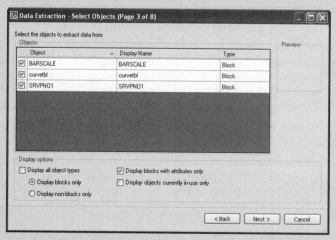

5. In the Select Properties dialog, locate the Point Number, Elevation, and Description, as well as X and Y. Click Next.

6. In the Refine Data screen of the Data Extraction dialog, rearrange the columns into a PNEZD format and remove any extra columns, such as Count and Name. Then click Next.

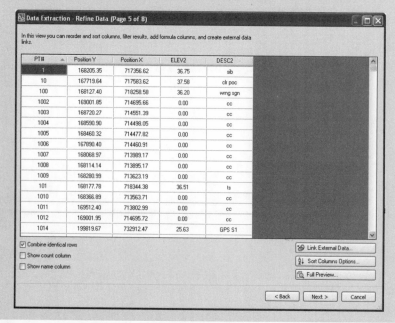

7. In the Choose Output screen of the Data Extraction dialog, choose Output Data To External File and save your extraction as an `.xls` (Microsoft Excel) file in a logical place. If you save it as a `.txt` file initially, the file will have extra spaces in the wrong places.

8. Open this file in Microsoft Excel and remove the first line of text (the header information). Use Save As to create a `.txt` file.

	A1	▼	✗ PT#					
	A	B	C	D	E	F	G	H
1	PT#	Position Y	Position X	ELEV2	DESC2			
2	1	168205.4	717356.62	36.75	sib			
3	10	167719.6	717583.62	37.58	clr poc			
4	100	168127.4	718258.58	36.2	wrng sgn			
5	1002	169001.9	714695.66	0	cc			
6	1003	168720.3	714551.39	0	cc			
7	1004	168590.9	714498.05	0	cc			
8	1005	168460.3	714477.82	0	cc			

9. In Civil 3D, use the Import Points tool in the Create Points dialog to import the `.txt` file.

CONVERTING POINTS

In this exercise, you will learn how to convert Land Desktop point objects and AutoCAD point entities into Civil 3D points:

1. Open the `Convert Points.dwg` file.

2. Use the List command or the AutoCAD Properties palette to confirm that most of the objects in this drawing are AECC_POINTs, which are points from Land Desktop. Also note a cluster of cyan-colored AutoCAD point objects in the western portion of the site.

3. Run the Land Desktop Point Conversion tool by choosing Points ➤ Utilities ➤ Convert Land Desktop Points. Note the Convert Autodesk Land Desktop Points dialog allows you to choose a default layer, point creation settings, styles, and so on and also add the points to a point group. Leave the defaults and click OK.

4. Civil 3D will scan the drawing looking for Land Desktop point objects.

5. Once Civil 3D has finished the conversion, zoom in on any of the former Land Desktop points. The points should now be AECC_COGO_POINTs in both the List command and in the AutoCAD Properties palette, confirming that the conversion has taken place. The Land Desktop points have been replaced with Civil 3D points, and the original Land Desktop points are no longer in the drawing.

6. Zoom in on the cyan AutoCAD point objects.

7. Run the AutoCAD Point Conversion tool by choosing Points ➤ Utilities ➤ Convert From AutoCAD points.

8. At the command-line prompt, enter a description of **GS** (Ground Shot) for each point.

9. Zoom in on one of the converted points and confirm that it has been converted to a Civil 3D point. Also note that the original AutoCAD points have been erased from the drawing.

10. The completed exercise is shown in the `Convert Points Finished.dwg` file.

Getting to Know the Create Points Dialog

In Civil 3D 2008, point creation tools can be found directly under the Points menu as well as in the Create Points dialog. The dialog is modeless, which means that it stays on your screen even when you switch between tasks.

Miscellaneous point creation options   The options in the Miscellaneous category are based on manually selecting a location or on an AutoCAD entity, such as a line, pline, and so on. Some common examples include placing points at intervals along a line or polyline, as well as converting Softdesk points or AutoCAD entities (see Figure 4.8 earlier in this chapter).

Intersection point creation options   The options in the Intersection category allow you to place points at a certain location without having to draw construction linework. For example, if you needed a point at the intersection of two bearings, you could draw two construction lines using the Bearing Distance transparent command, manually place a point where they intersect, and then erase the construction lines. Alternatively, you could use the Direction/Direction tool in the Intersection category (see Figure 4.9).

Alignment point creation options   The options in the Alignment category are designed for creating stakeout points based on a road centerline or other alignments. You can also set Profile Geometry points along the alignment using a tool from this menu. See Figure 4.10.

Surface point creation options   The options in the Surface category allow you to set points that harvest their elevation data from a surface. Note that these are points, not labels, and therefore are not dynamic to the surface. Points can be set manually, along a contour or a polyline, or in a grid. See Figure 4.11.

FIGURE 4.9
Intersection point
creation options

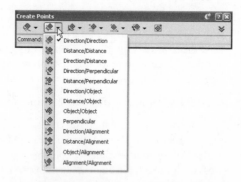

FIGURE 4.10
Alignment point
creation options

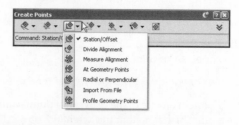

FIGURE 4.11
Surface point
creation options

Interpolation point creation options   The Interpolation category allows you to fill in missing information from survey data or establish intermediate points for your design tasks. For example, if your survey crew picked up centerline road shots every 100 feet, and you would like to interpolate intermediate points every 25 feet, instead of doing a manual slope calculation, you could use the Incremental Distance tool ![icon] to create additional points (see Figure 4.12).

Another use would be to set intermediate points along a pipe stakeout. You could set a point for the starting and ending invert, and then set intermediate points along the pipe to assist the field crew.

Slope point creation options   The Slope category allows you to set points between two known elevations by setting a slope or grade. Similar to the options in the Interpolate and Intersect categories, these tools save you time by eliminating construction geometry and hand calculations (see Figure 4.13).

The interpolation point creation options (a) and Intermediate points created using the Incremental Distance tool (b).

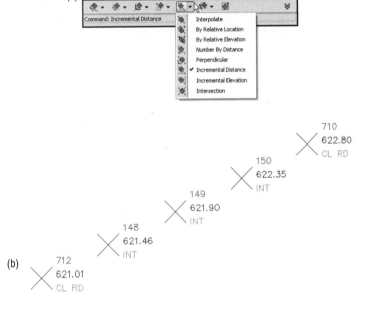

FIGURE 4.13
Slope point creation options

CREATING POINTS

In this exercise, you will learn how to create points along a parcel segment and along a surface contour:

1. Open the Create Points Exercise.dwg file. Note that there is an alignment, a series of parcels, and an existing ground surface in the drawing.

2. Open the Create Points dialog by selecting Points ➤ Create Points.

3. Click the down arrows at the far right side to expand the dialog.

4. Expand the Points Creation option and change the Prompt For Elevations value to None and the Prompt For Descriptions value to Automatic by clicking in the respective cell, clicking the down arrow, and selecting the appropriate option. Enter **LOT** for the Default Description (see Figure 4.14). This will prevent us from having to enter a description and elevation each time. Since we are setting stakeout points for rear lot corners, elevation is not important in this case.

5. Select the Automatic tool ⚙ under the Miscellaneous category to set points along the northern rear lot line. A point will be placed at each rear property corner.

6. Select the Measure Object tool ⚙ under the Miscellaneous category to set points along the southern rear lot line. This tool will prompt you for a starting and ending station (press ⏎ to accept the measurements), an offset (press ⏎ to accept 0), and an interval (enter **25**).

7. Experiment with other point creation tools as desired.

8. Go back into the Point Settings options and change Prompt For Elevations to Manual and change the Default Description to EG. The next round of points we will set will be based on the existing ground elevation.

9. Select the Along Polyline/Contour tool ⚙ in the Surface category to create points every 100 feet along any contour. The command line will prompt you to physically choose a surface, ask for a point spacing interval, and then pick a polyline or contour. Pick any contour on your surface and note points are placed at surface elevation along that contour.

10. The completed exercise can be seen in the `Create Points Exercise Finished.dwg` file.

FIGURE 4.14
Point Creation settings in the Create Points dialog

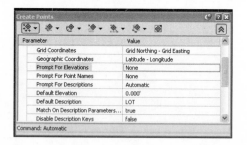

Basic Point Editing

Despite our best efforts, points are often placed in the wrong location or need additional editing after their initial creation. It is common for property-corner points to be rotated to match a different assumed benchmark or for points used in a grading design to need their elevations adjusted.

Physical Point Edits

Points can be moved, copied, rotated, deleted and more using standard AutoCAD commands and grip edits (see Figure 4.15).

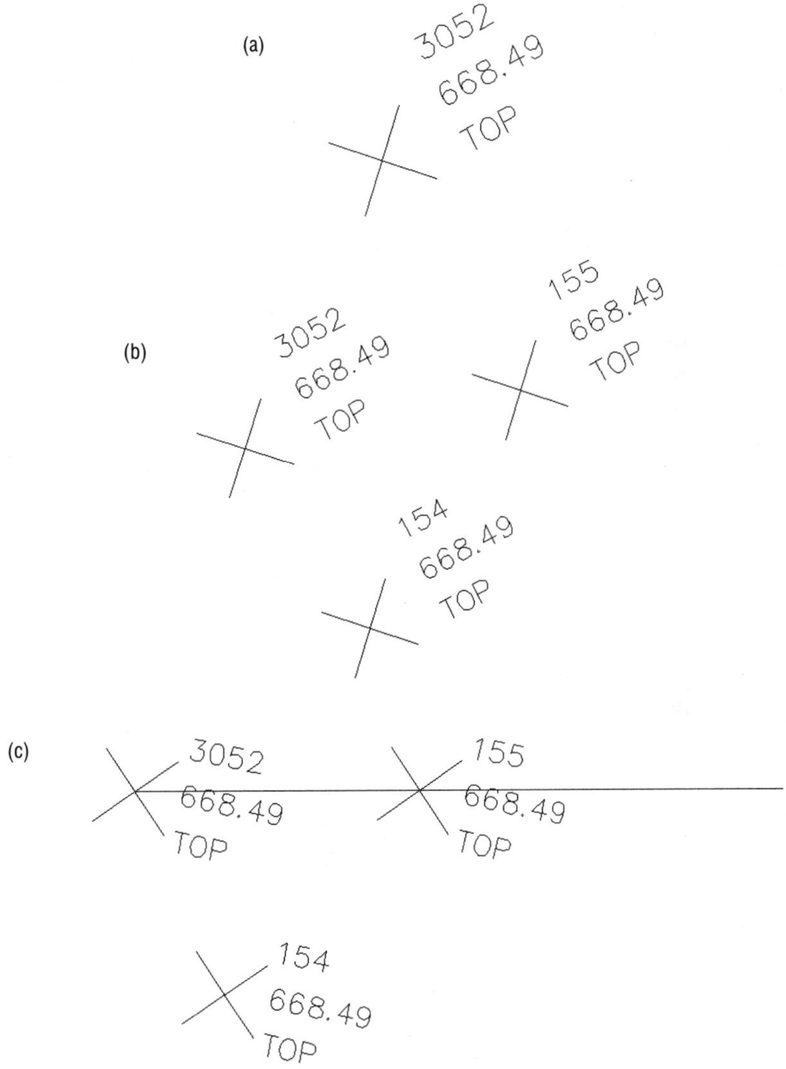

FIGURE 4.15

The AutoCAD Rotate command rotates (a), copies (b), and aligns (c) a Civil 3D point.

Properties Box Point Edits

Many point properties can be accessed through the AutoCAD Properties palette. Pick a point, right-click, and choose Properties (see Figure 4.2).

Panorama and Prospector Point Edits

Many point properties can be accessed through the Point Editor in Panorama. Choose a point (or points), right-click and choose Edit Points. The Panorama will bring up information for the selected point(s) (see Figure 4.16).

You can access a similar interface in the Prospector tab of Toolspace by highlighting the Points collection (Figure 4.17).

FIGURE 4.16
Edit points in
Panorama

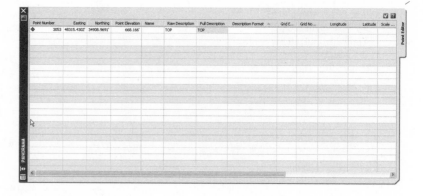

FIGURE 4.17
Prospector allows
you to view your
entire Points collec-
tion at once.

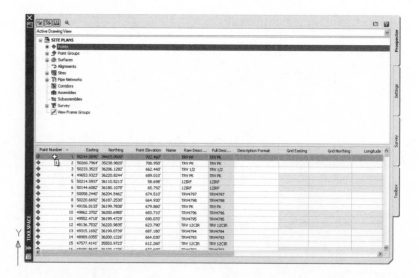

Real World Scenario

MOVING POINTS TO A DEED LOCATION

In this exercise, you will learn how use the Align command to move a group of points from an arbitrary location to where they belong on a deed.

Open the Moving Points Exercise.dwg file. Note that there are a series of parcels that overlay an existing ground surface and a series of points that are off to the side. Also note the text in the drawing calling out the desired locations of points 222 and 214 along the northern property line of Property:4.

Using the Align command, move and rotate the points to their correct location:

1. Type **ALIGN** at the command line.

2. Select Objects: Pick all point objects.

3. `Specify First Source Point:` Pick the node of point 222.

4. `Specify First Destination Point:` Pick the intersection of the two lot lines for the location of point 222.

5. `Specify Second Source Point:` Pick the node of point 214.

6. `Specify Second Destination Point:` Pick the intersection of the two lots lines for the location of point 214.

7. `Specify third source point or <continue>:` Press ↵ to continue the command.

8. `Scale Objects based on alignment points? [Yes/No] <N>:` Press ↵ to accept no.

Points should be aligned with lot corners.

Note that since this point label style was created to be oriented with the point object, you can use the AutoCAD Rotate command to spin the X about its node and therefore rotate the label at the same time. Also note that you can use the AutoCAD Move, Copy, Delete, and other commands to make adjustments to these points.

Changing Point Elevations

In addition to the basic point-editing functions, there are a few advanced tools for manipulating points (see Figure 4.18), in the Points ➤ Edit Points submenu.

We noted earlier that points can be created from a surface elevation, but if you already have a batch of points in your drawing that you would like to move up to a surface you can use Points ➤ Edit Points ➤ Elevations From Surface (see Figure 4.19).

Selecting Points ➤ Edit Points ➤ Datum allows you to raise or lower all of the points in a drawing.

If you would like to change the datum of only a certain selection of points, pick the points, right-click, and choose Edit Points. In Panorama, highlight the points, right-click, and choose Datum. This technique can be used for any point in Panorama or in the Preview pane of Prospector.

FIGURE 4.18
Advanced Point Editing commands in the Points menu

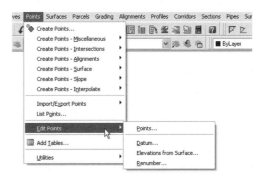

FIGURE 4.19
Tree points that were
moved up to surface
elevation

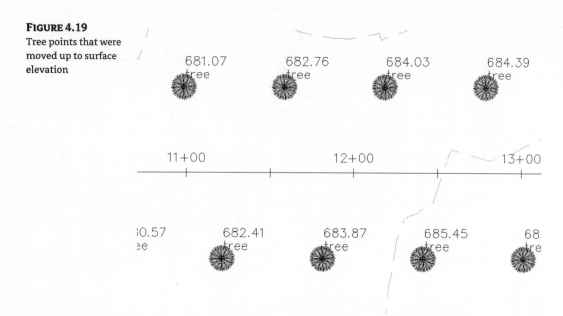

Point Styles

As with all other Civil 3D objects, the way that the point object itself appears is controlled by an object style. Point styles control the shape, size, location and visibility of the point marker (Figure 4.20) and the visibility of the point label.

Point styles appear on the Settings tab of Toolspace under the Point branch (see Figure 4.21).

FIGURE 4.20
The components
of a point object

FIGURE 4.21

Point styles on the Settings tab

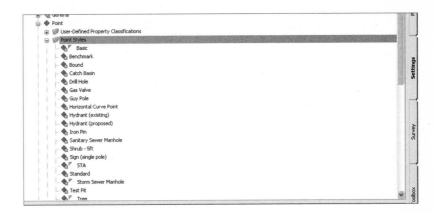

You can edit a point style by double-clicking on it. The Point Style dialog, which contains five tabs, appears. Each of these tabs are used to customize the point style:

Information Tab   The Information tab provides a place to name and describe your style (see Figure 4.22).

Marker Tab   The Marker tab (see Figure 4.23) allows you to customize the point marker. You can use an AutoCAD point, a custom marker (such as an X, +, or tick), or any AutoCAD block. The marker can have a fixed rotation.

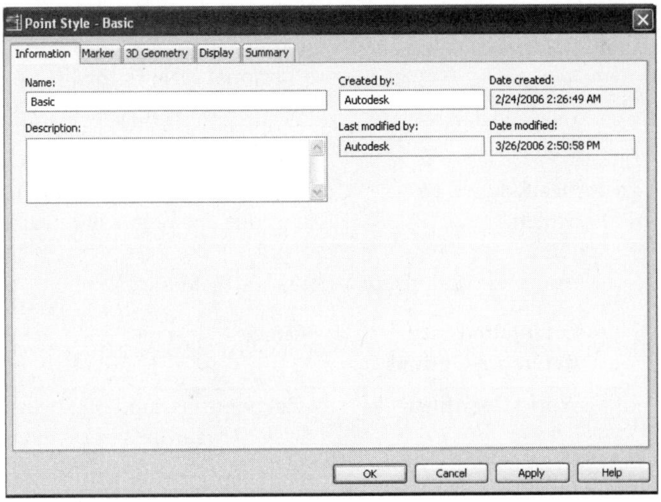

FIGURE 4.22

The Information tab in the Point Style dialog

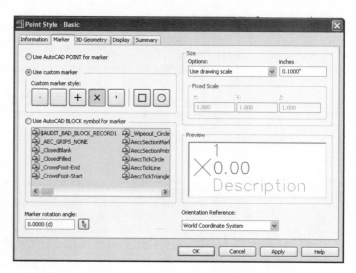

FIGURE 4.23
The Marker tab in the
Point Style dialog

You have these options for Size:

Size Options	Effect
Use Drawing Scale	Requires that you specify the plotted marker size in inches. Civil 3D will then scale the marker on the basis of your drawing or viewport scale.
Use Fixed Scale	Requires that you specify the actual size of the marker, then additional scale factors in the "Fixed Scale" area.
Use Size In Absolute Units	Requires that you specify an actual size for the marker.
Size Relative To Screen	Requires that you specify a percentage of the screen. As you zoom in or out, the points will resize when the screen is regenerated.

And these options for Orientation Reference:

Orientation Reference Options	Effect
World Coordinate System	The point marker will always relate to the World Coordinate System regardless of custom UCS changes or viewport orientation.
View	The point marker will respond to changes in viewport orientation.
Object	The point marker will be oriented with respect to the point location itself.

3D Geometry Tab If you would like to see your points drawn at the elevations they represent, you can set the Point Display Mode to Use Point Elevation. Most often, best practices would be to use Flatten Points To Elevation so that points are drawn at elevation zero with the balance of your normal linework.

This does not affect their intelligence, only where the actual points are physically drawn. For example, building points from surfaces uses the elevation value stored within the point intelligence, not the physical Z location of the point object.

This dialog also allows you to apply an exaggeration on the point object's location, if desired (see Figure 4.24).

Display Tab   The Display tab allows you to control visibility, layer mapping, and other properties in both 2D and 3D views of the Marker and Label components (see Figure 4.25).

Summary tab   The Summary tab provides a list of all of the point style properties (see Figure 4.26).

FIGURE 4.24
The 3D Geometry tab in the Point Style dialog

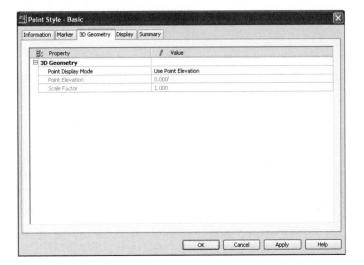

FIGURE 4.25
The Display tab in the Point Style dialog

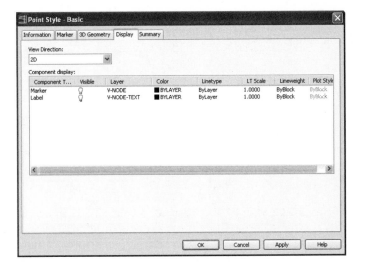

FIGURE 4.26
The Summary tab in
the Point Style dialog

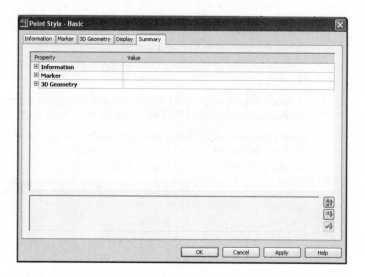

Point Label Styles

As with all other Civil 3D objects, the way that the point is labeled is controlled by the label style. Point label styles control which information is extracted from the point object for labeling purposes and how it is presented. This could be as simple as the point description in a standard font or as elaborate as several user-defined properties, coordinates, and more information in several colors and text styles.

Point label styles are composed much the same as all other labels in Civil 3D. For additional information about composing label styles, see Chapter 1 or the Civil 3D Users Guide.

Label styles appear on the Settings tab of Toolspace under the Point branch (see Figure 4.27).

FIGURE 4.27
Label styles on
the Settings tab

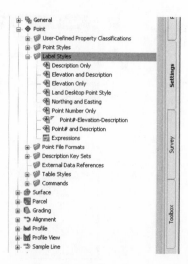

Edit a label style by double-clicking on it. The Label Style Composer dialog, which contains five tabs, appears. Each tab provides different options for customizing the label styles of the points in your drawing:

Information Tab The Information tab provides a place to name and describe your label style (see Figure 4.28).

General Tab The General tab provides options for setting text style, label visibility, layer, orientation, and readability (Figure 4.29).

Layout Tab The Layout tab in the Label Style Composer dialog is identical to the Layout tab of other label styles. Note that text, blocks, and lines can be added to the labels of points but there are no reference text options in points (see Figure 4.30).

Dragged State Tab The Dragged State tab is identical to the Dragged State tab of other label styles (see Figure 4.31).

Summary Tab This tab provides a list of all of the point style properties (see Figure 4.32).

FIGURE 4.28
The Information tab in the Label Style Composer dialog

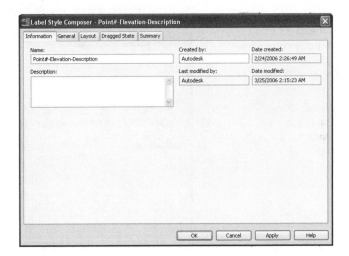

FIGURE 4.29
The General tab in the Label Style Composer dialog

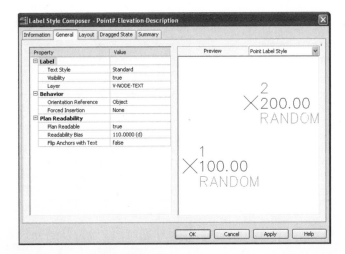

FIGURE 4.30
The Layout tab in the
Label Style Composer
dialog

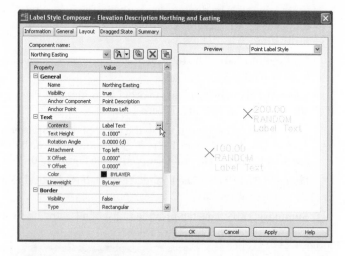

FIGURE 4.31
The Dragged State tab
in the Label Style
Composer dialog

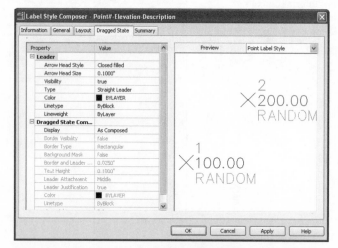

FIGURE 4.32
The Summary tab
in the Label Style
Composer

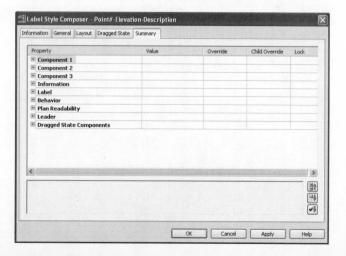

Creating More Complex Point and Point Label Styles

In this lesson, you will learn how to customize a point style to include a multiview block and to customize a point label style to include elevation, northing, and easting. Consider using points for objects you may have previously represented with AutoCAD blocks. Points are easier to label and edit, and you also gain the power of dynamic tables. Add the use of a 3D or multiview block and gain the ability to make 3D visualizations with little effort.

1. Open the file Point Style Exercise.dwg.

2. Expand the Point ➢ Point Styles branches of the Settings tab of Toolspace. Double-click the Tree point style to open the Point Style dialog.

3. Switch to the Marker tab. A 2D tree block is currently the marker for this style (you may have to scroll over to see the marker). Right-click in the white space of the Use AutoCAD BLOCK Symbol For Marker list box and click Browse, as shown in Figure 4.33.

4. Browse to C:\Program Files\AutoCAD Civil 3D 2008\Data\Symbols\Mvblocks\ Landscape. (Note that the path may vary depending on your OS or installation settings.)

5. Choose any tree multiview block in this directory, such as American Beech. Click Open to select this block as your point marker.

6. Switch to the Display tab of the Point Style dialog. Change the View Direction dropdown from 2D to 3D. Confirm that the Label component is turned off in 3D. Only the multiview tree block will be visible, and not the label text, when the drawing is rotated into isometric view.

7. Click OK to dismiss the Point Style dialog. Type **REGEN**↵ at the command line to see the changes in your point marker.

8. Select View ➢ 3D Views ➢ SW Isometric to change your drawing view from Top to SW Isometric. Zoom in on the site, and note that the trees appear as 3D trees in isometric.

9. Change back to Top view using View ➢ 3D Views ➢ Top.

FIGURE 4.33
Right-click in the block area and choose Browse.

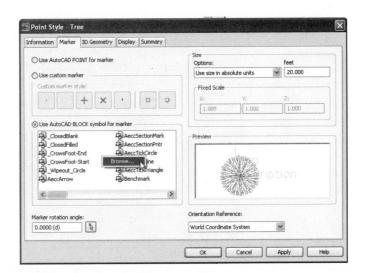

10. Expand the Point ≻ Label Styles branches on the Settings tab of Toolspace. Right-click the Elevation And Description label style and select Copy.

11. On the Information tab of the Label Style Composer, enter **Elevation Description Northing and Easting** in the Name text box.

12. Switch to the Layout tab. Click the down arrow next to the Create Text Component and choose Text from the dropdown menu, as shown in Figure 4.34.

13. Enter **Northing Easting** in the Text Component text box.

14. Change the Anchor Component to Point Description. This option will anchor the Northing Easting text to the Description text.

15. Change the Anchor Point to Bottom Left. This option will make sure that the label uses the bottom-left corner of the Point Description component as an attachment point.

16. Under the Text category, change the Attachment point to Top Left. This will ensure that the Northing Easting text uses the top-left corner to attach to the Point Description component. The Preview window should show the phrase Label Text lined up under the word RANDOM.

17. Click in the field for the Contents value to activate the ellipsis. Click the ellipsis button to open the Text Component Editor, as shown in Figure 4.35.

18. Use the Text Component Editor to add Northing, then Easting, to two decimal places separated by a comma. If you need more information about using the Text Component Editor, see Chapter 1 or the Civil 3D Users Guide.

19. Click OK to exit the Text Component Editor and again to exit the Label Style Composer.

20. Switch to the Prospector tab of Toolspace and locate the TREE point group under the Point Groups branch. Right-click and select Properties.

21. Select Elevation Description Northing and Easting from the dropdown menu in the Point Label Style selection box.

FIGURE 4.34
Adding a text component

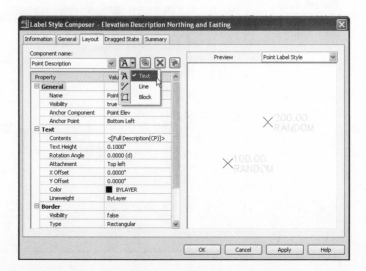

FIGURE 4.35
Click the ellipsis
button in the
Contents field.

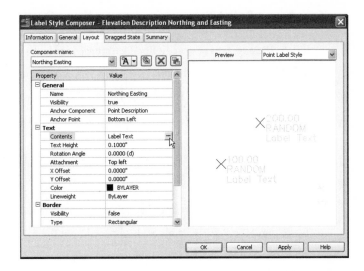

22. Zoom into one of your points and note the new label style. These labels can be dragged off to the site or the label style can be adjusted to have smaller text or different attachment points to ease readability.

23. The completed exercise is shown in the file `Point Style Exercise Finished.dwg`.

Point Tables

We've seen some of the power of dynamic point editing; now let's have a look at how those dynamic edits can be used to our advantage in point tables.

Most commonly, you may need to create a point table for survey or stakeout data; it could be as simple as a list of point numbers, northing, easting, and elevation. These types of tables are easy to create using the standard point table styles and the tools located in the Points menu under the Add Tables option.

Also consider that many plans require schedules and tables listing the locations and specifications of things like trees, signs, and light posts. Instead of representing these items with regular AutoCAD blocks labeled with quick leaders, consider building those blocks into your point object style and setting them as point objects instead. In the next exercise, we'll see how a tree schedule can be created from a customized point table style.

User-Defined Properties

Standard point properties include items such as number, easting, northing, elevation, name, description, and the other entries you see when examining points in Prospector or Panorama. But what if you would like a point to know more about itself?

It is common to receive points from a soil scientist that list additional information such as groundwater elevation or infiltration rate. Surveyed manhole points often include invert elevations or flow data. Tree points may also contain information about species or caliber measurements. All of this additional information can be added as user-defined properties to your point objects. User-defined properties can then be used in point labeling, analysis, point tables, and more.

Creating a Point Table and User-Defined Properties for Tree Points

In this exercise, you will learn how to create and customize a point table for tree location points, including the addition of user-defined properties for tree species:

1. Open the `Point Table.dwg` file. Note a series of points representing trees along an alignment.

2. Select Points ➤ Add Tables. The Point Table Creation dialog appears.

3. Click Select Point Groups on the right side of the middle of the dialog, next to the text that says No Point Group Selected, to open the Point Groups dialog. Select Tree, and click OK.

4. Leave all other options at their defaults, and click OK.

5. Place your table somewhere in the drawing off to the right side of the surface. Note that the table splits into three columns for readability. This table may be fine for many purposes, but let's customize it to be more suitable for a Tree schedule.

6. Expand the Point ➤ Table Styles branches on the Settings tab of Prospector.

7. Right-click the PNEZD table style and select Copy. The Table Style dialog appears.

8. On the Information tab, enter **Tree Table** in the Name text box.

9. Switch to the Data Properties tab.

10. Double-click the cell that says Point Table to display the Text Component Editor. Delete the words Point Table and enter **Tree Schedule**. Click OK.

11. Click to activate the Description column and click the red X to delete the Description column.

12. Click OK to exit the Table Style dialog.

13. Pan over to your table(s). Pick a table, right-click, and select Table Properties. The Table Properties dialog appears.

14. Select Tree Table (the style we just created) from the Table Style dropdown menu. Click OK.

Now let's create a user-defined property so that we can add a column for tree species:

1. Select the User-Defined Property Classifications entry under the Point branch on the Settings tab of Toolspace. Right-click and choose New. The User-Defined Property Classifications dialog appears.

2. Enter **Tree Properties** in the Classification Name text box.

3. Right-click the new entry under User-Defined Property Classification and select New. The New User-Defined Property dialog appears.

4. Enter **Species** in the Name text box, and make sure the Property Field Type selection box is set to String. Click OK. Note that we could continue to create additional properties such as diameter, canopy, or other extra tree values if we wanted.

5. Expand the Point ➤ Table Styles branches on the Settings tab. Double-click the Tree Table style to open the Table Style dialog.

6. Switch to the Data Properties tab (if not already there) and click in the Easting column to activate it. Click the blue + to add a new column.

7. Double-click the empty column header to open the Text Component Editor. Enter **Species** in the Preview screen to label the column. Click OK.

8. In the Column Value row, double-click under your Species column to open the Text Component Editor. Choose the user-defined property Species from the Properties dropdown menu, and click the blue arrow to move the name to the right side of the screen, as shown in Figure 4.36. (Sometimes it is necessary to save the drawing, exit Civil 3D, and reenter the drawing to see the User-Defined Properties as choices in the Text Component Editor and other places. If you do not see Species as a choice, click OK to exit the Text Component Editor, and again to exit the Table Style dialog. Save your drawing, close and reopen it, and come back to this point.)

9. Click OK to exit the Text Component Editor and OK again to exit the Table Style dialog. You should now see an empty Species column on the right side of your table in the drawing.

FIGURE 4.36

The Text Component Editor

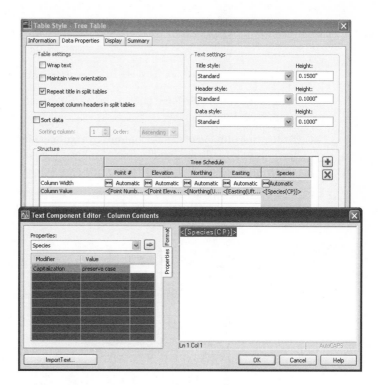

Next we need to assign the Species property to our Tree point group:

1. Highlight the Point Groups entry on the Prospector tab of Toolspace and look in the Preview pane to find the Classification column, as shown in Figure 4.37. (You may have to scroll to the right to see the Classification column.)

2. Click in the TREE Classification column and select the Tree Properties option from the drop-down menu. This tells the point group to add fields for any additional tree properties, such as our Species entry.

FIGURE 4.37

The Classification column in Prospector

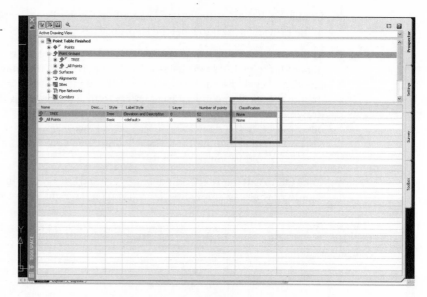

FIGURE 4.37

The Classification column in Prospector

3. Select TREE under the Point Group branch in Prospector. Species should now be the last column in the Preview pane.

4. Reduce the number of visible columns by right-clicking in a column header and unchecking the entries for latitude, longitude, and other columns that you aren't using right now, as shown in Figure 4.38. This will give us more room to work.

5. Enlarge the Species column by holding your mouse on the right side of the column header and dragging the column wider. Make a few entries in the Species column, such as **maple**, **oak**, **pine**, and so on.

FIGURE 4.38

Remove unnecessary columns from the Preview pane.

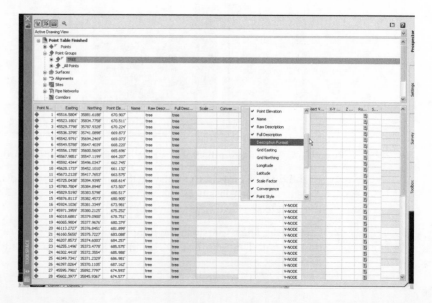

6. Go out to the Point Table and note the addition of these entries for user-defined properties, such as light post descriptions, hydrant specifications, and other proposed and existing features, as well as design elements.

7. The completed exercise can be seen in the `Point Table Finished.dwg`.

Creating a Point Group to Control Visibility and Moving a Point Group to Surface

Earlier we saw that default point styles and label styles could be assigned in the Command settings, but what happens when the points are already in our drawing or are accidentally placed with the wrong style? It would be tedious to select each point individually to make the change. Even making batch changes in Prospector would take a great deal of time.

Points often fit into categories. For example, topographic points could be grouped together for surface building, traverse points can be grouped to mark the path of surveyors, tree points can be separated into groups by specific species, and many other similar categories. These different categories can often be sorted and grouped for analysis, labeling, exporting, and other tasks. Point groups provide a tool for building sets of points that can be used not only to control visibility but also to organize points for more advanced applications, such as table creation.

You were introduced briefly to point groups in the section on point tables. This section, however, will more closely examine the options for point group creation and their uses.

Point groups can organize points on the basis of many different properties including, but not limited to, number (or range of numbers), elevations, descriptions, and names. Advanced query-building functions, overrides, exclusions, and other tools can also help fine-tune your point group.

In this exercise, you will learn how to use the Divide Alignment tool 🔘 to create a series of tree points, create a point group for them, and then use the Elevations From Surface tool to bring the tree points up to the existing ground surface elevation:

1. Open the drawing `Tree exercise.dwg`. Note that there is a surface and an alignment.

2. Choose Points ➢ Create Points. The Create Points dialog appears.

3. Click the down arrow on the Alignment category, and select the Divide Alignment tool.

4. At the command prompt, pick the alignment and enter **25**↵ at the segment prompt and **40**↵ at the offset prompt. This will place 25 points at equal intervals along the alignment at a 40′ offset. (When Civil 3D prompts for an offset, a positive number is a right offset.)

5. Enter **Tree**↵ as the point description and press ↵ at the elevation prompt. This will assign an initial elevation of zero to the points. Press ↵ to accept each point placement and note that red Xs, designating the points, are created at even intervals, as shown in Figure 4.39. Your drawing may show an elevation of zero or alternatively no elevation listing. Both cases are OK at this point. (Note that instead of pressing ↵ each time to accept the description and elevation, you could have also changed the default point settings as described in the "Creating Basic Points" section of this chapter.)

6. Repeat the process for the other side of the road. You can use the Divide Alignment tool, the Measure Alignment tool, or any other tool that appeals to you. Just remember that at this point, elevation is not important.

FIGURE 4.39
Using the Divide
Alignment tool to
place points

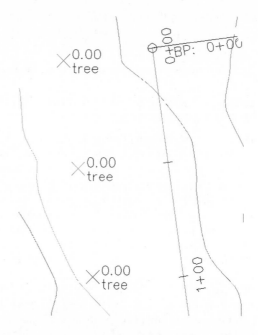

7. Right-click the Point Groups collection in Prospector and select New. The Point Group Properties dialog appears, and you can create a point group for your tree points.

8. Enter **Tree** in the Name text box. Select Tree from the dropdown menu in the Point Style selection box and Elevation And Description in the Point Label Style selection box.

9. Switch to the Include tab. Check the With Raw Description Matching box and type **TREE** into the text box, as shown in Figure 4.40.

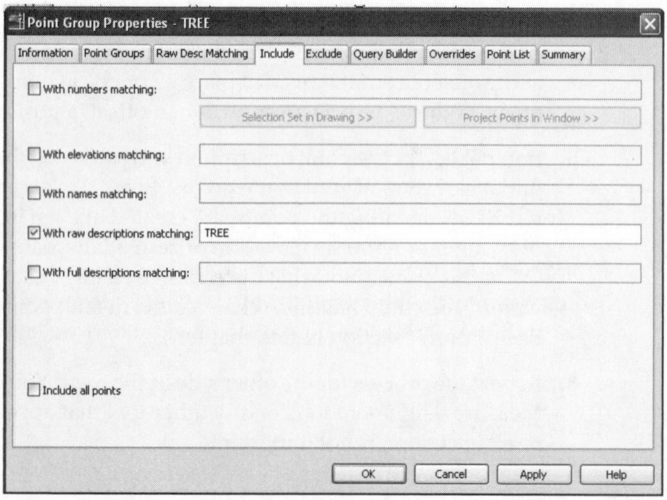

FIGURE 4.40
The Include tab of
the Point Group
Properties dialog

Point Group Properties - TREE

Information | Point Groups | Raw Desc Matching | Include | Exclude | Query Builder | Overrides | Point List | Summary

☐ With numbers matching:

    Selection Set in Drawing >>   Project Points in Window >>

☐ With elevations matching:

☐ With names matching:

☑ With raw descriptions matching: TREE

☐ With full descriptions matching:

☐ Include all points

OK   Cancel   Apply   Help

10. Click OK, and the point group will be created.

11. Zoom in on your points in the drawing. You should see the points as a tree block, as in Figure 4.41, with a label that reads *tree*. There are no elevations yet, but your drawing may list them as elevation zero.

12. Select Points ➢ Edit Points ➢ Elevations From Surface. The Select Surface dialog appears.

13. Choose EG from the dropdown menu and click OK.

14. The command line prompts for `Points [All/Numbers/Group/Selection]<All>`. Press `G↵ for Group`. The Point Groups dialog appears.

15. Select Tree, and click OK. Note that the tree points now have elevations reflecting the existing ground (EG) surface, as shown in Figure 4.41. If your EG changes, simply reapply the Elevations From Surface tool.

16. The completed exercise is shown in `Tree Exercise Finished.dwg`.

FIGURE 4.41
The completed exercise

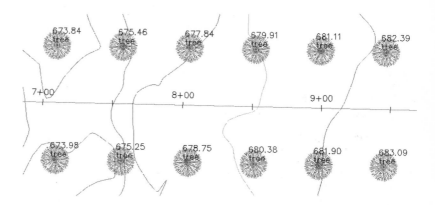

Working with Description Keys

Description keys are a tool that can be used to automatically control the visibility of points that meet certain criteria. Point groups control the style and labeling of the entire group of points, but description keys are applied to a single point as an override. In other words, a description key is an automated equivalent of manually choosing a point and changing its point style in Panorama.

If a new point is created when a description key set is active, the description key matches a point's raw description with a predefined set of style, label, format, and layer parameters. The example shown in Figure 4.42 indicates that all points created with the raw description of XTREE would be immediately identified by the description key as needing a tree style, a standard label style, and the existing tree format, and assigned to the layer V-NODE-TREE.

FIGURE 4.42

A tree description key

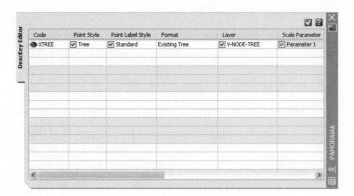

RAW DESCRIPTION VS. FULL DESCRIPTION

In Civil 3D vocabulary, the raw description as listed in Prospector and the code as listed in the DescKey Editor are identical. You can think of raw description or code as a field or machine-friendly string of characters that a surveyor would input while collecting points. These codes are used by the description key set to identify which description key to apply to a certain point. Typically, these codes are standardized by your company.

Along the same vein, full description and format are identical. Full description can "humanize" the raw description for use in labeling and identification purposes. For example, a code of BOTB might be difficult to understand if used in the point label. In that case, a format of "Bottom of Bank" can be applied in the BOTB description key and the full description used in the point label style.

In cases where you would like the format/full description to simply match the code/raw description, type ***$** in the Format column of the DescKey Editor.

The important thing to remember about description keys is that unlike point groups, they only work for points that are newly created, imported, or converted in the drawing when the description key set is active. If you already have points in your drawing, the description key will not scan the drawing to make changes to existing points.

CREATING A DESCRIPTION KEY SET

Description key sets appear on the Settings tab of Toolspace under the Point branch. A new description key set can be created by right-clicking on the Description Key Set collection and choosing New, as shown in Figure 4.43.

In the resulting Description Key Set dialog, give your description key set a meaningful name and click OK. You'll create the actual description keys in another dialog.

FIGURE 4.43
Creating a description key set

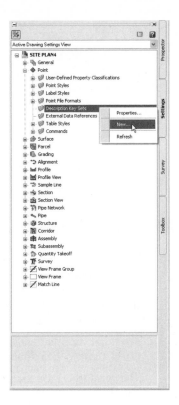

CREATING DESCRIPTION KEYS

The individual description key codes and parameters are entered by right-clicking your description key set, as illustrated in Figure 4.44, and selecting Edit Keys. The DescKey Editor in Panorama appears.

New codes can be entered by right-clicking on a row with an existing key in the DescKey Editor and choosing New or Copy from the shortcut menu, as shown in Figure 4.45.

FIGURE 4.44
Editing a description key set

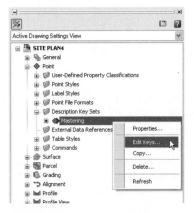

FIGURE 4.45

Creating or copying a description key

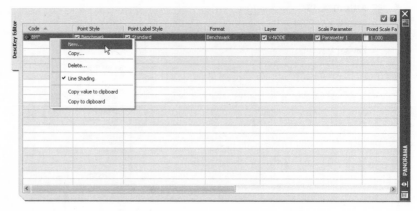

The first five columns in the DescKey Editor are the most commonly used:

Column	Use
Code	The raw description or "field" code entered by the person collecting or creating the points that works as an identifier for matching the point with the correct description key. Click inside this field to activate, then type your desired code. Wildcards are allowed.
Point Style	The point style that will be applied to points that meet the code criteria. Check the box, then click inside the field to activate a style selection dialog.
Point Label Style	The point label style that will be applied to points that meet the code criteria. Check the box, then click inside the field to activate a style selection dialog.
Format	The format or full description that will be applied to points that meet the code criteria. A value can be typed in this field, or use $* to match code.
Layer	The layer that will be applied to points that meet the code criteria. Click inside this field to activate a layer selection dialog.

Most firms will want to create a complete description key set for their standard field code list. Figure 4.46 shows an example of a short description key set using some common field codes, styles, and formats.

USING WILDCARDS

The asterisk (*) acts as a wildcard many places in Civil 3D. Two of the most common places to use a wildcard are the DescKey Editor and the Point Group Properties dialog. While a DescKey code of TREE will flag any points created with that raw description, a DescKey code of TREE* will also pick up raw descriptions of TREE1, TREE2, TREEMAPLE, TREEOAK, and so on. You can use the wildcard in the same way in the Point Group Properties dialog when specifying items to include or exclude.

There are more wildcard characters available for use in the DescKey Editor. See page 487 of the Civil 3D Users Guide PDF (found under the Help menu) for more information.

FIGURE 4.46

A simple description key set containing five description keys

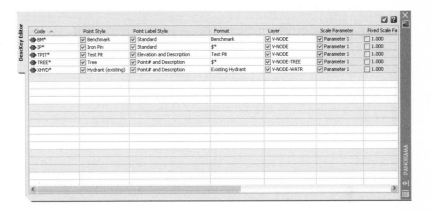

ADVANCED DESCRIPTION KEY PARAMETERS

After the first five columns, you will see additional columns containing advanced parameters. These parameters can be used to automatically scale and rotate your points based on information collected in the field. For more information and complete documentation on these features, see the Civil 3D Users Guide under the Help menu.

ACTIVATING A DESCRIPTION KEY SET

Once your description key set has been created, you must change the settings for your commands so that Civil 3D knows to match your newly created points with the appropriate key.

The Command ➤ CreatePoints branches are stored on the Settings tab of Toolspace under the Points branch. Edit these command settings by right-clicking, as shown in Figure 4.47.

In the Edit Command Settings dialog, ensure that Match On Description Parameters is set to True and Disable Description Keys is set to False, as shown in Figure 4.48.

If you have multiple description key sets in your drawing, you must specify matching search order for the sets. When a new point is created, Civil 3D will search through the first set on the list and work its way down through all the description keys in your drawing.

This search order can be accessed by locating the Description Key Sets collection on the Settings tab of Toolspace, right-clicking, and then choosing Properties. The dialog shown in Figure 4.49 appears. Use the arrows to move the desired description key set to adjust the search order.

FIGURE 4.47

The CreatePoints command settings

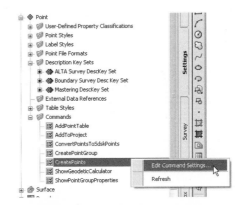

FIGURE 4.48
Set Disable Description Keys to False.

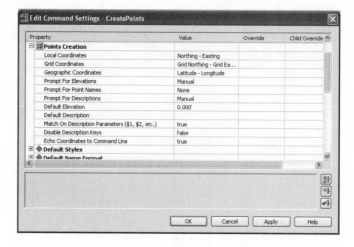

FIGURE 4.49
The Description Key Sets Search Order dialog

POINT GROUPS OR DESCRIPTION KEYS?

After reading through the last two sections, you're probably wondering which method is better for controlling the look of your points. There is no absolute answer to this question, but there are some things to take into consideration when making your decision.

Point groups are useful for both visibility control and sorting. They are dynamic and can be used to control the visibility of points that already exist in your drawing.

Both can be standardized and stored in your Civil 3D template.

Your best bet is probably a combination of the two methods. For large batches of imported points or points that require advanced rotation and scaling parameters, description keys are the better tool. For preparing points for surface building, exporting and changing the visibility of points already in your drawing, point groups will prove most useful.

The Bottom Line

Import points from a text file using description key matching. Most engineering offices receive text files containing point data at some point during a project. Description keys provide a way to automatically assign the appropriate styles, layers, and labels to newly imported points.

Master It Create a new drawing from _AutoCAD Civil 3D (Imperial) NCS Extended.dwt. Revise the Civil 3D description key set to use the following parameters:

Code	Point Style	Point Label Style	Format	Layer
GS	Standard	Elevation Only	Ground Shot	V-NODE
GUY	Guy Pole	Elevation and Description	Guy Pole	V-NODE
HYD	Hydrant (existing)	Elevation and Description	Existing Hydrant	V-NODE-WATR
TOP	Standard	Point#-Elevation-Description	Top of Curb	V-NODE
TREE	Tree	Elevation and Description	Existing Tree	V-NODE-TREE

Import the MasteringPointsPNEZDspace.txt file from the data location and confirm that the description keys made the appropriate matches by looking at a handful of points of each type. Do the trees look like trees? Do the hydrants look like hydrants?

Create a point group. Building a surface using a point group is a very common task. Among other criteria, you may want to filter out any points with zero or negative elevations from your Topo point group.

Master It Create a new point group called Topo that includes all points *except* those with elevations of zero or less.

Export points to LandXML and ASCII format. It is often necessary to export a LandXML or an ASCII file of points for stakeout or data-sharing purposes. Unless you want to export every point from your drawing, it is best to create a point group that isolates the desired point collection.

Master It Create a new point group that includes all of the points with a raw description of TOP. Export this point group via LandXML and to a PNEZD Comma Delimited text file.

Create a point table. Point tables provide an opportunity to list and study point properties. In addition to basic point tables that list number, elevation, description, and similar options, point table formats can be customized to include user-defined property fields.

Master It Create a point table for the Topo point group using the PNEZD format table style.

Chapter 5

The Ground Up: Surfaces in Civil 3D

While it's fun to play in fantasy land, designing in a void, at some point we have to get real to get things built. Once the survey has come in, the boundaries have been laid out, and the project has been defined, we have to start building a real model. One of the most primitive elements in a 3D model of any design is the surface. In this chapter, we'll look at various methods of surface creation and editing. Then we'll move into discussing ways to view, analyze, and label surfaces, and we'll explore how they interact with other parts of our project.

In this chapter, you will learn to:

- ◆ Create a preliminary surface using freely available data
- ◆ Modify and update a TIN surface
- ◆ Prepare a slope analysis
- ◆ Label surface contours and spot elevations

Digging In

A surface in Civil 3D is built on the basis of mathematical principles of planar geometry. Each face of a surface is based on three points defining a plane. Each of these triangular planes shares an edge with another, and a continuous surface is made. This methodology is typically referred to as a triangulated irregular network (TIN). On the basis of Delaunay triangulation, this means that for any given (x,y) point, there can be only one unique z value within the surface. What does this mean to you? It means surfaces in Civil 3D have two major limitations:

No thickness Operations on the basis of solid modeling are not possible. You cannot add or subtract surfaces or look for their unions as you can with a solid that has thickness in the vertical direction.

No vertical faces Vertical faces cannot exist in a TIN object since two points on the surface cannot have the same (x,y) coordinate pair. At a theoretical level, this limits the ability of Civil 3D to handle true vertical surfaces, such as walls or curb structures. In reality, the micro-miniscule amount of pitch required to keep a surface from going vertical is impossible to discern; it just has to be recognized and input to the system.

Beyond these basic limitations, surfaces are flexible and can describe any object's face in astonishing detail. The surfaces can range in size from a few square feet to square miles and generally process quickly.

There are two main categories of surfaces in Civil 3D: standard surfaces and volume surfaces. A standard surface is based on a single set of points, whereas a volume surface builds a surface by measuring distances between surfaces. Each of these surfaces can also be a grid or TIN surface. The grid version is still a TIN upon calculation of planar faces, but the data points are arranged in a regularly spaced grid of information. The TIN surface definition is made from randomly located points that may or may not follow any pattern to their location.

Creating Surfaces

Before we can analyze or do any other fun things with a surface, we have to make one! To the land development company today, this can mean pulling information from a large number of sources, including Internet sources, old drawings, and fieldwork. Working with each requires some level of knowledge about the reliability of the information and how to handle it in Civil 3D. In this section, we'll look at obtaining data from a couple of free sources and into your drawing, creating new surfaces in both TIN and grid formats, and making a volume surface.

Before moving on to creating the surface, let's look at the components that can be used as part of the definition:

LandXML files   These typically come from an outside source or are exported from another project. LandXML has become the lingua franca of the land development industry. These files include information about points and triangulation, making replication of the original surface a snap.

TIN files   Typically, a TIN file will come from a land development project that you or a peer worked on. These files contain the baseline TIN information from the original surface and can be used to replicate it easily.

DEM files   Digital Elevation Model (DEM) files are the standard format files from governmental agencies and GIS systems. These files are typically very large in scale, but can be great for planning purposes.

Point files   Point files work well when you're working with large data sets where the points themselves don't necessarily contain extra information. Examples include laser scanning or aerial surveys.

Point groups   Civil 3D point groups or survey point groups can be used to build a surface from their respective members and maintain the link between the membership in the point group and being part of the surface.

Boundaries   Boundaries are closed polylines that determine the visibility of the TIN inside the polyline. Outer boundaries are often used to eliminate stray triangulation, whereas others are used to indicate areas that could perhaps not be surveyed, such as a building pad.

Breaklines   Breaklines are used for creating hard-coded triangulation paths, even when those paths violate the Delaunay algorithms for normal TIN creation. These can describe anything from the top of a ridge to the flowline of a curb section.

Drawing objects   AutoCAD objects that have elevation can be used to populate a surface with points. It's important to remember that the objects themselves are not connected to the surface in any way.

Edits   Any manipulation after the surface is completed, such as adding or removing triangles or changing the datum, will be part of the edit history. These changes can be toggled on and off individually to make reviewing changes simple.

Working with all of these elements, you can model and render almost anything you'd find in the world—and many things you wouldn't. In the next section, we'll start actually building some surfaces.

Free Surface Information

You can find almost anything on the Internet, including information about your project site that probably includes level information you can use to build a surface.

One of the most common forms of free data is the Digital Elevation Model (DEM). These files have been used by the US Department of the Interior's United States Geological Survey (USGS) for years and are commonly produced by government organizations for their GIS systems. The DEM format can be read directly by Civil 3D, but USGS typically distributes the data in a complex format called Spatial Data Transfer Standard (SDTS). The files can be converted using a freely available tool (included on the companion CD). called `sdts2dem`. This DOS-based tool converts the files from the SDTS format to the DEM format we need. Once you are in possession of a DEM file, creating a surface from it is relatively simple, as you'll see in this exercise.

1. Start a new blank drawing from the NCS Imperial Extended template that ships with Civil 3D.

2. Switch to the Settings tab of Toolspace, right-click on the drawing name and select Drawing Settings. Set the coordinate system as shown in Figure 5.1 via the Drawing Settings dialog, and click OK. The coordinate system of the DEM file that we will import will be set to match the coordinate system of our drawing.

3. In Prospector, right-click the Surfaces collection and select the Create Surface option. The Create Surface dialog appears.

4. Accept the options in the dialog, and click OK to create the surface. This surface is added as Surface 1 to the Surfaces collection.

5. Expand the Surfaces ➢ Surface 1 ➢ Definition branch, as shown in Figure 5.2.

FIGURE 5.1
Civil 3D coordinate settings for DEM import

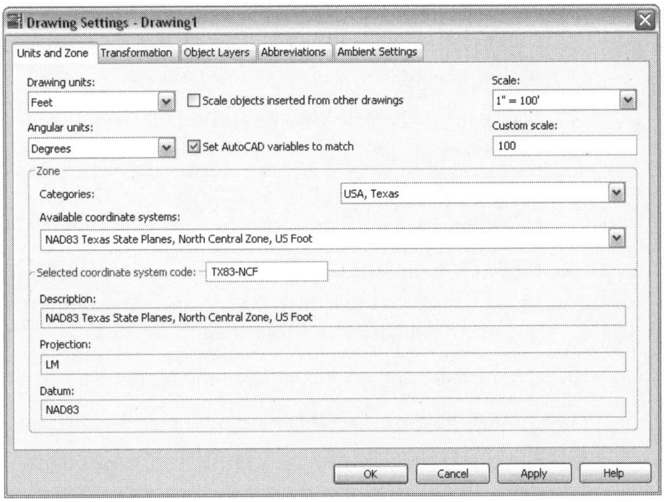

FIGURE 5.2
Adding DEM data
to a surface

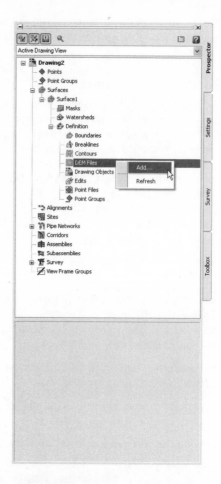

6. Right-click on DEM Files and select the Add option (see Figure 5.2). The Add DEM File dialog appears.

7. Navigate to the McKinneyWest.DEM file in the chapter data files on the book's CD, and click Open.

8. Set the values in the DEM File Properties dialog as shown in Figure 5.3 and click OK. This translates the DEM's coordinate system to the drawing's coordinate system.

9. Right-click on Surface 1 in Prospector and select Surface Properties. (You could also right-click on Surface 1 in Prospector and select Zoom To. Right-click on the surface in your drawing, and select Surface Properties.) The Surface Properties dialog appears.

10. On the Information tab, change the Name field to McKinney W, and close the dialog.

11. Change the Surface Style field to Standard (this displays a border only).

FIGURE 5.3
Setting the
McKinney
West.DEM file
properties

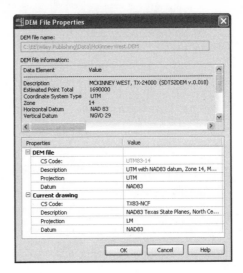

Once you have the DEM data imported, you can pause over any portion of the surface and see that Civil 3D is providing feedback through a tooltip. This surface can be used for preliminary planning purposes but isn't accurate enough for construction purposes. The main drawback to DEM data is the sheer bulk of the surface size and point count. A typical USGS DEM file contains 19,000 points and covers an area much larger than the typical site.

In addition to making a DEM a part of a TIN surface, you can build a surface directly from the DEM. The drawback to this is that no coordinate transformation is possible. Since one of the real benefits of using georectified data is pulling in information from differing coordinate systems, we're skipping this method to focus on the more flexible method shown here.

WHERE TO FIND FREE INFORMATION

Numerous websites contain free GIS information, but it can be hard to keep up with them. Scott McEachron has been a fan of free GIS data for years. His Autodesk University presentations on getting free data and using it were among our favorites—he always kept his list of sites up to date. Now you can find that list at his Civil 3D–related blog, `http://c3dpavingtheway.blogspot.com`.

Inexpensive Surface Approximations

Inexpensive is a relative term, but compared with on-the-ground surveying, a Google Earth Pro license or aerial and laser scanning services are inexpensive, especially in difficult terrain or over large tracts. In this section, we'll work with Google Earth information, elevations at polylines, and a large point cloud. These last two types are quite common, and historically it can be difficult making an acceptable surface from them.

SURFACES FROM GOOGLE EARTH PRO

Civil 3D 2008 includes an importing function that brings in surface and image information from Google Earth! In this first exercise, we'll look at importing a Google Earth location as a Civil 3D surface.

1. Download the latest version of Google Earth from http://earth.google.com and install it.

2. Launch Google Earth and get connected.

3. From the main menu, choose File ➤ Open.

4. Navigate to the Data directory and select the Efficiency Acres.kmz file on the CD to restore a view of a site in McKinney, Texas.

5. In Civil 3D, create a new drawing from the Imperial NCS Extended template and set the coordinate system as we did in the prior exercise.

6. From the main menu, choose File ➤ Import ➤ Import Google Earth Surface.

7. Press ↵ to accept the coordinate system.

8. From the main menu, choose View ➤ Zoom ➤ Extents to see something like Figure 5.4.

The interesting thing about surfaces built from Google Earth is that their accuracy is zoom-level dependent. This means that the tighter you are zoomed into a site in Google Earth, the better the surface you derive from that picture. Because of this dependence, you should attempt to zoom in as tightly as possible on the area of interest when using Google Earth for preliminary surface information.

FIGURE 5.4
Completed Google
Earth Pro surface
import

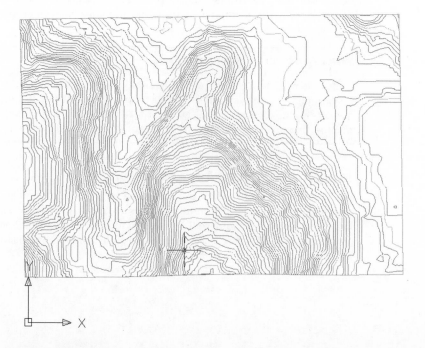

GOOGLE EARTH PRO?

You don't hear that name thrown out very often, but it's an important distinction if you're going to be using Google's surface information or surfaces in any way. The license for the free version explicitly states that it is not to be used for commercial purposes. Even if you never use the information beyond planning, you're a commercial user. Get licensed. At $400 a seat, Google Earth Pro is a steal for the information you get in return. Plus, you get some bonus functionality not found in the free version.

SURFACES FROM AERIAL CONTOUR INFORMATION

One of the common complaints of converting a drawing full of contours at elevation into a working Civil 3D surface is that the resulting contours don't accurately reflect the original data. With 2007, Civil 3D added a series of surface edits that work very well at matching the resulting surface to the original contour data. We'll look at those surface edits in this series of exercises.

1. Open the Aerial Contours.dwg file. Note that the contours in this file are composed of polylines.

2. In Prospector, right-click on the Surfaces branch, and select the Create Surface option. The Create Surface dialog appears.

3. Leave the Type field as TIN Surface but change the Name value to EG-Aerial.

4. Change the Description to something appropriate.

5. Change the Style value to Aerial and click OK to close the dialog

6. Expand the Surfaces ➢ EG-Aerial ➢ Definition branches.

7. Right-click on Contours and select the Add option. The Add Contour Data dialog appears.

8. Set the options as shown in Figure 5.5 and click OK. We will return to the Minimize Flat Areas By options in a bit, but for now, let's see what comes of the basic contour information.

9. Type **ALL** at the command line to select all of the entities in the drawing.

FIGURE 5.5
The Add Contour
Data dialog

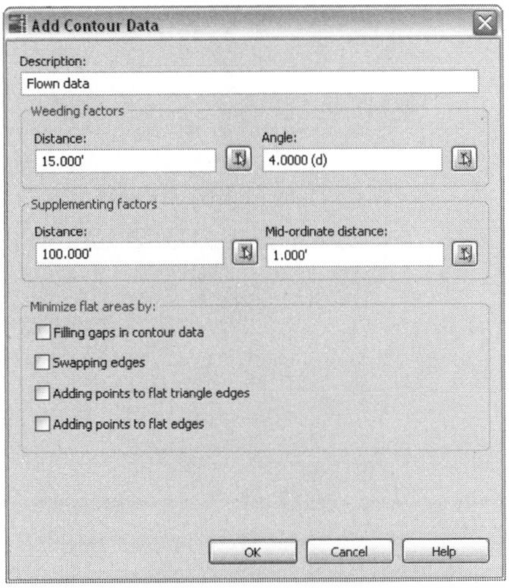

The contour data has some tight curves and flat spots where the algorithms simply fail. Zoom in to any portion of the site, and you can see these areas by looking for the red original contour not matching the new yellow or green Civil 3D-generated contour. Let's fix that now.

1. Expand the Definition branch and right-click on Edits. Select the Minimize Flat Areas option to open the Minimize Flat Areas dialog. Note that the dialog has the same options found in that portion of our original Add Contour Data dialog. We just did it as two steps to illustrate the power of these changes!

2. Click OK.

Now the contours displayed more closely match to the original contour information. There might be a few instances where there are gaps between old and new contour lines, but in a cursory analysis, none was off by more than 0.4′ in the horizontal direction—not bad when you're dealing with almost a square mile of contour information. Let's see how this was done in this quick exercise:

1. Zoom into an area with a dense contour spacing and select the surface.

2. Right-click and select the Surface Properties option. The Surface Properties dialog appears.

3. Change the Surface Style field to Contours With Points and click OK to see a drawing similar to Figure 5.6.

In Figure 5.6, we're seeing the points the TIN is derived from, with some styling applied to help understand the creation source of the points. Each point in red is a point picked up from the contour data itself. The blue points are all added data on the basis of the Minimize Flat Areas edits. These points make it possible for the Civil 3D surface to match almost exactly the input contour data.

FIGURE 5.6
Surface data points
and derived data
points

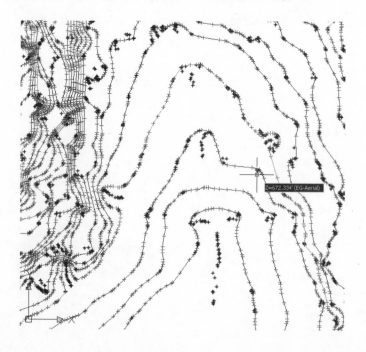

SURFACES FROM POINT CLOUDS OR TEXT FILES

Besides receiving polylines, it is common for an aerial surveying company to also send a simple text file with points. This isn't an ideal situation since we have no information about breaklines or other surface features, but it is better than nothing or using a Google Earth–derived surface. Because we have the same aerial surface described as a series of points, we'll add them to a surface in this exercise:

1. Create a new drawing using the NCS Extended Template.

2. From the main menu, choose Surfaces ➤ Create Surface. The Create Surface dialog appears.

3. Change the Name value to Aerial Points, and click OK to close the dialog.

4. In Prospector, expand the Surfaces ➤ Aerial Points ➤ Definition branches.

5. Right-click on Point Files and select the Add option. The Add Point File dialog appears.

6. Set the Format field to ENZ (Comma Delimited).

7. Click the Browse button shown in Figure 5.7. The Select Source File dialog opens.

8. Navigate to the Data folder, and select the `Point Cloud.txt` file. Click OK.

9. Click OK to exit the Add Point File dialog and build the surface.

10. Right-click on Aerial Points in Prospector and select the Zoom To option to view the new surface created.

This surface looks much like the one created from polylines, as it should. In both cases, we're making surfaces from the best information available. When doing preliminary work or large-scale planning, these types of surfaces are great. For more accurate and design-based surfaces, we typically have to get into field-surveyed information. We'll look at that next.

FIGURE 5.7
Adding a point file to the surface definition

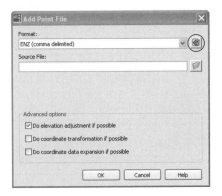

On-the-Ground Surveying

DEM and Google Earth are good starting points and aerial or laser-scanned data can be a solid addition, but most land development projects get built after the ground topographic (topo for short) work is performed. In this exercise, we'll look at building a surface from a point group created by surveyed points. Once we've completed basic surface building, it will be time to edit and refine it further.

1. Open the `Surface Points.dwg` file.

2. Right-click the Surfaces branch in Prospector and select the New option. The Create Surface dialog appears.

3. Change the Name to EG.

4. Click in the Style value field and click the ellipsis button to open the Select Surface Style dialog. Select the Contours 2′ and 10′ (Design) option, and then click OK to close the dialog.

5. Click OK again to close the Create Surface dialog.

6. In Prospector, expand the Surfaces ➤ EG ➤ Definition branches.

7. Right-click on Point Groups and select the Add option. The Point Groups dialog appears.

8. Select the Field Work point group and click OK. The dialog closes and your screen should look like Figure 5.8.

Simply adding surface information to a TIN definition isn't enough. To get beyond the basics, we need to look at the edits and other types of information that can be part of a surface.

FIGURE 5.8
Surface with just
point information

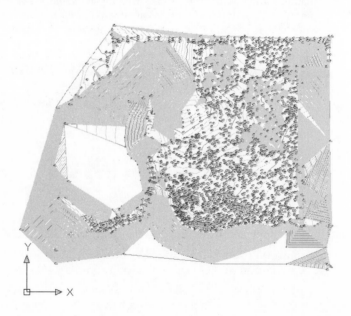

Refining and Editing Surfaces

Once a basic surface is built, and, in some cases, even before it is built, we can do some cleanup and modification to the TIN construction that make it much more usable and realistic. Some of these edits include limiting the input data, tweaking the triangulation, adding in breakline information, or hiding areas from view. In this section, we'll look at a number of ways to refine surfaces to give us the best possible model from which to build.

Surface Properties

The most basic steps we can perform in making a better model are right in the Surface Properties dialog. The surface object contains information about the build and edit operations, along with some values used in surface calculations. These values can be used to tweak our surface to a semi-acceptable state before more manual operations are needed.

In this exercise, we'll go through a couple of the basic surface-building controls that are available. We'll do them one at a time in order to measure their effects on the final surface display.

1. Open the Surface Properties.dwg file.

2. Expand the Surfaces branch.

3. Right-click EG and select Surface Properties. The Surface Properties dialog appears.

4. Select the Definition tab. Note the list at the bottom of the dialog.

5. Under the Definition Options at the top of the dialog, expand the Build option.

The Build options of the Definition tab allows us to tweak the way the triangulation occurs. The basic options are:

Copy Deleted Dependent Objects   When Yes is selected and an object that is part of the surface definition (like the polylines we used in our aerial surface, for instance) is deleted, the information derived from that object is copied into the surface definition. Setting this option to True in our aerial surface properties would let us erase the polylines from the drawing file while still maintaining the surface information.

Exclude Elevations Less Than   Setting this to Yes puts a floor on the surface. Any point that would be built into the surface, but is lower than the floor, is ignored. In our EG surface, there are calculated boundary points with zero elevations, causing real problems that can be solved with this simple click. The floor elevation is controlled by the user.

Exclude Elevations Greater Than   The idea is the same as with the preceding option, but a ceiling value is used.

Use Maximum Triangle Length   This setting attempts to limit the number of narrow "sliver" triangles that typically border a site. By not drawing any triangle with a length greater than the user input value, you can greatly refine the TIN.

Convert Proximity Breaklines To Standard   Toggling this to Yes will create breaklines out of the lines and entities used as proximity breaklines. We'll look at this more later.

Allow Crossing Breaklines   Determines what Civil 3D should do if two breaklines in a surface definition cross each other. As mentioned, an (x,y) coordinate pair cannot have two z values, so some decision must be made about crossing breaklines. If you set this to Yes, you can then select whether to use the elevation from the first or the second breakline or to average these elevations.

In this next portion of the exercise, we'll limit the build options in order to create a better model.

1. Set the Exclude Elevations Less Than value to Yes

2. Set the Value to 200 and click OK to exit the dialog. Elevations less than 200´ will be excluded.

3. A warning message will appear. Civil 3D is simply warning you that your surface definition has changed. Click Yes to rebuild the surface. When it's done, it should look like Figure 5.9.

FIGURE 5.9
EG surface after ignoring low elevations

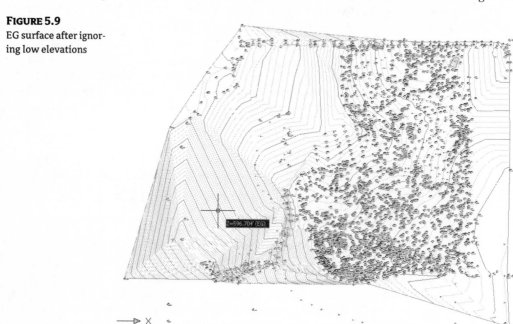

While this surface is better than our original, there are still huge areas being contoured that probably shouldn't be. By changing the style to review the surface, we can see where we still have some issues.

1. Bring up the Surface Properties dialog again, and switch to the Information tab.

2. Change the Surface Style field to Contours And Triangles.

3. Click Apply. This makes the changes without exiting the dialog.

4. Drag the dialog to the side so you can see the site. On the west side of the site, we can see some long triangles formed in areas where a survey was taken to pick up an offsite easement and tie into existing survey monuments.

5. Switch to the Definition tab.

6. Expand the Build option.

7. Set the Use Maximum Triangle Length value to Yes.

8. In the Maximum Triangle Length value field, there is a Pick On Screen button ⬚ ; click it and the dialog disappears.

9. Pick points as shown in Figure 5.10. The value should return around 850´. After picking the second point, the Surface Properties dialog should reappear.

10. Click OK to apply and exit the dialog.

11. Click Yes to rebuild and dismiss the warning message.

The value is a bit high, but it is a good practice to start with a high value and work down to avoid losing any pertinent data. Setting this value to 600´ will result in a surface that is acceptable because it doesn't lose a bunch of important points. Beyond this, we'll need to look at making some edits to the definition itself instead of modifying the build options.

FIGURE 5.10
Pick points for the Max Triangle Length

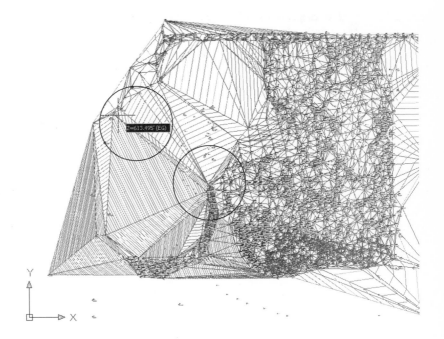

Surface Additions

Beyond the simple changes to the way the surface is built, we can look at modifying the pieces that make up the surface. In the case of our drawing so far, we have merely been building from points. While this is OK for small surfaces, we need to go further in the case of this surface. In this section, we'll add a few breaklines and a border and finally perform some manual edits to our site.

ADDING BREAKLINE INFORMATION

Breaklines can come from any number of sources. They can be approximated on the basis of aerial photos of the site that help define surface features or can be directly input from fieldbook files and the Civil 3D survey functionality. Five types of breaklines are available for use:

Standard breaklines are built on the basis of 3D lines, feature lines, or polylines. They typically connect points already included but can contain their own elevation data. Simple-use cases for connecting the dots include linework from a survey or drawing a building pad to ensure that a flat area is included in the surface. Feature lines and 3D polylines are often used as the mechanism for grading design and include their own vertical information. This might be the description of a parking lot area or a drainage swale behind a building, for instance.

Proximity breaklines allow you to force triangulation without picking precise points. These lines force triangulation but will not add vertical information to the surface.

Wall breaklines do just what they sound like: they define walls in surfaces. Because of the limitation of true vertical surfaces, a wall breakline will let you approximate a wall without having to create an offset. These are defined on the basis of an elevation at a vertex, then an elevation difference at each vertex.

Nondestructive breaklines are designed to maintain the integrity of the original surface while updating triangulation.

From File can be selected if a text file contains breakline information. This can be the output of another program and can be used to modify the surface without the creation of additional drawing objects.

In most cases, we'll build our surfaces from standard, proximity, and wall breaklines. In this example, we'll add in some breaklines that describe road and surface features:

1. Open the Surface Additions.dwg file.

2. In Prospector, expand the Surfaces ➢ EG ➢ Definition branches.

3. Right-click on Breaklines and select the Add option. The Add Breaklines dialog appears.

4. Enter a description and the settings as shown in Figure 5.11; then click OK to accept the settings and close the dialog.

5. Pick the two polylines along the north portion of the site and right-click to finish.

6. Right-click on Breaklines and select the Add option again.

7. In the Description field, enter **Gravel Road**, and click OK.

8. Zoom to the southwest portion of the site and pick the two longer polylines, as shown in Figure 5.12.

9. Right-click to finish the command.

FIGURE 5.11
Add Breaklines dialog

FIGURE 5.12
Selecting the gravel
road breaklines

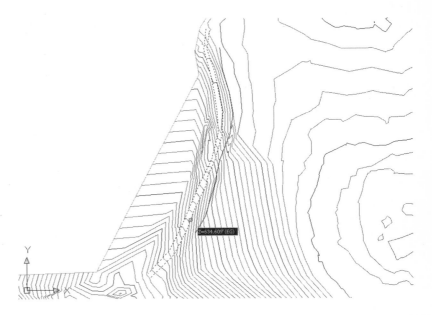

10. Add one more set of breaklines and enter **Slopes** in the Description field.

11. Pick the other polylines on the site. Our surveyors tagged these features with Toe and Top point descriptions, so we want to make sure the surface reflects the grade breaks that were found.

12. Right-click to complete the command.

The surface changes in this case are fairly subtle but are still visible. On sites with more extreme grade breaks, such as those that might follow a channel or a site grading, breaklines are invaluable in building the correct surface.

ADDING A SURFACE BORDER

In our case, the bigger issue is still the number of inappropriate triangles that are being drawn along the edge of the site. This is a common problem and can be solved by using a surface border. In prior versions of Civil 3D, we would sketch in a polyline to approximate a border. With the addition of the Extract Objects From Surface utility, we can use the surface itself as a starting point.

The Extract Objects From Surface utility allows you to re-create any displayed surface element as an independent AutoCAD entity. This can be the contours, grid, 3D faces, and so forth. In this exercise, we'll extract the existing surface boundary to give us a starting point for creating a more refined boundary that will limit triangulation.

1. From the main menu, choose View ➤ Zoom ➤ Extents to get the whole surface on screen.

2. From the main menu, choose Surfaces ➤ Utilities ➤ Extract Objects From Surface to bring up the Extract Objects From Surface dialog.

3. Deselect the Major and Minor Contour options, as shown in Figure 5.13.

FIGURE 5.13
Extracting the
border from the
surface object

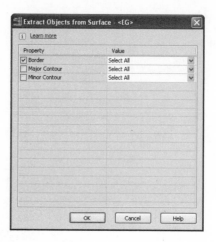

4. Click OK to finish the process.

5. Pick the green border line, and notice that you are no longer selecting the surface but a 3D polyline.

   This polyline will form the basis for our final surface boundary. By extracting the polyline from the existing surface, we save a lot of time playing connect the dots along the points that are valid. Now let's refine this polyline and add it to the surface as a boundary.

6. In Prospector, right-click on Point Groups and select the Properties option. The Point Groups dialog appears.

7. Move Field Work to the top of the list using the up and down arrows on the right.

8. Click OK to display all of our points on the screen.

9. Working your way around the site, grip-edit the polyline we made in the previous exercise to exclude some of the large triangles such as those on the eastern border. When complete, your polyline might look something like Figure 5.14.

Just like breaklines, there are multiple types of surface boundaries:

Outer boundaries are used to define the outer edge of the shown boundary. When the Non-destructive Breakline option is used, the points outside the boundary are still included in the calculations; then additional points are created along the boundary line where it intersects with the triangles it crosses. This trims the surface for display but does not exclude the points outside the boundary.

Hide boundaries are generally used to simply punch a hole in the surface display for things like building footprints or a wetlands area that are not to be touched by design. Hidden surface areas are *not* deleted but merely not displayed.

Show boundaries show the surface inside a hide boundary, essentially creating a donut effect in the surface display.

FIGURE 5.14
Revised surface
border polyline

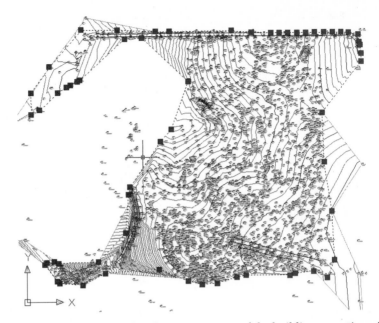

The addition of every boundary is considered a separate part of the building operations. This means that the order in which the boundaries are applied controls their final appearance. For example, a show boundary selected before a hide boundary will be overridden by that hide operation. To finish the exercise, we'll add the outer boundary twice, once as a nondestructive breakline and once with a standard breakline, and observe the difference.

1. In Prospector, expand the Surfaces branch.

2. Right-click on EG and select the Surface Properties option. The Surface Properties dialog appears.

3. Change the Surface Style to Contours And Triangles.

4. In Prospector, expand the Surfaces ➤ EG ➤ Definition branches.

5. Right-click on Boundaries and select the Add option. The Add Boundaries dialog opens.

6. Enter a name if you like and check the Non-destructive Breakline option.

7. Pick the polyline and notice the immediate change.

8. Zoom in on the southeast portion of our site, as shown in Figure 5.15.

Notice how the triangulation appears to include lines to nowhere. This is the nature of the nondestructive breakline. The points we attempted to exclude from the surface are still being included in the calculation; they are just excluded from the display. This isn't the result we were after, so let's fix it now:

1. In Prospector, expand the Surfaces ➤ EG ➤ Definition branches and select Boundaries.

2. A listing of the boundaries appears in the preview area.

3. Right-click on the border we just created and select Delete, as shown in Figure 5.16.

FIGURE 5.15
A nondestructive
border in action

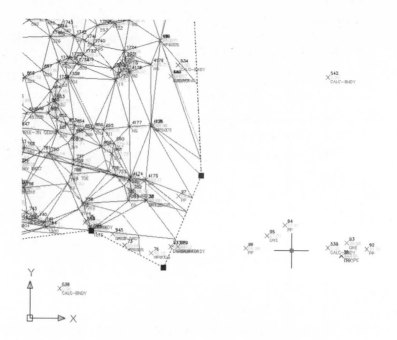

FIGURE 5.16
Deleting a surface
boundary

4. In Prospector, expand the Surfaces branch and right-click on EG. Select the Rebuild option to return to the prior version of the surface.

5. Right-click on Boundaries and select the Add option again. The Add Boundaries dialog appears.

6. This time, leave the Non-destructive Breakline option deselected and click OK.

7. Pick the border polyline on your screen. Notice that no triangles intersect our boundary now where it does not connect points.

8. On the main menu, choose View ➢ Zoom ➢ Extents to see the result of the border addition.

In spite of adding breaklines and a border, we still have some areas that need further correction or changes.

SURFACE MASKS

Surface masking is useful when you want to hide a portion of the surface or to create a rendering area. In this example, we'll use a closed polyline to create a rendering area for the surface:

1. Open the `Surface Masks.dwg` file.

2. Expand the Surfaces ➢ EG branches.

3. Right-click on Masks and select the Create Mask option.

4. Pick the magenta polyline on the southern half of the site and right-click to complete the selection. The Create Mask dialog appears.

5. Change the settings in the dialog as shown in Figure 5.17.

6. Click in the Render Material value field to activate the ellipsis button.

7. Click the ellipsis button, and the Select Render Material Style dialog appears. Select the Sitework.Planting Grass.Short material option.

8. Click OK to dismiss the Select Render Material Style dialog.

9. Click OK again to dismiss the Create Mask dialog.

10. In Prospector, right-click on EG and select the Surface Properties option to bring up the Surface Properties dialog.

FIGURE 5.17
Setting the options in the Create Mask dialog

11. Change the Surface Style field to Contours And Triangles. Click OK.

12. Select View ➤ Visual Styles ➤ Realistic to display the surface rendering. The main site will be displayed with a generic soil pattern, whereas our site will be rendered with a grass textural pattern, as shown in Figure 5.18.

Surface masks can be used to render surfaces with textures, to color large areas with solid colors for marketing purposes, or to hide information during surface presentation.

WHY CHANGE THE STYLE?

A Civil 3D surface must display triangles in order for rendering materials to be calculated and shown. You will inevitably forget this; it's just one of those frustrating anomalies in the program.

FIGURE 5.18
A realistic visual style with a rendering mask

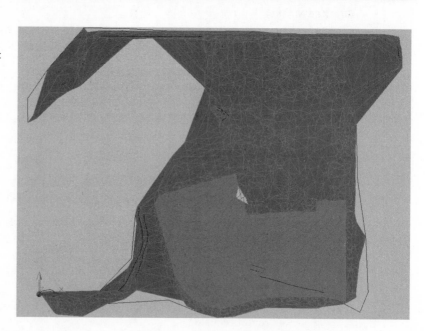

MANUAL SURFACE EDITS

In our surface, we have a few "finger" surface areas where the surveyors went out along narrow paths from the main area of topographic data. The nature of TIN surfaces is to connect dots, and so these fingers often wind up as webbed areas of surface information that's not really accurate or pertinent. A number of manual edits can be performed on a surface. These edit options are part of the definition of the surface and include the following:

Add Line connects two points where a triangle did not exist before. This essentially adds a breakline to the surface, so adding a breakline would generally be a better solution.

Delete Line removes the connection between two points. This is used frequently to clean up the edge of a surface or to remove internal data where a surface should have no triangulation at all. This can be areas like a building pad or water surface.

Swap Edge changes the direction of the triangulation methodology. For any four points, there are two solutions to the internal triangulation, and the Swap Edge edit alternates from one solution to the other.

Add Point does just what it sounds like: it allows for the manual addition of surface data. This function is often used to add a peak to a digitized set of contours that might have a flat spot at the top of a hill or mountain.

Delete Point is the opposite; it manually removes data from the surface points collection. Generally, it's better to fix the source of the bad data, but this can be a fix if the original data is not editable (in the case of a LandXML file, for example).

Modify Point and **Move Point** are variations on the same idea. Modify Point moves a surface point in the z direction, whereas a Move Point is limited to horizontal movement. In both cases, the original data input is not modified but merely the TIN point.

Minimize Flat Areas performs the edits we saw earlier in this chapter to add supplemental information to the TIN and to create a more accurate surface, forcing triangulation to work in the z direction instead of creating flat planes.

Raise/Lower Surface is a simple arithmetic operation that moves the surface in the z direction. This is useful for testing rough grading schemes for balancing dirt or for performing adjustment of entire surfaces after a new benchmark has been observed.

Smooth Surface presents a pair of methods for supplementing the surface TIN data. Both of these work by extrapolating more information from the current TIN data, but they are distinctly different in their methodology:

> **Natural Neighbor Interpolation (NNI)** works by adding points to a surface on the basis of the weighted average of nearby points. This data generally works well to refine contouring that is sharply angular because of limited information or long TIN connections. NNI only works within the bounds of a surface; it cannot extend beyond the original data.

> **Kriging** is based on one of five distinct algorithms to predict the elevations at additional surface points. These algorithms create a trending for the surface beyond the known information and can therefore be used to extend a surface beyond even the available data. Kriging is very volatile, and we suggest you understand the full methodology before applying this information to your surface. Kriging is frequently used in subsurface exploration industries such as mining where surface (or strata) information is difficult to come by and the distance between points can be higher than desired.

Paste Surface pulls in the TIN information from the selected surface and replaces the TIN information in the host surface with this new information. This is helpful in creating composite surfaces that reflect both the original ground and the design intent. We'll look more at pasting in Chapter 16 when we discuss grading.

Manual editing should always be the last step in updating a surface. Fixing the surface is a poor substitution for fixing the underlying data the TIN is built from, but in some cases, it is the quickest and easiest way to make a more accurate surface.

Point and Triangle Editing

In this section, we will remove triangles manually, and then finish our surface up by correcting what appears to be a blown survey shot.

1. Open the Surface Edits.dwg file.

2. In Prospector, expand the Surfaces ➢ EG ➢ Definition branches.

3. Right-click on Edits and select the Delete Line option.

4. Enter **C** at the command line to enter Crossing Selection Mode.

5. Start at the lower right of the pick area shown in Figure 5.19, and move to the upper-left corner as shown. Right-click to finish the selection.

6. Repeat this process in the upper right, then on the upper left, removing triangles until your site resembles Figure 5.20.

7. Zoom to the northeast corner of our site, and you'll notice a collection of contours that seems out of place.

8. Change the Surface Style to Contours And Points.

9. Right-click on Edits again and select the Delete Point option.

10. Select the red + marker in the middle of the contours, as shown in Figure 5.21.

11. Right-click to complete the edit, and notice the immediate change in the contouring.

FIGURE 5.19
Crossing the window
selection to delete
TIN lines

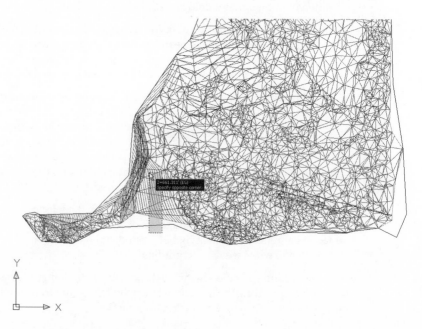

FIGURE 5.20
Surface after removal
of extraneous triangles

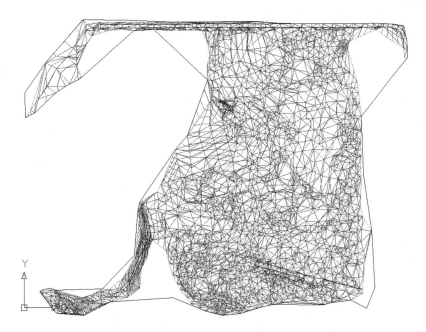

FIGURE 5.21
Blown survey shot
to be removed

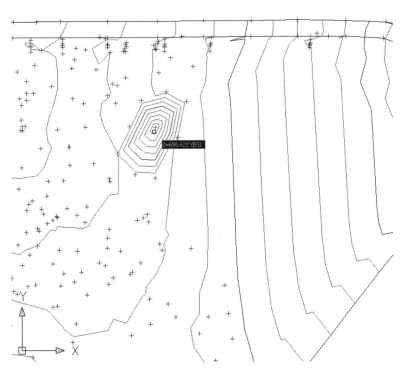

Surface Smoothing

One common complaint about computer-generated contours is that they're simply too precise. The level of calculations in setting elevations on the basis of linear interpolation along a triangle leg makes it possible for contour lines to be overly exact, ignoring contour line trends in place of small anomalies of point information. Under the eye of a board drafter, these small anomalies were averaged out, and contours were created with smooth flowing lines.

While we can apply object level smoothing as part of the contouring process, this smoothes the end result but not the underlying data. In this section, we'll use the NNI smoothing algorithm to reduce surface anomalies and create a more visually pleasing contour set:

1. Open the `Surface Smoothing.dwg` file. The area to be smoothed is shown in Figure 5.22.

2. In Prospector, expand the Surfaces ➢ EG ➢ Definition branches.

3. Right-click on Edits and select the Smooth Surface option. The Smooth Surface dialog opens.

4. Expand the Smoothing Methods branch, and select Natural Neighbor Interpolation for the Select Method value.

5. Expand the Point Interpolation/Extrapolation branch, and click in the Select Output Region value field. Click the ellipsis button.

6. Enter **S** at the command line to select the entire surface, and press ↵ to return to the Smooth Surface dialog.

7. Enter **20** for the Grid X-Spacing and Grid Y-Spacing values, and then press ↵. Note that Civil 3D will tell you how many points you are adding to the surface immediately below this input area by the value given in the Number Of Output Points field. It's grayed out, but it does change on the basis of your input values.

8. Click OK and the surface will be smoothed as shown in Figure 5.23.

FIGURE 5.22
Area of surface to
be smoothed

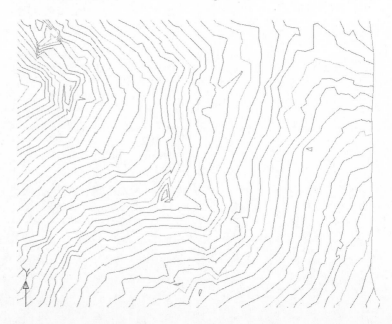

Note that we said for the *surface* to be smoothed—not the contours. To see the difference, change the Surface Style to Contours And Points to display your image as shown in Figure 5.24.

Note all of the points with a circle cross symbol. These points are all new, created by the NNI surface smoothing operation. These are part of your surface, and the contours reflect the updated surface information. The creation of a surface is merely the starting point. Once we have a TIN to work with, we have a number of ways to view the data using analysis tools and varying styles.

FIGURE 5.23
Using NNI to smooth
the surface

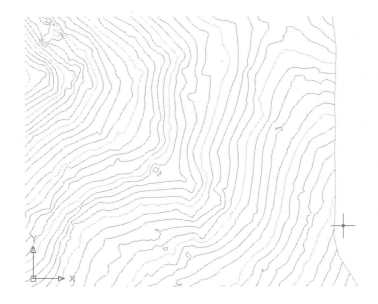

FIGURE 5.24
Points added via NNI
surface smoothing

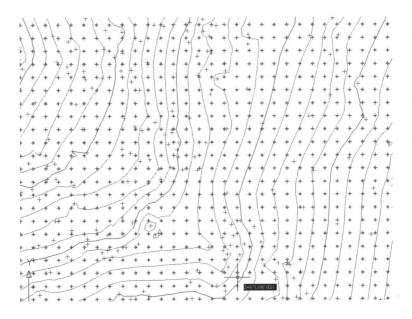

Surface Styling and Analysis

Once a surface is created, we can display information in a large number of ways. The most common so far has been contours and triangles, but these are the basics. By using varying styles, we can show a large amount of data with one single surface. Not only can we do simple things such as adjust the contour interval, but Civil 3D can apply a number of analysis tools to any surface:

Contours allows the user to specify a more specific color scheme or linetype as opposed to the typical minor-major scheme. Commonly used in cut-fill maps to color negative colors one way, positive contours another, and the balance or zero contours yet another color.

Elevations creates bands of color to differentiate various elevations. This can be a simple weighted distribution to help in creation of marketing materials, hard-coded elevations to differentiate floodplain and other elevation-driven site concerns, or ranges to help a designer understand the earthwork involved in creating a finished surface.

Direction Analysis draws arrows showing the normal direction of the surface face. This is typically used for aspect analysis, helping site planners review the way a site slopes with regard to cardinal directions and the sun.

Slopes Analysis colors the face of each triangle on the basis of the assigned slope values. While a distributed method is the normal setup, a common use is to check site slopes for compliance with Americans with Disabilities Act (ADA) requirements or other site slope limitations.

Slope Arrows displays the same information as a slope analysis, but instead of coloring the entire face of the TIN, this option places an arrow pointing in the downhill direction and colors that arrow on the basis of the specified slope ranges.

User-Defined Contours refers to those that typically fall outside the normal intervals. These user-defined contours are useful to draw lines on a surface that are especially relevant but don't fall on one of the standard levels. A typical use is to show the normal pool elevation on a site containing a pond or lake.

In the following exercises, we'll look at the basic style manipulations to get various contour and color schemes. Then we'll work through an elevation analysis using standard value distribution methods, a custom elevation analysis, and a slope analysis.

Surface Styles

Just like every other Civil 3D object, surfaces are displayed on the basis of styles. Like most other styles, the basic color and linetype controls are part of the style, but so are more specific surface components such as contour interval, the use of depression ticks, the colors used in elevation banding—and the list goes on. In this section, we'll look at the way the surface specific styles are built and some of their unique tricks. We'll start with adjusting surface contouring and then move into styles that are primarily focused on analysis.

THE CONTOURING BASICS

Contouring is the standard surface representation that land development plans are built on. But in past programs like Autodesk's Land Development, changing the contouring interval was akin to pulling teeth. With the use of styles in Civil 3D, we can have any number of styles prebuilt to allow us to quickly and painlessly change how contours are displayed. In this example, we'll copy an existing surface contouring style and modify the interval to a setting more suitable for commercial site design review.

1. Open the `Surface Styles.dwg` file. This surface is currently displayed with a 5′ minor contour and 25′ major contour.

2. Select the surface by picking any contour or the boundary, then right-click and select the Surface Properties option from the menu. The Surface Properties dialog appears.

3. On the Information tab, click on the down arrow next to the Style Editor button. Select the Copy Current Selection option as shown in Figure 5.25. The Surface Style dialog appears.

4. On the Information tab, change the Name field to Contours 0.25′ and 1′ and remove the description in place.

5. Switch to the Contours tab and expand the Contour Intervals property, as shown in Figure 5.26.

FIGURE 5.25
Copying the current style to create a new one

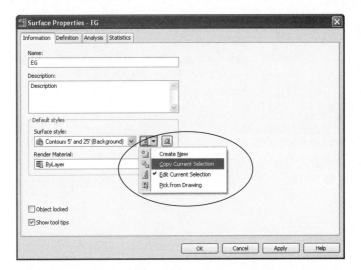

FIGURE 5.26
The expanded Contour Intervals setting

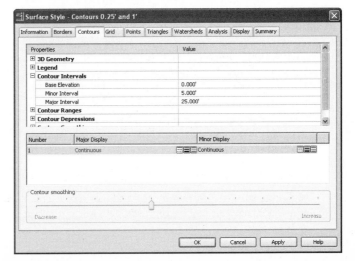

6. Change the Minor Interval value to 0.25´, and press ↵. The Major Interval value will jump to 1.25´, maintaining the ratio that was previously in place.

7. Change the Major Interval value to 1.0´, and press ↵.

8. Expand the Contour Smoothing property (you may have to scroll down). Select a Smooth Contours value of True, which activates the Contour Smoothing slider bar near the bottom. Don't change this Smoothing value, but keep in mind that this gives you a level of control over how much Civil 3D modifies the contours it draws.

9. Click OK to close this dialog and then click OK again to close the Surface Properties dialog.

The surface should be rendered faster than you can read this sentence even with the incredibly tight contour interval we've selected. This style doesn't make much sense on a site like this one but can be used effectively on something like a commercial site or highway entrance ramp where the low surface slope values make 1´ contours close to meaningless in terms of seeing what is going on with the surface.

We skipped over one portion of the surface contours that many people consider a great benefit of using Civil 3D: depression contours. If this option is turned on via the Contours tab, ticks will be added to the downhill side of any closed contours leading to a low point. This is a stylistic option, and usage varies widely.

Now let's look at a few of the other options and areas we ignored in creating this style. Taking a look at the component listing in Figure 5.27, we have some interesting changes from many other Civil 3D objects.

FIGURE 5.27
Listing of surface style components in the 2D direction

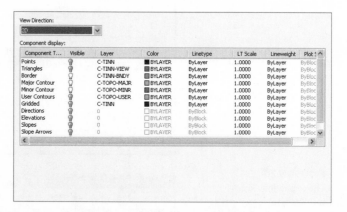

Under the Component Type column, Points, Triangles, Border, Major Contour, Minor Contour, User Contours, and Gridded are standard components and are controlled like any other object component. The 2D and 3D views are independent, and surfaces are one of the objects where different 2D and 3D views are common. The Directions, Elevations, Slopes, and Slope Arrows components are unique to surface styles. Note that the Layer, Color, and Linetype fields are grayed out for these components. Each of these components has its own special coloring schemes, which we'll look at in the next section.

Elevation Banding

Displaying surface information as bands of color is one of the most common display methods for engineers looking to make a high-impact view of the site. Elevations are a critical part of the site

---

SURFACE VS. CONTOUR SMOOTHING

Remember, contour smoothing is *not* surface smoothing. Contour smoothing applies smoothing at the individual contour level but not at the surface level. If you want to make your surface contouring look fluid, you should be smoothing the surface.

---

design process, and understanding how a site flows in terms of elevation is an important part of making the best design. Elevation analysis typically falls into two categories: showing bands of information on the basis of pure distribution of linear scales or showing a lesser number of bands to show some critical information about the site. In this first exercise, we'll use a pretty standard style to illustrate elevation distribution along with a prebuilt color scheme that works well for presentations.

1. Open the Surface Analysis.dwg file.

2. On the Settings tab of Toolspace, expand the Surface ➤ Surface Styles branches.

3. Right-click on Elevation Banding (2D) and select the Copy option. The Surface Style dialog appears.

4. On the Information tab, change the Name field to Elevation Banding (3D) and switch to the Analysis tab.

5. Expand the Elevations property to review the settings built into the style.

6. Set the Group By Value field to Equal Interval.

These distribution methods show up in nearly all of the surface analysis methods, so let's look at what they mean:

Quantile is often referred to as an equal count distribution and will create ranges that are equal in sample size. These ranges will not be equal in linear size but in distribution across a surface. This method is best used when the values are relatively equally spaced throughout the total range, with no extremes to throw off the group sizing.

Equal Interval is a stepped scale, created by taking the minimum and maximum values and then dividing the delta into the number of selected ranges. This method can create real anomalies when extremely large or small values skew the total range so that much of the data falls into one or two intervals, with almost no sampled data in the other ranges.

Standard Deviation is the bell curve that most engineers are familiar with and is well suited for when the data follows the bell distribution pattern. It generally works well for slope analysis, where very flat and very steep slopes are common and would make another distribution setting unwieldy.

For the elevation analysis, we'll use Equal Interval because our data is constrained to a relatively small range.

1. Change the Display Type value to 3D Faces to facilitate the isometric view we'll want to create later.

2. Change the Scheme value to Land.

3. Change the Elevations Display Mode value to Exaggerate Elevations. This will make the elevation differences more apparent when we select an isometric viewpoint.

4. Change the value of the Exaggerate Elevations By Scale Factor to 5. Your dialog should look like Figure 5.28.

5. Switch to the Display tab. The only component turned on is Elevations.

6. Change the View Direction field to 3D.

7. Turn off the Triangles and turn on Elevations by clicking on the lightbulb in the Visible field; then click OK.

8. Pick the surface on your screen.

9. Right-click and select Surface Properties. The Surface Properties dialog appears.

10. On the Information tab, change the Surface Style field to our new Elevation Banding (3D) style.

11. Switch to the Analysis tab.

12. Click the blue Run Analysis arrow in the middle of the dialog to populate the Range Details area.

13. Click OK to close the Surface Properties dialog.

14. On the main menu, choose View ➢ 3D Views ➢ SW Isometric.

15. Zoom in if necessary to get a better view.

16. On the main menu, choose View ➢ Visual Styles ➢ Conceptual to see a semi-rendered view that should look something like Figure 5.29.

FIGURE 5.28
Changes to the Elevation fields on the Analysis tab for better isometric views

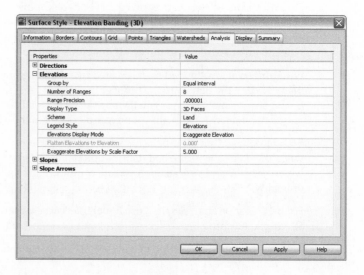

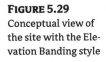

FIGURE 5.29
Conceptual view of the site with the Elevation Banding style

AUTOCAD VISUAL STYLES

The triangles seen are part of the view style and can be modified via the Visual Styles Manager. Turning the edge mode off will leave you with a nicely gradated view of our site. You can edit the visual style by clicking View ➢ Visual Styles ➢ Visual Style Manager on the main menu.

We'll look at more of the visualization techniques in Chapter 22. For now, let's move to using a 2D elevation to clearly illustrate portions of the site that cannot be developed. In this exercise, we'll manually tweak the colors and elevation ranges on the basis of design constraints from outside the program.

1. On the main menu, choose View ➢ 3D Views ➢ Top.

2. On the main menu, choose View ➢ Visual Styles ➢ 2D Wireframe.

3. On the main menu, choose View ➢ Zoom ➢ Extents to return to a triangle view of our site.

4. On the Settings tab, right-click the Elevation Banding (2D) style and select the Copy option. The Surface Style dialog appears.

5. On the Information tab, change the Name field to Zoning.

6. Switch to the Analysis tab and expand the Elevations property.

7. Change the Number field in the Ranges area to 3 and click OK to close the Surface Style editor.

8. This site has a limitation placed in that no development can go below the elevation of 664. Our analysis will show us the areas that are below 664, a buffer zone to 665, then everything above that.

9. Select the surface and right-click to select the Surface Properties option. The Surface Properties dialog appears.

10. On the Information tab, change the Surface Style field to Zoning.

11. On the Analysis tab, change the Number field in the Ranges area to 3.

12. Click the blue Run Analysis arrow in the Ranges area to populate the Range Details area.

13. Double-clicking in the Minimum and Maximum Elevations fields allows for direct editing. Double-clicking the color swatch field allows for manual picking. Modify your surface properties to match Figure 5.30. (The colors are red, yellow, and green from top to bottom, respectively.)

14. Click OK to exit the dialog.

Understanding surfaces from a vertical direction is helpful, but many times, the slopes are just as important. In the next section, we'll take a look at using the slope analysis tools in Civil 3D.

FIGURE 5.30
The Surface Properties dialog after manual editing

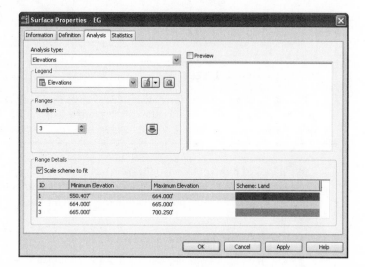

Slopes and Slope Arrows

Beyond the bands of color that show elevation differences in our models, we also have tools that display slope information about our surfaces. This analysis can be useful in checking for drainage concerns, meeting accessibility requirements, or adhering to zoning constraints. Slope is typically shown as areas of color as the elevations were or as colored arrows that indicate the downhill direction and slope. In this exercise, we'll look at a proposed site grading surface and run the two slope analysis tools.

1. Open the Surface Slope.dwg file.

2. Pick the surface and right-click. Select the Surface Properties option. The Surface Properties dialog appears.

3. On the Information tab, change the Surface Style field to Slope Banding (2D).

4. Change to the Analysis tab.

5. Change the Analysis Type field to Slopes.

6. Change the Number field in the Ranges area to 5 and click the blue Run Analysis button. The Range Details area will populate.

7. Click OK to close the dialog. Your screen should look like Figure 5.31.

FIGURE 5.31
Slope color
banding analysis

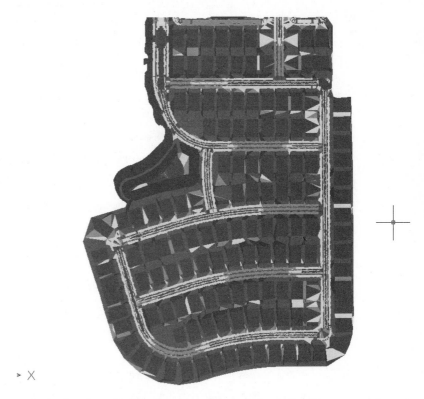

The colors are nice to look at, but they don't mean much, and slopes don't have any inherent information that can be portrayed by color association. To make more sense of this analysis, let's add a table.

1. On the main menu, choose Surfaces ➤ Add Legend Table.

2. Type **S** at the command line to select Slopes, and press ↵.

3. Press ↵ again to accept the default value of a Dynamic legend.

4. Pick a point on screen to draw the legend, as shown in Figure 5.32.

FIGURE 5.32
Slope legend table

Slopes Table

Number	Minimum Slope	Maximum Slope	Area	Color
1	0.00%	2.03%	829313.87	■
2	2.03%	3.27%	224037.88	■
3	3.27%	4.58%	173537.18	■
4	4.58%	20.70%	575088.48	■
5	20.70%	176874.45%	175598.72	■

By including a legend, we can actually make sense of the information presented in this view. Since we know what the slopes are, let's also see which way they go.

1. On the Settings tab of Toolspace, expand the Surface ➤ Surface Styles branches.

2. Right-click on Slope Banding (2D) and select Copy. The Surface Style dialog appears.

3. On the Information tab, change the Name field to Slope Arrows.

4. Switch to the Display tab and turn off the Slopes component by clicking on the lightbulb in the Visible field.

5. Turn on the Slope Arrows component by clicking on the lightbulb in the Visible field.

6. Click OK to close the dialog.

7. Right-click on the surface and select the Surface Properties option. The Surface Properties dialog appears.

8. On the Information tab, change the Surface Style field to Slope Arrows.

9. Change to the Analysis tab.

10. Change the Analysis Type field to Slope Arrows.

11. Change the Number field in the Ranges area to 5 and click the blue Run Analysis button.

12. Click OK to close the dialog.

The benefit of arrows is in looking for "birdbath" areas that will collect water. These arrows can also verify that inlets are in the right location as in Figure 5.33. Look for arrows pointing to the proposed drainage locations and you'll have a simple design verification tool.

With these simple analysis tools, we can show a client the areas of their site that meet their constraints. Visually strong and simple to produce, this is the kind of information that a 3D model makes available. Beyond the basic information that can be represented in a single surface, Civil 3D also contains a number of tools that let us compare surfaces. We'll compare this existing ground surface to a proposed grading plan in the next section.

FIGURE 5.33
FIGURE 5.33
Slope arrows pointing
to a proposed inlet
location

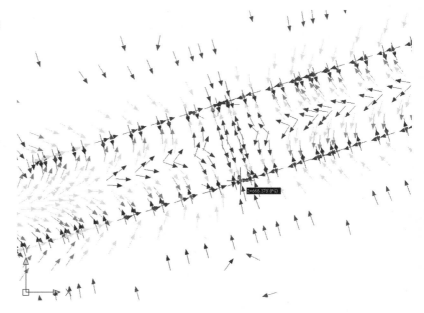

Comparing Surfaces

Earthwork is a major part of almost every land development project. The money involved with
earthmoving is a large part of the budget, and for this reason, minimizing this impact is a critical
part of the final design. Civil 3D contains a number of surface analysis tools designed to help in this
effort, and we'll look at them in this section. First, a simple comparison gives us feedback about the
volumetric difference; then, a more detailed approach lets us perform an analysis on this difference.

For years, civil engineers have performed earthwork using a section methodology. Sections
were taken at some interval, and a plot was made of both the original surface and the proposed surface. Comparing adjacent sections and multiplying by the distance between them yields an end-
area method of volumes that is generally considered acceptable. The main problem with this methodology is that it ignores the surfaces in the areas between sections. These areas could include areas
of major change, introducing some level of error. In spite of this limitation, this method worked
well with hand calculations, trading some accuracy for ease and speed.

With the advent of full-surface modeling, more precise methods became available. By analyzing
both the existing and proposed surfaces, a volume calculation can be performed that is as good as
the two surfaces. At every TIN vertex in both surfaces, a distance is measured vertically to the other
surface. These delta amounts can then be used to create a third volume surface representing the difference between the surfaces. Civil 3D uses this methodology to perform its calculations, but the
end-area method can still be used if desired.

Simple Volumes

When performing rough analysis, the total volume is the most important part. Once an acceptable
volume has been created, more refined analysis and comparison can be performed. In this exercise,

we'll compare two surfaces to simply pull a basic volume number, then modify the proposed grade to illustrate how quickly changes can be reviewed.

1. Open the Surface Volumes.dwg file.

2. On the main menu, choose Surfaces ➢ Utilities ➢ Volumes to display Panorama with the Composite Volumes tab, as shown in Figure 5.34.

3. Click the Create New Volume Entry button on the far left, as indicated in Figure 5.34, to create a new volume entry.

4. Click the <select surface> field under the Base Surface heading and select EG.

5. Click the <select surface> field under the Comparison Surface heading and select FG; Civil 3D will calculate the volume (Figure 5.35).

DON'T TOUCH THAT CLOSE BUTTON!

This utility's calculations will disappear if you close Panorama. This information can be exported to XML or copied and pasted into another document if a record is required.

---

6. Without closing Panorama, move to Prospector, and expand the Surfaces ➢ FG ➢ Definition branches.

7. Right-click on Edits and select the Raise/Lower Surface option.

8. Enter -0.25 at the Command line to drop the site 3″.

9. In Panorama, click the Recompute Volumes button (as shown in Figure 5.36) to update the calculations.

FIGURE 5.34
The Composite Volumes tab in Panorama

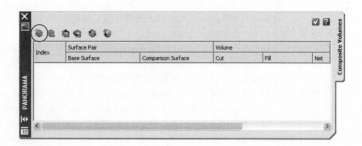

FIGURE 5.35
Composite volume calculated

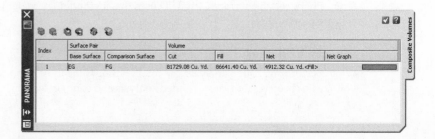

FIGURE 5.36
Recomputing the
composite volume

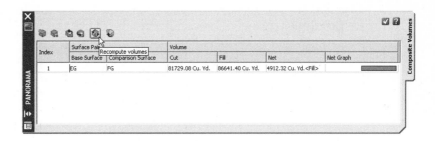

10. Right-click in the Edits list to remove the lowering edit and select Delete.

11. Return to Panorama and recompute to return to the original volume calculation.

The original design was quite good, so let's look at a more detailed analysis of the earthwork by using a TIN volume surface in the next section.

Volume Surfaces

Using the volume utility for initial design checking is helpful, but quite often, contractors and other outside users want to see more information about the grading and earthwork for their own uses. This requirement typically falls into two categories: a cut-fill analysis showing colors or contours, or a grid of cut-fill tick marks.

Color cut-fill maps are helpful when reviewing your site for the locations of movement. Some sites have areas of better material or can have areas where the cost of cut is prohibitive (such as rock). In this exercise, we'll use two of the surface analysis methods to look at the areas for cut-fill on our site.

1. Open the Surface Volumes.dwg file from the CD.

2. In Prospector, right-click the Surfaces branch and select Create Surface. The Create Surface dialog appears.

3. Change the Type field to TIN Volume Surface

4. Expand the Information property, and change the Name to Volume.

5. In the Style value, click the ellipsis button to open the Select Surface Style dialog. Select Elevation Banding (2D) and click OK.

6. Expand the Volume Surfaces property, and click in the Base Surface value field. Click the ellipsis button to open the Select Base Surface dialog. Select EG and click OK.

7. Click in the Comparison Surface value field. Click the ellipsis button to open the Select Comparison Surface dialog. Select FG and click OK. The dialog should look like Figure 5.37.

8. Click OK to complete the surface creation.

This new Volume surface appears in Prospector's Surfaces collection, but notice that the icon is slightly different, showing two surfaces stacked on each other. The color mapping currently shown is just a default set, though, and does not indicate much.

9. Right-click on Volume in Prospector and select the Surface Properties option. The Surface Properties dialog appears.

FIGURE 5.37
Creating a volume surface

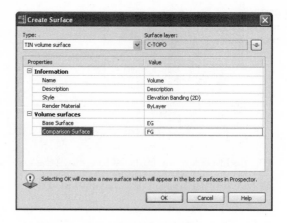

10. Switch to the Statistics tab and expand the Volume branch

The value shown for the Net Volume (Unadjusted) is what was calculated in the Surface Volume utility in the previous exercise. This information can be cut and pasted into other programs for saving or other analysis if needed.

11. Switch to the Analysis tab.

12. Change the Number field in the Ranges area to 3, and click the blue Run Analysis arrow.

13. Change the values in the cells by double-clicking and editing to match Figure 5.38.

14. Click OK to close the dialog.

The volume surface now clearly indicates areas of cut in green, fill in red, and areas near balancing in yellow, similar to Figure 5.39. If you leave a small range near the balance line, it's clearer to see the areas that are being left nearly undisturbed.

To show where large amounts of cut or fill could incur additional cost (such as compaction, or excavation protection), you would simply modify the analysis range as required.

FIGURE 5.38
Elevation analysis settings for earthworks

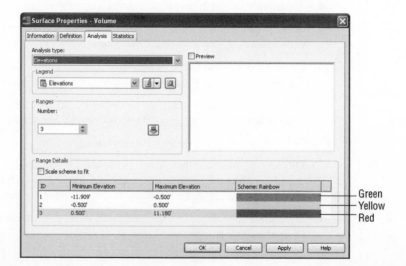

FIGURE 5.39
Completed elevation
analysis

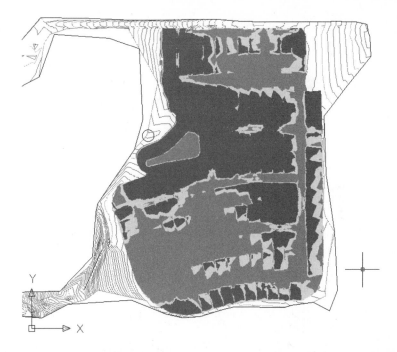

The Elevation Banding surface is great for onscreen analysis, but the color fills make it hard to plot or use in many applications. In this next exercise, we'll use the Contour Analysis tool to prepare cut-fill contours in these same colors.

1. Right-click on Volume and select the Surface Properties option to open the Surface Properties dialog again.

2. On the Analysis tab, set the Analysis Type field to Contours.

3. Change the Number field in the Ranges area to 3.

4. Click the blue Run Analysis button.

5. Change the ranges as shown in Figure 5.40. The contour colors are shades of green for cut, a yellow for the balance line, and shades of red for the fill areas. Click the small button shown in Figure 5.40 to display the AutoCAD Select Color dialog.

6. Leaving the Select Color dialog open, switch to the Information tab on the Surface Properties dialog, and change the Surface Style to Contours 1′ and 5′ (Design).

7. Click the down arrow next to the style dropdown and select the Copy Current Selection option. The Surface Style Editor appears.

8. On the Information tab, change the Name field to Contours 1′ and 5′ (Earthworks).

9. Switch to the Contours tab.

10. Expand the Contour Ranges branch.

FIGURE 5.40
Earthworks contour
analysis

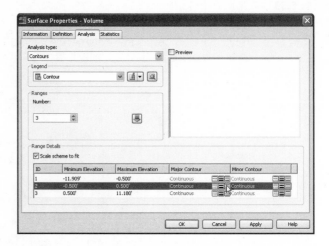

11. Change the value of the Use Color Scheme property to True. It's safe to ignore the values here since we hard-coded the values in our surface properties.

12. Click OK to close the Surface Style Editor and click OK again to close the Surface Properties dialog.

The volume surface can now be labeled using the surface-labeling functions, which we'll look at in the next section.

Labeling the Surface

Once you've created the surface model, it is time to communicate the model's information in various formats. This includes labeling contours, creating legends for the analysis we've created, or adding spot labels. These exercises will work through these main labeling requirements and building styles for each.

Contour Labeling

The most common requirement is to place labels on surface-generated contours. In Land Desktop, this was one of the last steps because of the simple fact that any change to the surface required erasing and replacing all the labels. Let's look at placing labels and then modifying the style of the labels themselves.

PLACING CONTOUR LABELS

Contour labels in Civil 3D are created by special lines that understand their relationship with the surface. Everywhere one of these lines crosses a contour line, a label is applied. This label's appearance is based on the style applied and can be a major, minor, or user-defined contour label. Each label can have styles selected independently, so using some AutoCAD selection techniques can be crucial to maintaining uniformity across a surface. In this exercise, we'll add labels to our surface and explore the interaction of contour label lines and the labels themselves.

1. Open the Surface Labeling.dwg file.

2. On the main menu, choose Surfaces ➢ Add Surface Labels ➢ Add Surface Labels to display the Add Labels dialog.

BUT THERE'S A MENU OPTION FOR THAT!

While there are direct commands available under the Add Surface Labels menu flyout, using the dialog offers us the chance to modify the styles used without going to the command settings for each of these commands.

---

3. Set the Label Type field to Contour - Single and click Add.

4. Pick any spot on a blue major contour to add a label.

5. Change the Label Type field to Contour - Multiple and click Add again.

6. Pick a point to the west of the northern edge of our site and then pick a second point due east, crossing a number of contours in the interval, as in Figure 5.41.

7. Change the Label Type field to Contour - Multiple At Interval and click Add again.

8. Pick a point near the middle left of the site and a second point across the site to the east.

9. Enter **400** at the command line for an interval value.

FIGURE 5.41
Placing multiple
surface labels

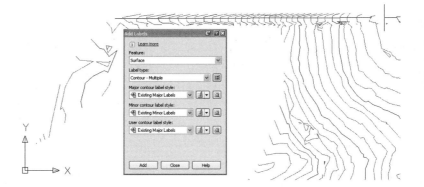

We've now labeled our site in three ways to give us contour labels in a number of permutations. We would need to add additional labels in the northeast and southwest to complete the labeling, as we did not cross these contour objects with our contour label line. We could add more labels by clicking Add, but we can also use the labels created already to fill in these missing areas. By modifying the contour line labels, we can manipulate the label locations and add new labels. In this exercise, we'll fill in the labeling to the northeast.

1. Zoom to the northeast portion of the site, and notice that some of the contours are labeled only along the boundary or not at all, as shown in Figure 5.42.

2. Zoom in to any contour label line, and pick the text. Three grips will appear. Our original contour label lines are quite apparent, but in reality, every label has a hidden label line beneath it.

3. Grab the northernmost grip and drag across an adjacent contour, as in Figure 5.43. New labels will appear everywhere your dragged line now crosses a contour.

4. Drop the grip somewhere to create labels as desired.

By using the created label lines instead of adding new ones, you'll find it easier to manage the layout of our labels.

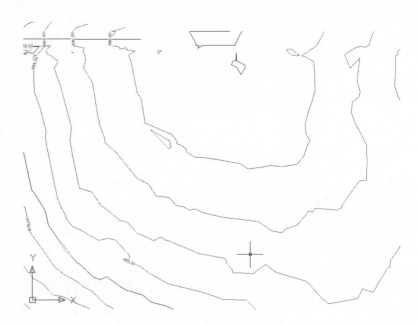

FIGURE 5.42
Contour labels applied

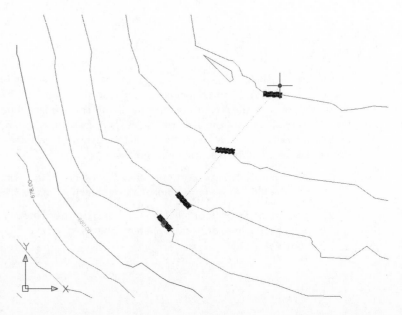

FIGURE 5.43
Grip-editing a contour label line

CONTOUR LABELING STYLES

The fewer label lines produced, the easier is it is to manage or modify them. Before we perform a change, let's build a new contour label style that uses a boundary around the text and has no decimal places.

1. Switch to the Settings tab of Toolspace, and expand Surface ➢ Label Styles ➢ Contour.

2. Right-click on Existing Major Label and select Copy. The Label Style Composer dialog appears.

3. On the Information tab, change the Name field to Existing With Box and switch to the Layout tab.

4. Under the Border property, set the Visibility to True.

5. Click in the Contents value, then click the ellipsis button to bring up the Text Component Editor.

6. Click in the preview area to select the text and delete it.

7. On the Properties tab, change the value of the Precision Modifier to 1 and click the blue insert arrow.

8. Click OK to close and zoom in on the preview, as shown in Figure 5.44, to verify your changes have stuck.

9. Click OK to close the Label Style Composer.

FIGURE 5.44
Completed Existing
With Box contour
label style

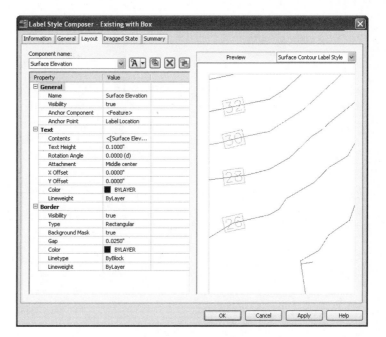

Now that we have a contour label style we're happy with, let's update all the label lines we've already created. In this exercise, we'll change the style used on our entire site.

1. Perform a zoom extents on your now labeled surface by selecting View ➤ Zoom ➤ Extents on the main menu.

2. Pick one of the visible contour label lines.

3. Right-click and choose Select Similar from the menu to pick all of the surface contour label lines. This pick is based on type and layer, so be careful that you don't pick up extraneous objects.

4. Right-click again and select Properties to open the AutoCAD Object Properties Manager dialog, shown in Figure 5.45.

5. Change the Display Contour Label Line value to True if you would like to see all the label lines created. Be sure to set it to False before continuing.

6. Change the Surface Contour Label Style Major value to Existing With Box.

7. Change the Display Minor Contour Labels value to False to turn off the minor contour labels.

8. Press the Esc key to dismiss the selection, and perform a zoom extents to see the results.

Even when the contour label lines are set to not display, selecting any label will activate the grips, allowing for the manipulation or selection of other contour label lines. Our site is generally labeled, so let's move on to more specific point labels.

FIGURE 5.45
Contour label group in the Object Properties Manager dialog box

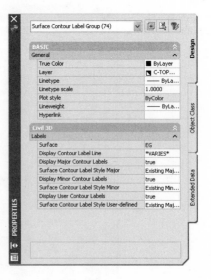

Surface Point Labels

In every site, there are points that fall off the contour line but are critical. In an existing surface, this can be the low point in a pond or a driveway that has to be matched. When we're working with commercial sites, the spot grade is the most common review element. One of the most time-consuming issues in land development is the preparation of grading plans with hundreds of individual spot grades. Every time a site grading scheme changes, these are typically updated manually, leaving lots of opportunities for error.

With Civil 3D's surface modeling, spot labels are dynamic and react to changes in the underlying surface. By using surface labels instead of points or text callouts, we can generate a grading plan early on in the design process and begin the process of creating sheets. In this section, we'll label surface slopes in a couple of ways, create a single spot label for critical information, and conclude by creating a grid of labels similar to many estimation software packages.

LABELING SLOPES

Beyond the specific grade at any single point, most grading plans use slope labels to indicate some level of trend across a site or drainage area. Civil 3D can generate the following two slope labels:

◆ One-point slope labels indicate the slope of an underlying surface triangle. These work well when the surface has large triangles, typically in pad or mass grading areas.

◆ Two-point slope labels indicate the slope trend on the basis of two points selected and their locations on the surface. A two-point slope label works by dividing the surface elevation distance between the points by the planar distance between the pick points. This works well in existing ground surface models to indicate a general slope direction but can be deceiving in that it does not consider the terrain between the points.

In this exercise, we'll apply both types of slope labels, and then look at a minor style modification that is commonly requested.

1. Open the `Surface Slope Labeling.dwg` file.

2. From the main menu, choose Surfaces ➢ Add Surface Labels➢ Slope.

3. At the command line, press ↵ to select a one-point label style.

4. Zoom in on the circle drawn on the western portion of the site and use a Center snap to place a label at its center, as shown in Figure 5.46.

FIGURE 5.46
A one-point
slope label

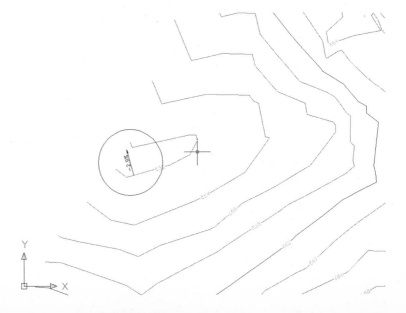

5. Press Esc to exit the command.

6. From the main menu, choose Surfaces ➤ Add Surface Labels ➤ Slope again.

7. At the command line, press T to switch to a two-point label style.

8. Pan to the southwest portion of the site, and pick the northern end of the line, as shown in Figure 5.47.

9. Select the other end of the line to complete the label.

FIGURE 5.47
First point in a two-
point slope label

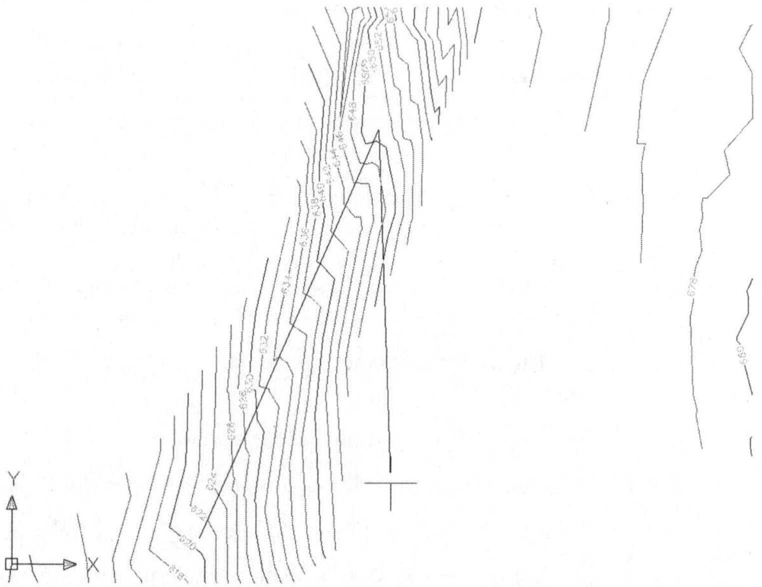

This second label indicates the average slope of a dirt road that is cut into the side of the site. By using a two-point label, we get a better understanding of the trend, as opposed to a specific point.

One concern for many users is the sign on the spot label. Because the arrow on the two-point label is always drawn from point one to point two, the arrow can point in both an upslope and a downslope direction, so the sign is important. On a one-point label, however, the arrow always points downhill, making the sign redundant. In this exercise, we will create a new style to drop the sign.

1. Select the one-point label created earlier.

2. Right-click and select Label Properties to display the AutoCAD Object Properties Manager palette.

3. Click the dropdown for Surface Slope Label Style and select Create/Edit at the bottom of the list to display the Style Selection dialog.

4. Select the dropdown on the right and select Create Child Of Current Selection to bring up the Label Style Composer.

5. On the Information tab, change the Name field to Percent-No Sign and change to the Layout tab.

6. Change the Component Name field to Surface Slope.

7. Click in the Contents value, then click the ellipsis button to bring up the Text Component Editor.

8. Delete the text in the preview area.

9. Change the Sign property to Drop Sign and click the blue arrow to insert the data field.

10. Click OK to close the Text Component Editor dialog. The preview should look like Figure 5.48.

11. Click OK to close the Style Selection dialog.

Note that the style is selected and the screen has updated already. Just a reminder: by creating a child style, we've built in a relationship between our Percent-No Sign label and the Percent label. A change in the Percent label style to layer, color, size, and so on will be reflected in our child.

FIGURE 5.48
Label Style Composer for the Percent-No Sign label

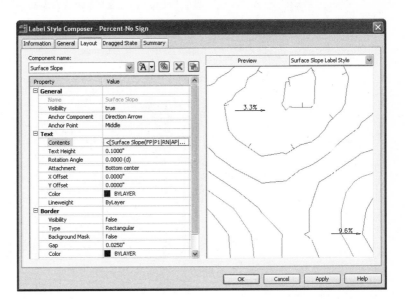

CRITICAL POINTS

A typical grading plan is a sea of critical points that drive the site topography. In the past, much of this labeling and point work was done by creating COGO points and simply displaying their properties. Although this is effective, it has two distinct disadvantages. First, these points are not reflective of the design but part of the design. This makes the sheet creation a part of the grading process, not a parallel process. Second, the addition of COGO points to any drawing and project when they're not truly needed just weighs down the design model. Point management is a mentally intensive task, and anything that can limit extraneous data is worth investigating.

Surface labels react dynamically to the surface and to the point of insertion. Moving any of these labels would update the information to reflect the surface underneath. This relationship makes it possible for one user to place labels on a grading plan while the final surface is still in flux. A change in the proposed surface is reflected in an update from the project, and an updated sheet can be on the plotter in minutes.

Real World Scenario

USING SURFACES TO DO MORE

In this exercise, we'll use a surface label to make a building pad label. By using surface information, we can also take advantage of Civil 3D's Expressions to include extra elevation information.

1. Open the Surface Spot Labeling.dwg file.

2. In the Settings tab of Toolspace, expand the Surfaces ➤ Label Styles ➤ Spot Elevation branches.

3. Right-click on Expressions and select the New option. The New Expression dialog appears.

4. Change the Name field to FF.

5. Change the Description to Finished Floor Elevation.

6. Click the Insert Property button and select Surface Elevation, as shown here.

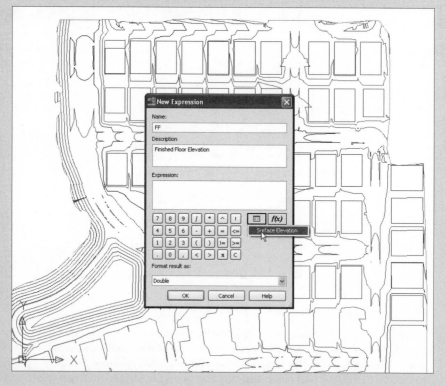

7. Click next to the Surface Elevation entry and type **+0.7**.

8. Click OK to close the dialog.

We use expressions throughout Civil 3D to label or modify labels with information that can be derived mathematically from a surface. These expressions can include some level of logic, but in this case, it's simple math to make two bits of information from one bit of data.

1. Right-click on the Spot Elevation branch and select the New option. The Label Style Composer dialog appears.

2. On the Information tab, change the Name field to Pad Label.

3. Switch to the Layout tab.

4. Click in the Contents value of the Surface Elevation component and click the ellipsis button to bring up the Text Component Editor.

5. Erase the text in the preview area, then type **FF**.

6. Select FF from the Properties dropdown list.

7. Change the Precision value to 0.1 and click the blue insert arrow.

8. Click to enter the text area, and press ⏎ to create a line return.

9. Type **FP**.

10. Select Surface Elevation from the Properties dropdown list.

11. Change the Precision value to 0.1 and click the blue insert arrow. Your label should look like this:

12. Click OK to close the Text Component Editor.

13. Change the Anchor Point value to Middle Center.

14. Change the Attachment value to Middle Center.

15. Click OK to close the dialog.

16. From the main menu, select Surfaces ➤ Add Surface Labels ➤ Add Surface Labels.

17. Change the Label Type field to Spot Elevation.

18. Change the Spot Elevation Label Style field to Pad Label.

19. Change the Marker Style: field to <none>.

20. Click the Add button.

21. Click in the middle of any of the red pads to insert the labels. Repeat a few times in adjacent pads to create something similar to what's shown here.

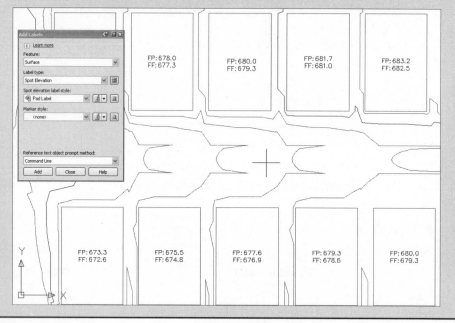

SURFACE GRID LABELS

Sometimes, more than a few points are requested. Estimation software typically creates a grid of point labels that can be easily reviewed or passed to a contractor for field work. In this exercise, we'll use the volume surface we generated earlier in this chapter to create a set of surface labels that reflect this requirement.

1. Open the Surface Volume Grid Labels.dwg file.

2. Select Surfaces ➤ Add Surface Labels ➤ Spot Elevations On Grid.

3. Click one of the red or green cut-fill contours to pick the Volume surface.

4. Pick a point in the southwest of the surface to set a base point for the grid.

5. Press ↵ to set the grid rotation to zero.

6. Enter **25** at the command line to set the X spacing.

7. Enter **25** at the command line to set the Y spacing.

8. Click to the northeast of the surface to set the area for the labels.

9. Verify the preview box contains the Volume surface and press ↵ at the command line to continue.

10. Wait a few moments as Civil 3D generates all the labels just specified. Your drawing should look similar to Figure 5.49.

FIGURE 5.49
Volume surface
with grid labels

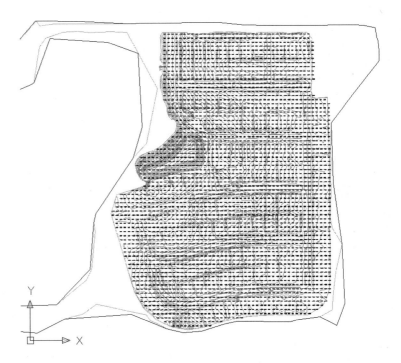

COLORING THE VOLUME LABELS

Most users immediately ask about coloring the labels based on cut and fill. We've modified enough styles in this chapter, so we'll point you to the Autodesk Civil Community at `http://civilcommunity` `.autodesk.com`, where Peter Funk was kind enough to walk through the expressions and label styles necessary to create a label that's one color in cut, another in fill. His example was for points, but the same technique works for surface labels.

Labeling the grid is imprecise at best. Grid labeling ignores anything that might happen between the grid points, but it presents the surface data in a familiar way for engineers and contractors. By using the tools available and the underlying surface model, we can present information from one source in an almost infinite number of ways.

The Bottom Line

Create a preliminary surface using freely available data. Almost every land development project involves a surface at some point. During the planning stages, freely available data can give you a good feel for the lay of the land, allowing design exploration before money is spent on fieldwork or aerial topography. Imprecise at best, this free data should never be used as a replacement for final design topography, but it's a great starting point.

Master It Create a new drawing from the Civil 3D Extended template and bring in a Google Earth surface for your home or office location. Be sure to set a proper coordinate system to get this surface in the right place.

Modify and update a TIN surface.   TIN surface creation is mathematically precise, but sometimes the assumptions behind the equations leave something to be desired. By using the editing tools built into Civil 3D, you can create a more realistic surface model.

   Master It   Modify your Google Earth surface to only show an area immediately around your home or office. Create an irregular shaped boundary and apply it to the Google Earth surface.

Prepare a slope analysis.   Surface analysis tools allow users to view more than contours and triangles in Civil 3D. Engineers working with nontechnical team members can create strong meaningful analysis displays to convey important site information using the built-in analysis methods in Civil 3D.

   Master It   Create an Elevation Banding analysis of your home or office surface and insert a legend to help clarify the image.

Label surface contours and spot elevations.   Showing a stack of contours is useless without context. Using the automated labeling tools in Civil 3D, you can create dynamic labels that update and reflect changes to your surface as your design evolves.

   Master It   Label the contours on your Google Earth surface at a 1´ and a 5´ interval.

Chapter 6

Don't Fence Me In: Parcels

Land-development projects often involve the subdivision of large pieces of land into smaller lots. Even when our projects do not directly involve subdivision, we are often required to show the legal boundaries of our site and the adjoining sites.

In previous CAD systems, we had few tools available for parcel management. We would create AutoCAD entities, such as lines and arcs, to represent the lot boundaries and then create a closed polyline to assist us in determining the parcel area. We would create static text labels for area, bearing, and distance. Even if we took advantage of some of the parcel-management tools in Land Desktop, the most minor change to the project, such as a road widening or a horizontal alignment adjustment, would require days of editing, adjustment, and relabeling.

Civil 3D parcels give us a dynamic way to create, edit, manage, and annotate these legal land divisions. If you edit a parcel segment to make a lot larger, all of the affected labels will update—including areas, bearings, distances, curve information, and table information.

By the end of this chapter, you will be able to:

◆ Create a boundary parcel from objects

◆ Create a right-of-way parcel using the right-of-way tool

◆ Create subdivision lots automatically by layout

◆ Add multiple parcel segment labels

Creating and Managing Sites

In Civil 3D, a site is a collection of parcels, alignments, grading objects, and feature lines that share a common topology. In other words, Civil 3D objects that are on the same site are related to, as well as interact with, each other. We will call these objects that react to each other *site geometry objects*.

Best Practices for Site Topology Interaction

At first glance, it may seem that the only uses for parcels would be subdivision lots, and therefore, you might think that you only need one site for your drawing.

However, once you begin working with parcels, you will find features like dynamic area labels to be useful for delineating and analyzing soil boundaries; paving, open-space, and wetlands areas; and any other region enclosed with a boundary. The automatic layer enforcement of parcel object styles also adds to the appeal of using parcels. Using additional types of parcels will require you to come up with a site-management strategy to keep everything straight.

It is important to understand how site geometry objects will react to on another. Figure 6.1 shows a typical parcel that might represent a property boundary.

When an alignment is drawn and placed on the same site as the property boundary, the parcel will be split into two parcels, as shown in Figure 6.2.

You must plan ahead to create meaningful sites based on interactions between the desired objects. For example, if you want a road centerline, a road right-of-way (ROW) parcel, and the lots in a subdivision to react to each other, they need to be on the same site (see Figure 6.3).

The alignment (or road centerline), ROW parcel, and lots all relate to one another. A change in the centerline of the road should prompt a change in the ROW parcel and the subdivision lots.

If you would like to avoid the interaction between site geometry objects, simply place them on different sites. Figure 6.4 shows an alignment that has been placed on a different site from the boundary parcel. Notice that the alignment does not split the boundary parcel.

FIGURE 6.1

A typical property boundary

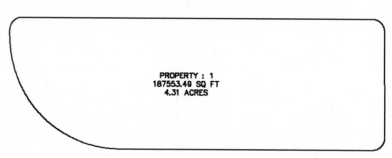

FIGURE 6.2

An alignment that crosses a parcel will divide the parcel in two if the alignment and parcel exist on the same site.

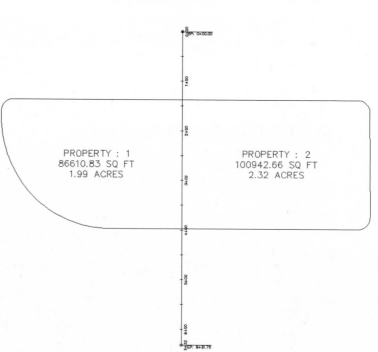

FIGURE 6.3
Alignments, ROW parcels, open space parcels, and subdivision lots will react to one another when drawn on the same site.

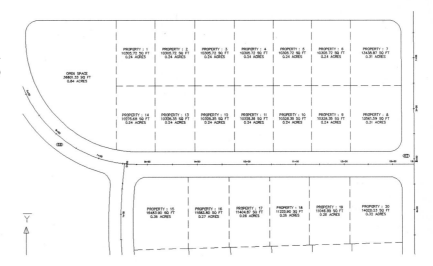

FIGURE 6.4
An alignment that crosses a parcel will not interact with the parcel if they exist on different sites.

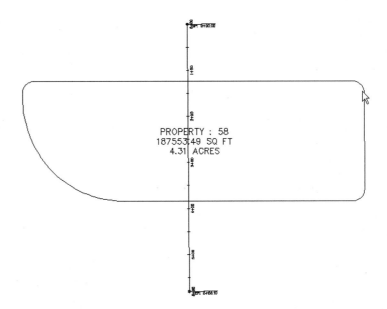

It is important that only objects that are intended to react to each other be placed on the same site. For example, in Figure 6.5, you can see parcels representing both subdivision lots and soils boundaries. Since it would not be meaningful for a soil boundary parcel segment to interrupt the area or react to a subdivision lot parcel, the subdivision lot parcels have been placed on a Subdivision Lots site, and the soil boundaries have been placed on a Soils Boundary site.

If you didn't realize the importance of site topology, you might create both your subdivision lot parcels and your soil boundary parcels on the same site and find your drawing looks similar to Figure 6.6. This figure shows the soil boundary segments dividing and interacting with subdivision lot parcel segments, which doesn't make any sense.

FIGURE 6.5
Parcels can be used for subdivision lots and soils boundaries as long as they are kept on separate sites.

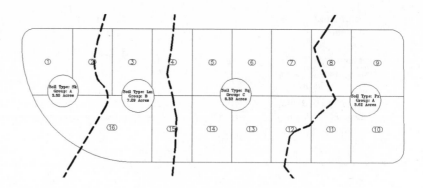

FIGURE 6.6
Subdivision lots and soils boundaries will react inappropriately when placed on the same site.

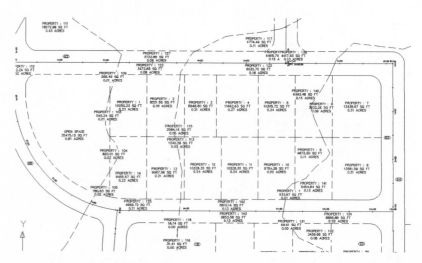

Another way to avoid site-geometry problems is to do site-specific tasks in different drawings and use a combination of external references and data references to share information.

For example, you could have an existing base drawing that housed the soil boundaries site, XRefed into a subdivision plat drawing that housed the subdivision lots site instead of separating the two drawings onto two different sites.

You will want to consider keeping your legal site plan in its own drawing. Because of the interactive and dynamic nature of Civil 3D parcels, it might be easy to accidentally grab a parcel segment when you meant to grab a manhole and unintentionally edit a portion of your plat.

We'll have a look at other workflow examples and drawing divisions later in this chapter, as well as in the chapters on data shortcuts (Chapter 17) and Vault (Chapter 19).

If you decide to have sites in the same drawing, here are ideas of some sites that you might want to create. These suggestions are meant to be used as a starting point. Use them to help find a combination of sites that works for your projects.

Roads and Lots This site could contain road centerlines, ROW, platted subdivision lots, open space, adjoining parcels, utility lots, and other aspects of the final legal site plan.

Grading Feature lines and grading objects are considered part of site geometry. If you are using these tools, you must make at least one site for them. You might even find it useful to have several grading sites.

Easements   If you would like to use parcels to manage, analyze, and annotate your easements, you may consider creating a separate site for easements.

Stormwater Management   If you would like to use parcels to manage, analyze, and annotate your stormwater subcatchment boundaries, you may consider creating a separate site for storm-water management.

As you learn new ways to take advantage of alignments, parcels, and grading objects, you may find additional sites that you would like to create at the beginning of a new project.

WHAT ABOUT THE "SITELESS" ALIGNMENT?

We mentioned in the previous section that alignments are considered site geometry objects. Civil 3D 2008 has introduced the concept of the "siteless" alignment or an alignment that is placed on the "<none>" site. An alignment that is created on the <none> site will not react with other site geometry objects or with other alignments created on the <none> site.

However, alignments can still be created on traditional sites, if desired, and will react to other site geometry objects. This may be desirable if you would like your road centerline alignment to bisect a ROW parcel, for example.

You will likely find that best practices for most alignments will be to place them on the <none> site. For example, if road centerlines, road transition alignments, swale centerlines, and pipe network alignments are placed on the <none> site, you will save yourself quite a bit of site geometry management.

See Chapter 7 for more information about alignments and sites.

Creating a New Site

You can create a new site in Prospector. You will find it to be easier if you brainstorm potentially needed sites at the beginning of your project and create those sites right away or, better yet, save them as part of your standard Civil 3D template. You can always add or delete sites later in the project.

The Sites collection is stored in Prospector, along with the other Civil 3D objects in your drawing.

The following exercise will lead you through creating a new site that you can use for creating subdivision lots:

1. Open the `Create Site.dwg` file. Note that the drawing contains alignments and soil boundary parcels, as shown in Figure 6.7.

2. Locate the Sites collection on the Prospector tab of Toolspace.

3. Right-click on the Sites collection and select New to open the Site Properties dialog (see Figure 6.8).

4. On the Information tab of the Site Properties dialog, enter **Subdivision Lots** for the name of your site.

FIGURE 6.7
The Create Site drawing contains alignments and soil boundary parcels.

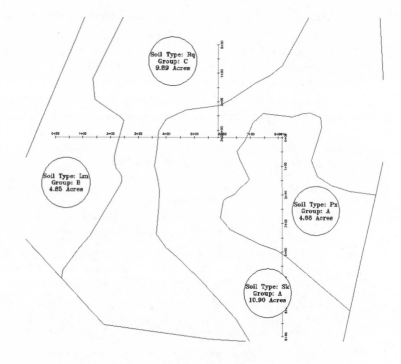

FIGURE 6.8
Right-click on the Sites collection and select New.

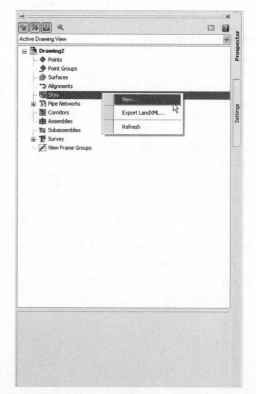

5. Confirm that the settings on the 3D Geometry tab match what is shown on Figure 6.9.

6. Confirm that the settings on the Numbering tab match Figure 6.10.

7. Locate the Sites collection on the Prospector tab of Toolspace and note that your Subdivision Lots site appears on the list.

You could repeat the process for all of the sites that you anticipate you will need over the course of the project, keeping in mind that you can always add or delete sites later. The next section will talk more about best practices for sites and give you some idea of sites you might need to create for your projects.

FIGURE 6.9
Confirm the settings on the 3D Geometry tab.

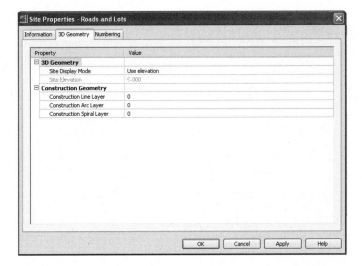

FIGURE 6.10
Confirm the settings on the Numbering tab.

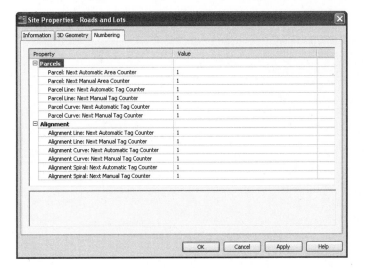

Creating a Boundary Parcel

The Create Parcel From Objects tool allows you to create parcels by choosing AutoCAD entities in your drawing or in an XRefed drawing. In a typical workflow, it is common to encounter a boundary created by AutoCAD entities, such as polylines, lines, and arcs.

When using AutoCAD geometry to create parcels, it is important that the geometry be created carefully and meet certain requirements. The AutoCAD geometry must be lines, arcs, polylines, or polygons. They cannot be 3D polylines, blocks, ellipses, circles, or other entities. Civil 3D may allow you to pick objects with an elevation other than zero, but you will find you get better results if you flatten the objects so that all objects have an elevation of zero. Sometimes the geometry will appear sound when elevation is applied, but you may notice that this is not the case once the objects are flattened. Flattening all objects before creating parcels can help you prevent frustration when creating parcels.

This exercise will teach you how to create a parcel from Civil 3D objects:

1. Open the `Create Boundary Parcel.dwg` file. This drawing has several alignments, which were created on the Subdivision Lots site, and some AutoCAD linework representing a boundary. In addition, parcels were formed when the alignments formed closed areas on the Subdivision Lots site.

2. Choose Parcels ➢ Create Parcel From Objects.

3. At the `Select lines, arcs, or polylines to convert into parcels or [Xref]:` prompt, pick the red polyline that represents the site boundary. Press ↵.

4. The Create Parcels – From Objects dialog will appear. Select Subdivision Lots; Property, and the Name, Square Foot, and Acres from the dropdown menu in the Site, Parcel Style, and Area Label Style selection box, respectively. Leave everything else as the defaults. Click OK to dismiss the dialog.

5. The boundary polyline will form parcel segments that react with the alignments. Area labels are placed at the newly created parcel centroids, as shown in Figure 6.11.

FIGURE 6.11
The boundary
parcel segments,
alignments, and
area labels

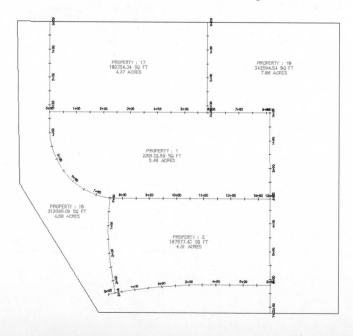

Creating a Wetlands Parcel

Although you may never have thought of things like wetlands areas, easements, and stormwater management facilities as parcels in the past, you can take advantage of the parcel tools to assist in labeling, stylizing, and analyzing these features for your plans.

This exercise will teach you how to create a parcel representing wetlands using the transparent commands and Draw Tangent-Tangent With No Curves tool from the Parcel Layout Tools toolbox:

1. Open the `Create Wetlands Parcel.dwg` file. Note that this drawing has several alignments, parcels, and a series of points that represent a wetlands delineation.

2. Choose Parcels ➤ Create Parcel By Layout. The Parcel Layout Tools toolbar will appear.

3. Click the Draw Tangent-Tangent With No Curves tool on the Parcel Layout Tools toolbar 🔳 . The Create Parcels – Layout dialog appears.

4. In the dialog, select Subdivision Lots, Property, and Name Square Foot & Acres from the dropdown menus in the Site, Parcel Style, and Area Label Style selection boxes, respectively. Keep the default settings for all other options. Click OK.

5. At the `Specify start point:` prompt, click the Point Object transparent command on the Transparent Commands toolbar 🔳 , and then pick point 1. Continue picking the wetlands points in numerical order, as shown in Figure 6.12.

6. Once you have reached point 9, be sure to pick point 1 again to close the loop. Press ↵ to exit the Point Object transparent command. Type **X, and** then press ↵ again to dismiss the Create Parcels – Layout dialog. Your result should look similar to Figure 6.13.

7. It is usually easier to change the appearance of the parcel and its area label after the parcel has been created. Change the style of the parcel by picking the parcel area label, right-clicking, and selecting Parcel Properties. The Parcel Properties dialog appears.

8. Select Wetlands from the dropdown menu in the Object Style selection box, and then click OK to dismiss the dialog. The parcel segments should turn green and a swamp hatch pattern should appear inside the parcel to match the Wetlands style.

FIGURE 6.12

Pick each wetlands point in numerical order.

FIGURE 6.13

The Wetlands parcel

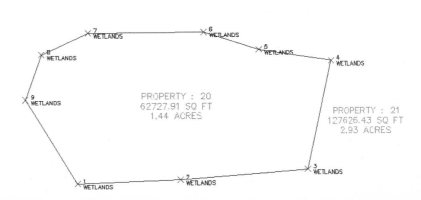

9. Change the style of the parcel area label by first selecting the Wetlands parcel area label, then right-click and select Label Properties. The Label Properties dialog appears.

10. In the Label Style row of the Label Properties dialog, click in the Value column. Click the ellipsis that appears. The Label Style dialog appears.

11. Select Wetlands from the dropdown list in the Area Label selection box. Click OK to dismiss the dialog, and click OK again to exit the Label Properties dialog. A label should appear labeling the wetlands as in Figure 6.14. Later sections will discuss parcel style and parcel area label style in more detail.

FIGURE 6.14
The Wetlands parcel with the appropriate label styles applied

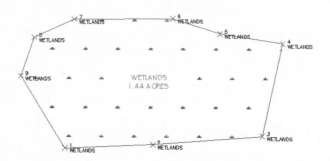

Creating a Right-of-Way Parcel

The Create ROW tool creates ROW parcels on either side of an alignment based on your specifications. The Create ROW tool can only be used when alignments are placed the same site as the boundary parcel, as in Figure 6.15.

FIGURE 6.15
An alignment on the same site as parcels

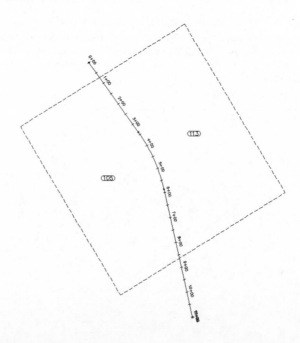

The resulting ROW parcel will look similar to Figure 6.16.

Options for the Create ROW tool include offset distance from alignment, fillet or chamfer cleanup at parcel boundaries, and alignment intersections. Figure 6.17 shows an example of chamfered cleanup at alignment intersections.

FIGURE 6.16
The resulting parcels
after application of
the Create ROW tool

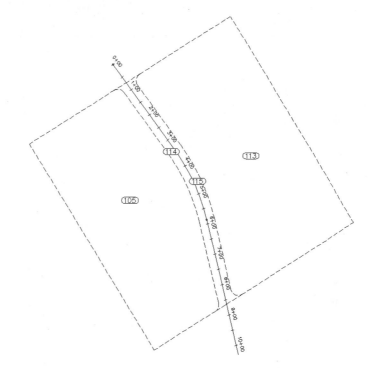

FIGURE 6.17
A ROW with chamfer
cleanup at alignment
intersections

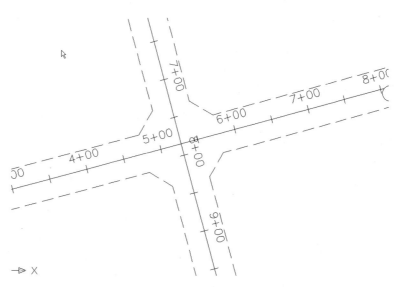

MAKE SURE YOUR GEOMETRY IS POSSIBLE

Make sure you are giving parameters that are possible. If the program cannot achieve your filleting requirements at any one intersection, a ROW parcel will not be created. For example, if you specify a 25´ filleting radius and the roads come together at a tight angle that would only allow a 15´ radius, then a ROW parcel will not be created.

Once the ROW parcel is created, it is no different from any other parcel. For example, it does not maintain a dynamic relationship with the alignment that created it. A change to the alignment will require the ROW parcel to be edited or, more likely, re-created.

This exercise will teach you how to use the Create ROW tool to automatically place a ROW parcel for each alignment on your site:

1. Open the `Create Right of Way Parcel.dwg` file. Note that this drawing has several alignments on the same site as the boundary parcel, resulting in several smaller parcels between the alignments and boundary.

2. Choose Parcels ➢ Create ROW.

3. At the `Select parcels:` prompt, pick Property: 1, Property: 2, Property: 3, and Property: 4 on screen. Press ↵ to stop picking parcels. The Create Right Of Way dialog appears, as shown in Figure 6.18.

4. Expand the Create Parcel Right Of Way parameter, and enter **25´** as the Value for the Offset From Alignment.

5. Expand the Cleanup At Parcel Boundaries parameter. Enter **25´** as the Value for the Fillet Radius At Parcel Boundary Intersections. Select Fillet from the dropdown menu in the Cleanup Method selection box.

6. Expand the Cleanup At Alignment Intersections parameter. Enter **25´** as the Value for the Fillet Radius At Alignment Intersections. Select Fillet from the dropdown menu in the Cleanup Method selection box.

7. Click OK to dismiss the dialog and create the ROW parcels. Your drawing should look like Figure 6.19.

FIGURE 6.18
The Create Right Of
Way dialog

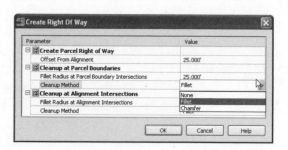

FIGURE 6.19
The completed
ROW parcels

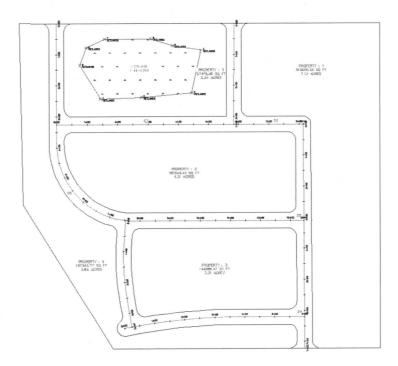

WHEN THE CREATE ROW TOOL ISN'T ENOUGH

The Create ROW tool works well for straightforward road plans that have even widths. If you need something a little more intricate for design elements, such as cul-de-sacs, width changes, or knuckles, you can do the same thing that the Create ROW tool does using the AutoCAD lines and curves commands and the Parcels ➢ Create Parcel From Objects menu command.

Creating Subdivision Lot Parcels Using Precise Sizing Tools

The precise sizing tools allow you to create parcels to your exact specifications. You will find these tools most useful when you have your roadways established and understand your lot depth requirements. These tools provide automatic, semiautomatic, and freeform ways to control frontage, parcel area, and segment direction.

Attached Parcel Segments

Parcel segments created with the precise sizing tools are called *attached segments.* Attached parcel segments have a start point that is attached to a frontage segment and an end point that is defined by the next parcel segment they encounter. Attached segments can be identified by their distinctive diamond-shaped grip at their start point and no grip at their end point (see Figure 6.20).

In other words, you establish their start point and their direction, but they seek another parcel segment to establish their end point. Figure 6.21 shows a series of attached parcel segments. You can tell the difference between their start and end points because the start points have the diamond-shaped grips.

The diamond-shaped grip can be dragged along the frontage to a new location, and the parcel segment will maintain its angle from the frontage. If the rear lot line is moved or erased, the attached parcel segments will find a new endpoint (see Figure 6.22) at the next available parcel segment.

FIGURE 6.20
An attached parcel segment

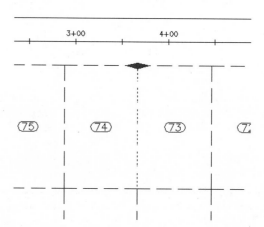

FIGURE 6.21
A series of attached parcel segments, with their endpoint at the rear lot line

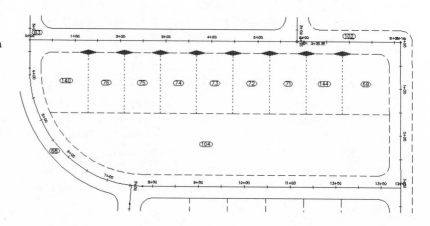

FIGURE 6.22
The end points of attached parcel segments will extend to the next available parcel segment if the initial parcel segment is erased.

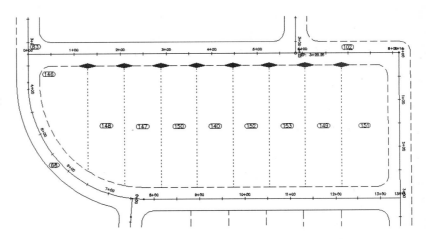

Precise Sizing Settings

The precise sizing tools consist of the Slide Angle, the Slide Direction, and the Swing Line tools (see Figure 6.23).

The Parcel Layout Tools toolbar can be expanded so that you can establish settings for each of the precise sizing tools (see Figure 6.24). Each of these settings is discussed in detail in the following sections.

FIGURE 6.23
The precise sizing tools on the Parcel Layout Tools toolbar

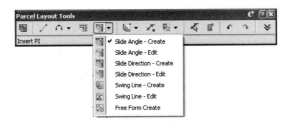

FIGURE 6.24
The settings on the Parcel Layout Tools toolbar

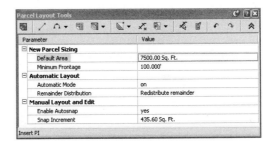

New Parcel Sizing

When you create new parcels, the tools will respect your default area and minimum frontage. The program will always use these numbers as a minimum; it will base the actual lot size on a combination of the geometry constraints (lot depth, frontage curves, and so on) and the additional settings that follow. Keep in mind that the numbers you establish under the New Parcel Sizing option must make geometric sense. For example, if you would like a series of 7500-square-foot lots that have 100′ of frontage, you must make sure that your rear parcel segment allows for at least 75′ of depth; otherwise, you may wind up with much larger frontage values than you desire or a situation where the software cannot return a meaningful result.

Automatic Layout

Automatic Layout has two parameters when the list is expanded—the Automatic Mode and the Remainder Distribution. The Automatic Mode parameter can have the following values:

On Automatically follows your settings and puts in all the parcels, without prompting you to confirm each one.

Off Allows you to confirm each parcel as it is created. In other words, this option provides you with a way to semiautomatically create parcels.

The Remainder Distribution parameter tells Civil 3D how you would like "extra" land handled. This parameter has the following options:

Create Parcel From Remainder Makes a last parcel with the leftovers once the tool has made as many parcels as it can to your specifications on the basis of the settings in this dialog. This parcel is usually smaller than the other parcels.

Place Remainder In Last Parcel Adds the leftover area to the last parcel once the tool has made as many parcels as it can to your specifications on the basis of the settings in this dialog.

Redistribute Remainder Takes the leftover area and pushes it back through the default-sized parcels once the tool has made as many parcels as it can to your specifications on the basis of the settings in this dialog. The resulting lots are not always evenly sized because of differences in geometry around curves and other variables, but the leftover area is absorbed.

In a typical subdivision workflow, you will use Create Parcel From Remainder and Place Remainder In Last Parcel most commonly on straight pieces and in places where parcel uniformity are important. You will use Redistribute Remainder most commonly around cul-de-sacs and in places that are tightly confined.

Slide Angle – Create Tool

The Slide Angle – Create tool creates an attached parcel segment based on an angle from frontage. You might find this tool most useful when your jurisdiction requires a uniform lot line angle from the right of way.

This exercise will lead you through using the Slide Angle – Create tool to create a series of subdivision lots:

1. Open the `Create Subdivision Lots.dwg` file. Note that this drawing has several alignments on the same site as the boundary parcel, resulting in several smaller parcels between the alignments and boundary.

2. Choose Parcels ➤ Create Parcel By Layout. The Parcel Layout Tools toolbar appears.

3. Expand the toolbar by clicking the Expand The Toolbar button, as shown in Figure 6.25.

4. Change the value of the following parameters by clicking in the Value column and typing in the new values:

   1. Default Area: **7500 Sq. Ft.**

   2. Minimum Frontage: **75´**

5. Change the following parameters by clicking in the Value column and selecting the appropriate option from the dropdown menu:

   1. Automatic Mode: On

   2. Remainder Distribution: Redistribute Remainder

6. Click the Slide Angle – Create tool (see Figure 6.26). The Create Parcels – Layout dialog appears.

7. Select Subdivision Lots, Single Family, and Name Square Foot & Acres from the dropdown menus in the Site, Parcel Style, and Area Label Style selection boxes, respectively. Leave the rest of the options as the default. Click OK to dismiss the dialog.

8. At the `Pick a point within the parcel to be subdivided:` prompt, pick any point inside Property: 29.

9. At the `Select start point on frontage:` prompt, use your Endpoint osnap to pick the point of curvature along the ROW parcel segment for Property: 29 (see Figure 6.27).

FIGURE 6.25
The Expand The Toolbar button

FIGURE 6.26
The Slide Angle – Create tool

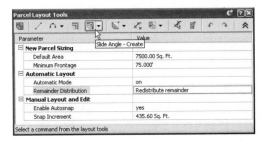

FIGURE 6.27
Pick the point of curvature along the ROW parcel segment.

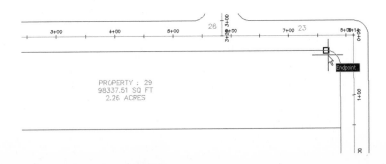

10. The parcel jig will appear. Move your mouse slowly along the ROW parcel segment and notice that the parcel jig follows the parcel segment. At the Select end point on frontage: prompt, use your Endpoint osnap to pick the point of curvature along the ROW parcel segment for Property: 29 (see Figure 6.28).

11. At the Specify angle at frontage: prompt, enter 90↵.

12. At the Specify area <7500 Sq. Ft.>: prompt, press ↵ to accept the default area of 7500 square feet. Press ↵ again to exit the command.

13. Your drawing should look like Figure 6.29. Note that Property: 29 still exists at the far left and has kept its original parcel style and area label style.

14. Repeat steps 4 through 12 for Property: 2, if desired. Try changing the Remainder Distribution option to something different or adjusting the area and frontage values.

FIGURE 6.28
Allow the parcel creation jig to follow the parcel segment, and then pick the point of curvature along the ROW parcel segment.

FIGURE 6.29
The automatically created lots

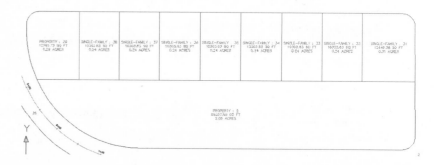

Slide Direction – Create Tool

The Slide Direction – Create tool leads you through a series of prompts identical to the Slide Angle – Create tool, except it prompts you for a direction in azimuth or bearing form instead of a frontage angle.

You might find this tool most useful when re-creating existing lots or when you would like to create a series of parallel lot lines with a known bearing.

Swing Line – Create Tool

The Swing Line – Create tool creates a "backwards" attached parcel segment where the diamond-shaped grip appears not at the frontage but at a different location that you specify. The tool will respect your minimum frontage, and it will adjust the frontage larger if necessary in order to respect your default area.

The Swing Line – Create tool is semiautomatic because it requires your input of the swing point location.

You might find this tool most useful around a cul-de-sac or in odd-shaped corners where you must hold frontage but have a lot of flexibility in the rear of the lot.

Creating Open Space Parcels Using the Free Form Create Tool

A site plan is more than just single-family lots. Areas are usually dedicated for open space, storm-water management facilities, parks, and public-utility lots. The Free Form Create tool can be useful when creating these types of parcels. The Free Form Create tool, like the precise sizing tools, creates an attached parcel segment with the special diamond-shaped grip.

In the following exercise, you will use the Free Form Create tool to create an open space parcel:

1. Open the `Create Open Space.dwg` file. Note that this drawing contains a series of subdivision lots.

2. Pan over to Property: 1. Property: 1 is currently 7.13 acres. Note the small marker point noting the desired location of the open space boundary.

3. Choose Parcels ➤ Create Parcel By Layout. Select the Free Form Create tool (see Figure 6.30). The Create Parcels – Layout dialog appears.

4. Select Subdivision Lots, Open Space, and Name Square Foot & Acres from the dropdown menus in the Site, Parcel Style, and Area Label Style selection boxes, respectively. Keep the default values for the remaining options. Click OK to dismiss the dialog.

5. Slide the Free Form Create attachment point around the Property: 1 frontage (see Figure 6.31). At the `Specify attachment point:` prompt, use your Node osnap to pick the point labeled Open Space Limit.

FIGURE 6.30
The Free Form
Create tool

FIGURE 6.31
Use the Free Form
Create tool to select an
attachment point.

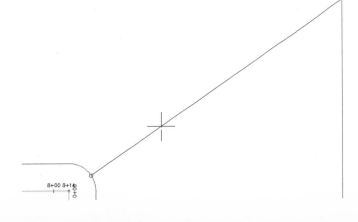

6. At the Specify lot line direction: prompt, press ↵ to specify a perpendicular lot line direction.

7. A new parcel segment has been created from your Open Space Limit point, perpendicular to the ROW parcel segment, as shown in Figure 6.32.

8. Note that a new Open Space parcel has formed and Property: 1 has been reduced from 7.13 acres to 3.54 acres.

9. Press ↵ to exit the Free Form Create command. Enter **X**, and then press ↵ to exit the toolbar.

10. Pick the new parcel segment so that you see its diamond-shaped grip. Grab the grip and slide the segment along the ROW parcel segment (see Figure 6.33).

11. Notice when you place the parcel segment at a new location that the segment endpoint snaps back to the rear parcel segment (see Figure 6.34). This is typical behavior for an attached parcel segment.

FIGURE 6.32
Attach the parcel segment to the marker point provided.

FIGURE 6.33
Sliding an attached parcel segment

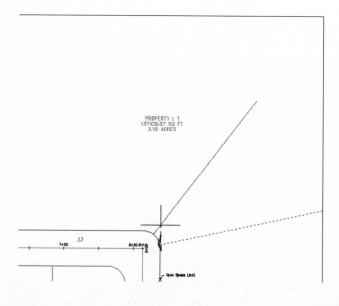

FIGURE 6.34
Attached parcel
segments will snap
back to the rear
parcel segment.

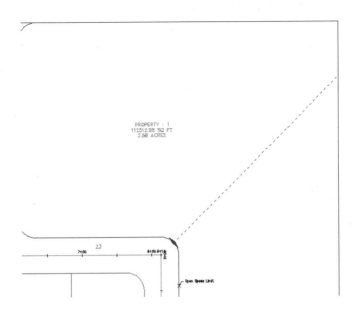

PROPERTY : 1
112512.99 SQ FT
2.58 ACRES

Editing Parcels by Deleting Parcel Segments

One of the most powerful aspects of Civil 3D parcels is the ability to perform many iterations of a site plan design. Typically, this design process involves creating a series of parcels, and then deleting them to make room for iteration with different parameters or deleting certain segments to make room for easements, public utility lots, and more.

Parcel segments can be deleted by using the AutoCAD Erase tool or the Delete Sub-Entity tool on the Parcel Layout Tools toolbar.

BREAK THE UNDO HABIT

You will find that parcels will behave better if you use one of the segment deletion methods described in this section to erase improperly placed parcels rather than using the Undo command.

It is important to understand the difference between these two methods. The AutoCAD Erase tool behaves as follows:

- If the parcel segment was originally created from a polyline (or similar parcel layout tools, such as the Tangent-Tangent No Curves tool), the AutoCAD Erase tool will erase the entire segment (see Figure 6.35).

- If the parcel segment was originally created from a line or arc (or similar parcel layout tools, such as the precise sizing tools), then AutoCAD Erase will erase the entire length of the original line or arc (see Figure 6.36).

The Delete Sub-Entity tool acts more like the AutoCAD Trim tool. The Delete Sub-Entity tool will only erase the parcel segments between parcel vertices. For example, if Parcel 76, as shown in Figure 6.37, must be absorbed into Parcel 104 to create a public utility lot with dual road access, you would want to only erase the segment at the rear of Parcel 76 and not the entire segment shown in Figure 6.36.

FIGURE 6.35

The segments indicated by the blue grips will be erased after using the AutoCAD Erase tool.

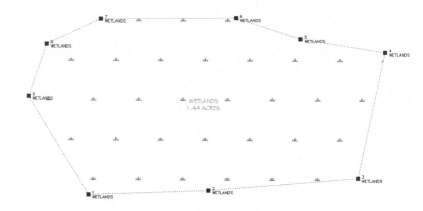

FIGURE 6.36

The AutoCAD Erase tool will erase the entire segment indicated by the blue grips.

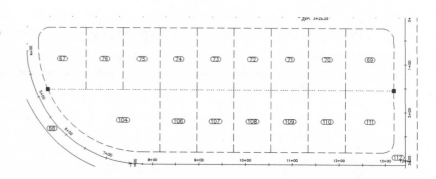

FIGURE 6.37

Use the Delete Sub-Entity tool to erase the rear parcel segment for Parcel 76.

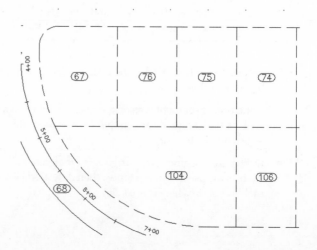

Choosing Parcels ➢ Edit Parcels ➢ Edit Parcel Segments and selecting the Delete Sub-Entity tool allows you to pick only the small rear parcel segment for Parcel 76. Figure 6.38 shows the result of this deletion.

The following exercise will lead you through deleting a series of parcel segments using both the AutoCAD Erase tool and the Delete Sub-Entity tool:

1. Open the `Delete Segments.dwg`. Note that this drawing contains a series of subdivision lots, along with a wetlands boundary.

2. Let's say you just received word that there was a mistake with the wetlands delineation and you need to erase the entire wetlands area. Use the AutoCAD Erase tool to erase the parcel segments that define the wetlands parcel. Note that the entire parcel disappears in one shot since it was created with the Tangent-Tangent No Curves tool (which behaves similarly to creating a polyline).

3. Next you discover that Parcel Single-Family: 29 needs to be removed and absorbed into Parcel Property: 2 to enlarge a stormwater management area. Choose Parcels ➢ Edit Parcel ➢ Edit Parcel Segments.

4. At the `Select lot line:` prompt, pick the rear lot line between Single-Family: 29 and Property: 2. The Parcel Layout Tools toolbar appears.

5. Click the Delete Sub-Entity tool (see Figure 6.39).

6. At the `Select subentity to remove:` prompt, pick the rear lot line between Single-Family: 29 and Property: 2. Press ↵ to exit the command, then enter **X**, and press ↵ to exit the Parcel Layout Tools toolbar.

7. The parcel segment will immediately disappear and the resulting parcel will have a combined area from Single-Family: 29 and Property: 2, as shown in Figure 6.40.

FIGURE 6.38

The rear lot line for Parcel 76 was erased using the Delete Sub-Entity tool, creating a larger Parcel 104.

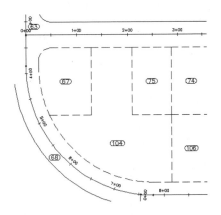

FIGURE 6.39

The Delete Sub-Entity tool

FIGURE 6.40
The parcel after eras-
ing the rear lot line

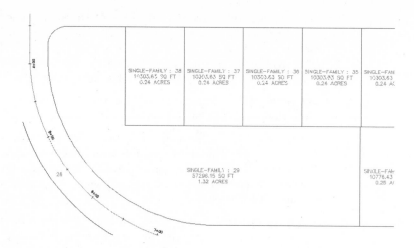

FIGURE 6.40
The parcel after eras-
ing the rear lot line

Best Practices for Parcel Creation

Now that you have an understanding of how objects on a site interact and have had some practice creating and editing parcels in a variety of ways, we can take a deeper look at how parcels them-selves must be constructed to achieve topology stability, predictable labeling, and desired parcel interaction.

Forming Parcels from Segments

In the earlier sections of this chapter, you saw that parcels are only created when parcel segments form a closed area (see Figure 6.41).

Parcels must always close. Whether you draw AutoCAD lines and use the Create Parcel From Objects menu command or use the parcel segment creation tools, a parcel will not form until there is an enclosed polygon. Figure 6.42 shows four parcel segments that do not close; therefore, no par-cel has been formed.

There are times in surveying and engineering where parcels of land do not necessarily close when created from legal descriptions. In this case, you must work with your surveyor to perform an adjustment or find some other solution to create a closed polygon.

You also saw that even though parcels cannot really be erased, if you erase the appropriate par-cel segments, the area contained within a parcel will be assimilated into neighboring parcels.

FIGURE 6.41
A parcel is created
when parcel segments
form a closed area.

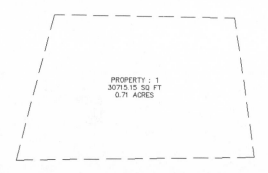

FIGURE 6.42

No parcel will be formed if parcel segments do not completely enclose an area.

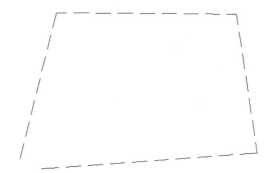

Parcels Reacting to Site Objects

Parcels require only one parcel segment to divide them from their neighbor (see Figure 6.43). This behavior eliminates the need for duplicate segments between parcels, and duplicate segments must be avoided.

As we saw in the section on site interaction, parcels understand their relationships to one another. When you create a single parcel segment between two subdivision lots, you have the ability to move one line and affect two parcels. Figure 6.44 shows the parcels from Figure 6.43 once the parcel segment between them has been shifted to the left. Note that both areas change in response.

A mistake that many people new to Civil 3D make is to create parcels from closed polylines, which results in a duplicate segment between parcels. Figure 6.45 shows two parcels created from two closed polylines. These two parcels may appear identical to the two seen in the previous example because they were both created from a closed polyline rectangle; however, the segment between them is actually two segments

FIGURE 6.43

Two parcels, with one parcel segment between them

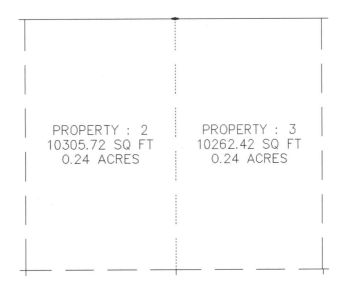

PROPERTY : 2
10305.72 SQ FT
0.24 ACRES

PROPERTY : 3
10262.42 SQ FT
0.24 ACRES

FIGURE 6.44
Moving one parcel segment affects the area of two parcels

FIGURE 6.45
Adjacent parcels created from closed polylines will create overlapping or duplicate segments.

The duplicate segment becomes apparent when attempting to grip-edit the parcel segments. Moving one vertex from the common lot line, as seen in Figure 6.46, reveals the second segment. Also note that a sliver parcel is formed. Duplicate site geometry objects and sliver parcels make it difficult for Civil 3D to solve the site topology and can cause drawing stability problems and unexpected parcel behavior. You must avoid this at all costs. Creating a subdivision plat of parcels this way almost guarantees that your labeling will not perform properly and could potentially lead to data loss and drawing corruption.

MIGRATE PARCELS FROM LAND DESKTOP? JUST DON'T DO IT!

The Land Desktop Parcel Manager essentially created Land Desktop parcels from closed polylines. If you migrate Land Desktop parcels into Civil 3D, your resulting Civil 3D parcels will behave poorly and almost universally result in drawing corruption.

Parcels will form to fill the space contained by the original outer boundary. We always begin a parcel division project with an outer boundary of some sort (see Figure 6.47).

We then add road centerline alignments to the site, which divides the outer boundary (see Figure 6.48).

It is important to note that the boundary parcel no longer exists intact. As we subdivide this site, parcel 1 is continually reallocated with every division. As road ROW and subdivision lots are formed from parcel segments, more parcels are created. Every bit of space that was contained in the original outer boundary is accounted for in the mesh of newly formed parcels (see Figure 6.49).

From now on, you will consider a ROW and wetlands, parkland, or open-space areas as "parcels," even if you didn't before. Custom label styles can be made to annotate these parcels however you decide, including a "no show" or none label.

FIGURE 6.46
Duplicate segment become apparent when they are grip-edited and a sliver parcel is formed.

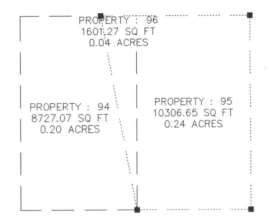

FIGURE 6.47
An outer boundary parcel

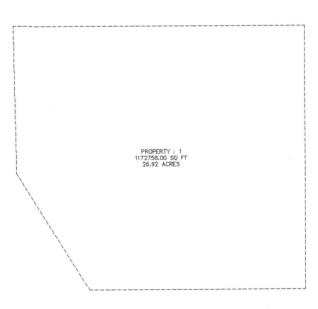

FIGURE 6.48
Alignments added to the same site as the boundary parcel will divide the boundary parcel.

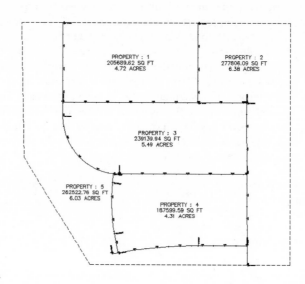

FIGURE 6.49
The total area of parcels contained within the original boundary will sum to equal the original boundary area.

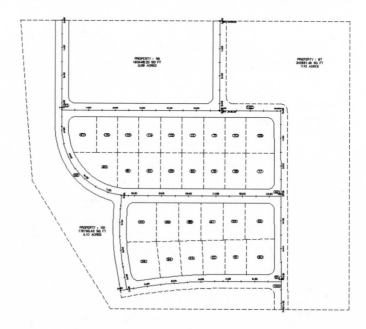

Real World Scenario

IF I CAN'T USE CLOSED POLYLINES, HOW DO I CREATE MY PARCELS?

How do you create your parcels if parcels must always close, but you aren't supposed to use closed polylines to create them?

In the earlier exercises in this chapter, you learned several techniques for creating parcels. These techniques included using AutoCAD objects and a variety of parcel layout tools. A summary of some of the best practices for creating parcels are listed here.

◆ Create closed polylines for boundaries and islands and then use the Create Parcel From Objects menu command—Closed polylines are suitable foundation geometry in cases where they will not be subject to possible duplicate segments. The following graphic shows a boundary parcel and a designated open-space parcel that were both created from closed polylines. Other examples of island parcels would include isolated wetlands, ponds, or similar features that do not share a common segment with the boundary parcel.

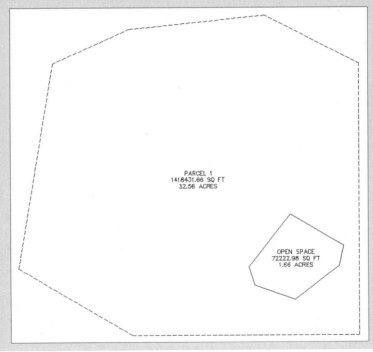

◆ Create trimmed/extended polylines for internal features and then use the Create Parcel From Objects menu command—For internal features such as easements, buffers, open space, or wetlands that share a segment with the outer boundary, draw a polyline that intersects the outer boundary, but be careful not to trace over any segments of the outer boundary. Use the Create Parcel From Objects menu command to convert the polyline into a parcel segment. This graphic shows the technique used for an easement:

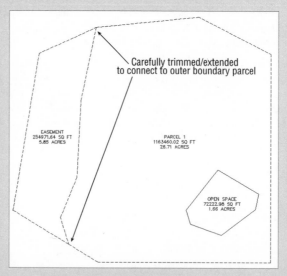

◆ Use the Create ROW tool or create trimmed/extended polylines and then use the Create Parcel From Objects menu command for ROW segments—in a previous exercise, we used the Create ROW tool. We also mentioned that even though this tool can be useful, it cannot create cul-de-sacs or changes in ROW width. In cases where you need a more intricate ROW parcel, use the AutoCAD Offset tool to offset your alignment. The resulting offsets will be polylines. Use circles, arcs, fillet, trim, extend, and other tools to create a joined polyline to use as foundation geometry for your ROW parcel. Use the Create Parcel From Objects menu command to convert this linework into parcel segments, as shown here:

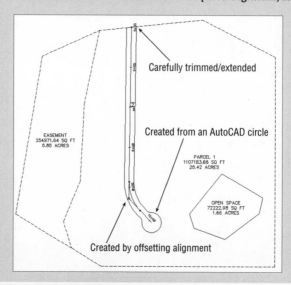

◆ Create trimmed/extended polylines for rear lot lines and then use the Create Parcel From Objects menu command—the precise sizing tools tend to work best when given a rear lot line as a target endpoint. Create this rear target by offsetting your ROW parcel to your desired lot depth. The resulting offset will be a polyline. Use trim, extend, and other tools to create a joined polyline to use as foundation geometry for your rear lot parcel segment. Use the Create Parcel From Objects menu command to convert this linework into parcel segments, as shown here:

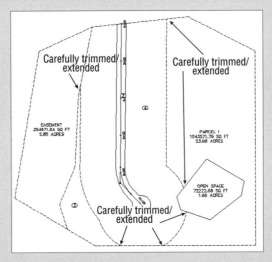

◆ Use the Create Parcel By Layout menu command with the attached segment tools for internal parcels—the precise sizing tools and Free Form Create automatically create just one attached segment between parcels, so using them to create your subdivision lot boundaries will ensure proper parcel geometry, as seen in Properties 1 through 19 in this graphic:

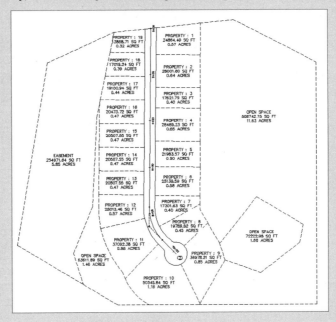

◆ Use line segments and the Create Parcel From Objects for final detailed segment work—surveyors often prefer to lay out straight-line segments rather than curves, so for the final rear-lot line cleanup, create AutoCAD lines across the back of each lot and then use Create Parcel From Objects to turn those lines into parcel segments, as shown here:

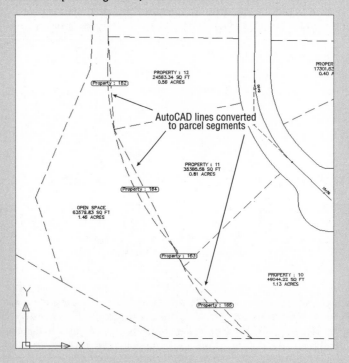

This final cleanup is best saved for the very end of the project. Parcel iterations and refinement work much better with a continuous rear lot line.

Constructing Parcel Segments with the Appropriate Vertices

Parcel segments should only have natural vertices where necessary and split-created vertices at all other intersections. A natural vertex, or point of intersection (PI), can be identified by picking a line, polyline, or parcel segment and noting the location of the grips (see Figure 6.50).

FIGURE 6.50
Natural vertices on
a parcel segment

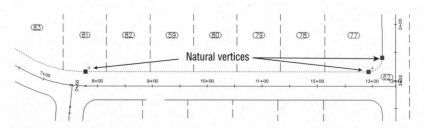

A split-created vertex occurs when two parcel segments touch or cross each other. Note that in Figure 6.51, the parcel segment does not show a grip even where each individual lot line touches the ROW parcel.

It is desirable to have as few natural vertices as possible. In the example in Figure 6.50, the ROW frontage line can be expressed as a single bearing and length from the end of the arc in Parcel 81 through the beginning of the arc in parcel 77 as opposed to having seven smaller line segments.

If the foundation geometry was drawn with a natural vertex at each lot line intersection as in Figure 6.52, then the resulting parcel segment would not label properly and could cause complications with editing and other functions. This subject will be discussed in more detail later in the section "Labeling Spanning Segments" later in this chapter.

Parcel segments must not overlap. Overlapping segments create redundant vertices, sliver parcels, and other problems that will complicate editing parcel segments and labeling. Figure 6.53 shows a segment created to form parcel 104 that overlaps the rear parcel segment for the entire block. This segment should be edited to remove the redundant parcel segment across the rear of parcel 76 to ensure good parcel topology.

FIGURE 6.51
Split-created vertices on a parcel segment

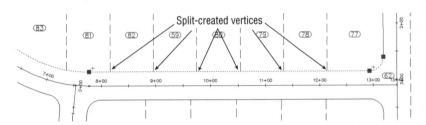

FIGURE 6.52
Unnecessary natural vertices on a parcel segment will create problems for labeling and editing.

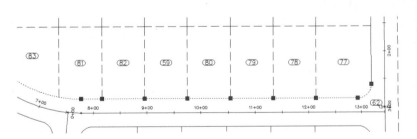

FIGURE 6.53
Avoid creating overlapping parcel segments.

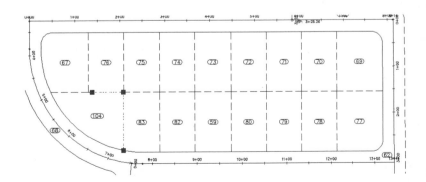

Parcel segments must not overhang. Spanning labels are designed to overlook the location of intersection formed (or T-shaped) split-created vertices. However, these labels will not span a crossing formed (X- or + [plus]-shaped) split-created vertex. Even a very small parcel segment overhang would prevent a spanning label from working and might even affect the area computation for adjacent parcels. The overhanging segment in Figure 6.54 would prevent a label from returning the full spanning length of the ROW segment it crosses.

FIGURE 6.54
Avoid creating
overhanging parcel
segments.

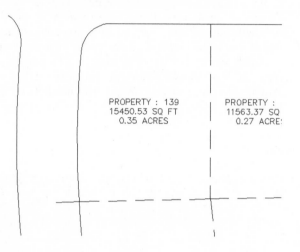

Labeling Parcel Areas

A parcel area label is placed at the parcel centroid by default, and it refers to the parcel in its entirety. When asked to pick a parcel, you will pick the area label. An area label does not necessarily have to include the actual area of the parcel.

Area labels can be customized to suit your fancy. Figure 6.55 shows a variety of customized area labels.

FIGURE 6.55
Sample area labels

Parcel area labels are composed like all other labels in Civil 3D. You can select the following default parcel properties for text components of the label from the dropdown menu in the Properties selection box in the Text Component Editor dialog (see Figure 6.56):

- Name
- Description
- Parcel Area
- Parcel Number
- Parcel Perimeter
- Parcel Address
- Parcel Site Name
- Parcel Style Name
- Parcel Tax ID

FIGURE 6.56

Text Component Editor showing the various properties that the text components of an area label can have

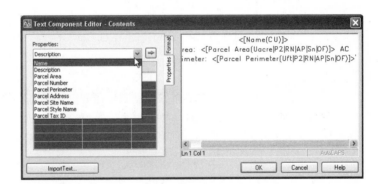

Area labels often include the parcel name or number. Parcels can be renamed or renumbered using the Parcels ➤Edit Parcel ➤ Rename/Renumber Parcels menu command.

The following exercise will teach you how to renumber a series of parcels:

1. Open `Change Area Label.dwg`. Note that this drawing contains many subdivision lot parcels.

2. Choose Parcels ➤ Edit Parcel ➤ Rename/Renumber Parcels. In the Renumber/Rename Parcels dialog, make sure Subdivision Lots is selected from the dropdown menu in the Site selection box. Change the value of the Starting Number selection box to 1. Click OK.

3. At the `Specify start point or [Polylines/Site]:` prompt, pick a point on the screen anywhere inside the Single-Family: 31 parcel, which will become your new Single-Family: 1 at the end of the command.

4. At the `End point or [Undo]:` prompt, pick a point on the screen anywhere inside the Single-Family: 29 parcel, almost as if you were drawing a line, then a point anywhere inside Property: 2, and then inside Single-Family: 39. Press ↵ to stop choosing parcels. Press ↵ again to end the command.

Note that your parcels have been renumbered from 1 through 16. Repeat the exercise with other parcels in the drawing for additional practice if desired.

The next exercise will lead you through using the Edit Parcel Properties dialog to change an area label:

1. Continue working in the `Change Area Label.dwg` file.

2. Choose Parcels ➤ Edit Parcel ➤ Edit Parcel Properties. At the `Specify start point or [Polylines/Site]:` prompt, pick a point on the screen anywhere inside the Single-Family: 1 parcel.

3. At the `End point or [Undo]:` prompt, pick a point on the screen anywhere inside Single-Family: 2, almost as if you were drawing a line. Press ↵ to stop choosing parcels. Press ↵ again to open the Edit Parcel Properties dialog (see Figure 6.57).

4. Click the + sign to open the Area Label Style dialog. Select Parcel Number from the drop-down list in the Area Label Style selection box. Click OK to dismiss the dialog.

5. In the Area Label Styles portion of the Edit Parcel Properties dialog, highlight the Name Square Foot & Acres entry. Click the red X to delete this label from the Single-Family: 1 parcel.

6. Click on the Next Parcel arrow ▣ in the upper-left corner of the dialog. The dialog will advance to the Single-Family: 2 parcel. Repeat steps 4 and 5 for this parcel.

7. Click OK to dismiss the Parcel Properties dialog.

FIGURE 6.57

The Edit Parcel Properties dialog

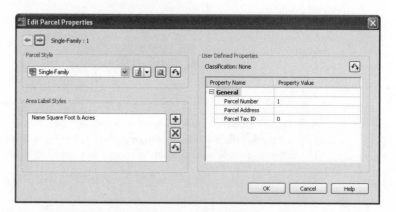

The two parcels now have parcel area labels that call out numbers only. Note that you could also use this interface to add a second area label to certain parcels if required.

This final exercise will show you how to use Prospector to change a group of parcel area labels at the same time:

1. Continue working in the `Change Area Label.dwg` file.

2. In Prospector, expand the Sites ➤ Subdivision Lots ➤ Parcels collection (see Figure 6.58).

3. In the Preview pane, click the Name column to sort the Parcel collection by name.

FIGURE 6.58
The Parcel collection in Prospector

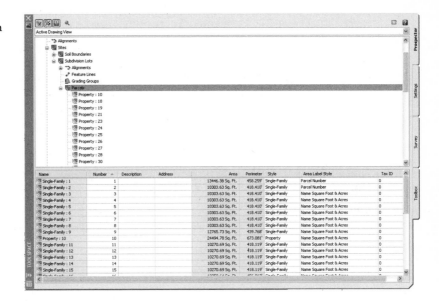

4. Hold down your Shift key and click each Single-Family parcel to select them all. Release the Shift key, and your parcels should remain selected.

5. Slide over to the Area Label Style column. Right-click on the column header and select Edit (see Figure 6.59).

6. In the Select Label Style dialog, select Parcel Number from the dropdown list in the Label Style selection box. Click OK to dismiss the dialog.

7. The drawing will process for a moment. Once the processing is finished, minimize Prospector and inspect your parcels. All the Single-Family parcels should now have the Parcel Number area label style.

FIGURE 6.59
Right-click on the Area Label Style column header and select Edit.

WHAT IF I NEED MY AREA LABEL SPLIT ONTO TWO LAYERS?

You may have a few different types of plans that show parcels. Since it would be awkward to have to change the parcel area label style before you plot each sheet, it would be best to find a way make a second label on a second layer so that you can freeze the area component in sheets or viewports when it is not needed. Here's an example where the square footage has been placed on a different layer so that it can be frozen in certain viewports:

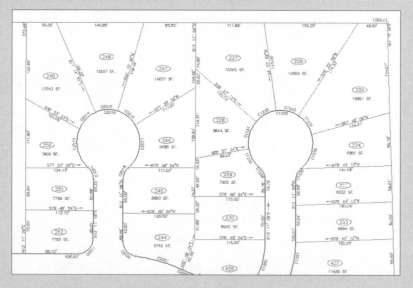

You can accomplish this by either creating a second parcel area label that calls out area only or a General Note label that contains parcel reference text.

Add a second parcel area label by choosing Parcel ➤ Add Parcel Labels ➤ Add Parcel Labels. Select Area from the dropdown menu in the Label Type selection box and then a second area label style. Click Add, and then pick your parcel on screen.

You can also create a General Note label that has reference text, which calls out the parcel area. Here's an example of how this label can be composed:

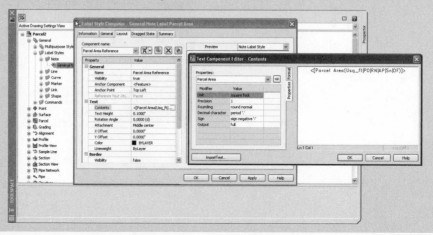

Choose General ➤ Add Labels. In the Add Labels dialog, select Note from the dropdown menu in the Feature selection box, and then select the Note label style. Click Add, and pick an insertion point for the label. You will be prompted to pick the parcel you would like to reference.

You will find a second parcel area label to be a little more automatic when you place it (it already knows what parcel to reference), but you will find the General Note label to be more flexible about location, easier to pin, and easier to erase.

Labeling Parcel Segments

Although we have seen parcels used for much more than just subdivision lots, most parcels you create will probably be used for concept plans, record plats, and other legal subdivision plans. These plans, such as the one shown in Figure 6.60, almost always require segment labels for bearing, distance, direction, crow's feet, and more.

Labeling Multiple Parcel Segments

The following exercise will teach you how to add labels to multiple parcel segments:

1. Open the Segment Labels.dwg file. Note that this drawing contains many subdivision lot parcels.

2. Choose Parcels ➤Add Parcel Labels ➤ Add Parcel Labels.

3. In the Add Labels dialog, select Multiple Segment, Bearing Over Distance, and Delta Over Length And Radius from the dropdown list in the Label Type, Line Label Style, and Curve Label Style selection boxes, respectively.

FIGURE 6.60
A fully labeled
site plan

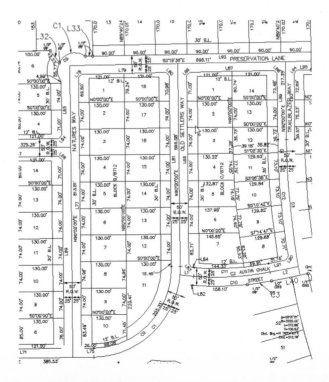

4. Click Add.

5. At the `Select parcel to be labeled by clicking on area label or [CLockwise/ COunterclockwise]<CLockwise>:` prompt, pick the area label for parcel 17.

6. Each parcel segment for parcel 17 should now be labeled. Continue picking parcels 18 through 28 in the same manner. Note that segments are never given a duplicate label, even along shared lot lines.

7. Press ↵ to exit the command.

The following exercise will teach you how to edit and delete parcel segment labels:

1. Continue working in the `Segment Labels.dwg` file.

2. Zoom in on the label along the frontage of Parcel 18 (see Figure 6.61).

3. Select the label. You will know your label has been picked when you see a diamond-shaped grip at the label midpoint (see Figure 6.62).

4. Once your label has been picked, right-click over the label to bring up the shortcut menu.

5. Select Flip Label from the shortcut menu. The label will flip so that the bearing component is on top of the line and the distance component is underneath the line.

6. Select the label again, then right-click and select Reverse Label. The label will reverse so that the bearing now reads NW instead of NE.

FIGURE 6.61
The label along the
frontage of Parcel 18

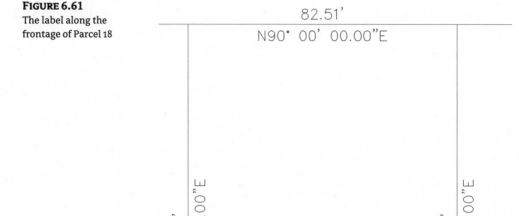

FIGURE 6.62
A diamond-shaped
grip appears when the
label has been picked.

82.51'

N90° 00' 00.00"E

7. Repeat steps 3 through 6 for several other segment labels and note their reactions.

8. Select any label. Once the label is picked, execute the AutoCAD Erase tool. Note that the label disappears.

Labeling Spanning Segments

Spanning labels are used where you need a label that spans the overall length of an outside segment, such as the example in Figure 6.63.

Spanning labels require that you use the appropriate vertices as discussed in detail in a previous section. Spanning labels have the following requirements:

◆ Spanning labels can only span across split-created vertices. Natural vertices will interrupt a spanning length.

◆ Spanning label styles must be composed to span the outside segment (see Figure 6.64).

◆ Spanning label styles must be composed to attach the desired spanning components (such as length and direction arrow) on the outside segment (as shown in Figure 6.63), with a small offset (see Figure 6.65).

FIGURE 6.63
A spanning label

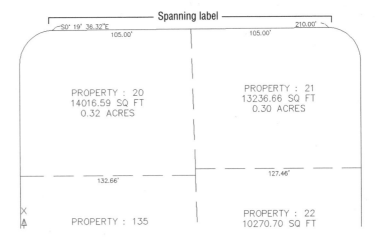

FIGURE 6.64
Set all components of a spanning label to span outside segments.

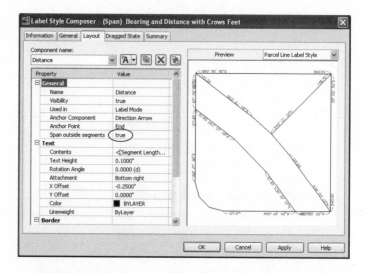

FIGURE 6.65
Give each component a small offset in the y direction.

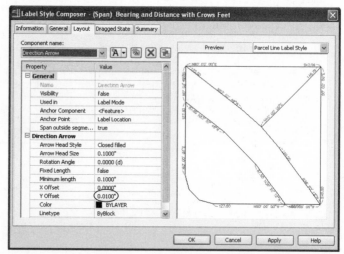

Once you have confirmed that your geometry is sound and your label is properly composed, you are set to span. The following exercise will teach you how to add spanning labels to single parcel segments:

1. Continue working in the Segment Labels.dwg file.

2. Zoom in on the ROW parcel segment that runs from Parcel 10 through Parcel 16.

3. Choose Parcels ➤ Add Parcel Labels ➤ Add Parcel Labels.

4. In the Add Labels dialog, select Single Segment, (Span) Bearing And Distance With Crow's Feet, and Delta Over Length And Radius from the dropdown list in the Label Type, Line Label Style, and Curve Label Style selection boxes, respectively.

5. Click Add.

6. At the Select label location: prompt, pick somewhere near the middle of the ROW parcel segment that runs from Parcel 10 through Parcel 16.

7. A label that spans the full length between natural vertices will appear (see Figure 6.66).

FIGURE 6.66
The spanning label

FLIP IT, REVERSE IT

If your spanning label doesn't seem to work on your first try and you have followed all the spanning label guidelines, try flipping your label to the other side of the parcel segment, reversing the label, or using a combination of both flipping and reversing.

Adding Curve Tags to Prepare for Table Creation

Surveyors and engineers often make segment tables to simplify plan labeling, produce reports, and facilitate stakeout. Civil 3D parcels provide tools for creating dynamic line and curve tables, as well as a combination of line and curve tables.

Parcel segments must be labeled before they can be used to create a table. They can be labeled with any type of label, but you will likely find it to be best practice to create a tag-only style for segments that will be placed in a table.

The following exercise will teach you how to replace curve labels with tag-only labels to single curve segments and renumber tags:

1. Continue working in the Segment Labels.dwg file. Note that the labels along curves, such as Parcels 17 and 22, would be better represented as curve tags.

2. Choose Parcels ➢Add Parcel Labels ➢ Add Parcel Labels.

3. In the Add Labels dialog, select Replace Multiple Segment, Bearing Over Distance, and Curve Tag Only from the dropdown list in the Label Type, Line Label Style, and the Curve Label Style selection boxes, respectively.

4. At the Select parcel to be labeled by clicking on area label or [CLockwise/COunterclockwise]<CLockwise>: prompt, pick the area label for Parcel 17. Note that the line labels for Parcel 17 are reset and the curve labels convert to tags.

5. Repeat step 4 for Parcels 18 through 28. Press ⏎ to exit the command.

Now that each curve label has been replaced with a tag, it is desirable to have the tag numbers sequential. The following exercise will teach you how to renumber tags:

1. Continue working in the Segment Labels.dwg file.

2. Zoom into the curve on the upper-left side of Parcel 22 (see Figure 6.67). Your curve may have a different number from the figure.

3. Choose Parcels ➢Add Tables ➢ Renumber Tags.

4. At the `Select segment type or [Line/Curve/End]<End>:` prompt, type **C** to select the curve type.

5. The Renumbering dialog appears (see Figure 6.68). Change the value in the Starting Number selection box to 1. Click OK.

6. Click each curve tag in the drawing at the `Select labels on Curves:` prompt. Each one will instantly renumber to the next available number in sequence. Press ↵ to exit the command.

FIGURE 6.67
Curve tags
on Parcel 22

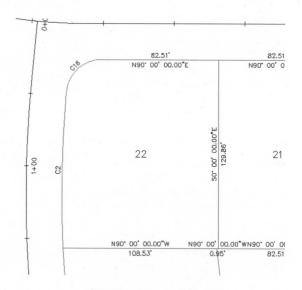

FIGURE 6.68
The Renumbering
dialog

Creating a Table for Parcel Segments

The following exercise will teach you how to replace curve labels on single-curve segments with tag-only labels and also how to renumber tags:

1. Continue working in the `Segment Labels.dwg` file.

2. You should have several curves labeled with the Curve Tag Only label.

3. Choose Parcels ➢Add Tables ➢ Add Curve.

4. In the Table Creation dialog, select Length, Radius & Delta from the dropdown menu in the Table Style selection box. In the Selection area of the dialog, check the Apply box for the Curve Tag Only entry under the Label Style Name. Keep the default values for the remaining options. The dialog should look like Figure 6.69. Click OK.

5. At the `Select upper left corner:` prompt, pick a location in your drawing for the table. A curve table appears, as shown in Figure 6.70.

FIGURE 6.69

The Table Creation dialog

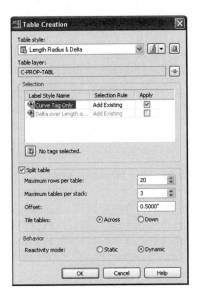

FIGURE 6.70

A curve table

Curve Table					
Curve #	Length	Radius	Delta	Chord Direction	Chord Length
C1	37.06	25.00	84.93	N47° 31' 58"E	33.76
C15	39.13	25.00	89.68	S45° 09' 28"E	35.26
C14	39.41	25.00	90.31	S44° 50' 33"W	35.45
C13	311.43	2025.00	8.81	S85° 35' 39"W	311.12
C12	311.43	2025.00	8.81	S85° 35' 39"W	311.12
C11	311.43	2025.00	8.81	S85° 35' 39"W	311.12
C8	311.43	2025.00	8.81	S85° 35' 39"W	311.12
C7	0.00	1.13	0.04	S81° 11' 18"W	0.00
C6	38.66	25.00	88.60	N54° 30' 36"W	34.92
C3	206.60	775.00	15.27	N2° 34' 19"W	205.99
C2	206.60	775.00	15.27	N2° 34' 19"W	205.99

The Bottom Line

Create a boundary parcel from objects.   The first step to any parceling project is to create an outer boundary for the site.

Master It   Open the `Mastering Parcels.dwg` file. Convert the polyline in the drawing to a parcel.

Create a right-of-way parcel using the right-of-way tool.   For many projects, the ROW parcel will serve as frontage for subdivision parcels. For straightforward sites, the automatic Create ROW tool provides a quick way to create this parcel.

Master It   Continue working in the `Mastering Parcels.dwg` file. Create a ROW parcel that is offset by 25′ on either side of the road centerline with 25′ fillets at the parcel boundary.

Create subdivision lots automatically by layout.   The biggest challenge when creating a subdivision plan is optimizing the number of lots. The precise sizing parcel tools provide a means to automate this process.

Master It   Continue working in the `Mastering Parcels.dwg` file. Create a series of lots with a minimum of 10,000 square feet and 100′ frontage.

Add multiple parcel segment labels.   Every subdivision plat must be appropriately labeled. Parcels can be quickly labeled with their bearings, distances, direction, and more using the segment labeling tools.

Master It   Continue working in the `Mastering Parcels.dwg` file. Place Bearing Over Distance labels on every parcel line segment and Delta Over Length And Radius labels on every parcel curve segment using the Multiple Segment Labeling tool.

Chapter 7

Laying a Path: Alignments

The world is 3D, but almost every design starts as a concept: a flat line on a flat piece of paper. Cutting a way through the trees, the hills, and the forests, we design around a basic layout to get some idea of horizontal placement. This horizontal placement is the alignment and drives much of our design. In this chapter, we'll look at how alignments can be created, how they interact with the rest of the design, how to edit and analyze them, how styles are involved with display and labeling, and finally, how they work with the overall project.

By the end of this chapter, you will be able to:

◆ Create an alignment from a polyline

◆ Create a reverse curve that never loses tangency

◆ Replace a component of an alignment with another component type

◆ Create a new label set

◆ Override individual labels with other styles

Alignments, Pickles, and Freedom

There are two major concepts that you have to understand before you can efficiently work with alignments: the interaction of alignments and sites, and the idea of geometry that is fixed, floating, or free.

Alignments and Sites

Prior to Civil 3D 2008, alignments were always a part of a site and interacted with the topology contained in that site. This interaction led to the pickle analogy: alignments are like pickles in a mason jar. You don't put pickles and pepper in the same jar unless you want hot pickles, and you don't put lots and alignments in the same site unless you want subdivided lots.

With the release of 2008, Civil 3D now has two ways of handling alignments: they can be contained in a site as before, or they can be independent of a site. Notice how Figure 7.1 shows Parker Place as a member of the Alignments collection directly under the drawing and Carson Court as a member of the Alignments collection that is part of the Rose Acres Sites collection, which is directly under the drawing.

FIGURE 7.1
Alignments in and out
of the site collection

Both the Parker Place and the Carson Court alignment can be used to cut profiles or control corridors, but only the Carson Court alignment will react with and create parcels as a member of a site topology.

Many users of versions prior to 2008 had real issues keeping alignments and sites straight. Unless you have good reason to have them interact, it makes sense to create alignments outside of any site object. They can be moved later if need be. For the purpose of the exercises in this chapter, we will not place any alignments in a site.

Alignment Entities and Freedom

Alignments can consist of three types of entities or segments: lines, arcs, and spirals. These segments control the horizontal alignment of your design. Their relationship to one another is described by the following terminology:

◆ Fixed segments are fixed in space. They are defined by connecting points in the coordinate plane and are independent of the segments that occur either before or after them in the alignment. Additionally, fixed segments may be created as tangent to other components, but their very independence from those objects will allow you to move them out of tangency during editing operations. This can be helpful when you're trying to match existing field conditions.

◆ Floating segments float in space but are attached to a point in the plane and to some segment to which they are maintaining tangency. Floating segments work well in situations where you have a critical point but the other points of the horizontal alignment are flexible.

◆ Free segments are functions of the entities that come before and after them in the alignment structure. Unlike fixed or floating segments, a free segment must have segments that come before and after it. Free segments will maintain tangency to the segments that come before and after them and will move as required to make that happen. Although some geometry constraints can be put in place, these constraints can be edited and are user dependent.

During the exercises in this chapter, we will use a mix of these entity types to understand them better. Autodesk has also published a drawing called Playground that can be found by searching on the Web. This drawing contains examples of most of the types of entities that you can create.

Creating an Alignment

Alignments in Civil 3D can be created from a polyline or by layout. In this section, we'll look at both ways to create an alignment and discuss the advantages and disadvantages of each. The exercise will use the street layout shown in Figure 7.2 as well as the different methods to achieve our designs.

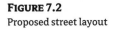

FIGURE 7.2
Proposed street layout

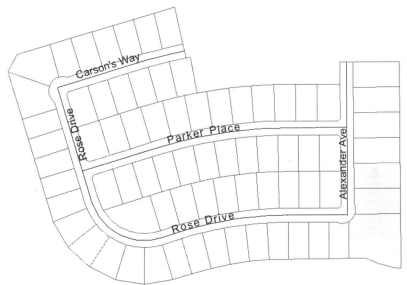

Creating from a Polyline

Most designers have used either polylines or lines and arcs in the past to generate the horizontal control of their projects. It's quite common for surveyors to generate polylines to describe the center of a right of way or for an environmental engineer to draw a polyline to show where a new channel should be constructed. These team members may or may not have Civil 3D, so they used their familiar friend—the polyline—to describe their design intent.

While polylines are good at showing where something should go, they don't have much data behind them. To make full use of these objects, they should be converted to native Civil 3D alignments that can then be shared and used for myriad purposes. In this exercise, we'll convert a polyline to an alignment.

1. Open the `Alignments From Polylines.dwg` file.

2. From the main menu, select Alignments ➤ Create Alignment From Polyline.

3. Pick the polyline labeled as Parker Place in Figure 7.2, and the Create Alignment – From Polyline dialog appears.

4. Change the Name field to Parker Place, as shown in Figure 7.3.

5. Accept the other settings and click OK.

FIGURE 7.3
The settings used to
create the Parker Place
alignment

You've created your first alignment and attached stationing and geometry point labels with the All Labels option selected in the Alignment Label Set field. We'll examine the labeling in a later portion of this chapter. Let's do some more by changing other settings in the dialog:

1. From the main menu, select Alignments ➢ Create Alignment From Polyline.

2. Pick the shorter polyline that will define Carson's Way on the northern end of our site.

3. In the Create Alignment – From Polyline dialog, do the following:

    ◆ Change the Name field to Carson's Way.

    ◆ Set the Alignment Style field to Layout.

    ◆ Set the Alignment Label Set field to Major And Minor Only.

4. Click OK.

Just like every other Civil 3D object, alignments and their labels are controlled by styles. In this case, setting the Alignment Label Set to Major And Minor Only means that only the labels for major and minor stations are displayed. We'll look at label sets a bit later in this chapter, but for now, let's see what other options we have for labeling alignments:

1. From the main menu, select Alignments ➢ Create Alignment From Polyline.

2. Pick the longer polyline wrapping around the southwest corner of our site. This polyline is Rose Drive in Figure 7.2.

3. In the Create Alignment – From Polyline dialog, do the following:

    ◆ Change the Name field to Rose Drive.

    ◆ Set the Alignment Style field to Select Proposed.

    ◆ Set the Alignment Label Set field to No Label.

4. Click OK.

No labels will be displayed when the Alignment Label Set is set to No Label.

Finally, we also have one street (Alexander Ave) that was drawn as a simple line. But the command is Create Alignment From Polyline, not Create Alignment From Lines or Create Alignment From Lines And Arcs. It's a simple matter of using some built-in, right-click functionality to convert the street first to a polyline and then to an alignment:

1. Pick the straight line, representing the street, on the eastern portion of our site.

2. Right-click and select Convert To Polyline, as shown in Figure 7.4.

3. From the main menu, select Alignments ➤ Create Alignment From Polyline.

4. Pick the polyline that was just created.

5. In the Create Alignment – From Polyline dialog, do the following:

   ◆ Change the Name field to Alexander Ave.

   ◆ Set the Alignment Style field to Basic.

   ◆ Set the Alignment Label Set field to All Labels.

6. Click OK.

Four street alignments were created from polylines, in under a minute, ready for use in corridors, in profiling, or for any number of other uses.

The only major issue with alignments made from polylines (especially if they already have nice sweeping arcs in them) is that all entities are fixed. They don't understand each other or try to maintain tangency when moved. To illustrate, follow these simple steps:

1. Zoom in on the Carson's Way alignment on the north end of our site. The style we selected, Layout, shows arcs and tangents as different colors, so it's easy to see what we're getting.

2. Pick the alignment to activate the grips.

3. Grab the circular grip on the right-hand end, and pull it away from its current location.

Notice how the line and arc, which make up Carson's Way, are no longer tangent. Both of these entities are fixed and independent of each other. This is the main drawback of using polylines when creating alignments. This issue is magnified when dealing with more complex alignments, which have multiple components that must all maintain tangency.

FIGURE 7.4
Converting a line
to a polyline

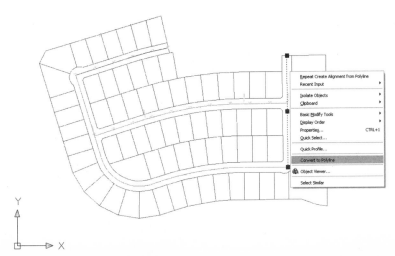

Creating by Layout

Now that we've made a series of alignments from polylines, let's look at the other creation option, Create By Layout. We'll use the same street layout (Figure 7.2) that was given to us by a planner, but instead of converting from polylines, we'll trace the alignments. Although this seems like duplicate work, it will actually pay dividends in the relationships created between segments.

1. Open the `Alignments By Layout.dwg` file.

2. From the main menu, select Alignments ➤ Create Alignment By Layout. The Create Alignment – Layout dialog appears, as shown in Figure 7.5.

3. Change the Name field to Parker Place, then click OK to accept the other settings. The Alignment Layout Tools toolbar appears, as shown in Figure 7.6.

4. Click on the down arrow next to the Draw Tangent-Tangent Without Curve tool on the far left, and select the Tangent-Tangent (With Curves) option. The tool will place a curve automatically, and we'll adjust the curve, watching the tangents extend as needed.

5. Pick the far left end of Parker Place using an Endpoint snap.

6. Pick just above the arc in the middle of the street; then pick the endpoint at the far right, as shown in Figure 7.7, to finish creating this alignment.

FIGURE 7.5
Creating an Alignment By Layout

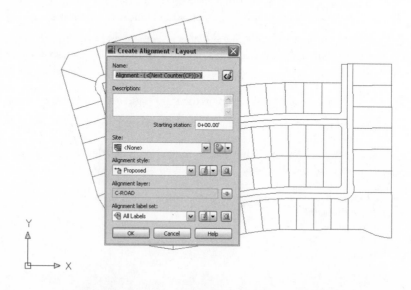

FIGURE 7.6
The Alignment Layout Tools toolbar

FIGURE 7.7
Competing the Parker
Place alignment

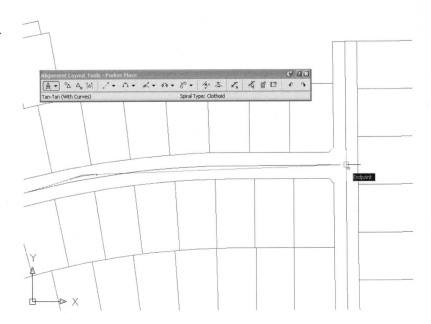

7. Right-click, and you'll be back at the command line, but the toolbar will still be open.

8. Click on the red X button in the upper right of the toolbar to close it.

Zoom in on the arc, and notice that it doesn't really match the arc that the planner put in for us to follow. That's OK—we'll fix it in just a few minutes. It bears repeating that in dealing with Civil 3D objects, it's good to get something in place and *then* refine. With Land Desktop or other packages, you didn't want to define the object until it was fully designed. In Civil 3D, design, then refine.

The alignment we just made is one of the most basic. Let's move on to some of the others and use a few of the other tools to complete our initial layout. In this exercise, we'll build the alignment at the north end of the site, but this time we'll use a floating curve to make sure that the two segments we create maintain their relationship.

1. From the main menu, select Alignments ➢ Create Alignment By Layout.

2. In the Create Alignment – Layout dialog, do the following:

♦ Change the Name field to Carson's Way.

♦ Set the Alignment Style field to Layout.

♦ Set the Alignment Label Set field to Major And Minor Only.

3. Click OK, and the Alignment Layout Tools toolbar appears.

4. Select the Draw Fixed Line – Two Points tool (see Figure 7.8).

5. Pick the two points circled in Figure 7.8, using Endpoint snaps and working left to right, to draw the fixed line. When complete, the command line will state, "Specify start point:".

6. Click the down arrow next to the Add Fixed Curve (Three Points) tool on the toolbar, and select the More Floating Curves ➤ Floating Curve (From Entity End, Through Point) option, as shown in Figure 7.9.

7. Pick the fixed line segment you drew in steps 4 and 5. A blue rubberband should appear, indicating that the alignment of the curve segment is being floated off the endpoint of the fixed segment (see Figure 7.10).

FIGURE 7.8

The Draw Fixed Line – Two Points tool

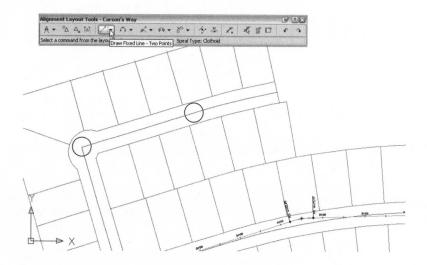

FIGURE 7.9

Selecting the Floating Curve tool

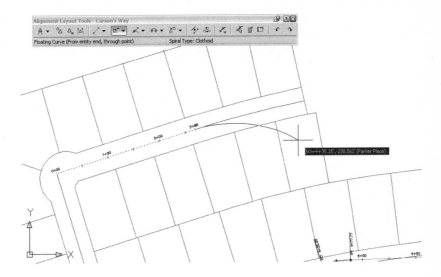

8. Pick the east end of the Carson's Way polyline.

9. Right-click to exit the command.

10. Close the toolbar to return to Civil 3D.

In our previous drawing, we picked a point on the Carson's Way alignment and pulled it away to illustrate the lack of connection between the two segments. This time, pick the grip near the western end and pull it away from its location in the cul-de-sac. Notice that the line and the arc move in sync and tangency is maintained (see Figure 7.11). Remember that, in the first drawing, the Carson's Way alignment was created from polylines, whereas, in this drawing, it was created by layout.

FIGURE 7.11

Floating curves main-
tain their tangency.

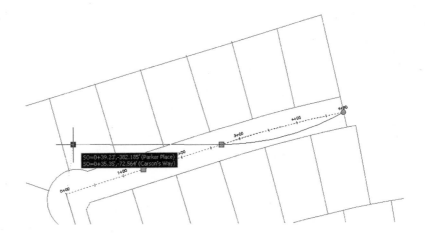

Next, let's look at a more complicated alignment construction—building a reverse curve where the planner left a short segment connecting two curves.

1. From the main menu, select Alignments ➢ Create Alignment By Layout.

2. In the Create Alignment – Layout dialog, do the following:

   ◆ Change the Name field to Rose Drive.

   ◆ Set the Alignment Style field to Layout,

   ◆ Set the Alignment Label Set field to No Labels.

3. Click OK, and the Alignment Layout Tools toolbar appears.

4. Start by drawing a fixed line from the north end of the western portion to its endpoint using the same Draw Fixed Line (Two Points) tool as before.

5. Now use the same Floating Curve (From Entity End, Through Point) tool to draw a curve from the end of this segment to the midpoint of the small tangent on the south end (see Figure 7.12).

6. Return to the toolbar and select the Draw Fixed Line (Two Points) tool again. Draw in the line on the east end of this proposed street. This segment will still be part of the alignment, in spite of not being connected!

FIGURE 7.12
Segment layout for
Rose Drive

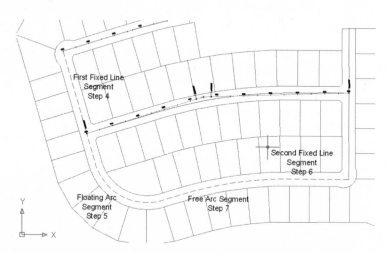

To finish our reverse curve, we need a free curve to tie the floating curve to the segment that was just drawn.

1. Click the down arrow next to the Add Fixed Curve (Three Points) tool, and select the Free Curve Fillet (Between Two Entities, Radius) option.

2. Pick the first arc drawn, as shown in Figure 7.13. The free curve will attach to this entity.

3. Pick the detached segment made a moment ago.

4. Press ↵ at the command line for a solution of less than 180 and draw a curve as opposed to a cloverleaf, which is the only other solution that will solve this geometry.

5. Enter **R** at the command line to select a reverse curve.

6. Use a Center snap to pick the center of the sketched polyline arc and then pick a point on the arc to set the radius. (If you'd like to cheat a bit, then enter **1380** at the command line.)

7. Right-click and close the toolbar.

The alignment now contains a perfect reverse curve. Move any of the pieces and you will see the other segments react to maintain the relationships shown in Figure 7.14. This flexibility in design simply isn't possible with the converted polylines we used previously. Additionally, the flexibility of our tools allows us to explore an alternate solution (the reverse curve) as opposed to the basic solution (two curves with a short tangent). Flexibility is one of Civil 3D's real strengths.

FIGURE 7.13
Adding the floating curve segment

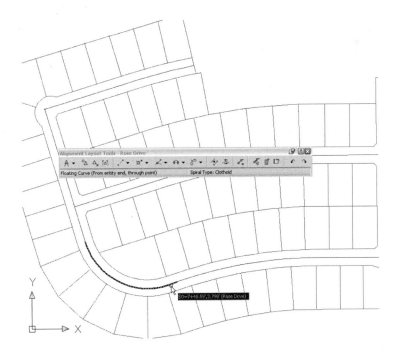

FIGURE 7.14
Curve relationships during a grip edit

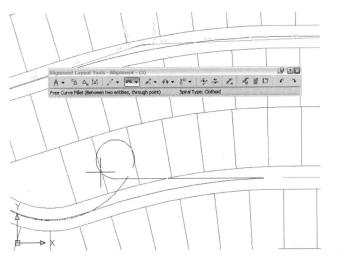

Let's do one more exercise and draw a simple straight line from south to north on the east portion of the site using the Alignment Layout Tools toolbar:

1. From the main menu, select Alignments ➤ Create Alignment By Layout.

2. In the Create Alignment – Layout dialog, do the following:

    ◆ Change the Name field to Alexander Ave.

    ◆ Set the Alignment Style field to Layout.

    ◆ Set the Alignment Label Set field to All Labels.

3. Click OK, and the Alignment Layout Tools toolbar appears.

4. Select the Draw Fixed Line tool again, and then pick the south and the north end of Alexander Ave to create a straight line.

5. Right-click and close the toolbar.

We've completed our initial layout (see Figure 7.15). There are some issues with curve sizes, and the reverse curve might not be acceptable to our designer, but we'll look at changing these things in the next section.

FIGURE 7.15
Completed
alignment layout

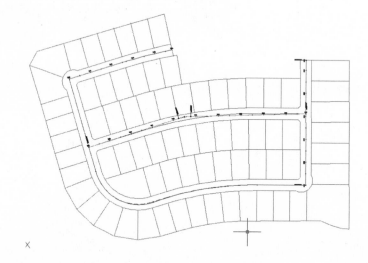

Editing Alignment Geometry

The general power of Civil 3D lies in its flexibility. The documentation process is tied directly to the objects involved, so making edits to those objects doesn't create hours of work in updating the documentation. With alignments, there are three major ways to edit the object's horizontal geometry without modifying the underlying construction:

Graphical Select the object and use the various grips to move critical points. This method works well for realignment, but precise editing for things like a radius or direction can be difficult without construction elements.

Tabular Use Panorama to view all the alignment segments and their properties, typing in values to make changes. This approach works well for modifying lengths or radius values, but setting a tangent perpendicular to a screen element or placing a control point in a specific location is better done graphically.

Segment   Use the Alignment Layout Parameters dialog to view the properties of an individual piece of the alignment. This method makes it easy to modify one piece of an alignment that is complicated and that consists of numerous segments, whereas picking the right field in a Panorama view could be difficult.

In addition to these methods, we can use the Alignment Layout Tools toolbar to make edits that involve removing components or adding to the underlying component count. We'll look at the three simple edits and then look at removing and adding components to an alignment without redefining it.

Grip Editing

We've already used graphical editing techniques when we created alignments from polylines, but the techniques can also be used with considerably more precision than we showed before. The alignment object has a number of grips (see Figure 7.16) that reveal important information about the elements creation.

The grips in Figure 7.16 can be used to do the following actions:

◆ The square grip at the beginning of the alignment, Grip 1, indicates a segment point that can be moved at will. This grip doesn't attach to any other components.

◆ The square grip in the middle of the tangents, Grip 2, allows the element to be translated. Other components will attempt to hold their respective relationships, but moving the grip to a location that would break the alignment will not be allowed.

◆ The triangular grip at the intersection of tangents, Grip 3, indicates a PI relationship. The curve shown is a function of these two tangents and is free to move on the basis of incoming and outgoing tangents, while still holding a radius.

◆ The triangular grip near the middle of the curve, Grip 4, allows the user to modify the radius directly. The tangents must be maintained, however, so any selection that would break the alignment geometry will not be allowed.

◆ Circular grips on the end of the curve, Grip 5, allow the radius of the curve to be indirectly changed by changing the point of the PC of the alignment. This change is made by changing the curve length, which in effect changes the radius.

FIGURE 7.16
Alignment grips

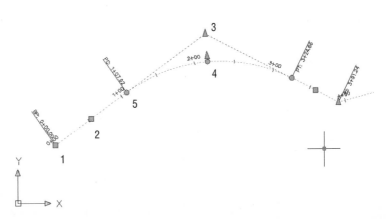

In the following exercise, we'll look at using grip edits to make one of our alignments match the planner's intent more closely:

1. Open the Editing Alignments.dwg file.

2. Expand the Alignments branch in Prospector, right-click on Parker Place, and select Zoom To.

3. Zoom in on the curve in the middle of the alignment. This curve was inserted using the default settings and does not match the guiding polyline very well.

4. Select the alignment to activate the grips.

5. Select the triangular grip that appears near the PI, and use your scroll wheel to zoom out. Careful; there will be two triangular grips here, so be sure to grab the PI one, not the curve radius one.

6. Use an Extended Intersection snap to place the PI at the intersection of the two straight polyline segments. This will place the PI in the location shown in Figure 7.17.

7. Zoom in again on the curve. Notice that the curve still doesn't follow the polyline.

8. Select the circular grip in the middle of the curve, and use a Nearest snap to place it on the dashed polyline. This changes the radius without changing the PI.

Your alignment now follows the planned layout. With no knowledge of the curve properties or other driving information, you've reproduced the intent of the design very quickly.

FIGURE 7.17
Grip-editing the Parker Place curve

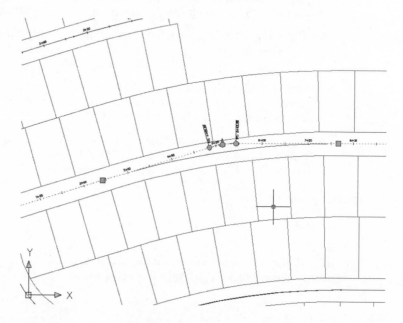

Tabular Design

When you're designing on the basis of governing requirements, one of the most important elements is meeting curve radius requirements. It's easy to work along an alignment in a tabular view, verifying that the design meets the criteria. In this exercise, we'll verify that our curves are suitable for our design.

1. Open the Editing Alignments.dwg file.

2. Zoom to the Carson's Way alignment, and select it in the drawing window to activate the grips.

3. Right-click and select Edit Alignment Geometry from the context menu. The Alignment Layout Tools toolbar opens.

4. Select the Alignment Grid View tool, as shown in Figure 7.18.

5. Panorama appears with the two elements of the alignment listed along the left. Use the scroll bar along the bottom to review the properties of the alignment. Note that the columns can be resized as well as toggled off by right-clicking on the column headers.

FIGURE 7.18
Selecting the Alignment Grid View tool

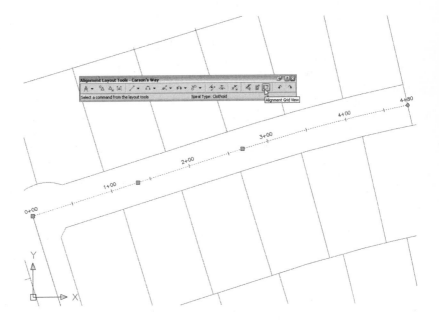

CREATING AND SAVING CUSTOM PANORAMA VIEWS

If you right-click on a column heading and select Customize near the bottom of the menu, you'll be presented with a Customize Columns dialog (new for 2008). This dialog allows you to set up any number of column views, such as Road Design or Stakeout, that will show different columns. These views can be saved, allowing you to switch between views very easily. This feature is a great change from previous versions where the column view changes were not held or saved between viewings.

6. The radius for the first curve cannot be edited. Remember that the location of the curve was based on the curve being tangent to the line before and passing through a point.

7. Click the green checkbox to dismiss Panorama, and then close the toolbar.

Panorama allows for quick and easy review of designs and for precise entering of data, if required. Grip editing is commonly used to place the line and curve of an alignment in an approximate working location, but then the tabular view in Panorama is used to make the values more reasonable—in other words, to change a radius of 292.56 to 300.00.

Component-Level Editing

Once an alignment gets a bit more complicated, the tabular view in Panorama can be hard to navigate, and deciphering which element is which can be difficult. In this case, reviewing individual elements by picking them on screen can be easier.

1. Open the `Editing Alignments.dwg` file.

2. Zoom to Rose Drive, and select it to activate the grips.

3. Right-click and select Edit Alignment Geometry from the context menu. The Alignment Layout Tools toolbar appears.

4. Select the Sub-Entity Editor tool, shown on Figure 7.19, to open the Alignment Layout Parameters dialog.

5. Select the Pick Sub-Entity tool (just to the left of the Sub-Entity Editor tool) on the Alignment Layout Tools toolbar.

6. Pick the first curve on the southwest corner of the site to display its properties in the Alignment Layout Parameters dialog (see Figure 7.20). The properties are mostly grayed out, which indicates that the values for this curve are being derived from other parameters. This curve was drawn so that it would be tangent to a line and would pass through a point (Pass Through Point3), which controls every other aspect of the curve.

FIGURE 7.19
The Sub-Entity
Editor tool

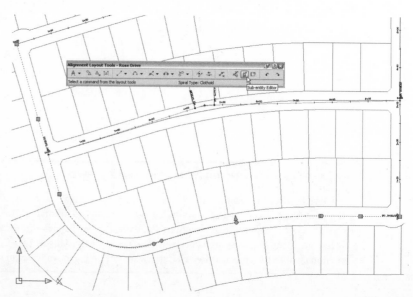

7. Zoom in and pick the second curve in the reverse curve. Notice that the Radius field is now black (see Figure 7.21) and is available for editing.

8. Change the value in the Radius field to 2000 and watch the screen update. This value is too far from the original design intent to be a valid alternative.

FIGURE 7.20

The Alignment Layout Parameters toolbar for the first curve on Rose Drive

Alignment Layout Parameters	
Parameter	**Value**
⊟ **Geometry**	
Number	2
Curve Group Index	
Curve Group Sub-E...	
Type	Curve
Constraint1	Float
Constraint2	Passthrough hol...
Length	326.874'
Radius	202.481'
Delta angle	92.4955 (d)
Start Station	4+20.00'
End Station	7+46.87'
Start Direction	S16° 56' 21"E
End Direction	N70° 33' 56"E
Start Point	(2448860.3721',...
End Point	(2449121.4388',...
Center Point	(2449054.0681',...
Pass Through Point1	
Pass Through Point2	
Pass Through Point3	(2449142.5662',...
Direction at Throug...	
Direction at Throug...	
Chord length	292.513'
Chord Direction	S63° 11' 12"E
Mid-Ordinate	62.457
External Tangent	211.493'
External Secant	90.315'
PI Included Angle	87.5048 (d)
Greater than 180	
PI Station	6+31.50'

FIGURE 7.21

The Alignment Layout Parameters toolbar for the second curve on Rose Drive

Alignment Layout Parameters	
Parameter	**Value**
⊟ **Geometry**	
Number	3
Curve Group Index	
Curve Group Sub-E...	
Type	Curve
Constraint1	Free
Constraint2	Radius
Length	468.087'
Radius	**1380.000'**
Delta angle	19.4344 (d)
Start Station	7+46.87'
End Station	12+14.96'
Start Direction	N70° 33' 56"E
End Direction	N90° 00' 00"E
Start Point	(2449121.4388',...
End Point	(2449580.6018',...
Center Point	(2449580.6018',...
Pass Through Point1	
Pass Through Point2	
Pass Through Point3	
Direction at Throug...	
Direction at Throug...	
Chord length	465.846'
Chord Direction	N80° 16' 58"E
Mid-Ordinate	19.799
External Tangent	236.314'
External Secant	20.087'
PI Included Angle	160.5656 (d)
Greater than 180	false
PI Station	9+83.19'

9. Change the value in the Radius field to 1400 and again watch the update. This value is closer to the design and is acceptable.

10. Close the Alignment Layout Parameters dialog and the Alignments Layout Tools toolbar.

By using the Alignment Layout Parameters dialog, we can concisely review all of the individual parameters of a component. In each of the editing methods discussed so far, we've just been modifying the elements that were already in place. Now let's look at changing the makeup of the alignment itself, not just the values driving it.

Changing Alignment Components

One of the most common changes is adding a curve where there was none before or changing the makeup of the curves and tangents already in place in an alignment. Other design changes can include swapping out curves for tangents or adding in a second curve to make a transition area smoother.

SOMETIMES THE PLANNER IS RIGHT

In this example, we'll go back to the design the planner gave us for the southwest corner of the site (Rose Drive) and place a tangent between the curves. It turns out that our perfect reverse curve isn't allowed by the current ordinances for subdivision design!

1. Open the `Editing Alignments.dwg` file.

2. Zoom to and select Rose Drive to activate the grips.

3. Right-click and select Edit Alignment Geometry. The Alignment Layout Tools toolbar appears.

4. Select the Delete Sub-Entity tool.

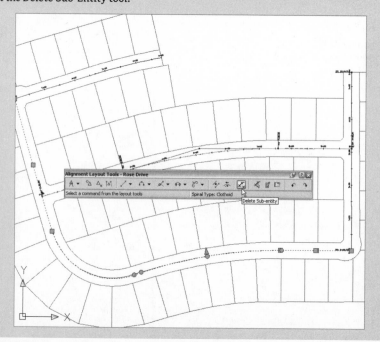

5. Pick the two curves in Rose Drive to remove them. Note that the last tangent is still part of the alignment; it just isn't connected.

6. Select the Draw Fixed Line - Two Points tool and snap to the endpoints of the short tangent in the red polyline. Be sure to pick from left to right to get the direction correct.

7. Click on the down arrow next to Add Fixed Curve - Three Points, and select the Free Curve Fillet (Between Two Entities, Through Point) option.

8. Pick the line on the western edge, then pick the short line just created. The blue arc shown indicates the placement of the proposed fillet.

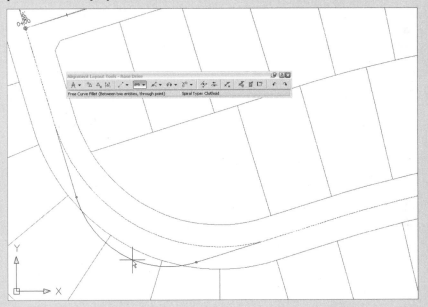

9. Use a Nearest snap and pick a point along the arc.

10. Repeat this process to complete the other curve and connect the full alignment.

11. When finished, close the Alignment Layout Tools toolbar.

We've created and modified the horizontal alignments, adjusted them onscreen to look like what our planner delivered, and tweaked the design using a number of different methods. Now let's look beyond the lines and arcs and get into the design properties of the alignment.

Alignments As Objects

Beyond the simple nature of lines and arcs, alignments represent other things such as highways, streams, sidewalks, or even flight patterns. All of these things have properties that help define them, and many of these properties can also be a part of our alignments. In addition to obvious properties like names or descriptions, functionality such as superelevation, station equations, reference points, and station control can be included. In this section, we'll look at other properties that can be associated with an alignment and how to edit them.

Renaming Objects

The default naming convention for alignments is flexible (and configurable) but not very descriptive. In previous sections, we ignored the descriptions and left the default names in place, but now let's modify them. In addition, we'll look at the easy way to change the object style and how to add a description.

Most of the basic properties of an alignment can be modified right in Prospector. In this exercise, we'll change the name in a couple of ways:

1. Open the `Alignment Properties.dwg` file, and make sure Prospector is open.

2. Expand the Alignments collection, and note that Alignment (1) through Alignment (4) are listed as members.

DIDN'T WE ALREADY DO THIS?

Yes, actually. The alignments were named in earlier exercises to make referencing them in the text simpler and easier to understand. Hope you'll forgive the rewind!

---

7. Click on the Alignments branch, and the individual alignments appear in a preview area (see Figure 7.22).

8. Click in the Name field for Alignment - (1) and pause briefly before clicking again. The text should highlight for editing

9. Change the name to **Parker Place**, and press ↵. The field will update, and Prospector will as well.

10. Click in the Description field and enter a description. Press ↵.

11. Click on the Style field, and the Select Label Style dialog appears. Select Layout from the dropdown menu and click OK to dismiss. The screen will update.

FIGURE 7.22
The Alignments collection listed in the preview area of Prospector

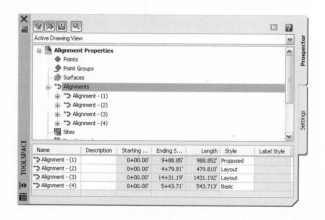

That's one method. The next is to use the AutoCAD Object Properties Manager (OPM) palette:

1. Open the OPM palette by using the Ctrl+1 shortcut command or some other method.

2. Select Alignment - (3) in the drawing. The OPM should look like Figure 7.23.

3. Click in the Name field and change the name to **Rose Drive**.

4. Click in the Description field and enter a description. Click OK.

5. Notice that the Style field for the alignment cannot be changed, which somewhat limits this method.

6. Press Esc on your keyboard to deselect all objects, and close the OPM dialog if you'd like.

FIGURE 7.23
Alignment (3) in the
AutoCAD Object Prop-
erties Manager palette

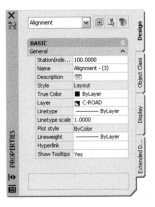

The final method involves getting into the Alignment Properties dialog, our access point to information beyond the basics:

1. In the main Prospector window, right-click on Alignment - (2) and select Properties. The Alignment Properties dialog for Alignment - (2) opens.

2. Change to the Information tab if it is not selected.

3. Change the name to **Carson's Way** and enter a description in the Description field as well.

4. Set Object Style to Existing.

5. Click Apply. Notice the dialog header updates immediately, as does the display style in the drawing.

6. Click OK to exit the dialog.

Now that we have updated our alignments, let's make them all the same style for ease of viewing. The best way to do this is in the Prospector preview window.

1. Pick the Alignments branch, and highlight one of the alignments in the preview area.

2. Press Ctrl+A to select them all, or pick the top and then Shift-click the bottom item. The idea is to pick *all* of the alignments.

3. Right-click on the Style column header and select Edit (see Figure 7.24).

FIGURE 7.24
Editing alignment
styles en masse via
Prospector

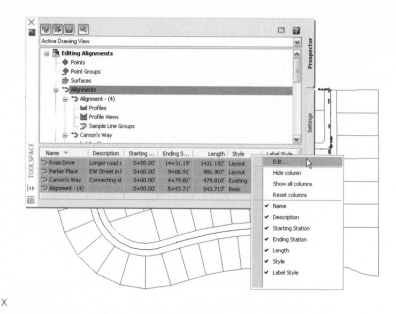

4. Select Layout from the dropdown list in the Select Label Style dialog that appears and click OK. Notice that all alignments have picked up this style.

5. While you're here, change the name of Alignment - (4) to **Alexander Ave.**

DON'T FORGET THIS TECHNIQUE

This technique works on every object that displays in the List Style preview. This means parcels, pipes, corridors, assemblies, and so on. It can be painfully tedious to change a large number of objects from one style to another using any other method.

The alignments now all look the same, and all but one have a name and description. Let's look beyond these basics at the other properties we can modify and update.

The Right Station

At the end of the process, every alignment has stationing applied to help locate design information. This stationing often starts at zero, but could also tie to an existing object and may start at some arbitrary value. Stationing can also be fixed in both directions, requiring station equations that help translate between two disparate points that are the basis for the stationing in the drawing.

One common problem is an alignment that was drawn in the wrong direction. Thankfully, Civil 3D has a quick edit command to fix that.

1. From the main menu, select Alignments ➢ Reverse Alignment Direction.

2. Pick Alexander Ave on the drawing window.

3. A warning message will appear, reminding you of the consequences of such a change. Click OK to dismiss it.

4. The stationing will reverse, with 0+00 now at the north end of the street.

This technique allows us to reverse an alignment almost instantly. The warning that appeared is critical, though! When an alignment is reversed, the information that was derived from its original direction may not translate correctly, if at all. One prime example of this is design profiles. They will not reverse themselves when the alignment is reversed, and this can lead to serious design issues if you are not paying attention.

Beyond simply reversing, it's quite common for alignments to not start with zero. For example, the Alexander Ave alignment is a continuation of an existing street, and it makes sense to set the starting station for this alignment with the end station from the existing street. In this exercise, we'll set the beginning station:

1. Select the Alexander Ave alignment.

2. Right-click and select Alignment Properties.

3. Switch to the Station Control tab. This tab controls the base stationing and allows for the creation of station equations.

4. Enter **456.79** in the Station field in the Reference Point area (see Figure 7.25) and click Apply.

5. Dismiss the warning message that appears, and click Apply again. The Station Information area will update. This area cannot be edited, but provides a convenient way to review the alignment's length and station values.

In addition to simply changing the value for the start of the alignment, you could also use the Pick Reference Point button, circled in Figure 7.25, to select another point as the stationing reference point.

FIGURE 7.25
Setting a new starting station on the Alexander Ave alignment

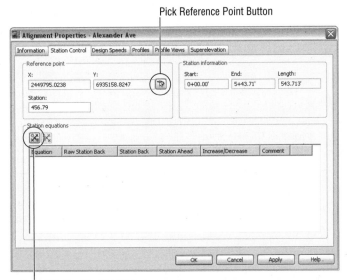

Pick Reference Point Button

Add Station Equation Button

Station equations can occur multiple times along an alignment. They typically come into play when plans must match existing conditions or when the stationing has to match other plans, but the lengths in the new alignment would make that impossible without some translation. In this exercise, we'll add a station equation about halfway down Alexander Ave just for illustrative purposes:

1. On the Station Control tab of the Alignment Properties dialog, click the Add Station Equation button (see the circled button in Figure 7.25).

2. Use an End snap to pick the intersection of the two alignments about halfway down Alexander Ave.

3. Change the Station Ahead value to **1000**. (Again, we're going for illustration, not reality!)

4. Click Apply, and notice the change in the Station Information area (see Figure 7.26).

5. Click OK to close the dialog, and review the stationing that has been applied to the alignment.

Stationing is constantly changing as alignments are modified during the initial stages of a development or as late design changes are pushed back into the plans. With the flexibility shown here, you can reduce the time you spend dealing with these minor changes that seem to ripple across an entire plan set.

FIGURE 7.26
Alexander Ave station equation in place

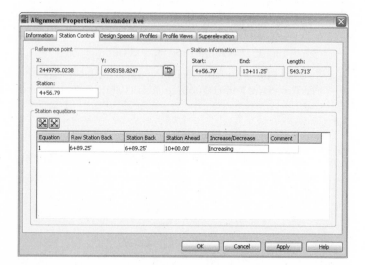

Assigning Design Speeds

One driving part of transportation design is the design speed. Civil 3D considers the design speed a property of the alignment, which can be used in labels or calculations as needed. In this simple exercise, we'll add a series of design speeds to Rose Drive. Later in the chapter, we'll label these sections of the road.

1. Bring up the Alignment Properties dialog for Rose Drive using any of the methods discussed.

2. Switch to the Design Speeds tab.

3. Click the Add Design Speed button on the top row.

4. Click in the Design Speed field for Station Number 1 and enter **30**. This speed is typical for a subdivision street.

5. Click the Add Design Speed button again.

6. Click in the Station field for Number 2. A small Pick On Screen button will appear to the right of the Station value, as shown in Figure 7.27.

7. Click the Pick On Screen button, then use a snap to pick the PC on the southwest portion of the site, near station 4+20.

8. Enter a value of **20** in the Design Speed field for Station Number 2.

9. Click the Pick On Screen button again to add one more design speed portion, and snap to the end of the short tangent.

10. Enter a value of **30** for this design speed. When complete, the tab should look like Figure 7.28.

FIGURE 7.27
Setting the design speed for a Station field

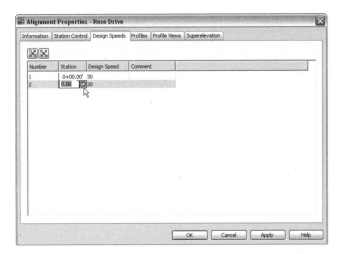

FIGURE 7.28
The design speeds assigned to Rose Drive

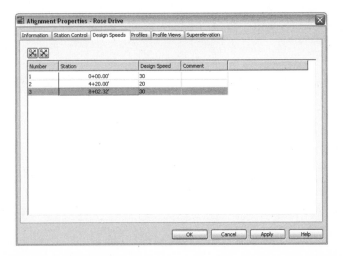

In a subdivision, these values could be simply inserted for labeling purposes. In a highway design, they can be used to drive the superelevation calculations that are critical to a working design. We'll look at that next.

Banking Turn Two

Once you move beyond the basic subdivision collector street, you move into the realm of thoroughfare and highway design. In the United States, this design is governed by American Association of State Highway and Transportation Officials (AASHTO) manuals that dictate equations for inserting superelevation and transition zones. In this brief exercise, we'll look at creating superelevation tables for an alignment.

1. Open the `Alignments With Superelevation.dwg` file. This drawing contains an alignment, with a design speed of 65 mph, that is more typical of highway design.

2. Pull up the Route 66 Alignment Properties dialog and switch to the Superelevation tab (see Figure 7.29).

3. Click the Set Superelevation Properties button (see Figure 7.29) to display the full range of options. The 2001 AASHTO manual is selected by default, but other criteria can be selected from this dialog.

4. Change the Superelevation Rate Table to AASHTO 2001 eMax 8% and click OK. On the basis of the curves in the alignment and the AASHTO 2001 specification, superelevation ranges, including runout areas, are created.

5. Click OK to close the dialog.

This information could now be used by corridor assemblies to determine cross slope for lanes, shoulders, or other areas of interest. Additionally, in simpler design cases, transitions can be accomplished by manually typing in slope amounts at critical stations.

All of the information applied to an alignment is great, but without putting that information to paper, it's pretty useless. Let's turn our focus to labeling all this information and making those labels efficiently.

FIGURE 7.29
Assigning superelevation to the Route 66 alignment

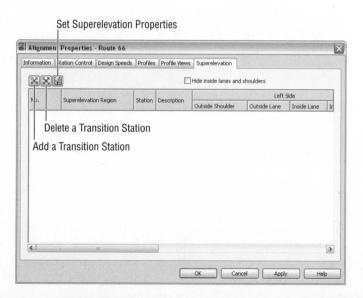

WE DON'T USE SUPERELEVATION, DO WE?

Don't get trapped into thinking that just because you don't do highway design, you can't use some of the same tools. One company even uses superelevation to help design waterslides. The fun in learning Civil 3D is in finding new ways to use the tools given to solve one problem to solve another problem entirely. You'll know you've mastered the software when you find yourself abusing the tools in this manner.

Styling Alignments

There are three major areas to deal with in setting up alignment styles:

◆ The alignment itself

◆ Alignment labels, including

   ◆ Label sets

   ◆ Station

   ◆ Station offsets

   ◆ Lines

   ◆ Curves

   ◆ Spirals

   ◆ Tangent intersections

◆ Table styles with options for

   ◆ Line

   ◆ Curve

   ◆ Spiral

   ◆ Segment

This breakdown follows exactly the same format as the Settings tab of Toolspace, so let's look at them in the same way. Each of these label styles can be manipulated in similar ways, so we won't examine every single one, but we'll cover most.

The Alignment Itself

The alignment style controls how the actual alignment appears. This is outside the scope of the labeling or layering that might be at play. As you've seen in the previous portions of this chapter, an alignment style can dramatically alter the appearance of the simplest alignments, such as when we used the Layout style to show lines in red and arcs in blue.

Civil 3D ships with a number of alignment styles, but they're pretty generic. In this exercise, let's copy the existing style and modify it to create a plot style that we might use in our construction documents:

1. Open the `Alignment Styles.dwg` file. All of the alignments currently have the Layout style applied.

2. On the Settings tab, expand the Alignment ➢ Alignment Styles branch.

3. Right-click on Existing and select Copy.

4. On the Information tab, change the name in the Name field to **Plot**, and enter a description. We will work our way through the tabs to build our style.

5. Switch to the Markers tab, where we have the option to display marker objects at all the major critical points. We'll add the Begin Of Alignment and the End Of Alignment points to the Alignment Geometry style.

6. Click on the small Style icon on the right-hand side of the Marker Style field for the Begin Of Alignment (see Figure 7.30), and select Alignment Geometry from the dropdown list in the Pick Marker Style dialog.

7. Click OK and close the dialog,

8. Repeat these three steps for the End Of Alignment,

9. Click OK to close the Alignment Style dialog.

Your new style should have appeared in the list of alignment styles. Go ahead and change all the alignments to use this style using the techniques we've covered earlier. Changing the alignment style is fairly straightforward. As you think about your office, you might build alignment styles for various types of roads, pipe networks, sidewalks or trails—any number of things!

FIGURE 7.30
Selecting the marker style

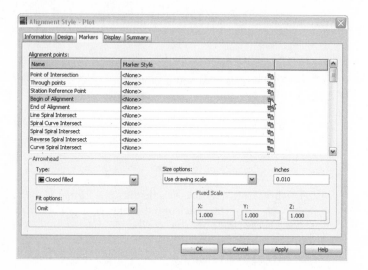

Labeling Alignments

Labeling in Civil 3D is one of the strengths of the program, but is also an easy place to get lost. There are myriad options for every type of labeling situation under the sun, and keeping them straight can be difficult. In this section, we'll begin by building label styles for stationing along an alignment, culminating in a label set. Then we'll create styles for station and offset labels, using reference text to describe alignment intersections. Finally, we'll add a street name label that makes it easier to keep track of things.

THE POWER OF LABEL SETS

When you think about it, any number of things can be labeled on an alignment, before getting into any of the adjoining objects. These include major and minor stations, geometry points, design speeds, and profile information. And each of these can have its own style to be applied. Keeping track of all of these individual labeling styles and options would be burdensome and uniformity would be difficult, so Civil 3D features the concept of *label sets*.

A label set allows the user to build up the labeling options for an alignment, picking styles for the labels of interest, or even multiple labels on a point of interest, and then save them as a set. These sets are available during the creation and labeling process, making the application of individual labels less tedious. Out of the box there are a number of sets, primarily designed for combinations of major and minor station styles along with geometry information. We'll create individual label styles over the next couple of exercises, then pull them all together with a label set. To end this section, we'll apply our new label set to the alignments.

Major Station

Major Station labels typically include a tick mark and a station callout. In this exercise, we'll build a style to show only the station increment and run it parallel to the alignment:

1. Open the Alignment Styles.dwg file.

2. Switch to the Settings tab and expand the Alignment ➤ Label Styles ➤ Station ➤ Major Station branch.

3. Right-click on the Parallel With Tick style and select Copy. The Label Style Composer dialog appears.

4. On the Information tab, change the Name field to **Station Index Only**.

5. Switch to the Layout tab.

6. Click in the Contents Value field, under the Text property, and then click the ellipsis button to open the Text Component Editor dialog.

7. Click in the preview area of the Text Component Editor dialog, and delete the text already there.

8. Click in the Output Value field, and click the down arrow to open the dropdown list.

9. Select the Left Of Station Character option, as shown in Figure 7.31. You may have to scroll down.

10. Click the blue insert arrow circled in Figure 7.31.

11. Click OK to close the Text Component Editor dialog.

12. Click OK to close the Label Style Composer dialog.

The label style will now show in your label styles, but it's not being applied to any alignments yet.

FIGURE 7.31
Modifying the Station
Value Output value in
the Text Component
Editor dialog

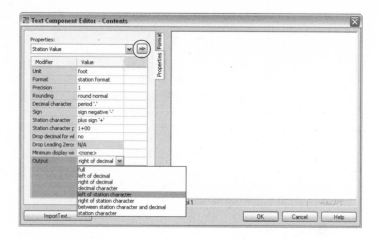

Geometry Points

Geometry points reflect the PC, PT, and other points along the alignment that define the geometric properties. The existing label style doesn't reflect a plan-readable format that we like, so we'll copy it and make this minor change in this exercise:

1. Expand the Alignment ➤ Label Styles ➤ Geometry Point branch.

2. Right-click on the Perpendicular With Tick And Line and select Copy to open the Label Style Composer dialog.

3. On the Information tab, change the name to **Perpendicular With Line**, and change the description, removing the circle portion.

4. Switch to the General tab.

5. Change the Readability Bias setting to **95**. This will force the labels to flip at a much earlier point.

6. Switch to the Layout tab.

7. Set the Component Name field to the Tick option.

8. Click the Delete Component button (the red X button).

9. Click OK to close the Label Style Composer dialog.

This new style simply flips the plan-readable labels a bit sooner and removes the circle tick mark.

Label Set

In contrast to the prebuilt styles, we'll build our label set on the basis of its designed use. As a result, it will be easier to pick it from a list than if it was being picked on the basis of a combination of its components. This exercise will build a Paving label set from scratch, but you could copy a similar label set and simply modify for future sets.

1. Expand the Alignment ➤ Label Styles ➤ Label Sets branch.

2. Right-click on Label Sets and select New to open the Alignment Label Set dialog.

3. On the Information tab, change the name to **Paving**.

4. Switch to the Labels tab.

5. Set the Type field to the Major Stations option, the Major Station Label Style field to the Station Index Only style that we just created, and click the Add button.

6. Set the Type field to the Minor Stations option, the Minor Station Label Style field to the Tick option, and click the Add button.

7. Set the Type field to Geometry Points, the Geometry Point Label Style field to Perpendicular With Line, and click the Add button.

8. Review the settings to make sure they match Figure 7.32; then click OK to dismiss the Alignment Label Set dialog.

FIGURE 7.32
The completed Paving alignment label set

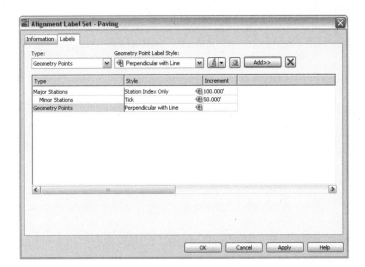

We've built a new label set that we can apply to Paving alignment labels. In previous versions of Civil 3D, the labels were a part of the alignment, and it made it difficult to sometimes get labels just the way we wanted. In 2008, the label set is a different object entirely. Enter the LIST command, and pick a label. You'll now see a reference to a label group instead of an alignment object. What does this mean to you as an end user? A couple of things: first you can use the AutoCAD properties to set label styles for individual groups; and second, the Labeling tab in the Alignment Properties dialog is no more. In this exercise, we'll apply our label set to all of our alignments, then show how an individual label can be changed from the set.

1. Select the Rose Drive alignment on screen.

2. Right-click and select Edit Alignment Labels to display the Alignment Labels dialog in Figure 7.33.

3. Click the Import Label Set button near the bottom of this dialog.

4. In the Select Style Set dropdown list, select the Paving Label Set and click OK.

FIGURE 7.33
The Alignment Labels
dialog for Rose Drive

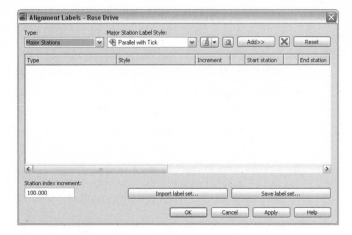

5. The Style field for the alignment labels will populate with the option we selected.

6. Click OK to dismiss the dialog.

7. Repeat this process across the rest of the alignments.

8. Once complete, zoom in on any of the major station labels.

9. Holding down the Ctrl key, select the label. Notice that a single label is selected, not the label set group.

10. Right-click and select Label Properties.

11. The Label Properties dialog appears, allowing you to pick another label style from the dropdown.

12. Change the Label Style value to Parallel With Tick, and change the Flip Label value to True.

13. Press Esc to deselect the label item and exit this dialog.

By using alignment label sets, you'll find it easy to standardize the appearance of labeling and stationing across alignments. Building label sets can take some time, but it's one of the easy, effective ways to enforce standards.

CTRL-CLICK? WHAT IS THAT ABOUT?

In Civil 3D 2007 as well as in previous versions, clicking on an individual label picked the label and the alignment. Because labels are part of a label set object in 2008, Ctrl-click is the *only* way to access the Flip Label and Reverse Label functions! This is a major change from 2007—don't let it befuddle you.

STATION OFFSET LABELING

Beyond labeling the basic stationing and geometry points of an alignment, we often want to label points of interest in reference to the alignment. Station offset labeling is designed to do just that. In addition to labeling the properties of the alignment, you can include references to other object types in your Station Offset labels. The objects available for referencing are:

- Alignments
- Cogo points
- Parcels
- Profiles
- Surfaces

In this exercise, we'll use an alignment reference to create a label suitable for labeling the intersection of two alignments. It will pick up the stationing information from both.

1. Open the `Alignment Styles.dwg` file.

2. On the Settings tab, expand Alignment ➤ Label Styles ➤ Station Offset.

3. Right-click on Station Offset and select Copy to open the Label Style Composer dialog.

4. On the Information tab, change the name of our new style to **Alignment Intersection**.

5. Change to the Layout tab. In the Component Name field, delete the Marker component.

6. In the Component Name field, select the Station Offset component.

7. Change the Name field to **Main Alignment**.

8. In the Contents Value field, click the ellipsis button to bring up the Text Component Editor.

9. Select the text in the preview area and delete it all.

10. Type **Sta.** in the preview area; be sure to leave a space after the period.

11. In the Properties dropdown field, select Station Value.

12. Click the blue insert arrow.

13. In the Properties dropdown field, select Alignment Name.

14. Click the blue insert arrow to add this bit of code to the preview.

15. Click your mouse in the preview area. Move to the end of the line and type an equal sign (=).

16. Click OK to return to the Label Style Composer dialog shown in Figure 7.34.

17. Under the Border Property, set the Visibility Value field to False

18. Click the down arrow next to the Add Component tool and select Reference Text from the dropdown list (see Figure 7.35).

19. In the Select Type dialog that appears, select Alignment and click OK.

20. Change the Name Value field to **Intersecting Alignment**.

21. In the Anchor Component Value field, select Main Alignment.

FIGURE 7.34
Alignment text
changed to the
new values

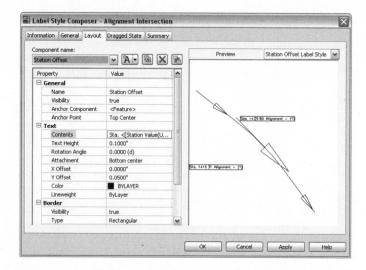

FIGURE 7.35
Adding a Reference
Text component to
a label

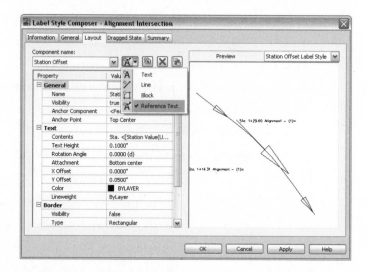

22. In the Anchor Point Value field, select Bottom Left.

23. In the Attachment Value field, select Top Left.

24. Click in the Contents Value field and click the ellipsis button to open the Text Component Editor.

25. Delete the generic "Label Text" that appears.

26. Type **Sta.** in the preview area; be sure to leave a space after the period.

27. In the Properties dropdown list, select Station Value.

28. Click the blue insert arrow.

29. In the Properties dropdown list, select Alignment Name.

30. Click the blue insert arrow to add this bit of code to the preview.

31. Click OK to exit the Text Component Editor and click OK again to exit the Label Style Composer dialog.

Wow, that seemed like a lot of work for one label! But if you never have to rebuild that label again, then it's worth it, right? With the Station Offset label type we have two options:

◆ Station Offset is used for labeling points that are important because of where they are along an alignment, such as a buffer area or setback. In these cases, the station along the alignment is the driving force in where the label occurs.

◆ Station Offset-Fixed Point type is used for labeling points that are fixed in space, like a fire hydrant or curb return. In the case of the Fixed Point option, the point being labeled isn't dependent on the alignment station for relevance but for location.

With those out of the way, let's test our new label and pick up all the intersections of the streets. We'll use Rose Drive as our main alignment and work our way along it.

1. From the main menu, select Alignment ≻ Add Alignment Labels ≻ Add Alignment Labels. The Add Labels dialog appears.

2. In the Label Type dropdown list, select Station Offset.

3. In the Station Offset Label Style dropdown list, select Alignment Intersection.

4. Leave the Marker Style field alone, but remember that you could use any of these styles to mark the selected point.

5. Click the Add button.

6. Pick the Rose Drive alignment.

7. Snap to the endpoint at the far northwest end.

8. Enter 0 for the offset amount and press ↵.

9. The command line will prompt you to Select Alignment For Label Style Component Intersecting Alignment. Pick the Carson's Way alignment.

10. Click the Add button again and repeat the process at the other two alignment intersections.

There are two things to note in this process: first, that you click Add between adding labels because Civil 3D will otherwise assume you want to use the same reference object for every instance of the label; second, the labels are sitting right on the point of interest. Drag them to a convenient location and you're set to go. When you do this, your label should look something like the one shown in Figure 7.36.

Making use of Station Offset labels and their reference object ability, you can label most site plans very quickly with information that dynamically updates.

FIGURE 7.36
The Alignment Inter-
section label style
in use

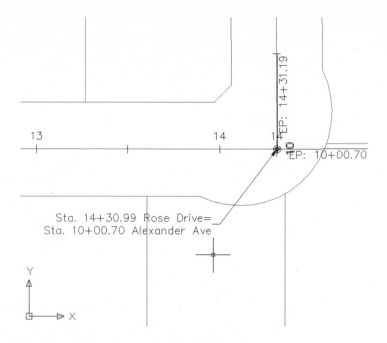

SEGMENT LABELING

Every land development professional has a story about the developer who named an entire subdivision after their kids/grandkids/dogs/golf buddies/favorite bars, etc. As these plans work their
way through reviewing agencies, there are inevitably changes, and the tedium of changing a street
name on 45 pages of construction documents cannot be described.

Thankfully, as you've already seen in the Station Offset label, we can access the properties of the
alignment to generate a label. In this exercise, we'll use that same set of properties to create street
name labels that are applied and always up to date.

1. Open the `Alignment Styles.dwg` file.

2. In the Settings tab, expand the Alignment ➤ Label Styles ➤ Line branch.

3. Right-click on Line and select New. The Label Style Composer dialog appears.

4. On the Information tab, change the Name field to **Street Names** and switch to the
   General tab.

5. Click in the Layer Value field and click the ellipsis button. The Layer Selection dialog
   appears.

6. Select the Layer C-ROAD-LABL and click OK to close the Layer Selection dialog.

7. Change the Readability Bias Value field to 95(d). Switch to the Layout tab.

8. In the Component Name dropdown list, delete the Direction Arrow and Distance components by clicking the red X button.

9. In the Component Name dropdown list, select the Bearing component, and change its name in the Value field to **Street Name**.

10. Click on the Contents Value field and click the ellipsis button. The Text Component Editor appears.

11. Delete the entire preview contents.

12. 12In the Properties dropdown list, select Alignment Name.

13. Set the Capitalization Value field to Upper Case. By forcing the capitalization here, we can standardize the way street names appear without having to double-check every bit of user input.

14. Click the blue insert arrow, then click OK to exit the Text Component Editor.

15. Click OK again to exit the Label Style Composer dialog.

16. From the main menu, select Alignments ➢ Add Alignment Labels ➢ Add Alignment Labels to display the Add Labels dialog shown in Figure 7.37.

17. In the Label Type field, select Single Segment from the dropdown list. Then in the Line Label Style field, select our Street Names style. Note that curves and spirals have their own set of styles. If you click on a curve during the labeling process, you won't get a street name— you'll get something else.

18. Click the Add button.

19. Pick various line segments around the drawing. Each street will be labeled with the appropriate name.

20. Click the Close button to close the Add Labels dialog.

Days of work averted! The object properties of an alignment can be invaluable in documenting your design. Creation of a collection of styles for all the various components and types will take some time, but will pay back in hours of work taken out of every job.

FIGURE 7.37
The Add Labels dialog

Alignment Tables

There simply isn't always room to label alignment objects directly on top of them. Sometimes it doesn't make sense to, or sometimes a reviewing agency wants to see a table showing the radius of every curve in the design. Documentation requirements never cease to amaze us in their disparity and seemingly random requirements. Beyond the labels that can be applied directly to the alignment objects, we can also create tables to meet these requirements and get plans out the door.

There are four types of tables:

◆ Lines

◆ Curves

◆ Spirals

◆ Segments

Each of these is self-explanatory except perhaps the Segments table. That table will generate a mix of all the lines, curves, and spirals that make up an alignment, essentially creating the alignment in a tabular format. In this section, we'll generate a new line table and simply draw the segment table that ships with the product.

All of the tables work in similar fashion. From the main menu, select Alignments ➢ Add Tables and then pick a table type that is relevant to your work. The Table Creation dialog appears (see Figure 7.38).

You can select a table style from the dropdown list or create a new one. Select a table layer by pressing the blue arrow. The Selection area determines how the table will be populated. All of the various label style names for the selected type of component will be presented, along with a checkbox to the right. Applying one of these styles enables the Selection Rule, which has the following two options:

Add Existing Any label using this style that currently exists in the drawing will be converted to a tag format, substituting a key number such as L1 or C27, and added to the table. Any labels using this style created in the future will *not* be added to the table.

FIGURE 7.38
The Table
Creation dialog

Add Existing And New   Any label using this style that currently exists in the drawing will be converted to a tag format and added to the table. Also, any labels using this style created in the future will be added to the table.

Beneath the Selection area is the Split Table area, which determines how the table is stacked up in Model space once it is populated. These values can be modified after a table is generated, so it's often easier to just leave them alone during the creation process.

Finally, the Behavior area provides two selections for the Reactivity Mode: Static and Dynamic. These selections determine how the table reacts to changes in the driving geometry. We've seen a few cases in surveying where this disconnect was used as a safeguard to the platted data, but in general, the whole point of a 3D model is to have live labels that dynamically react to changes in the object.

Before we draw any tables, we need to apply some labels so that the tables will have some data to populate. In this exercise, we'll throw some labels on all of our alignments very quickly; then we'll move on to drawing some tables in the next sections.

1. From the main menu, select Alignments ➢ Add Alignment Labels ➢ Add Alignment Labels to open the Add Labels dialog.

2. In the Label Type field, select Multiple Segment from the dropdown list. With this, we'll click each alignment one time, and every subcomponent will be labeled with the style selected here.

3. Verify that the Line Label Style field is set to Bearing Over Distance. We won't be left with these labels; we just want them for selecting elements later.

4. Click Add, and select all four of the alignments.

5. Click Close to close the Add Labels dialog.

Now that we've got some labels to play with, let's build some tables.

CREATING A LINE TABLE

Most line tables are pretty simple: a line tag, a bearing, and a distance. Just because we can, we'll also show how Civil 3D can translate units without having to change anything at the drawing level.

1. On the Settings tab, expand the Alignment ➢ Alignment Styles ➢ Table Styles branch.

2. Right-click on Line and select New to open the Table Style dialog.

3. On the Information tab, change the Name field to **Bearing & Distance (ft + m)** and switch to the Data Properties tab shown in Figure 7.39.

4. Click in the Start Point column header, and then click the red X button on the right edge of the screen to delete the column.

5. Repeat this step for the End Point column.

6. Double-click the Length column header to bring up the Text Component Editor.

7. Add a space, then **(ft.)** to the end of the text already in place.

8. Click OK to close the editor.

9. Click the blue + button on the bottom right of the Table Style dialog to add an additional column.

FIGURE 7.39
Before the table edits

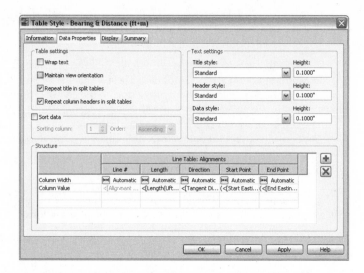

10. Double-click the header to bring up the Text Component Editor.

11. Title it **Length (m)** in the preview area. Click OK to close the editor.

12. Double-click the Column Value field under the new column to bring up the Text Component Editor.

13. Set the Properties dropdown list to Length and change the Units Value field to Meter and the Precision Value field to two decimal places.

14. Click the blue insert arrow and click OK to close the editor.

15. Click and drag the Direction column header to the left until a small table icon appears. This indicates a column rearranging. Place the Direction column as second. Your table should look like Figure 7.40.

FIGURE 7.40
Completed table edits

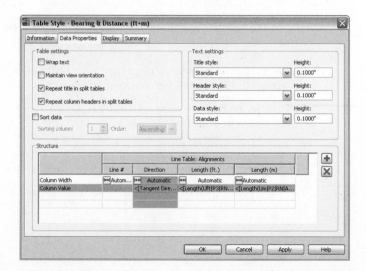

16. Switch to the Display tab and turn off the display of the three fill components by clicking on the lightbulbs.

17. Click OK to close the dialog.

18. From the main menu, select Alignments ➢ Add Tables ➢ Add Line to open the Table Creation dialog.

19. Set the dialog options as shown in Figure 7.41 and click OK.

20. Pick a point on screen and the table will generate.

Pan back to your drawing and you will notice that the line labels have turned into tags on the line segments. Once you've made one table, the rest are very similar. Be patient as you create tables—a lot of values will need to be tweaked to make them look just right. By drawing one on screen, then editing the style, you can quickly achieve the results you're after.

FIGURE 7.41
Creating a line table

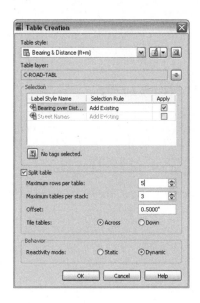

AN ALIGNMENT SEGMENT TABLE

An individual segment table allows a reviewer to see all the components of an alignment. In this exercise, we'll draw the Segment table for Rose Drive.

1. From the main menu, select Alignments ➢ Add Tables ➢ Add Segments.

2. In the Select Alignment field, choose the Rose Drive alignment from the dropdown list and click OK.

3. Pick a point on the screen and the table will be drawn.

Note that there seem to be a number of segments that are exactly the same! Because we made a table previously that changed the existing label styles and then built this table on the basis of the Rose Drive alignment, the lines have duplicate tags. If we erase some of these tags, we can update this table to be correct. We'll also renumber for ease of use.

1. Move along Rose Drive, making sure that each segment has one tag only. Remove any duplicated tags by simply erasing them.

2. From the main menu, select Alignments ➤ Add Tables ➤ Renumber Tags.

3. Enter **L** at the command line to select the Line option and press ↵. The Renumbering dialog appears.

4. Click OK in the Renumbering dialog; we'll renumber them from one.

5. Pick each of the line tags along the alignments.

6. Right-click to exit the command.

7. Both tables have updated to reflect the new numbering scheme and still reflect the properties of each segment.

The Bottom Line

Create an alignment from a polyline. Creating alignments based on polylines is a traditional method of building up engineering models. With Civil 3D's built-in tools for conversion, correction, and alignment reversal, it's easy to use the linework prepared by others to start your design model. These alignments lack the intelligence of crafted alignments however and should be used sparingly.

Master It Open the `Mastering Alignments.dwg` file and create alignments from the linework found there.

Create a reverse curve that never loses tangency. Using the alignment layout tools, we can build intelligence into the objects we design. One of the most common errors introduced to engineering designs is curves and lines that are not tangent, requiring expensive revisions and resubmittals. The free, floating, and fixed components can make smart alignments in a large number of combinations available to solve almost any design problem.

Master It Open the `Mastering Alignments.dwg` file and create an alignment from the linework on the right. Create a reverse curve with both radii equal to 200, and with a pass-through point in the center of the displayed circle.

Replace a component of an alignment with another component type. One of the goals in using a dynamic modeling solution is to find better solutions, not just a solution. In the layout of alignments, this can mean changing components out along the design path, or changing the way they are defined. Civil 3D's ability to modify alignments geometric construction without destroying the object or forcing a new definition allows the designer to experiment without destroying the data already based on an alignment.

Master It Convert the arc indicated in the `Mastering Alignments.dwg` file to a free arc that is a function of the two adjoining segments. The curve radius is 150′.

Create a new label set. Label sets allow us to determine the appearance of an alignment's labels and quickly standardize that appearance across all the objects of the same nature. By creating sets that reflect their intended use, we can make it easy for a designer to quickly label alignments according to specifications with little understanding of the requirement itself.

Master It Within the `Mastering Alignments.dwg` file, create a new label set containing only major station labels, and apply it to all of the alignments in that drawing.

Override individual labels with other styles. In spite of our desire to have uniform labeling styles and appearances between alignments within a single drawing, project, or firm, there are always exceptions. Using the AutoCAD Ctrl-click element selection methods, we can access commands that modify individual labels and let us modify our labels or even change their style completely.

Master It Create a copy of the Perpendicular With Tick Major Station style called Major With Marker. Change the Tick Block Name to Marker Pnt. Replace some of your major station labels with this new style, but not all.

Chapter 8

Cut to the Chase: Profiles

Profile information is the backbone of vertical design. Civil 3D takes advantage of sampled data, design data, and external input files to create profiles for a number of uses. Even the most basic designs require profiles, and in this chapter we'll look at creation tools, editing profiles, and display styles, and show you ways to get your labels just so. Profile views are a different subject and will be covered in more detail in the next chapter.

In this chapter, you will learn to:

◆ Sample a surface profile with offset samples

◆ Lay out a design profile on the basis of a table of data

◆ Add and modify individual components in a design profile

◆ Apply a standard label set

Elevate Me

The whole point of a three-dimensional model is to include that elevation element that's been missing for years. But to get there, designers and engineers still depend on a very flat 2D representation of the vertical dimension as shown in a profile view (see Figure 8.1).

A profile is nothing more than a series of data pairs in a station, elevation format. There are basic curve and tangent components, but these are purely the mathematical basis for the paired data sets. In Civil 3D, profile information can be generated in one of the following three basic ways:

◆ Sampling from a surface involves taking vertical information from a surface object every time the sampled alignment crosses a TIN line of the surface.

◆ Creating by a layout allows the user to input design information, setting critical station and elevation points, calculating curves to connect linear segments, and typically working within requirements laid out by a reviewing agency.

◆ Creating from a file allows the user to point to a specially formatted text file to pull in the station and elevation pairs. This can be helpful in dealing with other analysis packages or spreadsheet tabular data.

In this section, we'll look at all three methods of creating profiles.

FIGURE 8.1

A typical profile view of the surface elevation along an alignment

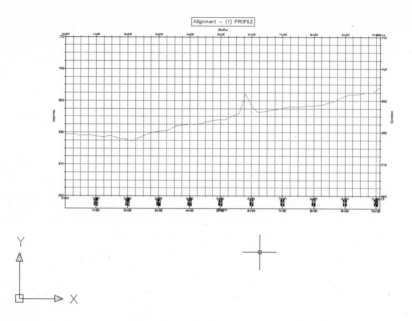

Surface Sampling

Working with surface information is the most elemental method of getting a profile created. This information can represent a simple existing or proposed surface, a river flood elevation, or any number of other surface derived data sets. Within Civil 3D, surfaces can also be sampled at offsets, as we'll see in this series of exercises:

1. Open the Profile Sampling.dwg file to arrive at Figure 8.2.

2. From the main menu, choose Profiles ➢ Create Profile From Surface to display the Create Profile From Surface dialog, shown in Figure 8.3.

   This dialog has a number of important features, so let's discuss how it breaks down:

   ◆ The upper-left quadrant is dedicated to information about the alignment. You can select the alignment from a dropdown list or by clicking the Pick On Screen button. The Station Range area is automatically set to run from the beginning to the end of the alignment, but can be manually controlled by entering the station ranges in the To Sample text boxes.

   ◆ The upper-right quadrant controls the selection of the surface and the offsets. You can select a surface from the list or by clicking the Pick On Screen button. Beneath the Select Surfaces list area, you'll see an option for Sample Offsets. The offsets are not applied in both the left and right direction uniformly. A negative value must be entered to sample to the left of the alignment, and a positive value must be entered to sample to the right. In all cases, the actual profile is not generated until you click the Add button.

   ◆ The Profile List box on the bottom displays all profiles associated with the alignment currently selected in the Alignment list box. This area is generally static (it will not change), but you can modify the Update Mode, Layer, and Style columns by clicking on the appropriate cells in this table. The columns can be stretched and rearranged to customize the view.

FIGURE 8.2
The drawing used
for the exercise on
profile sampling

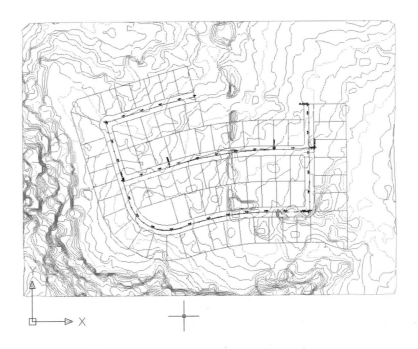

FIGURE 8.3
The Create Profile
From Surface dialog

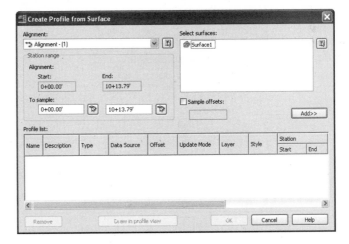

3. In the Alignment list box, select the Alignment - (1) option if it is not already selected.

4. In the Select Surfaces list area, select Surface1.

5. Click the Add button, and the Profile List area is populated with profile information for Surface1 on Alignment - (1).

6. Check the Sample Offsets box to make the entry box active, and enter **-25,25**.

7. Click the Add button again to achieve Figure 8.4.

FIGURE 8.4
The Create Profile From Surface dialog showing the profiles sampled on Surface1

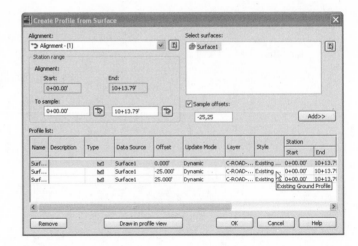

8. In the Profile List area, select the cell in the Style column that corresponds to the -25.000′ value in the Offset column (see Figure 8.4) to activate the Pick Profile Style dialog.

9. Select the Left Sample Profile option and click OK. The style changes from the Existing Ground Profile to the Left Sample Profile in the table.

10. Now select the cell in the Style column that corresponds to the 25.000′ value in the Offset column.

11. Select the Right Sample Profile option and click OK to achieve Figure 8.5.

12. Click OK to dismiss this dialog.

13. The Events tab in Panorama will appear telling you that you have sampled data or if an error in the sampling needs to be fixed. Click on the green checkmark or the X to dismiss.

Profiles are dependent on the alignment they are derived from, so they are stored as profile branches under their parent alignment on the Prospector tab, as shown in Figure 8.6.

FIGURE 8.5
The Create Profile From Surface dialog with styles assigned on the basis of the Off-set value

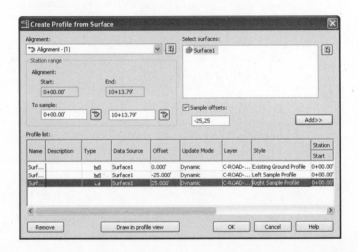

FIGURE 8.6

Alignment profiles on the Prospector tab

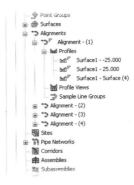

AREN'T YOU GOING TO DRAW THE PROFILE VIEW?

Under normal conditions, we would click the Draw In Profile View button to go through the process of creating the grid, labels, and the other components that are part of a completed profile view. We'll skip that step for now because we want to focus on the profiles themselves.

By maintaining the profiles under the alignments, it becomes somewhat simpler to review what has been sampled and modified for each alignment. Note that the profiles are dynamic and continuously update, as we'll see in this next exercise:

1. Open the Dynamic Profiles.dwg file. This drawing has profiles that were created in the first exercise from sampling the surface along Alignment - (1) and along offsets that were 25′ to the right and left of Alignment - (1).

2. From the main menu, select View ➢ Viewports ➢ 2 Viewports. Enter **H**↵ at the command line to split your screen into two horizontal viewports. If Dynamic Input is on, then select the Horizontal option from the Dynamic Input menu near the crosshairs.

3. Click in the top viewport to activate it.

4. On the Prospector tab, expand the Alignments branch and right-click on Alignment - (1). Select the Zoom To option, as shown in Figure 8.7.

5. Click in the bottom viewport to activate it.

6. Expand the Alignments ➢ Alignment - (1) ➢ Profile Views branches.

7. Right-click on Alignment - (1)3 and select the Zoom To option again. Your screen should now look like Figure 8.8.

FIGURE 8.7
The Zoom To option
on Alignment - (1)

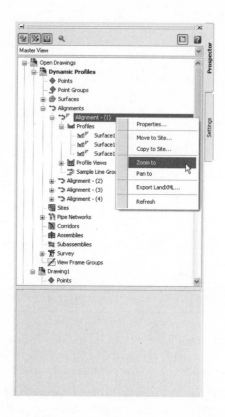

FIGURE 8.8
Splitting the screen
for plan and profile
editing

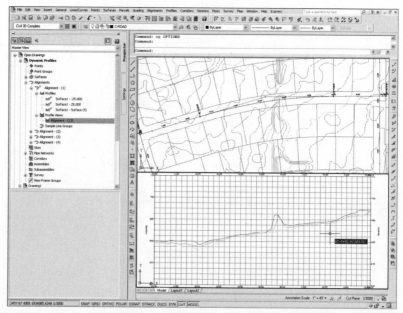

8. Click in the top viewport again.

9. From the main menu, select View ➤ Zoom ➤ Out. Notice a circle on the left-hand side, beyond the lot layout.

10. Pick the alignment to activate the grips, and stretch the beginning grip to the center of the circle, as shown in Figure 8.9.

11. Click to complete the edit, and the alignment profile (the green line) will automatically adjust to reflect the change in the starting point of the alignment. Note that the offset profiles (the yellow and red lines) move dynamically as well.

By maintaining the relationships between the alignment, the surface, the sampled information, and the offsets, Civil 3D creates a much more dynamic feedback system for designers. This can be useful when analyzing a situation with a number of possible solutions, where the surface information will be a deciding factor in the final location of the alignment. Once a location has been selected, this profile view can be used to create a vertical design, as we'll see in the next section.

FIGURE 8.9
Grip-editing the alignment

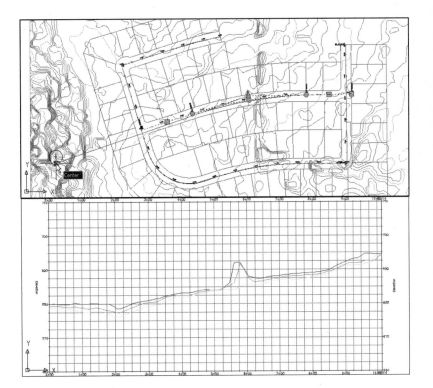

Layout Profiles

Working with sampled surface information is dynamic and the improvement over previous generations of Autodesk Civil design software is profound. Moving into the design stage, you'll see how these improvements continue as we look at the nature of creating design profiles. By working with layout profiles as a collection of components that understand their relationships with each other as opposed to independent finite elements, we can continue to use the program as a design tool instead of just a drafting tool.

Layout profiles can be created in two basic ways:

◆ PVI-based layouts are the most common, using tangents between points of vertical intersection (PVIs) and then applying curve parameters to connect them. PVI-based editing allows editing in a more conventional tabular format.

◆ Entity-based layouts operate like horizontal alignments in the use of free, floating, and fixed entities. The PVI points are derived from pass-through points and other parameters that are used to create the entities. Entity-based editing allows for the selection of individual entities and editing in an individual component dialog.

We will work with both methods in this series of exercises to illustrate a variety of creation and editing techniques. First we'll focus on initial layout, and then we'll look at editing the various layouts.

LAYOUT BY PVI

PVI layout is the most common methodology in transportation design. Using long tangents that connect PVIs by derived parabolic curves is a method most engineers are familiar with, and it's the method we'll use in our first example:

1. Open the Layout Profiles 1.dwg file.

2. From the main menu, choose Profiles ➢ Create Profile By Layout.

3. Pick the Alignment - (1) profile view by clicking on one of the grid lines; you'll see the Create Profile dialog in Figure 8.10.

4. Click OK to accept the default settings. (We'll explore the "Profile Label Sets" section of this chapter.) The Profile Layout Tools toolbar appears. Notice that the toolbar (see Figure 8.11) is modeless, meaning it will stay open even if you proceed to do other AutoCAD operations such as Pan or Zoom.

5. On the toolbar, click the down arrow next to the Draw Tangents Without Curves tool on the far left. Select the Curve Settings option, as shown in Figure 8.11. The Vertical Curve Settings dialog opens.

6. The Select Curve Type list box should be set to Parabolic and the Length values in both the Crest Curves and the Sag Curves areas should be 150.000´. Selecting a Circular or Asymmetric curve type activates the other options in this dialog.

FIGURE 8.10
The Create
Profile dialog

FIGURE 8.11

The Curve Settings option on the Profile Layout Tools toolbar

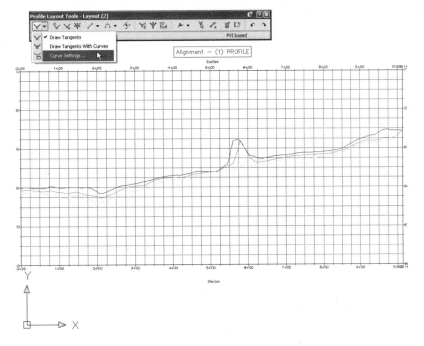

TO K OR NOT TO K

Resist the urge to toggle to a K value-based design. Even if K values are the driving force, you should still use a Length parameter. Otherwise, Civil 3D will solve the vertical curve for an exact value of K, resulting in curve lengths such as 273.87´. That value may work well in the digital world we model in, but it's not a value that would make a surveyor or plan reviewer happy.

1. Click OK to close the Vertical Curve Settings dialog.

2. On the Profile Layout Tools toolbar, click the down arrow next to the Draw Tangents Without Curves tool again. This time, however, select the Draw Tangents With Curves option.

3. Use a Center osnap to pick the center of the circle on the far left-hand side of the profile view. A rubberbanding line, which will be your layout profile, will appear.

4. Continue working your way across the profile view, picking the center of each circle with a Center osnap.

5. Right-click after selecting the center of the last circle; your drawing should look like Figure 8.12.

FIGURE 8.12

A completed layout profile with labels

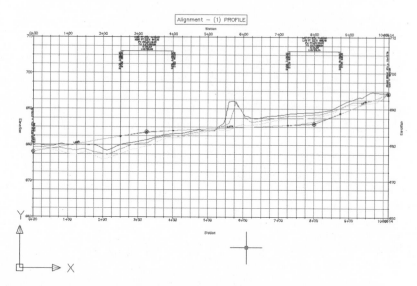

The layout profile is labeled with the Complete Label Set that was selected in the Create Profile dialog. As you would expect, this labeling and the layout profile are dynamic. If you click and then zoom in on this profile line, not the labels or the profile view, you will see something like Figure 8.13. Let's look at some of the unique grips available on PVI-based layout profiles.

♦ The red triangle at the PVI point is the PVI grip. Moving this will alter the inbound and outbound tangents, but the curve will remain in place with the same design parameters of length and type.

♦ The triangular grips on either side of the PVI are sliding PVI grips. Selecting and moving either will move the PVI, but the movement is limited to along the tangent of the grip selected. The curve length will not be affected by moving these grips.

♦ The circular grips near the PVI and at each end of the curve are curve grips. Moving any of these grips will make the curve longer or shorter without adjusting the inbound or outbound tangents or the PVI point.

Although this simple pick-and-go methodology works for preliminary layout, it does lack a certain amount of control typically required of final design. For that, let's look at another method of creating PVIs:

1. Open the Layout Profiles 1.dwg file if you have closed it. Make sure the Transparent Commands toolbar (Figure 8.14) is displayed somewhere on your screen. If the toolbar is not displayed, right-click in the gray area next to the other toolbars and from the context menu choose Civil ➢ Transparent Commands to open it.

FIGURE 8.13

The types of grips on a layout profile

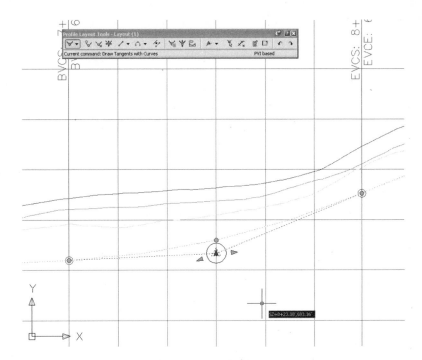

FIGURE 8.14

Transparent Commands toolbar

2. From the main menu, choose Profiles ➤ Create Profile By Layout.

3. Pick a grid line on the Alignment - (1) profile view to display the Create Profile dialog.

4. Click OK to accept the default settings.

5. On the Profile Layout Tools toolbar, click the down arrow next to the Draw Tangents Without Curves tool and select the Draw Tangents With Curves tool, as in the previous exercise. Use a Center osnap to snap to the center of the circle on the left edge of the profile view.

6. On the Transparent Commands toolbar, select the Profile Station Elevation command 🔧.

7. Pick a grid line on the profile view. If you move your cursor within the profile grid area, a vertical red line, or "jig," will appear, which moves up and down and from side to side. Note that there are two bits of information being fed back through the tooltips. The text in the white box shows the horizontal location of the cursor, and the text in the blue box shows the horizontal and vertical elevation along the jig.

8. Enter **245.**↵ at the command line for the station value. If you move your cursor within the profile grid area, a horizontal and vertical jig will appear (see Figure 8.15), but it can only move vertically along station 245. The text in the white box shows the elevation along the 245 jig, and the text in the black box shows the horizontal and vertical location of the cursor.

A JIG? BUT I DON'T REALLY DANCE!

A *jig* is a temporary line shown on screen to help you locate your pick point. Jigs work in a similar way to the Endpoint osnaps in that they give feedback during the command use but then disappear when the selection is complete. Civil 3D uses jigs to help you locate information on the screen for alignments and profile views.

FIGURE 8.15

A jig appears when you use the Profile Station Elevation transparent command.

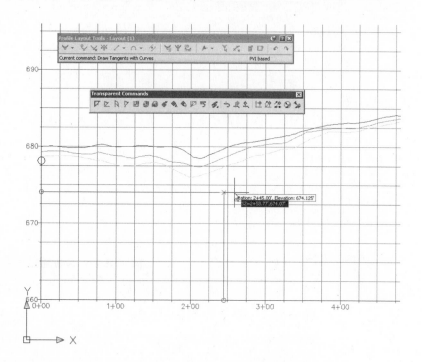

9. Enter 675↵ at the command line to set the elevation for the second PVI.

10. Press Esc. The Profile Station Elevation command is no longer active, but the Draw Tangents With Curves tool that was previously selected on the Profile Layout Tools toolbar continues to be active.

11. On the Transparent Commands toolbar, select the Profile Grade Station command ⚙.

12. Enter 3↵ at the command line for the profile grade.

13. Enter 650↵ for the station value at the command line. Press Esc to deactivate the Profile Grade Station command.

14. On the Transparent Commands toolbar, select the Profile Grade Length command ⚙.

15. Enter 2↵ at the command line for the profile grade.

16. Enter 300↵ for the profile grade length.

17. Press Esc to deactivate the Profile Grade Length command and to continue using the Draw Tangent With Curves tool.

18. Use a Nearest osnap to select a point along the far right-hand side of the profile view. Be careful to select a point on the grid or within the grid. Note that a curve has not been inserted between the last two tangents. The PVI at 9+50 doesn't leave room for a 150′ vertical curve to fit before the last PVI at 10+13.79.

19. Press ↵ to complete the profile. Your profile should look like Figure 8.16.

Using PVIs to define tangents and fitting curves between them is the most common approach to create a layout profile, but let's look at an entity-based design in the next section.

FIGURE 8.16

Using the Transparent Commands toolbar to create a layout profile

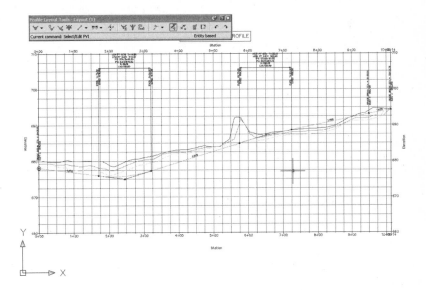

LAYOUT BY ENTITY

Working with the concepts of fixed, floating, and free entities as we did in Chapter 7 on alignments, we'll lay out a design profile in this exercise.

1. Open the Layout Profiles 3.dwg file.

2. From the main menu, choose Profiles ➢ Create Profile By Layout.

3. Pick a grid line on the Alignment - (1) profile view to display the Create Profile dialog.

4. Click OK to accept the default settings and open the Profile Layout Tools toolbar.

5. Click on the down arrow next to the Draw Fixed Tangent By Two Points tool, and select the Fixed Tangent (Two Points) option, as shown in Figure 8.17.

6. Using a Center osnap, pick the circle on the left-hand edge of the profile view. A rubber-banding line will appear.

FIGURE 8.17

Selecting the Fixed Tangent (Two Points) tool on the Profile Layout Tools toolbar

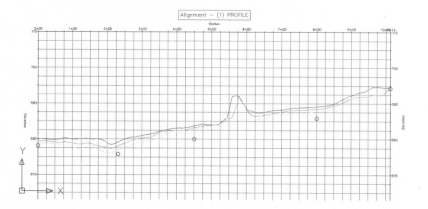

7. Using a Center osnap, pick the circle located at approximately station 2+30. A tangent will be drawn between these two circles.

8. Using a Center osnap, pick the circle located at approximately 8+00. Another rubberbanding line appears.

9. Using a Center osnap, pick the circle located on the right-hand edge of the profile view. A second tangent will be drawn. Right-click to exit the Fixed Line (Two Points) command, and your drawing should look like Figure 8.18. Note that there are no labels on the second tangent, since it is not yet tied to the first segment. The labeling begins at station 0 +00 and continues until there is a break, as there was at the end of the first tangent.

10. Select the down arrow next to the Draw Fixed Parabola By Three Points tool on the Profile Layout Tools toolbar. Choose the More Fixed Vertical Curves ➢ Fixed Vertical Curve (Entity End, Through Point) option, as shown in Figure 8.19.

11. Pick the left-hand tangent to attach the fixed vertical curve. Remember to pick the tangent line and not the end circle. A rubberbanding line appears.

12. Using a Center osnap, select the circle located at approximately station 4+50.

13. Right-click to exit the Fixed Vertical Curve (Entity End, Through Point) command and your drawing should look like Figure 8.20.

14. Click on the down arrow next to the Draw Fixed Tangent By Two Points tools, and select the Float Tangent (Through Point) option, as shown in Figure 8.21.

15. Pick the curve you just created, then pick the beginning of the tangent we'd created on the far right.

FIGURE 8.18
Layout profile with
two tangents drawn

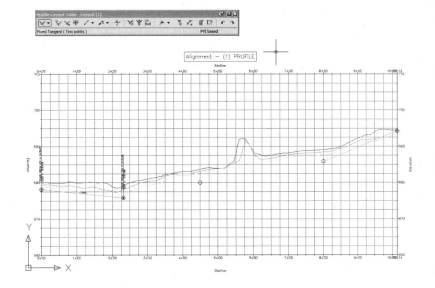

FIGURE 8.19
The Fixed Vertical
Curve (Entity End,
Through Point) tool on
the Profile Layout
Tools toolbar

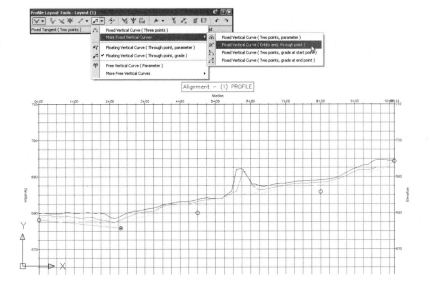

FIGURE 8.20
Completed curve
from entity end

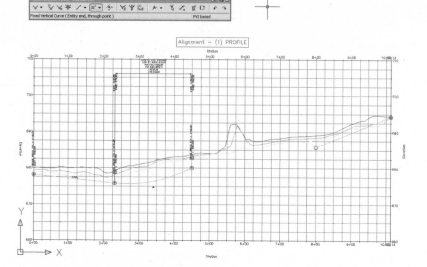

FIGURE 8.21
Selecting the Float
Tangent (Through
Point) tool on the
Profile Layout Tools
toolbar

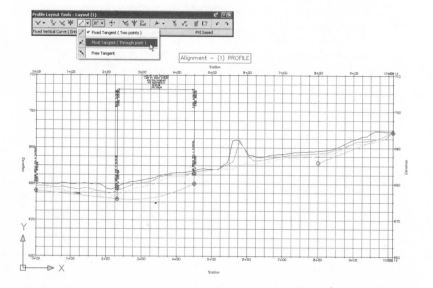

WE HATE TO CALL IT A BUG, BUT....

There's a quirk of the selection process with the Float Tangent (Through Point) tool. You have one chance to pick the endpoint, or Civil 3D will tell you the point is an invalid solution. If you miss the pick point described in the step and get a red glyph when you attempt to pick the tangent on the right, simply click the tool on the toolbar to reinitiate the command. It may be easier to have your osnap up and running, and then select the Float Tangent (Through Point) tool.

16. Click the down pointing arrow next to the Draw Fixed Parabola Tangential To End Of An Entity And Passing Through A Point tool, and select the Free Vertical Curve (Parameter) option, as shown in Figure 8.22.

17. Pick the tangent just created, then pick the tangent that ends our layout profile.

18. Enter **150⏎** at the command line for a curve length.

19. Right-click to complete the profile, and close the Profile Layout Tools toolbar by clicking on the red X button. Your drawing should look like Figure 8.23.

With the entity creation method, grip editing still works in a similar way to other layout methods. We'll look at more editing methods after looking at the final creation method.

FIGURE 8.22
Selecting the Free Vertical Curve (Parameter) tool on the Profile Layout Tools toolbar

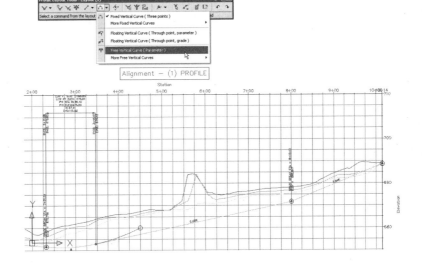

FIGURE 8.23
Completed layout profile created with entity tools

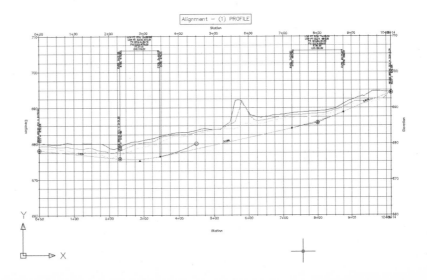

CREATING A PROFILE FROM A FILE

Working with profile information inside Civil 3D is nice, but it's not the only place where we can create or manipulate this sort of information. Many programs or analysis packages generate profile information. One common case is the plotting of a hydraulic grade line against a stormwater network profile of the pipes. In these cases, where the information is coming from outside the Civil 3D program, it can often be output in myriad formats. If this format can be converted to the required format for Civil 3D, the profile information can be input directly.

Civil 3D has a very specific format. Each line is a PVI definition (station and elevation). Curve information is an optional third bit of data on any line. Here's one example:

```
0 550.76
127.5 552.24
200.8 554 100
256.8 557.78 50
310.75 561
```

In this example, the third and fourth lines include the curve length as the optional third piece of information. The only inconvenience of using this input method is that the information in Civil 3D does not directly reference the text file, so once the profile data is imported, there is no dynamic relationship with the text file. In this simple exercise, we'll import a small text file to see how the function works:

1. Open the `Profile From File.dwg` file.

2. From the main menu, choose Profiles ➢ Create Profile From File.

3. Select the `TextProfile.txt` file and click Open. The Create Profile dialog appears.

4. In the dialog, set the Profile Label Set list box to Complete Label Set.

5. Click OK. Your drawing should look like Figure 8.24.

Now that we've looked at the three main ways of creating profile information, let's look at editing and modifying a profile.

FIGURE 8.24

A completed profile created from a file

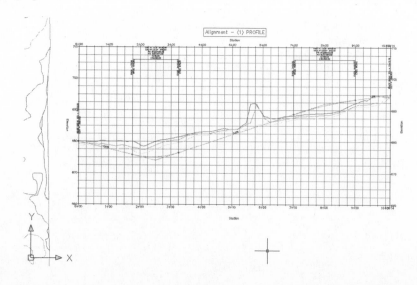

Editing Profiles

The three methods just reviewed allow for quick creation of profiles. We looked at how sampled profiles reflect changes in the parent alignment and how some grips are available on layout profiles, and we also imported a text file that could be easily modified. In all of these cases, the editing methods left something to be desired, from either a precision or dynamic relationship viewpoint.

In this section, we'll look at profile editing methods. The most basic is a more precise grip-editing methodology; then you'll look at how to modify the PVI-based layout profile, how to change out the components that make up a layout profile, and how to use some editing functions that don't fit into a nice category.

GRIP PROFILE EDITING

Once a layout is in place, sometimes a simple grip edit will suffice. But for precision editing, we can use a combination of the grips and the tools on the Transparent Commands toolbar, as in this short exercise:

1. Open the `Grip Editing Profiles.dwg` file.

2. Zoom in and pick the layout profile to activate its grips.

3. Pick the red triangular grip on the left-hand vertical curve to begin a grip stretch of the PVI, as shown in Figure 8.25.

4. On the Transparent Commands toolbar, select the Profile Station Elevation command.

5. Pick a grid line on the profile view.

6. Enter **275**↵ at the command line to set the profile station.

7. Enter **677**↵ to set the profile elevation.

8. Press Esc to deselect the layout profile object selected in step 2 and regenerate your view to complete the changes, as shown in Figure 8.26.

FIGURE 8.25

Grip-editing a PVI

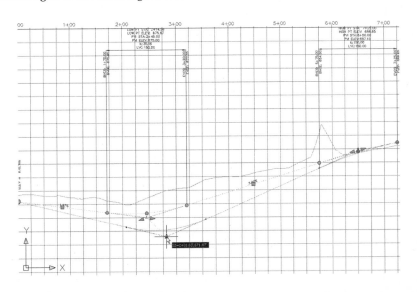

FIGURE 8.26
Completed grip
edit using the trans-
parent commands
for precision

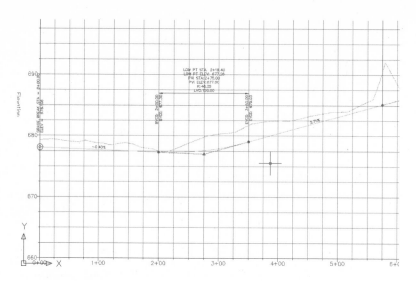

The grips can go from quick-and-dirty editing tools to precise editing tools when used in conjunction with the transparent commands in the profile view. They lack the ability to precisely control a curve length, though, so let's look at that change now.

PARAMETER AND PANORAMA PROFILE EDITING

Beyond the simple grip edits, but before changing out the components of a typical profile, we can modify the values that drive an individual component. In this exercise, we'll look at editing using the Profile Layout Parameter dialog and the Panorama palette set to modify the curve properties on our design profile:

1. Open the `Parameter Editing Profiles.dwg` file.

2. Pick the layout profile to activate its grips.

3. Right-click and select the Edit Profile Geometry option, as shown in Figure 8.27. The same result could be achieved by selecting Profiles ➤ Edit Profile Geometry from the main menu and then picking the layout profile, but we like right-click better!

4. On the Profile Layout Tools toolbar, click the Profile Layout Parameters tool ⬚ to open the Profile Layout Parameters dialog.

5. Click the Select PVI tool, as shown in Figure 8.28, and zoom in to click near the PVI at station 6+50 to populate the Profile Layout Parameters dialog.

   Values that can be edited are in black; the rest are mathematically derived values that can be of some design value but cannot be directly modified. A double chevron in the upper left will toggle the amount of information displayed.

FIGURE 8.27
The Edit Profile
Geometry option on
the right-click menu

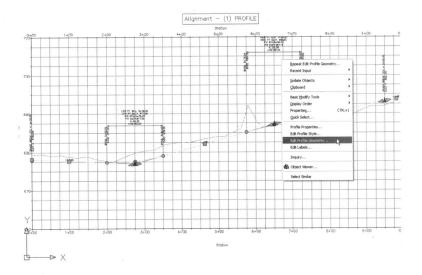

FIGURE 8.28
The PVI tool on the
Profile Layout Tools
toolbar and the Profile
Layout Parameters
dialog

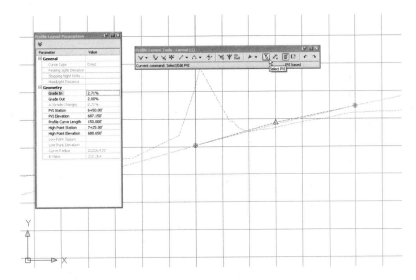

6. Change the Profile Curve Length in the Profile Layout Parameters dialog to **250.000′** (see Figure 8.29).

7. Close the Profile Layout Parameters dialog by clicking the small red X button in the upper-right corner. Then press the Esc key to deactivate the Select PVI tool.

FIGURE 8.29
Direct editing of
the curve layout
parameters

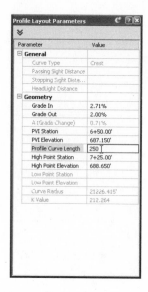

8. On the Profile Layout Tools toolbar, click the Profile Grid View tool 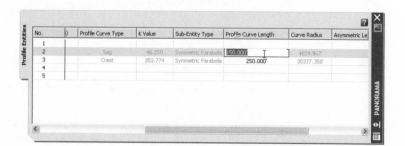 to activate the Pro-file Entities tab in Panorama. Panorama allows you to view all of the profile components at once, in a compact form.

9. Scroll right in Panorama until you see the Profile Curve Length column.

10. Double-click in the cell for the Entity 2 value in the Profile Curve Length column (see Figure 8.30), and change the value from 150.000′ to **250.000′**.

11. Close the Profile Layout Tools toolbar and zoom out to review your edits. Your complete profile should now look like Figure 8.31.

We can use these tools to modify the PVI points or tangent parameters, but they won't let us add or remove an entire component. We'll do that in the next section.

FIGURE 8.30
Direct editing of
the curve length
in Panorama

FIGURE 8.31
The completed editing
of the curve length in
the layout profile

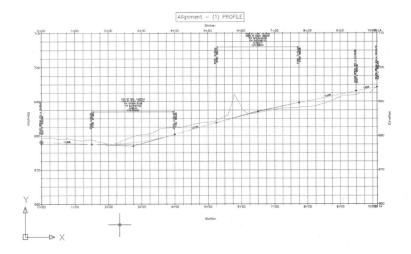

COMPONENT-LEVEL EDITING

Beyond the editing of basic parameters and locations, there are times when we have to add or remove entire components. In this exercise, we'll look at adding a PVI, removing a curve from an area that no longer requires one, and inserting a new curve into the layout profile:

1. Open the `Component Editing Profiles.dwg` file.

2. Select the layout profile to activate its grips.

3. Right-click and select the Edit Profile Geometry option, as in the previous exercise.

4. On the Profile Layout Tools toolbar, click the Insert PVI tool, as shown in Figure 8.32.

FIGURE 8.32
Click the Insert
PVI tool.

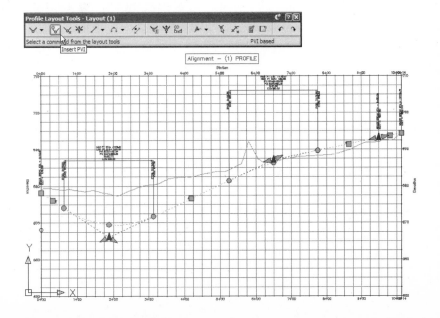

5. Using the tooltip to guide you, pick a point near the 3+50 station, with an approximate elevation of 680. The position of the tangents on either side of this new PVI is affected, and the profile is adjusted accordingly. The vertical curves that were in place are also modified to accommodate this new geometry.

6. On the Profile Layout Tools toolbar, click the Delete Entity tool ✕. Notice that the grips disappear and that the labels update.

7. Zoom in and pick the curve entity near station 2+00 to delete it, and then right-click to update the display.

8. On the Profile Layout Tools toolbar, click the down arrow next to the Draw Fixed Parabola By Three Points tool. Select the More Free Vertical Curves ➤ Free Vertical Parabola (PVI Based) option, as shown in Figure 8.33.

9. Pick near the PVI we just inserted (near the 3 + 50 station in step 5) to add a curve.

10. Enter 100⏎ at the command line to set the curve length.

11. Right-click to exit the command and update the profile display.

12. Close the Profile Layout Tools toolbar.

Editing profiles using any of these methods gives precise control of the creation and layout of your vertical design. Beyond these tools, though, are some tools on the Profile Layout Tools toolbar worth investigating that somewhat defy these categories. Let's look at them next.

FIGURE 8.33
The layout profile after curve deletion and selecting the Free Vertical Parabola tool on the Profile Layout Tools toolbar

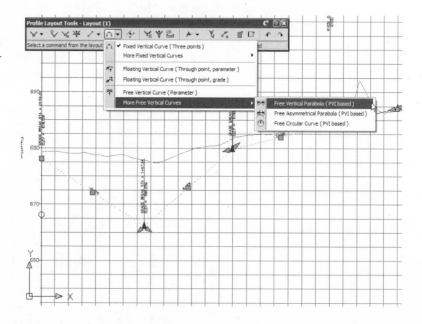

🌐 Real World Scenario

OTHER PROFILE EDITS

Some handy tools exist on the Profile Layout Tools toolbar for performing very specific actions. These tools aren't normally used during the preliminary design stage, but they come into play as you are working to create final design for grading or corridor design. They include raising or lowering a whole layout in one shot, as well as copying profiles.

1. Open the Other Profile Edits.dwg file.

2. Pick the layout profile to activate its grips.

3. Right-click on a grid line and select the Edit Profile Geometry option. The Profile Layout Tools toolbar will appear.

4. Click on the Raise/Lower PVIs tool. The Raise/Lower PVI Elevation dialog will appear.

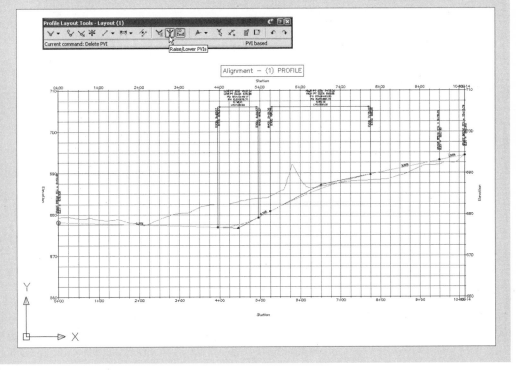

5. Set the Elevation Change to **4.000´**. Click the Station Range radio button and set the Start value to 0+ 10´ and the End value to 8+50.00´. We are moving the internal PVIs 4´ vertically while maintaining the endpoints of the design. Click OK.

6. Click the Copy Profile tool just to the right of the Raise/Lower PVIs tool to display the Copy Profile Data dialog.

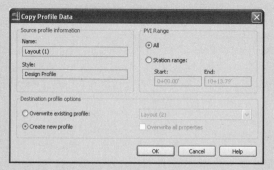

7. Click OK to create a new layout profile directly on top of Layout 1. Note that the Profile Layout Tools toolbar now references this newly created Layout (2) profile!

8. Use the Raise/Lower tool to drop Layout (2) by 0.5´ to simulate an edge of pavement design.

Using the layout and editing tools in these sections, you should be able to design and draw a combination of profile information presented to you as a Civil 3D user.

Profile Display and Stylization

No matter how profiles have been created, they need to be shown and labeled to make the information more understandable. In this section, we'll look at the style options for the profile linework itself, as well as options for the profile labels.

Profile Styles

Like every other object in Civil 3D, the display of profiles is controlled through styles. In this series of exercises, we'll look at the components that make up a profile display and prepare the display for plotting:

1. Open the Profile Styles.dwg file.

2. Zoom in on any BVC or EVC point and notice the double circles around the PVI points.

The style used for the layout profile and the style used to label the vertical curve both have small circles at the BVC and EVC points, creating the double circles seen in the drawing. These circles on the profile style are called *markers*, and you can be apply them at selected profile data points to illustrate various features on a profile, such as high or low points. In addition, just like any object in Civil 3D, the markers have their own style.

The double circles are not needed, so now we are going to modify the Design Profile style to remove the circles from the vertical curve points on the layout profile.

3. In Toolspace, switch to the Settings tab.

4. Expand the Profile ➤ Profile Styles branches to expose the styles already in this drawing.

5. Right-click on Design Profile and select the Copy option to open the Profile Style dialog.

6. On the Information tab, change the Name field to **Road Plot**.

7. Change to the Design tab (see Figure 8.34).

The 3D Chain Visualization is Civil 3D's way of displaying profile information in an isometric view. Profile information is displayed as a 3D polyline with X and Y information from the alignment and Z information from the profile data at that location. Since 3D polylines cannot accurately reflect a curve in space, the values are tessellated by using the distance in this dialog.

8. Switch to the Markers tab, as shown in Figure 8.35.

Note that the Alignment Geometry marker style, which places a small circle around each of the vertical curve points, is being used in our new Road Plot profile style.

9. Double-click the small icon on the right of the Marker field for the Vertical Tangent Curve Intersect to display the Pick Marker Style dialog.

10. Select <none> from the dropdown menu to remove the Alignment Geometry marker style, and click OK to close this dialog.

FIGURE 8.34
The Profile Style
Design tab

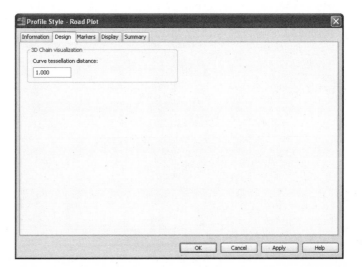

FIGURE 8.35

The Markers tab and
profile style circles

11. Repeat steps 8 and 9 for the Vertical Compound Curve Intersect, the Vertical Reverse Curve Intersect, and the Vertical Curve Tangent Intersect profile points. Your Profile Style dialog will look like Figure 8.36.

12. The Display tab works like it does in other dialogs we've explored, so we'll skip it in this exercise. Click OK to close the dialog. The new profile style will be listed under the Profile Styles branch in Prospector.

13. Pick the layout profile again, right-click, and select the Profile Properties option. The Profile Properties dialog appears.

14. On the Information tab, set the Object Style field to Road Plot and click OK. The double circles are gone and our profile is ready for plotting.

FIGURE 8.36

Marker styles set
to <none> for all
vertical profile
intersect points

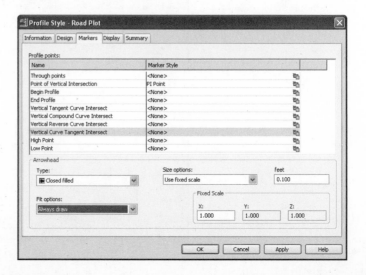

Take a few moments to check out the Layout Profile style in this exercise drawing. Remember, you need to pick the layout profile, right-click, and select the Profile Properties option, and then set the Object Style field to Layout Profile. This style uses different colors for the components that make up a layout profile, making it easy to visually discern a curve versus tangent on screen. This type of style is tailored for the design phase, when information is primarily displayed onscreen as opposed to plotted on paper. No matter how a profile is colored or marked with symbols, the labels really tell the story.

PROFILE LABELS

It is important to remember that the profile and the profile view are not the same thing. The labels we look at in this section are those that relate directly to the profile itself. This usually means station-based labels, individual tangent and curve labels, or grade breaks. We'll look at individual label styles for these components, then at the concept of the label set.

APPLYING LABELS

Like alignments, labels are applied as a separate group of objects from the profile itself. In this exercise, you'll learn how to add labels along a profile object.

1. Open the `Applying Profile Labels.dwg` file.

2. Pick the cyan layout profile to activate the profile object.

3. Right-click and select the Edit Labels option from the context menu to display the Profile Labels dialog (see Figure 8.37).

FIGURE 8.37
Empty Profile
Labels dialog

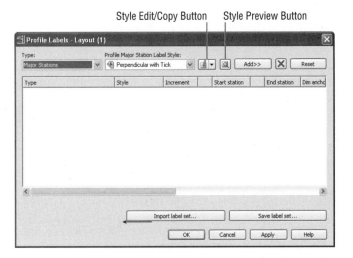

Two dropdown list boxes are on the top left of the dialog. Selecting the type of label from the Type dropdown changes the second dropdown to list the styles that are available for that label type. Next to this dropdown menu is the usual Style Edit/Copy button and a preview button. Once a style has been selected from the Style dropdown, clicking the Add button places it on the profile. The middle portion of this dialog displays information about the labels that are being applied to the profile selected; we'll look at that in just a moment.

4. Set the Type list box to the Major Stations option. The name of the second dropdown list box changes to Profile Major Station Label Style to reflect this option. Select the Perpendicular With Tick option for this list box.

5. Click Add to apply this label to the profile.

6. Change the Type list box to Horizontal Geometry Points.

7. The name of the Style list box changes to Unused Profile Geometry Point Label. Select the Standard option for this list box and click Add again.

8. Click the Apply button. Drag the dialog out of the way to view the changes to the profile (see Figure 8.38).

9. In the middle of the Profile Labels dialog, change the Increment value in the Major Stations row to **50**, as shown in Figure 8.39. This modifies the labeling increment only, not the grid or other values.

10. Click OK to close the Profile Labels dialog.

As you can see, applying labels one at a time could turn into a tedious task. After we look at the various types of labels available, we'll revisit this dialog and look at the two buttons on the bottom for dealing with label sets.

FIGURE 8.38

Labels applied to major stations and alignment geometry points

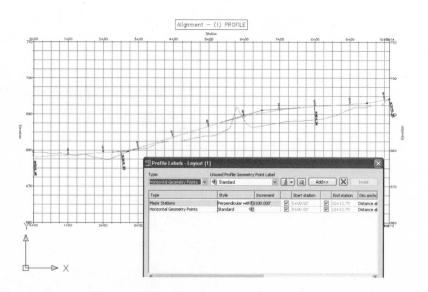

FIGURE 8.39
Modifying the major
station labeling
Increment

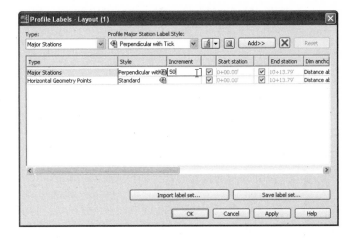

STATION LABELS

Labeling along the profile at major, minor, and alignment geometry points allows the user to insert labels similar to a horizontal alignment. In this exercise, we'll modify a style to reflect a plan-readable approach and remove the stationing from the first and last points along the profile.

1. Open the `Station Profile Labels.dwg` file.

2. Pick the layout profile and right-click and select the Edit Labels option to display the Profile Labels dialog.

3. Uncheck the Start and End station checkboxes for the Major Stations label.

4. Change the value for the Start Station to **50** and the value of the End Station to **1012**, as shown in Figure 8.40.

5. Click the icon in the Style field to display the Pick Label Style dialog.

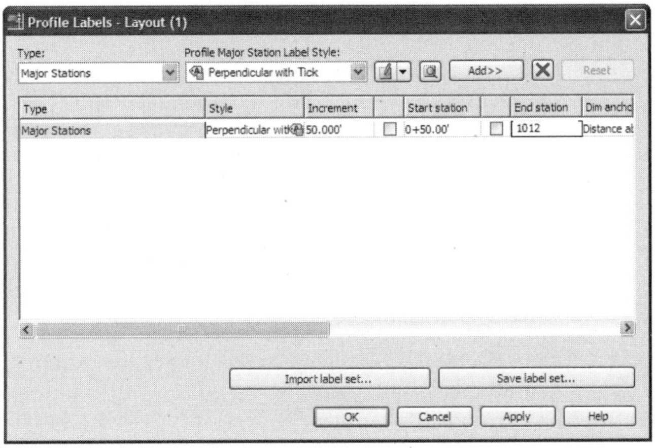

FIGURE 8.40
Modifying the values
of the starting and
ending stations for
the major labels

6. On the button to the right of the Style list box, click the down arrow and select the Edit Current Selection option. The Label Style Composer dialog appears.

7. On the General tab, change the value of the Orientation Reference to View, as shown in Figure 8.41.

8. Click OK to close the Label Style Composer dialog. Click OK again to close the Pick Label Style dialog.

9. Click OK to close the Profile Labels dialog. Instead of each station label being oriented so that it is perpendicular to the profile at the station, all station labels are now oriented vertically along the top of the profile at the station.

By controlling the frequency, starting and ending station, and label style, we can create labels for stationing or for conveying profile information along a layout profile.

FIGURE 8.41
Changing the orientation reference of a label

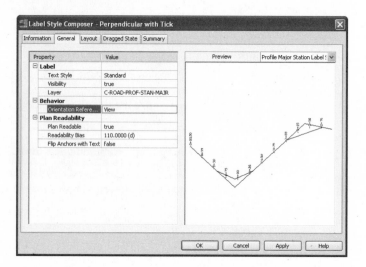

LINE LABELS

Line labels in profiles are typically used to convey the slope or length of a tangent segment. In this exercise, we'll add a length and slope to the layout profile.

1. Open the Line Profile Labels.dwg file.

2. Switch to the Settings tab of Toolspace.

3. Expand the Profile ➤ Label Styles ➤ Line branches

4. Right-click on Percent Grade and select the New option to open the Label Style Composer dialog and create a child style.

5. On the Information tab, change the Name field to Length And Percent Grade.

6. Change to the Layout tab.

7. Click in the cell for the Contents value and click the ellipsis button to display the Text Component Editor.

8. Change the Properties list box to the Tangent Slope Length option and the Precision value to 0.01, as shown in Figure 8.42.

9. Click the blue insert arrow, then add a foot symbol and the @ symbol in the preview pane of the editor so that it looks like Figure 8.42.

10. Click OK to close the Text Component Editor and click OK again to close the Label Style Composer dialog.

11. Pick the layout profile, right-click, and select the Edit Labels option to display the Profile Labels dialog.

12. Change the Type field to the Lines option. The name of the style list box changes to Profile Tangent Label Style. Select the Length And Percent Grade option for this list box.

13. Click the Add button and then click OK to exit the dialog. The profile view should look like Figure 8.43.

FIGURE 8.42

The Text Component Editor with the values for the Tangent Slope Length entered

Foot marker and @ symbol inserted here.

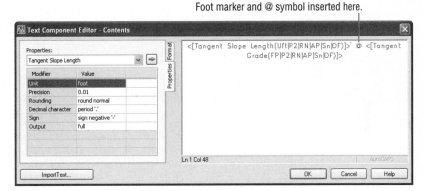

FIGURE 8.43

A new line label applied to the layout profile

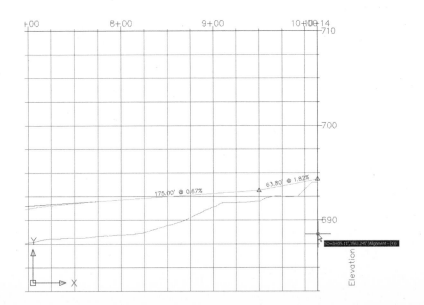

WHERE IS THAT DISTANCE BEING MEASURED?

The tangent slope length is the distance along the horizontal geometry between vertical curves. This value doesn't include the tangent extensions. There are a number of ways to label this length; be sure to look in the Text Component Editor if you're looking for a different measurement.

CURVE LABELS

Vertical curve labels are one of the most confusing aspects of profile labeling. Many people become overwhelmed rapidly because there's just so much that can be labeled and ways to get all the right information in the right place. In this quick exercise, we'll look at some of the special label anchor points that are unique to curve labels and how they can be helpful.

1. Open the `Curve Profile Labels.dwg` file.

2. Pick the layout profile. Right-click and select the Edit Labels option to display the Profile Labels dialog.

3. Change the Type field to the Crest Curves option. The name of the style list box changes to Profile Crest Curve Label Style. Select the Crest and Sag option for this list box.

4. Click the Add button to apply the label.

5. Change the Type field to the Sag Curves option. The name of the style list box changes to Profile Sag Curve Label Style. Click Add to apply the same label style.

6. Click OK to close the dialog, and your profile should look like Figure 8.44.

FIGURE 8.44
Curve labels applied with default values

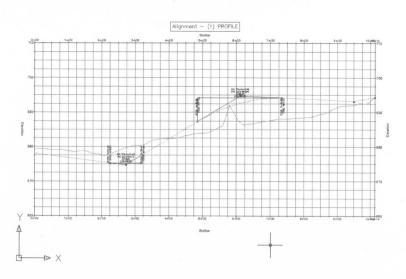

Most labels are applied directly on top of the object being referenced. Because typical curve labels have a large amount of information, putting the label right on the object can yield undesired results. Let's modify the label settings to review the options available for curve labels.

1. Pick the layout profile, right-click, and select the Edit Labels option to display the Profile Labels dialog.

2. Scroll to the right in the middle area of the dialog and locate the Dim Anchor Opt column.

3. Change the Dim Anchor Opt value for the Sag Curves to Distance Below.

4. Change its Dim Anchor Val to 2″.

5. Change the Dim Anchor Val value for the Crest Curves to 2″ as well. Your dialog should look like the one shown in Figure 8.45.

6. Click OK to close the dialog.

FIGURE 8.45
Curve labels with distance values inserted

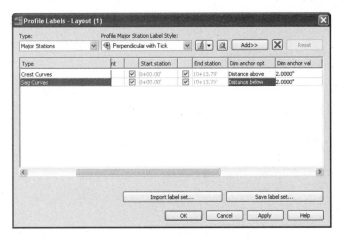

The labels can also be grip modified to move higher or lower as needed, but there is one more option we should review.

1. Pick the layout profile, right-click, and select the Edit Labels option to display the Profile Labels dialog.

2. Scroll to the right and change both Dim Anchor Opt values for the Crest and Sag Curves to Graph View Top.

3. Change the Dim Anchor Val for both curves to -1′ and click OK to close the dialog. Your drawing should look like Figure 8.46.

By using the top or bottom of the graph as the anchor point, you can apply consistent and easy labeling to the curve labels, regardless of the curve location or size.

FIGURE 8.46

Curve labels anchored to the top of the graph

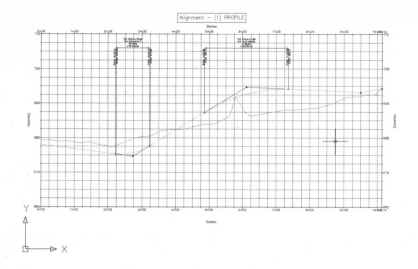

GRADE BREAKS

The last label style typically involved in a profile is a grade break label at PVI points that do not fall inside a vertical curve such as the beginning or end of the layout profile. Additional uses include things like water level profiling where vertical curves aren't part of the profile information or existing surface labeling. In this exercise, we'll add a grade break label and look at another option for controlling how often labels are applied to profile data.

1. Open the `Grade Break Profile Labels.dwg` file.

2. Pick the green surface profile. Right-click to select the Edit Labels option to display the Profile Labels dialog.

3. Set the Type list box to Grade Breaks and click the Add button.

4. Click Apply and drag the dialog out of the way to review the change. It should appear as in Figure 8.47.

   A sampled surface profile has grade breaks every time the alignment crosses a surface TIN line. So why didn't our view get completely coated with labels?

5. Scroll to the right, and change the Weeding value to 50´.

6. Click OK to dismiss the dialog, and your profile should look like the one in Figure 8.48.

Weeding allows the user to control how frequently grade break labels are applied. This makes it possible to label very dense profiles, such as a surface sampling, without overwhelming the user or cluttering the view beyond usefulness. As you've seen, there are a large number of ways to apply labeling to profiles, and applying these labels to each profile individually could be a tedious process. In the next section, we'll build a label set to make this process more efficient.

FIGURE 8.47
Grade break labels on
a sampled surface

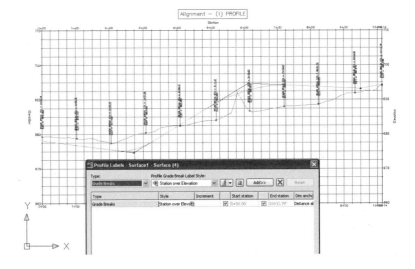

FIGURE 8.48
Grade break labels
with a 50´ Weeding
value

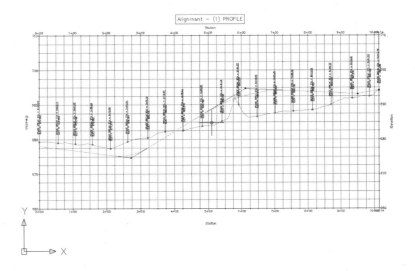

PROFILE LABEL SETS

Applying labels to both crest and sag curves, tangents, grade breaks, and geometry with the label style selection and various options could be tedious. Thankfully we have the ability to use label sets, as in alignments, to make the process quick and easy. In this exercise, we'll apply a label set, then make a few changes and export a new label set that can be then shared with other team members or imported to the Civil 3D template.

1. Open the Profile Label Sets.dwg file.

2. Pick the layout profile, right-click, and select the Edit Labels option to display the Profile Labels dialog.

3. Click the Import Label Set button near the bottom of the dialog to display the Select Style Set dialog.

4. Select the Standard option from the dropdown list and click OK.

5. Click OK again to close the Profile Labels dialog and view the profile view as in Figure 8.49.

6. Pick the layout profile, right-click, and select the Edit Labels option to display the Profile Labels dialog.

7. Click the Import Label Set button near the bottom of the dialog to display the Select Style Set dialog.

8. Select the Complete Label Set option from the dropdown list and click OK.

9. Double-click the icon in the style cell for the Lines label. The Pick Label Style dialog opens. Select the Length And Percent Grade option from the dropdown menu and click OK.

10. Double-click the icon in the style cell for both the Crest and Sag Curves labels. The Pick Label Style opens. Select the Crest And Sag option for both curves from the dropdown menu, and click OK.

11. Click the Apply button to see the changes reflected as in Figure 8.50.

12. Click the Save Label Set button to open the Profile Label Set dialog and create a new Profile label set.

13. On the Information tab, change the Name to Road Profile Labels and click OK to close the Profile Label Set dialog.

14. Click OK to close the Profile Labels dialog.

15. On the Settings tab of Toolspace, select Profile ➤ Label Styles ➤ Label Sets. Note that the Road Profile Labels set is now available for sharing or importing to other profile label dialogs.

FIGURE 8.49
Profile with the Standard label set applied

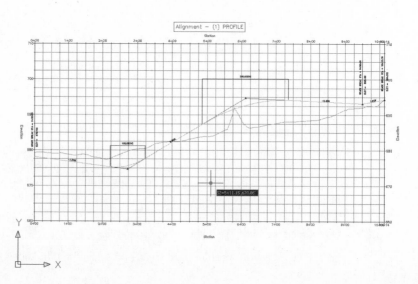

FIGURE 8.50

Applying a full
Road label set

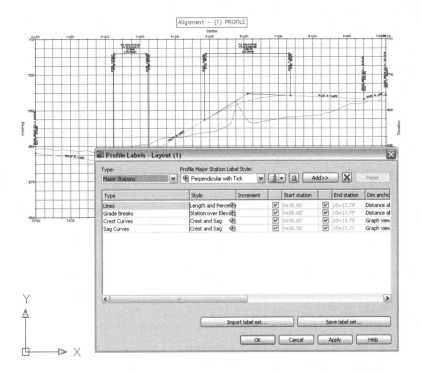

Label sets are the best way to get profile labeling applied uniformly. Working with a well-developed set of styles and label sets, it's quick and easy to go from sketched profile layout to plan-ready output.

The Bottom Line

Sample a surface profile with offset samples. Working with surface data to create dynamic sampled profiles is an important advantage in working with a three-dimensional model. Quick viewing of various surface slices with grip editing of alignments makes for a very effective preliminary planning tool. Combined with offset data to meet review agency requirements, profiles are robust design tools in Civil 3D 2008.

Master It Open the `Mastering Profile.dwg` file and sample the ground surface along Alignment - (2), along with offset values at 15´ left and 25´ right of the alignment.

Lay out a design profile on the basis of a table of data.   Many programs and designers work by creating pairs of station and elevation data. The tools built into Civil 3D allow the user to input this data precisely and quickly.

Master It   In the `Mastering Profiles.dwg` file, create a layout profile on Alignment (4) with the following information:

Station	PVI Elevation	Curve Length
0+00	694	
2+90	696.50	250´
5+43.16	688	

Add and modify individual components in a design profile.   The ability to delete, modify, and edit the individual components of the design profile while maintaining the relationships is an important concept in the 3D modeling world. The ability to tweak the design allows you to pursue a better solution, not just a working solution.

Master It   In the `Mastering Profile.dwg` file, move the third PVI (currently at 9+65, 687) to (9+50, 690). Then add a 175´ parabolic vertical curve at this point.

Apply a standard label set.   Standardization of appearance is one of the major benefits of using Civil 3D styles in labeling. By applying label sets, you can quickly create plot-ready profile views that have the required information for review.

Master It   In the `Mastering Profile.dwg` file, apply the Road Profiles label set to all layout profiles.

Chapter 9

Slice and Dice: Profile Views in Civil 3D

Although we work with profiles of all lengths while we're designing, that design profile eventually has to be printed for reviewers, contractors, and other project members. Converting the long profiles into workable chunks of data that fit nicely on the printed page with labeling and the important information placed in the right places is where profile views come into action.

By the end of this chapter, you'll be able to:

◆ Create a simple view as part of the sampling process

◆ Change profile views and band sets as needed

◆ Split profile views into smaller views

A Better Point of View

Working with vertical data is an integral part of building the Civil 3D model. Once profile information has been created in any number of ways, displaying it to make sense is another whole task. It can't be stated enough that profiles and profile views are not the same thing in Civil 3D. The profile view is the method that Civil 3D uses to display profile data. A single profile can be shown in an infinite number of views, with different grids, exaggeration factors, labels, or linetypes. In this first part of the chapter, we'll look at the various methods available for creating profile views.

Creating During Sampling

The easiest way to create a profile view is to draw it as an extended part of the surface sampling procedure. In this brief exercise, we'll sample a surface and then create the view in one series of steps.

1. Open the `Profile Views 1.dwg` file.

2. From the main menu, select Profiles ➤ Create Profile From Surface to display the Create Profile From Surface dialog.

3. In the Alignment text box, select Parker Place. In the Select Surfaces list box, select the EG surface. Click the Add button.

4. Click the Draw In Profile View button to move into the Create Profile View wizard, shown in Figure 9.1.

FIGURE 9.1
The Create Profile
View wizard

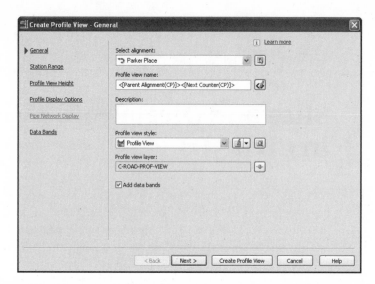

New for 2008, profile views are created with the help of a wizard. The wizard offers the advantage of stepping through all the options involved in creating a view or simply accepting the command settings and creating the profile view quickly and simply.

1. Uncheck the Add Data Bands option and click the Next button.

2. Verify that the Station Range area has the Automatic option selected and click Next.

3. Verify that the Profile View Height field has the Automatic option selected and click Next.

4. Click the Create Profile View button in the Profile Display Options window.

5. Pick a point on screen somewhere to the right of the site and surface to draw the profile view, as shown in Figure 9.2.

FIGURE 9.2
The completed profile
view for Parker Place

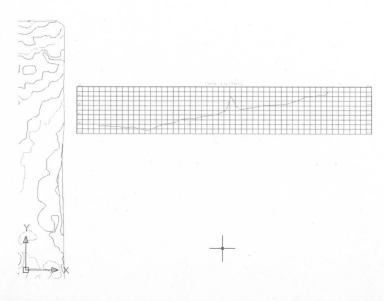

By combining the profile sampling step with the creation of the profile view, you have avoided one more trip to the menus. This is the most common method of creating a profile view, but let's look at a manual creation in the next section.

Creating Manually

Once an alignment has profile information associated with it, any number of profile views might be needed to display the proper information in the right format. To create a second, third, or tenth profile view once the sampling is done, it's necessary to use a manual creation method. In this exercise, we'll create a profile view manually for an alignment that already has a surface-sampled profile associated with it.

1. Open `Profile Views 1.dwg` file if you have not already done so.

2. From the main menu, select Profiles ➢ Create Profile View to display the Create Profile View wizard.

3. In the Select Alignment text box, select Carson's Way from the dropdown list. The profile was already sampled from the surface.

4. In the Profile View Style text box, select the Full Grid option.

5. Uncheck the Add Data Bands option.

6. Click the Create Profile View button and pick a point on screen to draw the profile view, as shown in Figure 9.3.

Using these two creation methods, we've made simple views, but let's look at a longer alignment in the next exercise, and some more of the options available in the Create Profile View wizard.

FIGURE 9.3
The completed profile
view of Carson's Way

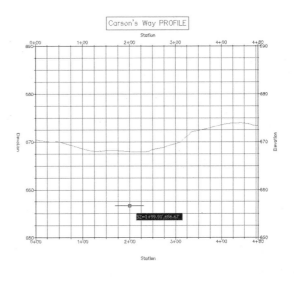

Splitting Views

Dividing up the data shown in a profile view can be time consuming. Civil 3D 2008 introduced the wizard for simple profile view creation, but the wizard can also be used to create manually limited profile views, staggered (or stepped) profile views, and multiple profile views with gaps between the views. We'll look at these three different variations on profile view creation in this section.

CREATING MANUALLY LIMITED PROFILE VIEWS

Continuous profile views like we made in the first two exercises work well for design purposes, but they are often unusable for plotting or exhibiting purposes. In this exercise, we'll sample a surface, then use the wizard to create a manually limited profile view. This variation will allow us to control how long and how high each profile view will be, thus making the views easier to plot or use for other purposes.

1. Open the Profile Views 2.dwg file.

2. From the main menu, select Profiles ➢ Create Profile From Surface to display the Create Profile From Surface dialog.

3. In the Alignment text box, select Rose Drive; in the Select Surface list box, select the EG surface, and click the Add button.

4. Click the Draw In Profile View button to enter the wizard.

5. In the Profile View Style text box, select the Full Grid option.

6. Uncheck the Add Data Bands option, and click the Next button.

7. In the Station Range area, select the User Specified Range option. Enter **0** for the Start station and 10+00 for the End station, as shown in Figure 9.4. Notice the preview picture shows a clipped portion of the total profile. Click Next.

FIGURE 9.4
The start and end stations for the user-specified profile view

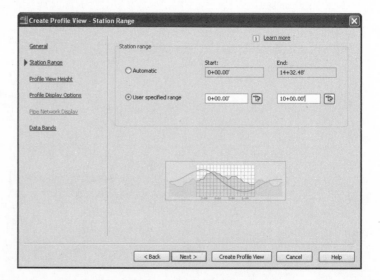

8. In the Profile View Height area, select the User Specified option. Set the Minimum height to 665 and the Maximum height to 705.

9. Click the Create Profile View button and pick a point on screen to draw the profile view (see Figure 9.5).

FIGURE 9.5

Applying user-specified station and height values to a profile view

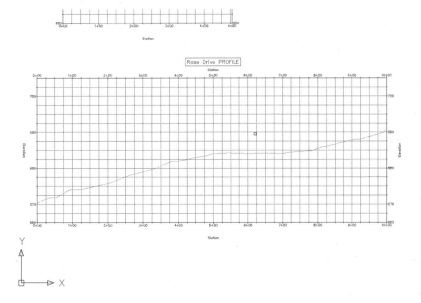

CREATING STAGGERED VIEWS

When large variations occur in profile height, the graph must often be split just to keep from wasting much of the page with empty gridlines. In this exercise, we'll use the wizard to create a staggered, or stepped, view.

1. Open the `Profile Views 2.dwg` file if you haven't already.

2. From the main menu, select Profiles ➤ Create Profile From Surface to display the Create Profile From Surface dialog.

3. In the Alignment text box, select Escarpment; in the Select Surface list box, select the EG surface and click the Add button.

4. Click the Draw In Profile View button to enter the wizard.

5. Uncheck the Add Data Bands option and click the Next button.

6. Click Next button in the Station Range window to allow the view to show the full length.

7. In the Profile View Height field, select the User Specified option and set the values as shown in Figure 9.6.

8. Check the Split Profile View options and set the view styles, as shown in Figure 9.6.

9. Click the Create Profile View button and pick a point on screen to draw the staggered display, as shown in Figure 9.7.

FIGURE 9.6
Split Profile
View settings

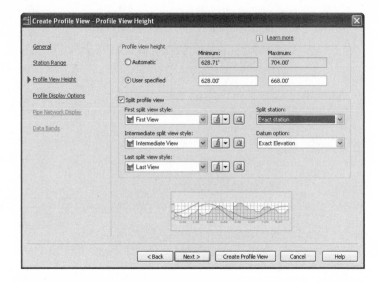

FIGURE 9.7
A Staggered (stepped)
profile view created
via the wizard

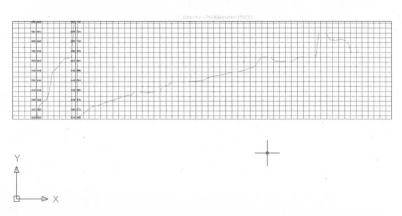

The profile view is split into three views according to the settings that were selected in the Create Profile View wizard in step 8. The first section is empty because of the grid padding built into the Profile View Style. The next section shows the profile from 0 to the station where the elevation change of the profile exceeds the limit for our height. The final section displays the rest of the profile. Each of these sections is part of the same profile view, and can be adjusted by visiting the Profile View Properties dialog.

CREATING GAPPED PROFILE VIEWS

Profile views must often be limited in length and height to fit a given sheet size. Gapped views are a way to show the entire length and height of the profile, by breaking the profile into different sections with "gaps" or spaces between each view. In this exercise, we'll use a variation of the Create Profile View wizard to create gapped views automatically.

1. Open the Profile View 2.dwg file if you haven't already.

2. *If you did the previous exercise, skip steps 3 and 4!*

3. From the main menu, select Profiles ➤ Create Profile From Surface to display the Create Profile From Surface dialog.

4. In the Alignment text box, select Escarpment; in the Select Surface list box, select the EG surface and click the Add button. Click OK to exit the dialog.

5. From the main menu, select Profiles ➤ Create Multiple Profile Views to display the Create Multiple Profile Views wizard (see Figure 9.8).

FIGURE 9.8
The Multiple Profile Views wizard

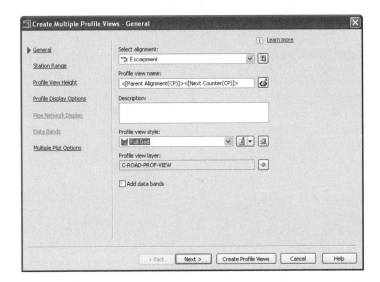

6. In the Select Alignment text box, select Escarpment, in the Profile View Style select the Full Grid option, and uncheck the Add Data Bands option, as shown in Figure 9.8. Click Next.

7. In the Station Range area, make sure the Automatic option is selected. This area is also where the Length Of Each View is set. Click Next.

8. In the Profile View Height area, make sure the Automatic option is selected. Note that we could use the Split Profile View options from the previous exercise here as well. Click Next.

9. Click Next again to move to the Multiple Plot Options window.

10. This step controls whether the gapped profile views will be arranged in a column, row, or a grid. The Escarpment alignment is fairly short, so the gapped views will be aligned in a row. However, it could be prudent with longer alignments to stack the profile views in a column or a compact grid, thereby saving screen space.

11. Click the Create Profile Views button and pick a point on screen to create a view similar to Figure 9.9.

The gapped profile views are the two profile views on the bottom of the screen and, just like the staggered profile view, show the entire alignment from start to finish. Unlike the staggered view, however, the gapped view is separated by a "gap" into two views. In addition, the gapped views are independent of each other so they have their own styles, properties, and labeling associated with them, making them useful when you don't want a view to show information that is not needed on a particular section. This is also the primary way to create divided profile views for sheet production.

Note that when using the Create Multiple Views option, every profile view is the full length as defined in the wizard, even if the alignment is not that long.

FIGURE 9.9
The staggered and gapped profile views of the Escarpment alignment

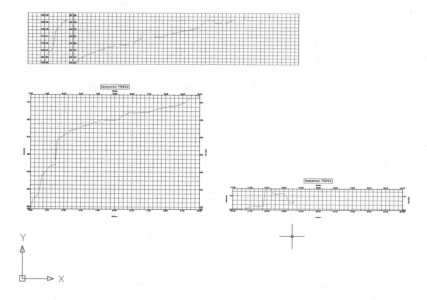

Profile Utilities

One common requirement is to compare profile data for objects that are aligned similarly but not parallel. Civil 3D builds in the ability to superimpose profile information from one profile view to another. The profile must be drawn in a profile view to be selected, so this utility is in this chapter. In this brief exercise, we'll superimpose one of our street designs onto the other to see how they compare over a certain portion of their length.

1. Open the Superimpose Profiles.dwg file. This drawing has two profile views created, one with a layout profile.

2. From the main menu, select Profiles ➤ Create Superimposed Profile.

3. Zoom into the Carson's Way profile view and pick the cyan layout profile.

4. Pick the Parker Place profile view to display the Superimpose Profile Options dialog.

5. Click OK to dismiss the dialog.

6. Zoom in on the left side of the Parker Place profile view to see the superimposed data, as shown in Figure 9.10.

Note that the vertical curve in the Carson's Way layout profile has been approximated on the Parker Place profile view, using a series of PVIs. Superimposing works by projecting a line from the target alignment (Parker Place) to an intersection with the other source alignment (Carson's Way).

The target alignment is queried for an elevation at the intersecting station and a PVI is added to the superimposed profile. See Figure 9.11 for a bit of clarification. Note that this superimposed profile is still dynamic! A change in the Carson's Way layout profile will be reflected on the Parker Place profile view.

FIGURE 9.10
The Carson's Way layout profile superimposed on the Parker Place profile view

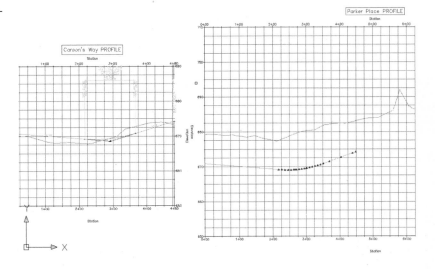

FIGURE 9.11
An example of profile sample lines that have been superimposed

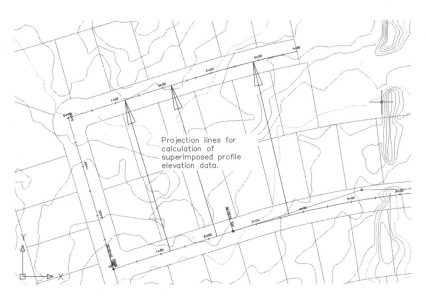

Editing Profile Views

Once profile views have been created, it gets interesting. The number of modifications to the view itself that can be applied, even before editing the styles, makes profile views one of the most flexible pieces of the Civil 3D package. In this series of exercises, we'll look at a number of changes that can be applied to any profile view in place.

Profile View Properties

Picking a profile view and right-clicking to access the Profile View Properties yields the dialog shown in Figure 9.12. The properties of a profile include the style applied, station and elevation limits, the number of profiles displayed, and the bands associated with the profile view.

FIGURE 9.12
Typical Profile View Properties dialog

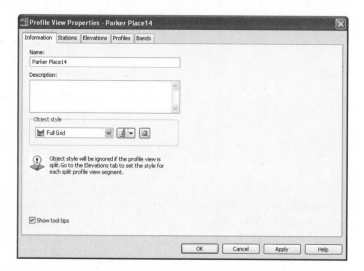

ADJUSTING THE PROFILE VIEW STATION LIMITS

In spite of the wizard, there are often times where manually adjusting a profile view is needed. For example, the most common change is to limit the length or height (or both) of the alignment that is being shown so it fits on a specific size of paper or viewport. You can make some of these changes during the initial creation of a profile view (as shown in a previous exercise), but you can also make changes after the profile view has been created.

One way to do this is to use the Profile View Properties dialog to make changes to the profile view. The profile view is a Civil 3D object, so it has properties and styles that can be adjusted through this dialog to make the profile view look like we need it to.

1. Open the `Profile View Properties.dwg` file.

2. Pick the Rose Drive profile view.

3. Right-click on a grid line, and select the Profile View Properties option to open the Profile View Properties dialog.

4. On the Stations tab, click the User Specified Range radio button, and set the value of the End station to 10+10, as shown in Figure 9.13.

FIGURE 9.13
Adjusting the end station values for Rose Drive

Profile View Properties - Rose Drive15

Information | Stations | Elevations | Profiles | Bands

Station range

	Start:	End:
◯ Automatic	0+00.00'	14+32.48'
◉ User specified range	0+00.00'	10+00.00'

5. Click OK to close the dialog. The profile view will now reflect the updated end station value.

One of the niceties in Civil 3D is that copies of a profile view retain the properties of that view, making a gapped view easy to create manually if they were not created with the wizard.

6. Enter **Copy**↵ on the command line. Pick the Rose Drive profile view we just modified.

7. Press F8 on your keyboard to toggle on the orthogonal mode, and then press ↵.

8. Pick a base point and move the crosshairs to the right. When the crosshairs reach a point where the two profile views do not overlap, pick that as your second point, and press ↵ to end the Copy command.

9. Pick the copy just created, right-click on a grid line, and select the Profile View Properties option. The Profile View Properties dialog appears.

10. On the Stations tab, change the stations again. This time, set the Start field to 10+00 and the End field to 14+32.48. The total length of the alignment will now be displayed on the two profile views, with a gap between the two views at station 10+00. Click OK, and your drawing will look like Figure 9.14.

In addition to creating gapped profile views by changing the profile properties, you can also show phase limits by applying a different style to the profile in the second view.

FIGURE 9.14
A manually created gap between profile views

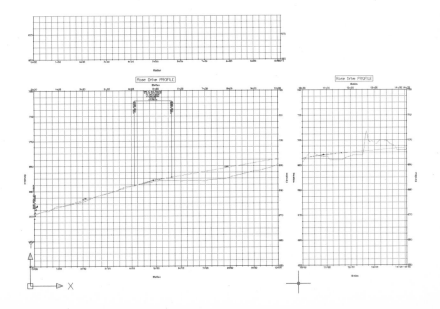

ADJUSTING THE PROFILE VIEW ELEVATIONS

Another common issue is the need to control the height of the profile view. Civil 3D automatically sets the datum and the top elevation of profile views on the basis of the data to be displayed. In most cases this is adequate, but in others, this simply creates a view too large for the space allocated on the sheet or wastes a large amount of that space.

1. Open the `Profile View Properties.dwg` file if you have not already done so.

2. Pick the Parker Place profile view.

3. Right-click on a grid line and select the Profile View Properties option. The Profile View Properties dialog opens.

4. Change to the Elevations tab.

5. In the Elevation Range area, check the User Specified Height radio button and enter the Minimum and Maximum heights, as shown in Figure 9.15.

6. Click OK to close the dialog. The profile view of Parker Place should reflect the updated elevations (see Figure 9.16).

The Elevations tab can also be used to split the profile view and create the staggered view that we previously created with the wizard.

1. Pick the Escarpment profile view, right-click on a grid line, and select the Profile View Properties option to open the Profile View Properties dialog.

2. Change to the Elevations tab.

3. In the Elevations Range area, click the User Specified Height radio button, Notice that the Height field is now active. Set the height to **40**.

4. Check the Split Profile View option.

5. Click OK to exit the dialog. The profile view should look like Figure 9.17.

FIGURE 9.15
Modifying the height of the profile view

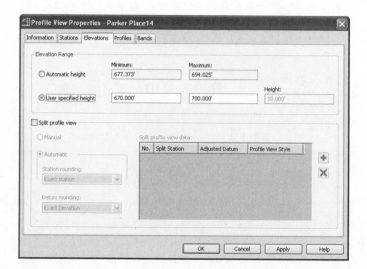

FIGURE 9.16

The updated profile view with the heights manually adjusted

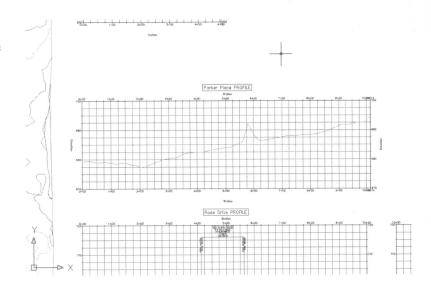

FIGURE 9.17

A split profile view for the Escarpment alignment

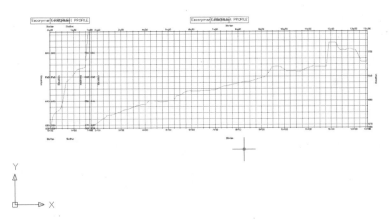

The automation gives us a rough idea of what our profile looks like, but it simply doesn't work or look as good as we'd like it. Let's look at tweaking this even further by manually splitting the view.

1. Pick the Escarpment profile view, right-click on a grid line, and select the Profile View Properties option to open the Profile View Properties dialog.

2. In the Split Profile View area, click the Manual radio button to turn on the Split Profile View Data table.

3. Click in the third row to highlight this profile view, then click the red X button shown in Figure 9.18 to remove it from the collection.

4. In the Split Profile View Data table, change the values of the Split Station, the Adjusted Datum, and the Profile View Style for profile views 1 and 2 so that they match Figure 9.19. Notice that we also had to change the Height field in the Elevation Range area.

5. Click OK to close the dialog.

By removing one of the views, we reduced the wasted space and made the view as efficient as possible. Automatically creating split views is a good starting point, but you'll often have to tweak them as we've done here. The selection of the proper profile view styles is an important part of the Split Profile View process. We'll look at styles in a later section of this chapter.

FIGURE 9.18
Removing a profile view from the Split Profile View Data table

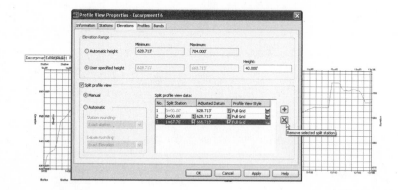

FIGURE 9.19
Updating the Elevations tab

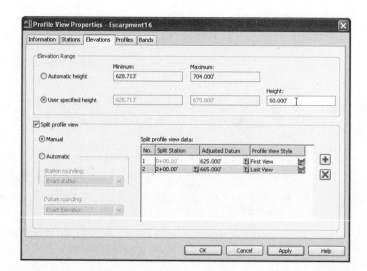

PROFILE DISPLAY OPTIONS

Civil 3D allows the creation of literally hundreds of profiles for any given alignment. This makes it easy to evaluate multiple design solutions but can also mean that profile views get very crowded. In this exercise, we'll look at some profile display options that allow the toggling of various profiles within a profile view.

1. Open the `Profile View Properties.dwg` file if you have not done so already.

2. Pick the Carson's Way profile view, right-click on a grid line, and select the Profile View Properties option. The Profile View Properties dialog opens.

3. Switch to the Profiles tab.

4. Uncheck the Draw option in the EG Surface row and click the Apply button.

5. Drag your dialog out of the way and your profile view should look similar to Figure 9.20.

   Toggling off the Draw option for the EG surface has created a profile view style in which a profile of the existing ground surface will not be drawn on the profile view. In addition, this style includes an option that removes, or "clips," the grid lines above the EG surface profile. In effect, the EG profile line acts as the grid-clipping line. Clipping is generally a reviewer requirement more than a user one.

6. Click the radio button in the Layout (1) row for the Clip Grid option.

7. Click OK to have a profile view similar to Figure 9.21.

The sampled profile from the EG surface still exists under the Carson's Way alignment; it simply isn't shown in the current profile view. Now that we've modified a number of styles, let's look at another option that is available on the Profile View Properties dialog: bands.

FIGURE 9.20

The Carson's Way profile view with the Draw option toggled off

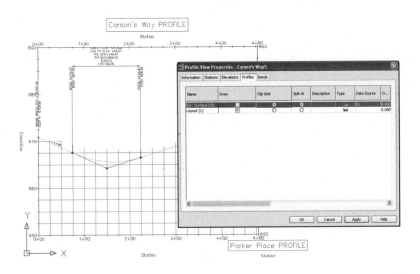

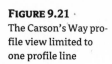

FIGURE 9.21 ·
The Carson's Way profile view limited to one profile line

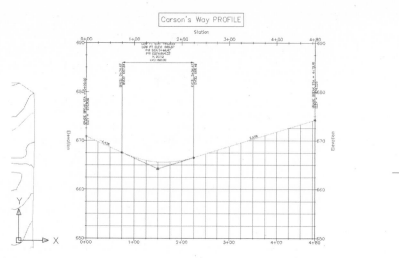

PROFILE VIEW BANDS

Data bands are horizontal elements that display additional information about the profile or alignment that is referenced in a profile view. Bands can be applied to both the top and bottom of a profile view, and there are six different band types:

Profile Data bands display information about the selected profile. This information can include simple elements such as elevation, or more complicated information such as the cut-fill between two profiles at the given station.

Vertical Geometry bands create an iconic view of the elements making up a profile. Typically used in reference to a design profile, vertical data bands make it easy for a designer to see where vertical curves are located along the alignment.

Horizontal Geometry bands create a simplified view of the horizontal alignment elements, giving the designer or reviewer information about line, curve, and spirals and their relative location to the profile data being displayed.

Superelevation bands display the various options for Superelevation values at the critical points along the alignment.

Sectional Data bands can display information about the sample line locations, distance between them, and other sectional-related information.

Pipe Data bands can show specific information about each pipe or structure being shown in the profile view.

In this exercise, we'll add bands to give feedback on the EG and layout profiles, as well as horizontal and vertical geometry.

1. Open the `Profile View Bands.dwg` file.

2. Zoom out and down to pick the Rose Drive profile view, right-click on a grid line, and select the Profile View Properties option to display the Profile View Properties dialog. Click the Bands tab, as shown in Figure 9.22.

FIGURE 9.22
The Bands tab of the
Profile View Proper-
ties dialog

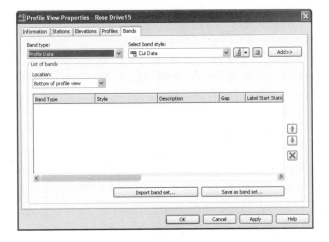

Set the Band Type list box to the Profile Data option and set the Select Band Style list box to the Elevations And Stations option. Click the Add button. The Profile Data band will be added to the table in the List Of Bands area.

3. Set the Location list box to the Top Of Profile View option.

4. Change the Band Type list box to the Horizontal Geometry option and the Select Band Style list box to the Geometry option. Click Add. The Horizontal Geometry band will now be added to the table in the List Of Bands area.

5. Change the Band Type list box to the Vertical Geometry option. Do not change the Select Band Style list box from its current option of Geometry. Click Add. The Vertical Geometry band will also be added to the table in the List Of Bands area.

6. Click OK to exit the dialog. Your profile view should look like Figure 9.23.

FIGURE 9.23
Applying bands
to a profile view

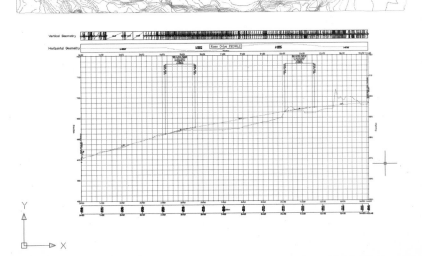

However, there are obviously problems with the bands. The Vertical Geometry band is a mess and is located above the title of the profile view, whereas the Horizontal Geometry band actually overwrites the title. In addition, the elevation information has two numbers with different rounding applied. Let's fix these issues.

1. Go to the Bands tab in the Profile View Properties dialog of the Rose Drive alignment.

2. Verify that the Location list box in the List Of Bands area is set to the Bottom Of Profile View option.

3. The Profile Data band is the only band currently listed in the table in the List Of Bands area. Scroll right in the Profile Data row and notice that there are two columns labeled Profile 1 and Profile 2. Change the value of Profile 2 to Layout (2).

4. Change the Location dropdown to the Top Of Profile View option.

5. The Horizontal and the Vertical Geometry bands are now listed in the table as well. Scroll to the right again, and set the value of Profile 1 in the Vertical Geometry band to Layout (2), as shown in Figure 9.24.

6. Scroll back to the left and set the Gap for the Horizontal Geometry band to 1.5″. This value controls the distance from one band to the next or to the edge of the profile view itself.

7. Click OK to close the dialog. Your profile view should now look like Figure 9.25.

Bands use the Profile 1 and Profile 2 designation as part of their style construction. By changing what profile is referenced as Profile 1 or 2, you change the values that are calculated and displayed. These bands are just one more item that is driven by styles, so let's move to looking at all the various styles in play with a profile view.

FIGURE 9.24

Setting the Profile View Bands to reference the Layout (2) profile

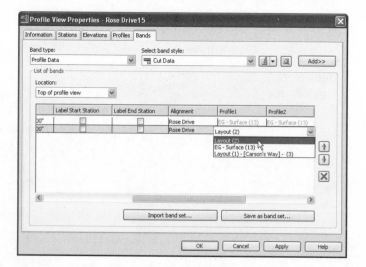

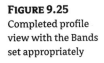

FIGURE 9.25
Completed profile
view with the Bands
set appropriately

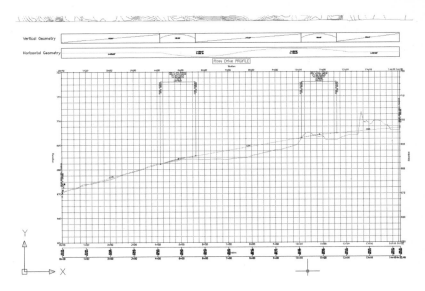

Profile View Styles

Profile view styles are among the most complicated to establish in Civil 3D, matched only by cross-sectional views. The style controls so many things, including annotation along all four axes, grid-and-tick spacing and clipping, and horizontal alignment information. The nice thing is that just like with every other stylized object, you have to go through the process only once and you can then apply the style to other views and share it.

PROFILE STYLE SELECTION

Selection of a profile view style is straightforward, but because of the large number of settings in play with a profile view style, the changes can be dramatic.

1. Open the `Profile View Styles.dwg` file.

2. Pick the Carson's Way profile view, right-click on a grid line, and select the Profile View Properties option. The Profile View Properties dialog opens.

3. On the Information tab, change the Object Style list box to Major Grids and click OK to arrive at Figure 9.26.

A profile view style includes information such as labeling on the axis, vertical scale factors, grid clipping, and component coloring. Using various styles lets us make changes to the view to meet requirements without changing any of the design information. Changing the style is a straightforward exercise, so let's look at what's happening behind the scenes when a profile view style is modified.

FIGURE 9.26

The Carson's Way profile view with the Major Grids style applied

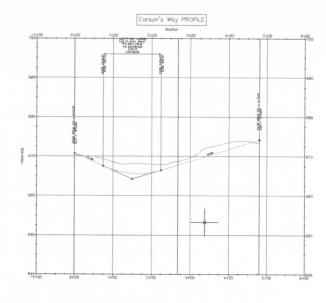

PROFILE STYLE EDITING

Like every other object, profile view styles control every aspect of how a profile view looks. In this series of exercises, we'll go in and out of the Profile View Style editor quite frequently so we can see each change individually.

1. Open the `Profile View Styles.dwg` file if you haven't already.

2. In the Settings tab on Toolspace, expand the Profile Views ➤ Profile View Styles branches.

3. Right-click on Full Grid and select the Copy option.

4. On the Information tab, change the Name field to **Mastering** and click OK to close the dialog.

5. Pick the Rose Drive profile view, right-click on a grid line, and select the Profile View Properties option. The Profile View Properties dialog opens.

6. On the Information tab, change the style name in the Object Style list box from the Full Grid profile view style to the new Mastering profile view style and click OK.

    We haven't truly changed anything, since the Mastering profile view style is still just a copy of the Full Grid profile view style. However, now that the Rose Drive profile view references our new style, we can step through a large number of changes and evaluate the results by simply clicking the Apply button in the dialog and reviewing the updated profile view.

7. In the Settings tab on Prospector, right-click on Mastering, and select the Edit option. The Profile View Style dialog opens.

8. Change to the Graph tab.

9. Change the Vertical Exaggeration field to 4. The Profile View Direction could also be modified here, but we'll leave it as Left To Right.

10. Click the Apply button, but do not close the dialog, to see the change in the Rose Drive profile view (see Figure 9.27).

11. Change to the Grid tab.

12. In the Grid Options area, check the Clip Vertical Grid option and then check the Clip To Highest Profile(s) option.

13. Click the Apply button so your figure looks like Figure 9.28. The vertical grid lines have been removed, or "clipped."

14. In the Grid Options area, check the Clip Horizontal grid option.

FIGURE 9.27
The Rose Drive profile view with an updated vertical exaggeration

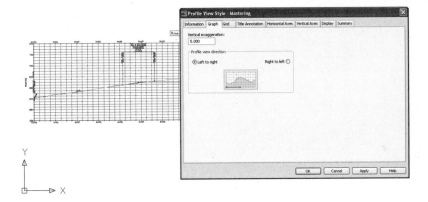

FIGURE 9.28
Clipping the vertical grid lines on the Rose Drive profile view

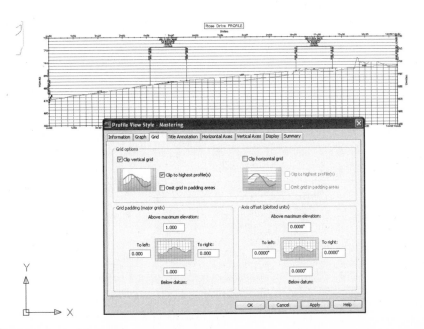

15. Click the Apply button and your view should look like Figure 9.29. By using the Apply button, we can verify changes without having to exit the dialog, and then reenter if we want to continue editing.

16. If the profile looks like it should, click OK to close the dialog. If not, review the prior steps, making changes as needed, and use the Apply button to check your work.

17. Zoom in on the left-hand axis to make the next changes easier to view.

18. Right-click on Mastering in the Settings tab again and select the Edit option. The Profile View Style dialog opens.

19. Still on the Grid tab, change the value of the To Left field in the Grid Padding (Major Grids) to 1 and click Apply to see the change in the profile view (see Figure 9.30).

FIGURE 9.29
The Rose Drive profile view with both the vertical and horizontal grids clipped

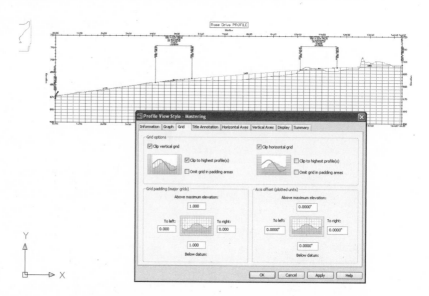

FIGURE 9.30
A grid padding applied to the left of the Rose Drive profile view

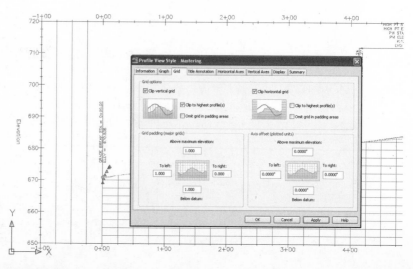

20. Change the value of the To Left field in the Grid Padding (Major Grids) area back to 0, and change the value of the To Left and To Right fields in the Axis Offset (Plotted Units) area to 0.5˝.

21. Click OK to close the dialog.

The padding and offset values are used to add extra grid and buffer space around the main portion of the profile view. By using various values in conjunction, almost any spacing requirement can be accommodated.

22. Zoom to the title of the Rose Drive profile view so we can more clearly see the changes about to be applied.

23. Right-click on Mastering again in the Settings tab and select the Edit option. The Profile View Style dialog opens.

24. Change to the Title Annotation tab, as shown in Figure 9.31.

FIGURE 9.31

The Title Annotation tab in the Profile View Style dialog

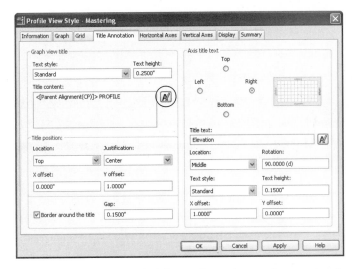

It's important to remember that in addition to all of the configurations we're stepping through, we also have the ability to turn on and off individual components on the Display tab as we do with other objects. We'll get there in a few more tabs. The left portion of the Title Annotation tab in Figure 9.31 is devoted to the title of the profile view, and the right portion is set up to control the annotation placed on each axis. The right axis settings are visible, as indicated by both the radio button and the different-colored text in the small preview picture.

1. Click the Edit Mtext button circled in Figure 9.31 to bring up the Text Component Editor for the title text.

2. Click in the preview area, change PROFILE to **Profile**, and press ↵ to create a line break.

3. In the Properties list box, select the Drawing Scale option and change the Precision value to 1.

4. Click the blue insert arrow button to add this property to the label. Press ↵ at the end of this new line to create a line break.

5. In the Properties list box, select the Graph View Vertical Scale option and change the Precision value to 1.

6. Click the blue insert arrow button as shown on Figure 9.32 to add this property to the label.

7. Highlight the second and third line in the preview screen, as shown on Figure 9.33. Right-click and select the Cut option.

8. Click OK to close the Text Component Editor.

9. At the bottom of the Graph View Title area (on the left-hand side of the dialog), uncheck the Border Around The Title checkbox. Click Apply to see the change.

FIGURE 9.32

Inserting the label components for the title of the profile view

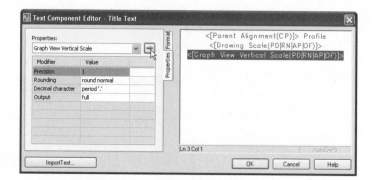

FIGURE 9.33

Cutting label components from the preview screen in the Text Component Editor

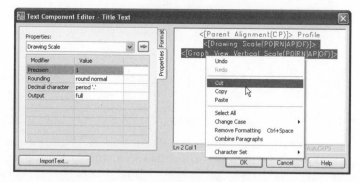

The Drawing Scale and the Graph View Vertical Scale properties, which were cut from the preview screen in step 7, aren't available for selection in the axis labels, only in the title label. But the program understands the field codes we just cut and will let us use them in the axis labels by pasting them in, even if they can't be selected directly. This is one of our favorite hacks for getting around the limitations that are in Civil 3D!

1. In the Axis Title Text (on the top right-hand side of the dialog) area, select the Bottom radio button.

2. Click the Edit Mtext button just to the right of the Title Text text box to enter the Text Component Editor for the Axis Title Text. Note that the scale labels aren't available from the Properties dropdown list shown in Figure 9.34.

3. Highlight Station in the preview area, right-click, and select the Paste option.

4. Click in the preview area and add text to match (Figure 9.35).

5. Click OK to close the Text Component Editor.

6. Set the Location list box to the Right option, the X Offset value to -1.25″, and the Y Offset value to 0.75″.

FIGURE 9.34
The Text Component Editor for the axis label text and its available properties

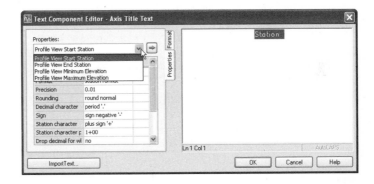

FIGURE 9.35
Hacked axis label with additional properties available!

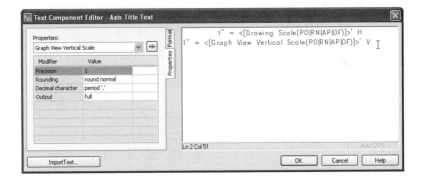

7. Click OK to exit the dialog, and Pan to the lower right of the profile view to see the change, as shown in Figure 9.36.

8. Right-click on the Mastering profile view style yet again on the Settings tab, and select the Edit option to open the Profile View Style dialog.

9. On the Horizontal Axes tab, set the options as follows:

   ◆ In the Select Axis To Control area, select the Top radio button and notice how the highlighted area in the preview picture changes.

   ◆ In the Minor Tick Details area, set the Interval value to 20′.

   ◆ In both the Major and Minor Tick Details area, set the Tick Justification field to the Top option.

FIGURE 9.36
Applied bottom axis label with scale inserted and border offsets

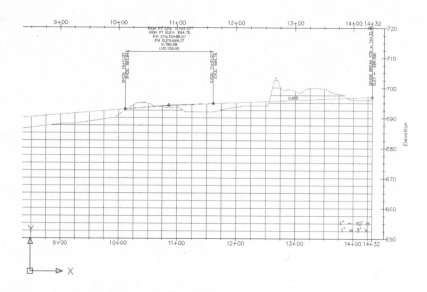

FIGURE 9.37
Horizontal ticks and vertical grid after modifications in step 9

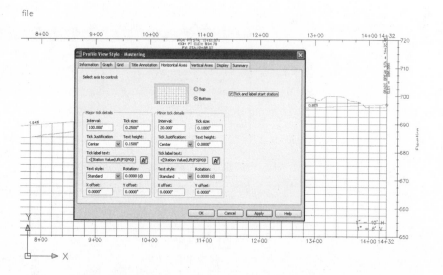

10. Click Apply to see the changes to the drawing, as shown in Figure 9.37.

11. Switch to the Vertical Axes tab, and set the Tick Justification field in both the Major and Minor Tick Details area to the Left option.

12. In the Major Tick Details area, set the following options to match the dialog in Figure 9.38:

    ◆ Tick Size: 0.5″

    ◆ X Offset: 0.1200″

    ◆ Y Offset: 0.1000″

FIGURE 9.38

Labeling of the vertical ticks using the settings shown on the Vertical Axes tab

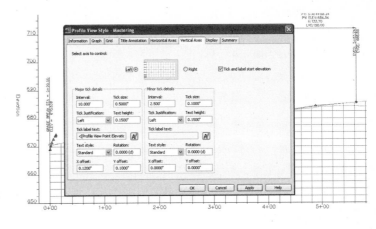

13. In the Select Axis To Control area on the top of the screen, click the Right radio button. Set the Tick Justification field in both the Major and Minor Tick Details area to the Right option.

14. In the Major Tick Details area, set the following options:

- Tick Size: 0.5″
- X Offset: -0.1200″
- Y Offset: 0.1000″

15. Switch to the Display tab and turn off the following additional components:

- Left Axis Title
- Right Axis Title
- Top Axis Title
- Top Axis Annotation Major
- Top Axis Ticks Minor

16. Click OK to close the Profile View Style dialog. Your profile view should look like Figure 9.39.

WHAT'S DRIVING THE MINOR AXIS VALUES?

For a long time, it wasn't documented, but the Minor Tick Interval on the Left Vertical and Bottom Horizontal axes is what controls the grid spacing. Even if you don't turn on the ticks on these axes, the spacing increment will be reflected in the minor grid lines.

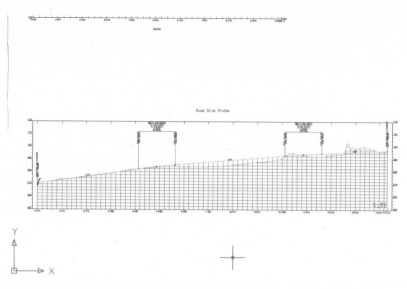

While that style took a long time to create and modify, it's not ready for use on any other profile view in the drawing, or to be moved to a drawing template file for sharing with other team members. Now that we have the grid looking how we like, we'll apply some more labels and see how the data bands are built.

Labeling Styles

Now that the profile is labeled, the profile view grid spacing is set, and the titles all look good, it's time to add some specific callouts and detail information. Civil 3D uses profile view labels and bands for annotating.

VIEW ANNOTATION

Profile view annotations label individual points in a profile view but are not tied to a specific profile object. These labels can be used to label a single point or the depth between two points in a profile. We say depth because the label recognizes the vertical exaggeration of the profile view and applies the scaling factor to label the correct depth. Profile view labels can be either station elevation or depth labels. In this exercise, we'll use demonstrate both.

1. Open the `Profile View Labels.dwg` file.

2. Zoom in on the Carson's Way profile view.

3. From the main menu, select Profiles ➤ Add Profile View Labels ➤ Add Profile View Labels. The Add Labels dialog opens.

4. In the Label Type list box, select the Station Elevation option, and in the Station Elevation Label Style list box, select the Station And Elevation option.

5. Click the Add button.

6. Right-click on a grid line in the Carson Way profile view. Zoom in on the right side so that you can see the point where the EG and layout profiles cross over.

7. Pick this profile crossover point by using an Intersection osnap to set the station, and then pick the same point to set the elevation. Your label should look like Figure 9.40.

8. In the Add Labels dialog, change the Label Type list box and the Depth Label Style list box to the Depth option. Click the Add button.

9. Click on a grid line on the Carson's Way profile view.

10. Pick a point along the layout profile and then pick a point along the EG profile. The depth between the two profiles will be measured as shown in Figure 9.41.

11. Close the Add Labels dialog.

FIGURE 9.40
An elevation label for a profile station

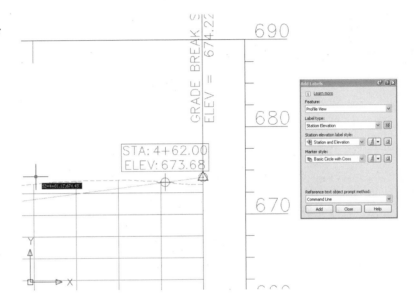

FIGURE 9.41
A depth label applied to the Carson's Way profile view

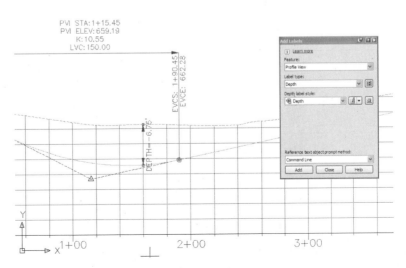

Depth labels can be handy in earthworks situations where cut and fill become critical, and individual spot labels are important to understanding points of interest, but most design documentation is accomplished with labels placed along the profile view axes in the form of data bands. Let's look at them in the next section.

 Real World Scenario

MAKING THE BAND

We looked at assigning bands to the profile view earlier in the chapter, but now let's look at how bands are composed. This really gets into how you'll use Civil 3D in your office, as making profile views look just like the reviewer wants them is one of the most important tasks. Setting up various bands for every agency can be time consuming, but pays dividends in uniformity and simple creation of the required views later on. Let's modify an existing band style and apply it to our Carson's Way profile view.

1. Open the `Profile View Labels.dwg` file if you haven't already.

2. On the Settings tab, expand the Profile View ➢ Band Styles ➢ Profile Data branches.

3. Right-click on the Elevations And Stations band style and select the Copy option. The Profile Data Band Style dialog opens.

4. On the Information tab, change the Name text box to **Elevations Only**.

5. Change to the Band Details tab as shown. The left side of this tab controls the various options for the title text for the band. These options were turned off on the Display tab in the style we copied, so we can ignore them. The right side controls the labeling of other critical points.

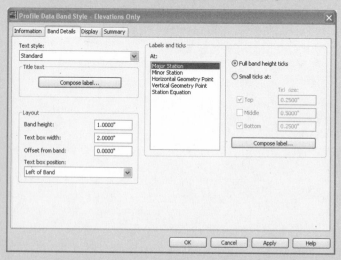

6. In the Labels And Ticks area, select the Major Station option in the At list box and click the Compose Label button to bring up the Label Style Composer.

7. In the Component Name list box, select the Station Value component and set the Visibility property to False.

8. Change to the EG Elevation component in the Component Name list box.

9. Click in the Contents value cell and click the More button to bring up the Text Component Editor.

10. Delete the text in the preview area, and type **EG:**, then select the Profile 1 Elevation property in the Properties list box with a Precision value of 0.1. Click the blue insert arrow button to insert these properties into the preview.

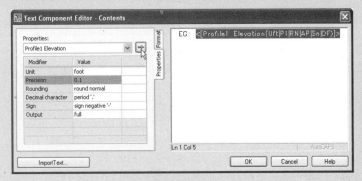

11. Click OK to close the Text Component Editor.

12. In the Label Style Composer, change the EG Elevation to the FG Elevation component in the Component Name list box. Click in the Contents value cell and click the More button to bring up the Text Component Editor.

13. Delete the text in the preview area, and type **FG:**, then select the Profile 2 Elevation property in the Properties list box with a Precision value of 0.01. Click the blue insert arrow button to insert these properties into the preview area.

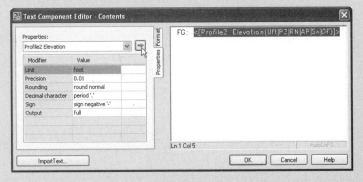

14. Click OK to exit the Text Component Editor, the Label Style Composer, and the Profile Data Band Style dialog.

15. Pick the Carson's Way profile view, right-click on a grid line, and select the Profile View Properties option. The Profile View Properties dialog opens.

16. Change to the Bands tab, and set the Band Type list box to Profile Data and the Select Band Style list box to Elevations Only. In the List Of Bands area, set the Location list box to the Bottom Of Profile View. Click Add to populate the List Of Bands table.

17. Add the Offsets band to the Bottom Of Profile View as well. This band will label the offset surface elevations.

18. Click OK to close the dialog and update your profile view.

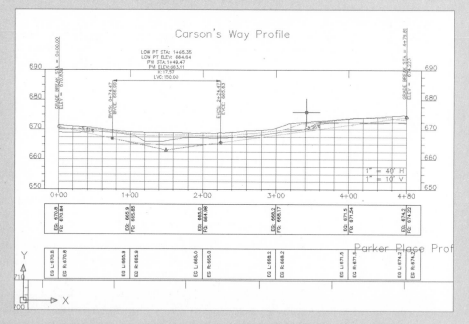

19. Select the profile view, right-click, and return to the Profile View Properties dialog.

20. Scroll to the right in the List Of Bands area, and change the Profile assignments as shown here.

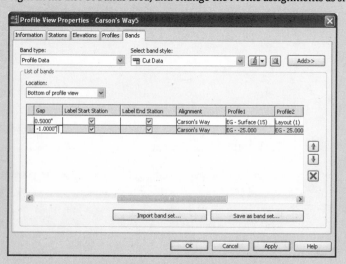

21. Change the Gap for the Offsets band to -1″ as shown. This superimposes the Offsets band on top of the Elevations Only band.

22. Click OK and update your profile view.

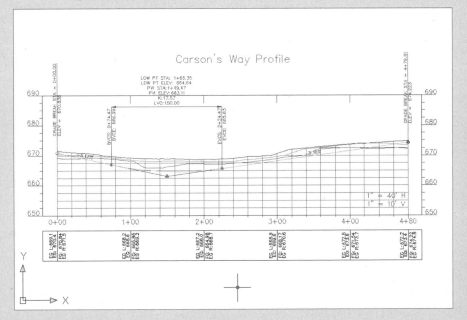

Band information can show any number of profiles, and by creatively using the offsets and profile assignments, you can apply labeling simply as well.

BAND SETS

Band sets are simply collections of bands, much like the profile label sets or alignment label sets. In this brief exercise we'll save a band set, then apply it to a second profile view.

1. Open the `Profile View Band Sets.dwg` file if you haven't already.

2. Pick the Carson's Way profile view, right-click, and select the Profile View Properties option. The Profile View Properties dialog opens.

3. Switch to the Bands tab.

4. Click the Save As Band Set button to display the Band Set dialog in Figure 9.42.

5. Change the Name field to **EG+FG And Offsets**.

6. Click OK to close the Band Set dialog.

7. Click OK to close the Profile View Properties dialog.

8. Pan to the Rose Drive profile view.

FIGURE 9.42
Information tab for
the Band Set dialog

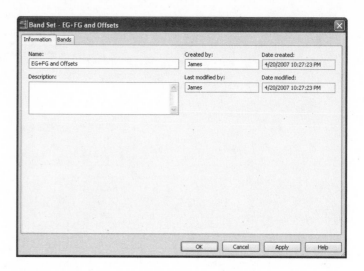

9. Pick the profile view, right-click, and select the Profile View Properties option. The Profile View Properties dialog opens.

10. Switch to the Bands tab.

11. Click the Import Band Set button, and the Band Set dialog opens.

12. Select the EG+FG And Offsets option from the dropdown and click OK.

13. Change the Alignment and Profile assignments for the Elevations Only and Offsets band style, as shown in Figure 9.43.

14. Click OK to exit the Profile View Properties dialog. Your profile view should look like Figure 9.44.

FIGURE 9.43
Assigning relevant
alignments and pro-
files to the bands

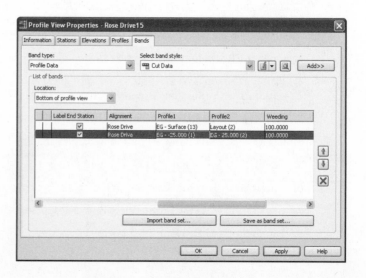

FIGURE 9.44
Completed profile
view after importing
the band set

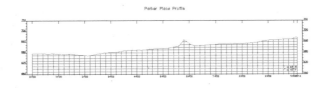

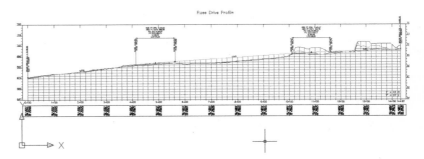

Our Rose Drive profile view now looks like the Carson's Way profile view. Band sets allows you to create uniform labeling and callout information across a variety of profile views. By using a band set, you can apply myriad settings and styles that you've assigned to a single profile view to a number of profile views. The simplicity of enforcing standard profile view labels and styles makes using profiles and profile views simpler than ever.

The Bottom Line

Create a simple view as part of the sampling process.   It's not very often that you want to sample a surface without creating a view of that data. By combing the steps into one quick process, you save time and effort as profile views are generated.

> **Master It**   Open the `Mastering Profile Views.dwg` file and create a view using the Full Grid profile view style for the Alexander Ave alignment. Display only the layout profile, the EG and offsets at 15´ left and 25´ right.

Change profile views and band sets as needed.   Using profile view styles and band sets allows for the quick customization and standardization of profile data. Since it's easy to change the styles and bands, many users find that they design using one style, and then change the style as required for submission.

> **Master It**   Change the Alexander Ave profile view to the Mastering style and assign the EG+FG And Offsets band set. Assign appropriate profiles to the bands.

Split profile views into smaller views.   Designing in one continuous profile view makes the designer's job easier, but plotting typically requires multiple views. Using the wizard or individual profile view properties makes it easy to split apart profile view information for presentation or submittal purposes.

> **Master It**   Create a new pair of profile views for the Parker Place alignment, each 600´ long. Assign the Mastering profile view style but no bands.

Chapter 10

Templates Plus: Assemblies and Subassemblies

Roads, ditches, trenches, and berms usually follow a predictable pattern known as a *typical section*. Assemblies are how we tell Civil 3D what these typical sections look like. Assemblies are made up of smaller components called subassemblies. For example, a typical road section assembly would contain subassemblies such as lanes, sidewalks, and curbs.

These typical sections, or assemblies, will be strung together into simple and complex corridor models in Chapters 11 and 12, so in this chapter our focus will be on understanding where these assemblies come from and how to build and manage them. Since it is difficult to understand the extensive applications of assemblies without seeing them in action in a corridor model, you may find it useful to work through the simple examples in this chapter, then come back and reread it after working through Chapters 11 and 12.

By the end of this chapter, you will be able to:

◆ Create a typical road assembly with lanes, curb, gutter, and sidewalk

◆ Edit an assembly

◆ Add daylighting to a typical road assembly

Subassemblies

A *subassembly* is a building block of a typical section, known as an *assembly*. Examples of subassemblies include lanes, curbs, sidewalks, channels, trenches, daylighting, and any other component required to complete a typical corridor section.

The Corridor Modeling Catalog

An extensive catalog of subassemblies has been created using the Microsoft .NET programming language for use in Civil 3D. (In previous releases, these subassemblies were programmed in Visual Basic for applications [VBA]. VBA subassemblies are still supported in the 2008 release, but .NET subassemblies perform much faster.) There are approximately 60 subassemblies available in the standard catalog, and each subassembly has a list of adjustable parameters. There are also about a dozen generic links that can be used to further refine your most complex assembly needs. The design possibilities included in the standard catalog are almost infinite.

It is possible to create additional subassemblies by programming in .NET, and by using Corridors ➤ Create Subassembly From Polyline. Since the Create Subassembly From Polyline tool is not intuitive, and it is rare to truly need a new subassembly, this chapter will focus on taking advantage and customizing subassembly parts from the standard catalog. If you have exhausted the possibilities in the standard catalog and still feel you need to create your own custom subassembly, you can find more information about creating them in the Help file.

ACCESSING THE CORRIDOR MODELING CATALOG

The Corridor Modeling Catalog is installed by default on your local hard drive. Choose Corridors ➤ Subassembly Catalog to open a content browser interface that will allow you to explore the entire collection of subassemblies that are available in each category (see Figure 10.1).

FIGURE 10.1

The front page of the Corridor Modeling Catalog

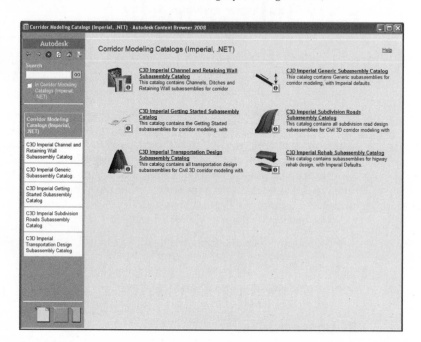

ACCESSING SUBASSEMBLY HELP

We will point out other shortcuts to access the extensive subassembly documentation later in the chapter, but you can get quick access to information by right-clicking on any subassembly entry on the Corridor Modeling Catalog page and selecting the Help option (see Figure 10.2).

FIGURE 10.2

Accessing the Help file through the Corridor Modeling Catalog

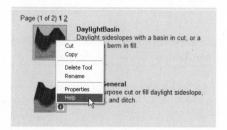

The Subassembly Reference in the Help file provides a detailed breakdown of each subassembly, examples for its use, its parameters, coding diagram, and more. While you are searching the catalog for the right parts to use, you will find the Subassembly Reference infinitely useful.

ADDING SUBASSEMBLIES TO A TOOL PALETTE

The creation of assemblies relies heavily on the use of tool palettes, as we will see later in this chapter. By default, Civil 3D has several tool palettes created for corridor modeling. You can access these tool palettes by selecting Corridors ➤ Subassembly Tool Palettes.

If you would like to add additional subassemblies to your tool palettes, or for some reason your default palettes did not get installed, you can use the i-drop to grab subassemblies from the catalog and drop them onto a tool palette. To use the i-drop, simply left-click on the small blue "i" next to any subassembly and continue to hold down your left mouse button until you are over the desired tool palette. Release the button and your subassembly should appear on the tool palette (see Figure 10.3)

FIGURE 10.3
Using the i-drop to add a subassembly to a tool palette

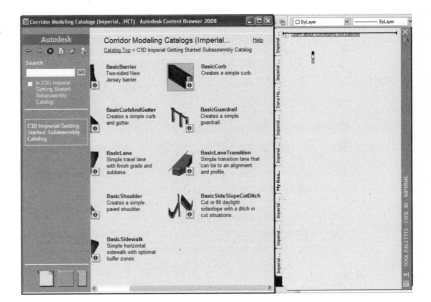

Building Assemblies

Assemblies are built by creating an assembly baseline by selecting Corridors ➤ Create Assembly and then adding subassembly components to that baseline from a tool palette. A typical assembly baseline is shown in Figure 10.4.

The process is extremely simple, much like building with interlocking blocks. Each component you add will have an understanding of how it needs to connect to the assembly. Though the creation of assemblies is easy, it takes a bit of practice to get into the rhythm and to understand all of the different subassembly parameters.

FIGURE 10.4
An assembly baseline

Creating a Typical Road Assembly

The most common assembly used in corridor modeling is a typical road assembly. This assembly will use the road centerline alignment and profile as its baseline.

The process for building an assembly requires the use of the tool palette and the AutoCAD Properties palette, both of which can be docked. You will quickly learn how to best orient these palettes with your limited screen real estate. If you run dual monitors, you may find it useful to place both of these palettes on your second monitor.

When you are creating your first few assemblies, it is common to miss a prompt or misplace a subassembly. To prevent these errors, proceed slowly, read the command line, and know that you can always erase misplaced subassemblies and replace them.

This exercise builds a typical assembly using the BasicLane, BasicCurbandGutter, and Basic-Sidewalk subassemblies (see Figure 10.5) to match a road section consisting of 10′ lanes, a curb and gutter, and a 5′ sidewalk with 2′ boulevard buffer strips on either side.

Let's have a more detailed look at each component we will use in the following exercise. A quick peek into the subassembly help will give us a breakdown of attachment options, input parameters, target parameters, output parameters, behavior, layout mode operation, and the point, link, and shape codes. (For more information about points, links, and shapes, see Chapter 11.)

FIGURE 10.5
A typical road
assembly

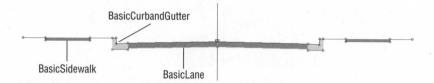

THE BASICLANE SUBASSEMBLY

The BasicLane subassembly creates a simple lane with only a few parameters. This is typically the best lane subassembly to use for your first attempts at corridor modeling as well as any situation where a straightforward lane is required. The BasicLane subassembly has parameters for customizing its side, width, and slope as well as depth of material (see Figure 10.6).

FIGURE 10.6
The BasicLane
subassembly

Corridors built using the BasicLane subassembly are most commonly used for building top and datum surfaces, rendering paved areas, and creating cross sections. They can also return quantities of excavated material. Keep in mind, however, that there is only one depth parameter, so this subassembly is not useful for a detailed breakdown of placed material, such as a road section that has a layer of asphalt, a layer of gravel, and so on.

The BasicLane cannot be superelevated, nor does it have targets for transitions.

THE BASICCURBANDGUTTER SUBASSEMBLY

The BasicCurbandGutter subassembly (Figure 10.7) is another simple component that creates an attached curb and gutter. Looking into the subassembly help, you will see a diagram of the Basic-CurbandGutter with callouts for its seven parameters: side; insertion point; gutter width and slope; and curb height, width, and depth. You can adjust these parameters to match many standard curb-and-gutter configurations.

Corridors built using the BasicCurbandGutter subassembly are most commonly used for building top and datum surfaces, rendering curb-and-gutter areas and creating cross sections. The Basic-CurbandGutter subassembly can return quantities of concrete (or other curb-and-gutter construction material) but not gravel bedding or other advanced material layers.

The BasicCurbandGutter does not have targets for transitions.

FIGURE 10.7
The BasicCurband-
Gutter subassembly

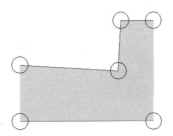

THE BASICSIDEWALK SUBASSEMBLY

The BasicSidewalk subassembly (Figure 10.8) will create a sidewalk and boulevard buffer strips. The Help file lists the following five parameters for the BasicSidewalk subassembly: side, width, depth, buffer width 1, and buffer width 2. These parameters allow the sidewalk width, material depth, and buffer widths to be adjusted to match your design specification.

FIGURE 10.8

The BasicSidewalk
subassembly

Corridors built using the BasicSidewalk subassembly are most commonly used for building top and datum surfaces and rendering concrete sidewalk areas. The BasicSidewalk subassembly can return quantities of concrete (or other sidewalk construction material), but not gravel bedding or other advanced material layers.

In the following exercise, we will build a typical road assembly using the subassemblies that we've discussed. Note that the BasicSidewalk is a flat sidewalk section. If your standard sidewalk detail requires a cross slope, use the UrbanSidewalk subassembly (which is discussed later in this chapter).

1. Create a new drawing from the _AutoCAD Civil 3D (Imperial) NCS Extended.dwt template.

2. Choose Corridors ➤ Create Assembly. The Create Assembly dialog opens.

3. Enter **Typical Road** in the Name text box. Make sure the Assembly Style text box is set to Basic and the Code Set Style text box is set to All Codes. Click OK.

4. Pick a location in your drawing for the assembly—somewhere in the center of your screen is fine.

5. Choose Corridors ➤ Subassembly Tool Palettes and locate the Imperial-Basic tool palette. Position the palette on your screen so that you can clearly see the assembly baseline.

6. Click the BasicLane button on the tool palette (see Figure 10.9). The AutoCAD Properties palette will appear. Position the palette on your screen so that you can clearly see both the assembly baseline and the Imperial-Basic tool palette.

7. Locate the Advanced section on the Design tab of the AutoCAD Properties palette. This section will list the BasicLane parameters. Make sure the Side parameter says Right and change the Width parameter to 10´. This will prepare you to place a 10´-wide lane on the right side of the assembly.

8. Note the command line states Select marker point within assembly or [RETURN for Detached]:. Click the assembly on the right side of the center point marker to place a 10´-wide lane on the right side of the assembly.

9. Return to the AutoCAD Properties palette and change the Side parameter to Left. Click the assembly on the left side of the center point marker to place a 10´ lane on the left side of the assembly. (Be sure to click the assembly baseline marker itself and not any part of the right BasicLane.) If you lost the AutoCAD Properties palette, you can resume the BasicLane subassembly placement by clicking the BasicLane button on your tool palette. Note you will have to change the Width parameter again.

FIGURE 10.9
BasicLane button on
the Imperial-Basic
tool palette

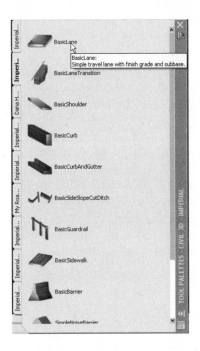

FIGURE 10.9
BasicLane button on
the Imperial-Basic
tool palette

10. Click the BasicCurbandGutter button on the tool palette. The Advanced section of the
    AutoCAD Properties palette Design tab will list the BasicCurbandGutter parameters.
    Change the Side parameter to Right. Note the Insertion Point parameter has been estab-
    lished at the Gutter Edge, meaning the curb will attach to our lane at the desired gutter edge
    location. This would typically be at our edge of the pavement.

11. Note the command line states `Select marker point within assembly or [RETURN for
    Detached]:`. Click the circular point marker on the right BasicLane subassembly that repre-
    sents the edge of the pavement to place a BasicCurbandGutter subassembly at the edge of
    the pavement (see Figure 10.10). If you misplace your BasicCurbandGutter, simply use the
    AutoCAD Erase command to erase the misplaced subassembly and return to step 10.

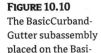

FIGURE 10.10
The BasicCurband-
Gutter subassembly
placed on the Basi-
cLane subassembly

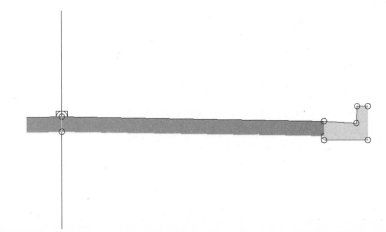

12. Change the Side parameter on the AutoCAD Properties palette to Left. Click the circular point marker on the left of the BasicLane subassembly that represents the edge of the pavement.

13. Click the BasicSidewalk button on the tool palette. In the Advanced section of the Design tab on the AutoCAD Properties palette, change the Side parameter to Right, the Width parameter to 5´, and the Buffer Width 1 and Buffer Width 2 parameters to 2´. This will create a sidewalk subassembly that has a 5´-wide sidewalk with 2´-wide boulevard strips on either side.

14. Note the command line states `Select marker point within assembly or [RETURN for Detached]:`. Click the circular point marker on the right BasicCurbandGutter subassembly that represents the top rear of the curb to attach the BasicSidewalk subassembly (see Figure 10.11). If you misplace the subassembly, use the AutoCAD Erase command to erase the misplaced subassembly and return to step 13.

15. Change the Side parameter on the AutoCAD Properties palette to Left. Click the circular point marker on the right of the BasicCurbandGutter subassembly that represents the top rear of the curb.

You have now completed a typical road assembly. Save your drawing if you would like to use it in a future exercise.

FIGURE 10.11

The BasicSidewalk subassembly placed on the BasicCurband-Gutter subassembly

Alternative Subassemblies

Once you gain some skills in building assemblies, you can explore the Corridor Modeling Catalog to find subassemblies that have more advanced parameters so that you can get more out of your corridor model. For example, if you must produce detailed schedules of road materials such as asphalt, coarse gravel, fine gravel, subgrade material, and so on, there are lane subassemblies in the catalog that allow you to specify those thicknesses for automatic volume reports.

The following list includes some examples of different components you could use in your typical road assembly. There are many more alternatives in the Corridor Modeling Catalog. The Help file provides a complete breakdown of each subassembly in the catalog that you will find useful as you search for your perfect subassembly.

Each of these subassemblies would be added to an assembly using exactly the same process specified in the first exercise in this chapter. Simply choose your alternative subassembly instead of the basic parts specified in the exercise, and adjust the parameters accordingly.

ALTERNATIVES TO THE BASICLANE SUBASSEMBLY

While the BasicLane is suitable for many roads, you may find you need a more robust road lane that provides an opportunity for superelevation, additional materials, or transitioning.

BasicLaneTransition

The BasicLaneTransition subassembly (Figure 10.12) can be used instead of the BasicLane. The BasicLaneTransition is limited to a few parameters and builds a corridor model that can have a top surface and a datum surface. However, this subassembly provides an opportunity for the lane to be widened or narrowed, as you will see in exercises in both Chapters 11 and 12. Refer to those exercises for more detailed examples.

The transition parameters for the BasicLaneTransition are as follows:

Hold Offset And Elevation behaves as a normal lane with no widening or narrowing.

Hold Elevation, Change Offset holds design elevation at edge of pavement and calculates a new grade to accommodate a stretch on the basis of a target alignment.

Hold Grade, Change Offset holds the lane grade as specified in the parameters, but calculates a new design elevation to accommodate a stretch on the basis of a target alignment.

Hold Offset, Change Elevation holds the lane width as specified in the parameters, but uses a design elevation as specified by a target profile.

Change Offset And Elevation determines both the elevation and grade at edge of pavement by a target alignment and profile.

FIGURE 10.12
The BasicLaneTransition subassembly

LaneParabolic

The LaneParabolic subassembly (Figure 10.13) is used for road sections that require a parabolic lane in contrast to the linear grade of the BasicLane. The LaneParabolic subassembly also adds options for two pavement depths and a base depth. This is useful in jurisdictions that require two lifts of asphalt and granular subbase material. Taking advantage of these additional parameters will give you an opportunity to build corridor models that can return more detailed quantity takeoffs and volume calculations.

Note that the LaneParabolic subassembly does not have a Side parameter. The parabolic nature of the component results in a single attachment point that would typically be the Assembly centerline marker.

FIGURE 10.13
The LaneParabolic subassembly

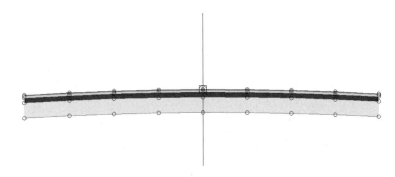

LaneBrokenBack

If your design calls for multiple lanes, and those lanes must each have a unique slope, investigate the LaneBrokenBack subassembly (Figure 10.14). This subassembly provides parameters to change the road crown location and specify the width and slope for each lane. Like the LaneParabolic, the LandBrokenBack subassembly also provides parameters for additional material thicknesses.

The LaneBrokenBack subassembly, like the BasicLaneTransition, allows for the use of target alignments and profiles to guide the subassembly horizontally and/or vertically.

FIGURE 10.14
The LaneBrokenBack subassembly

ALTERNATIVES TO THE BASICCURBANDGUTTER

There are many types of curbs, and the BasicCurbandGutter subassembly cannot model them all. There will be times that you may need to extract subbase quantities for your curbing or a more complicated set of curb dimensions, or perhaps you simply need a shoulder. In those cases, there are many alternatives to the BasicCurbandGutter in the Corridor Modeling Catalog.

BasicCurb

The BasicCurb subassembly (see Figure 10.15) is even simpler than the BasicCurbandGutter assembly. This subassembly is a straight-faced, gutterless curb that is typically attached to an outside edge of pavement. However, it can also be used on the inside edge of median or anywhere else a straight-faced curb component is required.

BasicShoulder

The BasicShoulder (see Figure 10.16) is another simple, yet effective, subassembly for use with road sections that require a shoulder.

FIGURE 10.15
The BasicCurb subassembly

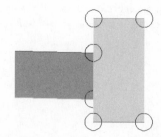

FIGURE 10.16
The BasicShoulder subassembly

UrbanCurbGutterGeneral

The UrbanCurbGutterGeneral subassembly (Figure 10.17) is very similar to the BasicCurbandGutter, except that it provides more dimension parameters and additional material parameters. If your jurisdiction specifies a curb that cannot be replicated using the simple dimensions of the BasicCurb-andGutter, investigate the Help file for this subassembly. Also, if your design requires detailed quantity takeoffs for the subbase used under your curb and gutter structures, this subassembly has parameters for subbase depth and slope.

FIGURE 10.17
The UrbanCurb-GutterGeneral subassembly

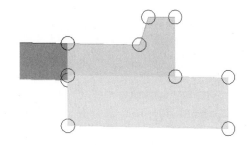

Alternatives to the BasicSidewalk Subassembly

The BasicSidewalk can reproduce many sidewalk designs, but it is not as customizable as the other sidewalk subassembly. In addition to the UrbanSidewalk discussed next, consider generic links, guardrails, and other roadside structures to enhance your corridor model.

UrbanSidewalk

While the BasicSidewalk produces a flat sidewalk and boulevard area, the UrbanSidewalk subassembly (see Figure 10.18) can assign a slope to its sidewalk and boulevards. Additionally, the sidewalk can be assigned alignment targets that would be useful in cases where your sidewalk or boulevard must be widened to accommodate a bus stop, lane widening, or other pedestrian feature.

FIGURE 10.18
The UrbanSidewalk subassembly

Editing an Assembly

When you first begin making assemblies, you will be tempted to erase components and begin again when you make a mistake such as specifying an incorrect lane width. Although there is no harm in starting over, it is very simple to make changes to a subassembly parameter.

EDITING A SINGLE SUBASSEMBLY

Once your assembly is created, you can edit individual subassemblies in the following way:

1. Pick the subassembly you would like to edit and right-click.

2. Select the Subassembly Properties option.

3. The Subassembly Properties dialog appears. Click the Subassembly Help button on the bottom right of the dialog if you would like to shortcut to the Help page that gives detailed information about the use of this particular subassembly.

4. Switch to the Parameters tab to access the same parameters you saw in the AutoCAD Properties palette when first placing the subassembly.

5. Click inside any field on the Parameters tab to make changes.

EDITING THE ENTIRE ASSEMBLY

Sometimes it is more efficient to edit all of the subassemblies in an assembly at once. Pick the assembly baseline marker, or any subassembly that is connected to the assembly you'd like to edit, and right-click. This time, however, select the Assembly Properties option from the shortcut menu.

RENAMING THE ASSEMBLY

The Information tab on the Assembly Properties dialog gives you an opportunity to rename your assembly and provide an optional description.

CHANGING PARAMETERS

The Construction tab on the Assembly Properties dialog houses each subassembly and its parameters. You can change the parameters for individual subassemblies by selecting the subassembly on the left side of the Construction tab and changing the desired parameter on the right side of the Construction tab.

RENAMING GROUPS AND SUBASSEMBLIES

Note that on the left side of the Construction tab, there is a list of groups. Under each group is a list of the subassemblies in use in your assembly. A new group is formed every time a subassembly is connected directly to the assembly marker.

For example, in Figure 10.19, we see Group - (13). The first subassembly under Group-(13) is the BasicLane - (74), and if we dig into its parameters on the right side of the dialog, it will tell us that this lane is attached to the right side of the assembly marker, a BasicCurbandGutter was attached to right side of the BasicLane, and a BasicSidewalk was attached to the right side of the BasicCurbandGutter. The next group, Group - (14), is identical, only attached to the left side of the assembly marker.

The automatic naming conventions are not terribly explanatory, and it would be convenient not to have to dig into the subassembly parameters to determine which side of the assembly a certain group may be. Later, when you are making complex corridors, you will be provided a list of subassemblies to choose from, and it would certainly be easier to figure out which BasicLane you need to choose when your choice is "Basic Lane Right" as opposed to "Basic Lane - (74)". Therefore, it is in your best interest to rename your subassemblies once you have built your assembly.

You can rename both groups and subassemblies on the Construction tab of the Assembly Properties dialog by selecting the entry you would like to rename, right-clicking, and selecting Rename.

There is no official best practice on renaming your groups and subassemblies, but you may find it useful if you designate what type of subassembly it is, what side of the assembly it falls on, and other distinguishing features, such as a Transition Lane (see Figure 10.20).

FIGURE 10.19

The Construction tab shows the default group and subassembly naming.

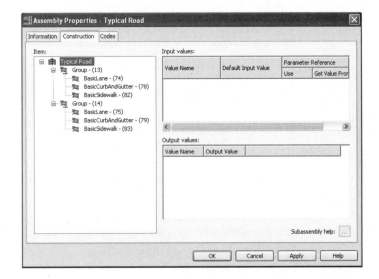

FIGURE 10.20

The Construction tab showing renamed groups and subassemblies

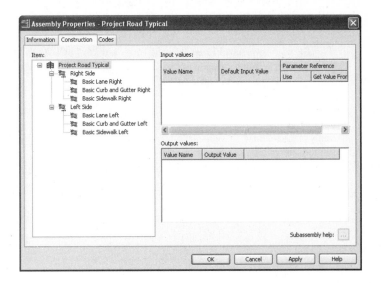

Creating Assemblies for Nonroad Uses

There are many uses for assemblies and their resulting corridor models aside from just road sections. The Corridor Modeling Catalog also includes components for retaining walls, rail sections, bridges, channels, pipe trenches, and much more. In Chapter 11, you will use a channel assembly and a pipe trench assembly to build corridor models. Let's investigate how those assemblies are put together by building a channel assembly for a simple stream section:

1. Create a new drawing from the _AutoCAD Civil 3D (Imperial) NCS Extended.dwt template, or continue working in your drawing from the first exercise in this chapter.

2. Choose Corridors ➢ Create Assembly.

3. Enter **Channel** in the Name text box. Confirm the Assembly Style text box is set to Basic and that Code Set Style is set to All Codes. Click OK.

4. Specify a location in your drawing for the assembly. Somewhere in the center of your screen where you have room to work is fine.

5. Choose Corridors ➢ Subassembly Tool Palettes and locate the Imperial-Channels And Ditches tool palette. Position your tool palette on your screen so that you can clearly see the assembly baseline.

6. Click the Channel button on the tool palette. The AutoCAD Properties palette appears. Position the palette on your screen so that you can clearly see both the assembly baseline and the tool palette.

7. Locate the Advanced section on the Design tab of the AutoCAD Properties palette. We'll place the channel with its default parameters and make adjustments through the Assembly Properties dialog, so don't change anything for now. Note that there is no Side parameter. This subassembly will be centered on the assembly marker.

8. The command line states Select marker point within assembly or [RETURN for Detached]:. Pick the assembly center point marker, and a channel will be placed on the assembly (see Figure 10.21).

FIGURE 10.21
The Channel subassembly placed on the assembly centerline marker

9. Press Esc to leave the assembly creation command and dismiss the palette.

10. Select the Assembly marker and right-click. Select the Assembly Properties option.

11. The Assembly Properties dialog appears. Switch to the Construction tab.

12. Select the Channel Assembly entry on the left side of the dialog. Click the Subassembly Help button located at the bottom right of the Construction tab of the dialog.

13. The Subassembly Reference portion from the AutoCAD Civil 3D 2008 Help file appears. Familiarize yourself with the diagram and input parameters for the Channel subassembly. Especially note the attachment point, bottom width, depth, and sideslope parameters. The attachment point indicates where our baseline alignment and profile will be applied.

14. Minimize the Help file.

15. We would like a simple stream section with a 6´-wide bottom, 6´-deep, 1:1 sideslopes, and no backslopes to match the engineer's specified design. Change the following parameters in the Assembly Properties dialog:

   ◆ Bottom Width: 6´

   ◆ Depth: 6´

   ◆ Left and Right Backslope Width: 0´

   ◆ Sideslope: 1:1

16. Click OK, and confirm that your completed assembly looks like Figure 10.22.

17. Save your drawing if you would like to use it in a future exercise.

FIGURE 10.22
A completed channel
assembly

 Real World Scenario

A PIPE TRENCH ASSEMBLY

Projects that include piping, such as sanitary sewers, storm drainage, gas pipelines, or similar structures, almost always include trenching. The trench must be carefully prepared to ensure the safety of the workers placing the pipe, as well as providing structural stability for the pipe in the form of bedding and compacted fill.

The corridor is an ideal tool for modeling pipe trenching. With the appropriate assembly combined with a pipe run alignment and profile, you can not only design a pipe trench, but also use cross-section tools to generate section views (Graphic), materials tables, and quantity takeoffs. The resulting corridor model can also be used to create a surface for additional analysis and use.

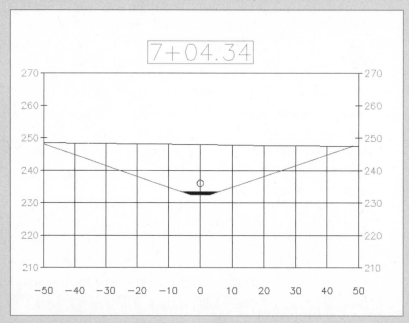

1. Create a new drawing using the _AutoCAD Civil 3D (Imperial) NCS Extended.dwt template, or continue working in your drawing from the previous exercise.

2. Choose Corridors ➤ Create Assembly.

3. Enter **Pipe Trench** in the Name text box to change the assembly's name. Confirm that the Assembly Style text box is set to Basic and Code Set Style is set to All Codes. Click OK.

4. Pick a location in your drawing for the assembly. Somewhere in the center of your screen where you have room to work is fine.

5. Choose Corridors ➤ Subassembly Tool Palettes and locate the Imperial-Channels And Ditches tool palette. Position the tool palette on your screen so that you can clearly see the assembly baseline.

6. Click the TrenchPipe1 button on the tool palette. The AutoCAD Properties palette appears. Position the AutoCAD Properties palette on your screen so that you can clearly see both the assembly baseline and the tool palette.

7. Locate the Advanced section on the Design tab of the AutoCAD Properties palette. This section will list the PipeTrench1 parameters. We'll place PipeTrench1 with its default parameters and make adjustments through the Assembly Properties dialog, so don't change anything for now. Note that there is no Side parameter. This subassembly will be placed centered on the assembly marker.

8. Note the command line states `Select marker point within assembly or [RETURN for Detached]:`. Pick the assembly center point marker. A PipeTrench1 subassembly will be placed on the assembly as shown.

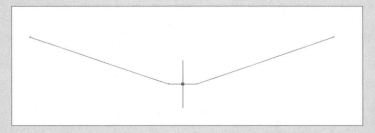

9. Press Esc to leave the assembly creation command and dismiss the AutoCAD Properties palette.

10. Select the assembly marker and right-click. Select the Assembly Properties option.

11. The Assembly Properties dialog appears. Switch to the Construction tab.

12. Select the TrenchPipe1 assembly entry on the left side of the dialog. Click the Subassembly Help button located at the bottom-right corner.

13. The Subassembly Reference portion of the AutoCAD Civil 3D 2008 Help file appears. Familiarize yourself with the diagram and input parameters for the TrenchPipe1 subassembly. In this case, the profile grade line will attach to a profile drawn to represent the pipe invert. Since the trench will be excavated deeper than the pipe invert to accommodate gravel bedding, we will use the bedding depth parameter in a moment. Also note under the Target Parameters that this subassembly needs a surface target to determine where the sideslopes terminate.

14. Minimize the Help file.

15. We would like a 3´-deep and a 6´-wide pipe trench with 3:1 sideslopes and 1´ of gravel bedding. Change the following parameters on the Assembly Properties dialog:

    ◆ Bedding Depth: 1´

    ◆ Offset To Bottom: -3´

    ◆ Sideslope: 3:1

16. Click OK.

17. Confirm that your completed assembly looks like the graphic shown here, and save your drawing.

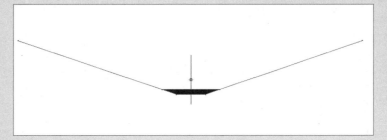

This assembly will be used to build a pipe trench corridor in Chapter 11.

Working with Generic Subassemblies

Despite the over 60 subassemblies available in the Corridor Modeling Catalog, there comes a time when you may not find the perfect component. Perhaps none of the channel assemblies exactly meet your design specifications and you'd like to make a more customized assembly, or neither of the sidewalk subassemblies allow for the proper boulevard slopes. Maybe you'd like to try to do some preliminary lot grading using your corridor, or mark a certain point on your subassembly so that you can extract important features easily.

All of the above items can be tackled by programming your own custom subassemblies, creating a custom subassembly from a polyline, but better yet they can all be handled using subassemblies from the Generic Subassembly Catalog (see Figure 10.23). These simple and flexible components can be used to build almost anything, although they lack the coded intelligence of some of the more intricate assemblies (such as knowing if they are paved, grass, or similar, and understanding things like subbase depth, and so on).

FIGURE 10.23
The Generic Subassembly Catalog

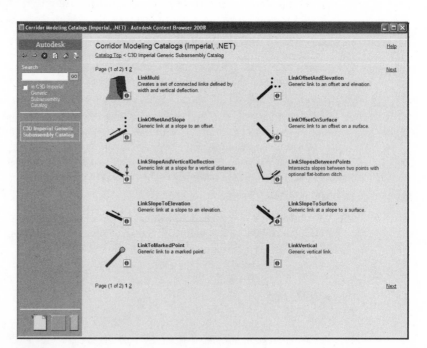

Enhancing Assemblies using Generic Links

Let's look at two examples where you might take advantage of generic links.

The first example involves the typical road section we built in the first exercise in this chapter. We saw that the BasicSidewalk does not allow for a sloped sidewalk or sloped buffer strips. The UrbanSidewalk does have a slope parameter, but each buffer strip has the same slope as the sidewalk itself. If we needed a 6´-wide buffer strip with a 3 percent slope, then a 5´ sidewalk with a

2 percent slope, followed by another buffer strip that is 10′ wide with a slope of 5 percent, we can use generic links to assist in the construction of the proper assembly.

1. Open the `Sidewalk Start.dwg` file or continue working in your drawing from the first exercise in this chapter.

2. Zoom in on the road section assembly. If you are working in your drawing from the first exercise in the chapter, erase the BasicSidewalk subassemblies from either side of your assembly.

3. Choose Corridors ➢ Subassembly Tool Palettes and locate the Imperial-Generic tool palette. Position the tool palette on your screen so that you can clearly see the assembly baseline.

4. Click the LinkWidthandSlope button, and the AutoCAD Properties dialog appears. Position the dialog on your screen so that you can clearly see both the assembly baseline and the tool palette.

5. Locate the Advanced section on the Design tab of the AutoCAD Properties dialog. This section lists the parameters for this subassembly. Change the parameters as follows to create the first buffer strip:

   ◆ Side: Right

   ◆ Width: 6′

   ◆ Slope: 3%

6. Note the command line states `Select marker point within assembly or [RETURN for Detached]:`. Select the circular point marker on the right BasicCurbandGutter subassembly, which represents the top rear of the curb. A Link subassembly appears, as shown in Figure 10.24.

7. Switch to the Imperial-Structures tab of the tool palette. Click the UrbanSidewalk button, and the AutoCAD Properties palette appears. Position the palette on your screen so that you can clearly see it, the assembly baseline, and the tool palette.

8. Locate the Advanced section on the Design tab of the AutoCAD Properties palette. This section lists the parameters for the UrbanSidewalk subassembly. Change the parameters as follows to create the sidewalk:

   ◆ Side: Right

   ◆ Width: 5′

   ◆ Slope: 2%

   ◆ Inside/Outside Boulevard Width: 0′

FIGURE 10.24
The Generic Link
subassembly

9. Note the command line states `Select marker point within assembly or [RETURN for Detached]:`. Select the circular point marker on the right LinkWidthandSlope subassembly. An Urban Sidewalk subassembly appears, as shown in Figure 10.25.

10. Switch to the Imperial-Generic tab of the tool palette. Click the LinkWidthandSlope, and the AutoCAD Properties palette appears. Position the palette on your screen so that you can still see the assembly baseline and the tool palette.

11. Locate the Advanced section on the Design tab of the AutoCAD Properties dialog. This section lists the parameters for the LinkWidthandSlope that we saw in step 5. Change the parameters as follows to create the second buffer strip:

    ◆ Side: Right

    ◆ Width: 10′

    ◆ Slope: 5%

    Your drawing should now look like Figure 10.26.

12. To complete the left side of the assembly, repeat steps 3 through 11 and change the Side parameter for each subassembly to the Left option. The completed assembly should look like Figure 10.27.

13. Save your drawing if you would like to use it in a future exercise.

We have now created a custom sidewalk boulevard for a typical road.

FIGURE 10.25
The urban sidewalk subassembly

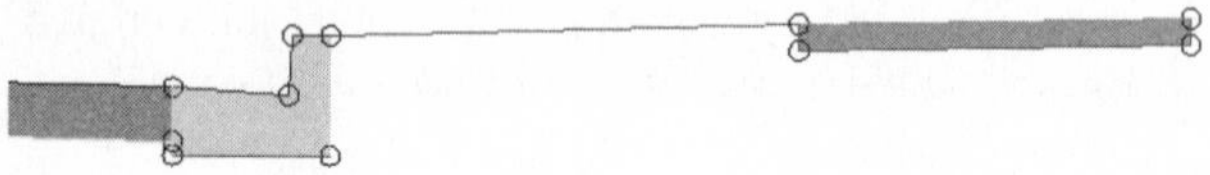

FIGURE 10.26
The sidewalk and buffer strips

FIGURE 10.27
The completed assembly

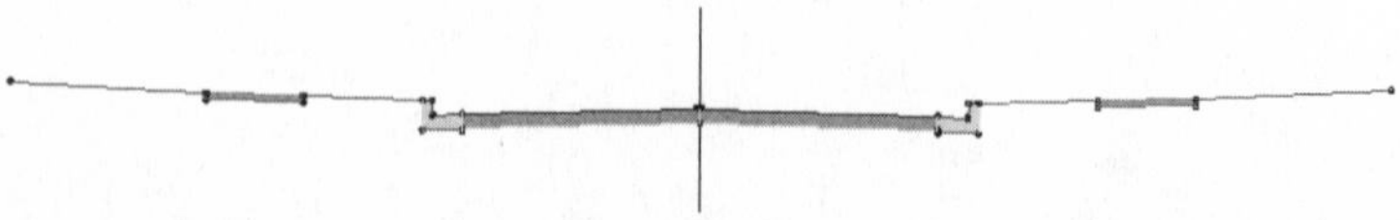

The second example involves the channel section we built earlier in this chapter. Although the TrenchPipe1 subassembly includes a surface target, the Channel assembly does not. This exercise will lead you through using the LinkSlopetoSurface subassembly, which will provide a surface target to the Channel assembly, that will seek the target assembly at a 25 percent slope. For more information about surface targets, see Chapters 11 and 12.

1. Open the `Channel Link Start.dwg` file or continue working in your drawing from the channel exercise in this chapter.

2. Zoom in on the Channel assembly.

3. Choose Corridors ➤ Subassembly Tool Palettes and locate the Imperial-Generic tool palette. Position the tool palette on your screen so that you can clearly see the assembly baseline.

4. Click the LinkSlopetoSurface button. The AutoCAD Properties palette appears. Position the palette on your screen so that you can still see both the assembly baseline and the tool palette.

5. Locate the Advanced section on the Design tab of the AutoCAD Properties palette. This section lists the parameters for the LinkWidthandSlope subassembly. Change the parameters as follows to create a surface target link:

   ◆ Side: Right

   ◆ Slope: 25%

6. Note the command line states `Select marker point within assembly or [RETURN for Detached]:`. Click the circular point marker in the upper right on the Channel subassembly that is farthest away. A surface target link appears (see Figure 10.28).

7. To complete the left side of the assembly, repeat steps 4 through 6, and change the Side parameter to the Left option.

8. The completed assembly should look like Figure 10.29.

Adding a surface link to a channel assembly provides a surface target for the assembly. When designing a channel, it is important to tie into existing ground. In its original form, the Channel subassembly does not include a target parameter that would allow you to choose an existing ground; therefore, you would need to do quite a bit of hand grading between the top of bank and existing ground. Now that you have added the LinkSlopetoSurface, you can simply specify your existing ground as the surface target, and the subassembly will grade between top of bank and the surface for you. Additional flexibility for connecting to existing ground can be achieved with the more complicated Daylight subassemblies, as discussed in the next section.

FIGURE 10.28
The attachment location for the LinkSlopetoSurface subassembly

FIGURE 10.29
The completed channel assembly

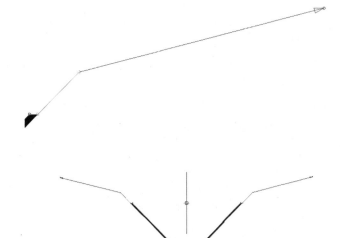

Working with Daylight Subassemblies

Most typical sections have many absolute requirements, such as a cross slope for a lane or a height of curb, but from that last engineered point on the left and right of a typical section, there are some design decisions to be made that often have some flexibility.

In the example of the typical road section from the first part of this chapter, the engineer needs to design the grade from the last buffer strip until the section ties into existing ground. The location where the design meets existing ground is known as *daylighting*.

Daylight subassemblies provide tools to assist the engineer in meeting their design intent between existing ground and the typical section. Some Daylight subassemblies are shown in Figure 10.30.

FIGURE 10.30
Some Daylight subassemblies in the Corridor Modeling Catalog

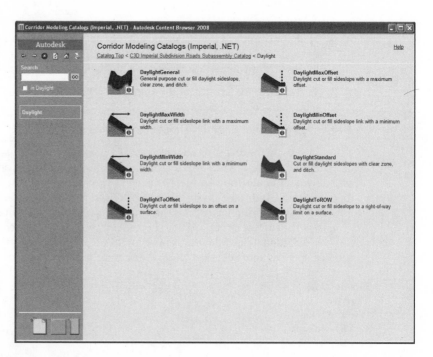

Enhancing an Assembly with a Daylight Subassembly

Using the typical road section from the first exercise in this chapter, our subdivision layout allows for grading 25′ from the end of the sidewalk buffer strip. This grading has a 4:1 maximum for both cut-and-fill situations. In the following exercise, we will use the DaylightMaxWidth subassembly, which contains parameters for specifying the grading width and the maximum cut-and-fill slopes.

1. Open the Daylight Start.dwg file or continue working in any drawing from this chapter that contains a typical road section.

2. Zoom in on the typical road section assembly.

3. Choose Corridors ➢ Subassembly Tool Palettes and locate the Imperial-Daylight tool palette. Position the tool palette on your screen so that you can clearly see the assembly baseline.

4. Click the DaylightMaxWidth button on the tool palette. The AutoCAD Properties palette appears. Position the palette on your screen so that you can still clearly see both the assembly baseline and the tool palette.

5. Locate the Advanced section on the Design tab of the AutoCAD Properties palette. This section lists the parameters for the DaylightMaxWidth subassembly. Change the following parameters to create the daylight as required:

   ◆ Side: Right

   ◆ Cut Slope: 6´

   ◆ Fill Slope: 3%

   ◆ Max Width: 25

6. Note the command line states Select marker point within assembly or [RETURN for Detached]:. Select the circular point marker on the farthest right link. The subassembly appears as in Figure 10.31.

7. Press Esc to exit the assembly creation command.

8. Pick the DaylightMaxWidth subassembly, then right-click. Select the Subassembly Properties option.

9. Switch to the Parameters tab in the Subassembly Properties dialog.

10. Click the Subassembly Help button in the lower-right corner. The Subassembly Reference should open in a new window. Familiarize yourself with the options for the DaylightMax-Width subassembly, especially noting there are optional parameters for a lined material, a mandatory daylight surface target, and an optional alignment target that can be used for the maximum width.

11. Minimize the Subassembly Reference window.

12. To complete the left side of the assembly, repeat steps 3 through 6, changing the Side parameter for each subassembly to the Left option. The completed assembly should look like Figure 10.32.

FIGURE 10.31
Placement of the
DaylightMaxWidth
subassembly

FIGURE 10.32
The completed
assembly

WHEN TO IGNORE PARAMETERS

The first time you attempt to use many Daylight subassemblies, you may become overwhelmed by the sheer number of parameters, as shown here.

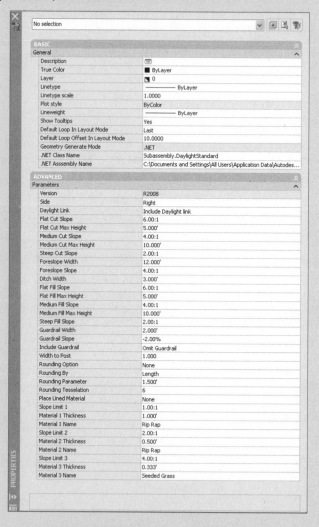

The good news is that many of these parameters are unnecessary for most uses. For example, many Daylight subassemblies, such as DaylightGeneral, include multiple cut-and-fill widths for complicated cases where the design may call for test scenarios. If your design does not require this level of detail, simply leave those parameters as zero. Some Daylight subassemblies include guardrail options. If your situation does not require a guardrail, leave the default parameter set to the Omit Guardrail option and ignore it from then on. Another common confusing parameter is the Place Lined Material option, which can be used for riprap or erosion-control matting. If your design does not require this much detail, simply ensure that this parameter is set to the None option and ignore the thickness, name, and slope parameters that follow.

One parameter that cannot be ignored, however, is the Target Surface. The entire function of daylighting is to tie into a target surface. Without that target, many of the daylight parameters have no point of reference, and often your Daylight subassembly will not work and you will get errors upon building your corridor.

That being said, the Daylight link can be temporarily omitted on subassemblies where ditch or bench construction occurs if your target surface isn't ready. An example of this might be if you are tying into an adjacent plot of land that is already under construction. When the construction is finished and you have obtained the final surface model, then you would want to change the parameter to include the Daylight link.

If you are ever in doubt about which parameters can be omitted, investigate the Help file for that subassembly.

ALTERNATIVE DAYLIGHT SUBASSEMBLIES

There are at least a dozen daylight subassemblies that vary from a simple cut-fill parameter to a more complicated benching or basin design. Your engineering requirements may dictate something more challenging than the exercise in this section. Here are some alternative Daylight subassemblies and the situations where you might use them. For more information on any of these subassemblies and the many other daylighting choices, see the AutoCAD Civil 3D 2008 Subassembly Reference in the Help file.

DaylightToROW

The DaylightToROW subassembly (see Figure 10.33) forces a tie-in to the target surface using the controlling parameter of ROW Offset From Baseline. Since this value is calculated from the baseline location, you can place lanes, sidewalks, curbs, and more between the baseline and the Daylight subassembly and not worry about recalculating the width of the Daylight subassembly like you would with DaylightMaxWidth. This subassembly is most useful in design situations where you absolutely must not grade outside of the ROW.

FIGURE 10.33
The DaylightToROW subassembly

BasicSideSlopeCutDitch

In addition to including cut-and-fill parameters, the BasicSideSlopeCutDitch subassembly (see Figure 10.34) is capable of creating a ditch when it detects a cut condition. This is most useful for road sections that require a roadside ditch through cut sections but omit it when passing through areas of fill. If your corridor model is revised in a way that changes the location of cut-and-fill boundaries, the ditch will automatically adjust.

FIGURE 10.34
The BasicSide-
SlopeCutDitch
subassembly

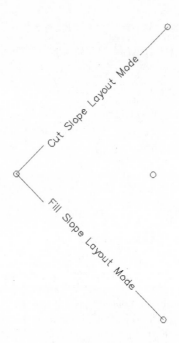

DaylightBasin

Many engineers must design berms to contain roadside swales when the road design is in the fill condition. The process for determining where these berms are required is often tedious. The DaylightBasin subassembly (see Figure 10.35) provides a tool for automatically creating these "false berms." The subassembly contains parameters for the specification of a basin (which can be easily adapted to most roadside ditch cross sections as well) and parameters for a containment berm that only appear when the subassembly runs into areas of roadside cut.

Saving Subassemblies and Assemblies for Later Use

Customizing subassemblies and creating assemblies are both simple tasks. However, you will save time in future projects if you store them for later use.

FIGURE 10.35
The DaylightBasin
subassembly

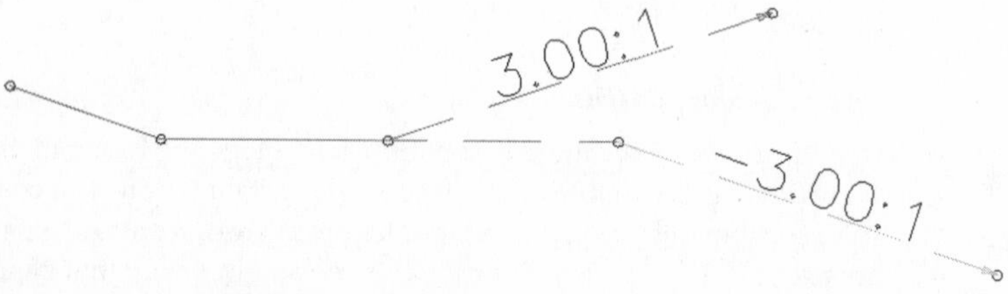

Storing a Customized Subassembly on a Tool Palette

A typical jurisdiction usually has a finite number of allowable lane widths, curb types, and other components. It would be extremely beneficial to have the right subassemblies with the parameters already set available on your tool palette.

The following exercise will lead you through storing a customized subassembly on a tool palette:

1. Open the `Storing Subassemblies and Assemblies.dwg` file.

2. Choose Corridors ➤ Subassembly Tool Palettes and locate the Imperial-Basic tool palette.

3. Right-click in the tool palette area and select New Palette to create a new tool palette. Enter **My Road Parts** in the Name text box.

4. Select the right lane from the assembly. You'll know it is selected when you can see it highlighted and the grip appears at the assembly baseline.

5. Left-click on the lane anywhere except the grip location until you see an arrow-shaped glyph appear. Once the arrow appears, continue to hold down the left mouse button, move your mouse to the tool palette, and release it once you are over the tool palette.

6. Upon release, an entry should appear on your tool palette for BasicLane. Right-click on this entry and select the Properties option. The Tool Properties dialog appears (Figure 10.36).

7. Enter **10-Foot Wide Basic Lane at 2%** in the Name text box. You can also change the image, description, and other parameters in this dialog. Click OK.

8. Repeat this process for each lane and each curb, if desired, in the drawing, Your resulting tool palette will look similar to Figure 10.37.

Note that the tool palette entries for each subassembly point to the location of the `Subassembly .NET` directory, and not to this drawing. If you share this tool palette, make sure that the subassembly directory is either identical or accessible to the person you are sharing with.

FIGURE 10.36

The Tool Properties dialog

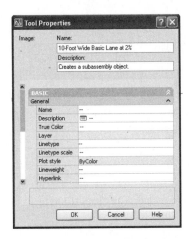

FIGURE 10.37
A tool palette with
three customized
subassemblies

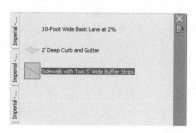

Storing a Completed Assembly on a Tool Palette

In addition to storing individual subassemblies on a tool palette, it would often be useful to warehouse entire completed assemblies. Many jurisdictions have several standard road cross sections and once each standard assembly has been built, you can save time on future similar projects by pulling in a prebuilt assembly.

The process for storing an assembly on a tool palette involves converting the assembly into a block with an insertion point at the assembly baseline. Then, you drag this block onto a tool palette. If you edit the tool palette entry to explode the block upon insertion, a new assembly is created in future drawings.

1. Open the `Storing Subassemblies and Assemblies.dwg` file.

2. Enter **block**⏎ in the command line.

3. The Block Definition dialog appears. Enter **Typical 50-Foot ROW Road Section** in the Name text box.

4. Click the Pick Point button to choose a base point at the intersection of the assembly baseline and the two lanes.

5. Click the Select Objects button to make a crossing window that includes the first assembly baseline and all associated subassemblies.

6. Uncheck Open in the Block Editor box. Click OK.

7. Enter **Insert**⏎ in the command line.

8. Insert the Typical 50-Foot ROW Road Section block into the drawing in any location where you have room to work. Do not explode this block.

9. Use the same technique from the previous exercise, and grab and drag the entire block from the drawing to the tool palette.

10. Select the new entry on your tool palette and right-click. Select the Properties option, and the Tool Properties dialog appears.

11. In the Tool Properties dialog, change the Explode option from No to Yes. This will automatically explode the block upon insertion to a new drawing so that it becomes an assembly in that drawing.

Other options in the Tool Properties dialog can be adjusted, including the name, description, and image. Also note under Source File that this tool references the drawing that houses the block. For this reason, it is usually a good idea to create a warehouse drawing in a shared network location for common completed assemblies and create all of your assembly blocks in that drawing before dragging them on to the tool palette.

The Bottom Line

Create a typical road assembly with lanes, curb, gutter, and sidewalk. Most corridors are built to model roads. The most common assembly used in these road corridors is some variation of a typical road section consisting of lanes, curb, gutter, and sidewalk.

Master It Create a new drawing from the `_AutoCAD Civil 3D (Imperial) NCS Extended .dwt` template. Build a symmetrical assembly using BasicLane, BasicCurbandGutter, and BasicSidewalk. Use widths and slopes of your choosing.

Edit an assembly. Once an assembly has been created, it can be easily edited to reflect a design change. Often, at the beginning of a project, you won't know the final lane width. You can build your assembly and corridor model with one lane width, then later change the width and rebuild the model immediately.

Master It Working in the same drawing, edit the width of each BasicLane to 14´, and change the cross slope of each BasicLane to -3.08%.

Add daylighting to a typical road assembly. Often the most difficult part of a designer's job is figuring out how to grade the area between the last hard engineered point in the cross section (such as the back of a sidewalk) and existing ground. There is an extensive catalog of daylighting subassemblies to assist with this task.

Master It Working in the same drawing, add the DaylightMinWidth to both sides of your typical road assembly. Establish a minimum width of 10´.

Chapter 11

Easy Does It: Basic Corridors

The corridor object is a three-dimensional road model that combines the horizontal geometry of an alignment, the vertical geometry of a profile, and the cross-sectional geometry of an assembly.

Corridors range from extremely simple roads to complicated highways and interchanges. This chapter will focus on building several simple corridors that can be used to model and design roads, channels, and trenches.

By the end of this chapter, you'll be able to:

◆ Build a single baseline corridor from an alignment, profile, and assembly

◆ Create a corridor surface

◆ Add an automatic boundary to a corridor surface

Understanding Corridors

It its simplest form, a corridor is a three-dimensional combination of an alignment, a profile, and an assembly (see Figure 11.1).

We can also build corridors with additional combinations of alignments, profiles, and assemblies to make complicated intersections, interchanges, and branching streams (see Figure 11.2).

FIGURE 11.1
A simple corridor

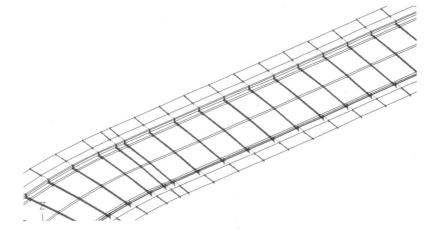

The horizontal properties of the alignment, the vertical properties of the profile, and the cross-sectional properties of the assembly are merged together to form a dynamic model that can be used to build surfaces, sample cross sections, and much more.

Most commonly, we think of corridors as being used to model roads, but they can also be adapted to model berms, streams, lagoons, trails, and even parking lots (see Figure 11.3).

FIGURE 11.2
An intersection modeled with a corridor

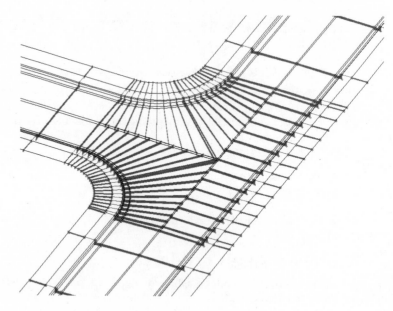

FIGURE 11.3
A complex stream modeled with a corridor

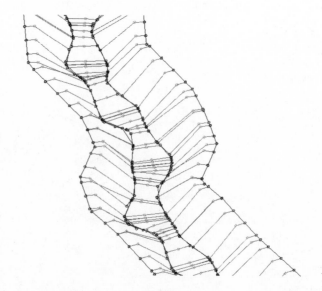

Creating a Simple Road Corridor

The first ingredient in any corridor is an alignment. This alignment is referred to as a *baseline*. A baseline requires a corresponding profile and an assembly. A corridor can have multiple baselines, and a baseline can be divided into *regions*. We'll see how regions are used a little later in this chapter. Corridors with multiple baselines will be discussed in Chapter 12.

Before building a corridor, even a simple corridor, it is important to make sure your alignments, profiles, assemblies, and subassemblies have good names. When we are creating and iterating our design, we often use its default name, such as Alignment-64 or Basic Lane-(3)(3), instead of a much more meaningful name.

If you get into the habit of giving your objects significant and meaningful names—even for the simplest corridor—you will be rewarded when you build larger corridors (see Figure 11.4).

FIGURE 11.4

Check the names of your alignments, profiles, assemblies, and subassemblies.

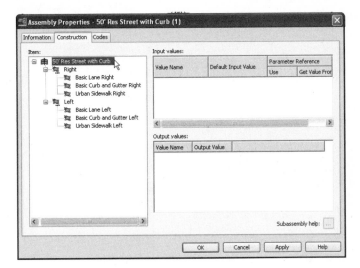

This exercise will give you hands-on experience in building a corridor model from an alignment, a profile, and an assembly:

1. Open the Simple Corridor.dwg file. Note that the drawing has an alignment, a profile view with two profiles, and an assembly, as well as an existing ground surface.

2. Choose Corridors ➤ Create Simple Corridor. The Create Simple Corridor dialog opens.

3. In the Name text box, give your corridor a meaningful name, such as **Project Road**. Keep the default values for Corridor Style and Corridor Layer (see Figure 11.5).

4. Click OK to dismiss the dialog.

5. At the Select baseline alignment <or press enter key to select from list>: prompt, pick the alignment in the drawing. Alternatively, you could press ↵ and select your alignment from a list.

6. At the `Select a profile <or press enter key to select from list>`: prompt, pick the Finished Ground profile in the drawing. Alternatively, you could press ↵ and select your profile from a list.

7. At the `Select an assembly <or press enter key to select from list>`: prompt, pick the assembly in the drawing. Alternatively, you could press ↵ and select your assembly from a list.

8. The program will process and build the corridor, which will appear over the road centerline alignment, as shown in Figure 11.6.

FIGURE 11.5
Change the corridor name to something meaningful for easy bookkeeping.

FIGURE 11.6
The completed simple corridor

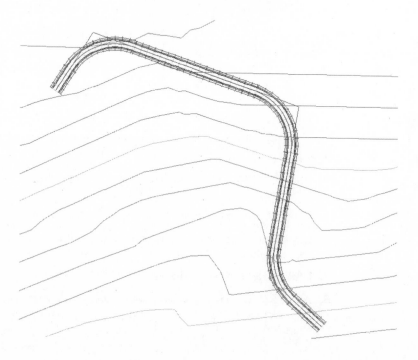

Utilities for Viewing Your Corridor

Once your corridor is built, chances are you will want to examine the corridor in section view and use 3D to view the model and check for problems. For a station-by-station look at a corridor, choose Corridors ➤ View/Edit Corridor Section Tools from the menu bar. Pick a corridor, and the View/Edit Corridor Section Tools toolbar opens (see Figure 11.7).

The View/Edit Corridor Section Tools toolbar allows you to move forward and backward through your corridor to see what each section looks like.

To view your corridor in an isometric view, use View ➤ 3D Views and choose one of the isometric choices.

FIGURE 11.7
The View/Edit
Corridor Section
Tools toolbar

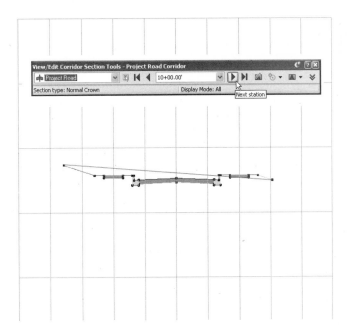

Rebuilding Your Corridor

A corridor is a *dynamic* model—which means if you modify any of the objects that were used to create the corridor, the corridor must be updated to reflect those changes. For example, if you make a change to the Finished Ground profile, the corridor needs to be rebuilt to reflect the new design. The same principle applies to changes to alignments, assemblies, target surfaces, and any other corridor ingredients or parameters.

You have two options for rebuilding corridors. The first is to manually rebuild your corridor by right-clicking on the corridor object itself and choosing Rebuild Corridor from the shortcut menu. The second option is to right-click on the corridor name in the Corridor collection in Prospector, and select Rebuild – Automatic (see Figure 11.8). Although Rebuild – Automatic is great for small corridors or while you are actively iterating a portion of your corridor and would like to see the results immediately, it is not a good idea to have this set as a general rule. Every time you make a change that even remotely affects your corridor, the corridor will go through a rebuilding process, during which you cannot work. If you have a large corridor or you need to make a series of changes, this can be extremely disruptive.

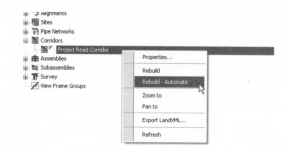

FIGURE 11.8
Right-click on the corridor name in the Corridor collection in Prospector to rebuild it.

Common Corridor Problems

When you build your first few corridors, many new users encounter several problems. Here is a list of some of the most typical problems and how to solve them:

Problem Your corridor seems to fall off a cliff, meaning the beginning or ending station of your corridor drops down to zero, as shown in Figure 11.9.

Typical Cause Your profile is not exactly the same length as the baseline alignment.

Fix Adjust your profile to be exactly as long as your alignment or edit your corridor region to begin/end before the trouble area. A good guide for determining if your profile is the same length as your alignment is by looking at the length of your Existing Ground profile. Unless your alignment goes off the surface, your Existing Ground line should be exactly the same length as your alignment. Using the Endpoint osnaps is a good way to check whether they are the same length. In Figure 11.10, you can see that the finished grade profile has been snapped to the endpoint of the Existing Ground profile.

Problem Your corridor seems to take longer to build and sample at a higher frequency that you intended. Also, your daylighting seems to be nonexistent (see Figure 11.11).

FIGURE 11.9
A corridor that drops down to zero

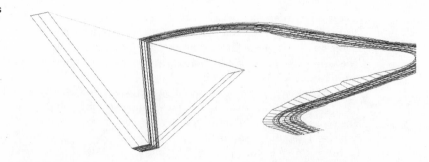

FIGURE 11.10
Your proposed profile and the Existing Ground profile must be the same length.

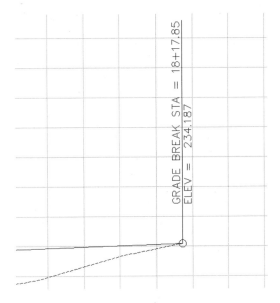

FIGURE 11.11
An example of unexpected corridor frequency

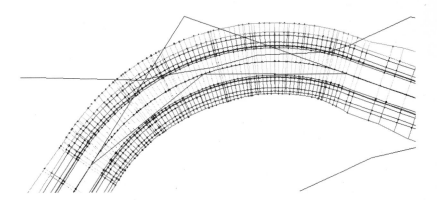

Typical Cause   You accidentally chose the Existing Ground profile instead of the Finished Ground profile for your baseline profile. Most corridors are set up to sample at every vertical geometry point, and a sampled profile, such as the Existing Ground profile, has many more vertical geometry points than a layout profile (in this case, the Finished Ground profile). These additional points on the Existing Ground profile cause the unexpected sample lines and flags that something is wrong.

Fix   Always use care to choose the correct profile. Either physically pick the profile on screen or make sure your naming conventions clearly define your finished grade as finished grade. If your corridor is already built, pick your corridor, right-click, and choose Corridor Properties. On the Parameters tab of the Corridor Properties dialog, change the baseline profile from Existing Ground to Finished Ground. Figure 11.12 shows the Parameters tab with Finished Ground properly listed as the baseline profile.

FIGURE 11.12

The Parameters tab of the Corridor Properties dialog

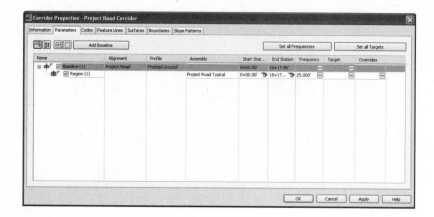

Corridor Anatomy

Corridors are made up of several components. If you explore the corridor you created in the last section, you should see the four components that make up every corridor. Points and links are coded into the subassemblies that comprise the assembly. Feature lines glue the points and links together along the baseline. Shapes, which are not required for the actual model building, add an additional visual cue for material type.

A corridor is a collection of cross sections at a given frequency. The cross section comes from the assembly. In Figure 11.13, you can see that a corridor cross section looks very much like an assembly. Note the location of points, links, and shapes in the cross section. Links connect the points, and the shapes fill in the areas created by links with color.

FIGURE 11.13

A single corridor section

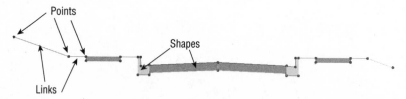

The cross sections are placed at intervals along the corridor baseline and then connected with corridor feature lines (see Figure 11.14). The corridor feature lines connect points from one cross section to the next.

Points

Not to be confused with Civil 3D COGO points or AutoCAD points, corridor points are at the foundation of a corridor section. They provide the first dimension of the corridor cross section.

As we discussed in Chapter 10, points are coded at the time of subassembly programming to have an understanding of their identity. A corridor point knows whether it is a Crown, an Edge Of Travel Way, an Edge Of Paved Shoulder, or one of 50 other standard point codes. These point codes indicate where the point can be found on the subassembly. For example, a point that has the Crown point code will appear at the crown of a road lane subassembly, and Crown-coded points will be placed in each cross section of the corridor model in the same location.

Figure 11.15 shows the same cross section from Figure 11.14, with only the points turned on.

FIGURE 11.14

A corridor is a collection of cross sections connected with feature lines.

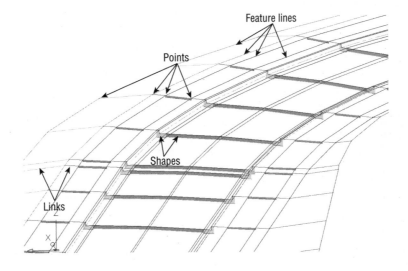

FIGURE 11.15

Corridor points in cross section

Links

Links provide the second dimension to the corridor cross section. Think of links as special, intelligent lines that connect the corridor points. Like points, links are coded at the time of subassembly programming to understand that they are a Top, Base, Pave, or one of the 18 other standard link codes. Similar to point codes, link codes indicate where the links are used. For example, links that are assigned to the Top link code connect points that are located at the finished grade surface regardless of whether they are paved or unpaved, whereas links assigned to the Pave link code are used to link points representing only the paved elements of the finished grade. A link can be assigned more than one code, if applicable. For example, a road lane would be assigned both Top and Pave, whereas a grassed buffer strip would only be assigned Top.

Figure 11.16 also shows the same cross section from Figure 11.14, except now both the points and links are shown.

FIGURE 11.16

A cross-sectional view of corridor points connected with links

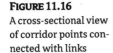

Feature Lines

Points and links come from subassemblies, but feature lines are created when the corridor is built. Feature lines are the third dimension that takes a corridor from being simply a collection of cross sections to being a model with meaningful flow (see Figure 11.17).

Corridor feature lines are similar to grading feature lines, which will be studied in detail in Chapter 16. Both types of feature lines are stylized using Feature Line styles. Corridor feature lines can also be used as breaklines when a corridor surface is built, much like grading feature lines can be added to a surface as breaklines.

Corridor feature lines are first drawn connecting the same point codes. For example, a feature line will work its way down the corridor and connect all the TopCurb points. If there are TopCurb points on the entire length of your corridor, then the feature line does not have any decisions to make. If your corridor changes from having a curb to having a grassed buffer or ditch, the feature line needs to figure out where to go next.

The Feature Lines tab of the Corridor Properties dialog has a dropdown menu called Branching (see Figure 11.18), with two options—Inward and Outward. Inward branching forces the feature line to connect to the next point it finds toward the baseline. Outward branching forces the feature line to connect to the next point it finds away from the baseline.

FIGURE 11.17
A three-dimensional view showing feature lines connecting each cross section

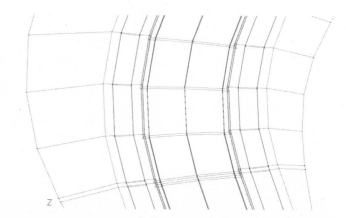

FIGURE 11.18
The Feature Lines tab of the Corridor Properties dialog

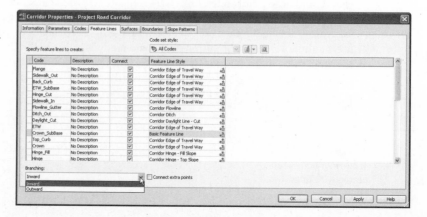

As mentioned earlier, a feature line will only connect the same point codes by default. However, the Feature Lines tab of the Corridor Properties dialog allows you to eliminate certain feature lines on the basis of the point code. For example, if there was some reason you did not want your TopCurb points connected with a feature line, you could toggle that feature line off.

Shapes

Like points and links, shapes are also coded as part of the subassembly. Shapes are defined from links that form a closed polygon, such as a course of pavement, a gravel-base course, or a thickness of sidewalk. Figure 11.19 shows shapes that represent a sidewalk, a curb, and pavement.

Shapes are not a critical part of the corridor model, but they do provide visual enhancement to assist in viewing sections of the corridor, as well as for use in cross-sectional views.

FIGURE 11.19
Shapes can represent pavement, a curb, and a sidewalk.

Adding a Surface Target for Daylighting

A road cross section between centerline and right-of-way is usually clearly defined by the local road–design specifications. The area between the right-of-way and the existing ground surface, however, is not always so straightforward. In Chapter 10, we talked about daylighting subassemblies that can assist in grading this in-between area.

A daylighting subassembly needs to understand which surface it is targeting. This exercise will teach you how to assign the target surface to a corridor:

1. Open the `Corridor Daylight.dwg` file. Note that the drawing contains an alignment, a profile view with two profiles, and an assembly, as well as an Existing Ground surface.

2. Pan over to the subassembly. In addition to the lanes, curbs, and sidewalk, there is a Daylight subassembly built into the assembly.

FIGURE 11.20
A rendered corridor showing daylighting between the sidewalk and existing ground

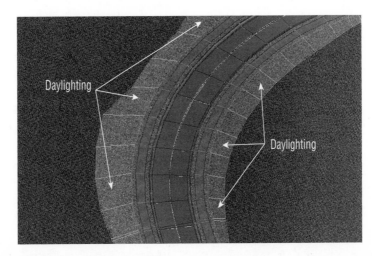

3. Choose Corridors ➤ Create Simple Corridor.

4. Create your corridor exactly as you did in the first exercise in this chapter. Follow the prompts to pick the alignment, profile, and assembly. The Target Mapping dialog appears after each object has been picked.

5. Click in the Object Name column field in the Target Mapping dialog. The Pick A Surface dialog appears and prompts you to choose a surface for the daylighting subassembly to target.

6. Select the Existing Ground surface. Click OK to dismiss the dialog. Click OK again to dismiss the Target Mapping dialog. Make sure Steps 5 & 6 are performed for both the left and right Daylight subassemblies.

7. The corridor will build and create daylighting points, links, and feature lines that show how it ties into the Existing Ground surface. The result should be similar to Figure 11.21.

FIGURE 11.21
The completed corridor with daylighting

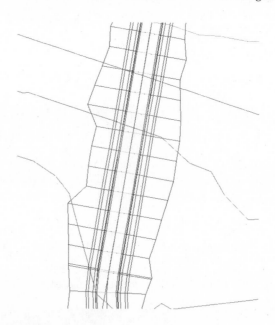

Common Daylighting Problems

Adding a surface target throws another variable into the mix. Here is a list of some of the most typical problems new users face and how to solve them:

Problem   Your corridor doesn't show daylighting even though you have a Daylight subassembly on your assembly. You may get a Target Object Not Found or a similar error message in Event Viewer.

Typical Cause   You forgot to set the surface target when you created your surface.

Fix   If your corridor is already built, pick your corridor, right-click, and select Corridor Properties. On the Parameters tab of the Corridor Properties dialog, click Set All Targets. The Target Mapping dialog opens, and its first entry is Surfaces. Click in the Object Name column field. This will prompt you to choose a surface for the daylighting subassembly to target.

Problem Your corridor seems to be missing patches of daylighting. You may also get an error message in Event Viewer.

Typical Cause Your target surface doesn't fully extend the full length of your corridor or your target surface is too narrow at certain locations.

Fix Add more data to your target surface so that it is large enough to accommodate daylighting down the full length of the corridor. If this is not possible, omit daylighting through those specific stations, and once your corridor is built, do hand grading using feature lines or grading objects. You can also investigate other subassemblies such as Link Offset To Elevation that will meet your design intention without requiring a surface target.

Problem Your corridor daylighting falls short of a tie-in to the existing ground surface. You may get an error message in Event Viewer, such as No Intersection With Link Found.

Typical Cause Your Daylight subassembly parameters are too restrictive to grade all the way to your target surface. The Daylight link cannot find the target surface within the grade, width, or other parameters you've set in the subassembly properties.

Fix Revisit your Daylight subassembly settings to give the program a wider offset or steeper grade. If your settings cannot be adjusted, you'll have to adjust your horizontal and/or vertical design to properly grade.

Applying a Hatch Pattern to Corridor

In this chapter and in Chapter 10, we learned that links have codes that give them intelligence about what part of the road they are on. These codes can be used to apply styles automatically. For example, if we wanted all of our paved areas to have a certain hatch pattern or render material, we could assign a style to the Pave link code, as in Figure 11.22.

A code set style can be created to enhance your corridor's appearance for things like exhibits at public hearings. Instead of spending time creating a series of hatch boundaries using polylines and then manually applying hatches to areas of paving, sidewalks, curbs, and so on, you can have the code set style automatically hatch those areas for you.

Another task that can be performed with a code set style is the application of render materials. This type of code set style will be studied in more detail in Chapter 22. Similar to a hatch pattern code set style, the render material code set style will automatically apply render materials to your corridor on the basis of link codes. For example, the corridor in Figure 11.23 was stylized with a code set that automatically assigned an asphalt render material to the Pave code, a concrete render material to the Curb and Sidewalk codes, and a grass render material to the Daylight code.

FIGURE 11.22
A corridor with a hatching code set style

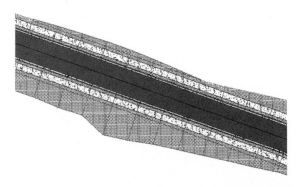

FIGURE 11.23

An image of a corridor with a render material code set style

You can view the Code Set Style collection on the Settings tab of Toolspace by expanding the General ➤ Multipurpose Styles ➤ Code Set Styles branches. The Code Set Style dialog is shown in Figure 11.24.

A code set style is a compilation of styles for links, points, shapes, and feature lines. A code set style could be thought of as similar to an Alignment label set. Since an alignment can have many different types of labels, the label set lets you collect and stylize them in one spot instead of having to assign each style individually.

FIGURE 11.24

The Code Set Style dialog

Just like you might create an Alignment label set for local roads, highways, streams, and other special situations, you can create different code set styles for different desired corridor looks. Some examples might be a code set style that applies elaborate hatching for preliminary site plans, another code set style that applies render materials for rendering and drive-throughs, and maybe another that applies a different hatch to designate that a road is already constructed for use in future road plans.

In addition to assigning fill material (hatching) and render material to specific links, the code set controls the appearance of all corridor components. If you would like to customize the color, layer, linetype, and so on of links, points, shapes, or feature lines, this is where you would do that. Figure 11.25 shows an example of a corridor where the color of each point, link, feature line, and shape has been customized in the code set style.

FIGURE 11.25

A corridor's appearance is controlled by link, point, shape, and feature line styles.

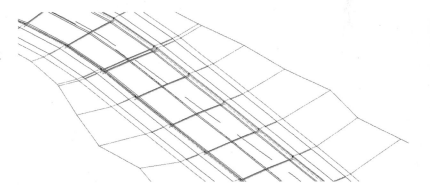

WHAT ABOUT THE FEATURE LINES?

When you build your corridor, the default code set style in your Command settings is applied to links, points, shapes, render materials, fill materials, and feature lines. Once the corridor is built, changes to the code set style will update all of these items except the feature lines. Changes to feature lines once the corridor is built must be made in the Corridor Properties dialog.

In this next exercise, we are going to examine a default code set style and apply it to our corridor to see the hatch pattern:

1. Open the Hatch Corridor.dwg file. Note that this drawing contains a corridor.

2. Pick the corridor and right-click. Select Corridor Properties.

3. In the Corridor Properties dialog, switch to the Codes tab. Select All Codes With Hatching from the dropdown list in the Code Set Style selection box.

4. Click OK to dismiss the dialog.

5. Your corridor should now have hatching applied as per the code set style, similar to Figure 11.22.

6. Expand the General ➤ Multipurpose Styles ➤ Code Set Styles branches on the Settings tab of Toolspace.

7. Double-click on the All Codes With Hatching code set style and the Code Set Style dialog opens. Switch to the Codes tab.

8. Scroll to the right until you see the Material Area Fill Style column. The Material Area Fill Style specifies the hatch pattern for each link code. You can customize these hatch patterns by clicking any entry in this column and modifying the style.

Creating a Corridor Surface

A corridor provides the raw material for surface creation. Just like you would make a surface from points and breaklines, a corridor surface uses corridor points as point data along with using feature lines and links like breaklines.

The Corridor Surface

Civil 3D does not automatically build a corridor surface when you build a corridor, because it needs more information about what you want to build. From examining subassemblies, assemblies, and the simple corridors we have built in the previous exercises, you have probably noticed that there are many "layers" of points, links, and feature lines. Some represent the very top of the finished ground of your road design, some represent subsurface gravel or concrete thicknesses, and some represent subgrade, among other possibilities. You can choose to build a surface from any one of these layers or from all of them. Figure 11.26 shows an example of a surface built from the links that are all coded Top, which would represent final finished ground.

When you first create a surface from a corridor, it is dependent on the corridor object. This means that if you change something that affects your corridor and then rebuild the corridor, the surface will also update. In Civil 3D 2007, and all subsequent versions since, this surface shows up as a true surface under the Surfaces branch in Prospector. After you create the initial corridor surface, you can create a static export of the surface using Corridors ➢ Utilities ➢ Create Detached Surfaces From Corridor. A detached surface will not react to corridor changes and can be used to archive a version of your surface.

FIGURE 11.26
A surface built from
Top code links

Creation Fundamentals

You create corridor surfaces on the Surfaces tab in the Corridor Properties dialog using the following two steps (which will be examined in detail later in this section):

1. Click Create A Corridor Surface to add a surface entry (see Figure 11.27).

2. Choose data to add, and then click the + sign.

DATA TYPES

You can choose to create your corridor surface on the basis of links, feature lines, or a combination of both.

Creating a Surface from Link Data

Most of the time, you will build your corridor surface from links. As we discussed earlier, links understand which "layer" they fit into on your corridor. Choosing to build a surface from Top links will create a surface that triangulates between the points at the link vertices that represent the final finished grade. The most commonly built link-based surfaces are Top, Datum, and Subbase; however, you can build a surface from any link code in your corridor. Figure 11.28 shows a corridor and its surface, which was created from link data. You can see the triangulation lines connecting the link vertex points.

FIGURE 11.27
The Create A Corridor Surface button

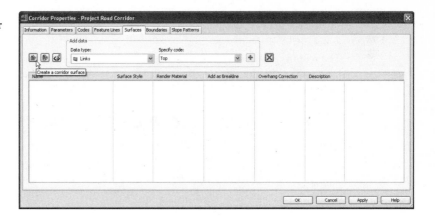

FIGURE 11.28
A corridor and its surface was created from link data.

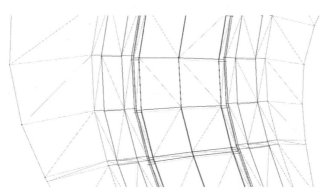

When building a surface from links, you have the option of checking a box in the Add As Breakline column. Checking this box will add the actual link lines themselves as additional breaklines to the surface. In most cases, especially in intersection design, checking this box forces better triangulation. It would be good practice to always check this box. If you find that you have an extremely large corridor and run into performance problems, then consider leaving this box unchecked.

Creating a Surface from Feature Lines

There might be cases where you would like to build a simple surface from your corridor—for example, by using just the crown and edge-of-travel way. If you build a surface from feature lines only or a combination of links and feature lines, you have more control over what Civil 3D uses as breaklines for the surface.

If you added each Top feature-line code to your surface entry and built a surface, you would get a very similar result as if you had added the Top link codes. Each feature line usually has a vertex where the corridor points would normally fall; therefore, triangulation occurs almost identically to a link-based surface. However, you would have to choose and add each feature line individually, which would take more time than building a link-based surface. Also, if your corridor is complex and has transitions, a feature line may not be continuous along the length of your corridor and would cause unexpected triangulation. For the most part, you will probably find that you rarely build a surface from feature lines alone. Feature lines are most useful when added to link-based corridor surfaces to reinforce triangulation.

Figure 11.29 shows what the Surfaces tab of the Corridor Properties dialog would look like if you chose to build a surface from the Back_Curb, Crown, Daylight, and Edge of Travel Way (ETW) feature lines.

The resulting surface can be seen in Figure 11.30. Although there are few applications for a feature line-only corridor surface, it is useful to understand what happens when feature lines are added to a corridor surface.

FIGURE 11.29
The Surfaces tab indicates that the surface will only be built from certain feature lines.

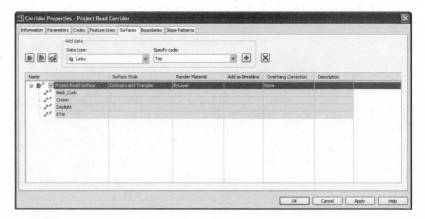

FIGURE 11.30

A surface built from only the Back_Curb, Crown, Daylight, and ETW feature lines

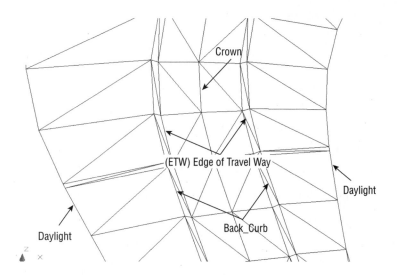

Creating a Surface from both Link Data and Feature Lines

A link-based surface can be improved by the addition of feature lines. A link-based surface does not automatically include the corridor feature lines, but instead uses the link vertex points to create triangulation. Therefore, the addition of feature lines ensures that triangulation occurs where desired. This is especially important for intersection design, curves, and other corridor surfaces where triangulation around tight corners is critical. Figure 11.31 shows the Surfaces tab of the Corridor Properties dialog where a Top link surface will be improved by the addition of Back_Curb, ETW, and Top_Curb feature lines.

If you are having trouble with triangulation or contours not behaving as expected, experiment with adding a few feature lines to your corridor surface definition.

FIGURE 11.31

The Surfaces tab indicates that the surface will be built from Top links as well as from several feature lines.

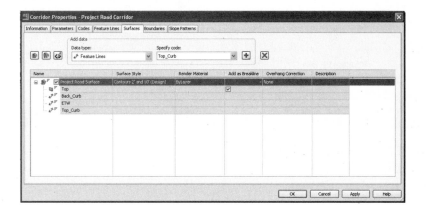

OTHER SURFACE TASKS

Several other tasks can be done on the Surfaces tab. You can set a Surface Style, assign a meaningful name, and provide a description for your surface. Alternatively, you can do all those things once the surface appears in the drawing and through Prospector.

Adding a Surface Boundary

Every surface should have a boundary, and a corridor surface is no exception. Tools that can automatically and interactively add surface boundaries, using the corridor intelligence, are available. Figure 11.32 shows a corridor surface before the addition of a boundary.

You can create corridor surface boundaries using the Boundaries tab of the Corridor Properties dialog. Figure 11.33 shows a corridor surface after the application of an automatic boundary. Notice how the extraneous triangulation has been eliminated.

FIGURE 11.32
A corridor surface before the addition of a boundary

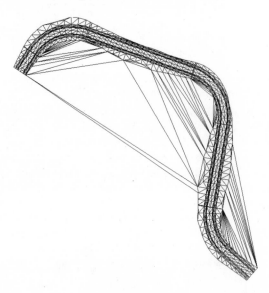

FIGURE 11.33
A corridor surface after the addition of an automatic daylight boundary

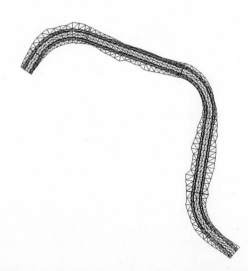

BOUNDARY TYPES

There are several tools to assist in corridor surface boundary creation. They can be automatic, semi-automatic, or manual in nature depending on your needs and the complexity of the corridor.

You access these options on the Boundaries tab of the Corridor Properties dialog by right-clicking on the name of your surface entry, as shown in Figure 11.34.

FIGURE 11.34
Corridor surface boundary options

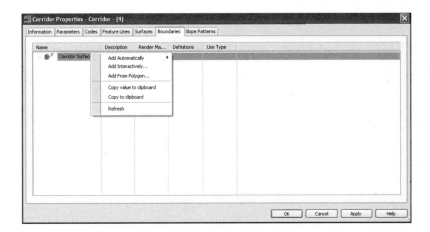

Add Automatically

The Add Automatically boundary tool allows you to pick a Feature Line code to use as your corridor boundary. This tool is only available for single baseline corridors. Since this tool is the most automatic and easiest to apply, you will use it almost every time you build a single baseline corridor.

Add Interactively

The Add Interactively boundary tool allows you to work your way around a multibaseline corridor and choose which corridor feature lines you would like to use as part of the boundary definition. You will probably find this option to be the most useful boundary creation tool, as it can be used regardless of corridor complexity. We will discuss this tool in detail in the next chapter.

Add From Polygon

The Add From Polygon tool allows you to choose a closed polyline or polygon in your drawing that you would like to add as a boundary for your corridor surface.

Now that you have studied the components of how corridor surfaces are built and how to create corridor surface boundaries, this next exercise will lead you through creating a corridor surface with an automatic boundary:

1. Open the `Corridor Surface.dwg` file. Note that there is a corridor in this drawing.

2. Open the Corridor Properties dialog and switch to the Surfaces tab.

3. Click Create A Corridor Surface on the far left side of the dialog ![icon]. You should now have a surface entry in the bottom half of the dialog. Click on the surface entry under the Name column and change the default name of your surface to **Project Road Corridor Surface**. The surface style can also be changed under the Surface Style column.

4. Confirm that Links has been selected from the dropdown menu in the Data Type selection box and that Top has been selected from the dropdown menu in the Specify Code selection box. Click the + button to add Top Links to the Surface Definition.

5. Click OK to leave this dialog, and examine your surface. The area inside the corridor model itself should look fine; however, since we have not yet added a boundary to this surface, undesirable triangulation is occurring outside our corridor area.

6. Expand the Surfaces branch in Prospector. Note that you now have a corridor surface listed.

7. Pick the corridor in your drawing, right-click, and select Corridor Properties.

8. In the Corridor Properties dialog, switch to the Boundaries tab.

9. Right-click on the surface entry. Select the Add Automatically flyout, and select Sidewalk_ Out as the feature line that will define the outer boundary of the surface. Note the Add Automatically option is only available on single baseline corridors.

10. Confirm that the Use Type column says Outside Boundary to ensure that the boundary definition will be used to define the desired extreme outer limits of the surface.

11. Click OK to dismiss the dialog. Examine your surface, and note that the triangulation terminates at the Sidewalk_Out point all along the corridor model.

12. Experiment with making changes to your finished grade profile, assembly, or alignment geometry and rebuilding both your corridor and finished ground surface.

REBUILD: LEAVE IT ON OR OFF?

Note that upon rebuilding your corridor, your surface will need to be updated. Typically, the best practice is to leave Rebuild – Automatic OFF for corridors and keeping Rebuild – Automatic ON for surfaces. This practice is usually OK for your corridor-dependent surfaces. The surface will only want to rebuild when the corridor is rebuilt. For very large corridors, this may become a bit of a memory lag, so try it both ways and see what you like best.

COMMON SURFACE CREATION PROBLEMS

Some common problems encountered when creating surfaces are as follows:

Problem Your corridor surface does not appear or seems to be empty.

Typical Cause You might have created the surface entry but no data.

Fix Open the Corridor Properties dialog and switch to the Surfaces tab. Select an entry from the dropdown menus in the Data Type and Specify Code selection boxes, and click the + sign. Make sure your dialog shows both a surface entry and a data type, as per Figure 11.35.

Problem Your corridor surface does not seem to respect its boundary after a change to the assembly or surface-building data type (in other words, you switched from link data to feature lines).

FIGURE 11.35
A surface cannot be
created without both
a surface entry and a
data type

Typical Cause   Automatic and interactive boundary definitions are dependent on the codes used in your corridor. If you remove or change the codes used in your corridor, the boundary needs to be defined.

Fix   Open the Corridor Properties dialog and switch to the Boundaries tab. Erase any boundary definitions that are no longer valid (if any). Redefine your boundaries.

Performing a Volume Calculation

One of the most powerful aspects of Civil 3D is having instant feedback on your design iterations. Once you create a preliminary road corridor, you can immediately compare a corridor surface to existing ground and get a good understanding of earthwork magnitude. When you make an adjustment to the finished grade profile and then rebuild your corridor, you can see the effect that this change had on your earthwork within a minute or two, if not sooner.

Even though volumes were covered in detail in Chapter 5, it is worth revisiting the subject here in the context of corridors.

This exercise uses a TIN-to-TIN composite volume calculation; average end area and other section-based volume calculations will be covered in Chapter 13.

1. Open the `Corridor Surface Volume.dwg` file. Note that this drawing has a corridor and a corridor surface.

2. Choose Surfaces ➢ Utilities ➢ Volumes.

3. The Composite Volume palette in Panorama appears.

4. Click the Create New Volume Entry. A Volume entry with an Index of 1 should appear in the palette.

5. Click inside the cell in the Base Surface column and select Existing Ground for the Volume entry with an Index of 1.

6. Click inside the cell in the Comparison Surface column and select the Project Road Corridor Surface.

7. A Cut/Fill breakdown should appear in the remaining columns, as shown in Figure 11.36. Make a note of these numbers.

8. Leave Panorama open on your screen (make it smaller, if desired), and pan over to your Finished Ground profile.

9. Pick the Finished Ground profile and grip-edit a PVI so that the profile changes drastically—in other words, so there would suddenly be a great deal more cut or fill.

10. Pick the corridor, right-click, and choose Rebuild Corridor. Notice that the corridor changes, and therefore the corridor surface changes as well.

11. Click Recompute Volume Entries in Panorama and note the new values for cut and fill.

FIGURE 11.36

Panorama showing the volume entry and the cut/fill results

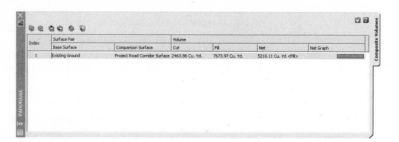

Common Volume Problem

A common volume problem is as follows:

Problem   Your volume number does not update.

Typical Cause   You might have forgotten to rebuild the corridor, rebuild the corridor surface, or click Recompute Volumes.

Fix   Check Prospector to see if either your corridor or corridor surface is out of date. First rebuild the corridor and then rebuild the corridor surface.

Creating a Corridor with a Lane Widening

So far, all of the corridor examples we have looked at have a constant cross section. Let's take a look at what happens when a portion of your corridor needs to transition to a wider section, and then transition back to normal.

Using Target Alignments

Earlier in this chapter, we discussed baselines and mentioned that baselines can be broken up into different regions. Regions will be examined in detail in Chapter 12.

In this section, we will apply another corridor parameter called a *target*. We mentioned the idea of targets when we added a surface target for a daylighting subassembly. In addition to surfaces, alignments and profiles can be used as targets.

Many subassemblies have been programmed to allow for not only a baseline attachment point but also additional attachment points on target alignments and/or profiles. Figure 11.37 shows a centerline alignment to be used as a baseline and an edge-of-travel way alignment to be used as a target.

The subassembly will be stretched, raised, lowered, and adjusted to reflect the location and elevation of the target. In this chapter, we will discuss target alignments. In Chapter 12, we will go into more detail about using profile targets.

For example, the BasicLaneTransition subassembly can be set up to hook on to an alignment and a profile. Think of the lane as a rubber band that is attached both to the baseline of the corridor (such as the road centerline) and the target alignment. As the target alignment, such as a lane widening, gets further from the baseline, the rubber band is stretched wider. As that target alignment transitions back toward the baseline, the rubber band changes to reflect a narrower cross section. Figure 11.38 shows a corridor built using the edge-of-travel way alignment shown in Figure 11.37 as a target.

FIGURE 11.37

A centerline alignment used as a baseline and an edge-of-travel way alignment used as a target

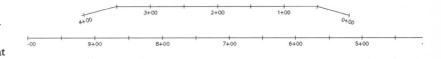

FIGURE 11.38

A corridor built using the centerline and the edge-of-travel way alignments

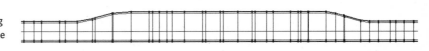

As we discussed in Chapter 10, the BasicLaneTransition subassembly has several options for how it will transition. For the next example, we will use Hold Grade, Change Offset. Hold grade means the subassembly will hold the default grade of -2% as it is stretched to change offset with the target alignment. Using the Hold Grade, Change Offset setting eliminates the need for a target profile, since the elevation at the edge-of-travel way will be determined by the default grade (-2%, in this case) and lane width at a given sampling location.

The following exercise will teach you how to use a transition alignment as a corridor target for a lane widening:

1. Open the `Corridor Widening.dwg` file. Note that this drawing has a corridor.

2. Freeze the layer C-ROAD-CORR. Note that the Widening EOP alignment represents the edge-of-pavement for a street parking zone.

3. Thaw the layer C-ROAD-CORR.

4. Pan over to the assembly in the drawing. Select the right lane subassembly, right-click, and choose Subassembly Properties. Switch to the Parameters tab on the Subassembly Properties dialog.

5. Note that the entry for the Transition field is Hold Grade, Change Offset, as shown in Figure 11.39. Click OK to dismiss the dialog.

6. Pan over to your corridor. Pick the corridor, right-click, and choose Corridor Properties. Switch to the Parameters tab on the Corridor Properties dialog.

FIGURE 11.39
Set the Default Input Value for the Transition field to Hold Grade, Change Offset.

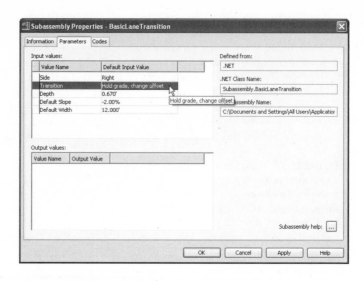

7. Click Set All Targets. The Target Mapping dialog opens. Click in the field next to Transition Alignment to select the Widening EOP alignment.

8. Click OK to dismiss the dialog. Click OK again to dismiss the Corridor Properties dialog.

9. The corridor will rebuild and reflect the wider lane where appropriate. The finished corridor should look similar to Figure 11.38.

Common Transition Problems

A common problem encountered when creating transitions is as follows:

Problem Your corridor does not reflect your lane widening.

Typical Cause No. 1 You forgot to set the targets.

Fix Refer to steps 6, 7, and 8 in the previous exercise

Typical Cause No. 2 Your subassembly isn't set to Change Offset.

Fix Examine your lane subassembly. Make sure it is a subassembly with a transition parameter, such as a BasicLaneTransition. Swap out the subassembly if necessary. Once you have confirmed the proper subassembly is in place, make sure that you have chosen a transition parameter that meets your design intent, such as Hold Grade, Change Offset.

Creating a Stream Corridor

Corridors can be used for far more than just road designs. We will explore some more advanced corridor models in Chapter 12, but there are plenty of simple, single-baseline applications for alternative corridors such as channels, berms, streams, retaining walls, and more. You can take advantage of several specialized subassemblies or build your own custom assembly using a combination of generic links. Figure 11.40 shows an example of a stream corridor.

FIGURE 11.40

A simple stream corridor viewed in 3D built from the Channel subassembly and a generic link subassembly

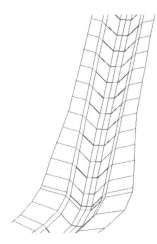

One of the subassemblies that we discussed in Chapter 10 is the Channel subassembly. The following exercise shows you how to apply this subassembly to design a simple stream.

1. Open the Corridor Stream.dwg file. Note that there is an alignment that represents a stream centerline, a profile that represents the stream normal water line, and an assembly created using the Channel and LinkSlopetoSurface subassemblies.

2. Choose Corridors ➢ Create Simple Corridor. The Create Simple Corridor dialog opens.

3. Name your corridor something appropriate, such as Project Stream. Click OK.

4. Follow the prompts, and pick the Stream CL alignment, the Stream NWL profile, and the Project Stream assembly. The Target Mapping dialog will appear after all objects have been picked.

5. In the Target Mapping dialog, choose the Existing Ground surface for all surface targets. Keep the default values for the additional targets. Click OK to dismiss the dialog.

6. The stream corridor will build itself and will look similar to Figure 11.41. Choose Corridors ➢ View/Edit Corridor Section Tools to open the toolbar and navigate through the stream cross sections.

This corridor can be used to build a surface for a TIN-to-TIN volume calculation or can be used to create sections and generate material quantities, cross-sectional views, and anything else that can be done with a more traditional road corridor.

FIGURE 11.41

The completed stream corridor

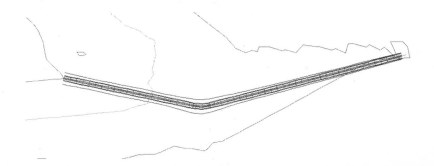

Real World Scenario

CREATING A PIPE TRENCH CORRIDOR

Another alternative use for a corridor is a pipe trench. A pipe trench corridor is useful for determining quantities of excavated material, limits of disturbance, trench-safety specifications and more. This graphic shows a completed pipe trench corridor:

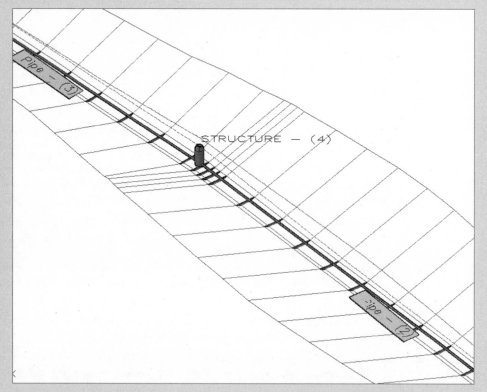

One of the subassemblies that we discussed in Chapter 10 is the TrenchPipe1 subassembly. The following exercise leads you through applying this subassembly to a Pipe Trench corridor.

1. Open the Corridor Pipe Trench.dwg file. Note that there is a pipe network, with a corresponding alignment, profile view, and pipe trench assembly. Also note that there is a profile drawn that corresponds with the inverts of the pipe network.

2. Choose Corridors ➢ Create Simple Corridor. Give your corridor a meaningful name, such as **Pipe Trench Corridor**. Click OK.

3. Follow the prompts, and pick the Pipe Centerline alignment, the Bottom Of Pipe profile, and the Pipe Trench assembly as your corridor components. Once these selections are made, the Target Mapping dialog appears.

4. In the Target Mapping dialog, choose Existing Ground as the target surface. Click OK.

5. The corridor will build itself. Choose Corridors ➢ View/Edit Corridor Section Tools from the menu bar. Pick the corridor to open the toolbar and view the cross sections through the trench. This corridor can be used to build a surface for a TIN-to-TIN volume calculation or can be used to create sections and generate material quantities, cross-sectional views, and anything else that can be done with a more traditional road corridor.

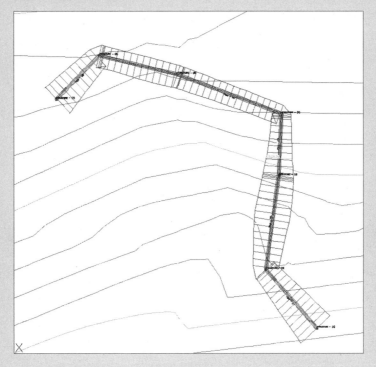

The Bottom Line

Build a single baseline corridor from an alignment, profile, and assembly. Corridors are created from the combination of alignments, profiles, and assemblies. While corridors can be used to model many things, most corridors are used for road design.

Master It Open the Mastering Corridors.dwg file. Build a corridor on the basis of the Project Road alignment, the Project Road Finished Ground profile, and the Project Typical Road Assembly.

Create a corridor surface. The corridor model can be used to build a surface. This corridor surface can then be analyzed and annotated to produce finished road plans.

Master It Continue working in the Mastering Corridors.dwg file. Create a corridor surface from Top links.

Add an automatic boundary to a corridor surface. Surfaces can be improved with the addition of a boundary. Single baseline corridors can take advantage of automatic boundary creation.

Master It Continue working in the `Mastering Corridors.dwg` file. Use the Automatic Boundary Creation tool to add a boundary using the Daylight code.

Chapter 12

The Road Ahead: Advanced Corridors

In Chapter 11, you built several simple corridors and began to see the dynamic power of the corridor model. While the focus of Chapter 11 was to get things started, it is unrealistic to think that a project would only have one road in the middle of nowhere with no intersections, no adjustments, and no complications. You may be having trouble visualizing how you will build a corridor to tackle your more complex design projects, such as the one pictured in Figure 12.1.

This chapter will focus on taking your corridor-modeling skills to a new level by introducing more tools to your corridor-building toolbox, such as intersecting roads, cul-de-sacs, advanced techniques, and troubleshooting. Keep in mind that this is only the beginning. There are so many ways to manipulate your assemblies, alignments, profiles, and the corridor itself to model anything you can imagine.

This chapter assumes that you have a worked through the examples in the alignments, profiles, profile view, assemblies and basic corridor chapters. Without a strong knowledge of the foundation skills, many of the tasks in this chapter may prove to be difficult.

By the end of this chapter, you will be able to:

◆ Add a baseline to a corridor model for a cul-de-sac

◆ Add alignment and profile targets to a region for a cul-de-sac

◆ Use the interactive boundary tool to add a boundary to the corridor surface

FIGURE 12.1
A corridor model
for a medium-sized
subdivision

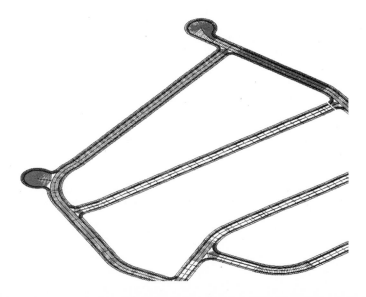

Getting Creative with Corridor Models

When working on live projects, we often get requests from new users to teach them how to design an intersection (or a cul-de-sac, or a site, or anything) using Civil 3D.

By the end of this chapter, you will understand why this request is not only unrealistic, but actually probably impossible. There are as many ways to design an intersection as there are intersections in the world.

The best you can do is to learn how the corridor tools can be applied to a few typical scenarios but do not take them as gospel. Take the skills you learn here to create a foundation for your own models in your own design situations. We have often seen users dismiss an intersection from being applicable to their situation because it did not include a turn lane or perhaps their intersection came together at an odd angle. This is truly unfortunate, because the same fundamental tools can be adapted to accommodate additional design constraints.

Another example that you may consider is adapting the corridor model for use in a parking lot or in a commercial site. As we saw in Chapter 11 with stream and pipe trench corridors, the corridor model is not a road-only tool.

Civil 3D, in general, and the corridor model, specifically, will not be of true use to you unless you can see it as a limitless, flexible model that you control to your design constraints. Build something, try something. If it doesn't work, look back through the chapter for more ideas and keep refining, improving, and learning.

Using Alignment and Profile Targets to Model a Roadside Swale

In the previous chapter, we had an example where the road lane used an alignment target to add a variable width to the lane without changing the vertical design.

In this chapter, we will look at a roadside swale that follows a variable horizontal alignment, as well as a vertical profile that does not follow the centerline of road. This happens frequently when there are existing culvert crossings that must be met or different slope requirements for the roadside swale.

Corridor Utilities

To create an alignment and profile for the swale, we will take advantage of some of the corridor utilities found on the menu bar under Corridors ➤ Utilities.

Create Polyline From Corridor   Extracts a 3D polyline from a corridor feature line. This polyline can be used as is or flattened to create road linework.

Create Grading Feature Line From Corridor   Extracts a grading feature line from a corridor feature line. Typically, this extracted feature line would be used as a foundation for some feature line grading or projection grading.

Create Alignment From Corridor   Creates an alignment that follows the horizontal path of a corridor feature line. This alignment can be used to create target alignments, profile views, special labeling, or anything else a traditional alignment could be used for.

Create Profile From Corridor   Creates a profile that follows the vertical path of a corridor feature line. This profile will appear in Prospector under the baseline alignment and will be drawn on any profile view that is associated with that baseline alignment. This profile is typically used to extract edge of pavement (EOP) or swale profiles for a finished profile view sheet or as a target profile for additional corridor design, as we will see in this section's exercise.

Create COGO Points From Corridor   Creates Civil 3D points that are based on corridor point codes. You select which point codes to use as well as a range of corridor stations. A Civil 3D point will be placed at every point code location in that range.

Create Detached Surfaces From Corridor   Copies a dynamic corridor surface and converts it into a static corridor surface. This tool is most useful for creating an archive surface that will not react to future corridor revisions.

The important thing to remember is that each of the entities created using corridor utilities *is a static snapshot of the corridor as it exists when you extract the entity.* For example, if you extract COGO points from your corridor, then revise your baseline profile and rebuild your corridor, your COGO points *will not update* to match the new corridor elevations.

This exercise will take you through revising a model from a symmetrical corridor with roadside swales to a corridor with a transitioning roadside swale centerline. You will also take advantage of some of the corridor utilities discussed in this section.

1. Open the `Corridor Swale.dwg` file. Note that the drawing contains a symmetrical corridor (see Figure 12.2), which was built using an assembly that includes two roadside swales. You can view the corridor in 3D by picking it, right-clicking, and choosing Object Viewer. You can also change your view of the corridor by using the 3D orbit tools.

2. Choose Corridors ➤ Utilities ➤ Create Alignment From Corridor. Pick the corridor feature line that represents the swale on the right side of the centerline, as shown in Figure 12.3, to create an alignment.

3. In the Create Alignment dialog, name the alignment **Swale CL**. Keep the default values for the Style and Label options, and uncheck the Create Profile box. We'll add the profile another way. Click OK to dismiss the dialog, and notice that an alignment has been created at the corridor feature line (see Figure 12.4).

FIGURE 12.2
The initial corridor with symmetrical roadside swales

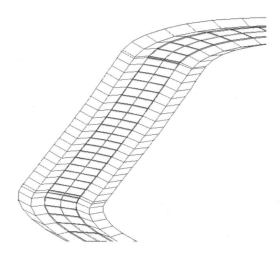

FIGURE 12.3
The corridor feature line that represents the swale on the right side of the centerline

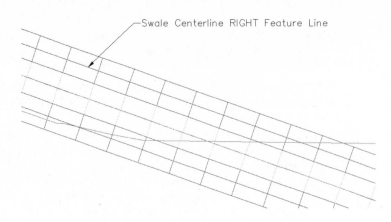

Swale Centerline RIGHT Feature Line

FIGURE 12.4
The resulting extracted alignment

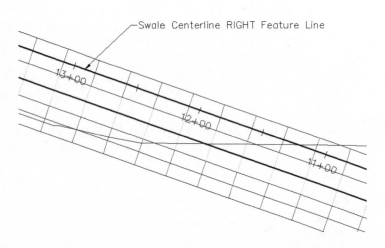

Swale Centerline RIGHT Feature Line

4. Choose Corridors ➤ Utilities ➤ Create Profile From Corridor. Pick the same corridor feature line to create the profile from. (Note that you may have to send your alignment to the back, so that you can pick the corridor feature line.) In the Create Profile dialog, keep the default values for the Style and Label options. Click OK to dismiss the dialog.

5. Pan over to the Project Road profile view to see the profile that was just created. The profile represents the vertical path of the swale centerline feature line, as shown in Figure 12.5.

6. Pan over to your newly extracted swale centerline alignment. Add a PI around Station 13+00 in plan. You can use the transparent commands to snap the PI to Station 13+00 exactly or just place it approximately at Station 13+00.

7. Grip-edit the PI and stretch it approximately 10′ to the right. Use the Station Offset transparent command if you would like to be precise.

8. Pan over to the profile view. Grip-edit the swale centerline profile to provide an exaggerated low spot around station 13+00, as shown in Figure 12.6.

9. Open the Corridor Properties dialog, and switch to the Parameters tab. Click Set All Targets to open the Target Mapping dialog.

10. Expand the Alignments option, and set the Ditch Foreslope RIGHT subassembly to target the Object Name Swale CL Alignment. Expand the Profiles option, and set the Ditch Foreslope RIGHT subassembly to target the Object Name Swale CL Profile. Figure 12.7 shows the Target Mapping dialog with the alignments and profiles appropriately mapped.

11. Click OK to dismiss the Target Mapping dialog. Click OK again to dismiss the Corridor Properties dialog and rebuild the corridor. The corridor should now look like Figure 12.8.

FIGURE 12.5
The resulting extracted profile

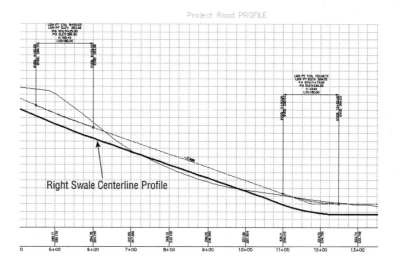

FIGURE 12.6
Stretch a PVI to provide an exaggerated low spot.

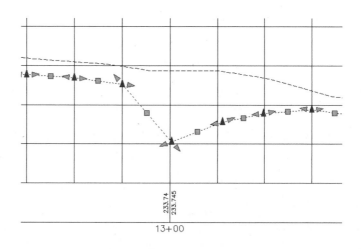

FIGURE 12.7
Set the Ditch Fore-
slope subassembly
to follow the swale
centerline alignment
and profile.

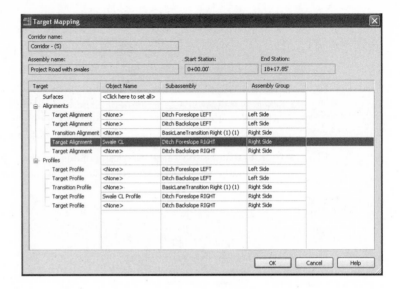

FIGURE 12.8
The adjusted corridor

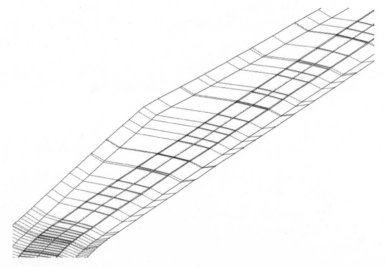

Note that the corridor has been adjusted to reflect the new target alignment and profile. Also note that you may want to increase the sampling frequency. You can view the sections using the View/Edit Corridor Section tools. You can also view the corridor in 3D by picking it, right-clicking, and choosing Object Viewer. Use the 3D orbit tools to change your view of the corridor.

Modeling a Peer-Road Intersection

One of the distinctions that is important to make when using the corridor model is that even though you are building a model, you aren't designing. Technically speaking, you could be building the model and designing the intersection simultaneously, but most users who attempt to have it "all figured out" as they are constructing the model find the task tedious and frustrating.

The first step is to figure out how your intersection works. Give yourself some modeling guidelines, trends, and design constraints (but *not* actual hard elevations just yet), either on screen or on a small plotted schematic (see Figure 12.9).

Next, plan what alignments, profiles, and assemblies you will need to create the right combination of baselines, regions, and targets to model an intersection that will interact the way you want.

Figure 12.10 shows a sketch of required baselines. Baselines are the horizontal and vertical foundation of a corridor, as we saw in Chapter 11. Each baseline will consist of an alignment and its corresponding finished ground (FG) profile. You may never have thought of edge of pavement (EOP) in terms of profile, but after building a few intersections, it will become second nature.

Figure 12.11 breaks each baseline into regions where a different assembly or different target will be applied. The next exercise will give you hands-on experience in adding regions to a corridor baseline.

FIGURE 12.9

Plan your intersection model in sketch form.

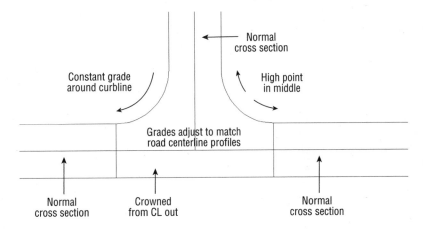

FIGURE 12.10

Required baselines for modeling a typical intersection

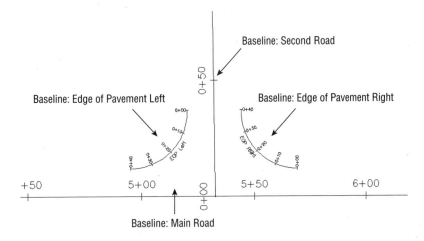

FIGURE 12.11
Required regions
for modeling an
intersection

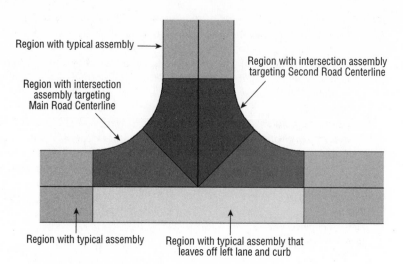

Region with typical assembly →

Region with intersection assembly
targeting Second Road Centerline

Region with intersection
assembly targeting
Main Road Centerline

Region with typical assembly

Region with typical assembly that
leaves off left lane and curb

Adding Regions to the Main Road

In Chapter 11, you learned briefly about regions. A baseline consists of a combination of an alignment and profile, while assemblies are applied to specific regions. By default, every baseline has one region, which you created in Chapter 11 whenever you made a new corridor. If certain zones of a baseline require the application of a different assembly, you simply split a baseline into multiple regions.

On the basis of the schematic you drew of your intersection, your main road will need two assemblies to reflect two different road cross sections. The first assembly, as shown in Figure 12.12, is the typical or "normal" case. The bulk of your neighborhood will use this typical assembly along straight pieces that aren't intersections, widening areas, or similar.

The next assembly (see Figure 12.13) is a right lane–only assembly that you will apply through the intersection. On the basis of your sketch, this particular main road won't maintain a full crown through the intersection; however, the right half of the road will be "normal."

FIGURE 12.12
A typical assembly
will be applied to all
"normal" regions.

FIGURE 12.13
Right lane–only
assembly

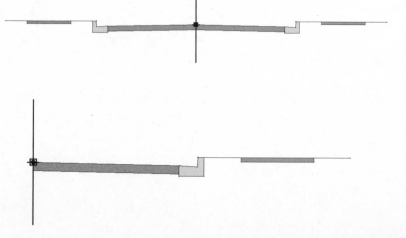

This exercise will take you through building a typical peer-road intersection shown in the figures in this section:

1. Open the `Corridor Peer Intersection.dwg` file. Note that the drawing contains four alignments, including two road alignments (Project Road and Second Road) and two alignments representing the EOP on either side of the intersection (EOP Right and EOP Left). The drawing also contains a single baseline corridor running down Project Road.

2. Open the Corridor Properties dialog and switch to the Parameters tab. Note that Baseline (1) uses the Project Road alignment and the Project Road FG profile. Also note there is currently one region for the Project Road typical assembly baseline. This baseline will require three total regions to match the schematic shown in Figure 12.11.

3. Adjust the End Station of Region (1) to meet the end of the EOP Left alignment. This occurs at Project Road Station 4+95.17. You can either type in **4+95.17** or click the Specify Station button (see Figure 12.14) and then pick a location in the drawing using your osnaps.

4. Right-click on Region (1) and choose Insert Region. Choose the Project Road Right Lane Only Assembly for the new region. We could build all the regions at once, but it is helpful when you first begin building complex corridors to see how each region affects the total corridor.

5. Adjust the End Station of this region to meet the beginning of the EOP Right alignment. This occurs at Project Road Station 5+69.18. Type in **5+69.18** or click the Specify Station button and then pick a location using your osnaps.

6. Right-click on Region (2) and select Insert Region. Choose the Project Road Typical Assembly for the new region. Region (3) should automatically extend to the end of the Project Road alignment.

7. Click OK to dismiss the Corridor Properties dialog and automatically rebuild your corridor. The corridor should look similar to Figure 12.15.

FIGURE 12.14
The Specify
Station button

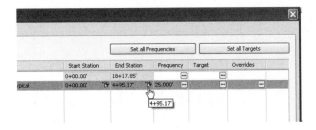

FIGURE 12.15
The Project Road
baseline with all three
regions applied

8. Notice the small gap that appears between Region (2) and Region (3) in Figure 12.15. Open the Corridor Properties dialog to repair the gap.

9. Switch to the Parameters tab, and enter **5+69.19** as the Start Station for Region (3). Click OK to dismiss the dialog and automatically rebuild your corridor. Your corridor should now look like Figure 12.16. Notice that the gap has been repaired.

FIGURE 12.16

The finished corridor

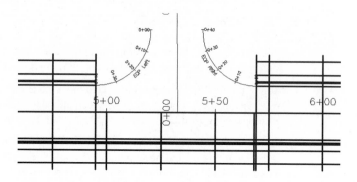

WHY THE GAP?

In the preceding example, a small gap appeared between Region (2) and Region (3), which was easily fixed by simply adding one hundredth of a foot to the Start Station in Region (3).

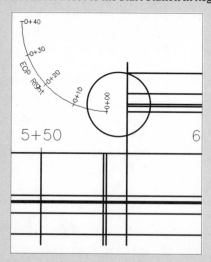

What is this gap and why does a hundredth of a foot make a difference? And why doesn't it happen between Region (1) and Region (2)? Without going into too much programming minutia, the basic idea is this:

Region (1) had a full width's worth of links and points and therefore had a full set of feature lines at its End Station. As a result, Region (2) knew where to connect its feature lines.

Region (2) had no links or points on the left side of the baseline, so when Region (2) came to an end, the corridor didn't create any points on the left side of the baseline at the End Station, leaving no connection points for Region (3)'s left-side feature lines.

Region (3) begins and sees that its Start Station, which is identical to Region (2)'s End Station, has already had points created, albeit only on the right side. It considers that station "taken care of" so it doesn't add any data at all and keeps moving along until it encounters its next sampling location. There, it starts building links, points, and feature lines for the full cross section. The result is a corridor feature line gap on the left side between the Start Station and the next sampling location. The feature lines on the left side simply had no points to connect to at the Start Station.

You can prevent this connection omission by changing the Start Station of Region (3) to the End Station of Region (2) and adding one hundredth of a foot (0.01´). Since this is a new station in the eyes of the corridor model, data is not there. Therefore, the software begins placing points and links immediately, which are then connected with feature lines.

So technically speaking, there is still a gap between your regions, but it is only one hundredth of a foot wide.

Adding a Baseline and Region for an Intersecting Road

A corridor is not limited to one baseline. Depending on the size of your project, you may build one corridor that includes many baselines. It is not uncommon to build a corridor with 60 or more baselines that represent road centerlines, transitions, swales, and more. In this example, you will add a baseline for an intersecting road to your corridor:

1. Open the `Corridor Peer Intersection 2.dwg` file, or continue working in your drawing from the previous exercise.

2. Open the Corridor Properties dialog and switch to the Parameters tab.

3. Click Add Baseline. The Pick Horizontal Alignment dialog opens.

4. Pick the Second Road alignment. Click OK to dismiss the dialog.

5. Click in the Profile field on the Parameters tab of the Corridor Properties dialog. The Select A Profile dialog opens.

6. Pick the Second Road FG. Click OK to dismiss the dialog.

7. In the Corridors Properties dialog, right-click on Baseline (2), and select Add Region.

8. In the Pick An Assembly dialog, select the Project Road Typical Assembly. Click OK to dismiss the dialog.

9. Expand Baseline (2) by clicking the small + sign and see the new region you just created.

10. Click OK to dismiss the Corridor Properties dialog and your corridor will automatically rebuild. Your corridor should now look like Figure 12.17.

FIGURE 12.17
The second
road baseline

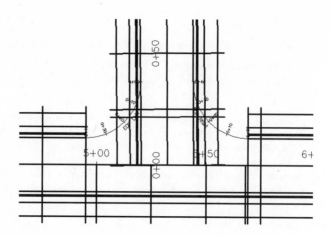

Notice that the region for the second baseline extends all the way to the end of the Second Road alignment. This must now be adjusted to match the EOP points of curvature.

1. Open the Corridor Properties dialog and switch to the Parameters tab. Adjust the Start Station of the region. You could also pick the corridor and use the triangular-shaped grip that represents the end of the region to adjust the station, as shown in Figure 12.18.

2. Once you move the region grip, you must rebuild your corridor. Pick your corridor, right-click, and choose Rebuild Corridor.

3. Your corridor should now match Figure 12.19.

FIGURE 12.18
Using the region grip
to move the region
End Station

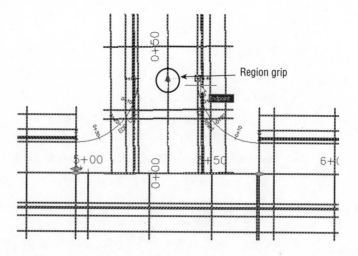

FIGURE 12.19

The finished corridor

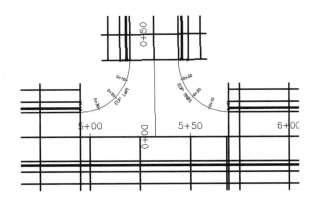

Creating an Assembly for the Intersection

You built several assemblies in Chapter 10, but most of them were based on the paradigm of using the assembly marker along a centerline. This next exercise leads you through building an assembly that attaches at the EOP.

The exercise uses the BasicLaneTransition subassembly (see Figure 12.20), but you are by no means limited to this subassembly in practice. You will find that the BasicLaneTransition is ideal for your first few intersections because it does not have many options for targeting or materials, which can often be confusing to new users.

The LaneOutsideSuper and LaneTowardCrown subassemblies can also be used, as well as any other lane with an alignment and profile target. Spend some time in the subassembly Help file to find your perfect subassembly.

1. Open the `Corridor Peer Intersection Assembly.dwg` file, or continue working in your drawing from the previous exercise.

2. Zoom in on the assemblies, and locate the Intersection Typical assembly. Note that it is incomplete.

3. Bring in your Tool palette and switch to the Imperial-Basic palette.

4. Click on the BasicLaneTransition subassembly. On the Properties palette, change the Transition parameter to the Change Offset And Elevation option (see Figure 12.21), which will allow the subassembly to react to both a target alignment and a target profile. Also change the value of the Default Slope to +2%.

FIGURE 12.20

The BasicLaneTransition subassembly

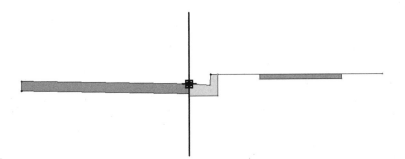

FIGURE 12.21
Change the Transition parameter to Change Offset And Elevation.

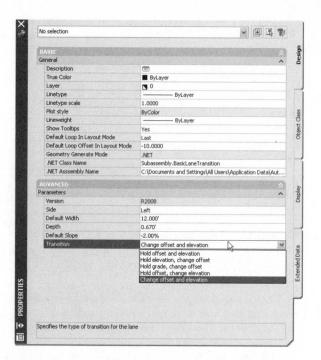

5. Add the BasicLaneTransition subassembly to the left side of the assembly.

6. Pick the subassembly, right-click and choose Subassembly Properties. On the Information tab of the dialog, change the name of the subassembly to **Intersection Transition Lane**.

Adding Baselines, Regions, and Targets for the Intersections

The Intersection assembly will attach to alignments created along the EOP. Since a baseline requires both horizontal and vertical information, we will also need to make sure that every EOP alignment has a corresponding finished grade (FG) profile.

It may first seem awkward to create alignment and profiles for things like the EOP, but after some practice you will start to see things differently. If you had been designing intersections using 3D polylines or feature lines, think of the profile as a vertical representation of a feature line and the profile grid view as the feature line elevation editor. If you designed intersections by setting points, think of alignment PIs and profile PVIs as points. So if you need a low point midway through the EOP as indicated in the sketch at the beginning of this section, you will simply add a PVI with the appropriate elevation to the EOP FG profile.

Here are some things to keep in mind:

Site Geometry Make sure any alignments you create are either "siteless" (placed on the <none> site) or placed on another appropriate site.

Naming Conventions Instead of just allowing your alignments and profiles to be named "Alignment-1", and so on, give each one a meaningful name that will help you keep it straight, so that you can identify it on a list and locate it in plan. The same rule applies for the FG profiles. If the alignment is named EOP Right, then name the profile EOP Right FG or something similar. Explore alignment and profile name templates to see if you can help yourself with some automation of the naming.

Organization   Figure out a way to keep your profile views organized. Perhaps line them up next to the appropriate road centerline or some other convention. If you just stick them anywhere, you will have a difficult time navigating and finding what you need.

Styles   Since you may not need to show these alignments and profiles on a plan sheet anywhere, consider making some design styles that give you the information you need. The style can also look different enough from your normal alignment and profile view styles so that you can look at it and, in a glance, identify it as an EOP profile view versus another type. The examples in this next exercise include smaller lettering, alignment name labels, tighter labeling intervals, and other style features to assist the designer.

You will build a corridor intersection in this next exercise. Along the way, you will examine the corridor in various stages of completion so that you understand what each step accomplishes. In practice, you will likely continue working until you build the entire model.

1. Open the `Corridor Peer Intersection 3.dwg` file, or continue working in your drawing from the previous exercise.

2. Zoom to the area where the profile views are located. Notice that there are existing and proposed ground profiles created for both EOP alignments (see Figure 12.22).

3. Open the Corridor Properties dialog and switch to the Parameters tab.

4. Click Add Baseline. The Pick Horizontal Alignment dialog opens.

5. Select the EOP Left alignment. Click OK to dismiss the dialog.

6. Click in the Profile field on the Parameters tab of the Corridor Properties dialog.

7. In the Select A Profile dialog, select EOP Left FG. Click OK to dismiss the dialog.

8. Right-click on Baseline (3) and select Add Region.

9. In the Pick An Assembly dialog, select the Intersection Typical Assembly. Click OK to dismiss the dialog.

10. Expand Baseline (3) and see the new region you just created.

11. Click OK to dismiss the Corridor Properties dialog and automatically rebuild your corridor. Your corridor should now look similar to Figure 12.23.

FIGURE 12.22
A profile view for the existing and proposed EOP profiles

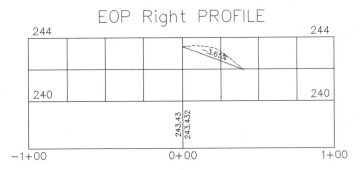

FIGURE 12.23
Your corridor after
applying the Intersec-
tion Typical Assembly

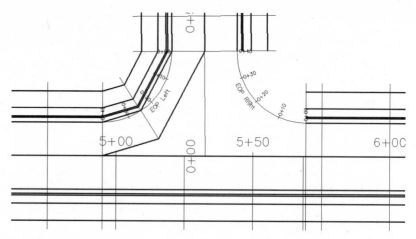

Notice that your assembly has been applied, but since you have not set the targets, the lane is only 12′ wide. You will need to target the Second Road centerline from Station 0+00 through approximately Station 0+20 and the Project Road centerline from approximately Station 0+20 through 0+40.

1. Open the Corridor Properties dialog and switch to the Parameters tab. Change the End Station of Baseline (3) Region (1) to **0+19.77**. The best way to do this is to click the Specify Station button and use your Intersection osnap to choose the intersection of Project Road and Second Road, as shown in Figure 12.24.

2. Click the ellipsis button in the Target column for the Baseline (3) Region (1) row, as shown in Figure 12.25.

3. In the Target Mapping dialog, choose Second Road for the Transition Alignment and Second Road FG for the Transition Profile. Click OK.

4. Click OK again to dismiss the Corridor Properties dialog and automatically rebuild your corridor. Your corridor should now look similar to Figure 12.26.

FIGURE 12.24
Use the Select
Station button and
the Intersection osnap
to change the End
Station.

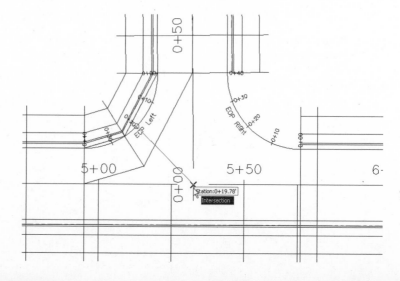

FIGURE 12.25
Click the
ellipsis button.

FIGURE 12.26
Your corridor after
setting the targets

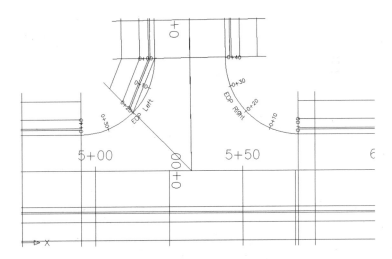

The target is set correctly for our first region, but the sampling frequency of the corridor is too far apart, resulting in a chunky appearance. We will now adjust the sampling frequency:

1. Open the Corridor Properties dialog and switch to the Parameters tab. Click the Frequency button for Baseline (3) Region (1).

2. In the Frequency To Apply To Assemblies dialog, change the Along Curves value to 2 and the At Profile High/Low Points value to Yes. Since our EOP alignments consist of a single curve, we can ignore the options for tangents and spirals. Click OK.

3. Click OK again to dismiss the Corridor Properties dialog and automatically rebuild your corridor. Your corridor should now look like Figure 12.27.

FIGURE 12.27
Your corridor after
changing the sam-
pling frequency

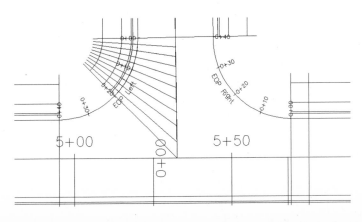

The first part of the EOP Left region is modeled properly. Now let's complete the left side of the corridor:

1. Open the Corridor Properties dialog and switch to the Parameters tab. Click on Region (1) under Baseline (3), and choose Insert Region. Use the Intersection Typical Assembly. The new region automatically picks up from station 0+19.77 and continues to the end of the EOP Left alignment.

2. Click the ellipsis button in the Target column for this region. In the Target Mapping dialog, change the Transition Alignment to Project Road and the Transition Profile to Project Road FG. Click OK.

3. Click the Frequency button for this region. In the Frequency To Apply To Assemblies dialog, change the Along Curves value to 2 and the At Profile High/Low Points value to Yes. Click OK.

4. Click OK to dismiss the Corridor Properties dialog and automatically rebuild your corridor. Your corridor should now look similar to Figure 12.28.

FIGURE 12.28

Your corridor after
mapping the targets

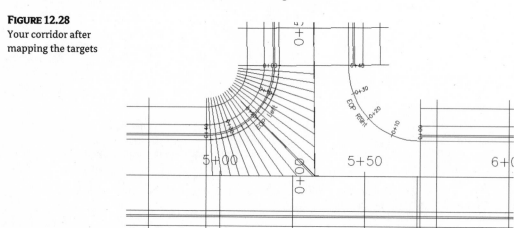

You must now repeat the process for the EOP Right baseline. To make it easier to work with your corridor, you can turn off baselines that you have finished building.

1. Open the Corridor Properties dialog again. Uncheck the boxes next to Baselines 1 through 3 on the Parameters tab, and click Apply.

2. Move the Corridor Properties dialog on your screen so that you can see the intersection alignments. Note that your corridor has temporarily disappeared since you have turned off all the baselines.

3. On the Parameters tab, click the Collapse All Categories button (see Figure 12.29) to "roll up" your baselines and regions and give you more room to work.

4. Add a baseline and appropriate regions, targets, and frequencies. A subtle, but important, difference for this side of the intersection is that the EOP Right alignment stationing is

reversed from the EOP Left, so you will first target the Project Road. Also note that if you would like to preview your work, you can click Apply and view the results without leaving the dialog.

5. The right side of your intersection should look like Figure 12.30.

6. On the Parameters tab, click Turn On All The Baselines to activate your corridor baselines (see Figure 12.31).

7. Click OK to dismiss the dialog and automatically rebuild your corridor. Your corridor should now look like Figure 12.32.

At this point, you have a properly modeled intersection, yet you have not even begun the design. The next few sections will lead you through some techniques to assist you in refining the model and beginning the design process.

FIGURE 12.29
The Collapse All
Categories button

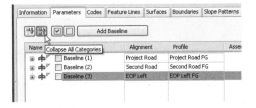

FIGURE 12.30
The right side of
the intersection

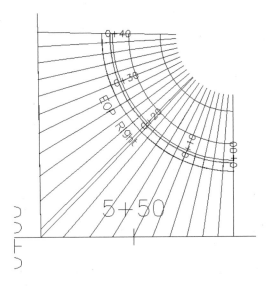

FIGURE 12.31
The Turn On All The
Baselines button

FIGURE 12.32
The properly modeled
intersection

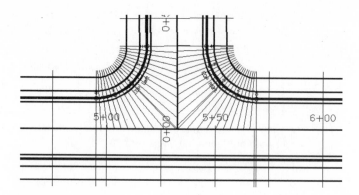

Troubleshooting Your Intersection

The best way to learn how to build advanced corridor components is to go ahead and build them, make mistakes, and try again. This section provides some guidelines on how to "read" your intersection to identify what steps you might have missed.

YOUR LANES APPEAR TO BE BACKWARDS

Occasionally, you might find that your lanes wind up on the wrong side of the EOP alignment, as in Figure 12.33. The most common cause for this is that the direction of your alignment is not compatible with your subassembly.

Fix this problem by reversing your alignment direction and rebuilding the corridor or editing your subassembly to swap the lane to the other side of the assembly. If you would like to minimize the number of assemblies in your drawing, simply note which directions the intersection alignments should run to accommodate one intersection assembly.

In the exercise, we used an intersection assembly with the transition lane on the left side, so we made sure that the left intersection EOP alignment ran clockwise and the right intersection EOP alignment ran counterclockwise. It is also easy enough to reverse an alignment and quickly rebuild the corridor if you catch the mistake after the corridor is built.

FIGURE 12.33
An intersection with
the lanes modeled
on the wrong side

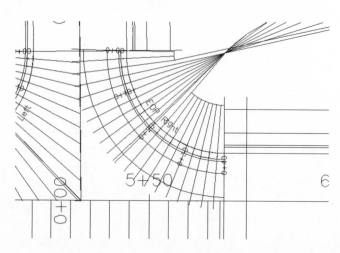

YOUR INTERSECTION DROPS DOWN TO ZERO

A common problem when modeling corridors is the "cliff" effect, where a portion of your corridor drops down to zero. You probably won't notice in plan view, but if you rotate your corridor in 3D using the Object Viewer (see Figure 12.34), you will notice the problem. If your baseline profile is not exactly as long as your baseline alignment, this will always occur.

Fix this problem by making sure that your baseline profile is exactly as long as your baseline alignment. The easiest way to ensure this is to use your osnaps to snap the proposed profile to the start and end points of the existing ground (EG) profile, and then use the profile grid view to refine the elevations. Alternatively, you can adjust your region limits to reflect the appropriate station range. You will find that it is much more foolproof just to make sure that your baseline alignment and profile match exactly.

YOUR LANES EXTEND TOO FAR IN SOME DIRECTIONS

There are several variations on this problem, but they all appear similar to Figure 12.35. All or some of your lanes extend too far down a target alignment, or they may cross one another, and so on. This occurs when the wrong target alignment and profile have been set for one or more regions.

FIGURE 12.34
A corridor viewed in 3D showing a drop down to zero

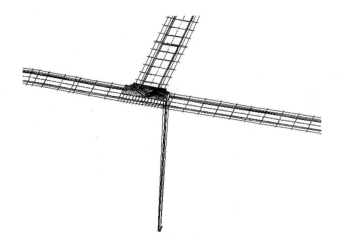

FIGURE 12.35
Intersection lanes extend too far down the main road alignment.

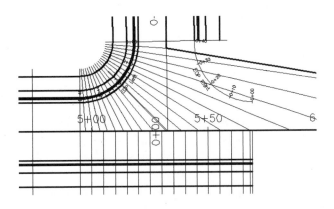

In the case of Figure 12.36, the first region of the EOP Left baseline was set to target the main road alignment instead of the secondary road alignment.

This problem can be fixed by simply opening the Target Mapping dialog for the affected regions and confirming that the appropriate targets have been set. Once the regions are targeting appropriately, your corridor should look like Figure 12.37.

FIGURE 12.36
Intersection lanes extend too far down the main road alignment.

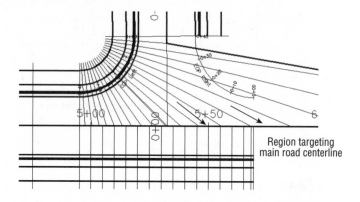

FIGURE 12.37
Intersection lanes have been repaired using the appropriate targets.

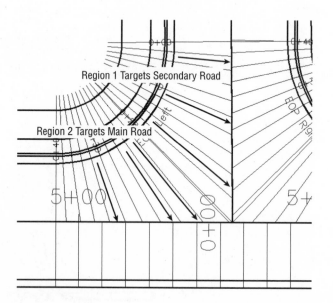

YOUR LANES DON'T EXTEND FAR ENOUGH

If your intersection or portions of your intersection look like Figure 12.38, you neglected to set the correct target alignment and profile.

This problem can be fixed by opening the Target Mapping dialog for the appropriate regions and double-checking that you assigned targets to the right subassembly. It is also common to accidentally set the target for the wrong subassembly if you used Map All Targets or if you have poor naming conventions for your subassemblies.

FIGURE 12.38
Intersection lanes
do not extend out
far enough.

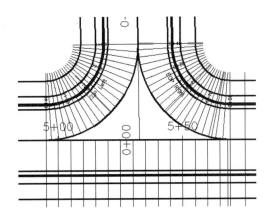

WHAT ABOUT OTHER TYPES OF INTERSECTIONS?

The corridor model is a tool that can be adapted to almost any design situation. There are many different ways to design an intersection and through a different combination of alignments, profiles, assemblies, and targets, you can create a model that will assist in the design of any intersection.

Another common method for intersection design occurs when the crowned section of the main road is held through the intersection. This type of intersection can be modeled with the same baselines as the peer-road intersection from the exercise in this chapter. There are a few differences, however.

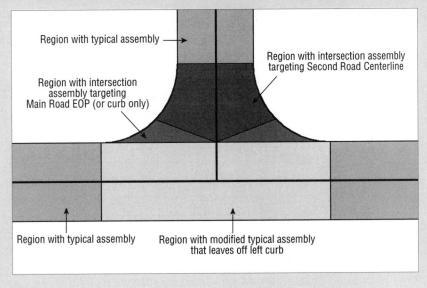

Instead of a "right-lane only" assembly, you'll need an assembly that is fundamentally the typical road section minus the left curb, sidewalk, and so on as in the following graphic.

The same intersection assembly can be used for the EOP baselines as in the exercise, but the region that would normally target the Main Road centerline now targets an alignment and corresponding profile that follows the edge of the Main Road left lane. The following graphic shows the location of this target alignment.

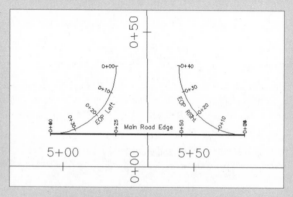

Once the region targets have been adjusted appropriately, the intersection corridor should look like this:

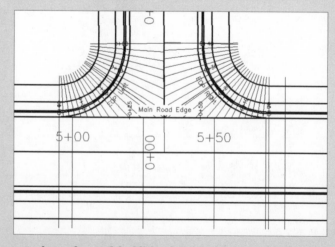

Similar techniques can be used to model additional design elements such as left-turn lanes, widening, asymmetrical intersections, and interchanges. The best way to tackle an intersection is to sketch the intersection layout and figure out how the components are related. Map out baselines, regions, targets, and subassemblies. Once you have a plan for your intersection, build all the required pieces and use the corridor to join your model together.

Building a First-Draft Corridor Surface

Once the initial model is built, the time comes to make sure that the elevations on the EOP profiles match your design intent. Since each end of the EOP alignment touches a portion of the "normal" cross section, it could be assumed that the elevations provided by a corridor surface at those locations would be your design intent. This information may change as you iterate the design, but those elevations, whatever they may be, will drive the design of the EOP profiles.

One technique for determining the elevations at those locations is to build a first-draft corridor surface. This surface will be ugly, and it will not contain any good information within the intersection area, but it will return solid elevations throughout the "normal" portions of our corridor.

Before beginning this exercise, review the basic corridor surface building sections in Chapter 11.

1. Open the `Corridor Peer Intersection Draft Surface.dwg` file, or continue working in your drawing from the previous exercise.

2. Open the Corridor Properties dialog and switch to the Surfaces tab.

3. Click Create A Corridor Surface. A Corridor Surface entry will appear.

4. Ensure that Links is selected as the Data Type and Top appears under Specify Code. Click the + button. An entry for Top should appear under the Corridor Surface entry.

5. Click OK, and your corridor will automatically rebuild. You should have a corridor surface that appears similar to Figure 12.39.

6. Pick the surface, right-click, and choose Surface Properties.

7. On the Information tab of the Surface Properties dialog, change the Surface Style setting to No Display. This will make the surface invisible so that you can use it for data but not be distracted by seeing it.

FIGURE 12.39
A first-draft
corridor surface

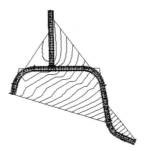

Perfecting Your Model to Optimize the Design

As stated in previous sections, your model can be built properly to reflect your desired trends and design constraints without having any real design information applied. Take the example in Figure 12.40. The corridor has been built to properly link all the components together, but Civil 3D does not automatically assign elevations to those relationships. The program depends on you to assign appropriate elevations to perfect your model and begin design iterations.

Once the appropriate elevations have been assigned, your corridor is ready for design iterations (see Figure 12.41).

FIGURE 12.40
A properly built corridor showing a location where the model needs to be corrected

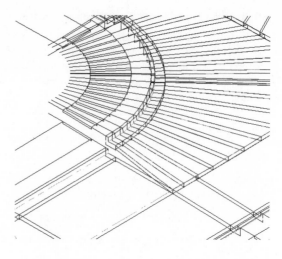

FIGURE 12.41
The same corridor after the model has been adjusted

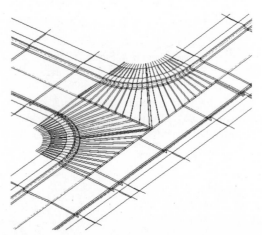

This exercise will lead you through placing some design labels to assist in perfecting your model, and then show you how to easily edit your EOP FG profiles to match the design intent on the basis of the draft corridor surface built in the previous section:

1. Open the `Corridor Peer Intersection 4.dwg` file, or continue working in your drawing from the previous exercise. You may find it easier to work if you freeze the C-ROAD-CORR layer. Thaw or freeze this layer as necessary to get a better view or to be able to osnap to your alignments more easily. If you have frozen your corridor, you can always access its properties by right-clicking the name of the corridor in Prospector. Also note that you can change the Corridor Surface style to No Display at any point during the exercise for the same reasons.

2. Open the Corridor Properties dialog and switch to the Parameters tab.

3. Uncheck the boxes next to the two intersection baselines—Baselines (3) and (4). By building the corridor (and therefore corridor surface) without these baselines, you eliminate the possibility of accidentally grabbing a bogus elevation produced by one of these yet-undesigned baselines.

4. Click OK and automatically rebuild your corridor. You should have a corridor that appears similar to Figure 12.42. Your model may also display contours. If desired, temporarily change the Surface Style to No Display to get a closer look at the corridor.

5. Your rough surface will also automatically rebuild, ignoring the intersection, as shown in Figure 12.43.

6. Add a label by choosing Alignments ➤ Add Alignment Labels ➤ Add Alignment Labels. In the Alignment Label dialog, confirm that the Main Road Profile and the Second Road Profile have identical elevations at their intersection point. It may be easier to use your osnaps if you freeze the C-ROAD_CORR layer for the next few steps.

FIGURE 12.42

The corridor model with the intersection baselines turned off and the Surface Style set to No Display

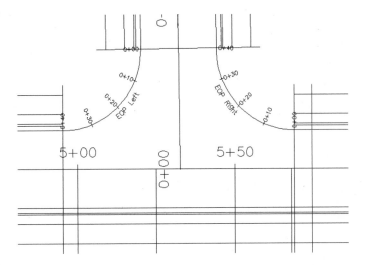

FIGURE 12.43

The corridor surface model with the intersection baselines turned off

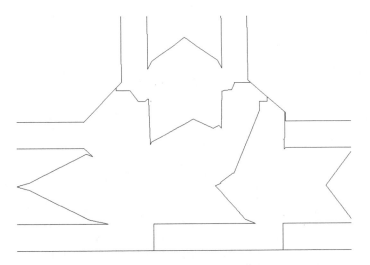

7. Select Station Offset for the Label Type, Intersection Centerline Label for the Station Offset label style, and Basic X for the Marker Style. Click Add.

8. This label was composed to reference two alignments and two profiles. At the `Select Alignment` command-line prompt, pick the Project Road alignment.

9. At the `Specify Station` command-line prompt, use your Intersection osnap to choose the intersection of the two alignments.

10. At the `Specify Station Offset` command-line prompt, type **0** (zero).

11. At the `Select profile for label style component Profile 1` command-line prompt, right-click to bring up a list of profiles and choose Project Road FG.

12. At the `Select alignment for label style component Alignment 2` command-line prompt, pick the Second Road alignment.

13. At the `Select profile for label style component Profile 2` command-line prompt, right-click to bring up a list of profiles and choose Second Road FG.

14. Press ↵, and then click OK to dismiss the Alignment Label dialog. Thaw the C-ROAD-CORR layer if it is frozen.

15. Pick the label, and use the square-shaped grip to drag the label somewhere out of the way. Your label should look like Figure 12.44.

Note that the elevations of the Project Road FG and Second Road FG are both equal to 233.792. If the label indicated that these elevations were not the same, you would need to edit your profile geometry to make sure they match. This label will be useful during later stages of the design process. As you iterate your FG profiles, this label will alert you to any adjustments that are required to make the profiles match at their intersection.

FIGURE 12.44
The Intersection Centerline design label

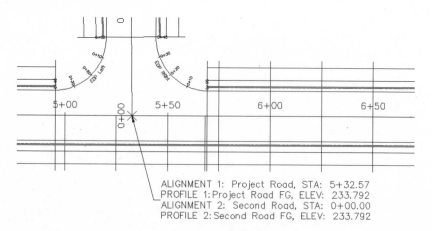

```
ALIGNMENT 1: Project Road, STA: 5+32.57
PROFILE 1: Project Road FG, ELEV: 233.792
ALIGNMENT 2: Second Road, STA: 0+00.00
PROFILE 2: Second Road FG, ELEV: 233.792
```

The next part of the exercise will guide you through the process of adding a label to help determine what elevations should be assigned to the Start and End stations of the EOP Right and EOP Left alignments:

1. Choose Alignments ➢ Add Alignment Labels ➢ Add Alignment Labels.

2. In the Alignment Label dialog, select Station Offset for the Label Type, Intersection EOP Label for the Station Offset label style, and Basic X for the Marker Style. Click Add.

3. These labels have been composed to be a label of the road centerline that references a surface elevation. At the `Select Alignment` command-line prompt, pick the Project Road alignment.

4. At the `Specify Station` command-line prompt, use your Endpoint osnap to pick the Start Station of the EOP Right alignment.

5. At the `Specify Station Offset` command-line prompt, use your Endpoint osnap to pick the Start Station of the EOP Right alignment.

6. At the `Select surface for label style component Corridor Surface` command-line prompt, right-click to bring up a list of surfaces and select the appropriate corridor surface.

7. Press ↵, and then click Ok to dismiss the Alignment Label dialog.

8. Pick the label and use the square-shaped grip to drag the label somewhere that is out of the way. Your label should look like Figure 12.45.

9. Repeat the previous steps to provide labels for the End Station of the EOP Right alignment and the Start and End stations of the EOP Left alignment. Note that you will have to exit the command when you need to switch the reference road centerline.

10. Once all the labels have been placed, your corridor should look like Figure 12.46.

FIGURE 12.45
The Intersection Centerline design label

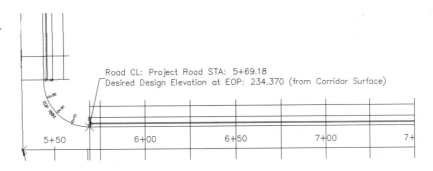

FIGURE 12.46
The corridor with all labels placed

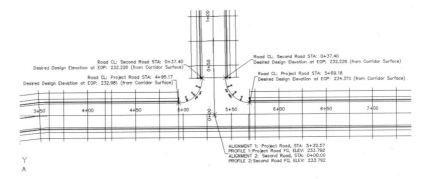

Now that you have added labels to the Start and End stations of the EOP Right and EOP Left alignments, let's add labels to the EOP Right and Left FG profiles and then view the contours from the corridor surface:

1. Choose View ➤ Viewports ➤ 2 Viewports to split your screen into two viewports so that you can easily see your EOP alignments and labels at the same time as the corresponding profiles. Press ↵ at the command line to specify a vertical split. Your screen should look similar to Figure 12.47.

2. Pick the EOP Right FG profile. Right-click and choose Edit Profile Geometry.

3. On the Profile Layout Tools toolbar, click Profile Grid View.

4. In the Profile Entities palette in Panorama, change the PVI elevations to match the values from the plan labels, as shown in Figure 12.48.

5. Dismiss Panorama. Repeat the previous steps for the EOP Left FG profile.

FIGURE 12.47

Use a split screen to see plan and profile simultaneously.

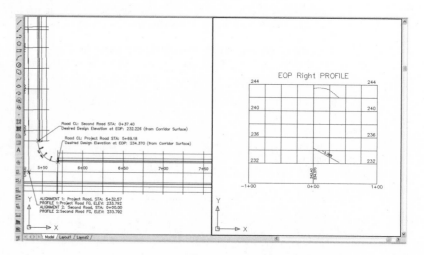

FIGURE 12.48

Edit the PVI elevations to match the desired EOP elevations.

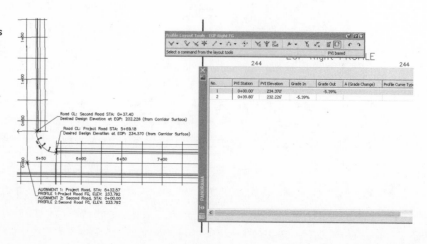

6. Open the Corridor Properties dialog and switch to the Parameters tab. Turn on all baselines. Click OK, and your corridor will automatically rebuild.

7. Pick your corridor. Right-click and choose Object Viewer.

8. Navigate through Object Viewer to confirm that your corridor model is now appropriately tied together at the EOP. Note that any changes in centerline will not automatically update your EOP alignments. Your corridor should look like Figure 12.49.

9. As you continue iterating your design and making edits to the centerline profiles, rebuild the corridor, and use your updated labels to refine the desired elevations on the EOP profiles.

10. Exit Object Viewer.

11. Select your corridor surface under the Surfaces branch in Prospector. Right-click and choose Surface Properties. The Surface Properties dialog opens. Change the Surface Style to Contours 1´ And 5´ (Design). Click OK to dismiss the dialog.

12. Pick the corridor surface and use Object Viewer to study the TIN in the intersection area.

Study the contours in the intersection area. Even though the contours may not necessarily be optimally designed at this point, you should have decent contours within the intersection area, with no "pits" or "holes" in the corridor surface. Ignore the contours outside the corridor limits.

FIGURE 12.49
The properly modeled intersection

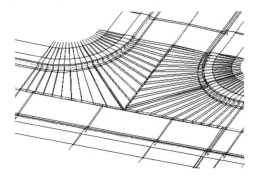

Refining a Corridor Surface

Once your model makes more sense, you can build a better corridor surface. Don't be confused into thinking this is your final design. You can continue to edit, refine, and optimize your corridor as you gain new information. From now on, however, it will take only a few minutes to edit the corridor and see the reaction of the corridor surface.

A few elements that will be used in this exercise include something mentioned in Chapter 11 about links as breaklines and adding feature lines. Be sure to review the section on surface building from corridors in Chapter 11.

When building a surface from links, you have the option of checking a box in the Add As Breakline column. Checking this box will add the actual link lines themselves as additional breaklines to the surface. In most cases, especially intersection design, checking this box forces better triangulation.

This next exercise will have you add a few meaningful corridor feature lines to the surface to force triangulation along important features like edge of travel way and top of curb.

The exercise also gives you hands-on experience in adding an interactive boundary to your corridor. In Chapter 11, we were able to use an automatic boundary. However, you no longer have the automatic boundary option for multiple baseline corridors. The Interactive Boundary tool provides an interface that allows you to choose a bounding feature line around your corridor.

The more appropriate data you add to the surface definition, the better your surface (and therefore your contours) will look—right from the beginning, which means fewer edits and less temptation to grade by hand.

1. Open the `Corridor Peer Intersection 5.dwg` file, or continue working in your drawing from the previous exercise.

2. Select the Corridor in the drawing or in Prospector. Right-click and choose Corridor Properties, then switch to the Surfaces tab. The Surface Properties dialog opens. Change the Surface Style to Contours 1′ And 5′ (Design). Change the Surface Style of Corridor - 5(5) to No Display so that you don't accidentally pick it when choosing a corridor boundary.

3. In the row for the Top, under Corridor Surface, check the box in the Add As Breakline column.

4. Select Feature Lines from the dropdown menu in the Data Type selection box.

5. Use the dropdown menu in the Specify Code selection box and the + button to add the Top, Back_Curb, Crown, ETW, Flange, Flowline_Gutter, and Top_Curb feature lines to the Corridor Surface, as shown in Figure 12.50.

6. Click Apply to add these feature lines, then switch to the Boundaries tab.

7. Pick your corridor surface and right-click. Choose Add Interactively.

8. Zoom down to the Start Station of Project Road. The command line will prompt you `To define boundary, select the first point on a corridor feature line`. Use your Endpoint osnap to pick the furthest left feature line on the corridor.

9. The command line will then prompt you to `Select next point on this feature line or click on another feature line or [Undo/Close]:`.

10. Move your mouse and notice that a red "jig" follows your cursor along the chosen feature line. It will continue to follow you until the end of a region.

FIGURE 12.50
Adding feature lines to the Corridor Surface

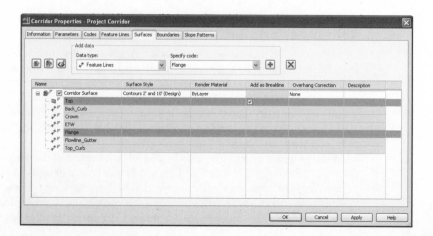

11. Once you reach the next region, simply pick the furthest left feature line in that region. Continue the process around the entire corridor. As you progress, the jig will continue to follow your cursor and picks, as shown in Figure 12.51.

12. When you come back to the Start Station of Project Road, type **C** to close the boundary.

13. The Boundaries tab of the Corridor Properties dialog will return.

14. Click OK to dismiss the dialog, and your corridor will automatically rebuild, along with your corridor surface.

15. Select your corridor surface under the Surfaces branch in Prospector. Right-click and choose Surface Properties. The Surface Properties dialog opens. Change the Surface Style to Contours 1′ And 5′ (Design), and click OK. Click OK to dismiss the Surface Properties dialog.

16. Note your surface is now limited to the area inside the interactive boundary. Use Object Viewer to examine your surface TIN. You may see some improvement in the triangulation because of adding the corridor links and feature lines as breaklines. In plan view, your surface contours should look like Figure 12.52.

FIGURE 12.51
The corridor
boundary jig

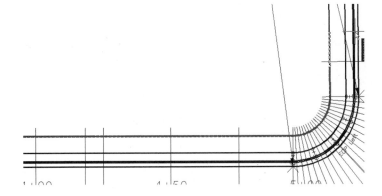

FIGURE 12.52
The finished corridor
surface contours

In isometric view, your surface TIN at the intersection should appear as shown in Figure 12.53. Additional, optional edits can be made to the TIN if you are still unhappy with your road surface. Edits that might prove useful would include increasing the corridor frequency in select regions, adjusting the starting and ending stations in a region, or using surface-editing commands to swap edges or delete points.

FIGURE 12.53
The surface TIN
viewed in 3D

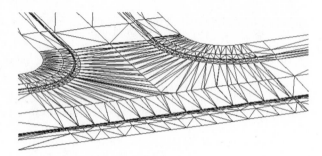

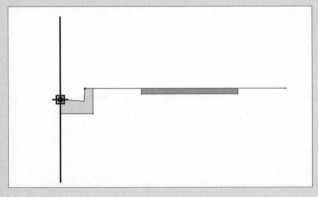

🌐 Real World Scenario

TAKE ADVANTAGE OF YOUR TIN

The corridor surface creation section in Chapter 11 and the corridor surface refinements in this chapter have given you a good understanding of how a corridor surface is built. There are many ways that you can take advantage of surface creation that allow the TIN to "fill in the blanks" for you and reduce the number of target alignments and profiles that you must create and maintain.

In a previous section, we mentioned a method for creating an intersection where the crown of the main road is held through the intersection. That method requires the creation and maintenance of a fifth alignment and profile that follows the main road EOP. In this example, you can use a curb-only assembly, similar to the following graphic, in the region that would have normally targeted the edge-of-lane alignment.

The resulting corridor will not have any links in this region, as in this graphic, which may seem strange until you build the corridor surface.

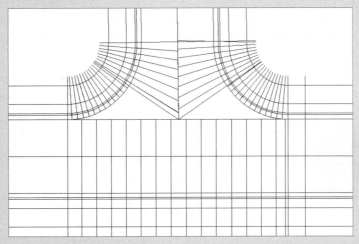

The resulting corridor surface uses the principles explained in the section "Building a First Draft Corridor Surface" in Chapter 11 to create the TIN, and therefore corridor points are connected to complete the lanes with TIN lines. The next image clearly shows the triangulation along the crowned section and no gaps anywhere in the intersection.

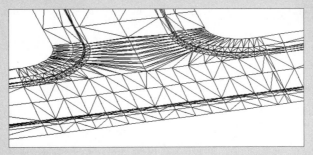

The resulting TIN occasionally needs more edge swapping than a corridor surface modeled with a complete set of links. Another thing to keep in mind is that since there are no links through part of the intersection, code set styles designed for hatching and rendering may not work through the linkless region and corridor-based material quantities may not be valid.

All things considered, this technique can be a major timesaver when modeling intersections.

Modeling a Cul-de-sac

Another common corridor design roadblock is the common cul-de-sac. While cul-de-sacs come in all shapes and sizes, you can apply and adapt the principles explained in this section in many design scenarios, including off-center cul-de-sacs, asymmetrical cul-de-sacs, knuckles, turnarounds, and other designs.

Adding a Baseline, Region, and Targets for the Cul-de-sac

As you would with an intersection, you sit down and plan your cul-de-sac before beginning the model. How does your cul-de-sac look? What is driving the elevations? Is there a crown in the cul-de-sac or does all of the pavement grade to one side? Answer these questions, and draw yourself a quick sketch. Then, as discussed in the section "Modeling a Peer-Road Intersection" earlier, plan your baselines, regions, targets, and subassemblies.

For this example, you will apply an assembly to a single baseline that traces the cul-de-sac EOP all the way around the bulb. We strongly recommended that you work through the intersection exercise before doing this exercise. Many of the techniques are identical and therefore will not be explained in the steps for this exercise.

1. Open the `Corridor Cul-de-sac.dwg` file. Note that there is an alignment that follows the EOP for a 38′ radius cul-de-sac, as well as a corresponding profile. There is also a corridor, a corridor surface, a few assemblies, and some Intersection EOP labels.

2. Choose View ➤ Viewports ➤ 2 Viewports. Press ⏎ in the command line to specify a vertical split. Use your Pan and Zoom commands so that you see the cul-de-sac plan on one side of your screen and the cul-de-sac EOP profile view on the other side.

3. Pick the cul-de-sac EOP FG profile. Open the Profile Layout Tools toolbar and use the Profile Grid View tool to confirm that the Start and End stations of the cul-de-sac EOP FG profile match the desired design elevations as listed in the plan view design labels. If the elevations do not match, make the necessary adjustments. Dismiss the grid view and the profile toolbar.

4. Choose View ➤ Viewports ➤ 1 Viewport to remove the split screen.

5. Zoom over to the cul-de-sac in plan view. Open the Corridor Properties dialog, and switch to the Parameters tab.

6. Click Add Baseline. Select the Cul-de-sac EOP as the baseline alignment in the Pick Horizontal Alignment dialog. Click OK.

7. Click in the Profile field. Select Cul-de-sac EOP FG as the baseline profile in the Select A Profile dialog. Click OK.

8. Right-click on the baseline you just created, and select Add Region. Select the Intersection Typical Assembly in the Pick An Assembly dialog. Click Ok.

9. Expand your baseline and see the new region you just created.

10. Click the Frequency button for your region. In the Frequency To Apply To Assemblies dialog, set all the frequency intervals to 5′, and change the At Profile High/Low Points to Yes. Click OK.

11. Click the Target button for your region. In the Target Mapping dialog, set the Transition alignment to Project Road and the Transition Profile to Project Road FG. Click OK.

12. Click OK again to dismiss the Corridor Properties dialog and automatically rebuild your corridor, along with your corridor surface. Your corridor should look similar to Figure 12.54.

13. Add a boundary to your corridor as detailed in the previous section. View your surface in Object Viewer or in a 3D view to check for triangulation problems and study the surface result. The corridor should look similar to Figure 12.55a in Object Viewer, whereas the corridor-surface contours and the corridor-surface TIN should look similar to Figures 12.55b and 12.55c, respectively.

FIGURE 12.54
The modeled
cul-de-sac

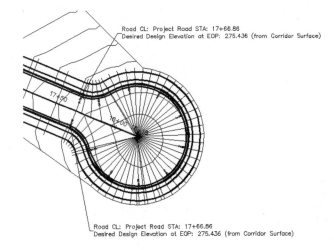

Road CL: Project Road STA: 17+66.86
Desired Design Elevation at EOP: 275.436 (from Corridor Surface)

Road CL: Project Road STA: 17+66.86
Desired Design Elevation at EOP: 275.436 (from Corridor Surface)

FIGURE 12.55
The corridor model
viewed in 3D (a),
the resulting corridor-
surface contours (b),
and the resulting cor-
ridor-surface TIN (c).

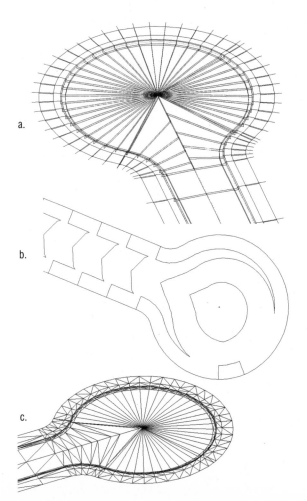

a.

b.

c.

Additionally, you may want to improve the quality of your corridor surface using some of the techniques described in the "Refining a Corridor Surface" section.

Troubleshooting Your Cul-de-sac

There are several common mistakes people make when modeling their first few cul-de-sacs.

YOUR CUL-DE-SAC APPEARS WITH A LARGE GAP IN THE CENTER

If your curb line seems to be modeling correctly but your lanes are leaving a large empty area in the middle (see Figure 12.56), chances are pretty good that you neglected to assign targets or perhaps assigned the incorrect targets.

FIGURE 12.56
A cul-de-sac
without targets

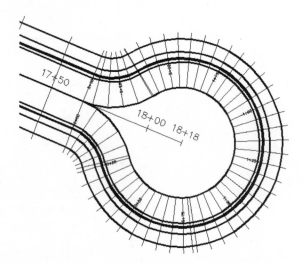

Fix this problem by opening the Target Mapping dialog for your region and checking to make sure you assigned the road centerline alignment and FG profile for your transition lane. If you have a more advanced lane subassembly, then you may have accidentally set the targets for another subassembly somewhere in your corridor instead of the lane for the cul-de-sac transition, especially if you have poor subassembly-naming conventions. Poor naming conventions become especially confusing if you used the Map All Targets button.

YOUR CUL-DE-SAC APPEARS TO BE BACKWARDS

Occasionally, you might find that your lanes wind up on the wrong side of the EOP alignment, as shown in Figure 12.57. The most common cause for this is that the direction of your alignment is not compatible with your subassembly.

You can fix this problem by reversing your alignment direction and rebuilding the corridor or editing your subassembly to swap the lane to the other side of the assembly.

FIGURE 12.57
A cul-de-sac with the
lanes modeled on the
wrong side

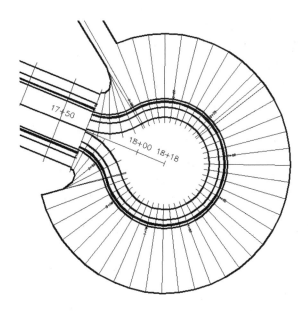

YOUR CUL-DE-SAC DROPS DOWN TO ZERO

A common problem when you first begin modeling cul-de-sacs, intersections, and other corridor components is that one end of your baseline drops down to zero. You probably won't notice the problem in plan view, but once you build your surface (see Figure 12.58a) or rotate your corridor in 3D (see Figure 12.58b), you will notice it. This problem will always occur if your baseline profile is not the exact length as your baseline alignment.

   This problem can be fixed by making sure that your baseline profile is the exact length as your baseline alignment. See the section "Troubleshooting Your Intersection" for more tips and information on fixing this problem.

FIGURE 12.58
Contours indicating
that the corridor
surface drops down
to zero (a) and a
corridor viewed in
3D showing a drop
down to zero (b).

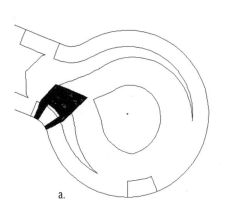

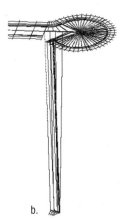

a.

b.

YOUR CUL-DE-SAC SEEMS FLAT

When first learning the concept of targets, it is easy to mix up baseline alignments and target alignments. In the beginning, you may accidentally choose your EOP alignment as a target instead of the road centerline. If this happens, your cul-de-sac will look similar to Figure 12.59.

You can fix this problem by opening the Target Mapping dialog for this region and making sure that the target alignment is set to the road centerline and the target profile is set to the road centerline FG profile.

FIGURE 12.59
A cul-de-sac with the wrong targets set

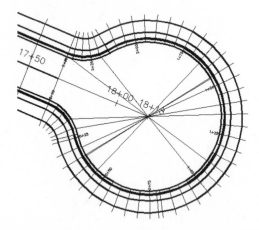

Modeling a Widening with an Assembly Offset

As you continue to improve your corridor-building skills, you will want to investigate increasingly more advanced methods for refining your model to better meet your design intent.

In Chapter 11, you did a road-widening example with a simple lane transition. Earlier in this chapter, you worked with a roadside-ditch transition, intersections, and cul-de-sacs. These are just a few of the combinations techniques for adjusting your corridor to accommodate a widening, narrowing, interchange, or similar circumstances. There is no one method for how to build a corridor model; every method we have discussed so far can be combined in a variety of ways to build a model that reflects your design intent.

Another tool in the corridor-building arsenal is the assembly offset. In the transition lane and transition ditch examples you have done, you may have noticed that every corridor link is modeled perpendicular to the baseline, as shown in Figure 12.60.

The assembly offset can be used when the elements outside your transition area are better modeled perpendicular to the transition alignment, as shown in Figure 12.61.

Typical examples of when you would use an assembly offset include transitioning ditches, widening roads, traffic-calming lanes, interchanges, and other applications. The assembly in Figure 12.62, for example, includes two assembly offsets. The assembly could be used for transitioning roadside swales, similar to the first exercise in this chapter.

In addition to adapting your assembly to include offsets, each offset requires a dedicated alignment and profile.

FIGURE 12.60
Modeling a
road widening

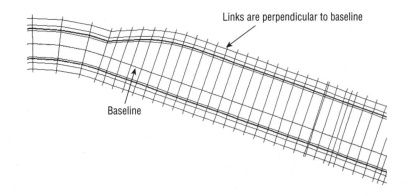

FIGURE 12.61
Modeling a road
widening with an
assembly offset

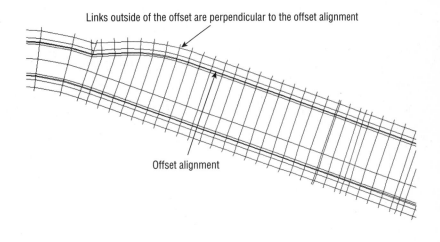

FIGURE 12.62
An assembly with
two offsets represent-
ing roadside swale
centerlines

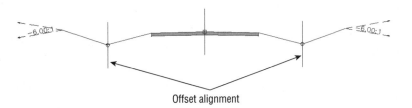

Even though each offset requires its own profile, it is not always necessary to use Profiles ➢ Create By Layout and design a profile from scratch. Use some creativity to figure out additional methods to achieve your design intent. Extracting a profile from a corridor, sampling a profile from a first draft surface, importing a profile from another source, copying a main road profile and moving it to different elevation, and superimposing profiles are all valid methods for creating profiles for targeting and assembly offsets.

In this exercise, you will improve the basic road-widening model from Chapter 11 with an assembly offset:

1. Open the `Offset Assembly Corridor.dwg` file. Note this is the same model you created in Chapter 11 using a simple transition with a target alignment. In addition to the road model, there is a profile view of the Widening EOP alignment.

2. Zoom to the area of the drawing where the assemblies are located. Note there is an incomplete assembly called Project Road Offset Assembly.

3. Choose Corridors ➢ Create Assembly Offset.

4. At the `Select an assembly <or press enter key to select from list>` command-line prompt, pick the Project Road Offset Assembly.

5. At the `Specify offset location` command-line prompt, pick the far-right point of the right lane on the Project Road Offset Assembly. Your result should look like Figure 12.63.

6. Use the AutoCAD Copy command to copy the Left Curb and Sidewalk subassemblies from one of the other assemblies. Place them near your Project Road Offset Assembly.

7. Pick the curb. Right-click and choose Add To Assembly, and then pick the assembly offset you placed on the Project Road Offset assembly.

8. Repeat step 6 with the Sidewalk subassembly, except attach the sidewalk to the appropriate place on the curb. Your result should look like Figure 12.64.

FIGURE 12.63
The Project Road Offset assembly

FIGURE 12.64
The Project Road Offset assembly with the Left Curb and Sidewalk subassembly

Now that the assembly is built, we need a profile representing EOP before we can adjust the corridor model. We have several options for creating this profile, such as using Profiles ➤ Create By Layout or any other valid profile creation technique. In this case, the corridor surface in this drawing can provide a valid profile for your offset.

1. Choose Profiles ➤ Create Profile From Surface. In the Create Profile From Surface dialog, select the Widening EOP Alignment and the Project Road Corridor Surface. Click Add to sample this surface.

2. In the Profile list, change the Update Mode of the profile to Static and the Style to Right Sample Profile. Click OK to dismiss the dialog. A surface profile should automatically appear in the Widening EOP profile view. If the Panorama window appears to notify you that a profile has been created, click the green check mark to dismiss it.

3. Now you must swap the more basic transition lane assembly for the more robust offset assembly you created earlier in the exercise. Open the Corridor Properties dialog and select the Project Road Corridor on the Parameters tab.

4. Change the Assembly for Region (2) from Project Road Transition Lane to Project Road Offset Assembly.

5. Expand Region (2) to list the offsets. Select Widening EOP under Alignment and Project Road Corridor Surface Profile under Profile.

6. Open the Target Mapping dialog for this region and confirm that the transition alignment for the left lane is still set to Widening EOP. Set this value if necessary. Click OK to close the dialog.

7. Click OK again to dismiss the Corridor Properties dialog and to automatically rebuild your corridor, along with your corridor surface.

If you examine the corridor model and the resulting surface, you will notice that there is a subtle, but potentially very important, difference in the curb and sidewalk. In the previous model, the curb and sidewalk links had been placed perpendicular to the baseline, which in this case was the Project Road centerline. In the offset assembly–based model, the links are perpendicular to the EOP alignment, which is often closer to your design intent. If you zoom in on the curb and sidewalk area, your corridor should look similar to Figure 12.65.

FIGURE 12.65
A close-up view of the completed corridor

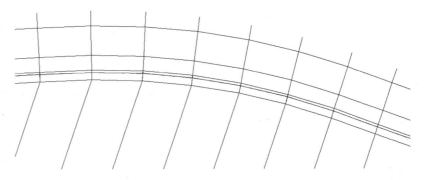

THE TROUBLE WITH BOWTIES

In your adventures with corridors, chances are pretty good that you will create an overlapping link or two. These overlapping links are known affectionately as "bowties." A mild example can be seen in the following graphic:

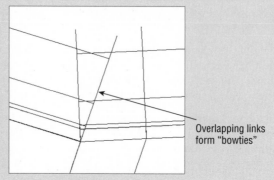

Overlapping links form "bowties"

An even more pronounced example can be seen in the following river corridor:

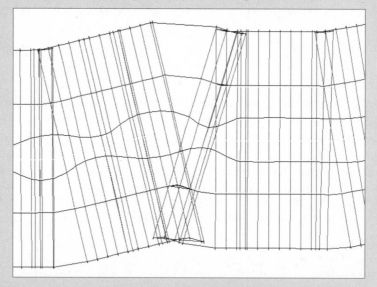

Bowties are problematic for several reasons. In essence, the corridor model has created two or more points at the same x and y locations with a different z, making it difficult to build surfaces, extract feature lines, create a boundary, and apply code set styles that render or hatch.

When your corridor surface is created, the TIN has to make some assumptions about crossing breaklines that can lead to strange triangulation and incoherent contours, such as in the following graphic:

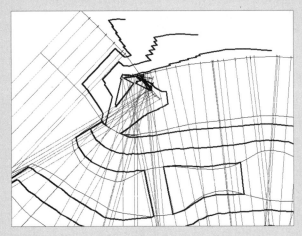

When you create a corridor that produces bowties, you will find your corridor will not behave as expected. Choosing Corridors ➤ Utilities to extract polylines or feature lines from overlapping corridor areas will yield an entity that will be difficult to use for additional grading or manipulation because of extraneous, overlapping, and invalid vertices. If the corridor contains many overlaps, you may have trouble even executing the extraction tools. The same concept applies to extracted alignments, profiles, and COGO points.

If you try to add an automatic or interactive boundary to your corridor surface, you will either get an error or the boundary jig will stop following the feature line altogether, making it impossible to create an interactive boundary.

Finally, in Chapter 22, we will explore some methods for applying code set styles to a corridor model for link-based rendering. The software goes through some superficial surface modeling to apply the render materials. Since the corridor has no inherent valid boundary when there are overlapping links, you will get undesirable results when rendering such a corridor, as in the following graphic, which shows a corridor similar to the one in the assembly offset exercise when the realistic visual style is applied.

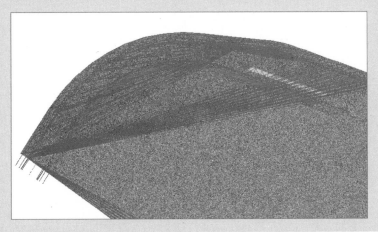

To prevent these problems, the best plan is to try to avoid link overlap. Be sure your baseline, offset, and target alignments do not have redundant or PI locations that are spaced excessively close.

If you initially build a corridor with simple transitions that produce a lot of overlap, try using an assembly offset and an alignment besides your centerline as a baseline. Another technique is to split your assembly into several smaller assemblies and to use your target assemblies as baselines, similar to using an assembly offset. This method was used to improve the river corridor seen in the previous graphics. This graphic shows the two assemblies that were created to attach at the top of bank alignments instead of the river centerline:

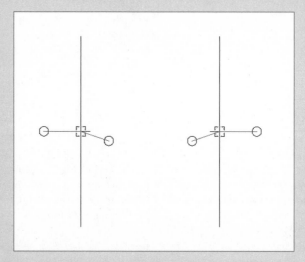

The resulting corridor is shown in the following graphic:

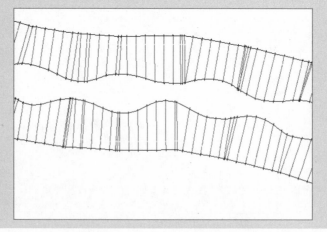

The TIN connected the points across the flat bottom and modeled the corridor perfectly:

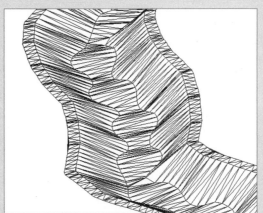

Another method for eliminating bowties is to notice the area where they seem to occur and adjust the regions. If your daylight links are overlapping, perhaps you can create an assembly that doesn't include daylighting and create a region to apply that new assembly.

If overlap cannot be avoided in your corridor, don't panic. If your overlaps are minimal, you should still be able to extract a polyline or feature line—just be sure to weed vertices and clean up the extracted entity before using it for projection grading. A boundary can be created for your corridor surface by drawing a regular polyline around your corridor and adding it as a boundary to the corridor surface under the Surfaces branch in Prospector. The surface-editing tools, such as Swap Edge, Delete Line, and Delete Point, can also prove useful for the final cleanup and contour improvement of your final corridor surface.

As you gain more and more experience building corridors, you will be able to prevent or fix most overlap situations, and you will also gain an understanding of when they are not having a detrimental effect on the quality of your corridor model and resulting surface.

The Bottom Line

Add a baseline to a corridor model for a cul-de-sac. Though for simple corridors you may think of a baseline as a road centerline, other elements of a road design can be used as a baseline. In the case of a cul-de-sac, the EOP, top of curb, or any other appropriate feature can be converted to an alignment and profile and used as a baseline.

Master It Open the `Mastering Advanced Corridors.dwg` file. Add the cul-de-sac alignment and profile to the corridor as a baseline. Create a region under this baseline that applies the Typical Intersection assembly.

Add alignment and profile targets to a region for a cul-de-sac. Adding a baseline isn't always enough. Some corridor models require the use of targets. In the case of a cul-de-sac, the lane elevations are often driven by the cul-de-sac centerline alignment and profile.

Master It Continue working in the `Mastering Advanced Corridors.dwg` file. Add the Second Road alignment and Second Road FG profile as targets to the cul-de-sac region. Adjust the Assembly Application Frequency to 5~FT and make sure the corridor samples at profile PVIs.

Use the interactive boundary tool to add a boundary to the corridor surface. Every good surface needs a boundary to prevent bad triangulation. Bad triangulation creates inaccurate and unsightly contours. Civil 3D provides several tools for creating corridor surface boundaries, including an Interactive Boundary tool.

Master It Continue working in the `Mastering Advanced Corridors.dwg` file. Create an interactive corridor surface boundary for the entire corridor model.

Chapter 13

Stacking Up: Cross Sections

Cross sections are used in Civil 3D to allow the user to have a graphic confirmation of design intent, as well as to calculate the quantities of materials used in a design. Sections must have at least two types of Civil 3D objects to be created: an alignment and a surface. Other objects, such as pipes, structures, and corridor components, can be sampled in a sample line group, which is used to create the graphical section that is displayed in a section view. These section views and sections remain dynamic throughout the design process, reflecting any changes made to the sampled information. This reduces potential errors in materials reports, keeping often costly mistakes from happening during the construction process.

In this chapter, you will learn how to:

◆ Create sample lines

◆ Create section views

◆ Define materials

◆ Generate volume reports

The Corridor

Before you create sample lines, you often start with a corridor. The corridor allows you to display the materials being used, as well as to show the new surface with cut-and-fill areas. In this chapter, the corridor is a relatively short roadway (1,340´) designed for a residential subdivision (see Figure 13.1).

This corridor has both a top surface and a base surface created for inclusion in the sample line group, as shown in Figure 13.2. Creating surfaces from the different links and feature lines in a corridor allow you to use sections to calculate volumes between those surfaces. These volumes are calculated by specifying which surfaces to compare when you create a materials list.

CREATING THE BEST POSSIBLE SURFACE FOR SAMPLING

Note that you can create corridor surfaces in two different ways—from links and from feature lines. Links will provide you with a total surface along the width of a corridor, such as the top of pavement, top of base, and top of subbase. Feature lines require selecting a few more objects to add into a corridor surface to accurately create the surface.

FIGURE 13.1
The Old Settlers
Way corridor

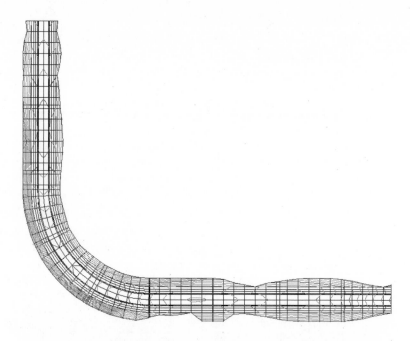

FIGURE 13.2
The Corridor
Properties dialog

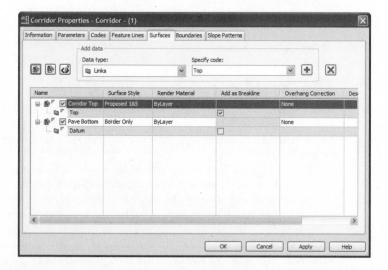

When you create your sample line group, you will have the option to sample any surface in your drawing, including corridor surfaces, the corridor assembly itself, and any pipes in your drawing. The sections are then sampled along the alignment with the left and right widths specified and at the intervals specified. Once the sample lines are created, you can then choose to create section views or to define materials.

Lining Up for Samples

Sample lines are the engine underneath both sections and materials and are held in a collection called sample line groups. One alignment can have multiple sample line groups, but a sample line group can only sample one alignment. Sample lines typically consist of two components: the sample lines and the sample line labels, as seen in Figure 13.3.

If you pick a sample line, you will see that it has three different types of grips, as shown in Figure 13.4. The diamond grip on the alignment allows you to move the sample line along the alignment. The triangular grip on the end of the sample line allows you to move the sample line along an extension of the line, either making it longer or shorter. The square grip on the end of the sample line allows you to not only move the sample line in or out, but also move it in any direction on the XY plane.

FIGURE 13.3
Sample lines consist of the lines and their labels

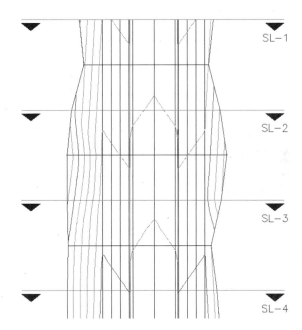

FIGURE 13.4
The three types of grips on a sample line

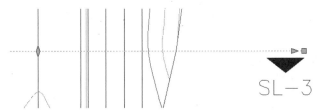

To create a sample line group, choose Sections ➤ Create Sample Lines from the menu bar. This will open the Create Sample Line Group dialog, shown in Figure 13.5. This dialog prompts you to name the sample line group, apply a sample line and label style, and choose what objects in your drawing you would like to sample. Every object that is available will be displayed in this box, with an area to set the section style, whether to sample the data, what layer each sampled item would be applied to, and a setting to specify whether the data should be static or dynamic. For example, you would typically select your existing ground (EG) surface to be sampled, displayed with an EG style, and be static. Your finished grade (FG) surface would also be sampled, but be displayed with a FG style and be dynamic.

Once the sample data has been selected, the Sample Line Tools toolbar will appear, as shown in Figure 13.6. This toolbar is context sensitive and only displays when you are creating sample lines. Once you have completed the sample line creation process, close the toolbar, and the command ends. Since most of the information is already set for you in this toolbar, the Sample Line Creation Methods button is the only one that is really needed. This gives you the following five options for creating sample lines:

◆ By Range Of Stations

◆ At A Station

◆ From Corridor Stations

◆ Pick Points On Screen

◆ Select Existing Polylines

In Civil 3D 2008, these options are listed in order from most used to least used. Because the most common method of creating sample lines is from one station to another at set intervals, the By Range Of Stations option is first. You can use At A Station to create one sample line at a specific station. From Corridor Stations allows you to insert a sample line at each corridor assembly insertion. Pick Points On Screen allows you to pick any two points to define a sample line. This option can be useful in special situations, such as sampling a pipe on a skew. The last option, Select Existing Polylines, lets you define sample lines from existing polylines.

FIGURE 13.5

The Create Sample Line Group dialog

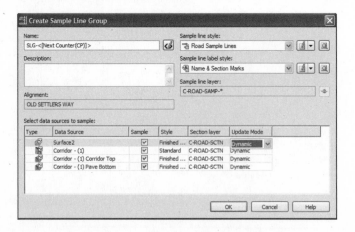

FIGURE 13.6

The Sample Line Tools toolbar

A WARNING ABOUT USING POLYLINES TO DEFINE SAMPLE LINES

Be careful when picking existing polylines to define sample lines. Any osnaps used during polyline creation can throw off the Z-values of the section, giving sometimes undesirable results.

To define sample lines, you need to specify a few settings. Figure 13.7 shows the settings that need to be defined in the Create Sample Lines By Station Range dialog. The Right Swath Width is the width from the alignment that you sample. Most of the time this distance is greater than the ROW distance. You also select your Sampling Increments, and choose whether to include special stations, such as horizontal geometry (PC, PT, and so on), vertical geometry (PVC, high point, low point, and so on), and superelevation critical stations.

FIGURE 13.7
Sample Line settings

Creating Sample Lines Along a Corridor

Before creating cross sections, you must sample the information that will be displayed. You do this by creating sample lines, which are part of a sample line group. Only one alignment can be sampled per sample line group. When creating sample lines, you will have to determine the frequency of your sections and the objects that you want included in the section views. In the following exercise, you will create sample lines for Old Settlers Way:

1. Open the `sections1.dwg` file.

2. Choose Sections ➢ Create Sample Lines.

3. Press ↵ to display the Select Alignment dialog.

4. Select the Old Settlers Way alignment and click OK. You can also pick the alignment in the drawing.

5. Notice the information selected for sampling. Deselect the Old Settlers Way Datum Surface.

6. Select Finished Ground from the dropdown menu in the Alignment Style selection box.

7. Click OK.

8. On the Sample Line Tools toolbar, click the Sample Line Creation Methods dropdown and click the By Range Of Stations button ![icon]. Observe the settings, but do not change anything.

9. Click OK, and press ↵ to end the command.

10. If you receive a Panorama view telling you that your corridor is out of date and may require rebuilding, dismiss it.

11. Close the drawing without saving.

The sample lines can be edited by using the grips as just described or by choosing Sections ➤ Edit Sample Lines from the menu bar to manually edit the sample lines. This command displays both the Sample Line Tools toolbar and the Edit Sample Line dialog, allowing you to pick your alignment. Once the alignment is picked, the sample lines can be edited individually or as a group. The Edit Sample Lines dialog allows you to pick a sample line and edit the information on an individual basis, but it is much more efficient to edit the sample lines at one time.

Editing the Swath Width of a Sample Line Group

There may come a time when you will need to show information outside the limits of your section views or not show as much information. To edit the width of a section view, you will have to change the swath width of a sample line group. These sample lines can be edited manually on an individual basis, or you can edit the entire group at once. In this exercise, we will edit the widths of an entire sample line group:

1. Open the sections2.dwg file.

2. Choose Sections ➤ Edit Sample Lines. The Sample Line Tools toolbar and the Edit Sample Line dialog appear.

3. Click the Alignment Picker button ☜ on the toolbar, and then pick the Old Settlers Way alignment.

4. Click OK.

5. Click the down arrow for the sample line editing tools on the toolbar and then click the Edit Swath Widths For Group button ⊞▾ . The Edit Sample Line Widths dialog appears.

6. Type **60** in both the Left and Right Swath Width text boxes. Click OK.

7. Press ↵ to end the command.

8. If you receive a Panorama view telling you that your corridor is out of date and may require rebuilding, dismiss it.

9. Examine your sample lines, noting the wider sample lines.

10. Close the drawing without saving.

Creating the Views

Once the sample line group is created, it is time to create views. Views can be created in three ways—single view, all views, or all views-by-page. Creating views-by-page allows you to lay out your cross sections on a sheet-by-sheet basis. This is accomplished by creating a page setup for your proposed sheet size and defining that page setup in your sheet style. You can arrange the section views by either rows or columns and specify the space between each consecutive section view. This even allows you to put a predefined grid on your cross-section sheet. Although the setup for this is quite tedious, the payoff is incredible if you plot many sheets' worth of cross sections at a time. Figure 13.8 shows a layout containing section views arranged to plot by page.

Section views are nothing more than a window showing the section. The view contains horizontal and vertical grids, tick marks for axis annotation, the axis annotation itself, and a title. Views can also be configured to show horizontal geometry, such as the centerline of the section, edges of pavement, and right-of-way. Tables displaying quantities or volumes can also be shown for individual sections. Figure 13.9 shows a typical section view with such a table.

FIGURE 13.8
Section views arranged to plot by page

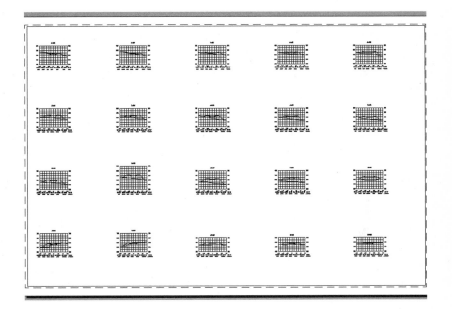

FIGURE 13.9
A table can be included in a section view.

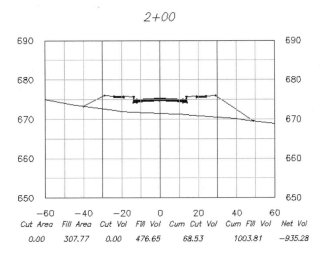

Cut Area	Fill Area	Cut Vol	Fill Vol	Cum Cut Vol	Cum Fill Vol	Net Vol
0.00	307.77	0.00	476.65	68.53	1003.81	−935.28

Creating a Single-Section View

There are occasions when all sections views are not needed. In these situations, a single-section view can be created. In this exercise, you will create a single-section view of station 3+00 from the sample lines created in the previous exercise.

1. Open the `sections3.dwg` file.

2. Choose Sections ➤ Create Section View. The Create Section View dialog appears.

3. Make sure the settings in the Create Section View dialog are the same as in Figure 13.10. Select Road Section from the dropdown menu in the Section View Style selection box, the Sample Line and Current Station selection boxes should be set to 3+00.00, and the boxes for the Add Data Bands and Add Volume Tables should not be checked. In the Select Sections To Be Drawn area, deselect Earthworks, and the Change Labels for each section should be set to No Labels.

4. Click OK.

5. Pick any point in the drawing area to place your section view.

6. Examine your section view. The display should match Figure 13.11.

7. Close the drawing without saving.

FIGURE 13.10

Settings for creating a single-section view

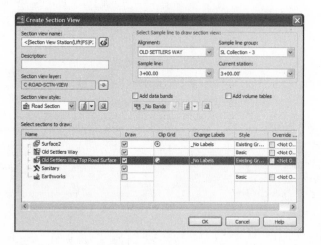

FIGURE 13.11

The finished section view

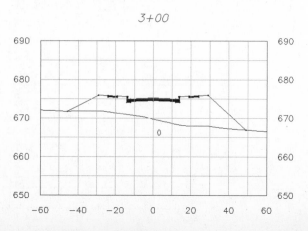

It's a Material World

Once alignments are sampled, volumes can be calculated from the sampled surface or from the corridor section shape. These volumes are calculated in a materials list and can be displayed as a label on each section view or in an overall volume table, as shown in Figure 13.12.

The volumes can also be displayed in an XML report, as shown in Figure 13.13.

FIGURE 13.12
A total volume table inserted into the drawing

Station	Fill Area	Cut Area	Fill Volume	Cut Volume	Cumulative Fill Vol	Cumulative Cut Vol
\multicolumn{7}{c}{Total Volume Table}						
0+50.00	97.77	38.27	0.00	0.00	0.00	0.00
1+00.00	132.28	17.87	213.01	51.99	213.01	51.99
1+50.00	207.01	0.00	314.15	16.55	527.16	68.53
2+00.00	307.77	0.00	476.65	0.00	1003.81	68.53
2+50.00	387.68	0.00	643.94	0.00	1647.75	68.53
3+00.00	446.32	0.00	772.22	0.00	2419.97	68.53
3+50.00	350.11	0.00	737.43	0.00	3157.41	68.53
4+00.00	383.68	0.00	679.43	0.00	3836.84	68.53
4+50.00	459.29	0.00	780.52	0.00	4617.36	68.53
5+00.00	431.67	0.00	824.96	0.00	5442.32	68.53
5+50.00	474.38	0.00	838.93	0.00	6281.25	68.53
6+00.00	543.49	0.00	942.47	0.00	7223.72	68.53
6+50.00	697.29	0.00	1148.87	0.00	8372.59	68.53
7+00.00	631.80	0.00	1230.65	0.00	9603.23	68.53
7+50.00	588.72	0.00	1130.12	0.00	10733.35	68.53
8+00.00	203.01	24.69	733.09	22.86	11466.44	91.39
8+50.00	116.07	49.97	295.44	69.13	11761.88	160.52
9+00.00	375.17	0.00	454.85	46.27	12216.73	206.79
9+50.00	293.14	0.00	618.81	0.00	12835.53	206.79
10+00.00	12.65	27.88	283.14	25.82	13118.68	232.60
10+50.00	0.00	157.91	11.71	172.03	13130.39	404.63
11+00.00	0.00	341.15	0.00	462.09	13130.39	866.72
11+50.00	0.00	447.02	0.00	729.78	13130.39	1596.50
12+00.00	0.00	443.95	0.00	824.97	13130.39	2421.47
12+50.00	0.00	316.31	0.00	703.95	13130.39	3125.42
13+00.00	0.00	127.75	0.00	411.17	13130.39	3536.59

FIGURE 13.13
A total volume XML report shown in Microsoft Internet Explorer.

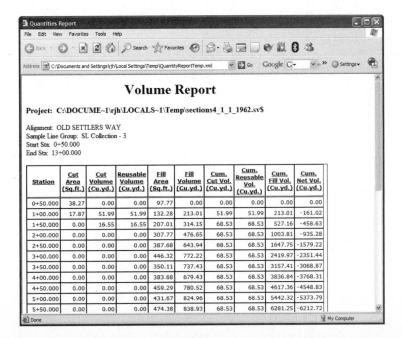

Volume Report

Project: C:\DOCUME~1\rjh\LOCALS~1\Temp\sections4_1_1_1962.sv$

Alignment: OLD SETTLERS WAY
Sample Line Group: SL Collection - 3
Start Sta: 0+50.000
End Sta: 13+00.000

Station	Cut Area (Sq.ft.)	Cut Volume (Cu.yd.)	Reusable Volume (Cu.yd.)	Fill Area (Sq.ft.)	Fill Volume (Cu.yd.)	Cum. Cut Vol. (Cu.yd.)	Cum. Reusable Vol. (Cu.yd.)	Cum. Fill Vol. (Cu.yd.)	Cum. Net Vol. (Cu.yd.)
0+50.000	38.27	0.00	0.00	97.77	0.00	0.00	0.00	0.00	0.00
1+00.000	17.87	51.99	51.99	132.28	213.01	51.99	51.99	213.01	-161.02
1+50.000	0.00	16.55	16.55	207.01	314.15	68.53	68.53	527.16	-458.63
2+00.000	0.00	0.00	0.00	307.77	476.65	68.53	68.53	1003.81	-935.28
2+50.000	0.00	0.00	0.00	387.68	643.94	68.53	68.53	1647.75	-1579.22
3+00.000	0.00	0.00	0.00	446.32	772.22	68.53	68.53	2419.97	-2351.44
3+50.000	0.00	0.00	0.00	350.11	737.43	68.53	68.53	3157.41	-3088.87
4+00.000	0.00	0.00	0.00	383.68	679.43	68.53	68.53	3836.84	-3768.31
4+50.000	0.00	0.00	0.00	459.29	780.52	68.53	68.53	4617.36	-4548.83
5+00.000	0.00	0.00	0.00	431.67	824.96	68.53	68.53	5442.32	-5373.79
5+50.000	0.00	0.00	0.00	474.38	838.93	68.53	68.53	6281.25	-6212.72

Once a material list is created, it can be edited to include more materials or to make modifications to the existing materials. For example, soil expansion (swell) and shrinkage factors can be entered to make the volumes more accurately match the true field conditions. This can make cost estimates more accurate, which can cause fewer surprises during the construction phase of any given project.

Creating a Materials List

Materials can be created from surfaces or from corridor shapes. Surfaces are great for earthwork since you can add cut or fill factors to the materials, whereas corridor shapes are great for determining quantities of asphalt or concrete. In this exercise, you will practice calculating earthwork quantities for the Old Settlers Way corridor:

1. Open the sections4.dwg file.

2. Choose Sections ➢ Compute Materials. The Select A Sample Line Group dialog appears.

3. In the Select Alignment field, verify that the alignment is set to Old Settlers Way, and in the Select Sample Line Group field, verify that the sample line group is set to SL Collection - 3.

4. Click OK. The Compute Materials dialog appears.

5. Select Earthworks from the dropdown menu in the Quantity Takeoff Criteria selection box.

6. Click in the Object Name cell for the Existing Ground surface, and select Surface2 from the dropdown menu.

7. Click in the Object Name cell for the Datum surface, and select Old Settlers Way Top Road Surface from the dropdown menu.

8. Verify that your settings match those shown in Figure 13.14.

9. Click OK.

10. Save the drawing.

FIGURE 13.14
The settings for the Compute Materials dialog

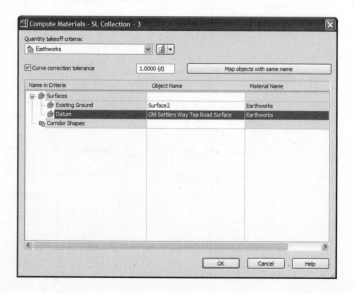

Creating a Volume Table in the Drawing

In the preceding exercise, materials were created that represent the total dirt to be moved or used in the sample line group. In the next exercise, we will insert a table into the drawing so we can inspect the volumes:

1. Continue using the `sections4.dwg` file.

2. Choose Sections ➢ Add Tables ➢ Total Volume. The Create Total Volume Table appears.

3. Verify that your settings match those shown in Figure 13.15. Pay close attention and make sure that Reactivity Mode at the bottom of the dialog is set to Dynamic. This will cause the table to update if any changes are made to the sample line collection.

4. Click OK.

5. Pick a point in the drawing to place the volume table. The table indicates a Cumulative Fill Volume of 13,256.27 cubic yards and a Cumulative Cut Volume of 3537.72 cubic yards, as shown in Figure 13.16. We will have to bring just over 9,718 cubic yards of dirt into the site to build our road.

6. Save the drawing.

FIGURE 13.15
The Create Total Volume Table dialog settings

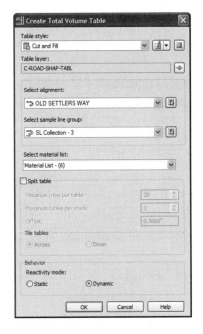

FIGURE 13.16

The total volume table

Station	Fill Area	Cut Area	Fill Volume	Cut Volume	Cumulative Fill Vol	Cumulative Cut Vol
0+50.00	97.77	38.27	0.00	0.00	0.00	0.00
1+00.00	132.28	17.87	213.01	51.99	213.01	51.99
1+50.00	207.01	0.00	314.15	16.55	527.16	68.53
2+00.00	307.77	0.00	476.85	0.00	1003.81	68.53
2+50.00	387.68	0.00	643.94	0.00	1647.75	68.53
3+00.00	446.32	0.00	772.22	0.00	2419.97	68.53
3+50.00	350.11	0.00	737.43	0.00	3157.41	68.53
4+00.00	383.68	0.00	687.84	0.00	3845.25	68.53
4+50.00	459.29	0.00	807.63	0.00	4652.88	68.53
5+00.00	431.67	0.00	848.33	0.00	5501.21	68.53
5+50.00	474.38	0.00	858.75	0.00	6359.96	68.53
6+00.00	543.49	0.00	960.20	0.00	7320.16	68.53
6+50.00	697.29	0.00	1168.84	0.00	8489.01	68.53
7+00.00	631.80	0.00	1245.37	0.00	9734.37	68.53
7+50.00	588.72	0.00	1134.80	0.00	10869.17	68.53
8+00.00	203.01	24.69	723.15	23.98	11592.32	92.51
8+50.00	116.07	49.97	295.44	69.13	11887.76	161.64
9+00.00	375.17	0.00	454.85	46.27	12342.61	207.91
9+50.00	293.14	0.00	618.81	0.00	12961.41	207.91
10+00.00	12.65	27.88	283.14	25.82	13244.56	233.73
10+50.00	0.00	157.91	11.71	172.03	13256.27	405.75
11+00.00	0.00	341.15	0.00	462.09	13256.27	867.84
11+50.00	0.00	447.02	0.00	729.78	13256.27	1597.62
12+00.00	0.00	443.95	0.00	824.97	13256.27	2422.60
12+50.00	0.00	316.31	0.00	703.95	13256.27	3126.55
13+00.00	0.00	127.75	0.00	411.17	13256.27	3537.72

Total Volume Table

Adding Soil Factors to a Materials List

Since this design obviously has an excessive amount of fill, the materials need to be modified to bring them closer in line with true field numbers. For this exercise, the shrinkage factor will be assumed to be 0.80 and 1.20 for the expansion factor (20% shrink and swell). These numbers are arbitrary—numbers used during an actual design will be based on soil type and conditions. In addition to these numbers (which Civil 3D represents as Cut Factor for swell and Fill Factor for shrinkage), a Refill Factor can also be set. This specifies how much cut can be reused for fill. For this exercise, we will assume a Refill Factor of 1.00:

1. Continue using drawing sections4.dwg.

2. Choose Sections ➤ Compute Materials. The Select A Sample Line Group dialog appears.

3. Select the Old Settlers Way alignment and the SL Collection - 3 sample line group, if not already selected.

4. Click OK. The Edit Material List dialog appears.

5. Enter a Cut Factor of **1.20**, a Fill Factor of **0.80**, and verify that all other settings are the same as in Figure 13.17. Click OK.

6. Examine the Total Volume table again. Notice that the new Cumulative Fill Volume is 10,605.02 cubic yards and the new Cumulative Cut Volume is 4245.26 cubic yards.

7. Save the drawing.

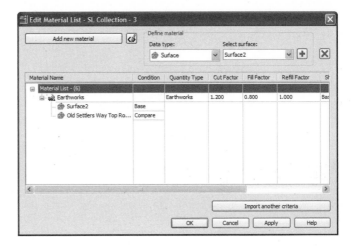

CAN I HAVE ACCURATE VOLUME NUMBERS WITHOUT SECTIONS?

Unfortunately, the only place in the program that can utilize cut-and-fill factors is in section volumes. Any other volumes that you calculate will be unadjusted numbers.

Volumes can also be created in a format that can be printed and put into a project documentation folder. This is accomplished by creating a volume report, which is populated through LandXML. This report will open and display in Internet Explorer, but can be put into Word or Excel format with a simple copy and paste from the XML report. The XML report style sheet can be edited, but the following is a sample of the default code:

```
<CrossSect name="1+00.00" number="2" sta="100" staEq="100"
areaCut="17.8692907698351" areaUsable="17.8692907698351"
areaFill="132.279872457422" volumeCut="62.3825333709404"
volumeUsable="51.9854444757837" volumeFill="170.406674689733"
cumVolumeCut="62.3825333709404" cumVolumeUsable="51.9854444757837"
cumVolumeFill="170.406674689733" massHaul="-108.024141318792">
- <MaterialCrossSects>
- <MaterialCrossSect name="Earthworks(Cut)" area="17.8692907698351"
volume="62.3825333709404" cumVolume="62.3825333709404">
- <MaterialCrossSectEnvelop area="0.136156978705912">
 <CrossSectPnt OE="-13.512209, 673.728273" />
 <CrossSectPnt OE="-12.263952, 673.582858" />
 <CrossSectPnt OE="-13.500000, 673.508695" />
 <CrossSectPnt OE="-13.512209, 673.728273" />
</MaterialCrossSectEnvelop>
```

This produces a table that looks like Table 13.1.

TABLE 13.1:   Output of the Volume Report

Station	Cut Area (Sq.Ft.)	Cut Volume (Cu.Yd.)	Reusable Volume (Cu.Yd.)	Fill Area (Sq.Ft.)	Fill Volume (Cu.Yd.)	Cum. Cut Vol. (Cu.Yd.)	Cum. Reusable Vol. (Cu.Yd.)	Cum. Fill Vol. (Cu.Yd.)	Cum. Net Vol. (Cu.Yd.)
0+50.000	38.27	0.00	0.00	97.77	0.00	0.00	0.00	0.00	0.00
1+00.000	17.87	62.38	51.99	132.28	170.41	62.38	51.99	170.41	-108.02
1+50.000	0.00	19.85	16.55	207.01	251.32	82.24	68.53	421.73	-339.49
2+00.000	0.00	0.00	0.00	307.77	381.32	82.24	68.53	803.05	-720.81
2+50.000	0.00	0.00	0.00	387.68	515.15	82.24	68.53	1318.20	-1235.96
3+00.000	0.00	0.00	0.00	446.32	617.78	82.24	68.53	1935.98	-1853.74
3+50.000	0.00	0.00	0.00	350.11	589.95	82.24	68.53	2525.92	-2443.69
4+00.000	0.00	0.00	0.00	383.68	550.27	82.24	68.53	3076.20	-2993.96
4+50.000	0.00	0.00	0.00	459.29	646.11	82.24	68.53	3722.30	-3640.07
5+00.000	0.00	0.00	0.00	431.67	678.67	82.24	68.53	4400.97	-4318.73
5+50.000	0.00	0.00	0.00	474.38	687.00	82.24	68.53	5087.97	-5005.73
6+00.000	0.00	0.00	0.00	543.49	768.16	82.24	68.53	5856.13	-5773.89

Generating a Volume Report

Volume reports can be included on a drawing but normally aren't because of liability issues. However, it is often necessary to know what these volumes are and have some record of them. Civil 3D provides you with a way to create a report that is suitable for printing or for transferring to a word processing or spreadsheet program. In this exercise, you will create a volume report for the Old Settlers Way corridor:

1. Open the sections5.dwg file.

2. Choose Sections ➤ Generate Volume Report.

3. Verify that your materials list is selected in the dialog, and if it is, click OK. If it is not, then select it from the dropdown menu and click OK.

4. You may get a warning message that says, "Scripts are usually safe. Do you want to allow scripts to run?" Click Yes.

5. Note the cut-and-fill volumes and compare them to your volume table in the drawing.

6. Close the drawing without saving.

Generating Section Views with Attached Volume Tables

Volumes can also be displayed on a section-by-section basis. This is accomplished with a volume table that shows only the volume at a selected station. You can see this more clearly in Figure 13.18.

One thing to note about attaching the volume tables to the section views is that a materials list has to be created prior to creating the section views. If a materials list exists, then the option to add volume tables will be displayed in the Create Multiple Views dialog. In this exercise, you will create section views and attach volume tables to the views:

1. Open the sections6.dwg file.

2. Choose Sections ➤ Create Multiple Section Views.

FIGURE 13.18
The section view with volume table attached

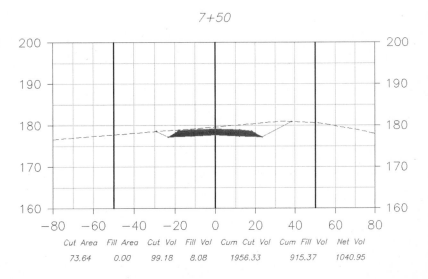

3. Set the Group Plot Style selection box to Plot By Page.

4. Clear the checkbox for the Add Data Bands, and select No Bands from the dropdown menu.

5. Verify that the Add Volume Table is checked.

6. In the Select Sections To Draw area, deselect Earthworks.

7. Set the Change Labels cell for both Surface 2 and Old Settlers Way Top Road Surface to No Labels.

8. Verify that the rest of the box matches the settings shown in Figure 13.19 and click OK.

9. Pick a point in the drawing to insert your section views. It is a good idea to select an area to the right of the drawing and away from the design area. The Section View Ancillary Data dialog appears.

10. Select Total Volume from the dropdown menu in the Type selection box and the Section Volume Table in the Select Table Style selection box.

11. Click Add.

12. Enter a value of **0.0001″** for the Gap Distance in the table. You will have to scroll to the right or resize the dialog to reach the setting.

13. Select Bottom Left from the dropdown menu in the Section View Anchor selection box.

14. Select Top Left from the dropdown menu in the Table Anchor selection box.

15. Enter an X and Y offset of **-0.2″**.

16. Verify that the rest of the box matches the settings shown in Figure 13.20 and click OK.

17. Examine your section views. Notice that two sheets were created, along with the volume table attached to each section view. Your sheets should look like those shown in Figure 13.21.

18. Close the drawing without saving.

FIGURE 13.19

The settings for the Create Multiple Section Views dialog

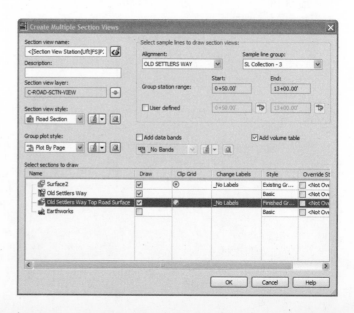

FIGURE 13.20

The settings for the Section View Ancillary Data dialog

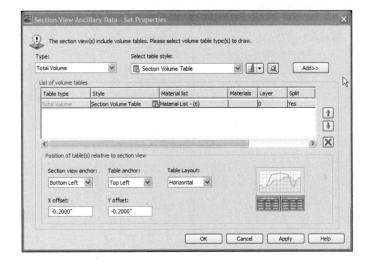

FIGURE 13.21

The completed section views

A Little More Sampling

Although it is good practice to create your section views as one of the last steps in your project, occasionally data is added that needs to be shown in a section view after the section views are created. To accomplish this, you need to add that data to the sample line group. This is accomplished by navigating to the sample line group and editing the properties of the sample line group. The Sections tab shown in Figure 13.22 shows the Sample More Sources button required to add more data to the sample line group.

Once you click Sample More Sources, the Section Sources dialog opens. This dialog allows you to either add more sample sources to or delete sample sources from the sample line group. In this example, you have a sanitary sewer network that was added to the project. Since you need to show the locations of the sanitary pipes with respect to the designed road, you need to add the sanitary sewer network to the Sample Line Group. To do this, simply select the sanitary sewer network and click Add, as shown in Figure 13.23.

FIGURE 13.22
The Sections tab of the
Sample Line Group
Properties dialog

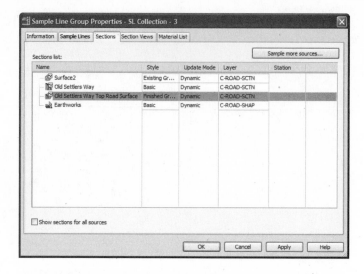

FIGURE 13.23
Adding a sanitary
sewer network to the
sample line group

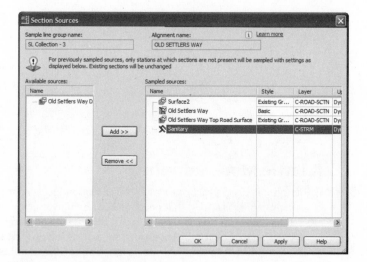

Adding a Pipe Network to a Sample Line Group

In prior releases of Civil 3D, it was difficult to add more information to a section view once the sample lines were created. Quite often, it was easier to delete the sample line group and create a new one from scratch, including the information that you wanted to show. With the 2008 release, it is much easier to sample additional information. In this exercise, you will add a pipe network to a sample line group and inspect the existing section views to ensure that the pipe network was added correctly:

1. Open the sections7.dwg file.

2. In Prospector, expand the Sites ➤ Site 1 ➤ Alignments ➤ Old Settlers Way ➤ Sample Line Groups ➤ SL Collection - 3 branches, as shown in Figure 13.24.

FIGURE 13.24
The location of the Sample Line Group, located deep under the Sites branch

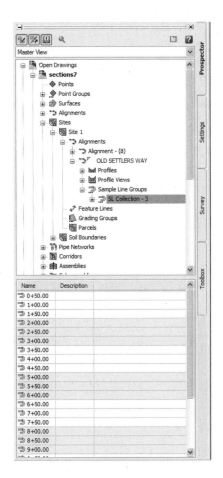

3. Right-click on the SL Collection - 3 and select Properties. The Sample Line Group Properties dialog appears.

4. Switch to the Sections tab.

5. Click Sample More Sources. The Section Sources dialog appears.

6. Select the Sanitary Network from the dropdown menu in the Available Sources selection box.

7. Click Add.

8. Click OK to dismiss the Section Sources dialog.

9. Click OK again to dismiss the Sample Line Group Properties dialog.

10. Review the section views. Notice that pipe sections are now displayed in the section view.

11. Close the drawing without saving.

Annotating the Sections

Now that the views are created, annotation is added to further explain design intent. Labels can be added through the code set style or by adding labels to the section view itself. These section labels can be used to label the section offset, elevation, or slope. You can see an example in Figure 13.25.

FIGURE 13.25
Labels added to a section view help to explain design intent

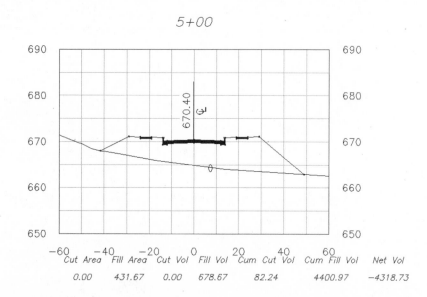

ADDING LABELS TO THE SECTION VIEW

There is often a need for labels to show what the various graphics mean in a section view. To show exact elevations, labels are much more efficient than scaling information from the grid. In this exercise, you will label the section-view elevation at the designed centerline of the road:

1. Open the sections8.dwg file.

2. Choose Sections ➤ Add Section View Labels ➤ Add Section View Labels. The Add Labels dialog appears.

3. Select Offset Elevation from the dropdown menu in the Label Type selection box.

4. Select CL Elevation from the dropdown menu in the Label Style selection box.

5. Click Add.

6. Pick a grid on the section view to select the view.

7. Pick the top centerline of the corridor in the view. It may be easier to pick using the Endpoint osnap.

8. Click Close in the Add Labels dialog. You now have labels reflecting the section-view elevation at the centerline.

9. Close the drawing without saving.

The Bottom Line

Create sample lines. Before any section views can be displayed, sections must be created from sample lines.

Master It Open `sections1.dwg` and create sample lines along the alignment every 50´.

Create section views. Just as profiles can only be shown in profile views, sections require section views to display. Section views can be plotted individually or all at once. You can even set them up to be broken up into sheets.

Master It In the previous drawing, you created sample lines. In that same drawing, create section views for all the sample lines.

Define materials. Materials are required to be defined before any quantities can be displayed. You learned that materials can be defined from surfaces or from corridor shapes. Corridors must exist for shape selection and surfaces must already be created for comparison in material lists.

Master It Using `sections4.dwg`, create a materials list that compares Surface2 with Old Settlers Way Top Road Surface.

Generate volume reports. Volume reports give you numbers that can be used for cost estimating on any given project. Typically, construction companies calculate their own quantities, but developers often want to know approximate volumes for budgeting purposes.

Master It Continue using `sections4.dwg`. Use the materials list created earlier to generate a volume report. Create an XML report and a table that can be displayed on the drawing.

Chapter 14

The Tool Chest: Parts Lists and Part Builder

Before you can begin modeling and designing your pipe network, which will be discussed in Chapter 15, consider what components you will need in your design. Civil 3D allows you to build a parts list that contains the specific pipes and structures that you will need at your fingertips while designing a pipe network. Civil 3D installs a large part catalog as well as an interface for customizing pipe network parts if necessary. In addition, the parts list will allow you to specify how each pipe and structure will look and behave in a design situation. This chapter explores creating a parts list for a typical sanitary sewer network.

By the end of this chapter, you'll be able to:

◆ Add pipe and structure families to a new parts list

◆ Create rule sets that apply to pipes and structures in a parts list

◆ Apply styles to pipes and structures in a parts list

Planning a Typical Pipe Network: A Sanitary Sewer Example

Before you begin designing your pipe network, it is important to brainstorm all of the parts that you will need to construct the network, how these objects will be represented in plan and profile, and the behavior of these parts (which you'll specify using the slope, cover, rim, and sump parameters). Once you have a list of the elements you need, you can locate the appropriate parts in the part catalog, build the appropriate rule sets, create the proper styles to match your CAD standard, and tie it all together in a parts list.

Let's have a look at a typical sanitary sewer design. You typically start by going through the sewer specifications for the jurisdiction you are working in. There is usually a published list of allowable pipe materials, manhole details, slope parameters, and cover guidelines. Perhaps you have concrete and PVC pipe manufacturer's catalogs that have pages of details for different manholes, pipes, headwalls, and junction boxes. There is usually also a recommended symbology for your submitted drawings, and, of course, you have your own in-house CAD standards. Assemble this information and make sure you address these issues:

◆ Recommended structures, including materials and dimensions (be sure to attach detail sheets)

◆ Structure behavior, such as required sump, drops across structures, surface adjustment

◆ Structure symbology

◆ Recommended pipes, including materials and dimensions (again, be sure to attach detail sheets)

◆ Pipe behavior, such as cover requirements; minimum, maximum, and recommended slopes; velocity restrictions; and so on.

◆ Pipe symbology

The following is an example of a completed checklist:

Sanitary Sewers in Sample County

Recommended Structures: Standard concentric manhole, small-diameter cleanout.

Structure Behavior: All structures have 1.5´ sump, rims, a 0.10´ invert drop across all structures, all structures designed at finished road grade.

Structure Symbology: Manholes are shown in plan view as a circle with an S inside and a diameter that corresponds to the actual diameter of the manhole. Cleanouts are shown as a solid, filled circle with a diameter, corresponding to the actual diameter of the cleanout. (See Figure 14.1.)

Manholes are shown in profile view with a coned top and rectangular bottom. Cleanouts are shown as a rectangle (see Figure 14.2).

FIGURE 14.1
Sanitary sewer manhole in plan view (a) and a cleanout in plan view (b)

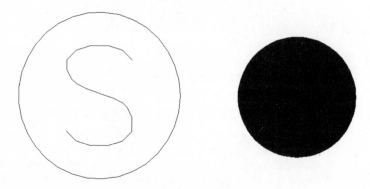

FIGURE 14.2
Profile view of a sanitary sewer manhole (on left) and a cleanout (on right)

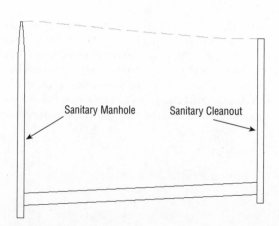

Sanitary Manhole   Sanitary Cleanout

Recommended Pipes: 8″, 10″, 12″ PVC pipe per manufacturer dimensions.

Pipe Behavior: Pipes must have cover of 4′ to the top of the pipe; the maximum slope for all pipes is 10%, although minimum slopes may be adjusted to optimize velocity per this table:

Sewer Size	Minimum Slope
8″	0.40%
10″	0.28%
12″	0.22%

Pipe Symbology: In plan view, pipes will be shown with a CENTER2 linetype line that has a thickness corresponding to the inner diameter of the pipe. In profile view, pipes will show both inner and outer walls, with a hatch between the walls to highlight the wall thickness (see Figure 14.3).

FIGURE 14.3

Sanitary pipe in plan view (a) and sanitary pipe in profile view (b)

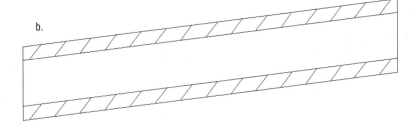

a.

b.

The Part Catalog

Once you know what parts you need, you will investigate the part catalog to make sure they (or a reasonable approximation of the parts you need) are available.

The part catalog is a collection of two "domains" that contain two catalogs each. Structures are considered one domain, and Pipes are the second. The Structures domain consists of a Metric Structures catalog and a US Imperial Structures catalog; the Pipes domain consists of a Metric Pipes catalog and a US Imperial Pipes catalog.

Though we can access the parts from the catalogs while creating our parts lists in Civil 3D, we cannot examine or explore the catalogs easily while in the Civil 3D interface. It is useful to understand where these catalogs reside and how they work.

The part catalog (see Figure 14.4) is installed locally by default at:

```
C:\Documents and Settings\All Users\
Application Data\Autodesk\C3D 2008\enu\Pipes Catalog\
```

FIGURE 14.4

The Pipes Catalog folder

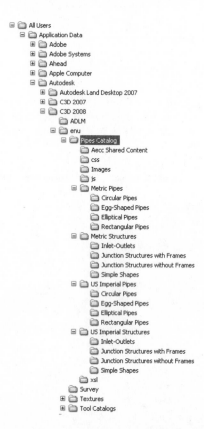

Note that all paths in this chapter are the Windows XP install paths. If you are running Civil 3D on Windows Vista, please check the Civil 3D Users Guide for information on the Pipes Catalog folder install location.

If you cannot locate the Pipes Catalog folder, it may be because your network administrator installed the catalogs at a network location when Civil 3D was deployed.

The Structures Domain

To learn more about how a catalog is organized, let's explore the US Imperial Structures folder.

The first file of interest in the US Imperial Structures folder is an HTML document called US Imperial Structures (see Figure 14.5).

Double-click this file and Internet Explorer will open with a window so you can explore the US Imperial Structures catalog. A tree with different structure types on the left is under the Catalog tab. Expanding the tree allows you to explore the types of structures that are available.

FIGURE 14.5

The US Imperial
Structures HTML
document

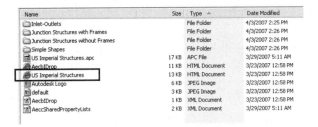

Structures that fall into the same type have behavioral properties in common but may vary in shape and proportion. The four types of structure in the default catalogs are:

◆ Inlet-Outlets

◆ Junction Structures With Frames

◆ Junction Structures Without Frames

◆ Simple Shapes

Under each structure type are several *shapes*. The shape spells out the details of how the structure is shaped and proportioned, and shows what happens to each dimension when the size increases. If you drill into the Junction Structures With Frames type and highlight the AeccStructConcentricCylinder_Imperial shape, you can see this in action (see Figure 14.6).

FIGURE 14.6

A closer look at the
structure type and
shape

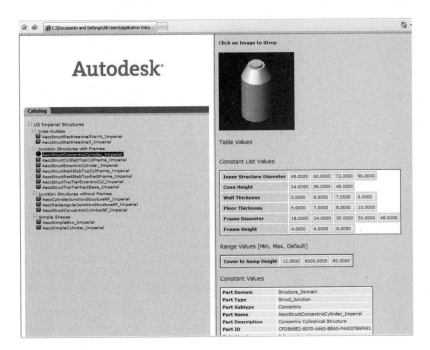

In this view, you can see the available sizes of the Concentric Cylindrical structure, such as 48″, 60″, 72″, and 96″. Follow the table to see what happens to the cone height, wall thickness, floor thickness, and frame diameter and height as the diameter dimension increases. The structure may get bigger or smaller, but its basic form remains the same and its behavior is predictable.

Explore the other structures of the Junction Structures With Frames type, and note why they are all considered to be the same type. Their shape changes, but their fundamental behavior and intent are similar. For example, each has a frame, each has a similar size range, or each is used as a junction for pipes.

Let's return to the example of a sanitary sewer network. We know we need a standard concentric manhole, and a simple, small-diameter cleanout, and most likely we have specification sheets from the concrete products company handy.

Exploring the different structures available, we see that both of our required structures have frames on their spec sheets, so we know we need a Junction Structure With Frames. Our manhole most closely resembles the Concentric Cylindrical structure, and the 48″ and 60″ match our allowable sizes. For the cleanout, the Cylindrical Slab Top structure is the appropriate shape and behavior, but we need a 6″ size. The smallest size available by default is 15″. Make notes on your checklist to add a part size for a 6″ Cylindrical Slab Top structure. We'll take care of that in the next section.

Something to keep in mind as you are searching for the appropriate structures to meet your standard is that the part you choose does not necessarily have to be an absolutely perfect match for your specified standard detail. The important things to look for are general shape, insertion behavior, and key dimensions.

Ask yourself the following:

◆ Will I be able to orient this structure in an appropriate way (is it round, rectangular, concentric, or eccentric)?

◆ Will I be able to label the insertion point (rim elevation) correctly?

◆ Will this structure look the way I need it to in the plan, profile, and section views? Does it look the same viewed from every angle, or would some views show a wider/narrower structure?

◆ Can I adjust my structure style in plan and profile views to display the structure the way I want to see it?

If you can find a standard shape that is conducive to all of these, it is worth your time to try it out before resorting to building custom parts with Part Builder.

For example, if you have a certain catch basin required in your town that has a unique frame and that is an elongated rectangle, try one of the standard rectangle frame structures first (see Figure 14.7). You probably already use a certain type of block in your CAD drawings to represent this type of catch basin, and that block can be applied to the structure style. It's not always necessary to build a custom part for small variations in shape. The important thing is that you model and label your rims and inverts properly. We'll discuss this more in the next few sections.

FIGURE 14.7
A Rectangular Slab
Top structure—each
catch basin can be
modeled with the
same Rectangular
Slab Top structure.

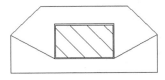

The Pipes Domain

The second part domain is named Pipes. Pipes have one only "type," which is also called Pipes.

Locate the catalog HTML file under the US Imperial Pipes folder (see Figure 14.8), and we'll explore this catalog the same way we explored the US Imperial Structures catalog.

FIGURE 14.8
The catalog HTML file
is in the US Imperial
Pipes folder.

Name	Size	Type ▲	Date Modified
Circular Pipes		File Folder	4/3/2007 2:25 PM
Egg-Shaped Pipes		File Folder	4/3/2007 2:25 PM
Elliptical Pipes		File Folder	4/3/2007 2:25 PM
Rectangular Pipes		File Folder	4/3/2007 2:25 PM
US Imperial Pipes.apc	9 KB	APC File	3/29/2007 5:11 AM
AecbIDrop	11 KB	HTML Document	3/23/2007 12:58 PM
US Imperial Pipes	13 KB	HTML Document	3/23/2007 12:58 PM
Autodesk Logo	6 KB	JPEG Image	3/23/2007 12:58 PM
default	3 KB	JPEG Image	3/23/2007 12:58 PM
AecbIDrop	1 KB	XML Document	3/23/2007 12:58 PM
AeccSharedPropertyLists	1 KB	XML Document	3/29/2007 5:11 AM

Double-click the HTML file and Internet Explorer will open with a window that allows you to view the US Imperial Pipes catalog. A tree with different pipe shapes appears on the left under the Catalog tab. Expanding the tree allows you to explore the pipe shapes that are available. Pipe shapes are broken into smaller categories by material (in the case of a circular pipe) or orientation (for an elliptical pipe).

The four pipe shapes in the default catalogs are:

◆ Circular Pipes (Concrete, Ductile Iron, Polyvinyl Chloride)

◆ Egg-Shaped Pipes (Concrete)

◆ Elliptical Pipes (Concrete Vertical, Concrete Horizontal)

◆ Rectangular Pipes (Concrete)

Drill into the Circular Pipes shape and highlight the AeccCircularConcretePipe_Imperial material, and let's dig into this a bit more (see Figure 14.9).

In this view, we can see the different inner pipe diameters and their corresponding wall thicknesses. Explore the other pipe shapes to get a feel for what is available.

We need 8″, 10″ and 12″ pipe for our sanitary sewer example. The spec sheet from our PVC pipe supplier indicates that the inner diameters and corresponding wall thicknesses are appropriate for our design.

Again, keep in mind as you are searching for the appropriate pipes to meet your standard that the pipe you choose does not necessarily have to be an absolutely perfect match for your specified standard detail. For example, your storm drainage system might have the option to use high-density polyethylene (HDPE) pipe. Since there is no standard catalog entry for HDPE, you might think you would have to build a custom pipe type using Part Builder.

FIGURE 14.9
A closer look at the pipe shape and material

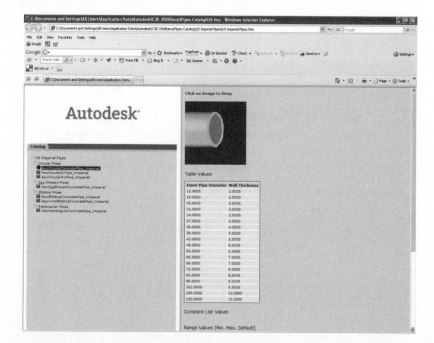

However, examine your symbology and labeling requirements a little further before jumping into building a custom part. The wall thickness of HDPE pipe is different from the same size PVC, but that may not be important for your drawing representation or labeling.

If you show HDPE as a single line, or a double line representing inner diameter, wall thickness is irrelevant. You can create a custom label style to label the pipe HDPE instead of PVC.

If you show HDPE represented as its outer diameter or have very particular requirements to show wall thickness in crossing and profile views, then building a custom pipe in Part Builder may be your best option (see Figure 14.10).

The important things to consider are general shape and wall thickness. Ask yourself:

♦ Does this pipe approximate the shape of my specified pipe?

♦ Does this pipe offer the correct inner diameter choice?

♦ How important is wall thickness to my model, plans, profiles, and sections?

♦ Can I adjust my pipe style in plan and profile views to display the pipe the way I need to see it?

♦ Can I create a pipe label that will label this pipe the way I need it labeled?

Again, if you can find a standard pipe that is conducive to all of these, it is worth your time to try it out before resorting to building custom pipes with Part Builder.

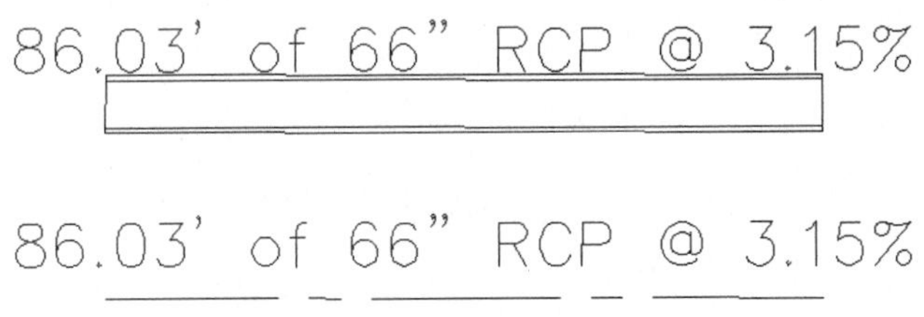

FIGURE 14.10
The top pipe must specify the outer diameter exactly. The bottom pipe, which uses a centerline to represent the inner diameter, does not.

86.03' of 66" RCP @ 3.15%

86.03' of 66" RCP @ 3.15%

The Supporting Files

For each part family in the catalog, there are three corresponding files, located here:

    C:\Documents and Settings\All Users\Application Data\Autodesk\C3D 2008\enu\Pipes
    Catalog\

Two files are mandatory sources of data required for the part to function properly, and one is an optional bitmap that provides the preview image you see in the catalog browser and parts list interface.

Digging into the folder

    C:\Documents and Settings\All Users\Application Data\Autodesk\C3D 2008\enu\Pipes
    Catalog\US Imperial Pipes\Circular Pipes

reveals these files for Imperial Circular Pipe:

partname.dwg   The part drawing file contains the geometry that makes up the part as well as the definition of the parametric relationships.

partname.xml   The part XML file is created as soon as a new part file is started in Part Builder. This file contains information on the parameter sizes, such as wall thickness, width, and diameter.

partname.bmp   The part image file is used as a visual preview for that particular part in the HTML catalog (as you saw in the previous section). This file is optional.

We will study some of these files in greater detail in the next section.

Mark on your checklist which parts you would like to use from the standard catalog, and also note the parts that we may have to customize using Part Builder.

Part Builder

Part Builder (which you access by choosing Pipes ➤ Part Builder) is an interface that allows you to build and modify pipe network parts. At first, you may use Part Builder to add a few missing pipes or structure sizes. As you become more familiar with the environment, you may build your own custom parts from scratch.

This section is intended to be an introduction to Part Builder and a primer in some basic skills required to navigate the interface. It is not intended to be a robust "how-to" for creating custom parts. For more details on building custom parts, please see the Civil 3D Users Guide—which you can access through the Civil 3D Help interface, as well as in .pdf format under Help ➤ Users Guide (pdf).

BACK UP THE PART CATALOGS

Here's a warning: before exploring Part Builder in any way, it is critical that you make a backup copy of the part catalogs. This will protect you from accidentally removing or corrupting default parts as you are learning and provide a means of restoring the original catalog for any reason.

The catalog (as discussed in the previous section) can be found by default at:

```
C:\Documents and Settings\All Users\Application Data\Autodesk\C3D 2008\enu\Pipes
Catalog\
```

To make a backup, simply copy this entire directory and save that copy to a safe location, such as another folder on your hard drive or network, or to a CD.

Parametric Parts

The parts in the Civil 3D pipe network catalogs are *parametric*. Parametric parts are dynamically sized according to a set of variables, or parameters. In practice, what this means is that we can create one part and use it in multiple situations.

For example, in the case of circular pipe, if we didn't have the option of using a parametric model, we would have to create a separate part for each diameter of pipe we wanted, even if all other aspects of the pipe remained the same. If we had ten pipe sizes to create, that would mean ten sets of *partname*.dwg, *partname*.xml, and *partname*.bmp, as well as an opportunity for mistakes and a great deal of redundant editing if one aspect of the pipe needed to change.

Fortunately, we can create one parametric model that understands how the different dimensions of the pipe are related to each other and what sizes are allowable. When a pipe is placed in a drawing, you can simply change its size and the pipe understands how that change in size affects all the other pipe dimensions such as wall thickness, outer diameter, and more, instead of having to sort through a long list of individual pipe definitions.

Part Builder Orientation

The Civil 3D pipe network catalogs are drawing specific. If you are in a metric drawing, you will want to make sure that the catalog is mapped to metric pipes and structures, whereas if you are in an imperial drawing, you'll want the imperial. By default, the Civil 3D templates should be appropriately mapped, but it is worth the time to check. Set the catalog by choosing Pipes ➤ Set Pipe Network Catalog, then choose the appropriate folder and catalog for your drawing units in the Pipe Network Catalog Settings dialog (see Figure 14.11).

UNDERSTANDING THE ORGANIZATION OF PART BUILDER

The vocabulary used in the Part Builder interface is related to the vocabulary in the HTML catalog interface that we examined in the previous section, but there are several differences that are sometimes confusing.

The first screen that appears when you choose Pipes ➤ Part Builder is the Getting Started – Catalog Screen (see Figure 14.12).

FIGURE 14.11
Choose the appropriate folder and catalog for your drawing units.

FIGURE 14.12
The Getting Started – Catalog Screen

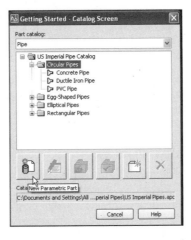

At the top of this window is a dropdown menu for selecting the pipe catalog. The choices, in this case Pipe or Structure, are based on what has been set for the drawing (either Metric or Imperial).

Below the Part Catalog input box is a listing of chapters. (In terms of Part Builder vocabulary, a *pipe chapter* is roughly equivalent to the catalog interface term *shape*.) US Imperial Pipe Catalog has four default chapters: Circular Pipes, Egg-Shaped Pipes, Elliptical Pipes, and Rectangular Pipes. We can create new chapters for different-shaped pipes, such as Arch Pipe.

US Imperial Structure Catalog also has four default chapters: Inlets-Outlets, Junction Structures With Frames, Junction Structures Without Frames, and Simple Shapes. We can create new chapters for custom structures. (In terms of Part Builder vocabulary, a *structure chapter* is roughly equivalent to the catalog interface term *type*.)

Each chapter folder can be expanded to reveal one or more part families. US Imperial Pipe Catalog has three default families (Concrete Pipe, Ductile Iron Pipe, and PVC Pipe) under the Circular Pipes chapter. Pipes that reside in the same family typically have the same parametric behavior, with only differences in size.

US Imperial Pipe Catalog has three default families (Concentric Cylindrical Structure NF, Cylindrical Junction Structure NF, and Rectangular Junction Structure NF) under the Junction Structures Without Frames chapter. Like pipes, structures that reside in the same family typically have the same parametric behavior, with only differences in size.

As Table 14.1 shows, there are a series of buttons on the Getting Started – Catalog Screen for performing various edits to chapters, families, and the catalog as a whole.

TABLE 14.1: The Part Builder Catalog Tools

ICON	FUNCTION
	The New Parametric Part button creates a new part family.
	The Modify Part Sizes button allows you to edit the parameters for a specific part family.
	The Catalog Regen button refreshes all the supporting files in the catalog when you have finished making edits to the catalog.
	The Catalog Test button validated the parts in the catalog when you have finished making edits to the catalog.
	The New Chapter button creates a new chapter.
	The Delete button deletes a part family. Use this button with caution, and remember that if you accidentally delete a part family, you can restore your backup catalog as mentioned in the beginning of this section.

EXPLORING PART FAMILIES

The best way to get oriented to the Part Builder interface is to explore one of the standard part families. In this case, we will examine the US Imperial Pipe Catalog ➤ Circular Pipe Chapter ➤ Concrete Pipe Family by highlighting Concrete Pipe and clicking the Modify Part Sizes button.

A Part Builder task pane will appear with `AeccCircularConcretePipe_Imperial.dwg` on the screen, as shown in Figure 14.13.

The Part Builder task pane, or Content Builder (Figure 14.14), is well documented in the Civil 3D Users Guide. Please refer to the Users Guide for detailed information about each entry in Content Builder.

FIGURE 14.13
The Parametric Build-
ing environment

FIGURE 14.13

The Parametric Build-
ing environment

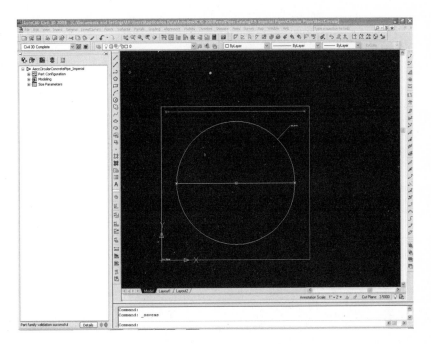

FIGURE 14.14

Content Builder

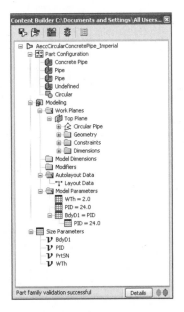

Adding a Part Size Using Part Builder

Our hypothetical municipality requires a 12″ sanitary sewer cleanout. After studying the catalog, we decide that the Concentric Cylindrical Structure With No Frames is the appropriate shape for our model, but the smallest inner diameter size in the catalog is 48″. The following tutorial will give you some practice in adding a structure size to the catalog—in this case, a 12″ structure to the US Imperial Structures catalog:

1. Changes to the US Imperial Structures catalog can be made from any drawing that is mapped to that catalog, which is probably any imperial drawing you have open. For this exercise, start a new drawing from the _AutoCAD Civil 3D (Imperial) NCS Base.dwt.

2. Choose Pipes ➤ Part Builder.

3. Choose Structure from the dropdown list in the Part Catalog selection box.

4. Expand the Junction Structure Without Frames chapter.

5. Highlight the Concentric Cylindrical Structure NF (no frames) part family.

6. Click the Modify Part Sizes button.

7. The Part Builder interface opens the AeccStructConcentricCylinderNF_Imperial.dwg along with the Content Builder task pane.

8. Expand the Size Parameters tree.

9. Right-click the SID (Structure Inner Diameter) parameter and choose Edit. The Edit Part Sizes dialog appears.

10. Locate the SID column (Figure 14.15). Double-click inside the box and note there is a drop-down menu showing the available inner diameter sizes: 48, 50, 72, 96.

11. Locate the Edit button (see Figure 14.16). Make sure you are still active in the SID column cell, and then click the Edit button. The Edit Values dialog appears. Click Add and type **12**. Click OK to close the Edit Values dialog, and click OK again to close the Edit Part Sizes dialog.

FIGURE 14.15

Choosing a part size

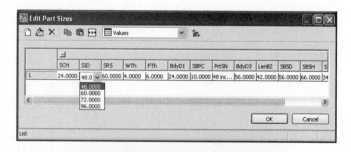

FIGURE 14.16

Click the Edit button to open the Edit Values dialog.

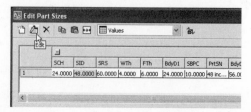

12. Click the small "x" in the top-right corner of the Content Builder task pane to exit Part Builder. When prompted with Save Changes To Concentric Cylindrical Structure NF, click Yes. (You could also click Save in Content Builder to save the part and remain active in the Part Builder interface.)

13. You are back in your original drawing. If you created a new parts list in any drawing that references the US Imperial Structures catalog, the 12″ structure would now be available for selection.

Sharing a Custom Part

You may find that you need to go beyond adding pipe and structure sizes to your catalog and build custom part families or even whole custom chapters. Perhaps instead of building them yourself, you are able to acquire them from an outside source.

The following section will lead you through the process of adding a custom part to your catalog from an outside source, as well as sharing custom parts that you have created. The key to sharing a part is to locate the three files we mentioned earlier.

Adding a custom part size to your catalog requires these steps:

1. Locate the *partname*.dwg, *partname*.xml, and (optionally) the *partname*.bmp of the part you would like to obtain.

2. Make a copy of the *partname*.dwg, *partname*.xml, and (optionally) the *partname*.bmp.

3. Insert the *partname*.dwg, *partname*.xml, and (optionally) the *partname*.bmp in the correct folder of your catalog.

4. Run the **partcatalogregen** command in Civil 3D.

ADDING ARCH PIPE TO YOUR PART CATALOG

This exercise will teach you how to add a premade custom part to your catalog:

1. Changes to the US Imperial Pipes catalog can be made from any drawing that is mapped to that catalog, which is probably any imperial drawing you have open. For this exercise, start a new drawing from the _AutoCAD Civil 3D (Imperial) NCS Base.dwt.

2. Create a new folder:

   ```
   C:\Documents and Settings\All Users\Application Data\Autodesk\
   C3D 2008\enu\Pipes Catalog\US Imperial Pipes\Arch Pipe
   ```

   There should now be five folders in this directory: Arch Pipe, Circular Pipe, Egg-Shaped Pipe, Elliptical Pipes, and Rectangular Pipes.

3. From the companion CD, copy Concrete Arch Pipe.dwg, Concrete Arch Pipe.xml, and Concrete Arch Pipe.bmp into the Arch Pipe folder.

4. Return to your drawing and enter **PARTCATALOGREGEN** in the command line. Press P to regenerate the Pipe catalog. A dialog appears alerting you to a successful regeneration.

5. If you created a new parts list at this point in any drawing that references the US Imperial Pipes catalog, the arch pipe would be available for selection.

6. To confirm the addition of the new pipe shape to the catalog, locate the catalog HTML file at

```
C:\Documents and Settings\All Users\Application Data\Autodesk\
C3D 2008\enu\Pipes Catalog\US Imperial Pipes\US Imperial Pipes.htm
```

and explore the catalog as we did in the "Part Catalog" section earlier.

Part Styles

The catalog defines how parts will be modeled, and styles define how the part will be represented in the drawing. Styles can be a true reflection of the model itself, or more commonly, they can be customized and enhanced with items such as AutoCAD blocks.

Your company or municipality should have a CAD standard that spells out the symbology you need to represent your pipes and structures. Prepare a list of blocks, layers, and other specifications that you need to compose the appropriate styles.

Creating Structure Styles

On the basis of our hypothetical sanitary sewer example, we will need to create structure styles to reflect the conventions shown earlier in Figures 14.1 and 14.2. You need a different structure style for each type shown. With your list of specifications, explore the style options to plan how best to build your styles. You access the Structure Style dialog by expanding Structure Styles on the Settings tab of Toolspace and double-clicking an existing style or creating a new style.

THE MODEL TAB

This tab (Figure 14.17) controls what represents your structure when you are working in 3D. Typically, you want to leave this as Use Catalog Defined 3D Part so that when you look at your structure, it looks like your concentric manhole or whatever you have chosen in the parts list.

FIGURE 14.17
The Model tab on the Structure Style dialog,

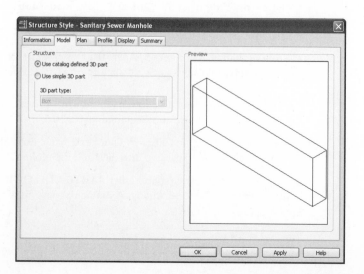

THE PLAN TAB

During your brainstorming session, you figured out how you need your structure represented in the plan. The Plan tab (Figure 14.18) enables you to compose your object style to match that specification. Options on the Plan tab include the following:

Use Outer Part Boundary uses the actual limits of your structure from the parts list and shows you an outline of the structure as it would appear in the plan.

User Defined Part uses any block you specify. In the case of your sanitary manhole, you chose a symbol to match the CAD Standard.

Size Options has several options. Click Help to learn more about the specifics of each option.

Enable Part Masking creates a wipeout or mask inside the limits of the structure. Any pipes that connect to the center of the pipe appear trimmed at the limits of the structure.

FIGURE 14.18

The Plan tab in the Structure Style dialog

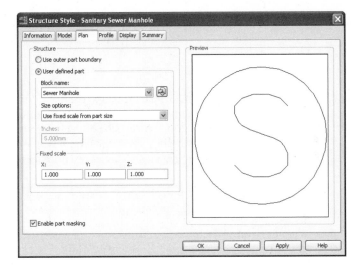

THE PROFILE TAB

Once you know what your structure must look like in the profile, you use the Profile tab (Figure 14.19) to create the style. Options on the Profile tab include the following:

Display As Solid uses the actual limits of your structure from the parts list and shows you the mesh of the structure as it would appear in profile view.

Display As Boundary uses the actual limits of your structure from the parts list and shows you an outline of the structure as it would appear in profile view. You will use this option for the sanitary manhole.

Display As Block uses any block you specify. You will use this option for the sanitary cleanout.

Size Options has several options. Click Help to learn more about the specifics of each option.

Enable Part Masking creates a wipeout or mask inside the limits of the structure. Any pipes that connect to the center of the pipe appear trimmed at the limits of the structure.

FIGURE 14.19
The Profile tab in the
Structure Style dialog

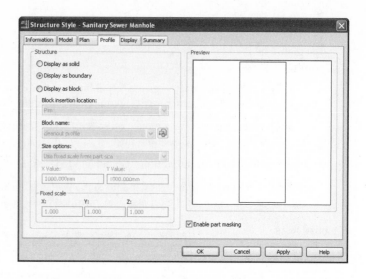

THE DISPLAY TAB

The Display tab (Figure 14.20) enables you to control the visibility and display properties of all possible structure style elements. Note that the same settings apply for both View Directions settings, 2D and 3D. Make sure you check both view directions for your desired visibility in both top view (2D) and any isometric views or 3D rotations.

The display options for Structure styles have a number of components that need to be reviewed and understood.

Plan Structure controls if the structure is visible in plan view and allows for layer mapping and color/linetype overrides.

Plan Structure Hatch controls the visibility of any structure hatch in plan view and also allows for layer mapping and color/linetype overrides.

FIGURE 14.20
The Display tab in the
Structure Style dialog

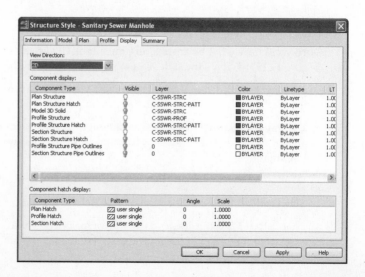

Model 3D Solid controls the visibility of the 3D model in plan view and allows for layer mapping and color/linetype overrides. In the 2D view direction, this is most commonly set to not visible.

Profile Structure controls if the structure is visible in profile view and allows for layer mapping and color/linetype overrides.

Profile Structure Hatch controls the visibility of any structure hatch in profile view and allows for layer mapping and color/linetype overrides.

Section Structure controls if the structure is visible in a section view and allows for layer mapping and color/linetype overrides.

Section Structure Hatch controls the visibility of any structure hatch in a section view and allows for layer mapping and color/linetype overrides.

Profile Structure Pipe Outlines controls the visibility of incoming connected pipes in profile view and allows for layer mapping and color/linetype overrides.

Section Structure Pipe Outlines controls the visibility of incoming connected pipes in a section view and allows for layer mapping and color/linetype overrides.

CREATING STRUCTURE STYLES FOR A SANITARY MANHOLE AND SANITARY CLEANOUT

In this exercise, you will create the structure styles for our sanitary sewer project:

1. Create a new drawing from the _AutoCAD Civil 3D (Imperial) NCS Base.dwt.

2. Expand the Structures ➤ Structures Styles trees on the Settings tab of Toolspace. Right-click the Sanitary Sewer Manhole style and choose Edit. The Structure Style dialog appears.

3. Switch to the Plan tab, and note that the User Defined Part option is selected. Note that the Block Name selection box has a dropdown menu you can use to choose any block contained in the drawing.

4. Under Size Options, use the dropdown menu to change the size from the Use Drawing Scale option to the Use Fixed Scale From Part Size. This will automatically size the block to reflect the modeled structure size. A 48″ manhole will be represented smaller than a 72″ manhole, and so on. Note that the Enable Part Masking box is checked.

5. Switch to the Profile tab.

6. Confirm that the Display As Boundary option is selected. This will make an outline in profile view that reflects the true shape of the model (ignore the preview window at this point). Since we will specify that our sanitary manholes be concentric cylindrical structures when we build the parts list, this boundary will be a conical topped structure with a square bottom, as required by our CAD standard. Note that the Enable Part Masking box is checked.

7. Switch to the Display tab. Confirm that the structure will be visible in plan, profile, and section views. Confirm that all hatches are set to not be visible.

8. Click OK.

9. Right-click the Sanitary Sewer Manhole style that we just edited, and choose Copy.

10. On the Information tab, rename the copied style to **Sanitary Sewer Cleanout**.

11. Switch to the Plan tab and change the selection to the Use Outer Part Boundary option (ignore the preview window at this point), which will make an outline around the outer limits of the model, as seen in plan view. Since we are using a circular structure to represent our cleanouts, this option will return a circle that corresponds with the diameter of our cleanout.

12. Switch to the Profile tab and select the Display As Block option; select Rim from the dropdown menu in the Block Insertion Location selection box; and then click the button next to the dropdown menu in the Block Name selection box to choose a block that is outside the drawing (see Figure 14.21). Navigate to the drawing found on the companion CD called `cleanout profile.dwg`. Select this drawing to be the block that will represent our cleanout in profile.

13. Select the Use Fixed Scale From Part Size option from the dropdown menu in the Size Options selection box. This option will stretch the block to accommodate the depth of the structure when our simple rectangular block is inserted at the structure rim location.

14. Switch to the Display tab. Leave everything the same, except make the Plan Structure Hatch visible. Then click in the Plan Hatch pattern column at the bottom of the dialog and the Hatch Pattern dialog appears. Select Solid Fill (see Figure 14.22) from the dropdown menu in the Type selection box. This will fill in our circle with a solid hatch to match our CAD Standard. Click OK.

FIGURE 14.21
Choose a block from outside the drawing.

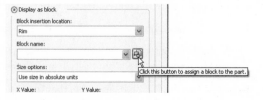

FIGURE 14.22
The Hatch Pattern dialog

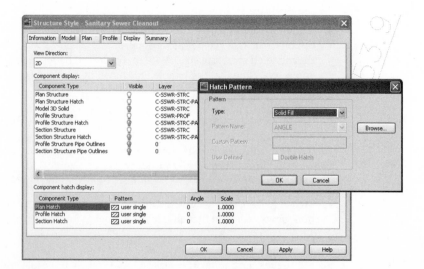

15. Click OK to close the Structure Style dialog. We will use these styles later when we define our parts list.

16. Save your drawing to use in the next exercise.

Creating Pipe Styles

On the basis of our hypothetical sanitary sewer example, we will need to create pipe styles to reflect the pipes shown earlier in Figure 14.3.

You need one pipe style to handle your sanitary sewer pipe. In your real projects, you will need to do similar brainstorming for your storm drainage, water, and any other pipes you may be designing. With your list of specifications, explore the style options to plan how best to build your styles. You access the Pipe Style dialog by expanding Pipe Styles on the Settings tab of Toolspace and double-clicking an existing style or creating a new style.

THE PLAN TAB

This tab (see Figure 14.23) controls what represents your pipe when you are working in plan view. Click Help at any time for a detailed breakdown of each option.

Pipe Wall Sizes: You have a choice of having the program apply the part size directly from the catalog part (i.e., the literal pipe dimensions as defined in the catalog), or you can specify your own constant or scaled dimensions.

Pipe Hatch Options: If you choose to show pipe hatching (see the Display tab), this part of the dialog gives you options to control that hatch. You can hatch the entire pipe to the inner or outer walls, or you can hatch the space between the inner and outer walls only, as shown in Figure 14.24.

FIGURE 14.23
The Plan tab in the Pipe Style dialog

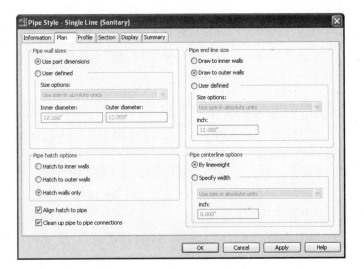

Pipe End Line Size: If you choose to show an end line (see the Display tab), you can control its length with these options. An end line can be drawn connecting the outer walls (see Figure 14.25), the inner walls, or you can specify your own constant or scaled dimensions.

Pipe Centerline Options: If you choose to show a centerline (see the Display tab), you can display it by the lineweight established in the Display tab, or you can specify your own part-driven, constant, or scaled dimensions. Use this option for your sanitary pipes in places where the width of the centerline widens or narrows on the basis of the pipe diameter.

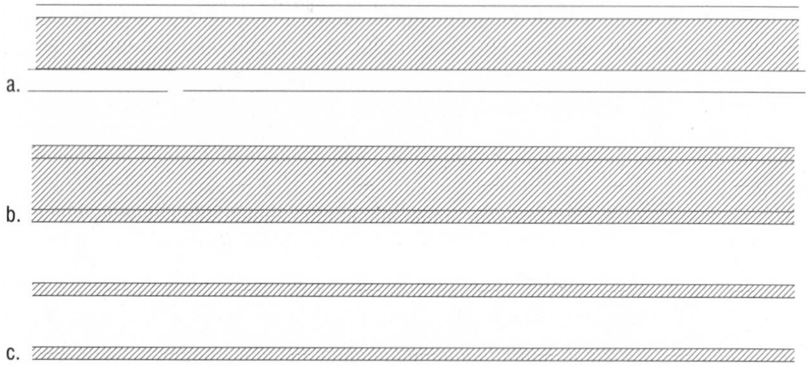

FIGURE 14.24

Pipe hatch to inner walls (a), outer walls (b), and hatch walls only (c)

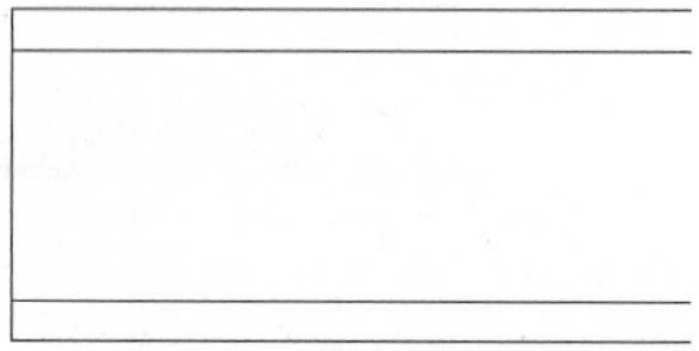

FIGURE 14.25

Pipe end line shown to outer walls

THE PROFILE TAB

The Profile tab (see Figure 14.26) is almost identical to the Plan tab, except the controls here determine what your pipe looks like in profile view. The only additional settings on this tab are the crossing pipe hatch options. If you choose to display crossing pipe with a hatch, these settings control the location of that hatch.

THE SECTION TAB

If you choose to show a hatch on your pipes in section, you control the hatch location on this tab (see Figure 14.27).

THE DISPLAY TAB

The Display tab (see Figure 14.28) enables you to control the visibility and display properties of all possible pipe style elements. Note that the same settings apply for both the 2D and 3D View Direction settings. Make sure you check both view directions for your desired visibility in both top view (2D) and any isometric views or 3D rotations.

FIGURE 14.26

The Profile tab in the Pipe Style dialog

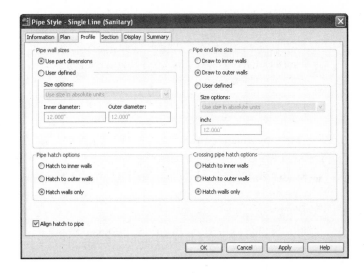

FIGURE 14.27

The Section tab in the Pipe Style dialog

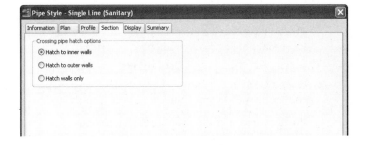

FIGURE 14.28

The Display tab in the Pipe Style dialog

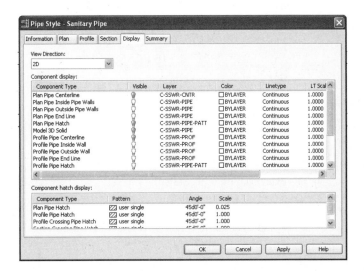

Just like the structure styles, the pipe styles have a long list of display components that can be adjusted and modified to suit your needs.

Plan Pipe Centerline/Inside Pipe Walls/Outside Pipe Walls controls if the pipe centerline/inside walls/outside walls are visible in plan view and allows for layer mapping and color/linetype overrides.

Plan Pipe End Line controls the visibility of the end line specified on the Plan tab and allows for layer mapping and color/linetype overrides.

Plan Pipe Hatch controls the visibility of the hatch specified on the Plan tab and allows for layer mapping and color/linetype overrides.

Model 3D Solid controls the visibility of the 3D model in plan view and allows for layer mapping and color/linetype overrides. In the 2D View Direction, this is most commonly set to not visible.

Profile Pipe Centerline/Inside Wall/Outside Wall controls if the pipe centerline/inside walls/outside walls are visible in profile view and allows for layer mapping and color/linetype overrides.

Profile Pipe End Line controls the visibility of the end line specified on the Profile tab and allows for layer mapping and color/linetype overrides.

Profile Pipe Hatch controls the visibility of the hatch specified on the Profile tab and allows for layer mapping and color/linetype overrides.

Profile Crossing Pipe Inside Wall is a control to be used for viewing the inside walls of pipes that CROSS profile views and allows for layer mapping and color/linetype overrides. Most commonly will be not visible except in a specific pipe crossing style.

Profile Crossing Pipe Outside Wall is a control to be used for viewing the outside walls of pipes that CROSS profile views and allows for layer mapping and color/linetype overrides. Most commonly will be not visible except in a specific pipe crossing style.

Profile Crossing Pipe Hatch is a control to be used for viewing hatch of pipes that CROSS profile views and allows for layer mapping and color/linetype overrides. Most commonly will be not visible except in a specific pipe crossing style.

Section Pipe Inside Walls controls the visibility of the inside pipe walls in section view and allows for layer mapping and color/linetype overrides.

Section Crossing Pipe Hatch controls the visibility of the outside pipe walls in section view and allows for layer mapping and color/linetype overrides.

CREATING A PIPE STYLE FOR A SANITARY SEWER

In this exercise, you will create the pipe styles for our sanitary sewer:

1. Continue working in your drawing from the last exercise.

2. Expand the Pipes ➤ Pipe Styles tree on the Settings tab on Toolspace. Right-click the Single Line Sanitary style and choose Edit. The Pipe Styles dialog appears.

3. Switch to the Plan tab and locate the Pipe Centerline Options area in the lower-right corner of the dialog. Select the Specify Width option, then use the dropdown list to change the

selection to the Draw To Inner Walls option. This will stretch the linetype of the specified layer to be equally as wide as the pipe inner diameter. For example, an 8″ pipe will have a thinner linetype than a 12″ pipe.

4. Switch to the Profile tab. Locate Pipe Hatch Options in the lower-left corner of the dialog. Confirm that the Hatch Walls Only option is selected.

5. Switch to the Display tab.

6. Note the Plan Pipe Centerline is mapped to the C-SSWR-CNTR layer. We will change its linetype in the Layer Manager dialog.

7. Make sure that the following options are visible: Plan Pipe Centerline, Profile Pipe Inside Wall, Profile Pipe Outside Wall, and Profile Pipe Hatch. The rest should be set to not visible.

8. Click OK.

9. Open the Layer Manager dialog (see Figure 14.29) and change the linetype on C-SSWR-CNTR to CENTER2. Click OK.

10. Save your drawing—you will use it in the next exercise.

FIGURE 14.29
Change the linetype in the Layer Manager dialog.

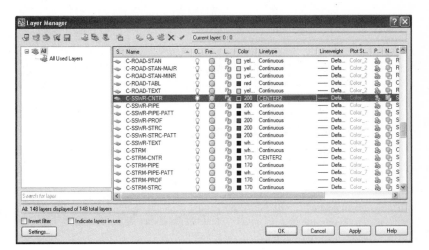

Part Rules

In the beginning of this chapter, we made notes about our hypothetical municipality having certain requirements for how our structures and pipes will behave—things like minimum slope, sump depths, and pipe invert drops across structure. Depending on the type of network and the complexity of your design, there might be many different constraints on your design. Civil 3D allows you to establish structure and pipe rules that will assist in respecting these constraints during initial layout and edits. Some rules do not change the pipes or structures during layout but provide a "violation only" check that can be viewed in Prospector.

Rules are separated into two categories—structure rules and pipe rules—and are collected in rule sets that you can then add to specific parts in your parts list, which we will build at the end of this chapter.

Structure Rules

Structure rule sets are located on the Settings tab of Toolspace, under the Structure tree.

For a detailed breakdown of structure rules and how they are applied, including images and illustrations, please see the Civil 3D Users Guide.

Click the Add Rule button on the Rules tab in the Structure Rule Set dialog. The Add Rule dialog appears, which allows you to access all the various structure rules (see Figure 14.30).

FIGURE 14.30

The Add Rule dialog

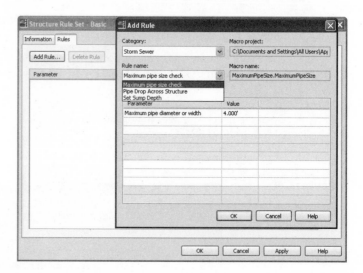

MAXIMUM PIPE SIZE CHECK

The Maximum Pipe Size Check rule (see Figure 14.31) examines all pipes connected to a structure and flags a violation in Prospector if any pipe is larger than your rule. This is a violation-only rule; it will not change your pipe size automatically.

FIGURE 14.31

The Maximum Pipe
Size Check rule option

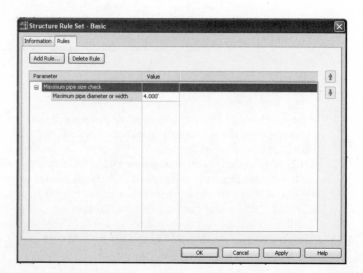

PIPE DROP ACROSS STRUCTURE

The Pipe Drop Across Structure rule (see Figure 14.32) places a piece of intelligence onto the structure that tells any connected pipes how their inverts (or alternatively their crowns or centerlines) must relate to one another.

FIGURE 14.32

The Pipe Drop Across Structure rule options

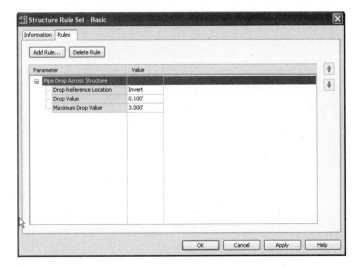

When a new pipe is connected to a structure that has the Pipe Drop Across Structure rule applied, the following checks will take place:

◆ A pipe drawn to be exiting a structure will have an invert equal to or lower than the lowest pipe entering the structure.

◆ A pipe drawn to be entering a structure will have an invert equal to or higher than the highest pipe exiting the structure.

◆ Any minimum specified drop distance is respected between the lowest entering pipe and the highest exiting pipe.

In our hypothetical sanitary sewer example, we are required to maintain a 0.10´ invert drop across all structures. We will use this rule in our structure rule set in the next exercise.

SET SUMP DEPTH

The Set Sump Depth rule (Figure 14.33) establishes a desired sump depth for structures. It is very important to add a sump depth rule to all your structure rule sets, otherwise Civil 3D will assume a sump for you that is most often undesirable and difficult to modify once your structures have been drawn.

In our hypothetical sanitary sewer example, all of our structures have a 1.5´ sump depth. We will use this rule in our structure rule set in the next exercise.

FIGURE 14.33

The Set Sump Depth
rule options

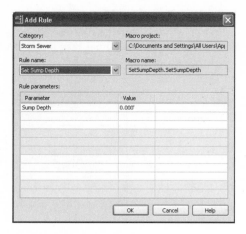

Pipe Rules

Pipe rule sets are located on the Settings tab of Toolspace, under the Pipe tree. For a detailed break-down of pipe rules and how they are applied, including images and illustrations, please see the Civil 3D Users Guide.

All of the pipe rules can be accessed by clicking the Add Rule button on the Rules tab of the Pipe Rule Set dialog.

COVER AND SLOPE RULE

The Cover And Slope rule (Figure 14.34) allows you to specify your desired slope range and cover range. We will create one cover and slope rule for each size pipe in our hypothetical sanitary sewer example.

FIGURE 14.34

The Cover And Slope
rule options

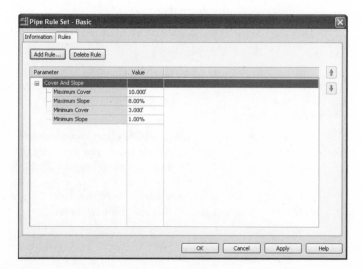

COVER ONLY RULE

The Cover Only rule (Figure 14.35) is designed for use with pressure-type pipe systems where slope can vary or is not a critical factor.

FIGURE 14.35
The Cover Only
rule options

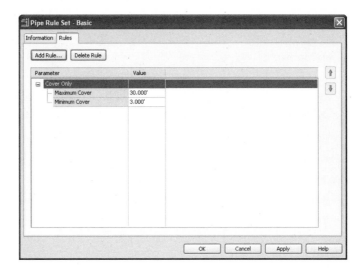

PIPE TO PIPE MATCH RULE

The Pipe To Pipe Match rule (Figure 14.36) is also designed for use with pressure-type pipe systems where there are no true structures (only null structures), including situations where pipe is placed to break into an existing pipe. This rule determines how pipe inverts will be assigned when two pipes come together, similar to the Pipe Drop Across Structure rule.

FIGURE 14.36
The Pipe To Pipe
Match rule options

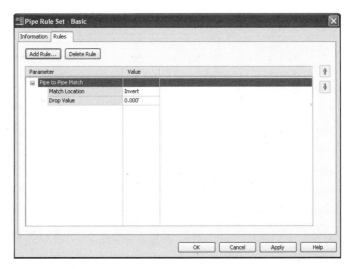

LENGTH CHECK

Length Check is a violation-only rule; it will not change your pipe length size automatically. The Length Check options (see Figure 14.37) allow you to specify a minimum and maximum pipe length.

FIGURE 14.37
The Length Check rule options

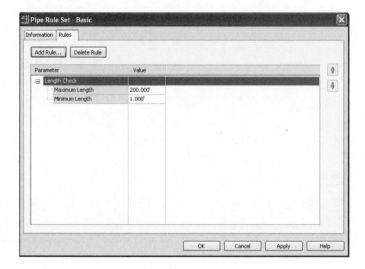

Creating Structure and Pipe Rule Sets

This exercise will have you create one structure rule set and three pipe rule sets for a hypothetical sanitary sewer project.

1. Continue working in your drawing from the previous exercise.

2. Locate the Structure Rule Sets on the Settings tab of Toolspace under the Structure tree. Right-click the rule set and choose New.

3. On the Information Tab, enter **Sanitary Structure Rules** in the Name text box.

4. Switch to the Rules tab. Click the Add Rule button.

5. In the Add Rule dialog, choose Pipe Drop Across Structure in the Rule Name dropdown list. Click OK. (You cannot change the parameters.)

6. Change the parameters on the Structure Rule Set dialog to the following:

Drop Reference Location	Invert
Drop Value	0.1′
Maximum Drop Value	3′

These parameters establish a rule that will match our hypothetical municipality's standard for the drop across sanitary sewer structures.

7. Click the Add Rule button.

8. In the Add Rule dialog, choose Set Sump Depth in the Rule Name dropdown list. Click OK. (You cannot change the parameters.)

9. Change the Sump Depth parameter to 1.5′ on the Structure Rule Set dialog to meet our hypothetical municipality's standard for sump in sanitary sewer structures.

10. Click OK.

11. Locate the Pipe Rule Set on the Settings tab of Toolspace under the Pipe tree. Right-click the Pipe Rule Set and choose New.

12. On the Information tab, enter **8 Inch Sanitary Pipe Rules** for the name.

13. Switch to the Rules tab. Click Add Rule.

14. In the Add Rule dialog, choose Cover And Slope in the Rule Name dropdown list. Click OK. (You cannot change the parameters.)

15. Modify the parameters to match the constraints established by our hypothetical municipality for 8″ pipe.

Maximum Cover	10′
Maximum Slope	10%
Minimum Cover	4′
Minimum Slope	0.40%

16. Click OK.

17. Select the rule set you just created (8 inch Sanitary Pipe Rules). Right-click and choose Copy.

18. On the Information tab, enter **10 Inch Sanitary Pipe Rules** in the Name text box.

19. Modify the parameters to match the constraints established by our hypothetical municipality for 10″ pipe:

Maximum Cover	10′
Maximum Slope	10%
Minimum Cover	4′
Minimum Slope	0.28%

20. Repeat the process to create a rule set for the 12″ pipe using the following parameters:

Maximum Cover	10′
Maximum Slope	10%
Minimum Cover	4′
Minimum Slope	0.22%

21. You should now have one structure rule set and three pipe rule sets.

22. Save your drawing; we will use it in the next exercise.

Parts List

When you know what parts you need, what they need to look like, and how you want them to behave, you can standardize your needs in the form of a parts list. If you think of the part catalog, the styles in your template and the rule sets as being your well-stocked workshop, the parts list is the toolbox that you fill with only the equipment you need to get the job done. Parts lists are stored in your standard Civil 3D template, so they will be at your fingertips when new jobs are created.

For example, when you are designing a sanitary sewer system, you may only need a small spectrum of PVC pipe sizes and manhole types that follow a few sets of rules and need only a style or two. You wouldn't want to have to sort through your entire collection of parts, rules, and styles every time you created a sanitary sewer network. So you will make a parts list called Sanitary Sewers or a similar name and stock it with the pipes, structures, styles, and rules that you will need to get the job done.

Similarly, depending on the type of work you do, you'll want at least a Storm Drainage parts list with concrete pipe, catch basins, storm manholes, applicable rule sets and styles, and a Water Network parts list containing PVC pipe and null structures as well as some cover-only rule sets. As you begin your first few pilot projects, you will begin to see which parts lists are most useful and you can continue to build them as part of your standard template.

The parts lists are located on the Settings tab of Toolspace under the Pipe Network tree. You can create parts lists by right-clicking the Parts Lists entry and choosing New. You can edit parts lists by choosing a specific parts list, right-clicking, and choosing Edit.

Adding Part Families on the Pipes Tab

When you create a parts list, the Pipes tab will initially be blank. You can add pipe families by right-clicking the entry on the Pipes tab (it may say New Parts List, or the name of your newly created parts list) and choosing Add Part Family (Figure 14.38).

FIGURE 14.38

Adding a part family

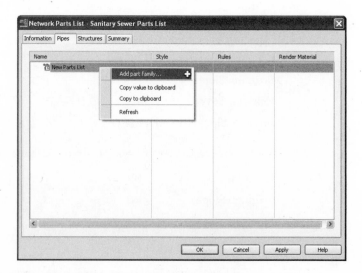

In the Part Catalog dialog (see Figure 14.39), you are given the opportunity to choose one or more part families to add to your parts list. You will recognize these choices from the catalog HTML interface as well as from the Part Builder interface. Note that the preview image comes from the *partname*.bmp located in the catalog folder.

Once the part family has been added to your Pipes tab, you must choose the appropriate sizes. Choose the Part Family entry, right-click, and choose Add Part Size.

Part sizes can be added individually, or you can check the Add All Sizes box to add every part size available for that part family. Sometimes it is easier to add all of the sizes and delete a few that you don't need rather than add many sizes individually.

Also note that in the Part Size Creator dialog (Figure 14.40) you can assign optional properties such as the Manning Coefficient or the Hazen Williams Coefficient. This optional property will be applied any time this particular pipe is added to your network using this parts list.

Once pipe sizes have been added to the Pipes tab, as shown in Figure 14.41, you can change their default descriptions by clicking in the first column. You can also delete an entry by selecting the size, right-clicking, and choosing Delete.

FIGURE 14.39

The Part Catalog dialog

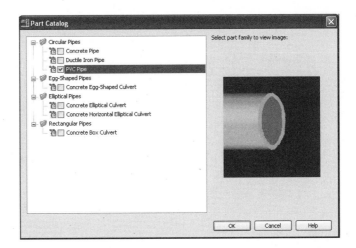

FIGURE 14.40

The Part Size Creator

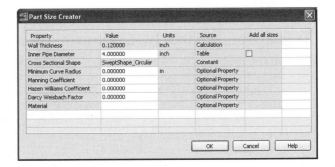

FIGURE 14.41
Pipe sizes added with descriptions edited. Note that style and rules remain to be changed.

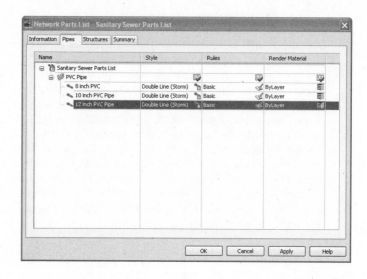

MODIFYING STYLES AND RULES

Next to each pipe size is an entry for style and rules. If you have different styles and rules for each size of pipe, they can be assigned individually. If you are applying the same style or rule set to all of your sizes, click the button across from the Part Family entry (see Figure 14.42) to assign style or rules to all sizes in that part family.

FIGURE 14.42
A completed Pipes tab for our hypothetical sanitary sewer project

Adding Part Families on the Structures Tab

When you create a parts list, the Structures tab will initially contain a null structure. You can add additional structure families by right-clicking the entry on the Pipes tab (it may say New Parts List, or the name of your newly created Parts List) and choosing Add Part Family.

In the Part Catalog dialog (see Figure 14.43), you are given the opportunity to choose one or more part families to add to your parts list. You will recognize these choices from the catalog HTML interface as well as the Part Builder interface. Note that the preview image comes from the *partname*.bmp located in the catalog folder.

Once the part family has been added to your Structures tab, you must now choose the appropriate sizes. Choose the entry for the part family, right-click, and choose Add Part Size.

Part sizes can be added individually, or you can check the Add All Sizes box to add every part size available for that part family. Sometimes it is easier to add all of the sizes and delete a few that you don't need rather than add many sizes individually.

Also note that in the Part Size Creator dialog (see Figure 14.44) you can assign optional properties such as Grate, Frame, and Cover Types. These properties will then be applied any time this particular structure is added to your network using this parts list.

Once pipe sizes have been added to the Structures tab (see Figure 14.45), you can change their default descriptions by clicking in the first column. You can also delete an entry by selecting the size, right-clicking, and choosing Delete. The null structure cannot be deleted. It serves as a placeholder between two pipes that are directly connected. In a gravity system, a null structure may never be necessary, but it must remain part of the Structures list in the case of two pipes being connected.

FIGURE 14.43
Adding the Concentric Cylindrical Structure part family to your parts list

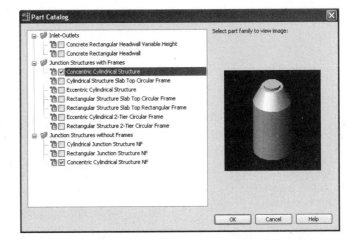

FIGURE 14.44
Part Size Creator with additional properties

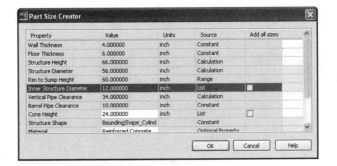

FIGURE 14.45

Pipe sizes added with descriptions edited. Note that their style and rules remain to be changed.

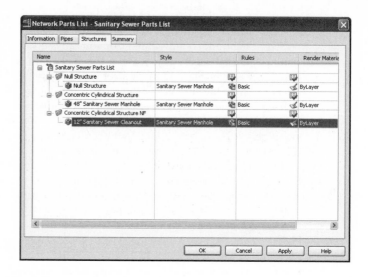

MODIFYING STYLES AND RULES

Next to each structure entry is an entry for style and rules (see Figure 14.46). If you have different styles and rules for each structure, these can be assigned individually. If you are applying the same style or rule set to all of your structures, click the button across from the Part Family entry to assign style or rules to all sizes in that part family.

FIGURE 14.46

A completed Structures tab for our hypothetical sanitary sewer project

Creating a Parts List for a Sanitary Sewer

In this exercise, you will combine the parts, styles, and rules created in the previous exercises:

1. Continue working in your drawing from the previous exercise.

2. Locate the Parts List entry on the Settings tab of Toolspace.

3. Locate the default Sanitary Sewer Parts List that is part of the default template. Select this parts list, right-click, and choose Delete. Parts lists must have unique names, and since we are about to create a list called Sanitary Sewers, we need to delete this one.

4. Select the Parts Lists entry under the Pipe Network tree, right-click, and choose Create Parts List. The Create Parts List dialog appears.

5. Enter **Sanitary Sewer** in the Name text box on the Information tab.

6. Switch to the Pipes tab. Right-click the New Parts List entry under the Name column, and choose Add Part Family. In the Part Catalog dialog, check the box next to PVC Pipe and click OK.

7. Expand the New Parts List tree on the Network Parts List dialog to see the entry for PVC Pipe. Note that you have added the part family but you have not yet added any pipe sizes.

8. Right-click the PVC Pipe entry and choose Add Part Size.

9. In the Part Size Creator dialog, click in the Value field next to Inner Pipe Diameter to activate the dropdown list, and choose 8.00 (Figure 14.47). Click OK to add the pipe size. Repeat the process to add 10″ and 12″ pipes.

10. Once you have returned to the Pipes tab, click inside the description field for your 8″ pipe. It probably says something like "8 inch PVC Pipe MCR_0.000000 ACMan_0.000000 ACHW_0.000000 ACDW_0.000000 Material_" by default. Edit the description so that it reads "8 inch PVC Pipe."

11. Repeat step 10 for the 10″ and 12″ pipes.

12. Follow the procedures found in the "Modifying Styles and Rules" subsection under "Adding Part Families on the Pipes Tab" earlier to change the pipe style to Single Line (Sanitary) and the rules to the appropriate rule set, respectively, for each size pipe.

13. Switch to the Structures tab. Right-click the New Parts List entry in the Name field and choose Add Part Family. In the Part Catalog dialog, check the boxes next to Concentric Cylindrical Structure and Concentric Cylindrical Junction Structure NF. Click OK.

14. Right-click the Concentric Cylindrical entry in the Network Parts List dialog and choose Add Part Size.

15. Following the same method used to add the different pipe sizes, add a 48″ and a 60″ structure size to the list.

16. Following the same method that was used in step 15, add a 12″ Concentric Cylindrical Junction Structure NF to the list. (Note that if you did not do the Part Builder exercise where we added the 12″ structure diameter, you will not have this choice. You may substitute any size in its place.)

17. Once you have returned to the Structures tab, click inside the Description field for your 48″ Structure. It probably says something like "Concentric Structure 48 dia 18 frame 24 cone 5 wall 6 floor Mat_Reinforced Concrete SF_Standard SG_Standard SC_Standard." Edit the description to say "48 inch Sanitary Sewer Manhole."

FIGURE 14.47
Choose a part size.

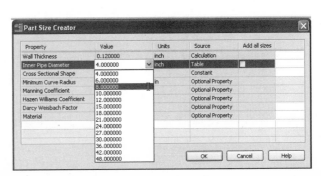

18. Repeat step 17 for the other structure types, giving each an appropriate description.

19. Follow the procedures found in the "Modifying Styles and Rules" subsection under "Adding Part Families on the Structures Tab" earlier to change the structure style to Sanitary Sewer Manhole and Sanitary Sewer Cleanout and the rules to Sanitary Structure Rules, respectively.

20. Check to make sure your Pipes and Structures tabs look like Figure 14.42 and Figure 14.46 earlier.

 Real World Scenario

WATER NETWORK RULES AND PARTS LIST

The example in this chapter has been a gravity sanitary sewer network. While a storm or other gravity network would have different parts, styles, and rules, the fundamental process is the same for all gravity pipe systems.

Pressure systems, however, need to take advantage of different parts, styles, and rules:

Parts   In Civil 3D, pipes cannot truly be connected without a structure between them. The structure acts like a "glue" that holds the pipes together. In the case of pipes-only networks, such as water, *null structures* are automatically placed wherever two or more pipes are directly connected. Null structures are part of every new parts list by default.

Styles   When water pipe is joined together, there is often no visible structure in plan or profile view. Therefore, it is important to create a style for your null structures that is either invisible or No Plot. Some people prefer the cleaner look of an Invisible style, knowing that they can always go into Prospector to locate and select the null structure. You can create a No Show style by turning off all the items in the Display tab of the Structure Style dialog.

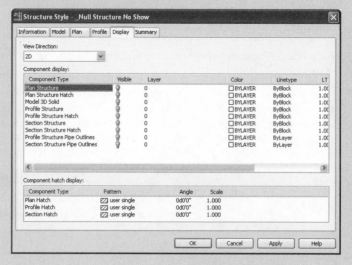

Once you apply this Invisible style to your null structure, the pipe connection will appear as if there is no structure present.

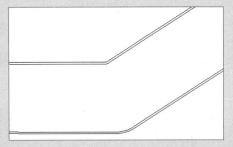

Some people prefer to use the No Plot style because it allows them to grab and grip-edit the location of the pipe connection; then they can either ignore or freeze the No Plot layer for plan production.

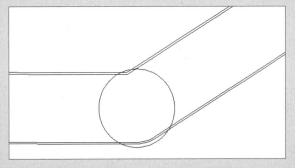

If inside or outside walls (or both) are shown when a pipe is drawn in plan view, there is an option that allows for cleanup at pipe connections.

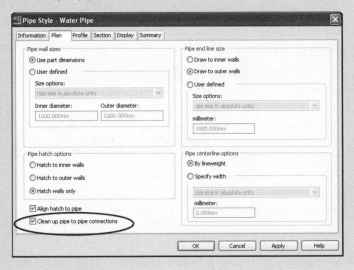

Rules   In most water network design situations, the driving design factor is minimum cover. There are often no slope restrictions. In this case, you would use the Cover Only rule instead of the Slope And Cover rule.

A second rule that may be added in a pipes-only situation is the Pipe To Pipe Match rule. This rule specifies what happens when two pipes are directly connected at a null structure.

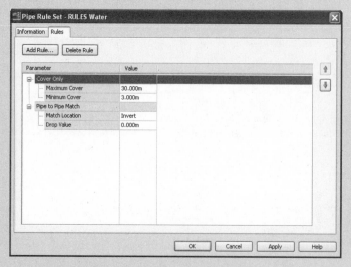

The process for creating a Water Network parts list is the same as creating one for a Sanitary parts list: identify all the parts that you will need to construct the network, identify how these parts will be represented in plan and profile views, and determine how these parts will behave.

Building your parts list using null structures, the appropriate style settings, and rules designed for a pipes-only network will ensure a smooth water network design.

The Bottom Line

Add pipe and structure families to a new parts list.   Before you can begin to design your pipe network, you must ensure you have the appropriate pipes and structures at your disposal.

   Master It   Create a new drawing from the _AutoCAD Civil 3D (Imperial) NCS Extended.dwt. Create a new parts list called Typical Storm Drainage. (There is already a Storm Sewer parts list in this template. Ignore it or delete it, but do not use it. Create your own for this exercise.)

   Add 12″, 15″, 18″, 24″, 36″, and 48″ Concrete Circular Pipe to the parts list.

   Add a Rectangular Structure Slab Top Rectangular Frame with an inner structure width and length of 15″ and a Rectangular Structure Slab Top Rectangular Frame with an inner structure width of 15″ and a length of 18″ and a Concentric Cylindrical Structure with an inner diameter of 48″ to the parts list.

Create rule sets that apply to pipes and structures in a parts list.   Municipal standards and engineering judgment determine how pipes will behave in design situations. Considerations include minimum and maximum slope, cover requirements, and length guidelines. For structures, there are regulations regarding sump depth and pipe drop. These considerations can be applied to pipe network parts through the creation of rule sets.

Master It Create a new structure rule set called Storm Drain Structure Rules. Add the following rules:

Pipe Drop Across Structure

Drop Reference Location: Invert

Drop Value: 0.01´

Maximum Drop Value: 2´

Set Sump Depth

Sump Depth: 0.5´

Create a new pipe rule set called Storm Drain Pipe Rules, and add the following rules:

Cover and Slope:

Max Cover 15´,

Max Slope 5%

Min Cover 4´

Min Slope .05%

Length Check:

Max Length 300´

Min Length 8´

Apply these rules to all pipes and structures in your Typical Storm Drainage parts list.

Apply styles to pipes and structures in a parts list. The final drafted appearance of pipes and structures in a drawing is controlled by municipal standards and company CAD standards. Civil 3D object styles allow you to control and automate the symbology used to represent pipes and structures in plan, profile, and section views.

Master It Apply the following styles to your parts list:

1. Single Line (Storm) to the 12˝, 15˝, 18˝ Concrete Circular Pipe

2. Double Line (Storm) to the 24˝, 36˝, 48˝ Concrete Circular Pipe

3. Storm Sewer Manhole to the Concentric Cylindrical Structure with an inner diameter of 48˝

4. Catch Basin to both sizes of the Rectangular Structure Slab Top Rectangular Frame

Chapter 15

Running Downhill: Pipe Networks

Once you've understood the parts used to design and construct pipe networks, it's time to assemble those parts into a system or network.

In this chapter, you'll learn to:

◆ Create a pipe network by layout

◆ Create an alignment from network parts and draw parts in profile view

◆ Label a pipe network in plan and profile

◆ Create a dynamic pipe table

Exploring Pipe Networks

Parts in a pipe network have relationships that follow a network paradigm. A pipe network can have many branches, like the one in Figure 15.1a. In most cases, the pipes and structures in your network will be connected to each other; however, they don't necessarily have to be physically touching to be included in the same pipe network.

Land Desktop with civil design and some other civil engineering-design programs do not design piping systems using a network paradigm; instead, they use a branch-by-branch or "run" paradigm (see Figure 15.1b). Though it is possible to separate your branches into their own separate pipe networks in Civil 3D, you will find the most power and flexibility in your design if you change your thinking from a "run-by-run" to a network paradigm.

Pipe Network Object Types

Pipes are components of a pipe network that primarily represent pipes but can be used to represent any type of conduit such as culverts, gas lines, or utility cables. They can be straight or curved, and though primarily used to represent gravity systems, they can be adapted and customized to represent pressure and other types of systems such as water networks and force mains. The standard catalog has pipe shapes that are circular, elliptical, egg-shaped, and rectangular and are made of materials ranging from PVC, RCP, and DI. Part Builder (see previous chapter) can be used to create your own shapes and materials if the default shapes and dimensions cannot be adapted for your design.

FIGURE 15.1
A typical Civil 3D pipe
network (a) and a
pipe network with a
single pipe run (b)

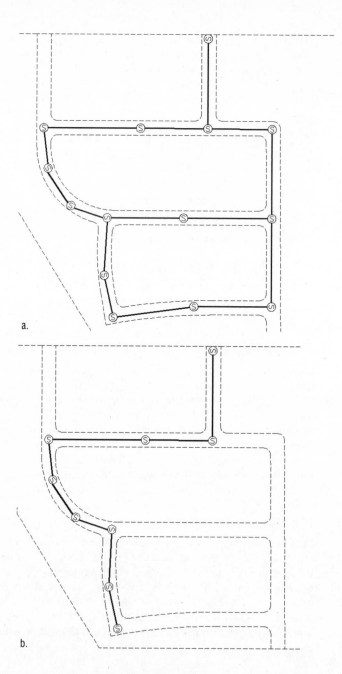

a.

b.

    Structures are components of a pipe network that represent manholes, catch basins, inlets, joints, and any other type of junction between two pipes. The standard catalog includes inlets, outlets, junction structures with frames (such as manholes with lids or catch basins with grates) and junction structures without frames (such as simple cylinders and rectangles). You can again take advantage of Part Builder to create your own shapes and materials if the default shapes and dimensions cannot be adapted for your design.

Null structures are created automatically when two pipes are joined together without a structure and act as a placeholder for a pipe endpoint. They have special properties, such as allowing pipe cleanup at pipe intersections. Most of the time, you will create a style for them that doesn't plot or is invisible for plotting purposes.

Creating a Sanitary Sewer Network

In Chapter 14, you prepared a parts list for a typical sanitary sewer network. This chapter will lead you through several methods for using that parts list to design, edit, and annotate a pipe network.

There are several ways to create pipe networks. You can create a pipe network using the Civil 3D pipe layout tools. There are also limited tools for creating pipe networks from certain AutoCAD and Civil 3D objects, such as lines, polylines, alignments, and feature lines.

Creating a Pipe Network with Layout Tools

Creating a pipe network with layout tools is very much like creating other Civil 3D objects, such as an alignment. After naming and establishing the parameters for your pipe network, you will be presented with a special toolbar, which you can use to lay out pipes and structures in plan, which will also drive a vertical design.

Establishing Pipe Network Parameters

Choose Pipes ➤ Create Pipe Network By Layout to begin creating your pipe network (see Figure 15.2). The Create Pipe Network dialog appears.

Before you can create a pipe network, you must give your network a name, but more importantly, you need to assign a parts list for your network. As you saw in Chapter 14, the parts list provides a toolkit of pipes, structures, rules, and styles to automate the pipe network design process. It is also important to select a reference surface in this interface. This surface will be used for rim elevations and rule application.

FIGURE 15.2
The Create Pipe
Network dialog

When creating a pipe network, you will be prompted for the following options:

Network Name Choose a name for your network that is meaningful and that will help you identify it in Prospector and other locations.

Network Description The description of your pipe network is optional. You might make a note of the date, the type of network, and any special characteristics.

Network Parts List Choose the parts list that contains the parts, rules, and styles you desire to use for this design (see Chapter 14).

Surface Name Choose the surface that will provide a basis for applying cover rules, as well as providing an insertion elevation for your structures (in other words, rim elevations). This surface can be changed later or for individual structures. For proposed pipe networks, this surface will usually be a finished ground surface.

Alignment Name Choose an alignment that will provide station and offset information for your structures in Prospector, as well as any labels that call for alignment stations and/or offset information. Since most pipe networks have several branches, it may not be meaningful for every structure in your network to reference the same alignment. Therefore, you might find it better to leave your Alignment option set to None in this dialog and set it for individual structures later using the layout tools or structure list in Prospector.

Using the Network Layout Creation Tools

After establishing your pipe network parameters in the Create Pipe Network dialog, click OK and the Network Layout Tools toolbar appears (see Figure 15.3). No other command can be executed while the toolbar is active.

Clicking the Pipe Network Properties tool displays the Pipe Network Properties dialog, which contains the settings for the entire network. If you mistyped any of the parameters in the original Create Pipe Network dialog, you can change them here. In addition, you can set the default label styles for the pipes and structures in this pipe network.

The Pipe Network Properties dialog contains the following tabs:

Information On this tab, you can rename your network, provide a description, and choose whether or not you would like to see network-specific tooltips.

Layout Settings Here you can change the default label styles, the parts list, reference surface and alignment, master object layers for plan pipes and structures, as well as name templates for your pipes and structures (see Figure 15.4).

Profile On this tab, you can change the default label styles and master object layers for profile pipes and structures (see Figure 15.5).

Section Here you can change the master object layers for network parts in a section (see Figure 15.6).

Statistics This tab gives you a snapshot of your pipe network information, such as elevation information, pipe and structure quantities, and references in use (see Figure 15.7).

FIGURE 15.3
The Network Layout
Tools toolbar

FIGURE 15.4
The Layout Settings tab of the Pipe Network Properties dialog

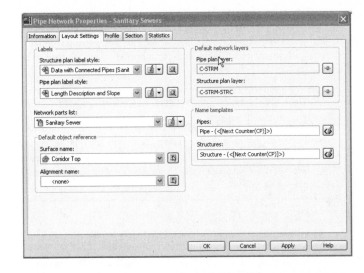

FIGURE 15.5
The Profile tab of the Pipe Network Properties dialog

FIGURE 15.6
The Section tab of the Pipe Network Properties dialog

FIGURE 15.7
The Statistics tab of the Pipe Network Properties dialog

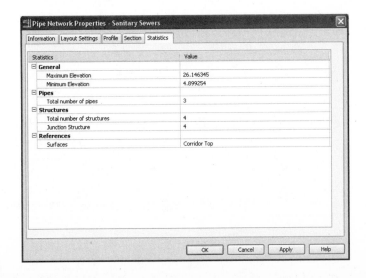

The Select Surface tool ⊕ on the Network Layout Tools toolbar allows you to switch between reference surfaces while you are placing network parts. For example, if you are about to place a structure that needs to reference the existing ground surface yet your network surface had been set to a proposed ground surface, you could click this tool to switch to the existing ground surface.

USING A COMPOSITE FINISHED GRADE SURFACE FOR YOUR PIPE NETWORK

It is cumbersome to constantly switch between a patchwork of different reference surfaces while designing your pipe network. You might want to consider creating a finished grade composite surface that includes components of your road design, finished grade, and even existing ground. This finished grade composite surface can be created by pasting surfaces together so that it is dynamic and changes as your design evolves.

The Select Alignment tool ⇥ on the Network Layout Tools toolbar allows you to switch between reference alignments while you are placing network parts, similar to the Select Surface tool. The Parts List tool 🗋 allows you to switch parts lists for the pipe network.

The dropdown menu in the Structure List box (see Figure 15.8a) allows you to choose which structure you would like to place next, and the Pipes dropdown (see Figure 15.8b) allows you to choose which pipe you would like to place next. Your choices come from the network parts list.

The options for the Draw Pipes And Structures category allows you to choose what type of parts you would like to lay out next. You can choose Pipes And Structures, Pipes Only, or Structures Only.

FIGURE 15.8
The Structure drop-
down list (a) and
The Pipes dropdown
list (b)

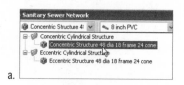
a.

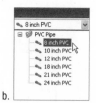
b.

PLACING PARTS IN A NETWORK

Parts are placed very much like other Civil 3D objects or even AutoCAD objects such as polylines. You can use your mouse, transparent commands, dynamic input, object snaps, and other drawing methods when laying out your pipe network.

If you choose Pipes And Structures, every place you click will place a structure, and the structures will be joined by pipes. If you place Structures Only, every place you click will place a Structure. If you choose Pipes Only, you can connect previously placed structures. If you are placing Pipes Only and there is no structure where you click, a null structure will be placed to connect your pipes.

While you are actively placing pipes and structures, you may want to connect to a previously placed part.

If you are placing parts and would like to tie into a structure, you will get a circular connection marker, shown in Figure 15.9a, when your cursor comes within connecting distance to that structure. If you click to place your pipe when this marker is visible, a structure to pipe connection will be formed, as shown in Figure 15.9b.

If you are placing parts and you would like to connect to a pipe, hover over the pipe you would like to connect to until you observe a connection marker that has two square shapes. Clicking to connect to the pipe will break the pipe in two pieces and place a structure (or null structure) at the break point.

The Toggle Upslope/Downslope tool ![tool icon] changes the flow direction of your pipes as they are placed. In Figure 15.10, Structure 9 was placed before Structure 10.

FIGURE 15.9

The Structure Connection marker (a) and the Pipe Connection marker (b)

FIGURE 15.10

Using the downslope toggle (a) and the upslope toggle (b) to create a pipe network leg

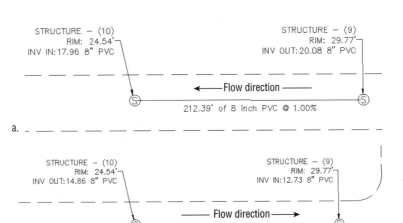

OPTIMIZE COVER BY STARTING UPHILL

If you are using the Cover And Slope rule for your pipe network, you will achieve better cover optimization if you begin your design at an upstream location and work your way down to the connection point.

The Cover And Slope rule prefers to hold minimum slope over optimal cover. In practice this means that as long as minimum cover is satisfied, the pipe will remain at minimum slope. If you start your design from the upstream location, the pipe is forced to use a higher slope to achieve minimum cover. The following graphic shows a pipe run that was created starting from the upstream location (right to left):

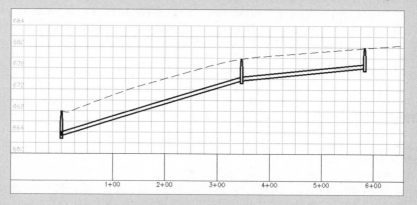

When you start from the downhill side of your project, the Minimum Slope Rule is applied as long as minimum cover is achieved. The following graphic shows a pipe run that was created starting from the downstream location (left to right):

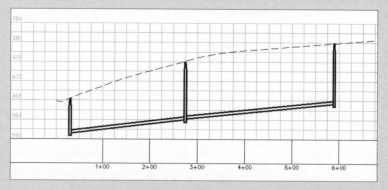

Notice how the slope remains constant even as the pipe cover increases. Maximum cover is a "violation only" rule, which means that it never forces a pipe to increase slope to remain within tolerance; it only provides a warning that maximum cover has been violated.

Click Delete Pipe Network Object 🗑 to delete pipes or structures of your choice. AutoCAD Erase can also delete network objects, but it would require you to leave the Network Layout Tools toolbar.

Clicking Pipe Network Vistas 🗗 brings up Panorama (see Figure 15.11), which allows you to make tabular edits to your pipe network while you are active in the Network Layout Tools toolbar.

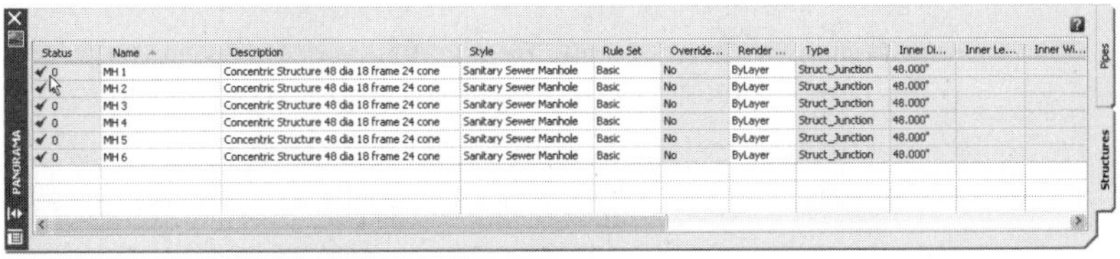

FIGURE 15.11

Pipe Network Vistas
via Panorama

The Pipe Network Vistas interface is similar to what you encounter in the Pipe Networks branch of Prospector. Many people think that the Pipe Network Vistas is not as user friendly as the Prospector interface because it does not remember your preferred column order like Prospector. The advantage to using the Pipe Network Vistas is that you can make tabular edits without leaving the Network Layout Tools toolbar. Pipe properties, such as invert and slope, can be edited on the Pipes tab, while structure properties, such as rim and sump, can be edited on the Structure tab.

CREATING A SANITARY SEWER NETWORK

This exercise will apply the concepts taught in this section and give you hands-on experience using the Network Layout Tools toolbar:

1. Open `Pipes-Exercise 1.dwg`.

2. Expand the Surfaces branch on Prospector and notice that there are two surfaces in this drawing, an existing ground and a proposed ground, both of which have a _No Display style applied to simplify our drawing. Expand the Alignments tab and notice that there are several road alignments.

3. Choose Pipes ➢ Create Pipe Network By Layout.

4. In the Create Pipe Network dialog, give your network the following information:

   ◆ Name: Sanitary Sewer Network

   ◆ Description: Sanitary Sewer Network created by (your name) on (today's date)

   ◆ Network Parts List: Sanitary Sewer

   ◆ Surface Name: Finished Ground

   ◆ Alignment Name: Nature's Way

   ◆ Structure Label Style: Data With Connected Pipes (Sanitary)

   ◆ Pipe Label Style: Length Material And Slope

5. Click OK. The Network Layout Tools toolbar should appear. If you press ↵ or Esc right now, you will lose this toolbar before you create anything.

6. Choose the Concentric Structure 48 Dia 18 Frame 24 Cone from the dropdown list in the Structure menu and 8 Inch PVC from the dropdown menu in the Pipe list.

7. Click the Draw Pipes And Structures tool. Place two structures (which will also place one pipe between them) along Nature's Way somewhere between the road centerline and the right of way by picking structure locations on your screen. Note that the command line gives you additional options for placement. You can refer to the sections on pipe network creation and editing for additional methods of placement.

8. Without exiting the command, go back to the Network Layout Tools toolbar and change the pipe dropdown from 8 Inch PVC to 10 Inch PVC, and then place another structure. Notice that the length of pipe between your second and third structures is a 10″ pipe.

9. Without exiting the command, go back to the Network Layout Tools toolbar and change the pipe dropdown to 8 Inch PVC. Add a structure off to one side of the road, and then connect to one of your structures within the road right-of-way. You will know you are about to connect to a structure when you see the connection marker (a round, golden-colored glyph shaped like the one in Figure 15.12) appear next to your previously inserted structure.

10. Press ↵ to exit the command. Observe your pipe network, including the labeling that automatically appeared as you drew the network.

11. Drill into the Pipe Networks branch in Prospector of Toolspace. and locate your sanitary sewer network. Click the Pipes branch and notice that the list of pipes appears in the Preview pane. Click the Structures branch and notice that the list of structures appears in the Preview pane.

12. Investigate the other sections of this chapter to experiment with tabular and graphical edits, drawing parts in profile view, and other tasks.

FIGURE 15.12
The connection marker appears when your cursor is near the existing structure.

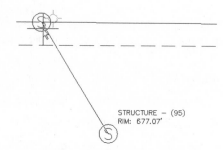

STRUCTURE – (95)
RIM: 677.07′

Creating a Storm Drainage Pipe Network from a Feature Line

If you already have an object in your drawing that represents a pipe network (such as a polyline, an alignment, or a feature line), you may be able to take advantage of Pipes ➤ Create Pipe Network From Object.

This option can be used for applications such as converting surveyed pipe runs into pipe networks or bringing forward legacy drawings that had used AutoCAD linework to represent pipes. It is not a good idea to use this in lieu of Create Pipe Network By Layout for new designs because of some limitations described later in this section.

It is often tempting in Civil 3D to rely on your former drawing habits and try to "convert" your AutoCAD objects into Civil 3D objects, but you will find that the effort you spend learning the Create Pipe Network By Layout pays off very quickly with a better-quality model and easier revisions.

The Create Pipe Network From Object option will create a pipe for every linear segment of your object and place a structure at every vertex of your object. For example, the polyline with four line segments and two arcs, shown in Figure 15.13, will be converted into a pipe network containing four straight pipes, two curved pipes, and seven structures—one at the start, one at the end, and one at each vertex.

FIGURE 15.13

A polyline showing
vertices (a) and a pipe
network created from
the polyline (b)

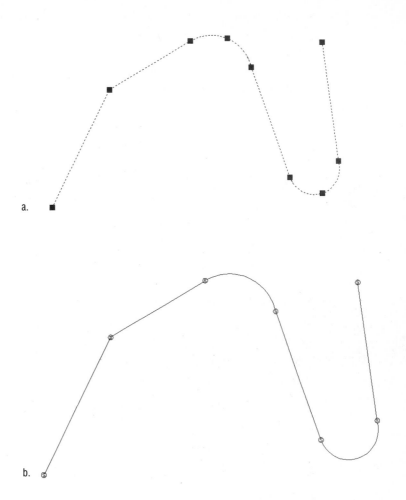

This option is most useful for creating pipe networks from long, single runs. It cannot build branching networks or append objects to a pipe network. For example, if you create a pipe network from one feature line, then a few days later receive a second feature line to add to that pipe network, you will have to use the pipe network editing tools to trace your second feature line, since there is no tool that can be used to add AutoCAD objects to an already created pipe network.

Keep in mind that pipe networks cannot be merged, and parts from one pipe network cannot be connected to parts on another pipe network, so it is not typically to your advantage to create a separate pipe network for each object. Best practice is simply to use your longest object to start the pipe network and use the layout tools to trace and re-create the rest.

CREATING A STORM DRAINAGE NETWORK FROM A FEATURE LINE

This exercise will give you hands-on experience building a pipe network from a feature line with elevations:

1. Open the Pipes-Exercise 2.dwg file. (It is important to start with this drawing rather than using the drawing from an earlier exercise.)

2. Expand the Surfaces branch on Prospector and notice that there are two surfaces in this drawing, an existing ground and a proposed ground, both of which have a _No Display style applied to simplify our drawing.

3. Expand the Alignments branch and notice that there are several road alignments. Notice in the drawing that there is a yellow feature line that runs a loop around the northern portion of the site. This feature line represents utility information for an existing storm drainage line. The elevations of this feature line correspond with centerline elevations that we'll apply to our pipe network.

4. Choose Pipes ➤ Create Pipe Network From Object.

5. At the Select Object or [Xref]: prompt, pick the yellow feature line. You are given a preview (see Figure 15.14) of pipe flow direction that is based on the direction in which the feature line was originally drawn.

6. At the Flow Direction [OK/Reverse] <Ok>: prompt, press ↵ to choose OK. The Create Pipe Network From Object dialog appears.

7. In the dialog, give your pipe network the following information:

   ◆ Name: Storm Network

   ◆ Description: Storm Network created by (your name) on (today's date) from Feature Line

   ◆ Network Parts List: Storm Network Parts List

   ◆ Pipe To Create: 15 Inch Concrete Pipe

   ◆ Surface Name: Finished Ground

   ◆ Alignment Name: <none>

   ◆ Erase Existing Entity: Checked

   ◆ Use Vertex Elevations: Checked

   The two checkboxes at the bottom of the dialog allow you to erase the existing entity and to apply the object's vertex elevations to the new pipe network.

   If you check Use Vertex Elevations, the pipe rules for your chosen parts list will be ignored. The elevations from each vertex will be applied as a center elevation of each pipe endpoint and not the invert as you may expect. For example, if you had a feature line that you created from survey shots of existing pipe inverts and used this method, your newly created pipe network would have inverts that were off by an elevation equal to the inner diameter of your newly created pipe.

8. Click OK, and a pipe network is created.

FIGURE 15.14
Flow direction
preview

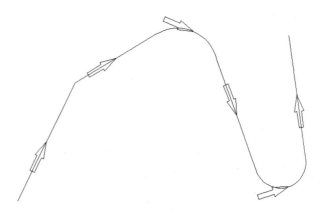

FIGURE 15.14
Flow direction
preview

Changing Flow Direction

Choosing Pipes ➤ Change Flow Direction allows you to reverse the pipe's understanding of which direction it flows, which comes into play when using the Apply Rules command and when annotating flow direction with a pipe label slope arrow.

Changing the flow direction of a pipe does not make any changes to the pipe's invert. By default, a pipe's flow direction depends on how the pipe was drawn and how the Toggle Upslope/Downslope tool was set when the pipe was drawn:

◆ If the toggle was set to Downslope, the pipe flow direction will be set to Start To End, which means the first endpoint you placed would be considered the start of flow and the second endpoint established as the end of flow.

◆ If the toggle was set to Upslope when the pipe was drawn, the pipe flow direction will be set to End To Start, which means the first endpoint placed is considered the "end" for flow purposes and the second endpoint the "start."

After pipes are drawn, there are two additional flow options—Bi-directional and By Slope—that can be set in Pipe Properties.

Start To End A pipe label flow arrow will show pipe direction from first pipe endpoint drawn to second endpoint drawn regardless of invert or slope.

End To Start A pipe label flow arrow will show pipe direction from second pipe endpoint drawn to first pipe endpoint drawn regardless of invert or slope.

Bi-directional Typically a pipe with zero slope that is used to connect two bodies that can drain into each other, such as two stormwater basins, septic tanks, or overflow vessels. The direction arrow is irrelevant in this case.

By Slope A pipe label flow arrow will show pipe direction as a function of pipe slope. For example, if end A has a higher invert than end B, the pipe will flow from A to B. If B is edited to have a higher invert than A, the flow direction will flip to be from B to A.

Editing a Sanitary Sewer Network

Pipe networks can be edited several ways:

- Using drawing layout edits such as grip, move, and rotate

- Grip-editing the pipe size

- Using vertical-movement edits using grips in profile (see profile section)

- Using tabular edits in the Pipe Networks branch in Prospector

- Right-clicking a network part to access tools such as swap part or pipe/structure properties

- Returning to the Network Layout Tools toolbar either by right-clicking the object and choosing Edit Network or by choosing the Pipes ➤ Edit Network menu option

Each of these methods is explored in the following sections.

Editing Your Network in Plan View

When selected, a structure has two types of grips, shown in Figure 15.15. The first is a square-shaped grip located at the structure insertion point. This grip can be used to grab the structure and stretch/move it to a new location using the insertion point as a basepoint. Stretching a structure will result in the movement of the structure, as well as any connected pipes. You can also scroll through stretch, move, and rotate by using your spacebar once you have the structure grabbed by this grip.

The second structure grip is a rotational grip that you can use to spin the structure about its insertion point. This will be most useful for aligning eccentric structures, such as rectangular junction structures.

Also note that common AutoCAD Modify commands work with structures. You can execute the following commands normally (such as from a toolbar or keyboard macro): Move, Copy, Rotate, Align, and Mirror (Figure 15.16a). (Scale does not have an effect on structures.) Keep in mind that the Modify commands are applied to the structure model itself, so depending on how you have your style established, it may not be clear that you have made a change. For example, if you execute the Mirror command, you can pick the structures to see the results or use a 3D visual style, such as in Object Viewer, to see the modeled parts, as shown in Figure 15.16b.

The AutoCAD Erase command can be used to erase network parts. Note that erasing a network part in plan completely removes that part from the network. Once erased, the part will disappear from plan, profile view, Prospector, and so on.

FIGURE 15.15
Two types of
structure grips

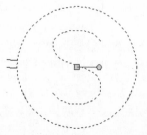

FIGURE 15.16

Mirrored structures seen in plan by their style (a) and in 3D wireframe visual style using Object Viewer (b)

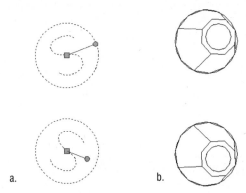

a.   b.

When selected, a pipe end has two types of grips (see Figure 15.17). The first grip is a square-shaped endpoint location grip. Using this grip, you can change the location of the pipe end without constraint. You can move it in any direction; make it longer or shorter, and take advantage of Stretch, Move, Rotate, and Scale by using your spacebar.

The second grip is a pipe length grip. This grip will allow you to extend a pipe along its current bearing.

A pipe midpoint also has two types of grips (see Figure 15.18). The first grip is a square location grip that allows you to move the pipe using its midpoint as a basepoint. As before, you can take advantage of Stretch, Move, Rotate, and Scale by using your spacebar.

The second grip is a triangular-shaped pipe diameter grip. Stretching this grip will give you a tooltip showing allowable diameters for that pipe, which is based on your parts list. Use this grip to make quick, visual changes to the pipe diameter.

FIGURE 15.17

Two types of pipe end grips

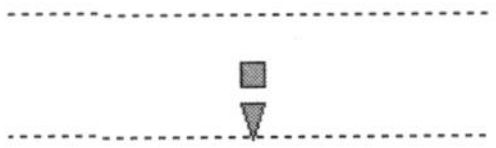

FIGURE 15.18

Two types of pipe midpoint grips

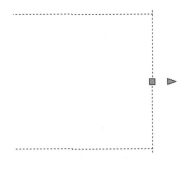

Also note that common AutoCAD Modify commands work with pipes. You can execute the following commands normally (such as from a toolbar or keyboard macro): Move, Copy, Rotate, Align, Scale, and Mirror. One thing to remember is that executing one of these commands will often result in the modified pipe becoming disconnected from its structures. Once a Modify command has been completed, be sure to right-click your pipe and choose Connect To Part to remedy any disconnects.

The AutoCAD Erase command can be used to erase network parts. Note that erasing a network part in plan completely removes that part from the network. Once erased, the part will disappear from plan view, profile view, Prospector, and so on.

DYNAMIC INPUT AND PIPE NETWORK EDITING

Dynamic Input (DYN) has been in AutoCAD-based products since the 2006 release, but many Civil 3D users aren't familiar with it. For some of the more command line–intensive Civil 3D tasks, DYN is not always useful, but for pipe network edits, it provides a visual way to interactively edit your pipes and structures.

To turn DYN on or off at any time, click DYN at the bottom of your Civil 3D window.

Structure Rotation   While DYN is active, you will get a tooltip that tracks rotation angle.

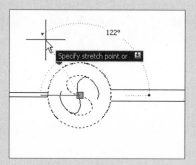

Press your down arrow key to get a shortcut menu that will allow you to specify a basepoint, followed by a rotation angle, as well as options for Copy and Undo. DYN combined with the Rotate command is beneficial when rotating eccentric structures for proper alignment.

Pipe Diameter   When using the pipe-diameter grip edit, DYN will give you a tooltip to assist you in choosing your desired diameter. Note that the tooltip depends on your drawing units, so in this example the tooltip diameter is shown as 1.5′.

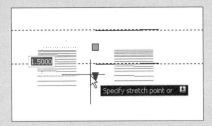

Pipe Length   This is probably the most common reason you would use the DYN for pipe edits. Choosing the pipe length grip when DYN is active will show tooltips for the pipe current length and pipe preview length, as well as fields for entering a desired pipe total length or pipe delta length. Use your Tab key to toggle between the total length and delta length fields. One of the benefits to using DYN in this interface is that even though you can't visually grip-edit a pipe to be shorter than its original length, you can enter a total length that is shorter than the original length. Note that the length shown and edited in the DYN interface is the 3D center-to-center length.

Pipe Endpoint Edits   Similar to pipe length, pipe endpoint location edits can benefit from using DYN. The active fields give you an opportunity to input X and Y.

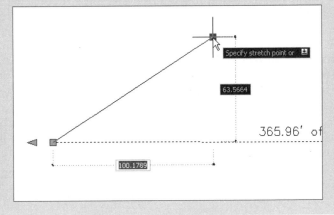

Pipe Vertical Grip Edits in Profile   Using DYN in profile view will allow you to set exact invert, centerline, or top elevations without having to enter the Pipe Properties dialog or Prospector. Choose the appropriate grip, and note that the active DYN field is tracking profile elevation. Enter your desired elevation, and your pipe will move as you specify.

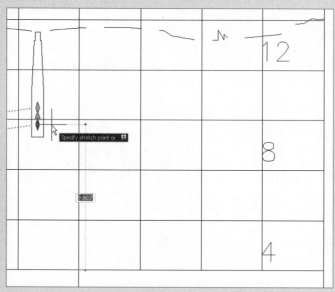

Making Tabular Edits to Your Sanitary Sewer Network

Another method for editing pipe networks is in a tabular form using the Pipe Networks branch in Prospector (see Figure 15.19).

To edit pipes in Prospector, highlight the Pipes entry under the appropriate pipe network. For example, if you want to edit your sanitary sewer pipes, expand the Sanitary Sewers branch and select the Pipes entry. You should get a Preview pane that lists the names of your pipes and some additional information in a tabular form. The same procedure can be used to list the structures in the network.

White columns can be edited in this interface. Gray columns are considered calculated values and therefore cannot be edited.

You can adjust many things in this interface, but you will find it cumbersome for some tasks. This interface is best used for the following:

Batch Changes to Styles, Render Materials, Reference Surfaces, Reference Alignments, Rule Sets, and So On   Use your Shift key to select the desired rows, then right-click the column header of the property you would like to change. Choose Edit, and then select the new value from the dropdown menu. If you find yourself doing this on every project for most network parts, confirm that you have the correct values set in your parts list and in the Pipe Network Properties dialog.

FIGURE 15.19

The Pipe Networks branch in Prospector

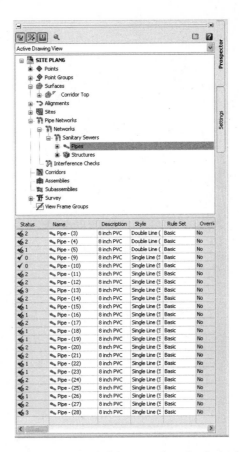

Status	Name	Description	Style	Rule Set	Overri
2	Pipe - (3)	8 inch PVC	Double Line (	Basic	No
2	Pipe - (4)	8 inch PVC	Double Line (	Basic	No
1	Pipe - (5)	8 inch PVC	Double Line (	Basic	No
0	Pipe - (9)	8 inch PVC	Single Line (S	Basic	No
0	Pipe - (10)	8 inch PVC	Single Line (S	Basic	No
2	Pipe - (11)	8 inch PVC	Single Line (S	Basic	No
2	Pipe - (12)	8 inch PVC	Single Line (S	Basic	No
3	Pipe - (13)	8 inch PVC	Single Line (S	Basic	No
2	Pipe - (14)	8 inch PVC	Single Line (S	Basic	No
1	Pipe - (15)	8 inch PVC	Single Line (S	Basic	No
1	Pipe - (16)	8 inch PVC	Single Line (S	Basic	No
2	Pipe - (17)	8 inch PVC	Single Line (S	Basic	No
1	Pipe - (18)	8 inch PVC	Single Line (S	Basic	No
1	Pipe - (19)	8 inch PVC	Single Line (S	Basic	No
2	Pipe - (20)	8 inch PVC	Single Line (S	Basic	No
2	Pipe - (21)	8 inch PVC	Single Line (S	Basic	No
1	Pipe - (22)	8 inch PVC	Single Line (S	Basic	No
1	Pipe - (23)	8 inch PVC	Single Line (S	Basic	No
2	Pipe - (24)	8 inch PVC	Single Line (S	Basic	No
2	Pipe - (25)	8 inch PVC	Single Line (S	Basic	No
1	Pipe - (26)	8 inch PVC	Single Line (S	Basic	No
2	Pipe - (27)	8 inch PVC	Single Line (S	Basic	No
3	Pipe - (28)	8 inch PVC	Single Line (S	Basic	No

Batch Changes to Pipe Description Use your Shift key to select the desired rows, then right-click the Description column header. Choose Edit, and then type in your new description. If you find yourself doing this on every project for most network parts, check your parts list. If a certain part will always have the same description, you can add it to your parts list and prevent the extra step of changing it here.

Changing Pipe or Structure Names You can change the name of a network part by simply typing in the Name field. If you find yourself doing this on every project for every part, check that you are taking advantage of the Name templates in your Pipe Network Properties dialog (which can be further enforced in your Pipe Network command settings).

You can Shift-select and copy the table to your clipboard for insertion into Microsoft Excel for sorting and further study. (Note that this is a static capture of information; your Excel sheet will not update along with changes to the pipe network.)

This interface can be useful for changing pipe inverts, crown, and centerline information. It's not always useful for changing part rotation, insertion point, start point, or end point. The reason it is not as useful as many people would think is because the pipe inverts will not "react" to each other. If Pipe A and Pipe B are connected to the same structure and Pipe A flows into Pipe B, changing the end invert of Pipe A does *not* affect the start invert of Pipe B automatically. If you are used to creating pipe design spreadsheets in Excel using formulas that automatically drop connected pipes to ensure flow, this can be frustrating.

Shortcut Menu Edits

Many edits can be done at the individual part level by using your right-click shortcut menu.

If you realized you placed the wrong part at a certain location, in other words, if you placed a catch basin where you needed a drainage manhole, use the Swap Part option on the shortcut menu (see Figure 15.20). You will be given a list of all the parts from all the parts lists in your drawing.

The same properties listed in Prospector can be accessed on an individual part level using your right-click shortcut menu and choosing Pipe Properties or Structure Properties. A dialog, like the Structure Properties dialog in Figure 15.21, will open with several tabs that you can use for editing that particular part.

FIGURE 15.20

Right-clicking a network part brings up a shortcut menu with many options, including Swap Part.

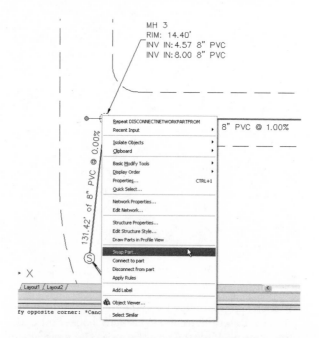

FIGURE 15.21

The Part Properties tab on the Structure Properties dialog gives you the opportunity to perform many edits and adjustments.

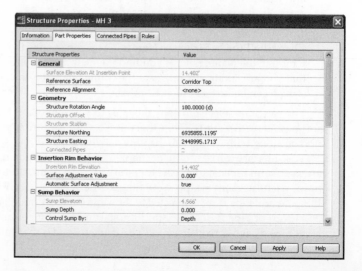

Editing with the Network Layout Tools Toolbar

You can also edit your pipe network by retrieving the Network Layout Tools toolbar. This is accomplished by picking a pipe network object, right-clicking, and choosing Edit Network, or by selecting Pipes ➢ Edit Pipe Network from the menu bar and then choosing any part in the network you'd like to edit.

Once the toolbar is up, you can continue working exactly the way you did when you originally laid out your pipe network.

This exercise will give you hands-on experience in making a variety of edits to a sanitary and storm-drainage pipe network:

1. Open the `Editing Pipes Plan.dwg` file. Note that there is a sanitary sewer network and a storm drainage network in this drawing, as well as two surfaces and some alignments.

2. Select STM STR 2 in the drawing. Right-click and choose Swap Part. Select the 24 X 48 Rect Slab Top Structure from the Swap Part Size dialog. Click OK.

3. Select the newly placed catch basin so that you see the two structure grips. Use the rotational grip and your Nearest osnap to align the catch basin with the pink property line.

4. Use the AutoCAD Erase command to erase Structure-(5).

5. Click DYN to turn it on, and pick Pipe-(4). Use the triangular endpoint grip and the DYN tooltip to lengthen Pipe-(4) to a total length of 310 feet. (Note that this is the 3D Center To Center Pipe Length).

6. Pick any pipe in the network. Right-click, and choose Edit Network

7. Select Draw Structures Only from the dropdown menu in the Draw Pipes And Structures selection box. Place a structure at the end of Pipe-(4).

8. Select Structure-(1) in the drawing. Right-click and choose Structure Properties. Switch to the Part Properties tab. Scroll down to the Sump Depth field and change the value to 0´.

9. Expand the Pipe Networks ➢ Sanitary Sewer Network branches on Prospector in Toolspace, and select the Structures entry. Use the tabular interface in the Preview pane area of Prospector to change the names of Structures (1) through (4) to MH1 through MH4.

Creating an Alignment from Network Parts

There are occasions where certain legs of a pipe network require their own stationing. Perhaps most of your pipes are shown on a road profile, but the legs that run offsite or through open space require their own profiles. Whatever the reason, it is often necessary to create an alignment from network parts.

1. Open the `Alignment From Network Parts.dwg` file.

2. Choose Pipes ➢ Utilities ➢ Create Alignment From Network Parts.

3. The command line prompts you to `Select first Network Part (Pipe or Structure):`. Pick Structure-(1).

4. The command line then prompts you to `Select next Network Part or [Undo]:`. Pick Structure-(5).

5. Press ↵, and a dialog appears that is almost identical to the one you see when you create an alignment from the Alignments menu. Name and stylize your alignment as appropriate. Notice the Create Profile And Profile View checkbox in the last line of the dialog. Leave the box checked and click OK.

6. The Create Profile From Surface dialog (see Figure 15.22) appears. This dialog is identical to the one that appears when you select Profiles ➤ Create Profile From Surface. Choose both the Existing Ground and Finished Ground surfaces, and click Draw In Profile View. (See Chapter 8 for further information about sampling profiles from surface.)

7. Next you'll see the General screen in the Create Profile View wizard (see Figure 15.23). Click Create Profile View and place the profile view to the right of the site plan.

8. You will see five structures and four pipes drawn in a profile view, which is based on the newly created alignment (see Figure 15.24).

FIGURE 15.22
The Create Profile From Surface dialog

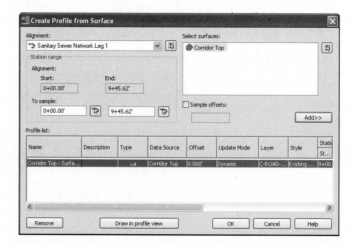

FIGURE 15.23
The General screen in the Create Profile View wizard

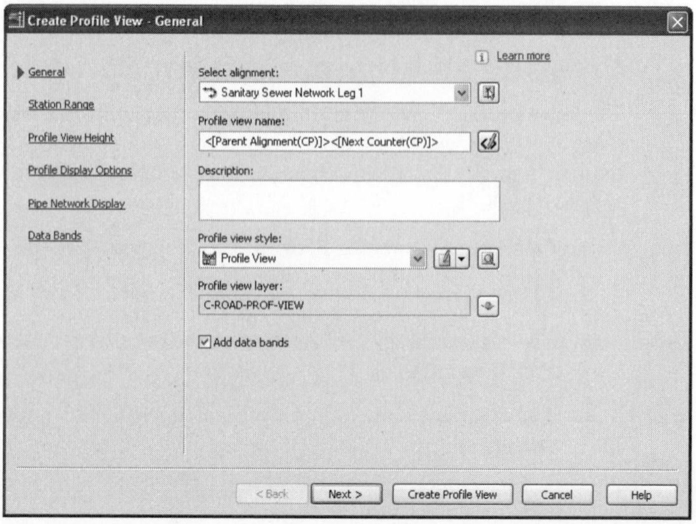

FIGURE 15.24

Creating a profile view

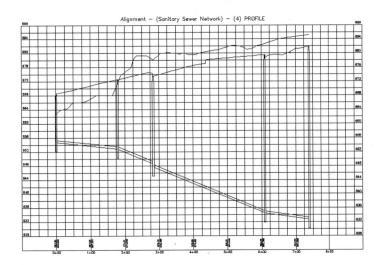

Drawing Parts in Profile View

If you already have an alignment and profile view created, for example, if you are going to show your pipes on the same profile view as your road design, choose Pipes ➢ Draw Parts In Profile View from the menu bar. When using this command, it is important to note that the default selection draws every pipe in the entire network in your chosen profile view.

This means that the command will add the entire pipe network to your profile view unless you only designate selected parts. Most of the time, you will want to designate specific parts to be drawn, especially if your network is a true "web." If you neglect to choose specific parts that are meaningful to show on your profile view, you will end up with a result like the one shown in Figure 15.25.

Another thing that you need to keep in mind when adding parts to your profile view is that depending on the location of your alignment with respect to your pipes and structures, the labeled length from the model may not be the same as a pipe length that you scale or measure from the profile view.

FIGURE 15.25

A profile view with inappropriate pipe network parts drawn on it

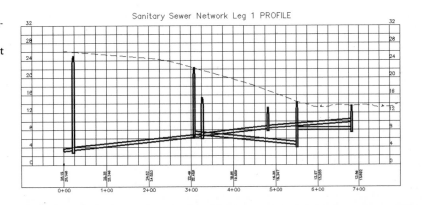

Profiles and profile views are always cut with respect to an alignment. Therefore, pipes are shown on the profile view on the basis of how they appear along that alignment or how they cross that alignment. Unless your alignment *exactly follows the centerline of your network parts*, your pipes will likely show some drafting distortion.

Let's look at Figure 15.26 as an example. This particular jurisdiction requires that all utilities be profiled along the road centerline. We have a curved road centerline, a sanitary network that jogs across the road to connect with an existing manhole in the middle, and a storm drain that crosses both the road centerline and our sanitary pipe.

FIGURE 15.26

These pipe lengths will be distorted in profile view.

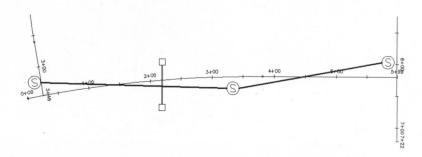

There are at least two potentially confusing elements that will show up in our profile view. First, our distance between structures (2D Length – Center To Center) will not be the same in plan and profile (see Figure 15.27) since the sanitary pipe does not run parallel to the alignment. Because the labeling reflects the network model, all labeling will be true to the 2D Length – Center To Center or any other length you specify in your label style.

The second potential issue is that the invert of our crossing storm pipe will be shown at the point where the storm pipe *crosses the alignment* and not at the point where it crosses the sanitary pipe (see Figure 15.28). Therefore, if you are looking to ensure that your pipes have certain minimum crossing clearances, plotting this pipe in profile view will not give you the information you are seeking. It would be best to use interference checking for this application.

1. Open the `Draw Parts In Profile.dwg` file. Note that the drawing has a sanitary pipe network, a storm drainage pipe network, and a profile view that is based on Nature's Way in the drawing.

2. Choose Pipes ➤ Draw Parts In Profile View.

3. The command line prompts you to `Select network(s) to add to profile view or [Selected parts only]:`. Enter **S** for Selected Parts Only, and then pick Structure-(3), Pipe-(3), Structure-(4), Pipe-(4), and Structure-(5). Press ⏎.

4. The command line will now prompt you to `Select profile view:`. Pick the Nature's Way profile view.

5. Three structures and two pipes appears in profile view.

FIGURE 15.27
Pipe labels in plan view (a) and in profile view (b)

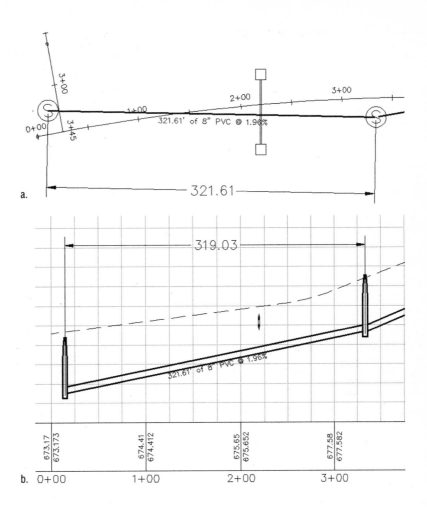

FIGURE 15.28
The invert of a crossing pipe is drawn at the location where it crosses the alignment.

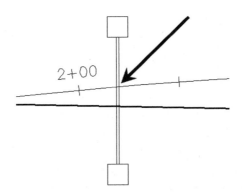

Vertical Movement Edits Using Grips in Profile

Although you cannot make changes to certain part properties, such as pipe length, in profile view, pipes and structures both have special grips for changing their vertical properties in profile view. When selected, a structure has two grips in profile view (see Figure 15.29).

FIGURE 15.29
A structure has two grips in profile view.

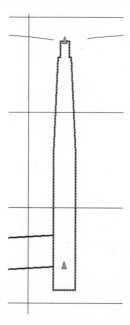

The first grip is a triangular-shaped grip representing a rim insertion point. This grip can be dragged up or down and will affect the model structure insertion point. There are two ways that moving this grip could be affecting your structure insertion point depending on how your structure properties were established:

◆ If your structure has the Automatic Surface Adjustment set to True, grip editing this rim insertion point grip will change the Surface Adjustment Value. If our reference surface changes, then our rim will change along with it, plus or minus that surface adjustment value.

◆ If your structure has the Automatic Surface Adjustment set to False, grip editing this rim grip modifies the insertion point of the rim. No matter what happens to our reference surface, the rim will stay locked in place.

Typically, you would only use the rim insertion point grip in cases where you do not have a surface for your rims to target to or if you know that there is a desired surface adjustment value. It is very tempting to just come in here and make a "quick change" instead of making the improvements to your surface that are fundamentally necessary to get the desired rim elevation. One quick change often grows in scope. Making the necessary design changes to your target surface will keep your model dynamic and, in the long run, will make editing your rim elevations easier.

The second grip is a triangular-shaped grip located at the sump depth. This grip does not represent structure invert. In Civil 3D, only pipes truly have invert elevation. The structure uses the connected pipe information to determine how deep it should be. In the case when the sump has been set at a depth of zero, the sump elevation would equal the invert of the deepest connected pipe. This grip can be dragged up or down and will affect the modeled sump depth in one of two ways depending on how your structure properties are established:

◆ If your structure is set to control sump by depth, editing with the sump grip will change the sump depth. The depth is measured from the structure insertion point. For example, if the original sump depth was zero, grip-editing the sump 0.5′ lower would be the equivalent of creating a new sump rule for a 0.5′ depth and applying the rule to this structure. This sump will react to hold the established depth if your reference surface changes, your connected pipe inverts change, or something else is modified that would affect the invert of the lowest connected pipe. This triangular-shaped grip is most useful in cases where most of your pipe network will follow the sump rule applied in your parts lists, but selected structures will need special treatment.

◆ If your structure is set to control sump by elevation, adjusting the sump grip will change that elevation. When sump is controlled by elevation, sump is treated as an absolute value that will hold regardless of the structure insertion point. For example, if we grip-edit our structure so its depth is 8.219′, the structure will remain at that depth regardless of what happens to the inverts of our connected pipes. The Control Sump By Elevation parameter might best be used for existing structures that have surveyed information of absolute sump elevations that won't change with the addition of new connected pipes.

When picked, a pipe end has three grips in profile view (see Figure 15.30). You can grip-edit the invert, crown, and centerline elevations at the structure connection using these grips, resulting in the pipe slope changing to accommodate the new endpoint elevation.

When picked, a pipe in profile view has one grip at its midpoint (see Figure 15.31). You can use this grip to move the pipe vertically while holding the slope of the pipe constant.

You can access pipe or structure properties by choosing a part, right-clicking, and choosing Pipe Properties.

FIGURE 15.30
Three grips for a pipe end in profile view

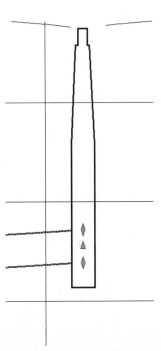

FIGURE 15.31
Use the midpoint
grip to move a pipe
vertically.

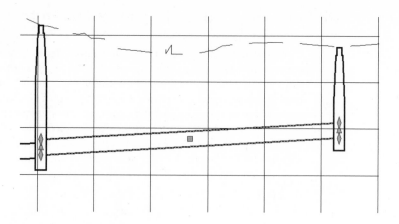

Removing a Part from Profile View

If you find you have a part in profile view that you would like to remove from the view but not delete it from the pipe network entirely, you have a few options.

AutoCAD Erase can remove a part from a profile view; however, that part will then be removed from every profile view it had appeared in. If you only have one profile view or if you are trying to delete the pipe from every profile view, this is a good method to use.

A better way to remove parts from a particular profile view is through the profile view properties. You can access these properties by picking the profile view, right-clicking, and choosing Profile View Properties.

The Pipe Networks tab of the Profile View Properties dialog (see Figure 15.32) provides a list of all pipes and structures that are shown in that profile view. You can uncheck the boxes next to parts you would like to omit from this view. Also note that you can add additional parts to your view by unchecking the Show Only Parts Drawn In Profile View box and making changes in the Draw column.

FIGURE 15.32
Uncheck parts to omit
them from a view.

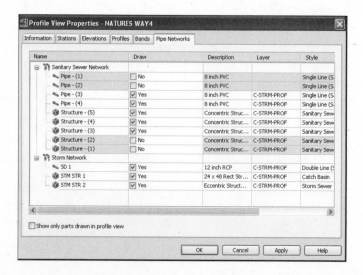

Showing Pipes That Cross the Profile View

If you have pipes that cross the parent alignment of your profile view, you can show them with a crossing style. Note that a pipe must cross the parent alignment to be shown as a crossing in profile, and the vertical location of the pipe will be shown where it crosses that alignment (see Figure 15.33).

For example, if you created an alignment directly from your network parts and then created a profile view for that alignment, any crossing pipes would be shown at the elevation where they cross the main run because your alignment and pipes coincide (see Figure 15.34).

If you have a leg of a pipe network that runs offset from the road centerline, such as that shown in Figure 15.35, yet you are showing those pipes in profile along the centerline alignment, any crossing pipes will be shown where they *intersect the road centerline alignment*.

FIGURE 15.33
A pipe shown crossing a profile

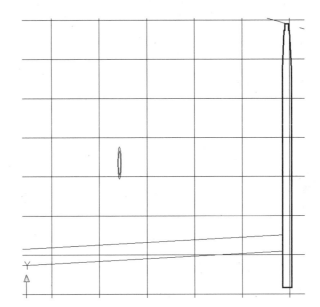

FIGURE 15.34
The invert of a storm crossing that runs along an alignment will be shown in profile at the elevation that it crosses the sanitary line.

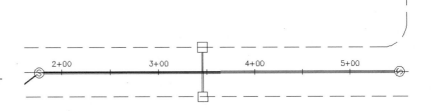

FIGURE 15.35
The invert of a storm crossing that is offset from the alignment will be shown in profile at the elevation that it crosses the alignment.

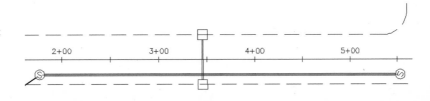

When pipes enter directly into profiled structures, they can be shown as an ellipse through the Display tab of the Structure Style dialog (see Figure 15.36). See Chapter 14 for more information about creating structure styles.

The first step to display a pipe crossing in profile is to add the pipe that crosses your alignment to your profile view using either the Pipes ➤ Draw Parts In Profile View menu option (be sure to type **S** in the command line so that you can choose single parts) or by using the checkboxes on the Pipe Network tab of the Profile View Properties dialog. When the pipe is added, it will be distorted when it is projected onto your profile view—in other words, it will be shown as if you wanted to see the entire length of pipe in profile (see Figure 15.37).

The next step is to override the pipe style *in this profile view only*. Changing the pipe style through pipe properties will not give you the desired result. You must override the style in the Pipes tab of the Profile View Properties dialog (see Figure 15.38).

FIGURE 15.36

Pipes that cross directly into a structure can be shown as part of the structure style (a). Crossing pipes can be shown by changing the Profile and Section Structure Pipe Outlines (b).

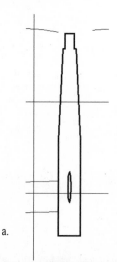

a.

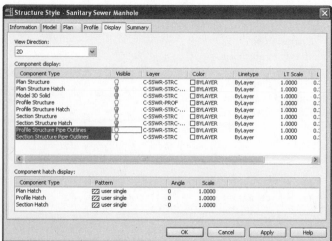

b.

FIGURE 15.37
The pipe crossing
is distorted.

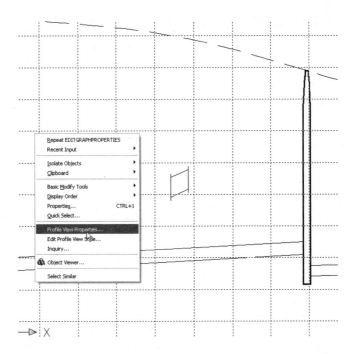

FIGURE 15.38
Correct the representation in the Profile
View Properties
dialog.

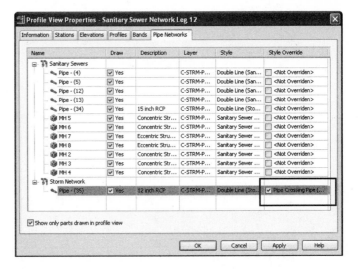

Locate the pipe you just added to your profile view and scroll to the last column on the right called Style Override. Check the Style Override box and choose your pipe crossing style. Click OK. Your pipe should now appear as an ellipse.

If your pipe appears as an ellipse but suddenly seems to have disappeared in the plan and other profiles, chances are good that you did not use the Style Override but accidentally changed the pipe style. Go back to the Profile View Properties dialog and make the necessary adjustments, and your pipes appear as you expect.

Adding Pipe Network Labels

Once you have your network designed, it is important to annotate the design in a pleasing way.

In this section, we will focus on pipe network-specific label components in plan and profile views (see Figure 15.39).

Like all Civil 3D objects, the Pipe and Structure label styles can be found in the Pipe and Structure branches of the Settings tab on Toolspace.

FIGURE 15.39

Typical pipe network labels in plan view (a) and profile view (b)

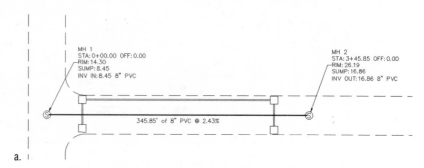

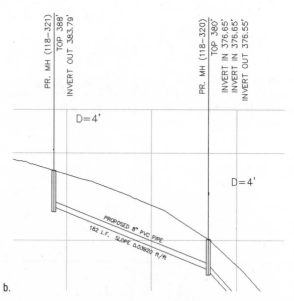

Creating a Labeled Pipe Network Profile Including Crossings

This exercise will apply several of the concepts in this chapter to give you hands-on experience producing a pipe network profile that includes pipes that cross the alignment:

1. Open the Pipes-Exercise 3.dwg file. (It is important to start with this drawing rather than using the drawing from an earlier exercise.)

2. Explore the drawing. Notice that the drawing has two pipe networks: a sanitary network that does not follow the road centerline and a small storm network that crosses the road and the sanitary network.

3. Choose Pipes ➢ Utilities ➢ Create Alignment From Network Parts.

4. At the command-line prompt, first pick Structure-5 and then Structure-1 to create an alignment from the entire sanitary sewer network, with station zero being at the outlet point (Structure 5).

5. Choose the following options in the Create Alignment From Network Parts dialog:

◆ Site: <none>

◆ Site: <none>

◆ Name: Sanitary Network Alignment

◆ Description: Alignment from Structure 5 through Structure 1

◆ Alignment Style: Proposed

◆ Alignment Label Set: All Labels

◆ Create Profile And Profile View: Checked

Click OK.

6. Sample both the Existing Ground and the Finished Ground surfaces in the Create Profile From Surface dialog.

7. Click Draw In Profile View to open the Create Profile View dialog.

8. Click Create Profile View, and choose a location in the drawing to place the profile view. Notice that Station 0+00 is the deepest end. Refer to previous sections for ideas on how to edit your pipes in profile view.

9. Choose Pipes ➢ Add Pipe Network Labels ➢ Entire Plan Profile.

10. Choose any pipe in your profile view to add pipe network labels.

11. Note that the alignment information is missing from your structure labels because the alignment was created after the pipe network. Expand the Sanitary Sewer Network branch on Prospector in Toolspace to set our new alignment as the reference alignment for these structures. Click the Structures entry and find the Structures list in the Preview pane.

12. Select all of the structures in the Preview pane using a shift-click. Scroll to the right until you see the Reference Alignment column. Right-click the column header and select Edit. Choose your Sanitary Network Alignment from the dropdown list (see Figure 15.40).

13. Once your reference alignment has been changed, you should see your structure labels update immediately.

14. Add the storm crossing by choosing the Pipes ➢ Draw Parts In Profile View menu option. Be careful to type **S** in the command line so that you just pick the crossing pipe and not the entire storm network. Override the pipe style in this profile view only by following the procedure in the "Showing Pipes That Cross the Profile View" section earlier in this chapter.

FIGURE 15.40
Change the alignment of all structures at once.

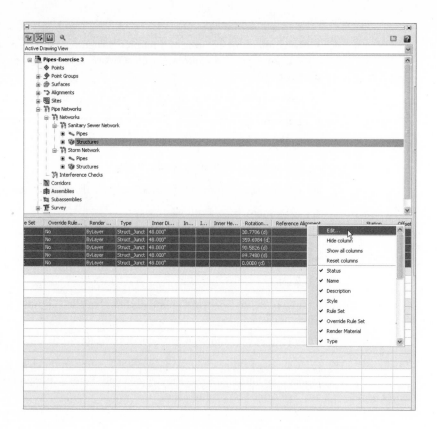

Pipe Labels

Civil 3D makes no separate distinction between a plan pipe label and a profile pipe label. The same label can be used both places.

In addition to single-part labels, pipes shown in plan view can be labeled using the Spanning Pipes option. This feature allows you to choose more than one pipe, and the length that will be reported in the label is the cumulative length of all pipes you chose. Unlike Parcel spanning labels, there is no special label style setting required to use this tool, which can be accessed through Pipes ➤ Add Pipe Network Labels ➤ Spanning Pipes.

A pipe label is composed identically to most other labels in Civil 3D. In addition to text, line, and block, structure labels can also have a flow arrow and reference text, as shown in Figure 15.41.

There are a large number of pipe properties that can be derived from the model and used in your label. If it's part of the design, it can probably be labeled. Spend some time in the Text Component Editor of your pipe label styles to fully explore all the information available.

FIGURE 15.41
A flow direction arrow
and reference text are
available in pipe and
structure label styles.

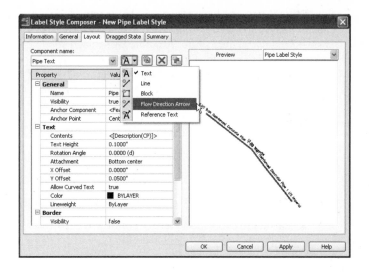

Structure Labels

As with pipes, Civil 3D makes no separate distinction between a plan structure label and a profile structure label. The same label can be used both places.

A structure label is composed identically to most other labels in Civil 3D. In addition to text, line, and block, structure labels can also have reference text and a component called Text For Each. Text For Each refers to text that pulls information from each connecting pipe. We mentioned earlier that structures don't have an understanding of invert. Therefore, if you want to label things like connected pipe inverts, connected pipe diameter, and so forth you need to add a Text For Each component to your label style.

SPECIAL PROFILE ATTACHMENT POINTS FOR STRUCTURE LABELS

Though we mentioned that Civil 3D makes no distinction between plan labels and profile labels, structure labels have two special attachment points in profile view that need to be understood before you can harness their power.

Typical structure labels from the default template have limited flexibility, such as the label shown in Figure 15.42.

FIGURE 15.42
An example of a
standard structure
label from the default
template

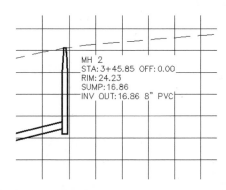

What if you wanted a structure profile label with a line that could grow longer when you stretched it? If you go into the Label Composer for any structure label, you'll see two options for anchor points on the feature: Structure Dimension and Label Location. You can change and control the locations of both the Structure Dimension point and Label Location point.

If you drill into the settings (right-click Pipe Networks in the branch and select Edit Feature Settings), you can see some options for customizing the locations of those two points (see Figure 15.43).

The Edit Feature Settings dialog has a rather cryptic batch of settings under Default Profile Label Placement. In a nutshell, these settings give your labels profile view attachment points that you can customize. We will examine the structure labels closely. Note the default settings:

◆ Dimension Anchor Option For Structures: Fixed

◆ Dimension Anchor Elevation Value For Structures: 0

◆ Dimension Anchor Plot Height Value For Structures: 0″

◆ Structure Label Placement: At Middle Of Structure

FIGURE 15.43
Accessing the
Edit Feature
Settings dialog

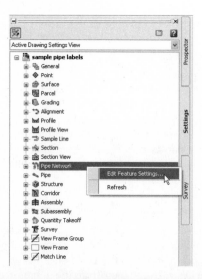

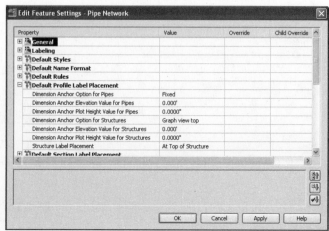

If you highlight a structure label in profile, two cyan-colored grips appear. The lower grip appears at Profile View Elevation Zero. This is the Structure Dimension. Right now, it is fixed at elevation zero, which makes sense on the basis of the default settings. The location of the Structure Dimension is based on the profile view, and it can be grip-edited and stretched vertically after placement.

The second cyan-colored grip is the Structure Label Location. Right now, it is set to At Middle Of Structure (see Figure 15.44) per the default settings. The Structure Label Location is always tied to the top, middle, or bottom of the structure and cannot be grip-edited after placement.

If you go back into the Edit Feature Settings dialog, you can change the values as follows:

♦ Dimension Anchor Option For Structures: Graph View Top

♦ Dimension Anchor Elevation Value For Structures: 0

♦ Dimension Anchor Plot Height Value For Structures: 0″

♦ Structure Label Placement: At Top Of Structure

You must erase and replace your label to see the new attachment points, but once you do, it is clear that the Structure Dimension is now at the Graph View Top, and the Label Location is set to At Top Of Structure, as shown in Figure 15.45.

FIGURE 15.44
Structure Label
Location

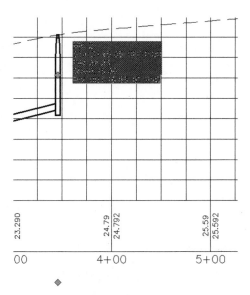

FIGURE 15.45
Structure Label Location set to At Top Of Structure, and Structure Dimension Location set to Graph View Top

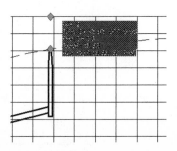

For label composition, adjusting the Structure Label Location and Structure Dimension Location is powerful because you can now attach and orient lines, blocks, and text to these two points.

The foundation of the label shown in Figure 15.46 is the vertical line that runs from the top of the structure to the Graph View Top.

Confirm that your feature settings have the Label Location set to At Top Of Structure and the Structure Dimension set to Graph View Top, and then make a new label style.

In the Label Style Composer, add a line that uses the Label Location as its start and the structure dimension as its end, as shown in Figure 15.47.

FIGURE 15.46
A structure label with a flexible line

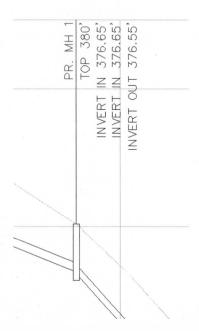

FIGURE 15.47
Add a line component anchored to Label Location and Structure Dimension.

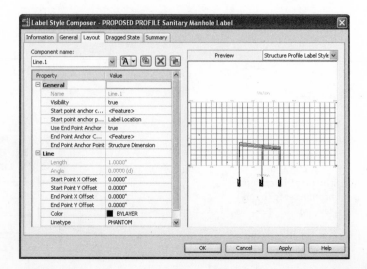

Add any other desired components, and examine your label. If you want to revise your label so that the vertical line goes all the way down to the bottom of the structure, you don't have to change the label style composition. In fact, going in to edit the label style wouldn't give you the desired results at all. The key is to change that Structure Label location to At Bottom Of Structure (see Figure 15.48).

Changing the feature settings requires you to reset the label, but once you replace the label you should see the line go all the way down to the bottom of the structure.

We said earlier that the Structure Dimension could be grip-edited to override the feature settings. If you grip-edit the Structure Dimension, you can drag the line vertically (see Figure 15.49).

FIGURE 15.48

Change the Structure Label Placement option to achieve a line that connects to the bottom of structure.

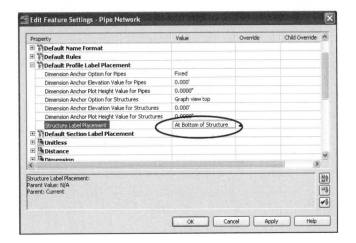

FIGURE 15.49

Use the grip to stretch the line and label.

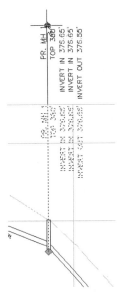

If you ever need to reset or customize the placement of this label, you can select the label, right-click, and choose Label Properties.

In the Properties dialog shown in Figure 15.50, you see the Structure Dimension Anchor Option from the feature settings and a Dimension Anchor Value, which is equal to the distance you stretched the grip. Therefore, if you want the line to shorten back to touch the Graph View Top, change the Dimension Anchor Value to 0.

FIGURE 15.50

The AutoCAD Properties palette showing the Dimension Anchor Option

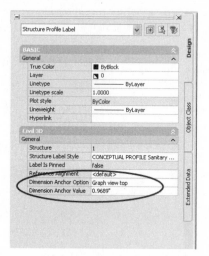

 Real World Scenario

ADDING EXISTING GROUND ELEVATION TO STRUCTURE LABELS

In design situations, it is often desirable to track not only the structure rim elevation at finished grade, but also the elevation at existing ground. This gives the designer an additional tool for optimizing earthwork balance.

This exercise will lead you through creating a structure label that includes surface reference text. We assume that you are familiar with Civil 3D label composition in general.

1. Open the Pipes-Exercise 4.dwg file, or continue working in any previous drawing.

2. Locate the Structure Label Styles branch on the Settings tab of Toolspace. (Choose General ➢ Toolspace and make the Settings tab active.)

3. Right-click Label Styles and select New. Set the options as follows:

   ◆ On the Information tab, name your label.

   ◆ On the General tab, note that you can choose your company text style and layer, as well as change the label orientation and readability behavior.

◆ On the Layout tab, note that there is a default text component called Structure Text. Click in the contents box to bring up the Text Component Editor.

◆ Use the Properties dropdown to add the <Name> and RIM <Insertion Rim Elevation> (two decimal places).

4. Click OK to leave the Text Component Editor.

5. In the Label Style Composer, choose Reference Text from the Add Component dropdown.

6. In the Select Type dialog, choose Surface.

7. Rename the component from Reference Text.1 to **Existing Ground**.

8. Click in the contents box to bring up the Text Component Editor.

9. Use the Properties dropdown to add the EG <Surface Elevation> (two decimal places).

10. Click OK to dismiss the Text Component Editor.

11. In the Label Style Composer, change the Anchor Component for Existing Ground to Structure Text, the Anchor Point to Bottom Center, and the Attachment to Top Center.

12. Pull down the Add Component dropdown and choose Text For Each.

13. In the Select Type dialog, choose Structure All Pipes.

14. Click in the Contents box to bring up the Text Component Editor.

15. Use the Properties dropdown to add the INV <Connected Pipe Invert Elevation> (two decimal places).

16. Click OK to dismiss the Text Component Editor.

17. In the Label Style Composer, change the Anchor Component for Text for Each.1 to Existing Ground and the Anchor Point to Bottom Center. Then change the Attachment to Top Center.

18. Click OK to dismiss the Label Style Composer.

19. Go into the drawing and select one or more structure labels.

20. Right-click and choose Properties. In the Properties dialog, pull down the Structure Label Style field and choose your new label from the list.

21. Exit the Properties dialog and clear your selections by pressing Esc. Look in the drawing and note that the Existing Ground part of the label is marked with "???".

22. Choose one or more labels again, right-click, and select Label Properties. This time you will be given a Reference Text Objects dropdown where you can choose the Existing Ground surface.

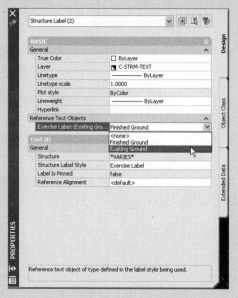

Look at the drawing and note that the Existing Ground part of the label is now populated.

```
Structure — (2)
RIM 672.61
EG 671.25
INV 652.87
INV 652.81
```

Explore label options to customize the layout and arrangement of your label using tools mentioned in this and other chapters. Choose Pipes ➢ Add Tables to add a pipe or structure table.

Creating an Interference Check between a Storm and Sanitary Pipe Network

In design, you must make sure that pipes and structures have appropriate separation. You can make some visual checks by rotating your modeling into 3D and plotting pipes in profile and section views (see Figure 15.51). Civil 3D also provides a tool called an Interference Check that will make a 3D sweep of your pipe networks and let you know if anything is too close for comfort.

FIGURE 15.51

Two pipe networks may interfere vertically where crossings occur (a). Viewing your pipes in profile view can also help identify conflicts (b).

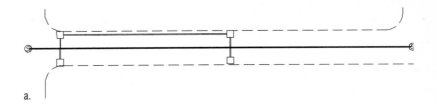

a.

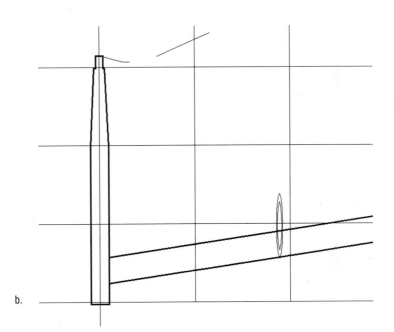

b.

The following exercise will lead you through creating a pipe network Interference Check to scan your design for potential pipe network conflicts.

1. Open the `Interference Start.dwg` file. Note that there is a sanitary sewer pipe network and a storm drainage network in this drawing.

2. Choose Pipes ➤ Utilities ➤ Create Interference Check and you'll see this command prompt: `Select a part from the first network:`. Choose a part from either the storm or sanitary pipe network.

3. The command line now reads `Select a part from the same network or different network`. Pick a part from the network not chosen in step two.

4. The Create Interferences dialog appears. Name the Interference Check **Exercise** and confirm that Sanitary Sewer Network and Storm Network appear in the Network 1 and Network 2 boxes.

5. Click 3D Proximity Check Criteria, and the Criteria dialog appears (see Figure 15.52).

FIGURE 15.52
Criteria for the 3D
proximity check

You are interested in finding all network parts that are within a certain tolerance of one another, so enter **3´** in the distance box. This setting will create a buffer to help find parts in all directions that might interfere.

(If you were interested only in physical, direct collisions between parts in your networks, you would leave the Apply 3D Proximity Check box empty and dismiss this dialog.)

AN INTERFERENCE "CLOUD"?

Think of the Interference Check as if each part is surrounded by a 3D "cloud." When that cloud touches another part, interference is flagged. If you specify distance, such as 2´, your cloud is created 2´ in all directions around each part. When you specify scale, such as 1.5, your cloud makes each part 1.5 times larger than its actual size.

---

6. Click OK to exit the Criteria dialog, and click OK to run the Interference Check. You will see a dialog that alerts you to one interference. Click OK to dismiss this dialog.

7. Zoom in on the crossing of pipe SD-1 and Pipe-3. Note a small marker has appeared, as in Figure 15.53.

8. Choose View ➢ 3D Views ➢ SW Isometric. Zoom in on the crossing of pipe SD-1 and Pipe-3. Note the interference marker in 3D, as shown in Figure 15.54.

FIGURE 15.53
The interference
marker in plan view

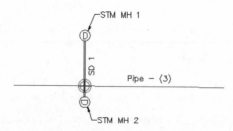

FIGURE 15.54
The interference
marker in 3D

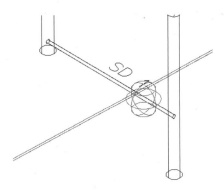

9. Choose View ➢ 3D Views ➢ Top to return to a normal plan view.

10. Drill into the Pipe Networks branch of Prospector, and you will see an entry for Interference Checks. Note that each instance of interference is listed in the preview pane for further study. Making edits to your pipe network will flag the interference check as "out of date." You can rerun Interference Checks simply by right-clicking the Interference Check in Prospector. Also note that you can edit your criteria in this right-click menu.

CREATING INTERFERENCE STYLES

You can create your interference style to give you a visual cue in both plan and 3D views. You can find interference styles on the Settings tab under Pipe Network ➢ Interference Styles. The Interference Style dialog has several options on both the Plan tab and the Model tab that control how you see the interference graphically.

Plan (2D) Options allows you to pick a marker style. You can choose one of the defaults, or create your own marker style by expanding General ➢ Marker Styles on the Settings tab. Marker styles are similar to Point styles and are used many places in Civil 3D.

Model (3D) Options allows you to choose between a "true interference solid" or a sphere.

A true interference solid assumes the shape of the exact overlap of the parts in question.

An interference sphere simply marks the location of the interference. You can control its size and behavior in this box. Choosing Diameter By True Solid Extents limits the size of the sphere to the overlap of the interference, similar to the true interference solid.

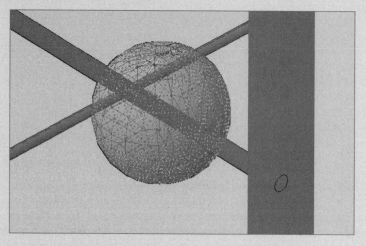

The Display tab allows you to control visibility in plan and model views. Typically, you will want to make sure that the plan symbol is visible in 2D and the model symbol is visible in 3D, as shown in the Interference Check exercise.

The Bottom Line

Create a pipe network by layout.   After you have created a parts list for your pipe network, the first step toward finalizing the design is to create a Pipe Network By Layout.

> **Master It**   Open the `Mastering Pipes.dwg` file. Choose the Pipes ➢ Create Pipe Network By Layout menu option to create a sanitary sewer pipe network.
>
> Use the Finished Ground surface, and name only structure and pipe label styles. Do not choose an alignment at this time. Create 8″ PVC pipes and concentric manholes.
>
> There are blocks in the drawing to assist you in placing manholes. Begin at the "START HERE" marker and place a manhole at each marker location. You can erase the markers when you have finished.

Create an alignment from network parts and draw parts in profile view.   Once your pipe network has been created in plan view, you would typically either add the parts to a profile view on the basis of either the road centerline or the pipe centerline.

> **Master It**   Continue working in the `Mastering Pipes.dwg` file. Create an alignment from your pipes so that station zero is located at the START HERE structure. Create a profile view from this alignment and draw the pipes on the profile view.

Label a pipe network in plan and profile.   Designing your pipe network is only half of the process. Engineering plans must be properly annotated.

> **Master It**   Continue working in the `Mastering Pipes.dwg` file. Add the Length Material And Slope style to profile pipes and the Data With Connected Pipes (Sanitary) style to profile structures.

Create a dynamic pipe table.   It is very common for municipalities and contractors to request a pipe or structure table for cost estimates or simply to make it easier to understand a busy plan.

> **Master It**   Continue working in the `Mastering Pipes.dwg` file. Create a pipe table for all pipes in your network.

Chapter 16

Working the Land: Grading

Beyond creating streets and sewers, cul-de-sacs, and inlets, much of what happens to the ground as a site is being designed must still be determined. Describing the final plan for the earthwork of a site is a crucial part of bringing the project together. In this chapter, we'll look at feature lines and grading groups, which are the two primary tools of site design. These two functions work in tandem to provide the site designer with tools for completely modeling the land.

By the end of this chapter, you will be able to:

◆ Convert existing linework into feature lines

◆ Model a simple linear grading with a feature line

◆ Create custom grading criteria

◆ Model planar site features with grading groups

Working with Feature Lines

Most work on a site can be broken down into a series of lines that connect important points. In Land Desktop (LDT) and other software, this is often done with the use of native 3D polylines. In Civil 3D, the creation of the feature line object adds a level of control and complexity not available to 3D polylines. In this section, we'll look at the Feature Lines toolbar, various methods of creating feature lines, some simple elevation edits, planar editing functionality, and labeling of the newly created feature lines.

The Feature Lines Toolbar

When you first fired up Civil 3D, you were confronted with the Feature Lines toolbar shown in Figure 16.1. Unlike any other component of the Civil 3D toolbox, the Feature Line tools were built onto a standard AutoCAD toolbar. In the default Civil 3D workspaces, this toolbar is presented front and center. Most users immediately dock it or turn it off.

One thing to remember when working with feature lines is that they do belong in a site. Feature lines within the same site snap to each other in the vertical and can cause some confusion when you're trying to build surfaces. If you're experiencing some weird elevation data along your feature line, be sure to check out the parent site.

FIGURE 16.1
The Feature
Lines toolbar

ACCESSING THE TOOLBAR

If you've put away the Feature Lines toolbar, you can get it back by restoring the Civil 3D Complete or Design workspace or by simply right-clicking in the gray areas surrounding your other toolbars (not on a toolbar) and selecting Civil ➤ Feature Lines. Additionally, most of these tools are available from the Grading menu, but we'll use the toolbar for most of this chapter.

In the next few sections, we'll break down the various tools in detail. We'll use almost all of them in this chapter, so in each section we'll spend some time getting familiar with the available tools and the basic concepts behind them. The toolbar is broken into three main areas: creation, elevation editing, and planar editing.

Creating Feature Lines

There are two methods of creating feature lines. They generate similar results but have some differences:

- The Create Feature Line tool ⌇ allows you to create a feature line from scratch, assigning elevations as you go. These elevations can be based on direct data input at the command line, slope information, or surface elevations.

- The Create From Objects tool ⌇ converts lines, arcs, polylines, and 3D polylines into feature lines. This process also allows elevations to be assigned from a surface or grading group.

Let's take a look at both methods in the next two exercises.

1. Open the Creating Feature Lines.dwg file. This drawing has the base line of a detention pond drawn already, along with a couple of critical points for drainage.

2. Click the Draw Feature Line tool to display the Create Feature Lines dialog, shown in Figure 16.2. We could assign a feature line style in this dialog, but will skip that process for now.

3. Click OK. Note that a new site will be created when you click OK to step forward. Grading objects and feature lines within the same site will react to each other. Keep an eye on your sites when you are dealing with large collections of these entities.

4. Use a Center osnap to pick the small circle on the right. (The pick order is shown in Figure 16.3.)

5. Enter S↵ at the command line to use a surface to set elevation information.

6. Press ↵ to accept the elevation offered.

7. Use a Center osnap to pick the center of the middle circle.

8. Enter -2↵ to set the grade between points.

9. Use a Center osnap to pick the center of the left-hand circle.

10. Enter SU↵ at the command line to set the elevation from the surface.

11. Press ↵ to accept the elevation.

12. Press ↵ again to exit the command. Your screen should look like Figure 16.3.

FIGURE 16.2
The Create Feature
Lines dialog

FIGURE 16.3
Completed breakline
with pick order

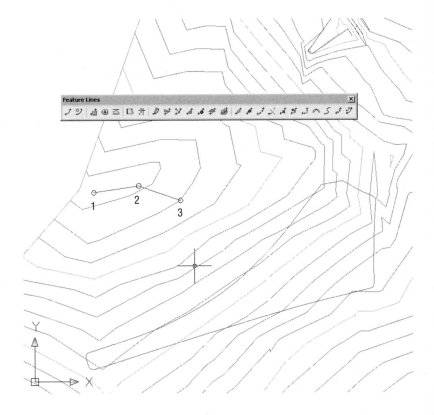

This method of creating a feature line connecting a few points seems pretty tedious to most users. In this next exercise, we'll convert an existing polyline to a feature line and set its elevations on the fly.

1. Open the `Creating Feature Lines.dwg` file if you closed it.

2. Click the Create From Objects tool from the Feature Lines toolbar.

3. Pick the closed polyline representing the pond basin.

4. Right-click and select Enter, or press ↵. The Create Feature Lines dialog will appear. This dialog is similar to Figure 16.2; however, the lower Conversion Options are now active, so let's look at the options presented:

    ◆ Erase Existing Entities removes the object onscreen and replaces it with a feature line object. This avoids the creation of duplicate linework, but could be harmful if you wanted your linework for planimetric purposes.

    ◆ Use Selected Entity Layers places the feature line on the same layer as the object being converted.

    ◆ Weed Points decreases the number of nodes along the object. This is handy when you're converting digitized information into feature lines.

    ◆ Assign Elevations lets you set the feature line PI (point of intersection) elevations from a surface or grading group, essentially draping the feature line on the selected object.

    ◆ Insert Intermediate Grade Break Points adds feature line elevation points at every crossing of the surface or grading group TIN with the object being converted.

5. Check the Assign Elevations box, leaving the From Surface option selected. The Erase Existing Entities option is on by default, and we will not select the Use Selected Entity Layers or Weed Points options in this case. Insert Intermediate Grade Break Points inserts a PI at every point along the feature line where it crosses an underlying TIN line.

6. Click OK.

7. Pick the pond outline, and the grips will look like Figure 16.4.

ANOTHER POND?

Yes, ponds are used entirely too frequently when demonstrating grading and feature line tools. They also happen to be one type of design that suits the demonstrating of myriad tools. We will use a pond to illustrate the concepts in this chapter. Yes, it could even be modified as a corridors, but there's almost always more than one approach in Civil 3D.

Note that in Figure 16.4 there are two types of grips. Feature lines offer feedback via the grip shape. A square feature line grip indicates a full PI. This node can be moved in the X, Y, and Z directions, manipulating both the layout and vertical design. Circular grips are elevation points only. Elevation points can only be slid along a given feature line segment, adjusting the vertical design, but cannot be moved in a horizontal plane. This combination of PIs and elevation points makes it easy to set up a long element with numerous changes in design grade that will maintain its linear design intent if the end points are moved. This is a huge advantage over 3D polylines! Now that we've created a couple of feature lines, we'll edit and manipulate them some more.

FIGURE 16.4
Conversion to a
feature line object

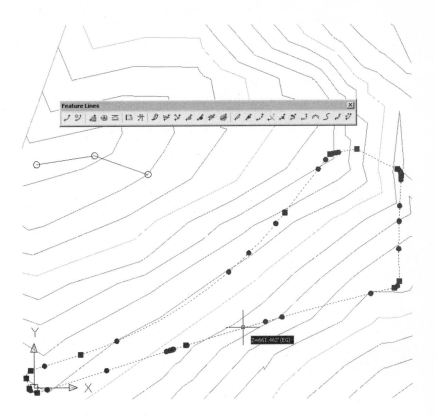

Editing Feature Line Elevation Information

Creating feature lines is straightforward. It's the editing and elevation tools that make them considerably more powerful than a standard 3D polyline. Let's continue our look at the Feature Lines toolbar shown in Figure 16.1. Moving across the toolbar, we find tools for modifying or assigning elevations to feature lines.

- The Feature Line Properties tool ⊞ displays the properties as you would expect. The unusual thing about this is that none of the design information is considered a property of the feature line; only the style is available for editing.

- The Add Labels tool ⊕ allows labeling of individual points or slopes along a feature line on the basis of line and curve labeling styles. Feature lines do not have their own labeling styles, but do have their own display styles.

- The Quick Profile tool ⊠ generates a temporary profile view along the feature line, sampling surfaces as selected in the dialog.

- The Elevation Editor tool ⊡ activates a palette in Panorama to display station, elevation, length, and grade information about the feature line selected.

- The Quick Elevation Edit tool ⌗ allows you to use onscreen cues to set elevations and slopes quickly between PIs on the feature line.

◆ The Edit Elevations tool ⟋ steps through the selected feature line, much like working through a polyline edit at the command line.

◆ The Set Grade/Slope Between Points tool ⟆ sets a continuous slope along the feature line between selected points.

◆ The Set Elevation By Reference tool ⟆ sets the elevation of a selected point along the feature line by picking a reference point, and then establishing a relationship to the selected feature line point. This relationship isn't dynamic!

◆ The Insert Elevation Point tool ⟆ inserts an elevation point at the point selected. Note that this point can only control elevation information; it does not act as a horizontal control point.

◆ The Delete Elevation Point tool ⟆ deletes the selected elevation point; the points on either side then become connected linearly on the basis of their current elevations.

◆ The Insert High/Low Elevation Point tool ⟆ places a new elevation point on the basis of two picked points and the forward and backward slopes. This calculated point is simply placed at the the intersection of two vertical slopes.

◆ The Elevations From Surface tool ⟆ sets the elevation at each PI and elevation point on the basis of the selected surface. It will also add elevation points at any point where the feature line crosses a surface TIN line.

We won't use all of the tools, but at least you have some concept of what is available. Let's look at a number of them in the next few exercises.

1. Open the Editing Feature Line Elevations.dwg file. Make sure the Feature Lines toolbar is visible.

2. Pick the shorter single feature line.

3. Right-click and select Feature Line Properties to display the dialog in Figure 16.5. As mentioned earlier, the Feature Line Properties dialog only controls the display of the feature line and none of the elevations.

4. Click OK.

5. Click the Quick Profile tool on the Feature Lines toolbar, and pick the shorter single feature line. The Create Quick Profiles dialog opens.

6. Select the Layout option from the dropdown list in the 3D Entity Profile Style selection box and click OK.

7. Click to the left of the contours to place a temporary profile view, as shown in Figure 16.6. A few notes on this operation: Civil 3D assigns an alignment number to perform the Quick Profile function, so your number might be different from that shown; a closed feature line will generate a parcel when the quick profile is executed; and finally, Panorama will display a message to tell you a profile view has been generated.

FIGURE 16.5
The Feature Line
Properties dialog

FIGURE 16.6
Quick profile of
the feature line

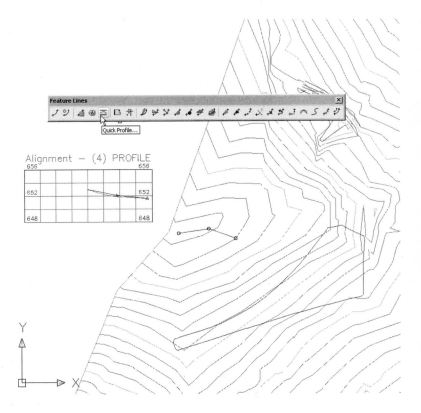

8. Pick the feature line again, right-click, and select Elevation Editor. The Grading Elevation Editor in Panorama will open. You could also click the Elevation Editor tool on the toolbar or select it from the Grading menu.

9. Click in the Grade Ahead column for the first PI. It's hard to see in the images, but as a row is selected in the Grading Elevation Editor, the PI or the elevation point that was selected will be highlighted on the screen with a small glyph.

10. Change the value to **-1.5**, as shown in Figure 16.7. Once the edit is complete, the quick profile will immediately update, reflecting the change in the object.

11. Click the green checkmark to dismiss Panorama.

FIGURE 16.7
Manual edits in the
Grading Elevation
Editor

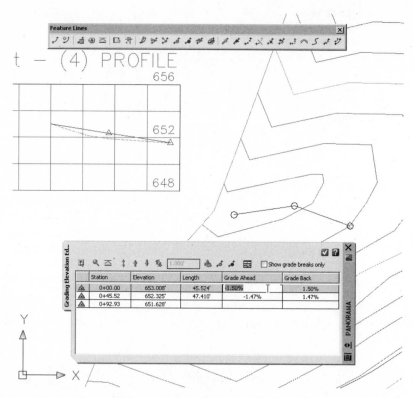

This is the most basic way to manipulate elevation information. We'll use it again to set the basic bottom of our pond, and then use the other tools to refine that part of our design. In this exercise, we'll remove some extraneous data points, and then set an elevation point for the inflow:

1. Pick the outline of the pond bottom.

2. Zoom in on the northern edge, as shown in Figure 16.8.

3. Click the Delete Elevation Point tool on the Feature Lines toolbar.

4. Pick near the three circular grip points on the feature line to remove these points.

5. Right-click to exit the Grading Elevation Editor.

6. Press ↵ or right-click again to exit the command. If you pick the feature line again, you'll see something like Figure 16.9. Notice that the three circular grips are gone, leaving two PIs at the segment ends.

7. Enter **655.0**↵ for a proposed elevation.

By using an elevation point instead of a PI, we can control the vertical without modifying the horizontal in any way. We will revisit this pond to explore using the Insert Elevation tool as well as other methods of grading along a feature line.

FIGURE 16.8
Elevation points
to be deleted

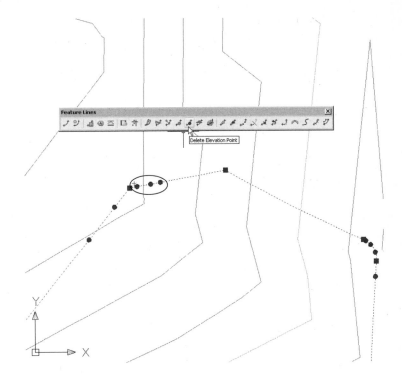

FIGURE 16.9
The feature line after
deleting elevation
points

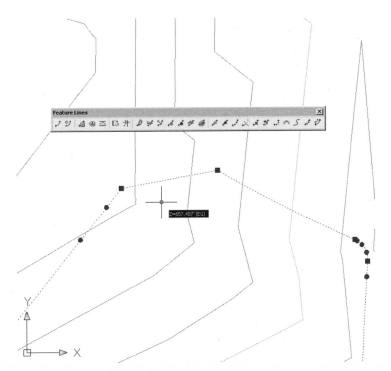

Editing Feature Line Horizontal Information

The final third of the Feature Lines toolbar is devoted to horizontal information. Grading revisions often require adding PIs, breaking apart feature lines, trimming, and performing other planar operations without destroying the vertical information. Let's take a look at the tools left on the Feature Lines toolbar:

◆ The Insert PI tool 🖉 allows you to insert a new PI, controlling both the horizontal and vertical design.

◆ The Remove PI tool 🖉 removes a PI. The feature line will mend the adjoining segments if possible, attempting to maintain similar geometry.

The next few tools act like their AutoCAD counterparts, but understand that elevations are involved and add PIs accordingly:

◆ The Break tool 🖉 operates similar to the AutoCAD Break command, allowing two objects or segments to be created from one. Additionally, if a feature line is part of a surface definition, both new feature lines are added to the surface definition to maintain integrity. Elevations at the new PIs are assigned on the basis of an interpolated elevation.

◆ The Trim tool 🖉 acts like the AutoCAD Trim command, adding a new end PI on the basis of an interpolated elevation.

◆ The Join tool 🖉 creates one feature line from two, making editing and control easier.

◆ The Reverse tool 🖉 changes the direction of a feature line.

◆ The Fillet tool 🖉 inserts a curve at PIs along a feature line and will connect feature lines sharing a common PI that are not actually connected.

The last few tools refine feature lines, making them easier to manipulate and use in surface building:

◆ The Fit Curve tool 🖉 analyzes a number of elevation points and attempts to define a working arc through them all. This is often used when the corridor utilities are used to generate feature lines. These derived feature lines can have a large number of unnecessary PIs in curved areas.

◆ The Smooth tool 🖉 turns a series of disjointed feature line segments and creates a best-fit curve. This tool is great for creating streamlines or other natural terrain features that are known to curve, but there's often not enough data to fully draw them that way.

◆ The Weed tool 🖉 allows the user to remove elevation points and PIs on the basis of various criteria. This is great for cleaning up corridor-generated feature lines as well.

◆ The Stepped Offset tool 🖉 allows offsetting in a horizontal and vertical manner, making it easy to create stepped features like stairs or curbs.

By using these controls, it's easier to manipulate the design elements of a typical site while still using feature lines for surface design. In this exercise, we'll manipulate a number of feature lines that were created by corridor operations:

1. Open the Horizontal Feature Line Edits.dwg file. A number of feature lines in the area of our detention pond have been brought into this drawing for editing and refinement (see Figure 16.10).

2. Click the Break tool on the Feature Lines toolbar.

3. Pick Feature Line A, as shown in Figure 16.10. Enter **F↵** to pick the first point of the break.

4. Using an Endpoint osnap, pick the end point on A just to the northwest of Feature Line B. Using an Endpoint osnap, pick the next end point on A to the east, leaving a gap, as shown in Figure 16.11.

FIGURE 16.10

Corridor-derived feature lines

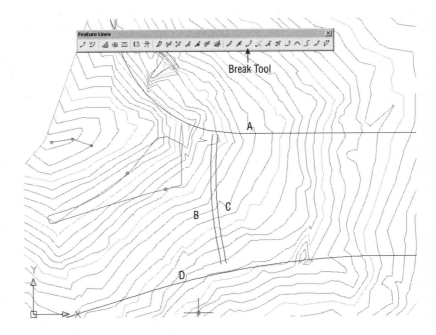

FIGURE 16.11

The feature line after executing the Break command

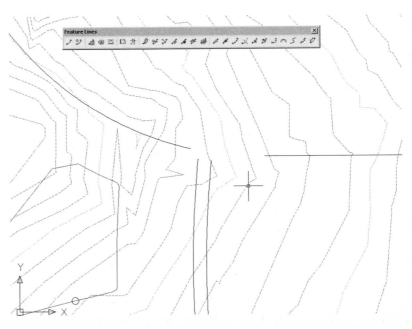

5. Click the Weed tool from the Feature Lines toolbar.

6. Pick Feature Line B to display the Weed Vertices dialog.

7. Enter 25´ for the Length, and then press Tab to register the value. The dialog changes to reflect the number of vertices that will be removed from the feature line. Additionally, the glyphs on the feature line itself will change from green to red to reflect nodes that will be removed under the current setting. Click OK to complete the command and OK again to dismiss the Weed Vertices dialog.

8. Pick Feature Lines B and C to activate grips on both lines, as shown in Figure 16.12.

9. Using a standard AutoCAD Extend command, extend Feature Line B to Feature Line D.

10. Click the Trim tool from the Feature Lines toolbar. A standard AutoCAD Trim will not work in this case. Pick Feature Line B as the cutting edge and right-click to complete the cutting-edge selection.

11. Pick the right-hand side of Feature Line D to trim it back to the intersection with Feature Line B, as shown in Figure 16.13.

12. Click the Fillet tool on the Feature Lines toolbar.

13. Pick Feature Line B. Enter J↵ to join two feature lines. Pick Feature Line D near the intersection to complete the Fillet command, as shown in Figure 16.14. Note that Feature Lines B and D have now joined as one feature line.

14. Right-click to exit the command.

There are almost 20 ways to modify feature lines on the Feature Lines toolbar. Take a few minutes and experiment with them to understand the options and tools available for this essential grading element. By manipulating the various pieces of the feature line collection, it's easier than ever to create dynamic modeling tools that match the designer's intent.

FIGURE 16.12
Feature lines after weeding (left) and before (right)

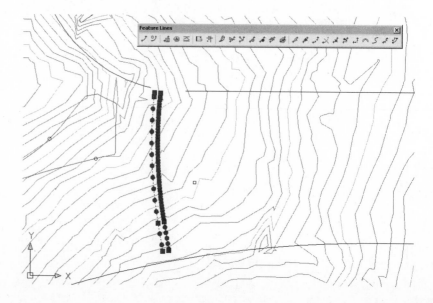

FIGURE 16.13
Feature Line D
trimmed

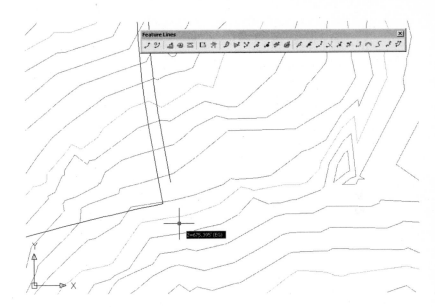

FIGURE 16.14
Filleted feature lines

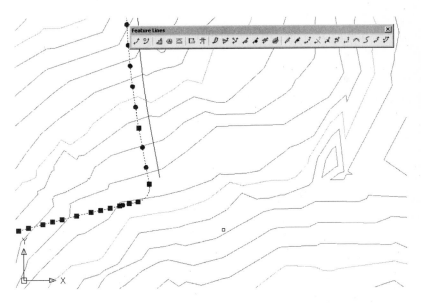

🌐 Real World Scenario

DRAINING THE POND

We need to use a combination of feature line tools and options to pull our pond together, and give us the most flexibility should we need to update the bottom area or manipulate the pond's general shape. Let's take a look at the methods that were used when this pond was designed:

1. Open the Pond Drainage Design.dwg file. The storm designer gave us a little bit more information about the pond design, as shown below.

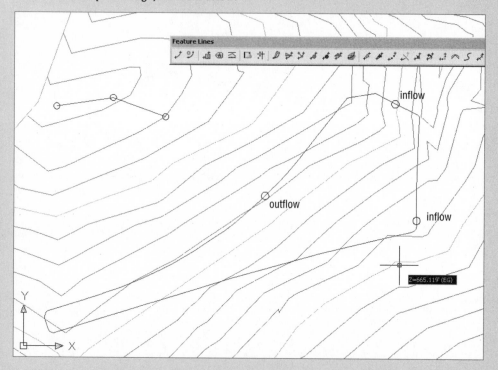

2. Click the Insert PI tool on the Feature Lines toolbar.

3. Pick the pond basin outline.

4. Use the Center osnap to insert the PIs in the center of each circle. Enter **655.5**↵ as the elevation of the inflow PIs. Press ↵ to accept the default for the elevation of the outflow PI; we'll be setting it in a moment.

5. Draw a polyline, like the one shown here, from the southern inflow point across the bottom of the pond, through the outflow, and snap to the endpoint of the drainage channel feature line created earlier. Be sure to place a PI at the center of the circle designating the outflow point. This polyline will be the layout for the pilot channel.

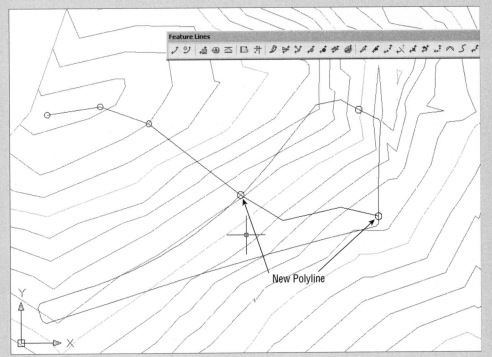

New Polyline

6. Click the Create From Objects tool on the Feature Lines toolbar, and pick the polyline just drawn.

7. Click OK to complete the conversion without changing any options.

8. Click the Fillet tool on the Feature Lines toolbar.

9. Pick our Pilot Channel feature line.

10. Enter **R**↵, and enter **25**↵ for the radius.

11. Enter **A**↵ to fillet all PIs.

12. Press ↵ to exit the Fillet command.

13. Click the Set Grade/Slope Between Point tool.

14. Pick the Pilot Channel feature line.

15. Pick the PI at the inflow.

16. Press ↵ to accept the elevation. Notice that this PI has picked up the elevation from the pond outline PI by virtue of being in the same site.

17. Pick the other end of the feature line as shown here. All the PIs will highlight, and Civil 3D will display the total length, elevation difference, and average slope at the command line.

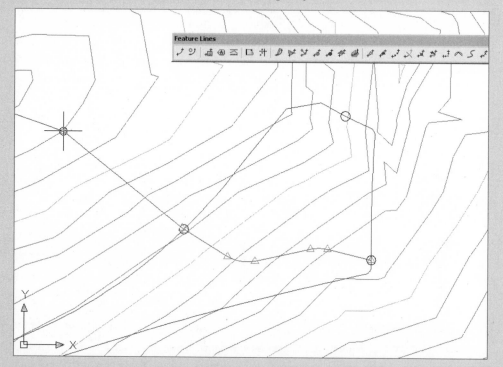

18. Press ↵ again to accept the grade. This completes a linear slope from one end of the feature line to the other, ensuring drainage through the pond and outfall structure.

19. Press ↵ to exit the Fillet command.

20. Pick the Pilot Channel feature line.

21. Right-click on the pilot channel and select Elevation Editor to open the Grading Elevation Editor in Panorama.

22. Click in the Station cells in the Grading Elevation Editor to highlight and ascertain the elevation at the outfall, as shown here. In this case, the elevation is 654.096´. Some minor variation might occur depending on your pick points and the length of your pilot channel.

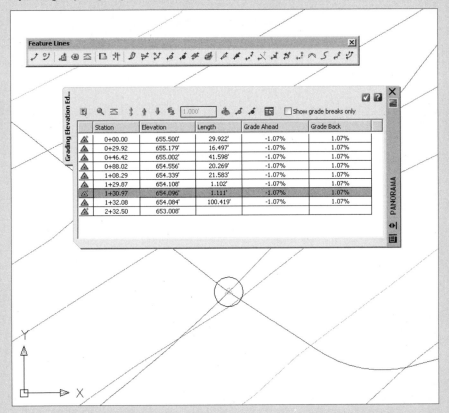

23. Close Panorama.

24. Click the Set Grade/Slope tool, and then pick the pond bottom again.

25. Pick the PI near the southwest corner of the pond bottom. Enter **656.**⏎ for the elevation.

26. Pick the PI at the southern inflow. This should register an elevation of 655.50.

27. Press ⏎ to accept the grade. This sets the elevations between the two selected PIs to all fall at the same grade.

28. Pick the pond bottom again.

29. Pick the same initial PI. Press ⏎ to accept the elevation of 656.

30. Moving your mouse clockwise to set the direction of the grading change we're about to make, pick the PI near the outflow shown here:

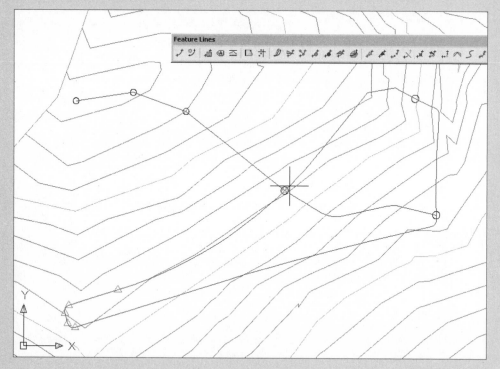

31. Enter **E** to input an elevation value. Enter the elevation ascertained in step 22. In our case, we enter **654.096**↵ as the elevation to tie to the pilot channel elevation.

32. Pick the pond bottom again. Pick the PI at the northern inflow, and press ↵ to accept the elevation (it should be 655.5).

33. Pick the outfall PI.

34. Enter **E** to accept the elevation value. The entire outline of the pond bottom is graded except the area between the two inflows. Because we want to avoid a low spot, we'll now force a high point.

35. Click the Insert High/Low Elevation Point tool.

36. Pick the pond outline.

37. Pick the PI near the north inflow as the start point, and pick the PI near the southern inflow as the end point. Enter **0.5**↵ as the grade ahead.

38. Enter **0.5↵** as the grade behind. A new elevation point will be created as shown here:

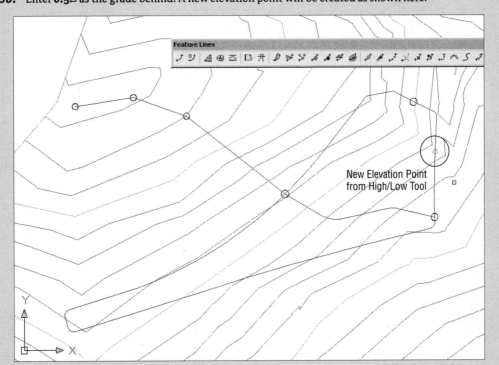

New Elevation Point from High/Low Tool

By using all the tools in the Feature Lines toolbar, you can quickly grade elements of your design and pull them together. This procedure seemed to involve a lot of steps, but it takes less than a minute in practice.

Stylizing and Labeling Feature Lines

While it's not common, feature lines can be stylized to reflect particular uses, and labels can be applied to help a reviewer understand the nature of the object being shown. In the next couple of exercises, we'll create a feature line style, then label a few critical points on our pond design to help understand the drainage patterns better.

FEATURE LINE STYLES

Feature line styles are among the simplest in the Civil 3D program. Feature lines have options only for the display of the feature line itself, 2D and 3D, respectively. Many users never stylize their feature lines because there's so little to gain, but let's look at the options:

1. Open the `Labeling Feature Lines.dwg` file. This is the completed Pond Pilot Channel exercise from the previous section.

2. Pick the Pilot Channel feature line, as shown in Figure 16.15.

FIGURE 16.15
Picking the Pilot
Channel feature line

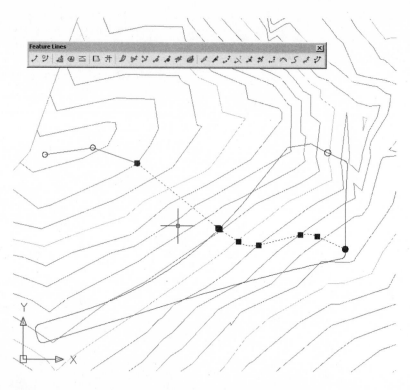

3. Right-click and select Feature Line Properties.

4. Check the Style box and click the down arrow to open the dropdown menu.

5. Select Create New, as shown in Figure 16.16, and the Feature Line Style dialog appears.

6. On the Information tab, enter **Pilot Channel** in the Name text box.

7. Switch to the Display tab.

8. Click the Linetype cell to open the Select Linetype dialog, and select Hidden. Click OK to dismiss the dialog.

9. Enter **3** in the LT Scale cell.

FIGURE 16.16
Creating a new
Feature Line style

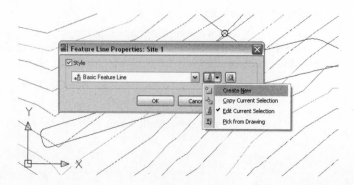

10. Click OK to dismiss the Feature Line Style dialog.

11. Click OK again to dismiss the Feature Line Properties dialog. Your screen should look like Figure 16.17.

The style helps convey that this is a flow path for water, but we don't have much help in determining the actual slope or distances involved.

FIGURE 16.17
Pilot channel after
styling the feature line

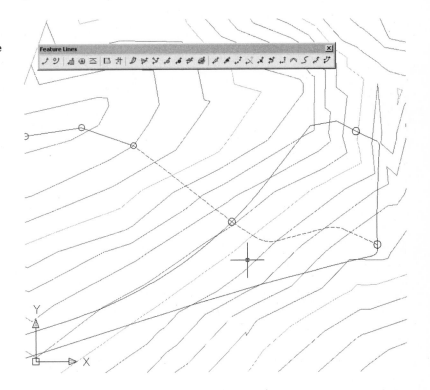

FEATURE LINE LABELS

Feature lines do not have their own unique label styles but instead share with general lines and arcs. The templates that ship with Civil 3D 2008 contain styles for labeling segment slopes, so let's label the critical slopes in our next exercise:

1. Open the Labeling Feature Lines.dwg file if you closed it.

2. Choose Grading ➤ Add Feature Line Labels ➤ Add Feature Line Labels.

3. Change the Line Label Style and Curve Label Style to Grade Only, as shown in Figure 16.18.

4. Click Add.

5. Pick a few points along the Pilot Channel feature line to create labels as shown in Figure 16.18.

FIGURE 16.18
Adding feature
line grade labels

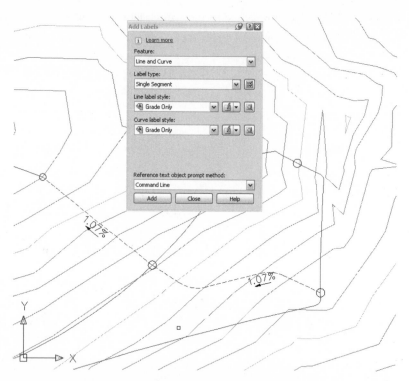

Although it would be convenient to label the feature line elevations as well, there's no simple method for doing so. In practice, you would want to label the surface that contains the feature line as a component.

Grading Objects

Once a linear feature line is created, there are two main uses. One is to incorporate the feature line itself directly into a surface object as a breakline; the other is to create a grading object (referred to hereafter as simply a grading or gradings) using the feature line as a baseline. A grading consists of some baseline with elevation information, and a criteria set for projecting outward from that baseline based on distance, slope, or other criteria. These criteria sets can be defined and stored in grading criteria sets for ease of management. Finally, gradings can be stylized to reflect plan production practices or convey information such as cut or fill.

In this section, we'll start with defining a criteria set, use a number of different methods to create gradings, edit those gradings, stylize the grading, and finally convert the grading group into a surface.

Defining Criteria Sets

Criteria sets are merely collections of grading criteria organized for ease of use. These criteria might be something along the lines of "Grade at 3:1 to a Surface" or "Grade at 100% for 6" Elevation Change." These criteria can be built as mere guides, or can act as straightforward commands offering little user interaction in the process. In this exercise, let's create a new criteria set and add a few grading criteria:

1. Open the `Defining a Criteria Set.dwg` file. The typical section can be seen in Figure 16.19. To achieve this section, we'll create a grading criteria set for the various slopes, the ledges, and the surface tie-in.

2. Switch to the Settings tab.

3. Expand the Grading ➢ Grading Criteria Sets branches.

4. Right-click on Grading Criteria Sets and select New. The Grading Criteria Set Properties dialog opens.

5. Enter **Pond Grading** in the Name text box and click OK.

6. Expand the Grading Criteria Sets branch, then right-click on the Pond Grading grading criteria set and select New.

7. Enter **3:1 to Elevation** in the Name text box.

8. Switch to the Criteria tab.

9. Change the values as shown in Figure 16.20.

10. Click OK.

FIGURE 16.19

Typical pond section

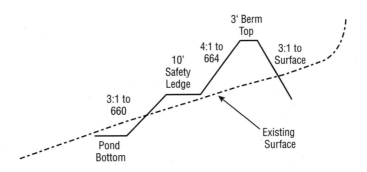

FIGURE 16.20

Creating a grading criteria

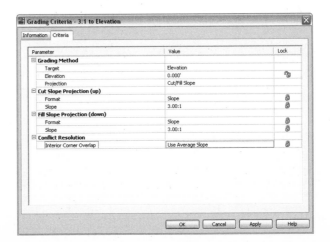

Let's take a few moments to review the options available on the Criteria tab:

◆ Grading Method controls the projection method used. The Target cell lets you set the target type. Surface, Elevation, Relative Elevation, and Distance are the valid options, and as each is selected, options appear directly underneath.

◆ Slope Projection allows the selection of slopes (X:1) or grades (X%) as the format for specifying the grading projections.

◆ Conflict Resolution determines how Civil 3D will handle overlapping projection lines on interior corners. Use Average Slope is the typical answer, cleaning up the grading object most cleanly when conflicts arise.

Note that each of the rows has a padlock to the far right. If you lock any individual piece, the user will not be prompted for that value or be allowed to change it. In the case of Figure 16.20, the only user input required will be the Target Elevation for the grading. Let's complete the rest of the Grading criteria set for our pond design:

1. Expand the Pond Grading branch, right-click on the 3:1 To Elevation branch, and select Copy, as shown in Figure 16.21.

FIGURE 16.21
Copying a Grading criteria set

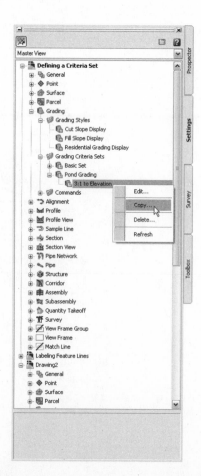

2. Enter **4:1 to Elevation** in the Name text box.

3. Switch to the Criteria tab.

4. Change the Cut Slope Projection and Fill Slope Projection to 4:1.

5. Click OK.

6. Right-click on 3:1 Elevation in the Pond Grading branch and select Copy.

7. Enter **3:1 to Surface** in the Name text box.

8. Switch to the Criteria tab.

9. Select Surface from the dropdown list in the Target selection box, and unlock the Slope values for both Cut and Fill Slope Projections, as shown in Figure 16.22.

10. Click OK.

11. Right-click on Pond Grading and select New.

12. Enter **Flat Ledge** in the Name text box.

13. Switch to the Criteria tab.

14. Select Surface from the dropdown list in the Target selection box.

15. Select Grade from the dropdown list in the Slope Projection Format selection box, as shown in Figure 16.23.

16. Enter **2%** for the Grade value.

17. Lock the Grade row.

18. Click OK.

FIGURE 16.22

3:1 to Surface Grading Criteria settings

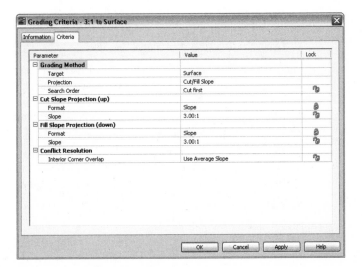

FIGURE 16.23

Flat ledge grading
criteria settings

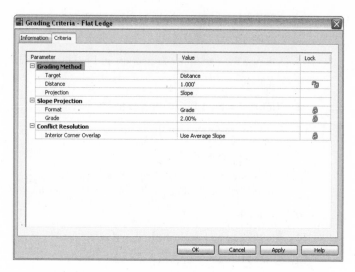

With this criteria set, we've locked many of the user inputs, making grading a fast and easy process with minimal opportunity for user input error. We'll put these grading criteria to use in the next section.

Creating Gradings

With criteria set in place, we can now look at grading the pond as designed. In this section, we'll look at grading groups and then create the individual gradings within the group. Grading groups act as a collection mechanism for individual gradings and let Civil 3D understand the daisy chain of individual gradings that are related and act in sync with each other.

One thing to be careful of when working with gradings is that they are part of a site. Any feature line within that same site will react with the feature lines created by the grading. For that reason, the exercise drawing has a second site called Pond Grading to be used for just the pond grading.

1. Open the `Grading the Pond.dwg` file.

2. Pick the pond bottom.

3. Right-click and select Move To Site. The Move To Site dialog appears.

4. Click OK to change the Pond feature line to the Pond Grading site. This will avoid interaction between the pond banks and the pilot channel we laid out earlier.

5. Choose Grading ➢ Create Grading. The Grading Creation Tools toolbar, shown in Figure 16.24, appears. This toolbar is similar to the toolbar used in pipe networks. The left section is focused on settings, the middle on creation, and the right on editing.

6. Click the Set The Grading Group tool ![icon] to display the Create Grading Group dialog.

FIGURE 16.24

The Grading Creation
Tools toolbar

7. Click OK to accept Pond Grading in the Move To Site dialog.

8. Enter **Pond** in the Name text box and click OK. We'll revisit the surface creation options in a bit.

9. Click the Select A Criteria Set tool 🔲 to display the Select A Criteria Set dialog.

10. Select Pond Grading from the dropdown list and click OK.

11. Click the Create Grading tool on the Grading Creation Tools toolbar, or click the down arrow next to the Create Grading tool and select Create Grading, as shown in Figure 16.25.

12. Pick the pond outline.

13. Pick a point on the outside of the pond to indicate the direction of the grading projections.

14. Press ↵ to apply the grading to the entire length of the pond outline.

15. Enter **660**↵ at the command line as the target elevation. The first grading is complete. The lines on screen are part of the Grading style.

16. In the Select A Grading Criteria dropdown list on the Grading Creation Tools toolbar, select Flat Ledge.

17. Click the Create Grading tool again.

18. Pick the upper boundary of the grading made in step 15, as shown in Figure 16.26.

FIGURE 16.25
Creating a grading using the 3:1 to Elevation criteria

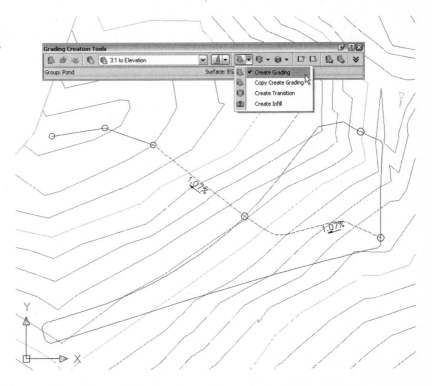

FIGURE 16.26
Creating a daisy
chain of gradings

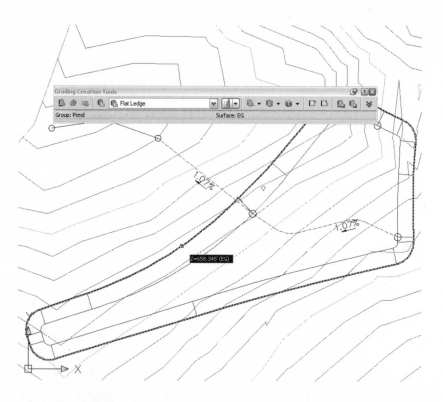

19. Press ↵ to apply to the whole length.

20. Enter **10**↵ for the target distance to build the safety ledge.

21. In the Select A Grading Criteria dropdown list on the Grading Creation Tools toolbar, select 4:1 to Elevation.

22. Click the Create Grading tool again.

23. Pick the outer edge of the safety ledge just created.

24. Press ↵ to apply to the whole length.

25. Enter **664**↵ as the target elevation.

26. In the Select A Grading Criteria dropdown list on the Grading Creation Tools toolbar, select Flat Ledge one more time.

27. Click the Create Grading tool again.

28. Pick the outside edge of the slope just made.

29. Press ↵ to apply to the whole length.

30. Enter **3**↵ for the target distance. The interior of the pond banking is complete, and your drawing should look like Figure 16.27.

FIGURE 16.27
Complete pond
interior grading

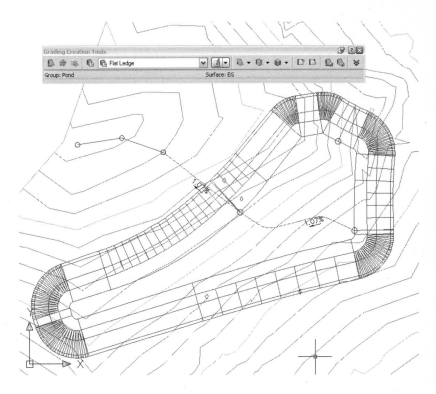

31. In the Select A Grading Criteria dropdown list on the Grading Creation Tools toolbar, select 3:1 To Surface.

32. Click the Create Grading tool again.

33. Pick the outside edge of the top berm just created.

34. Press ↵ to apply to the whole length.

35. Press ↵ to accept the default Cut Slope of 3:1.

36. Press ↵ to accept the default Fill Slope of 3:1.

37. Wait for the berm to complete the daylighting calculations. Your design should look similar to Figure 16.28.

Each piece of this pond is tied to the next, creating a dynamic model of our pond design on the basis of the designer's intent. What if that intent changes? Let's look at editing the various gradings in the next section.

FIGURE 16.28

Completed pond grading with groups

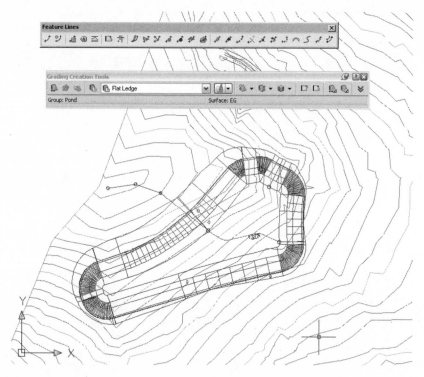

Editing Gradings

Once you've created a grading, you often need to make changes. A change can be as simple as changing the slope or changing the geometric layout. In this exercise, we'll make a simple change, but the concept applies to all the gradings we've created in our pond. Because our grading criteria were originally locked to make life easier, we'll now unlock them before modifying the daylight portion of the pond.

1. Open the Editing Grading.dwg file.

2. On the Settings tab, expand the Grading ➤ Grading Criteria Sets ➤ Pond Grading branches.

3. Right-click on the 3:1 To Surface criteria under Pond Grading, and select Edit. The Grading Criteria dialog opens.

4. On the Criteria tab, unlock the Slope values for both the Cut and Fill Slope Projections, as shown in Figure 16.29. Click OK.

5. Pick one of the daylight lines by picking a projection line or the small diamond on the outside of the pond.

6. Right-click and select Grading Editor. The Grading Editor in Panorama appears.

7. Enter **4:1** for a Fill Slope Projection. Panorama appears with an information message.

8. Close Panorama. Your display should look like Figure 16.30.

FIGURE 16.29
Modifying the 3:1
To Surface Grading
criteria

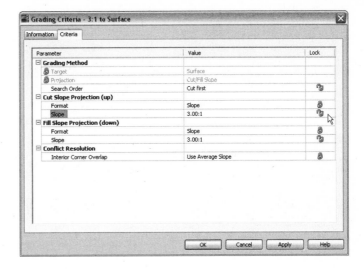

FIGURE 16.30
Completed
grading edit

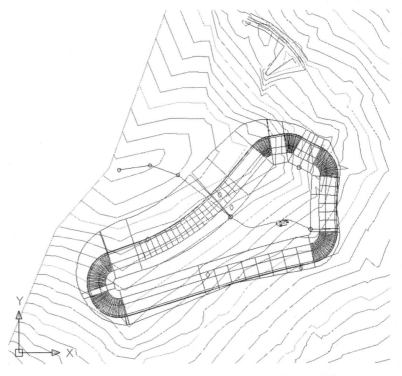

Editing any aspect of the grading will reflect instantly, and if other gradings within the group are dependent on the results of the modified grading, they will recalculate as well. Now that we have a working design, let's look at a better view of the pond on the basis of stylizing the gradings.

Grading Styles

The stock grading styles work fairly well, but we'd like to show the slopes using some pretty typical civil engineering symbology. This information gives immediate feedback about the gradings without you having to pull up a Properties dialog or inquire about slopes.

1. Open the Grading Styles.dwg file.

2. Expand the Grading ➤ Grading Styles branches on the Settings tab.

3. Right-click on Grading Styles and select New. The Grading Style dialog appears.

4. On the Information tab, enter **Pond Slopes** in the Name text box.

5. Switch to the Slope Patterns tab. Check the Slope Pattern box in the Options area.

6. Click the down arrow next to the Slope Pattern dropdown list box, as shown in Figure 16.31, and select Create New. The Slope Pattern Style dialog appears.

FIGURE 16.31
Creating a new
slope pattern style

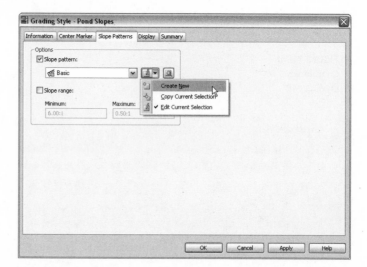

YES, WE'RE GOING AROUND THE LONG WAY

Slope pattern styles are contained in the Multipurpose styles collection under the General branch near the top of the Settings tree. Because we want to use this in direct correlation with a grading style, we're going through the Grading Style dialog to reach that same point. It's merely a reminder that there are a multitude of approaches to working within Civil 3D, and everyone will have his or her own favorite methods.

7. On the Information tab, enter **Full Slopes** in the Name text box.

8. Switch to the Layout tab. Change the values for Component 1, as shown in Figure 16.32. There are a large number of options for creating varied slope indicators, but this simple indicator works well for many cases.

FIGURE 16.32
Slope Pattern
Style Layout tab

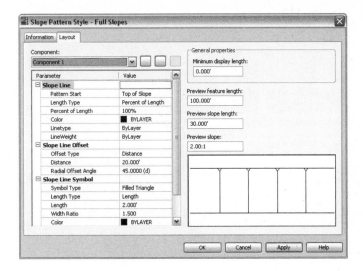

9. Click Apply.

10. Select Component 2 from the dropdown list in the Component selection box.

11. Click the red X button to delete Component 2, and click OK to dismiss the dialog.

12. Check the Slope Range box in the Options area. This option set limits for when the slope pattern will be applied. The default values will conveniently *not* put slope patterns on our benching and berm gradings, leaving a cleaner appearance. Leave the default values in place.

13. Switch to the Display tab. Turn the Projection Line component off in the 2D View Direction, and click OK to dismiss the dialog.

14. Pick one of the gradings by picking a projection line or the small diamond.

15. Right-click and select Grading Properties to display the Grading Properties dialog.

16. Select Pond Slopes from the dropdown lists in the Cut Style and Fill Style selection boxes, as shown in Figure 16.33. Click OK to dismiss the dialog.

17. Repeat this process for the other four gradings. The Ledges will only have one slope style to pick from, but you should still use the Pond Slopes option. Your completed work should look similar to Figure 16.34.

Although there are still some issues in the curve areas because of the way the gradings build feature lines, this view of our pond gives immediate feedback about the basic design. Note that the southeast corner contains slope arrows coming back to the pond area, indicating that the design is actually in a cut situation in this area. How much cut? Let's see in the next section.

FIGURE 16.33
Changing
grading styles

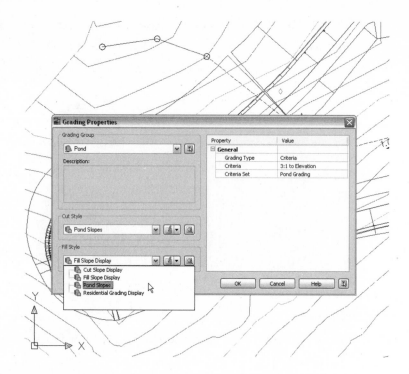

FIGURE 16.34
Completed grading
style changes

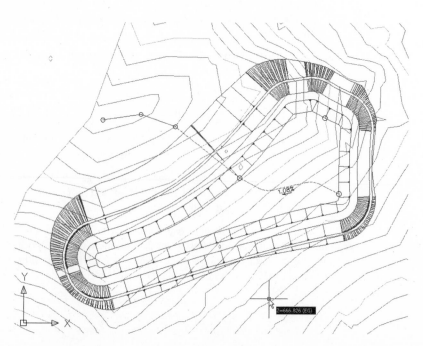

Creating Surfaces from Grading Groups

Grading groups work well for creating the model, but we have to use a TIN surface to go much further with them. In this section, we'll look at the conversion process, and then use the built-in tools to understand the impact of our grading group on site volumes.

1. Open the `Creating Grading Surfaces.dwg` file.

2. Pick one of the diamonds in the grading group.

3. Right-click and select Grading Group Properties. The Grading Group Properties dialog opens.

4. Switch to the Information tab if needed. Check the box for Automatic Surface Creation.

5. In the Create Surface dialog that appears, enter **Pond Surface** in the Name field.

6. Click in the Style field, and then click the ellipsis button. The Select Surface Style dialog appears. Select Contours 1′ And 5′ from the dropdown list in the selection box, as shown in Figure 16.35. Click OK.

FIGURE 16.35

Creating a grading group surface

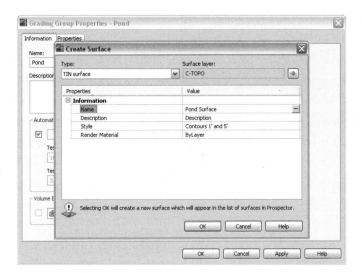

We're going through this process now because we didn't turn on the Automatic Surface Creation option when we created the grading group. If you're performing straightforward gradings, that option can be a bit faster and simpler. There are two options available when creating a surface from a grading group. They both control the creation of projection lines in curved area:

♦ The Tesselation Spacing value controls how often frequently along an arced feature line TIN points are created and projection lines calculated. A TIN surface cannot contain any true curves like a feature line can because it is built from triangles. The default values typically work for site mass grading, but might not be low enough to work with things like parking lot islands where the 10′ value would result in too little detail.

◆ The Tesselation Angle value is the degree measured between outside corners in a feature line. Corners with no curve segment have to have a number of projections swung in a radial pattern to calculate the TIN lines in the surface. The tesselation angle is the angular distance between these radial projections. The typical values work most of the time, but in large grading surfaces, a larger value might be acceptable, lowering the amount of data to calculate without significantly altering the final surface created.

Now let's complete our exercise:

7. In the Grading Group Properties dialog, check the Volume Base Surface option to perform a volume calculation.

8. Click OK, and dismiss Panorama if need be. Your drawing should look like Figure 16.36.

9. Zoom in if needed and pick the diamond again to select one of the gradings. Make sure you grab one of the gradings and not the surface contours that are being drawn on top of them.

10. Right-click and select Grading Group Properties.

11. Switch to the Properties tab to display the Volume information for the pond, as shown in Figure 16.37. This tab also allows you to review the criteria and styles being used in the grading group.

FIGURE 16.36
Complete grading
group surface

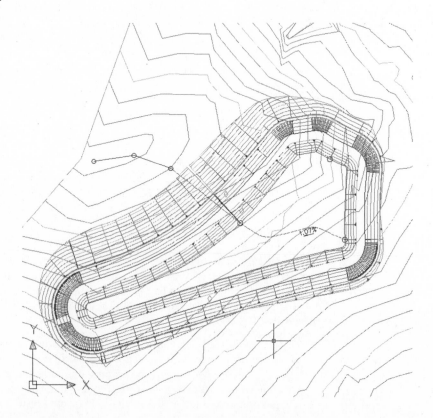

FIGURE 16.37
Reviewing the
grading group
volumes

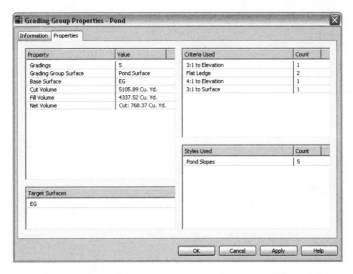

This new surface is listed in Prospector and is based on the gradings created. A change to the gradings would affect the grading group, which would, in turn, affect the surface and these volumes. Let's take a look at pulling it all together in one more exercise:

1. Open the `Creating Composite Surfaces.dwg` file.

2. Right-click on Surfaces in Prospector and select Create Surface.

3. In the Create Surface dialog, enter **Composite** in the Name text box. Click in the Style field, and then click the ellipsis to open the Select Surface Style dialog. Select the Contours 2´ And 10´ (Design) option from the dropdown list box, and click OK.

4. Click OK to dismiss the Create Surface dialog and create the surface in Prospector.

5. Change the surface style of the EG and Pond surfaces to No Display.

6. In Prospector, expand the Surfaces ➤ Composite ➤ Definition branches.

7. Right-click on Edits and select Paste Surface. The Select Surface To Paste dialog appears.

8. Select EG from the list and click OK. Dismiss Panorama if it appears.

9. Right-click on Edits again and select Paste Surface one more time.

10. Select Pond Surface and click OK. The drawing should look like Figure 16.38.

By creating a composite surface consisting of pasted together surfaces, the TIN triangulation cleans up any gaps in the data, making contours that are continuous from the original grade, through the pond, and out the other side. With the grading group still being dynamic and editable, this composite surface reflects a dynamic grading solution that will update with any changes.

FIGURE 16.38
Completed
composite surface

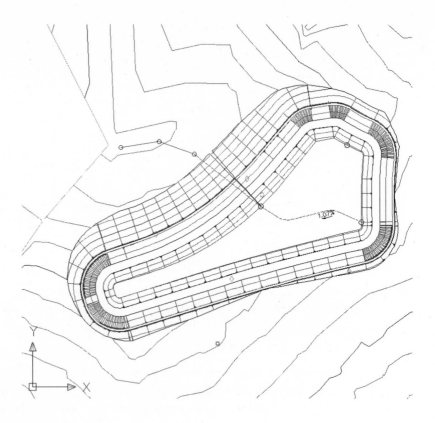

The Bottom Line

Convert existing linework into feature lines. Many site features are drawn initially as simple linework for the 2D plan. By converting this linework to feature line information, you avoid a large amount of rework. Additionally, the conversion process offers the ability to drape feature lines along a surface, making further grading use easier.

Master It Open the `Mastering Grading.dwg` file from the data location. Convert the polyline describing a proposed temporary drain into a feature line and drape it across the EG surface to set elevations.

Model a simple linear grading with a feature line. Feature lines define linear slope connections. This can be the flow of a drainage channel, the outline of a building pad, or the back of a street curb. These linear relationships can help define grading in a model, or simply allow for better understanding of design intent.

Master It Add 200′ radius fillets on the feature line just created. Set the grade from the top of the hill to the circled point to 5%, the remainder to a constant slope to be determined in the drawing. Draw a temporary profile view to verify the channel is below grade for most of its length.

Create custom grading criteria.   Using grading criteria to limit the amount of user input can help cut down on input errors and design mistakes. Defining a set to work with for a given design makes creating gradings a straightforward process.

   Master It   Continuing with the `Mastering Grading.dwg` file, create two new grading criteria: the first to be named Bottom, with a criteria of 5′ at 2% grade, the second to named Sides with criteria of daylight to a surface at 6:1 slope in cut areas only; in fill, do not grade.

Model planar site features with grading groups.   Once a feature line defines a linear feature, gradings collected in grading groups model the lateral projections from that line to other points in space. These projections combine to model a site much like a TIN surface, resulting in a dynamic design tool that works in the Civil 3D environment.

   Master It   Use the two grading criteria just used to define the pilot channel, with grading on both sides of the sketched centerline. Calculate the difference in volume between using 6:1 side slopes and 4:1 side slopes.

Chapter 17

Sharing the Model: Data Shortcuts

No man is an island, and it's the rare designer who gets to work alone. Even in a one-person design team, breaking the project into finite elements, such as grading, paving, and utilities, makes sense from a plan production and management standpoint. To do this effectively, your design software has to understand and have some method for sharing the design information behind the drawing objects. Civil 3D has two mechanisms for creating a project environment with project information sharing: data shortcuts and Vault. In this chapter, we will look at data shortcuts as a project-management scheme.

By the end of this chapter, you will be able to:

◆ List the project elements available for sharing through data shortcuts and those that cannot

◆ Create a data shortcut file from Civil 3D objects

◆ Import a data shortcut and create references

What Are Data Shortcuts?

Data shortcuts allow the cross referencing of design data between drawings. To this end, the data is what is made available, and it's important to note that the appearance can be entirely different between host and any number of data shortcuts. We will use the term *data shortcut* or, more simply, *shortcut* when we discuss selecting, modifying, or updating these links between files.

WHAT ABOUT VAULT?

This chapter will focus strictly on the creation and use of data shortcuts. In Chapter 19, we'll look at how using Vault compares and discuss the relative advantages of each method. We'll also look at a possible project-management methodology. The same techniques can generally be used with shortcuts.

There are two primary situations when you need data or information across drawings, and they are addressed with external references (XRefs) or shortcuts. These two options are similar but not the same. Let's compare:

XRef Functionality Used when the goal is to get a picture of the information in question. XRefs can be changed by using the layer control, XRef clips, and other drawing-element controls. They don't bring any design information, though, so XRefs are limited in labeling or querying situations.

Shortcut functionality Brings over the design information, but generally ignores the display. Shortcuts only work with Civil 3D objects, so they will have their own styles applied. This may seem like duplicitous work since you have already assigned styles and labels in one drawing and have to do it again, but it offers the advantage in that you can have completely different views of the same data in different drawings.

As we just noted, only Civil 3D objects can be used with shortcuts, and even then some objects are not available through shortcuts. The following objects are available for use through data shortcuts:

♦ Alignments

♦ Surfaces

♦ Profile data

♦ Pipe networks

♦ View frame groups

You might expect that corridor, parcel, assembly, point or point group information would be available through the shortcut mechanism, but they are not. The corridor object is available for use through XRefs curiously enough, but it is the only object that is exposed in that manner. Now that we've looked at what objects we can tackle with shortcuts, let's explore how to create them.

A NOTE ABOUT THE EXERCISES IN THIS CHAPTER

Many of the exercises in this chapter, as well as in Chapters 18 and 19 on Vault, assume you've stepped through the full chapter. It's difficult to simulate the large number of variables that come into play in a live environment. To that end, many of these exercises build on the previous one. Don't close any files until the end of the chapter for the easiest workflow.

Additionally, you'll have to make some saves to data files throughout this chapter. Remember that you can always get the original file from the media that came with your book.

Creating Data Shortcut Files

Shortcut files are simply XML files that contain pointers back to the drawing containing the object in question. There are two main approaches to creating shortcut files: breaking apart the shortcuts on the basis of the host drawing or on object type. In this section, we'll create shortcut files with both methods and examine each file using XML Notepad to understand the file pointers.

Drawing-Based Shortcut Files

Drawing-based shortcut files have the advantage of being easy to create and easy to update. They are also easy to manage in that you have little risk of overwriting a shortcut file inadvertently. This also makes it difficult to easily discern what shortcut file you should be linking to when it's time to create references to these objects. In this exercise, we'll look at creating one of these files and then examine its structure with XML Notepad.

MY SCREEN DOESN'T LOOK LIKE THAT!

Many of the screen captures and paths shown in this chapter reflect the author's working folders during the creation of the data. Your screen will be different depending on how you have installed the data, network permissions, and so on. Just focus on the content and don't let the different paths fool you—you're doing the right steps.

1. Open the `Creating Shortcuts.dwg` file. This drawing contains samples of each shortcut-ready object, as shown in Figure 17.1.

2. Select General ➤ Data Shortcuts ➤ Edit Data Shortcuts to display the Data Shortcuts palette in Panorama. A set of data shortcut tools is displayed on the top of the palette, as shown on Figure 17.2.

FIGURE 17.1
The Creating Short-cuts drawing file

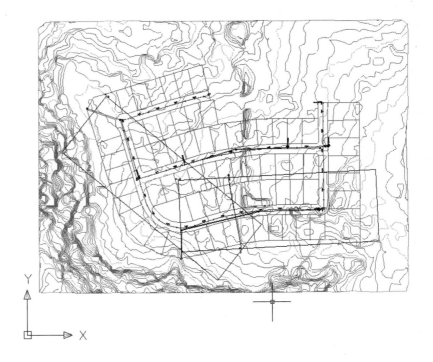

FIGURE 17.2
Tools on the Data Shortcuts palette in Panorama

Let's spend some time working our way across the tools at the top of Panorama before creating our shortcut file:

Icon	Function
	Import Data Shortcuts From File loads shortcuts from an external file. We'll look at this in the next section of this chapter.
	Export Data Shortcuts To File creates the shortcut file from the objects selected in the current drawing.
	Validate Data Shortcuts checks the integrity of the shortcut file. This process involves backtracking all of the shortcuts and making sure that an actual Civil 3D object exists on the other end and is available for referencing.
	Create Data Shortcut By Selection lets you pick items that will then be placed in the shortcut file. Unfortunately, these items have to be picked one at a time.
	Create Reference makes a reference in your current drawing from a shortcut file. This process creates the actual reference in the active drawing.
	Open Source Drawing opens the host file of a particular object listed in a shortcut file.
	Expand All Categories expands the list of shortcuts loaded and available in the current drawing.
	Collapse All Categories collapses the list of shortcuts loaded and available in the current drawing
	Delete Data Shortcuts removes selections from the Data Shortcuts palette so they are not part of any export command.

3. Click Create Data Shortcut By Selection and pick a surface by selecting any of the contours.

4. Repeat this step and pick the alignments one at a time (there are four).

5. Repeat the step again, picking the layout profiles from the Carson's Way and Rose Drive profile views.

6. Repeat this step one more time, picking the two pipe networks.

7. Repeat for the last time, picking either of the view frames to make the Data Shortcuts palette look like Figure 17.3.

8. Click Export Data Shortcuts To File

9. Browse to the desktop, and click Save to create the `Creating Shortcuts.xml` file.

Congratulations, you have now created a shortcut file. Selecting individual items is tedious and can be difficult when multiple objects exist in the same confined space.

FIGURE 17.3

The Data Shortcuts palette in Panorama

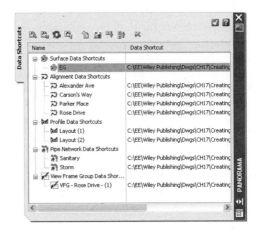

XML NOTEPAD

XML Notepad is a free and easy way to view and edit XML files. Although XML files are readable in any text editor, XML Notepad (or any other XML reader) understands the headers and will break apart the various data branches accordingly. It makes the process of understanding the file much easier.

Now, we'll examine the shortcut file.

1. Open the `Creating Shortcuts.xml` file with XML Notepad.

2. Expand the first Shortcut ➤ Criteria ➤ Object branches, as shown in Figure 17.4.

3. Expand the other shortcut branches, and you can review all of the pointers to the profiles, surface, and pipe networks, and view the frame groups.

FIGURE 17.4

Exploring the Creating Shortcuts.xml file in XML Notepad

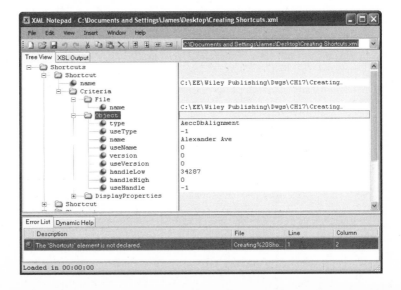

The XML file contains not only the name of the parent drawing, but also pointer information to the specific object. The object type describes the object, and the object handleLow describes the object within the host drawing's database of AutoCAD objects. It's this combination of data attributes that allows another drawing file to point back to the parent for information. Interestingly enough, changing the object name in the source Civil 3D file will change the object name in destination files, but the link will still point to the correct original object.

This file is self-contained, but two problems come to mind with this organization scheme. First, it's difficult to tell what is in the XML file on the basis of its name. Second, all of these shortcuts will load into a destination file. Even if references are not created, this is more information than is needed to pull out the pipes or alignments individually. Let's look at another way of creating and managing shortcuts.

Object Type-Based Shortcuts

The second common approach to data shortcuts is to break apart the shortcuts by object type or purpose. This means creating more XML shortcut files, but each one serves a distinct purpose. In this exercise, we'll create a second data shortcut file:

1. Open the Creating Shortcuts.dwg file if you've closed it.

2. Select General ➤ Data Shortcuts ➤ Edit Data Shortcuts to display the Data Shortcuts palette in Panorama.

3. Delete any shortcuts from the previous exercise by using the Delete Data Shortcut tool ✖ . Don't delete the alignments! They have to be deleted one at a time, just like they were added.

4. Add the alignments using the Create Data Shortcut By Selection tool 🔲 . Your palette should look like Figure 17.5.

5. Click Export Data Shortcuts To File 🔲 on the Data Shortcut palette.

6. Browse to the desktop and change the filename to **Alignments.xml**.

7. Click Save to create the new Alignments.xml shortcut file.

8. Remove the alignments from the shortcut list.

FIGURE 17.5
Data shortcuts with
only alignments
selected

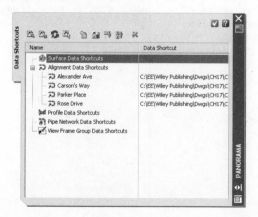

9. Add the EG surface to the shortcut list.

10. Export to the desktop again, creating `Surfaces.xml`.

By using separate shortcut files for each component of the design, it is easier for someone else to pick a relevant file and create the required shortcuts. We'll step through making shortcuts in the next section.

Using Data Shortcuts

Now that you've created the shortcut XML files to act as pointers back to the original drawing, let's use them in other ways and locations. Once a reference is in place, it's a simple matter to update the reference and see any changes in the original file reflected in the reference object. In this section, we'll look at creating and exploring these references, and then learn about updating or editing them.

Creating Shortcut References

Shortcut references are made using the same palette as we used to create the shortcut XML file. In this exercise, we'll import the previously made XML files to a new drawing and then create references:

1. Create a new drawing from the Imperial Extended template, and save it as **References.dwg** in a convenient location.

2. Select General ➢ Data Shortcuts ➢ Edit Data Shortcuts to display the Data Shortcuts palette in Panorama.

3. Click Import Data Shortcuts From File .

4. Navigate to the desktop and select the `Alignments.xml` file made in the previous exercise.

5. Expand the Alignment Data Shortcuts branch and your palette should look like Figure 17.6.

6. Right-click Alexander Ave and select Create Reference. The Create Alignment Reference dialog appears.

7. Set the Alignment style to Proposed and the Alignment Label Set to Major Minor And Geometry Points.

FIGURE 17.6
The Alignments.xml shortcut file loaded into a new file

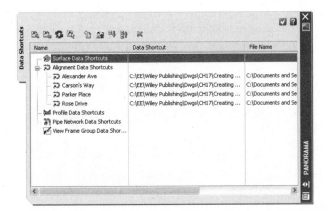

8. Click OK.

9. Perform a Zoom Extents to find this new alignment.

10. Repeat steps 6–8 for the other three alignments in the shortcuts list. When complete, your screen should look similar to Figure 17.7.

FIGURE 17.7
Completed creation of
alignments references

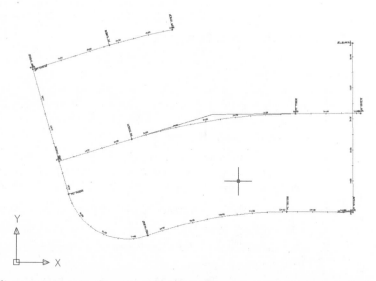

Each of these alignments is a simply a pointer back to the original file. They can be stylized, stationed, or labeled, but the definition of the alignment cannot be changed. This is more clearly illustrated in a surface, so let's add a surface reference now.

1. If you have closed the Data Shortcut palette, select General ➢ Data Shortcuts ➢ Edit Data Shortcuts to display the Data Shortcuts palette in Panorama.

2. Click Import Data Shortcuts From File .

3. Select the Surfaces.xml file from the desktop. Your palette should look like Figure 17.8. Note that the alignment files are still listed. You can load as many shortcut files as you like in a drawing to create the data you need.

4. Right-click the EG surface and select Create Reference. The Create Surface Reference dialog appears.

WHAT'S IN A NAME?

We mentioned earlier that the name in the XML file doesn't seem to have much effect on the creation of references; however, it does seem to have some effect on their maintenance. Some users have reported issues with broken references when they changed the name of an object during the Create Reference part of the process. No one seems to have a good feel for why it happens, but we wouldn't test it out. Leave the name alone during the Create Reference step!

FIGURE 17.8

Surfaces.xml loaded into the active drawing

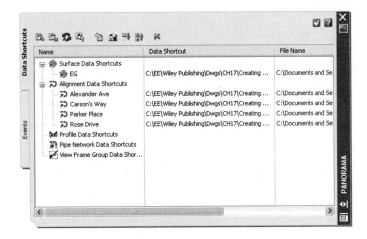

5. Change the Surface Style to Contours 1 & 5 Background, and then click OK. Your screen should look like Figure 17.9.

6. Close the Data Shortcuts palette by clicking the green checkbox.

7. Expand the Surfaces branch of Prospector and the EG surface as shown in Figure 17.10.

8. Right-click the EG surface and select Surface Properties.

FIGURE 17.9

The EG surface reference

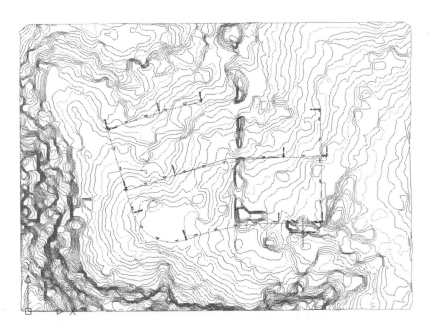

FIGURE 17.10

The EG surface in
Prospector and
the EG Surface
Properties dialog

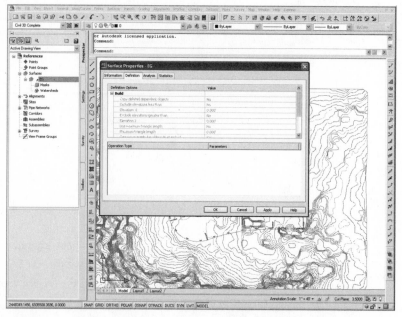

Here are a couple of important things to note:

♦ The small arrow next to the EG surface name indicates that the surface is a shortcut.

♦ There's no Definition branch under the EG surface. Additionally, in the Surface Properties dialog, the entire Definition tab is grayed out, making it impossible to change by using a shortcut.

To make a reference into a live object in the current drawing, simply right-click its name and select Promote. This breaks the link to the source information and creates an editable object in the current drawing.

Now that we've created a file with a group of references, we will look at how changes in the source drawing are reflected in this file.

 Real World Scenario

DO I NEED TO KNOW THIS?

Yes, actually you do. We generally prefer to use Vault as our project-management scheme, but there are times and situations where using data shortcuts is the only real solution. Let's look at a couple of cases where in spite of using Vault, we've used data shortcuts to pull the proverbial rabbit out of the hat.

When working with Vault, a drawing is typically attached to a particular project. While this generally isn't a problem, it does limit your resources somewhat. When you have a multiphase project that has been divided in Vault, it is impossible to use the Vault mechanism to grab information from a drawing that is not part of the set project.

To get around this limitation, use a shortcut! Go into the file containing the desired object and export out a shortcut. Then, in the target file, you can import the data shortcut and reference the data accordingly. As the source file changes, the shortcut will update, keeping the two phases in synchronization.

Many firms just starting out with Civil 3D will try to put too much in one drawing. Since the program can handle it, why shouldn't they? This is fine until they run into a deadline at the end of the project. With no real sharing methodology in place, it becomes almost impossible to split up the work.

Even if you don't want to get into sharing data at that point in the job, you can use the data shortcut mechanism to break out individual pieces to other files. Once a shortcut has been created in the target file, right-click on the object name in Panorama and select Promote, as shown in the graphic.

The act of promoting a shortcut breaks the link with the original data, and isn't a recommended practice, but sometimes the deadlines win. When it's time to get the project out the door, you do what works!

Updating and Managing References

As it is, if the reference were just a copy of the original data, we'd have done nothing more than cut and paste the object from one drawing to another. The benefit of using shortcuts is just like XRefs: when a change is made in the source, it's reflected in the reference drawing. In this section, we'll make a few changes and look at the updating process, then we'll see how to add to the shortcut XML files and how to avoid mistakes in that process.

UPDATING THE SOURCE AND REFERENCE

When it's necessary to make a change, it can be sometimes be confusing to remember which file we were in when we originally created a now-referenced object. Thankfully, we can use the tools in the Data Shortcut palette to jump back to that file, make the changes, and refresh the reference all very simply:

1. Still in the drawing with our references created, reopen the Data Shortcut palette.

2. Right-click Alexander Ave (the north-south alignment on the right-hand side of the drawing), and select Open Source Drawing.

3. Make a grip-edit to Alexander Ave's northern end, dragging it up and further north, as shown in Figure 17.11.

4. Save the drawing.

   Once a change is made in the source drawing, Civil 3D will synchronize references the next time they are opened. In the current exercise, the reference drawing is already open. Let's see how that the alert mechanism works in this situation.

5. Using the Window menu, select the `References.dwg` to make it active. An alert bubble like Figure 17.12 should appear.

6. Click Synchronize in the alert bubble to bring your drawing current with the design file. Your drawing will update, and the Alexander Ave alignment will reflect the change in the source.

This change is simple enough and works well once file relationships are established. But suppose there is a change in the file structure of the source information and you need to make a change? We'll look at that in the next section.

FIGURE 17.11
Grip-editing
Alexander Ave

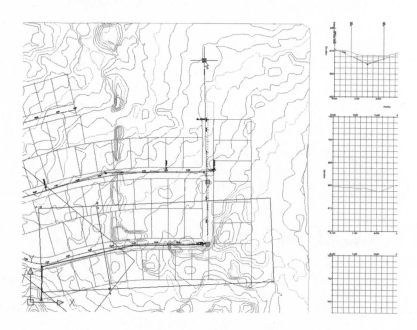

FIGURE 17.12
Data reference change
alert bubble

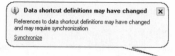

MANAGING CHANGES IN THE SOURCE DATA

Designs change often—there's no question about that. And using shortcuts to keep all the members of the design team on the same page is a great idea. But in the scene we're playing out, what happens if new, additional alignment data is added to the source file? We'll explore that in this exercise.

1. Return to the `Creating Shortcuts.dwg`.

2. Create a new alignment, named Carson Extension, extending from the end of Carson's Way to intersect with the now extended Alexander Ave. Your screen should look like Figure 17.13, with the new alignment circled.

3. Save the file.

FIGURE 17.13

Carson Extension
alignment drawn
and completed

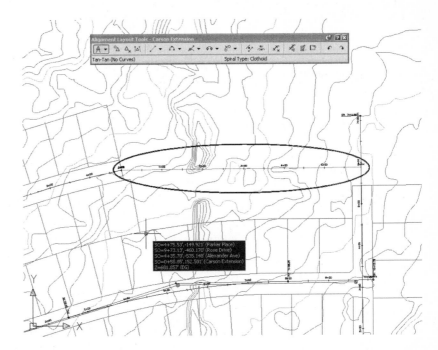

If we were to simply create a shortcut file for this new entry, it would possibly overwrite the original shortcut information, something we want to avoid. There are two ways to handle the problem. We can create a new Alignments.xml, being sure to include all of the original data, or we can make a new XML file and then append that to the original Alignments.xml file using XML Notepad. Pick *one* of the approaches shown here, and follow the instructions to complete the exercise.

Option A: Overwrite the Alignments.xml file:

1. Open the Data Shortcuts palette.

2. Remove the EG surface shortcut.

3. Import Alignments.xml as we did when creating references. Remember, XML files are just text, and importing the original file into the current file ensures that we don't forget any alignments when we export it again.

4. Click Create Data Shortcut By Selection 🔲 , and pick the Carson Extension. Your dialog should look like Figure 17.14. Note that the Carson Extension doesn't have information in the File Name column since it has not been exported yet.

5. Click Export Data Shortcuts To File 🔲 and select the Alignments.xml file. Confirm the overwriting of the existing file to complete the action.

FIGURE 17.14

Import the Alignments.xml file and then add the Carson Extension alignment.

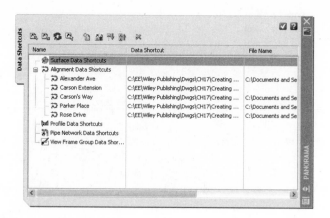

Option B: Append `Alignments.xml` with XML Notepad:

1. Open the Data Shortcuts palette.

2. Remove the EG surface shortcut.

3. Click Create Data Shortcut By Selection 📇 , and pick the Carson Extension.

4. Export a new shortcut file to the desktop. Call it **`Align2.xml`**.

5. Open `Alignments.xml` and `Align2.xml` in XML Notepad.

6. In the `Align2.xml` file, right-click the shortcut branch and select Copy.

7. In the `Alignments.xml` file, right-click the Shortcuts branch and select Paste to add the Carson Extension information to the `Alignments.xml` file.

8. Save and close both XML files.

Both of these methods wind up with an `Alignments.xml` that contains the same information. It is purely a matter of choice. This is also a good demonstration of how easy it is to make changes to the XML files with XML Notepad. Now that `Alignments.xml` is updated, we'll refresh the file in the references drawing:

1. Switch to the `References.dwg` and open the Data Shortcuts palette.

2. Click Import Data Shortcuts From File 📇 and select `Alignments.xml`.

3. The Carson Extension is now an option under the Alignments branch on the Data Shortcuts palette.

4. Right-click the Carson Extension alignment and select Create Reference as before.

By using shortcuts to handle and distribute design information, it's quite simple to keep adding information to the design as it progresses. It's important to remember that saving a file does not update the shortcut files created from the objects it contains.

The Bottom Line

List the project elements available for sharing through data shortcuts and those that cannot. The ability to load design information into a project environment is an important part of creating an efficient team. The main design elements of the project are available to the data shortcut mechanism, but some still are not.

Master It   List the top-level branches in Prospector that cannot be shared through data shortcuts.

Create a data shortcut file from Civil 3D objects.   Just creating a Civil 3D object isn't enough to share it using data shortcuts. You still have to go through the process of creating a shortcut file and exporting the linking information to allow other users to reference and analyze your data.

Master It   Open the `Creating Shortcuts.dwg` file and create an `Utility.xml` shortcut file for both of the pipe networks contained in that drawing.

Import a data shortcut and create references.   Once a shortcut has been created to a design element, references can be made and managed. Team members should be communicating that these files have been created and cognizant of not overwriting them with bad information. Creating and managing references is the most critical part of keeping project team members in sync with one another.

Master It   Create a new drawing, and create references to both the EG surface and a pipe network.

Chapter 18

Behind the Scenes: Autodesk Data Management Server

Data sharing in Civil 3D 2008 can be accomplished with two methods: the data shortcuts reviewed in Chapter 17, or via Vault and Autodesk Data Management Server. Vault brings true project management into play but requires a fair amount of behind-the-scenes machinery. In this chapter, we'll look at the server component of this equation. The Autodesk Data Management Server (ADMS) handles much of the file interaction that data shortcuts require but brings its own set of criteria to the table.

In this chapter, you'll learn to:

◆ Recommend a basic ADMS and SQL installation methodology

◆ Create multiple vaults, users, and user groups

◆ Manage working folders

What Is Vault?

Vault is a document management system initially created by Autodesk for the manufacturing industry. As Civil 3D evolved and a more robust project management tool was required beyond the Data Shortcut mechanism in Civil 3D 2006, the Autodesk developers decided that the concepts and mechanics of Vault could be applied across the board. The adoption of Vault as a platform-wide project management system meant that each product team could take the platform tool and use it to make their product stronger. Autodesk created ADMS to be the solution for all the products. Let's first take a look at how ADMS operates at a high level, and then we'll explore some of the options in the creation of an ADMS server and the database it runs on.

SPECIAL NOTE ABOUT THIS CHAPTER AND THE NEXT

ADMS and Vault are very specific and process oriented. In each of these chapters, each exercise will build on the previous. In some figures, you might note that the author is using a second machine to handle ADMS duties instead of installing to the local machine. In cases where this makes a difference in the images, we will attempt to note this. Finally, the installation of ADMS requires Windows permissions and may require making changes to your local Windows system configuration. We'll attempt to note these areas, but in a corporate environment, please visit your systems administrator before making these changes.

ADMS and Vault

Civil 3D uses the Vault mechanism to handle the standard document management issues such as versioning and user rights, but also to handle creating and managing the links between project data items such as alignments, surfaces, and pipe networks. Vault is the front end to ADMS that most users will see and use.

The basic breakdown is as shown in Figure 18.1. Data created on Vault clients is "checked in" to the project. This data is copied to the ADMS file store, and a record of the transaction is stored in the database. As another client requests that data, a lookup is made in the database and the relevant information is pulled from the file store and "checked out" to the requesting client. ADMS handles the tracking of these transactions as well as security and version issues, and acts as the management tool for both the file store and the database. It's important to note that in most installations, ADMS, the file store, and the database are all on one machine. They can be distributed to other machines, but that is an advanced installation and will not be covered in this text.

ADMS? WHAT HAPPENED TO VAULT SERVER?

With 2008, the naming convention changed, and Vault Server became ADMS. Vault is the front end that Civil 3D uses to interact with the ADMS. Nothing quite like a straightforward naming convention.

FIGURE 18.1
ADMS and Vault
client schematic

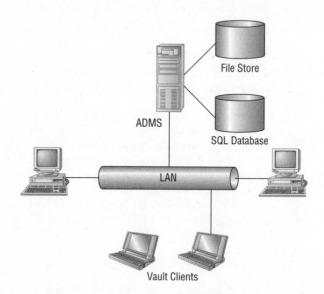

ADMS and SQL

The ADMS platform has two main options for installation. The first is based on Microsoft SQL Server Express 2005 (which we'll refer to as Express from now on) and is designed for individuals or small groups. This alternative is free, and is included on the Civil 3D installation media. The second option is to use a full Microsoft SQL Server in one of its dedicated flavors: Workgroup, Standard, or Enterprise. Let's take a look at the main differences:

Express   Limited to one processor and can access only 1GB of RAM. The database itself is limited to 4GB in size. Express will allow a fair number of users, but the performance limits of the processor and RAM make using it beyond 30–40 users a pretty undesirable state. Additionally, because Express is often installed on spare workstations or on a user's workstation, the Windows XP limit of 10 concurrent users comes into play. In spite of these limits, most small engineering firms find that using Express is a fine solution, especially when just getting into the process.

Workgroup, Standard, or Enterprise Edition   Designed for larger firms. These incarnations typically sit on dedicated servers with multiple processors where the memory is limited only by the OS. The database size is unlimited, and the functional limits of the database are dependent on hardware more than the software.

Because the nature of full SQL installations reaches beyond the scope of this text, we will use the default ADMS installation of Express in both this chapter and Chapter 19. For more information on the various flavors of SQL Server, visit Microsoft's website as well as Autodesk's. Both offer great information pertaining to the SQL Server version selection.

HOW MUCH SERVER DO I REALLY NEED?

The hardware requirements for ADMS are surprisingly low. Many firms become scared off of looking at Vault and ADMS because their trusted advisors in the hardware and software realm are telling them they need to invest in these huge dedicated servers built for launching the space shuttle. Don't buy it. Express in a pilot project environment or small workgroup can be run from an old AutoCAD workstation! The "second" machine that this chapter's ADMS is installed on is actually a virtual machine running XP, and there are engineering firms using virtual servers to run larger installations. You can also upgrade if you outgrow the Express edition. Don't let the misinformation out there scare you from using Vault!

With the growth of the open software movement, one common complaint is that ADMS will only function on a Microsoft SQL platform. While there have been numerous inquiries about using Oracle or MySQL databases along with ODBC connections, these are not supported solutions. You *might* be able to get it to run, but you are definitely in unsupported territory, and will have no help available if something goes wrong. Stick with Microsoft on this one, even if you don't on other Enterprise solutions.

Installing ADMS

ADMS installation is included on the Civil 3D installation disc. The process is straightforward but requires a few things be in place: Internet Information Services (IIS), .NET Framework 2.0, MSXML 6, and the Microsoft WSE 3.0 Runtime. Don't worry if none of these sound familiar! Most of these components are installed as part of the ADMS process, and if there are issues, you will receive a warning during the preinstall system checks. Let's perform a standard Vault install, walking through the settings:

1. Load the Civil 3D media and launch `Setup.exe`.

2. Click Install Products, and then click Next.

3. Select the Autodesk Data Management Server 2008 option, as shown in Figure 18.2. If you are adding to an existing Civil 3D installation on your local machine, the other options will already be checked and unavailable. Then click Next to begin installation.

4. Accept the License Agreement and click Next.

5. Enter a first and last name and organization and click Next.

6. Click Configure, shown circled in Figure 18.3, to display the ADMS Server 2008 installation options.

Because ADMS can be used in a variety of scenarios, ranging from the single engineer office to the multinational design firm, there are a number of configuration options that can be set during the installation. The configuration process allows for customization on the basis of your needs. In our case, we won't be modifying many settings since the default is for the small local user, but let's take a look at them.

Figure 18.4 shows the first page of the ADMS installation options. There are two pages of options and a confirmation page. The first page features these major options:

Use Local SQL or Use Remote SQL The only instance where using remote SQL is an option is when used in conjunction with Autodesk Product Stream Replicator. This is a new product for 2008 that allows the distribution of project data across a WAN. Replicator is outside the scope of this text, but you can find more information at Autodesk's website or by contacting qualified consultants.

FIGURE 18.2
Select the ADMS installation.

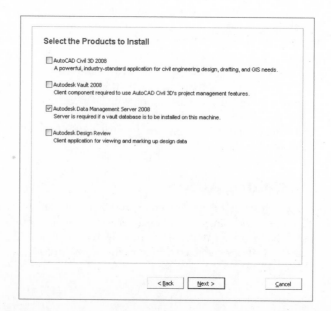

Select the Products to Install

☐ AutoCAD Civil 3D 2008
   A powerful, industry-standard application for civil engineering design, drafting, and GIS needs.

☐ Autodesk Vault 2008
   Client component required to use AutoCAD Civil 3D's project management features.

☑ Autodesk Data Management Server 2008
   Server is required if a vault database is to be installed on this machine.

☐ Autodesk Design Review
   Client application for viewing and marking up design data

                             < Back   Next >   Cancel

Specify Location Of SQL Installation Folder and Specify Location Of SQL Database You can change the location of the installation folder, but doing so will make it more difficult for any support personnel to assist. Don't change these values unless you have a very good reason.

Use My SQL Credentials If you are using another SQL installation or you are in a Replicator environment, it may be necessary to sign into the SQL database using something other than the default Autodesk security values. Enter this information here if needed. Again, don't change it unless you must.

FIGURE 18.3
The ADMS
Configuration
screen

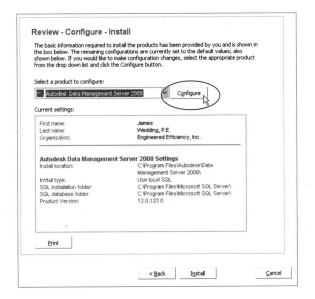

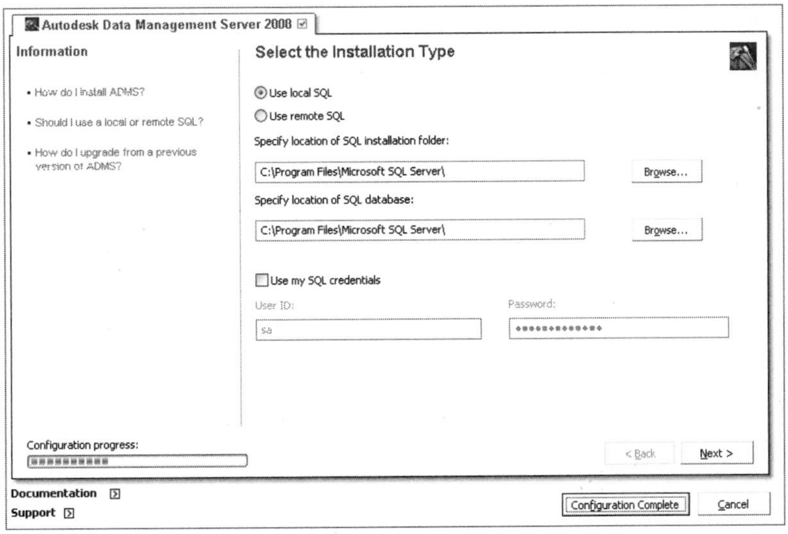

FIGURE 18.4
ADMS configuration
options

Clicking Next will take you to the second page of the ADMS configuration (Figure 18.5), which deals with ADMS preferences. The only option requiring explanation is the Interactive Mode For 'ADMS System Check.' There are three options: always showing interactive mode, only at failure, or only at failure and warnings. This setting determines the amount of feedback given to you during the installation process. As ADMS attempts to install, if it finds issues or fails at any point, it offers a message to alert you. This is definitely worth watching!

1. Let's continue with the installation:

2. Change the Interactive Mode For 'ADMS System Check' to Always Show Interactive Interface, then click Next.

3. Click Configuration Complete.

4. Verify your settings on the screen and click Install to begin copying the files to the local machine. ADMS will install the list of components shown in Figure 18.6. Because we selected Always Show Interactive Interface, the install process stops midway through to give the report shown in Figure 18.6.

5. Verify there are no actions required and that the warnings shown are acceptable. There are a large number of possible issues here—be sure to read and understand them! The ADMS documentation is quite good; refer to it for more detailed troubleshooting.

6. Click Continue if the results are acceptable.

7. Get a cup of coffee. This can take a few minutes. You might have time to run to Starbucks, depending on your system speed.

FIGURE 18.5
More ADMS configuration options

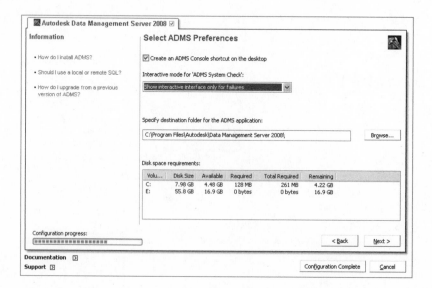

8. When the install completes, Figure 18.7 will appear. Uncheck the option View The Autodesk Data Management Server 2008 Readme, unless you'd like to read it now.

9. Click Finish to exit the installation program.

ADMS is now installed, ready to manage all of your Civil 3D projects.

FIGURE 18.6
ADMS Installation and System Readiness results

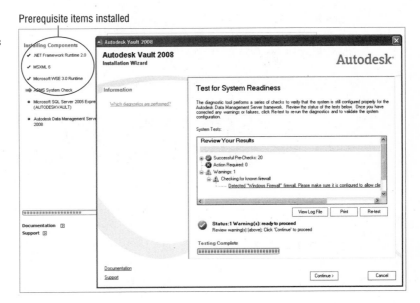

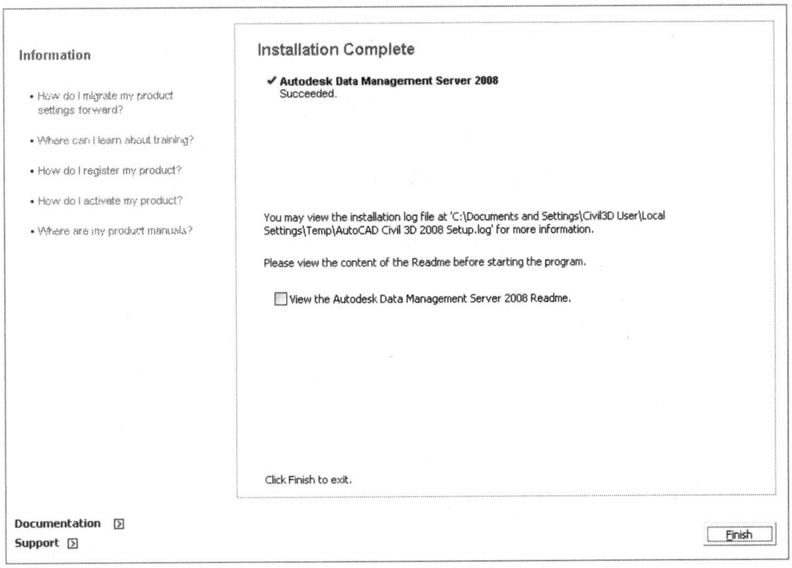

FIGURE 18.7
Completed ADMS installation

🌐 Real World Scenario

OPENING THE DOORS TO ADMS

At its heart, ADMS uses standard Internet protocols to communicate. This is why IIS is a requirement and part of the system check. This change to your OS basically creates a web server that handles much of the communication back and forth between ADMS and the Vault clients. This is great when you're installing on a server; they're typically set to perform this communication anyway. In the case of the small office or a test case like we're building here, however, XP is often used as the host OS. In this case the Windows XP Firewall that came with SP2 will probably get in the way. Let's take care of that now.

1. On the ADMS computer, select Start ➢ Control Panel ➢ Security Center to open the Windows Security Center dialog.

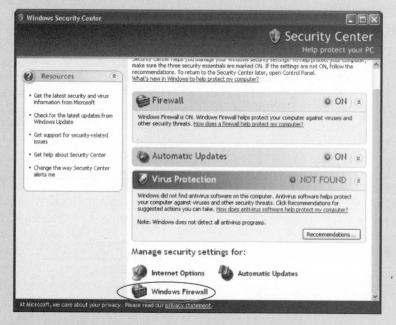

2. Click on the Windows Firewall option to open the Windows Firewall dialog.

3. Switch to the Exceptions tab.

4. Click the Add Port button to display the Add A Port dialog. Enter **ADMS** in the Name text box and **80** in the Port Number text box.

5. Click OK once to close the Add A Port dialog, and then again to close the Windows Firewall dialog.

ADMS should now be accessible from other machines on your network. We'll verify that using Vault Explorer later in this chapter.

Managing ADMS

Two components that allow interaction with ADMS are ADMS Console and Vault Explorer. These two programs focus on different management tools within the system, so we'll look at them independently in the next few sections.

ADMS Console

ADMS Console is only installed during the ADMS installation. This program manages the ADMS and starts and stops the Windows services behind the scenes, creates vaults, and performs data auditing at the database level. ADMS Console is a complex program, and there are a large number of functions that simply fall outside the scope of this book. Let's look at the pieces to getting a Civil 3D vault and project up and running.

1. Launch ADMS by selecting the desktop icon or by selecting Start ➢ All Programs ➢ Autodesk ➢ Autodesk Data Management ➢ ADMS Console 2008.

2. The program will present a login when launched. The default settings are a username of Administrator and no password. We will use these settings for this book, but you should probably change them before you go live with ADMS. Allowing normal users access to the Administrator is not a good security policy.

3. Click OK to log in and you'll be presented with the screen of the active ADMS as shown in Figure 18.8. Note that the text "on MASTERING" near the top center of the figure refers to the name of the host computer. Your install will be different.

FIGURE 18.8
The ADMS Console
2008 screen

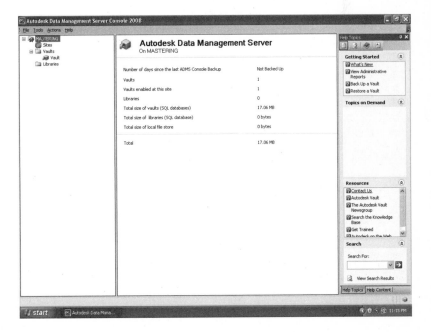

The main things to note on this screen are the Total Size of Vaults and Total Size Of Local File Store values. When the total size of the vaults begins to get near 3GB, it's time to consider moving to a full SQL version instead of Express. When the server itself begins to complain about file storage or disk space, take a look at Total Size Of Local File Store. This is the storage being used by record copies of all the files checked into the ADMS.

When the total size begins to grow to a level that makes the IT folks unhappy, it's time to purge the vault. This can be done manually or with scripts. Because of the complex nature of the operation, we're going to point you to the excellent help and online resources for dealing with ADMS and vault maintenance. Within ADMS Console, search Help for backup and you'll be in the right direction.

CREATING AND MANAGING VAULTS

In the left pane of Figure 18.10 is an Explorer-like interface to help navigate through the various vaults on the ADMS machine. Sites are only involved with Replicator-based installations, and Civil 3D does not use libraries, so we will ignore them in these exercises. During installation, a vault is created in the ADMS. This default vault is named Vault, which can lead to some confusion, so let's create another.

1. Select Vaults in the left pane.

2. Select Actions ➢ Create to display the Create Vault dialog, shown in Figure 18.9.

3. In the New Vault Name text box, enter the name **Melinda**.

MELINDA?

Yes, Melinda. When you are creating vaults for your office, you can name them anything you like. It doesn't matter too much as long as you and the other users know which vault is which. Common practice involves naming vaults for office locations, clients, or years. It's entirely up to you.

---

4. Click OK and wait for a confirmation message that "Vault 'Melinda' was successfully created."

5. Click OK again to dismiss the message. Melinda will now show in the Vaults collection in the left pane.

6. Select Melinda to display the summary pane in the middle of the console, as shown in Figure 18.10.

FIGURE 18.9
Creating a new vault

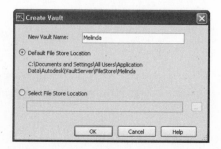

FIGURE 18.10
Summary of the
Melinda vault

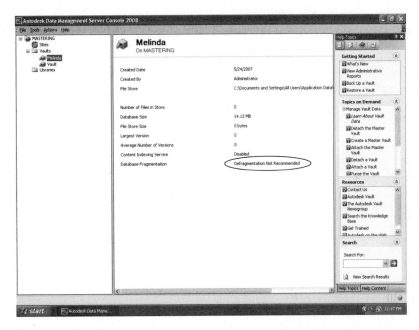

The information displayed in the summary pane can help determine the strategy for purging or defragmenting this vault. Purging is only required when the File Store Size value becomes unacceptable to the IT staff that allocates drive space. The need for defragmenting of the vault database will be indicated by a message in the lower right. This area is circled in Figure 18.10, indicating that defragmentation is not recommended at this time. This makes sense because we just created the vault. Vault-specific tasks are available by right-clicking the vault name in the left pane and selecting from the context menu.

CREATING AND MANAGING USERS

One of the primary functions of implementing ADMS and Vault is to create a log of changes and version tracking within the Civil 3D environment. To perform these types of data audits, transactions must be tied to individual users. In this exercise, we'll make a series of users so that we can use them in other exercises and in Chapter 19, when we're interacting with the vault from within Civil 3D.

1. From the ADMS Console 2008, select Tools ➤ Administration to display the Administration dialog.

2. Select the Security tab and click Users to display the User Management console.

3. Click New User on the right side to display the User Profile dialog, shown in Figure 18.11.

4. Enter the user information as shown in Figure 18.11 for the new user Jolene. Enter **jolene**, all lowercase, as the password.

5. Click Roles to display the Add Roles dialog.

6. Check the Vault Editor role. We want all Civil 3D users to be able to check files in and out of the vault, so they need to be vault editors. Then click OK.

7. Click Vaults, check the Melinda vault, then click OK.

8. Click OK.

9. Repeat the process and create a user named Jim as a vault editor in the Melinda vault.

10. In the User Management dialog, select the Card radio button in the View area on the upper right to get the User Management screen shown in Figure 18.12.

11. Click OK once to close the User Management dialog and then again to close the Administration dialog.

FIGURE 18.11
Creating a
new vault user

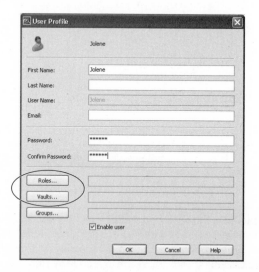

FIGURE 18.12
Users created and
assigned to roles
and vaults

ADMS isn't the place to try and manage security. All too often it happens that a user will leave the office for what's expected to be a short period and is gone all day. In this situation, you should make it easy for one of their peers to check a drawing back in without involving the full IT staff by changing passwords or other things. For this reason, vault passwords are commonly made simple. Windows or network passwords should be your security method!

CREATING GROUPS

Civil 3D can also limit certain users from accessing certain folders from within the project. It's common for surveyors and engineers to want to limit the amount of access the other group has to their information. In the case of items such as a plat, it can be a legal issue. Instead of having to control access by individual user (not bad with 10, inconceivable with 1,000), you can use groups to handle security levels. Let's make a few groups to help manage our design teams:

1. Select Tools ➤ Administration to display the Administration dialog.

2. Click Groups to display the Groups dialog.

3. Click New on the right to display the Group dialog, shown in Figure 18.13.

4. Enter **Engineering** for a group name.

5. Click Roles and select Vault Editor as we did with the users earlier.

6. Click Vaults and select Melinda as we did with the users earlier.

7. Click Add to select members in the Add Members dialog, shown in Figure 18.14.

8. Select Jim and click Add.

9. Select Jolene and click Add. You could also use Ctrl-click to select multiple users at once.

10. Click OK to close each dialog.

FIGURE 18.13
Completed
Group dialog

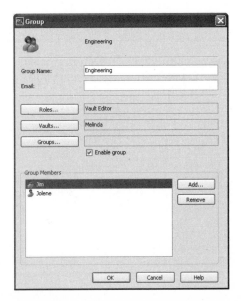

FIGURE 18.14

Add Members dialog

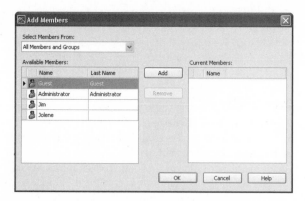

The creation of a single group will suffice for now. Most ADMS computers are managed by IT staff, where the CAD management group may or may not have access to the console. For this reason, we'll complete building our User and Groups objects via the control that is installed with Civil 3D: Vault Explorer.

Accessing Vaults via Vault Explorer

Most user interaction with ADMS will be through the Vault Explorer (VE) program. In addition to controlling users and groups, VE allows for other file-level management and review. We'll first look at more user administration and then file management.

VE is installed with Civil 3D, if it was selected during the initial installation. If not, you can add it by using Add/Remove Programs and selecting the Autodesk Vault product, as shown in Figure 18.15. Once Autodesk Vault is installed, you should have a desktop icon for Autodesk Vault Explorer 2008.

Logging into the vault is where the firewall issue can rear its head in a small office installation, so let's verify our connection before we go any further:

1. Double-click the Autodesk Vault Explorer icon on your desktop, or select Start ➤ All Programs ➤ Autodesk ➤ Autodesk Data Management ➤ Autodesk Vault Explorer 2008.

2. At VE startup, you'll see a Welcome screen similar to Figure 18.16. The three large buttons on the left are short help files that point you in other directions. Click Log In on the lower right to display the Log In dialog.

FIGURE 18.15

Adding Autodesk Vault to an existing Civil 3D install

> Select the Products to Install
>
> ☑ AutoCAD Civil 3D 2008
> A powerful, industry-standard application for civil engineering design, drafting, and GIS needs.
>
> ☑ Autodesk Vault 2008
> Client component required to use AutoCAD Civil 3D's project management features.
>
> ☐ Autodesk Data Management Server 2008
> Server is required if a vault database is to be installed on this machine.
> Autodesk Data Management Server 2008 is already installed.
>
> ☑ Autodesk Design Review
> Client application for viewing and marking up design data

FIGURE 18.16
Vault Explorer Welcome splash screen

3. In the User Name text box, enter **Administrator**. The password is blank for now.

4. In the Server text box, enter the name of your ADMS computer, or local host if you have installed it locally.

5. Click the ellipsis button circled in Figure 18.17 to bring up the Databases dialog. At this point, if all is well with the world, you will see Melinda and Vault both listed as options.

6. Select Melinda and click OK to return to the Log In dialog.

7. Click OK to log in.

LOGGING IN AUTOMATICALLY

In Figure 18.17, there is an option for Automatically Log In Next Session that we do not check. Because we are logging in as the vault administrator, this is probably not an option we want to leave on. It opens up a security hole because anyone with access to the computer could log into VE with full privileges. For most day-to-day users, that isn't a problem. It's a good suggestion to have users check this option on their personal workstations so they don't have to go through the login process every time. The same option is available when logging in via the Civil 3D interface.

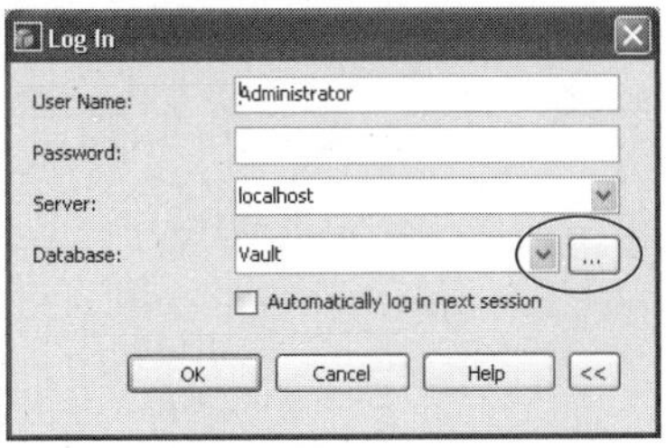

FIGURE 18.17
Vault Log In dialog

VE looks similar to the console application, but because it is focused on one vault instead of the server, you can only see information about a single vault and the project it contains. Managing users and groups is similar to the methods employed in the console, so we won't repeat them here. In the next section, we'll look at vault management through the VE interface.

Vault Management via Vault Explorer

Most of your daily interactions will be with the vaults, not the ADMS. Using VE from any station on the network, you can handle common management tasks such as managing users, project folders, and reviewing file versions. In this section, we'll look at a couple of important options in the VE interface, explore how to reach the same user and group functions as we did in the ADMS Console, and discuss Vault working folders.

Vault Options

Beyond the database side, there are a number of options available in how users interact with data in the vault. Vault options control many of the options, so let's look at what is available. Figure 18.18 shows the Options dialog accessed by selecting Tools ➤ Options.

The only one we'll concern ourselves with is the Show Working Folder Location option. Toggling this option displays the path of the working folder (discussed in the next section) in the head of the VE pane. The other options for dialog suppression can be set to let you blow past some warnings and dialogs while working in a vault environment. Once you are comfortable with the vault interface, you can consider shutting down some of these options, but it's not critical.

FIGURE 18.18
Options dialog with
two common options
selected

Vault Administration and Working Folder

The Administration panel in VE is similar to the ADMS Console, but it's not exactly the same. Because Vault and ADMS are used with a variety of programs, there are some options available that simply don't make complete sense in the Civil 3D market. Most users won't use the Enforce Unique File Names, Status, DWF Attachment Options, or File Properties option. Understanding the working folder is crucial to how Civil 3D with Vault works.

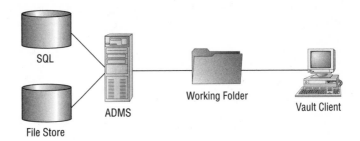

Figure 18.19 shows that the working folder acts as an intermediary between the ADMS and the Vault client. When a client requests a file from Vault, a query is made to the SQL database to check the status of that file (available for check-out, protected, and so on). If the request is allowable, then the file is copied to the working folder from the ADMS file store. The file store records that the file is checked out to the requesting user. The user can work with that file in the working folder as long as they like—opening, closing, making changes, saving as needed, all the normal tasks.

At the end of the day or when a critical part of the design has changed, the user checks the file back in. This check-in is what triggers the copying of the file in the working folder to the ADMS file store, and a new record is added to the SQL database. Now, let's set the options:

1. Launch and log into the Melinda vault.

2. Select Tools ➤ Administration to display the Administration dialog.

3. Switch to the Files tab (Figure 18.20).

4. Click Define, next to the Working Folder section, to display the Working Folder Options dialog, shown in Figure 18.21.

FIGURE 18.20
The Files tab in VE's
Administration dialog

FIGURE 18.21
Setting the
working folder

5. Select the Enforce Consistent Working Folder For All Clients radio button.

6. Set the path to C:\Mastering Projects\, as shown in Figure 18.21. This folder might not exist; typing it in will create it.

7. Click OK to close the dialog.

8. On the Administration dialog, change to the Security tab. Note that the options here are the same as they were on the console. Any user with a role of vault administrator can add users via this panel.

9. Close the Administration dialog.

MORE ON THE WORKING FOLDER

There are two schools of thought in setting the working folder. The first is to set it as in this process, letting each user have a local path to aid in speedy operations. The other idea is to set all users to point to a shared working folder, creating a common project repository. This creates a project structure similar to what more firms have in place prior to adopting ADMS, and is the authors' preferred methodology.

It's important to note that a change in the working folder enforcement will only kick in when a user logs out, then logs in again. When a login occurs after the enforcement has been set, users will receive an alert dialog that the path has been set. The administration panel of VE is similar to ADMS because it's still dealing with the database side at heart. There are some other Vault Explorer functions that we'll look at in Chapter 19 as we pull it all together.

The Bottom Line

Recommend a basic ADMS and SQL installation methodology. The complexity of corporate networks makes selecting the right combination of ADMS and Microsoft SQL software part of the challenge. Understanding the various flavors of SQL Server 2005 at a basic level, along with some limitations of the ADMS, will aid in selecting the right combination for your own needs.

Master It For each of the following descriptions, make some general recommendations for a general setup for their ADMS and SQL needs—for example, a 30-person engineering firm with two offices that rarely share project data. The solution might be a pair of SQL Express machines, one for each office, running a flavor of Windows Server to get around any limits on concurrent connections.

1. A 100-person engineering firm with one office.

2. A 15-person firm with three offices equally split. They share data constantly.

3. A 5-person engineering firm with one office.

Create multiple vaults, users, and user groups. The enterprise nature of ADMS means it can handle multiple sets of data and user inputs at once. By creating multiple vaults to help manage data, you can make life easier on end users. Creating logins to the ADMS for each user allows the tracking of file transactions, and creating groups makes security easier to handle.

Master It Create a new vault titled EE; add Mark, James, Dana, and Marc as users to this new vault. Additionally, make Marc a vault consumer, Mark and Dana vault editors, and James an administrator. Add an architecture group. Marc is the only architect; add the other new users to the engineering group.

Manage working folders. The working folder acts as your local desktop version of the file. Drawings are saved and edited within the working folder until checked back into the Vault. Enforcing the working folder will create a constant path for XRef information and make support easier.

Master It Set the working folder for the new EE vault to C:\EE Projects\. *Be sure to set this back to* C:\Mastering Projects *before beginning Chapter 19.*

Chapter 19

Teamwork: Vault Client and Civil 3D

Now it's time to pull it all together. Every chapter to this point has been focused on individual tasks or design elements. In this chapter, we'll look at using Vault to assemble the pieces into a complete set of plans. Although we won't create every single note on every sheet, we will attempt to look at the various plans and how they come together. We will discuss one possible workflow that has succeeded, and then look at the mechanics of populating the vault with design data for sharing, how changes and updates are handled, and finally, version tracking and restoration.

In this chapter, you'll learn to:

◆ Describe the differences between using Vault and data shortcuts

◆ Insert Civil 3D data into a vault

◆ Create data references

◆ Restore a previous version of a design file

Vault and Project Theory

When users begin to look into using Vault as their project management methodology, there can be a large number of questions. We looked at some of the infrastructure and setup concerns in Chapter 18, but let's focus on the two big questions that are left: Why use Vault instead of data shortcuts? And how does my team come together with Vault?

SPECIAL NOTE ABOUT THIS AND THE PREVIOUS CHAPTER

ADMS and Vault are very specific and process oriented. In each of these chapters, each exercise builds on the previous. In some figures, you might note that the author is using a second machine to handle ADMS duties instead of installing to the local machine. In cases where this makes a difference in the images, we will attempt to note this. Finally, the installation of ADMS requires Windows permissions and may require making changes to your local Windows system configuration. We'll attempt to note these areas, but in a corporate environment, please visit your systems administrator before making these changes.

Vault vs. Data Shortcuts

For many people this choice is the sticking point. They look at the low overhead of data shortcuts as discussed in Chapter 17 and see a simple solution that just works. Prior to Civil 3D 2007, data shortcuts were the only option for sharing data, so many users got comfortable with that model and have stuck with it. However, as you can see in Table 19.1, some functions simply aren't available in shortcuts.

Many users consider these differences trivial, but it is good to be aware of them. There are more apparent differences in the use and operation of the data once you're inside Civil 3D.

TABLE 19.1:   Vault Compared with Data Shortcuts

PRODUCT SHARING MECHANISM	VAULT	DATA SHORTCUTS
Reference of Civil 3D objects	X	X
Synchronizing of changes	X	X
Labeling of references	X	X
Locking source objects	X	X
Multioffice support	X	
Management of non-CAD data	X	
User controls	X	
Archives and backups	X	

Project Timing

Timing tends to be the biggest hurdle for people when making the transition to Civil 3D. You have myriad options for pulling it all together! XRefs, data shortcuts, and Vault all come into play. At the end of the day, it's likely you'll use all three to create your complete project. Let's look at the general schematic of the project before we get into the mechanics of using data references later in this chapter.

BUT THAT'S NOT HOW WE DO IT!

Before we wade too far into this discussion, remember, we're talking about one workflow that has worked for a fair number of Civil 3D users. It might not mesh perfectly with your office or project requirements. Workflow and data management are the most complex and flexible parts of the program and the reasons that we suggest getting qualified assistance when you take this task on. The adoption period of Civil 3D is a good time to evaluate the way that your office *does* do it and see if it still makes sense. Civil 3D really changes the game from a design side—is it any surprise it changes the way engineering teams work together?

Most engineering firms operate in a team environment, dividing labor as it makes sense from a training and cost-perspective angle:

◆ The project manager operates with very little knowledge of the CAD systems, but understands design, submittal requirements, and general project management.

◆ Designers do the bulk of the heavy lifting during the design process and generally have some level of CAD knowledge, but they may not be comfortable in using it as a design tool. These are typically highly experienced technicians that have moved to focus more on design or engineering.

◆ Technicians typically have less design knowledge but know how to put together a good set of plans. They are intimately familiar with the CAD system, creating most of the CAD work within the firm.

There are obviously exceptions to this broad generalization, but this breakdown of roles lets us examine the standard project timelines, conceptually illustrated in Figure 19.1.

In the past, using typical software meant that design processes wound up in a very linear state. Technicians didn't get involved until very late in the process because any change to the design would change so much of the labeling and other plan-level information that the technician's time would be wasted. Project managers had to wait until the documentation process was moving along to get a feel for the project and make sure the team members were on track. With this sort of project timeline, nothing was more dreaded than the last-minute change since it meant throwing out so much work. Lost work means lost time and lost profitability.

Working in the Civil 3D environment lets this timeline break apart and run in parallel. Because of the dynamic nature of the object model and labeling in Civil 3D, the technician can begin documentation shortly after the designer starts. Plans can be prepared for project manager review at a concept stage, understanding that the design is still in flux but looking for thoroughness of documentation, and adherence to and review of agency standards. The whole project timeline can be reduced, cutting days, weeks, or even months off the complete project timeline.

FIGURE 19.1
Comparing Civil 3D and other design software timelines

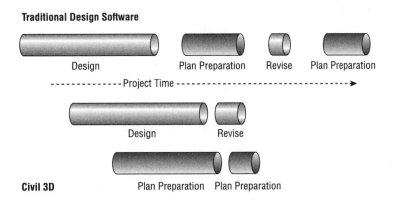

Project Workflow with Vault and Civil 3D

To achieve the shortening of the project timeline just discussed, the workflow has to change as well. Changing to a process where the tasks are running concurrently requires a different breakdown from prior software solutions. To make this process as efficient as possible, a breakdown of the process is more like that shown in Figure 19.2.

The concept is that design staff creates and models the Civil 3D design elements in the respective files. Upon pushing these files into the vault, design elements become available to project team members through Vault data references in addition to the standard AutoCAD XRef functionality. By using the Civil 3D objects to feed the creation of plan files, the technician can begin creating and labeling plans as soon as the first iteration of the design has been checked into the vault. Now let's take all this theory and put it to work using Vault inside of Civil 3D.

FIGURE 19.2
File and design infor-
mation breakdown

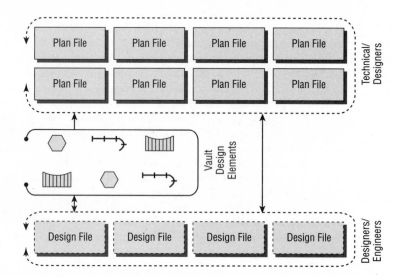

Feedback from the Vault

There's one last thing to look at before we step into actually working with Vault. While you use Vault in a project, you will often see icons next to drawing names. These icons indicate the status of the file in the working folder vs. the ADMS file store. Table 19.2 shows the possible icons and explains their meaning.

A similar table exists in the Civil 3D Help files. One good suggestion is printing that chart and placing it next to your monitor until you're familiar with these icons and what they mean to you.

Working in Vault

Using Vault with Civil 3D requires some mental effort. It is simply a new process for moving and sharing data within the team. In this section, we'll look at the mechanics of all this interaction, including setting up the project, checking data into the vault, and creating some data references.

TABLE 19.2:   Civil 3D Vault Status Icons

STATUS ICON	IS FILE CHECKED OUT?	FILE STORE VS. WORKING FOLDER	NOTES
○	No	In sync	
● (Green fill)	No	Working folder is newer	Usually means someone edited the file out of turn. Also known as a "dirty edit."
● (Red Fill)	No	File store is newer	Usually occurs when a previous version has been restored.
✓	Yes, to you	No working folder copy	
✓	Yes, to you	In sync	Occurs when you check out a file but have not made a save yet to update the local copy.
✓ (Green Fill)	Yes, to you	Working folder is newer	Occurs when you perform a local save on a checked-out drawing.
✓ (Red Fill)	Yes, to you	File store is newer	Occurs when restoring a previous version of the file.
✖	Yes, to someone else	No working folder copy	
✖	Yes, to someone else	In sync	
✖ (Green Fill)	Yes, to someone else	Working folder is newer	Can occur when someone else performs a save on a checked out drawing, and you are sharing a working folder on the network.
✖ (Red Fill)	Yes, to someone else	File store is newer	Someone else has checked this file out and then checked it back in. Your working folder is local, so you don't have the latest version in your working folder.

Preparing for Projects in Civil 3D

For most of the AutoCAD-based products, creating a folder in Vault Explorer is enough to generate a project available in the program. Not so with Civil 3D. Because of the project mechanism used to pass information from one drawing to another in Civil 3D, certain files must exist in a Vault folder for Civil 3D to recognize it as a valid project. First, let's set up a project template that matches our desired workflow; then we'll move to creating a project.

ESTABLISHING A PROJECT TEMPLATE

Civil 3D 2008 includes a mechanism for creating a typical project folder structure when working with Vault. By creating a blank copy of the folder structure we'd like to have in place for typical projects, we can use that as the starting point when a new project is created within Civil 3D.

1. Open Windows Explorer and navigate to C:\Civil 3D Project Templates.

2. Create a new folder titled Mastering.

3. Inside Mastering, create folders called Survey, Engineering, Architecture, Word, and Con Docs, as shown in Figure 19.3.

This structure will show inside Civil 3D, in the Working Folder when a project is created, and in Vault Explorer. We've included a Word folder as an example of other, non–Civil 3D–related folders you might have in your project setup for users outside the CAD team, such as accountants or the project manager. If you have any files in these folders, such as a project checklist spreadsheet, a blank contract, or images, they will be checked into new projects as they are created.

FIGURE 19.3
Creating a project template

CREATING A NEW CIVIL 3D PROJECT

With our project template in place, we can now use the Projects section of Prospector to create a project. Just a reminder: Projects created via Vault Explorer or any other clients will not appear in Prospector, since they are missing the magic files that we'll examine in the last part of this exercise.

1. Launch Civil 3D. Within Prospector, change the View dropdown at the top of the palette to Master View if it is not already.

2. Right-click the Projects branch in Prospector and select Log In.

3. Select your server or local host as appropriate and select the Melinda Database created in Chapter 18. Click OK to return to Civil 3D.

4. Right-click Projects again and notice the host of new options. Select New to bring up the New Project dialog shown in Figure 19.4.

5. Enter **Niblo** in the Name text box and select the `Mastering` Project Template as shown. Click OK to create the new Niblo project.

6. Expand Projects to reveal the project structure, as shown in Figure 19.5.

7. Launch Autodesk Vault Explorer and log in to the Melinda vault.

8. Select the `Niblo` folder, as shown in Figure 19.6.

FIGURE 19.4
Creating the
Niblo project

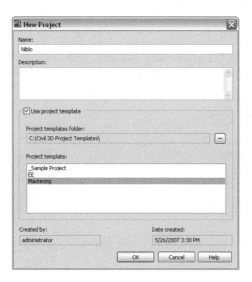

FIGURE 19.5
Prospector after creat-
ing the Niblo project
from the Mastering
project template

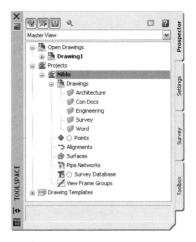

FIGURE 19.6
Niblo project viewed
in Autodesk Vault
Explorer

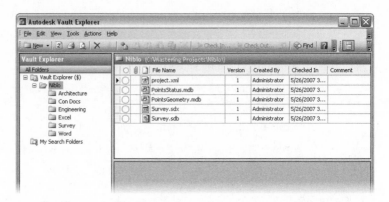

The files shown in the top-right pane of Autodesk Vault Explorer are the critical files for Civil 3D. Each file manages part of the project information that Civil 3D requires to operate. These files are the reason that you cannot simply create folders in Vault Explorer and expect them to show up in the Civil 3D Projects collection. However, once a project is created and these files exist, you can add folders if needed to flesh out a project structure.

1. Right-click Niblo in Vault Explorer and select New Folder.

2. Enter **Excel** for the name and click OK.

3. In Civil 3D, right-click Niblo in Prospector and select Refresh.

Note that the Excel folder just made in Vault Explorer now appears in the folder list within Prospector. The two programs are working from the ADMS, so they will stay in sync. Now that we have a project created, let's pull in some information.

Populating Vault with Data

Projects are useless without design files. In this section, we'll discuss the Civil 3D elements available for sharing through Vault and insert some of these design elements into our project.

VAULT ELIGIBILITY

Although there are more than a dozen Civil 3D specific object types that are used in modeling our designs, only certain ones are available for sharing as data objects in the Vault. The rest are typically used as components to other pieces of the model, but a few objects simply haven't been implemented as Vault data as of yet.

The objects that can be shared via Vault ("vaultable") are:

◆ Point databases

◆ Alignments

◆ Surfaces

◆ Pipe networks

◆ Survey database

◆ View Frame groups

Parcels are an obvious candidate for project-level sharing but are unfortunately not accessible at this time except via XRefs.

LOADING UP THE VAULT

All drawings related to a project should be part of the Vault. As drawings are added to the Vault, four steps take place:

1. The drawing is copied to the working folder if it's not in there already.

2. A copy of the file is made to the ADMS file store.

3. The SQL database is updated to reflect the existence of the file within the scope of the project.

4. Depending on the options selected during this process, the file is checked in and closed or checked out and left open.

New drawings, existing internal drawings, or drawings coming from external sources are three common sources for data we want to put into a Vault. Let's take a look at getting each of them into the Vault project.

Loading New Drawings

New drawings are the simplest to add, but be aware of some nuances to avoid any issues with duplicate data later. Let's take a look at the steps involved with adding a new drawing to the vault.

1. In Civil 3D, create a new file using the file NCS Extended template.

2. Choose File ➤ Save As and navigate to C:\Mastering Projects\Niblo\Engineering.

3. Name the file XStorm.dwg and click Save. By saving the file into the working folder, we avoid creating a duplicate copy when the file is checked in to the Vault.

4. Right-click the drawing name in Prospector, and select Add To Project, as shown in Figure 19.7.

5. Click Yes to go through the warning about the drawing being saved. This will display the Add To Project dialog.

6. Select the Niblo project and click Next.

7. Verify the Engineering folder is selected and click Next. Notice this tree matches our other views of the Vault project.

8. Uncheck the Create DWF column and click Finish. Prospector will add a project status icon as in Figure 19.8.

FIGURE 19.7
Adding a drawing
to a project

FIGURE 19.8
Drawing added to
the Niblo project

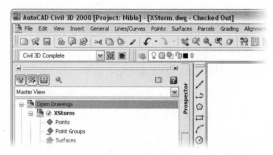

Some things to note on that last step: We removed the DWF option because the DWF created is quite often limited in its usefulness. It is used as a preview within Prospector, but does not plot a DWF of the full model or paper space—only the current view at check-in. Additionally, many users are not comfortable with DWF and are surprised to see a plot dialog appear when they thought they were saving their file. We also did not include a comment at this point, but comments can be used to indicate major milestones or indicate what was changed. These comments would then show up when browsing through the project files in Vault Explorer.

There are a couple of things to notice in Figure 19.8. First, the drawing name in Prospector now has a Vault status icon next to it. Second, the application window now reflects the attachment of a project and gives feedback on the drawing's status. Blank drawings are easy; now, let's add some existing data.

IT BEARS REPEATING

Be careful where you save those files when you're loading external data into the Vault! It's quite easy to save a copy to the root of a project but check it into a subfolder in the project. This will leave a file sitting within the project that other users might find and assume is good data. If you find you've made this mistake, erase *both* files, and then get the latest version from the Vault. This will ensure that the right file, in the right version, is in the right place.

Loading Existing Drawings

When project information exists in various file locations around the office, adding it to the project is an important part of data management. In this exercise, we'll add in some of the files we've worked with in earlier chapters and look at the data being made available to the project team:

1. Open the XTopo.dwg file.

2. Right-click the drawing name and select Add To Project as before.

3. Click Yes at the warning about the file being saved.

4. Select the Niblo project and click Next.

5. Select the Engineering folder and click Next.

6. Uncheck the Keep Files Checked Out and Create DWF options, as shown in Figure 19.9, and click Next.

7. Check the Surfaces checkbox, as shown in Figure 19.10.

8. Click Finish, and the drawing will be added to the Vault, and then closed.

FIGURE 19.9
Setting options for
DWF creation and
file check-in

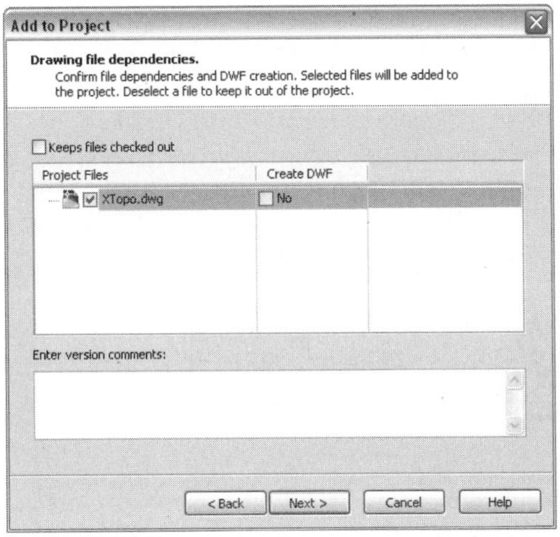

FIGURE 19.10
Selecting to share the
EG surface within the
project

Let's look at a few things that were different in this process. We had to select a project folder this time because the drawing was not stored in the working folder before being added to the project. If this drawing were coming from an outside source, such as another consultant, it would be wise to save it in the working folder as part of the data acceptance process. This would help with avoiding duplicate files. As it is, we now have a copy of the drawing in the data location from which we opened it and in the working folder. This type of duplicity could lead to errors later.

The second major change was deselecting the Keep Files Checked Out option in Figure 19.9. This option means that once the check-in is complete, we no longer want to keep that file open and reserved to us. If you think of this as a library where only one person can check out a book at a time, it can help.

Finally, the biggest change was the option to share the surface data. Because surfaces are among our vaultable objects, the check-in process offers the option of sharing this data. This screen will display each time a vaultable object is in the drawing and it has not been shared previously. Unfortunately, if you do not want to share something, you'll have to go through these options every time you check the drawing into the Vault.

Populating the Vault with Vault Explorer

There is one more method of adding information to the Vault that we have not considered. Vault Explorer can be used to add objects to the Vault via drag and drop or the file system. The major limitation of this method is that Vault Explorer does not recognize the Civil 3D objects that could be shared in the Vault. If any vaultable objects are in drawings added directly through Vault Explorer, these objects will be unavailable until the drawing is checked out and back in through the Civil 3D interface. Let's add a drawing file to the Vault using this method in a short exercise.

1. Launch Vault Explorer, and log in to the Melinda vault.

2. Expand the Niblo project, select the Engineering folder, and wait for the grid to populate, as shown in Figure 19.11.

3. Open Windows Explorer and navigate to the XPlat.dwg file. Drag the drawing file into Vault Explorer, dropping it on the Survey folder, as shown in Figure 19.12.

4. Add a comment stating "Linework Only" since this is just a sketch of the lot layout; then click OK.

5. Read the warning that appears; then click Yes.

FIGURE 19.11
Vault Explorer view of the Engineering folder in the Niblo project

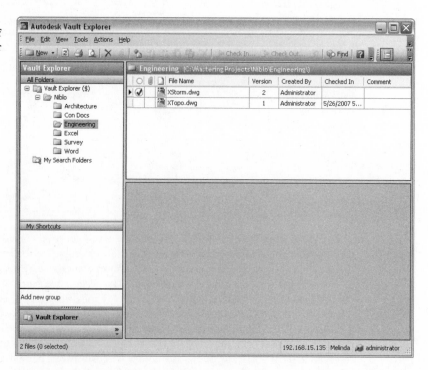

FIGURE 19.12

Adding the Xplat drawing file to the Niblo project via drag and drop to Vault Explorer

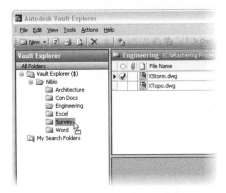

The drawing is added to the Vault and is available for checkout by the surveyors for creating true Civil 3D parcels. Finally, let's add in one more drawing just to repeat the process:

1. Open the XRoad.dwg file in Civil 3D.

2. Right-click and select Add To Project.

3. Add the Xroad drawing file to the Niblo project, in the Engineering folder. Do not keep it checked out, but do share all the alignments. Click Finish to complete the drawing.

4. In Prospector, expand Projects ➤ Niblo ➤ Drawings ➤ Engineering, Niblo ➤ Alignments, and Niblo ➤ Surfaces. Prospector should look like Figure 19.13.

The blank drawing we made is still open and checked out to us, so let's use it to design and create data references in this next section.

FIGURE 19.13

Niblo project shown in Prospector

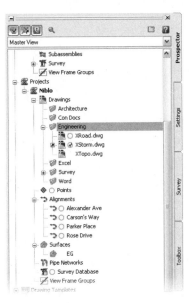

Working with Vault Data References

Similar to XRefs or data shortcuts, data references allow us to access the *data* in other drawings while applying styles and labels as required for the current drawing. The use of data references instead of XRefs brings into play all the design information, allowing us to not only paint a pretty picture of that data but also use it for design or inquiry. In this section, we'll look at creating some basic references for labeling or information and then make some changes to see how it all plays together.

CREATING A DATA REFERENCE

Data references work by backtracking through the project interface to find the original design information in its host drawing, and then displaying that data on the basis of the current drawing's style requirements. This sounds more complicated than it is, so let's do a simple exercise:

1. Switch to the XStorm.dwg file created earlier.

2. In Prospector, expand Projects ➤ Niblo ➤ Surfaces.

3. Right-click on the EG surface and select Create Reference to display the Create Surface Reference dialog. Click OK.

4. Expand XStorm ➤ Surfaces ➤ EG, as shown in Figure 19.14.

It's important to note the small shortcut arrow on the EG surface and that the Definition branch no longer appears under the EG surface as it did. Because EG in this drawing is a reference to another drawing, the definition cannot be changed. But the cursor is giving feedback about the surface, indicating an elevation in the tooltip. The data is available, and reference objects can be stylized as needed.

1. Change the EG surface style to Border Only.

2. Click Save.

FIGURE 19.14
EG data reference created in the XStorm drawing

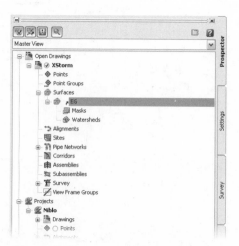

SAVE? I THOUGHT THIS WAS VAULT?

It is. A save at this point simply saves to the working folder. The version in the ADMS file store has not changed and is actually still the blank drawing we added earlier in this chapter. It's not necessary to check in a drawing every time you make a change or are heading to lunch. Actually, it's a bad idea to do so. ADMS stores a *full* copy of the drawing every time a new version is checked in, so the file store can fill quickly if you check in your 10MB file every time you change a single piece of text or a line. Saving gives you a failsafe point, leaves the file checked out for editing to you, and doesn't cause file store bloat.

UPDATING THE SOURCE

When design objects have been referenced, the original file is still available for checkout. Any changes that are then checked into the Vault will be communicated to drawings that reference that data, and those drawings can be updated as needed. Let's modify a surface and update the vaulted version by checking it back in.

1. Expand Projects ➤ Niblo ➤ Surfaces.

2. Right-click EG and select Check Out Source Drawing.

3. Click OK to get the latest version from the vault and place it in the working folder.

4. Draw a polyline like the one shown in Figure 19.15. Because we're dealing with only part of our site, we can place a boundary on the surface to limit the amount of data being shown.

5. Expand Xtopo ➤ Surfaces ➤ Definition.

FIGURE 19.15
Approximate surface boundary to be added

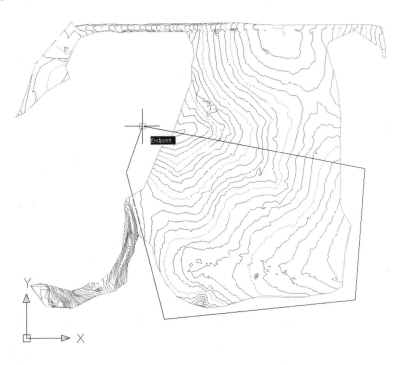

6. Right-click Boundaries and select Add. Check the Non-Destructive Breakline option, and then click OK.

7. Right-click XTopo in Prospector and select Check In.

8. Uncheck the Keep Files Checked Out and Create DWF options and click Finish.

This process actually saved the file to the working folder and created a second full copy in the file store. Although our EG file is relatively small, you can see how the file store size could bloat very quickly if you checked in a file every time you made even a minute change.

UPDATING THE REFERENCE

When source information changes, the `project.xml` file (one of those magic, Civil 3D required files) is updated. As each session of Civil 3D that is accessing a particular project communicates with the Vault, out-of-date items will be flagged as needing to be updated. Now we can go update the surface reference that was modified in the last exercise.

1. Switch back to the XStorm drawing.

2. In Prospector, expand `Surfaces`, as shown in Figure 19.16.

3. Right-click EG and select Synchronize. The surface updates, and the out-of-date warning is removed, as shown in Figure 19.17.

4. Right-click the XStorm drawing name in Prospector, and select Check In.

5. Check the Keep Checked Out option, and then click Finish to complete the process.

UM, I DIDN'T KEEP IT CHECKED OUT...

If you miss this checkbox at any point along the way, simply expand Projects ➤ Niblo ➤ Drawings ➤ Engineering, right-click the needed file, and select Check Out. This is how you'll access files on a daily basis, so it's good to know.

FIGURE 19.16
EG surface out-of-date warning and the Synchronize option

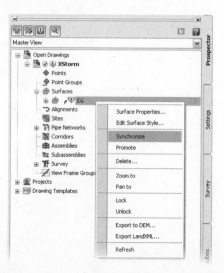

FIGURE 19.17
XStorm drawing after synchronizing project information

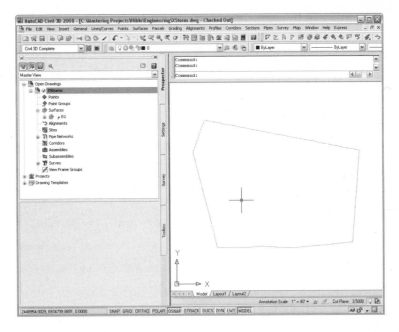

Taking this idea to the next level, the engineer could begin working with road-and-paving design and checking in the initial layout and profile information as soon as it is created. A technician could begin creating references, labeling things in the styles, and doing the formatting required to meet submittal specifications as the design is little more than a sketch. Using the preliminary design, sheets could be plotted for project manager review, looking for the level of detail that suits the need. As the design is updated, labels and entire sheets are updated with a simple synchronization and replotted.

BREAKING THE REFERENCE

Occasionally, reference objects need to become part of the drawing they are being referenced in, with no connection to the original design. This can be done to consolidate data, to explore design alternatives, or to prepare a file for sharing with an outside source:

1. Switch to the XStorm drawing if need be.

2. Expand XStorm ➤ Surfaces.

3. Right-click EG and select Promote.

4. Expand EG and notice that the Definition branch is now available.

5. Check in XStorm.dwg again, but, this time, do not keep it checked out. On the Share Data page of the Check In Drawing dialog, you will see a warning that EG cannot be checked in. Vault will not allow duplicate object names in the same project, but you can check the drawing in without sharing that surface.

At this point, the EG in XStorm.dwg has nothing to do with the EG in the project. It's a copy of the data but will not reflect any changes to the source information. That's a dangerous situation to be in if you want to keep using this as a design file. We'll look at restoring previous versions in a later section of this chapter.

Pulling It Together

Using a single reference is fairly straightforward; the complication comes when trying to understand how these references, XRefs, design files, and sheets all come together. Let's attempt to look at how we can use all of the tools in Civil 3D and Vault to create a plan and profile sheet for one road. This is a longer series of exercises, but it illustrates the full nature of the connections that can be handled in Vault. Additionally, this section acts as a mini-exam of all the skills you've learned throughout the book.

PULLING THE NEEDED REFERENCES

To begin your design, you need a file that will be used to explore design ideas for creating a road corridor:

1. Create a new drawing using the NCS Extended template.

2. Save As **XCorridor.dwg** in C:\Mastering Projects\Niblo\Engineering.

3. Right-click the drawing name in Prospector and select Add To Project.

4. Add to the Niblo project, but keep this drawing checked out.

5. In Prospector, expand Projects ➢ Niblo ➢ Surfaces.

6. Right-click EG and select Create Reference. Set the style to Border Only; then click OK.

7. Expand Niblo ➢ Alignments.

8. Right-click Rose Drive and select Create Reference to display the Create Alignment Reference dialog shown in Figure 19.18. Note the Source Alignment selection box at the top of the figure. Occasionally, Vault will get lost and choose the wrong alignment. You should always verify the correct file and alignment are listed.

9. Set the Alignment Style and Alignment Label Set as shown, and then click OK to create the alignment reference.

FIGURE 19.18
The Create Alignment
Reference dialog

GOING VERTICAL WITH DESIGN

Now that we have a surface and needed horizontal alignments, let's pull together some vertical information:

1. Sample the EG surface using the Rose Drive alignment.

2. Sample left and right offsets at 25´.

3. Set the profile styles as shown in Figure 19.19.

4. Click Draw In Profile View to display the Create Profile View wizard.

5. Set the Profile View style to Full Grid and click Create Profile View.

6. Pick a point to the right of the surface boundary to place the profile view.

    At this point, we're going to cheat a bit. Within the data files is a profile design for Rose Drive.

7. Select Profile ➢ Create Profile From File. In the dialog, select the `Rose Drive Prof.txt` file from the Chapter 19 folder. Change the Profile Name to **Rose Drive TC**, the Profile Style to Design, and the Label Set to Complete Label Set.

8. Click OK. Your drawing should look like Figure 19.20.

FIGURE 19.19
Creating profiles within the design file

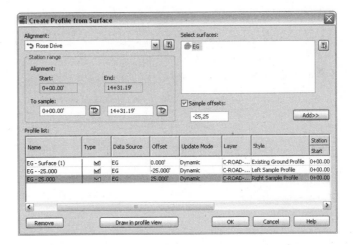

FIGURE 19.20
Sampled profiles from referenced alignment and surface data

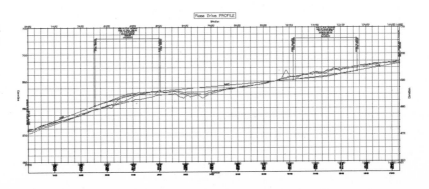

BUILDING A ROAD MODEL

We've got horizontal and vertical elements for our design. So, now let's build the road. To do this, we have another shortcut. We've already created a typical 27′ street assembly with sidewalks.

1. Insert the `Assembly.dwg` file using the AutoCAD Insert command. Use the Explode option to leave yourself with an assembly named 27 B-B-50′ROW.

2. Create a basic corridor using the Rose Drive alignment, the Rose Drive TC profile, and this assembly to arrive at the view in Figure 19.21.

PREPARING THE SHEETS

Now that some level of design is completed, we can bring on another team member. This team member can begin working with the sheet files to create plans that match reviewer requirements. In this exercise, we'll break out some plan sheets and add them to the project.

1. Choose General ➤ Plan Production Tools ➤ Create View Frames to display the Create View Frames wizard.

2. Click the Create View Frames button. (We're accepting the defaults of the wizard. See Chapter 20 for a full explanation of this new feature.) Your drawing should look like Figure 19.22.

FIGURE 19.21
Completed corridor model in our design file

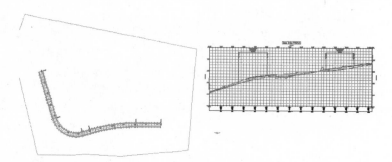

FIGURE 19.22
View frames created for Rose Drive

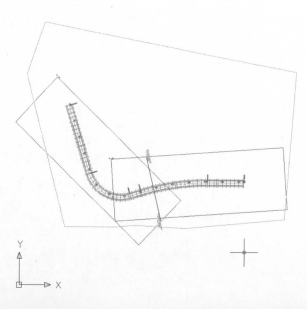

3. Choose General ➤ Plan Production Tools ➤ Create Sheets.

4. Select the radio button for All Layouts In One New Drawing, as shown in Figure 19.23, and then click Next to move to the Sheet Set step.

5. Click the ellipsis button next to the Sheet Set File (.DST) Storage Location text box shown in Figure 19.24. Select the Con Docs folder, and click OK. (There are two ellipsis buttons; we'll do this step twice.)

6. Click the other ellipsis button (next to the Sheet Files Storage Location text box) and select the Con Docs folder again. This sets the folder in Vault for the sheets to be stored.

7. Change the Sheet File Name to **ROAD**. The naming scheme uses X as a prefix to designate design files; no X means a sheet file.

FIGURE 19.23
Controlling the placement of new sheet layouts

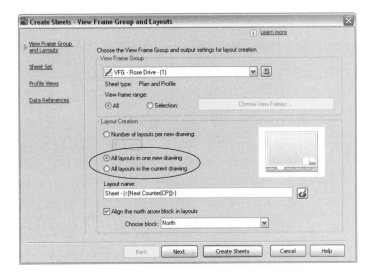

FIGURE 19.24
Setting paths for files and Vault storage

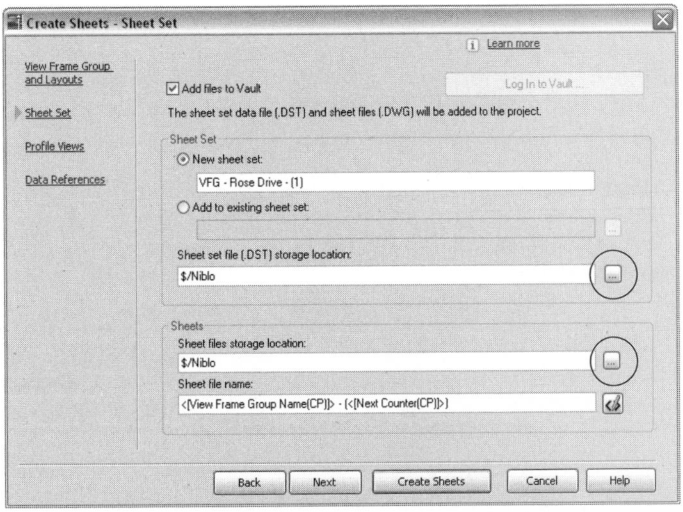

8. Click Next to complete the Sheet Set step and move to the Profile Views step. Click Next to accept the settings in the Profile Views step and move to the Data References step.

9. Click the EG surface, as shown in Figure 19.25.

10. Click Create Sheets, and click OK at the warning that appears.

11. Pick a point to the right of the profile view already in the drawing to set an origin for the sheet profile views to be created.

12. Close the Sheet Set Manager palette that appears and close Panorama if it's over your drawing.

13. In Prospector, expand Projects ➢ Niblo ➢ Drawings ➢ Con Docs. You should see the Road.dwg file (see Figure 19.26).

14. Check in your XCorridor drawing and do not keep it checked out.

15. Check the View Frame Groups option on the Share Data step, and click Finish.

At this point, we've effectively shortened the design and plan production process. Our technician can check out the Road drawing and begin to make any additional labels, titles, legends, notes, style changes, and so on as needed to complete the plans. A change in our design will be reflected via the updating mechanism, and the design and plan sheets will always stay in sync.

FIGURE 19.25
Selecting data references for the sheet file

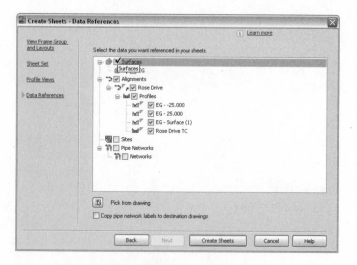

FIGURE 19.26
Sheet file created, added to the project, and checked in

One last *very* cool thing to notice: In 2007, profile information had to be created in the same drawing file as the alignment object to share it project wide. However, Vault 2008 blows past this limit, allowing us to design the vertical in a different file from the horizontal. This means that the surveyor who wants to lay out the street centerline to drive right-of-way calculation can share those alignments to keep the site designer in sync with the legal docs. That's one more step in the process that can be shared and split to make the project workflow more efficient.

Team Management in Vault

One of the common concerns with using Civil 3D is that the surveyor, engineer, technician, and project manager all have access to the design data. Many firms have taken this to the extreme in the past, creating separate projects for engineering versus surveying versus landscape architecture. In this section, let's take a look at how we can use Vault to keep permissions straight, and what we can do when something does get changed by mistake.

Vault Folder Permission

ADMS and Vault 2008 brought a new level of functionality and security to the groups and users they manage. Previous versions basically depended on Vault roles to handle data access control. Thankfully, this has changed, and now users and groups can manage access, similarly to Windows Users and Groups.

 Real World Scenario

KEEP THEM OUT OF MY DRAWINGS!

We've heard it a hundred times. The nature of CAD and engineering work means that sometimes you just need to keep files to certain groups or individuals. Now that we have files spread throughout our project, let's look at using these new functions to clearly delineate data access.

1. Launch Vault Explorer and log in to the Melinda vault.

2. Right-click the Engineering folder and select Properties to display the Properties For 'Engineering' dialog.

3. Switch to the Security tab and click Add near the bottom of this tab to display the Add Members dialog.

4. Select Jolene and click Add. Select Jim and click Add again. Then click OK to dismiss the dialog.

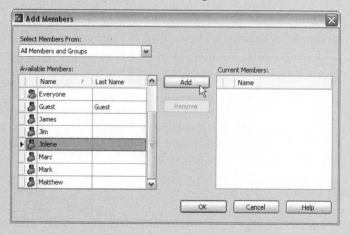

5. On the Properties For 'Engineering' dialog, click the dropdown list next to Jim and select Read Only. Then click OK to dismiss the dialog.

6. Switch back to Civil 3D. In Prospector, right-click Projects and select Log Out.

7. Select the Melinda vault, but log in as Jim.

8. Expand Projects ➢ Niblo ➢ Drawings ➢ Engineering and select XCorridor.

9. Right-click and select Check Out.

10. Click OK in the dialog. Vault will do some quick checking and present you with this alert. Click OK.

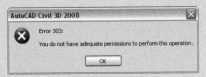

11. Right-click Projects and log out as Jim.

Although we used individuals, a more corporate approach would be to use groups to manage permissions. This type of security should go a long way in reassuring surveyors, engineers, and technicians that they can coexist in harmony on design projects. But what about when someone with the right permissions makes a change that isn't desired?

Restoring Previous Versions

Every time a drawing is checked into Vault, a full copy is made in the file store. Although this makes the bloat factor a real concern, it also means that it's relatively simple to pull any version of a file that was ever used out of the file store and bring it back to current status:

1. In Vault Explorer, expand Niblo ➤ Engineering and select XTopo.dwg, as shown in Figure 19.27.

2. Switch to the Where Used tab in the lower pane to review where this file is being referenced.

FIGURE 19.27
XTopo.dwg history in the Vault

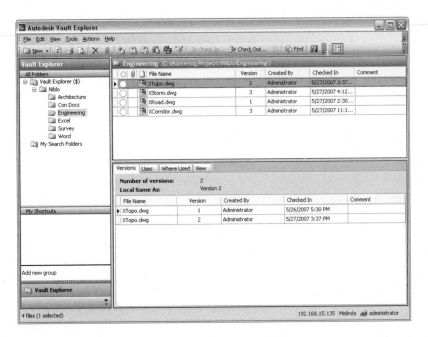

3. Right-click XTopo in the top pane and select Get Previous Version to display the Get Previous Version of 'XTopo.dwg' dialog, shown in Figure 19.28.

4. Select Version 1 from the dropdown list in the Version selection box (see Figure 19.28), and click OK to dismiss the dialog. Notice the XTopo status icon changes in Vault Explorer. Remember, the working folder is merely a temporary holding location as files are edited. Overwriting the version in the working folder does nothing to what is in the Vault and what is considered current.

5. Switch to Civil 3D.

6. Right-click Projects and select Log In. Use the Jolene account for this example.

7. Expand Project ➢ Niblo ➢ Engineering, and select Xtopo.

8. Right-click and select Check Out.

9. In the Check Out Drawing dialog, uncheck the Get Latest Version option, as shown in Figure 19.29. *This step is crucial!*

FIGURE 19.28
Use the Get Previous Version dialog to restore a version of a file.

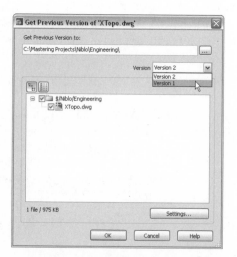

FIGURE 19.29
Do not get the latest version when attempting to restore a previous version.

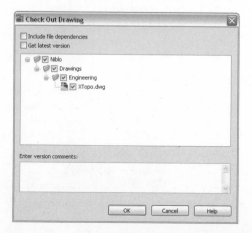

10. Click OK to dismiss the dialog. Your screen will regenerate, and the original version of the surface will be displayed.

11. Right-click XTopo in Prospector and select Check In. Uncheck the Keep Files Checked Out option in the Check In Drawing dialog if necessary. Click Finish.

12. Jump back over to Vault Explorer and press F5 to refresh the display.

13. Select XTopo one more time and note that version 3 is now in the Vault, with Jolene as the creator, as shown in Figure 19.30.

By placing an older version in the working folder, checking out without pulling the latest version from the file store to the working folder, but then checking back in the older version, we've effectively brought a file back from the past. In this case, it was a simple surface, but consider the sea of changes that sometimes occur when laying out a site. Being able to go back to the first conceptual design with almost no downtime is an enviable position to be in as a design firm.

FIGURE 19.30
Jolene has checked in version 3.

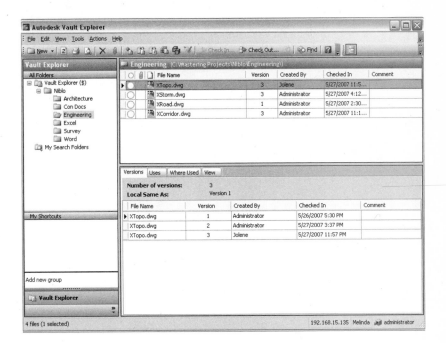

The Bottom Line

Describe the differences between using Vault and data shortcuts. The two mechanisms in Civil 3D for sharing data are quite similar. Every firm has their nuances, and it's important to evaluate both methods of sharing data to see which one would be a better fit for the team's workflow. Recognizing the differences will allow you to make these recommendations with confidence.

Master It Describe at least three major differences between the two data-sharing methods.

Insert Civil 3D data into a vault. Creating a project in Vault requires some care to make sure all the pieces go in the right place. Using the project template to create organizational structures similar to what is already in place is a good way to start. Adding individual components to the Vault as they fit into this structure makes for clean data organization and easy integration of new team members.

> **Master It** Create a new project titled Bailey in the Melinda vault using the `Mastering` project template. Add the `Bailey's Run.dwg` file to the project in the `Engineering` folder, sharing all of the data within it.

Create data shortcuts. Creating duplicate data is never good. By creating links to original data instead of working with copies, you maintain the integrity of the project information. Using data references instead of XRefs allows you to use the data behind the object instead of just the picture. This means styling and label changes can be part of the end file and allow team members to work on separate parts of the job at the same time.

> **Master It** Create a new drawing called **Mastering Vault**, add it to the Bailey project in the `Engineering` folder, and create references to the FG surface and to the Natures Way and Old Settlers Way alignments. Use a Contours 2′ And 10′ (Design) style for the surfaces.

Restore a previous version of a design file. One of the major advantages of using a database-driven system is the ability to track file changes and restore them if necessary. Vault has a mechanism for moving data in and out of the file store. By using the restoration tools and checking in the proper files, it's easy to roll back to a prior version of a file.

> **Master It** Erase the Founders Court alignment from the Bailey's Run file and check it in. Then use the Vault tools to restore the previous version containing the Founders Court alignment. What version number of the Bailey's Run drawing is listed when this is complete?

Chapter 20

Out the Door: Plan Production

So you've toiled for days, weeks, and maybe months creating your design in Civil 3D and now it's time to share it with the world—or at least your corner of it. Even in this digital age, paper plan sets still play an important role. You generate these plans in Civil 3D using the Plan Production feature. In this chapter, we'll examine the steps necessary to create a set of sheets, from initial setup, to framing and generating sheets, to data management and plotting.

In this chapter, you'll learn to:

◆ Create view frames

◆ Create sheets and use Sheet Set Manager

◆ Edit sheet templates and styles associated with plan production

Preparing for Plan Sets

Before you start generating all sorts of wonderful plan sets, there are a few concepts and prerequisites you must address first. Civil 3D takes advantage of several features and components to build a plan set. Some of these components have existed in AutoCAD and Civil 3D for years, such as layout tabs, drawing templates, alignments, and profiles. Others are new properties of existing features, like Plan or Profile viewport types. Still others are entirely new objects, including view frames, match lines, and view frame groups. Let's look at what you need to have in place before you can create your plotted masterpieces.

Prerequisite Components

The plan production feature draws upon several components to create a plan set. Here is a list of these components and a brief explanation of each. Later in this chapter, we'll explore these elements in greater detail.

Drawing Template   Plan production creates new layouts for each sheet in a plan set. To do this, the feature uses drawing templates with predefined viewports. These viewports have their Viewport Type property set to either Plan or Profile.

Object and Display Styles   Like every other feature in Civil 3D, plan production uses objects. Specifically, these objects are view frames, view frame groups, and match lines. Before creating plan sheets, you'll want to make sure you have styles set up for each of these objects.

Alignments and Profiles   In Civil 3D 2008, the plan production feature is designed primarily for use in creating plan and profile views. To that end, your drawing must contain (or reference) at least one alignment. If you are creating sheets with both plan and profile views, a profile must also be present.

With these elements in place, you're ready to dive in and create some sheets. The general steps to creating a set of plans follow:

1. Meet the prerequisites listed earlier.

2. Create view frames.

3. Create sheets.

4. Plot (hardcopy or DWF).

We'll next look at this process in detail and the tools used in plan production.

Using View Frames and Match Lines

When you create sheets using the plan production tool, Civil 3D first automatically helps you divide your alignment into sections that will fit on your plotted sheet and display at the desired scale. To do this, Civil 3D creates a series of rectangular frames placed end to end (or slightly overlapping) along the length of alignment, like those in Figure 20.1. These rectangles are referred to as *view frames* and are automatically sized and positioned to meet your plan sheet requirements. This collection of view frames is referred to as a *view frame group.* Additionally, where the view frames abut one another, Civil 3D creates *match lines* that establish continuity from frame to frame by referring to the previous or next sheet in the completed plan set. View frames and match lines are created in model space, using the prerequisite elements described in the previous section.

FIGURE 20.1
View frames and
match lines

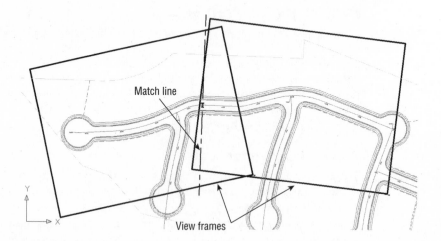

The Create View Frames Wizard

The first step in the process of creating plan sets is to generate view frames. Civil 3D provides a very intuitive wizard that walks you through each step of the view frame-creation process. Let's look at the wizard and the various page options. After we walk through each page, you'll run through an exercise to put what you've learned into practice.

The Create View Frames wizard (Figure 20.2) is launched from the General dropdown menu. Selecting General ➤ Plan Production Tools ➤ Create View Frames launches the Create View Frames wizard. The wizard consists of several pages. A list of these pages is shown along the left side, and an arrow indicates which page you are currently viewing. You move among the pages using the Next and Back navigation buttons along the bottom of each page. Alternately, you can jump directly to any page by clicking its name from the list on the left. Let's walk through the pages of the wizard and explain the features of each.

FIGURE 20.2

Create View
Frames wizard

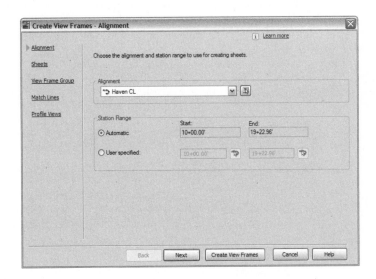

ALIGNMENT PAGE

The first page is used to select the alignment and station range along which the view frames will be created.

Alignment   In the first section of this page, you select the alignment along which you want to create view frames. You can either select it from the dropdown menu or click the Select From The Drawing button ⬛ to select the alignment from the drawing.

Station Range   In the Station Range section, you define the station range over which the frames will be created. Selecting Automatic creates frames from the alignment Start to the alignment End. Selecting User Specified lets you define a custom range, by either keying in Start and End station values in the appropriate box or by clicking the button to the right of the station value fields ⬛ and graphically selecting the station from the drawing.

SHEETS PAGE

The second page of the wizard (Figure 20.3) is used to establish the sheet type and the orientation of the view frames along the alignment. A plan production "sheet" is a layout tab in a drawing file. To create the sheets, Civil 3D references a predefined drawing template (.dwt) file. As mentioned earlier, the template must contain layout tabs and in each tab have the viewport's extended data properties set to either Plan or Profile. Later in this chapter you'll learn about editing and modifying templates for use in plan production.

FIGURE 20.3
Create View
Frames – Sheets

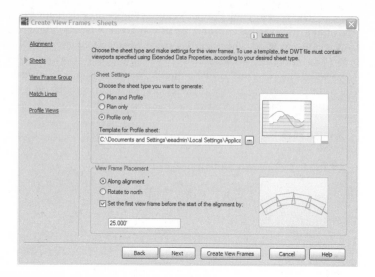

Sheet Settings   In Civil 3D 2008, the plan production feature provides options for creating three types of sheets:

Plan and Profile   This option generates a sheet with two viewports; one viewport shows a plan view and the other shows a profile view of the section of the selected alignment segment.

Plan Only   As the name implies, this option creates a sheet with a single viewport showing only the plan view of the selected alignment segment.

Profile Only   Similar to Plan Only, this option creates a sheet with a single viewport, showing only the profile view of the selected alignment segment.

GRAPHICS

Did you notice the nifty graphic to the right of the sheet type options in Figure 20.3? This image changes depending on the type of sheet you've selected. It provides a schematic representation of the sheet layout to further assist you in selecting the appropriate sheet type. You'll see this type of graphic image throughout the Create View Frame wizard and in other wizards used for plan production in Civil 3D.

After choosing the sheet type, you must define the template file and the layout tab within the selected template that Civil 3D will use to generate your sheets. Several predefined templates ship with Civil 3D and are part of the default installation.

Clicking the ellipsis button ⬚ displays the Select Layout As Sheet Template dialog. This dialog provides the option to select the DWT file itself and the layout tab within the template. Clicking the ellipsis button in that dialog lets you browse to the desired template location. Typically, the default template location is:

```
C:\Documents and Settings\<username>\Local Settings\Application
Data\Autodesk\C3D 2008\enu\Template\Plan Production\
```

After selecting the template you wish to use, a list of the layouts contained in the DWT file appears in the Select Layout As Sheet Template dialog (Figure 20.4). Here you can choose the appropriate layout tab.

FIGURE 20.4

Select Layout As Sheet Template dialog

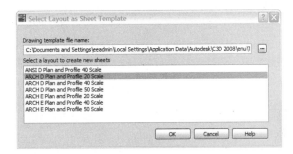

View Frame Placement   Your view frames can be placed in one of two ways: either along the axis or rotated north. Use the bottom section of the Sheets page of the wizard to establish the placement.

Along Alignment   This option aligns the long axes of the view frames parallel to the alignment. Refer to the graphic to the right for a visual representation of this option.

Rotate To North   As the name implies, this option aligns the view frames so they are rotated to the north directions (straight up), regardless of the changing rotation of the alignment centerline. "North" is defined by the orientation of the drawing. Again, refer to the graphic.

Set The First View Frame Before The Start Of The Alignment By   Regardless of the view frame alignment you choose, you have the option to place the first view frame some distance before the start of the alignment. This is useful if you want to show a portion of the site, such as an existing offsite road, in the plan view. When this option is selected, the text box becomes active, letting you enter the desired distance.

VIEW FRAME GROUP PAGE

The third page of the Create View Frames wizard (Figure 20.5) is used to define creation parameters for your view frames and the view frame group to which they'll belong. The page is divided into two sections, one for the view frame group and the other for the view frames themselves.

View Frame Group   Use these options to set the name and an optional description for the view frame group. The name can consist of a manually entered text; text automatically generated based on the Name Template settings (click the Edit View Frame Name button [icon] to open the Name Template dialog to adjust the name template); or a combination of both. In this example, the feature settings are such that the name will include manually defined prefix text (VFG-) followed by automatically generated text, which inserts the alignment name and a sequential counter number. For this example, this will result in a view frame group name of VFG – Haven CL - 1.

The Name Template dialog is not unique to the Plan Production feature of Civil 3D. However, the property fields available vary depending on the features to be named. If you need to reset the incremental number counter, use the options in the lower area of the Name Template dialog (Figure 20.6).

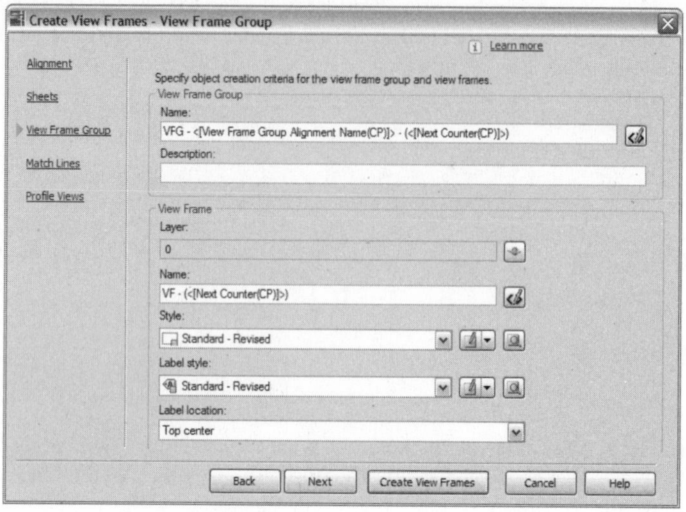

FIGURE 20.5

Create View Frames –
View Frame Group

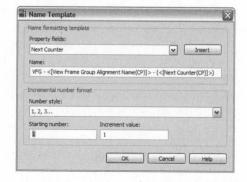

FIGURE 20.6

Name Template dia-
log. Use the options
in the Incremental
Number Format sec-
tion to adjust auto-
matic numbering.

View Frame These options are used to set various parameters for the view frames, including the layer for the frames, view frame names, view frame object and label styles, and the label location. Each view frame can have a unique name, but the other parameters are the same for all view frames.

Layer This option defines the layer on which the view frames are created. This layer is defined in the drawing settings, but you can override it by clicking the layer button ⬛ and selecting a different layer.

Name The Name setting is nearly identical in function to that for the view frame group name discussed earlier. In this example, the default name results in VF-1, VF-2, etc.

Style Like nearly every object in Civil 3D, view frames have styles associated with them. The view frame style is very simple, with only one component, the view frame border. You use the dropdown to select a predefined style.

Label Style Also like most other Civil 3D objects, a view frame has a label style associated with it. And like other label styles, the view frame labels are created using the Label Style

Composer and can contain a variety of components. The label style used in this example includes the frame name and station range placed at the top of the frame.

Label Location   The last option on this page lets you set the label location. The default feature setting is set so the label is placed at the Top Center of the view frame. Other options include Top Left, Top Right, Bottom Left, Bottom Right, and so on.

All view frame labels are placed at the top of the frame. However, the term "top" is relative to the orientation of the frames. For alignments that run left to right across the page, the top of the frame points toward the top of the screen. However, for alignments that run right to left, the top of the frame points toward the bottom of the screen. You can make the view frame label display along the frame edge closest to the top of the screen by using a large Y-offset value when defining your view frame label style.

Match Lines Page

The next page of the Create View Frames wizard (Figure 20.7) is used to establish settings for match lines. Match lines are used to maintain continuity from one sheet to the next. They are typically placed at or near the edge of a sheet, with instructions to "see sheet XX" for continuation. You have the option whether or not to automatically insert match lines. Match lines are used only for plan views, so if you are creating Plan and Profile or Profile Only sheets, the option is automatically selected and can't be deselected.

Positioning   The Positioning options are used to define the initial location of the match lines and provide the ability to later move or reposition the match lines.

Snap Station Value Down To The Nearest   By selecting this option, you override the drawing station settings and define a rounding value specific to match line placement. In this example, a value of 1 is entered, resulting in the match lines being placed at the nearest whole station. This feature always rounds down.

Allow Additional Distance For Repositioning   Checking this option activates the text box, allowing you to enter a distance by which the views on adjacent sheets will overlap and the maximum distance that you can move a match line from its original position.

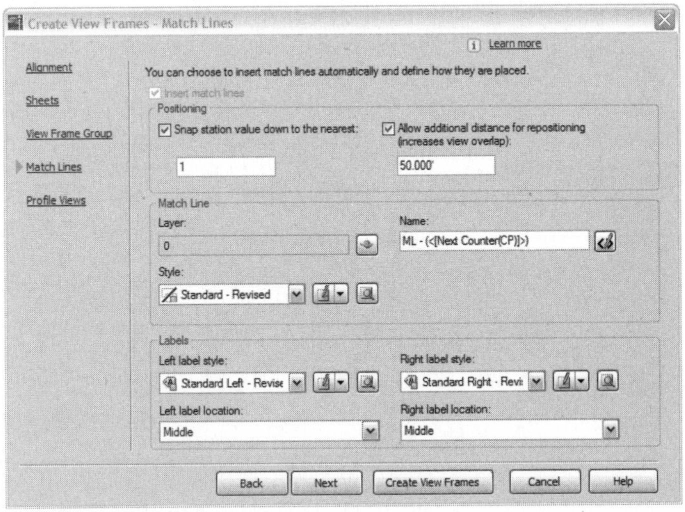

FIGURE 20.7

Create View Frames – Match Lines

Match Line   The options for the match line are similar to those for view frames described on the previous page of the wizard. You can define the layer, the name format, and the match line style.

Labels   These options are also similar to those for view frames. Different label styles are used to annotate match lines located at the left and right side of a frame. This allows you to define match line labels styles that reference either the previous or next station adjacent to the current frame. The location of each label can also be set independently using the Left and Right label location dropdown menus. You have options for placing the labels at the start, end, or middle, or at the point where the match line intersects the alignment.

PROFILE VIEWS PAGE

The final page of the Create View Frames wizard is the Profile Views page (Figure 20.8). This page is optional and will be disabled and skipped if you chose to create Plan Only sheets on the second page of the wizard. The Plan Production feature needs to know what profile view and band set styles you intend to use for the profile views. This allows the correct positioning to be applied. Use the dropdown menus to select both the Profile View style and the Band Set style.

Civil 3D has difficulty determining the proper extents of profile views. If you find that your profile view is not positioned correctly in the viewport (e.g., the annotation along the sides or bottom is clipped), you may need to create "buffer" areas. The _Autodesk Civil 3D NCS Extended dwt (both Imperial and Metric) file contains styles with these buffers created. See the readme.chm file contained in C:\program files\AutoCAD Civil 3D 2008\Setup\Docs for additional information. This is a Windows Help file and has some additional information on the subject.

There is no Next button on this last page of the wizard. To complete the wizard, click the Create View Frames button.

FIGURE 20.8
Create View Frames –
Profile Views

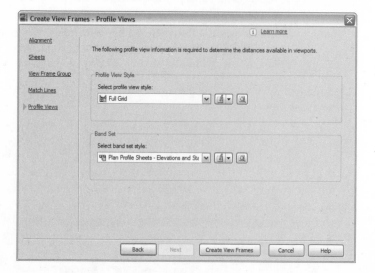

Creating View Frames

Now that you've got an understanding of the wizard pages and available options, let's practice with them:

1. Open View_Frame_Wizard.dwg. This drawing contains several alignments and profiles as well as styles for view frames, view frame groups, and match lines.

2. Select General ➤ Plan Production Tools ➤ Create View Frames. This launches the Create View Frames wizard.

3. On the Alignment page, for Alignment select Haven CL from the dropdown menu. For Station Range, verify Automatic is selected and click Next to advance to the next page.

4. On the Sheet page, select the Plan And Profile option. Next, click the ellipsis ⬚ to display the Select Layout As Sheet Template dialog. Click the next ellipsis ⬚ and browse to the Plan Production subfolder in the default template file location. Typically, this is:

   ```
   C:\Documents and Settings\<username>\Local Settings\Application
    Data\Autodesk\C3D 2008\enu\Template\Plan Production\
   ```

5. Select the template named Civil 3D (Imperial) Plan and Profile.dwt and click Open.

6. A list of the layouts in the DWT file appears in the Select Layout As Sheet Template dialog. Select the layout named ARCH D Plan and Profile 20 Scale and click OK.

7. In the View Frame Placement sections, select the Along Alignment option; check the box adjacent to Set The First View Frame Before The Start Of The Alignment By. Note that Feature Settings for this particular drawing default this value to 25′. Click Next to advance to the next page.

8. On the View Frame Group page, confirm that all settings are as follows (these are the same settings shown back in Figure 20.5) and then click Next to advance to the next page:

Setting	Value
View Frame Group Name	VFG - <[View Frame Group Alignment Name(CP)]> - (<[Next Counter(CP)]>)
View Frame Name	VF - (<[Next Counter(CP)]>)
Style	Standard - Revised
Label Style	Standard - Revised
Label Location	Top Center

9. On the Match Lines page, review the default settings and click Next to advance to the next page.

10. On the last page of the wizard, confirm the settings are as follows (these are the same settings shown back in Figure 20.8) and then click Create View Frames:

Setting	Value
Select Profile View Style	Full Grid
Select Band Set Style	Plan Profile Sheets - Elevations and Stations

The view frames and match lines are created and are displayed as a collection in the Prospector, as shown in Figure 20.9a and 20.9b.

Your view frames, view frame groups, and match lines numbering may not identically match those shown in the images. This is due to the incremental counting Civil 3D performs in the background. Each time you create one of these objects, the counter increments. You can reset the counter by modifying the name template.

FIGURE 20.9

Finished view frames, in the drawing (a) and in the Prospector (b)

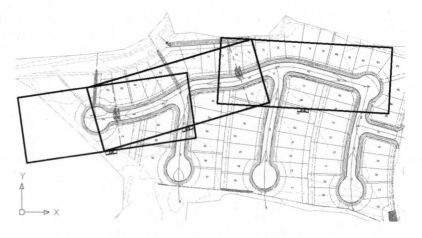

Editing View Frames and Match Lines

After you've created view frames and match lines, it is possible that you may need to edit them. Edits to some view frame and match line properties can be made via the Prospector tab in the Toolspace palette. For both view frames and match lines, you can only change the object's name and or style via the Information tab in the Properties dialog. All other information displayed on the other tabs is read-only.

Changes to geometry and location are made graphically using special grip edits (Figure 20.10). Like many other Civil 3D objects with special editing grips (e.g., Profiles; Pipe Network objects), view frames and match lines also have editing grips used to modify the location, rotation, and geometry of the object. Let's look at each separately.

View frames can be graphically edited in two ways. They can be moved along the alignment and they can be rotated:

To move a view frame: The first grip is the standard square grip that is used for most of the typical edits, including moving the object.

To slide a view frame: Select the view frame to be edited and then select the diamond-shaped grip at the center of the frame. This grip allows you to move the view frame in either direction along the alignment while maintaining the orientation (Along Alignment or Rotated North) that was originally established for the view frame when it was created.

To rotate a view frame: A view frame can be rotated by first selecting the frame and then selecting the circular "handle" grip. This grip works like the one on pipe network structures. Using this grip, the frame can be rotated about its center.

FIGURE 20.10
View frame and match line grips

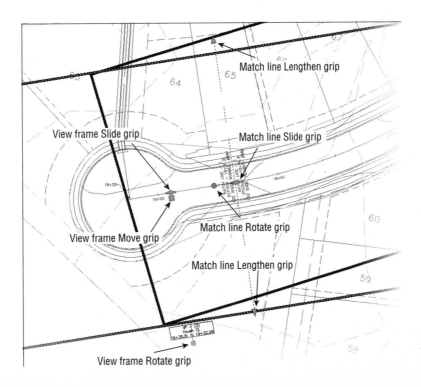

🌐 Real World Scenario

DON'T FORGET YOUR AUTOCAD FUNCTIONS!

While you're getting wrapped up in learning all about Civil 3D and its great design tools, it can be easy to forget you're sitting on an incredibly powerful CAD application.

AutoCAD features add functionality beyond what you can do with Civil 3D commands alone. First, make sure the DYN (Dynamic Input) option is turned on. This gives you additional functionality when moving a view frame. With DYN active, you can key in an exact station value to precisely locate the frame where you want it. Similar to view frame edits, with DYN active, you can key in an exact rotation angle. Note that this rotation angle is relative to your drawing settings (e.g., 0 degrees is to the left, 90 degrees is straight up, and so on). Also, selecting multiple objects and then selecting their grips while holding Shift makes each grip "hot" (usually a red color). This allows you to grip-edit a bunch of objects at once, like sliding a group of view frames along the alignment.

Whether you're learning Civil 3D yourself or training a group, it's a good idea to spend some time looking at the new features of AutoCAD with every new release. You never know when you'll discover some nugget that cuts hours off your workday!

A match line's location and length can be edited using special grips. Like view frames, they can be slid along the alignment and rotated. They can also be lengthened or shortened. Unlike view frames, they cannot be moved to an arbitrary location.

To slide a match line: Select the match line to be edited and then select the diamond-shaped grip at the center of the match line. This grip allows you to move the match line in either direction along the alignment while maintaining the orientation (Along Alignment or Rotated North) that was originally established for the view frame. Note that the match line can only be moved in either direction a distance equal to or less than that entered on the Match Line page of the wizard at the time the view frames were created. For example, if you entered a value of 50´ for the Allow Additional Distance For Repositioning option, your view frames are overlapped 50´ to each side of the match line and the match line can only be slid 50´ in either direction from its original location.

To rotate a match line: A match line can be rotated by first selecting the match line and then selecting the circular "handle" grip. This grip works like the one on the view frames.

To change a match line's length: When selected, a triangular grip is displayed at each end of the match line. These grips can be used to increase or decrease the length of each half of the match line. For example, moving the grip on the top end of the match line changes the length of only the top half of the match line. The other half of the match line remains unchanged. See the sidebar "Don't Forget Your AutoCAD Functions," for tips on using AutoCAD features.

Let's now work through an exercise and put what you've learned into practice. Make sure DYN is active.

1. Open `Edit ViewFrames and MatchLines.dwg` from the book's companion CD. This drawing contains view frames and match lines. You'll change the location and rotation of a view frame and change the location and length of a match line.

2. Select the middle view frame, VF-2, and select its diamond-shaped sliding grip. Let's slide this to the left, so that the overlap with VF-1 is not so large. Either graphically slide it to station 17+25 or enter **1725** in the DYN text box. Notice that the view frame label is updated with the revised stations.

3. Next, select the circular rotation grip. Rotate the view frame slightly to better encompass the road. In the DYN text box, enter **282**. Then press Esc to clear the grips from VF - (2).

4. Now you'll adjust the match line location and length. First select ML-1 and then select its diamond sliding grip. Either graphically slide it to station 14+70 or enter **1470** in the DYN text box. Notice that the match line label is updated with the revised station.

5. Next, you'll lengthen the lower half of the match line so it extends the width of the view frame. Select the triangular lengthen grip at the lower end of the ML-1 and either graphically lengthen it to 140´ or enter **140** in the DYN text box.

Using Sheets

Civil 3D's Plan Production feature uses the concept of *sheets* to generate the pages that make up a set of plans. Simply put, *sheets* are layout tabs with viewports showing a given portion of your design model, based on the view frames previously created. The viewports have special properties set, defining then as either Plan or Profile viewports. These viewports must be predefined in a template (DWT) file. The sheets are managed using the standard AutoCAD Sheet Set Manager feature, and the sheet drawings and the drawing sheet set file (DST) can be added to your project in Vault. (See Chapter 19 for more information on Vault.)

The Create Sheets Wizard

After you've created view frames and match lines, you can proceed to the next step of creating sheets. Like view frames, sheets are created using a wizard too. Let's look at the wizard and the various page options. After we walk through each page, you'll perform an exercise to put what you've learned into practice.

You launch the Create Sheets wizard by selecting General ➤ Plan Production Tools ➤ Create Sheets. A list of the wizard's pages is shown along the left side, and an arrow indicates which page you are currently viewing. You move among the pages using the Next and Back navigation buttons along the bottom of each page. Alternately, you can jump directly to any page by clicking its name from the list on the left. Let's walk through the pages of the wizard and explain the features of each.

VIEW FRAME GROUP AND LAYOUTS PAGE

The first page of this wizard (Figure 20.11) is used to select the view frame group for which the sheets will be created. It is also used to define how the layouts for these sheets will be generated.

View Frame Group   In the first section of this page, you select the view frame group from either the dropdown menu or by choosing the Select From The Drawing button 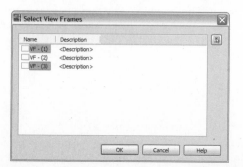 to select the view frame group from the drawing. After you've selected the group, you use the View Frame Range option to create sheets for all frames in the group or only for specific frames of your choosing.

All Frames   Select this option when you want sheets to be created for all view frames in the view frame group.

Selection   Selecting this option activates the Choose View Frames button. Click this button to select specific view frames from a list. A range of view frames can be selected by using the standard Windows selection technique of clicking the first view frame in the range and then holding Shift while you select the last view frame in the range. You can also select individual view frames in nonsequential order by holding Ctrl while you make your view frame selections. Figure 20.12 shows two of the three view frames selected in the Select View Frames dialog.

FIGURE 20.11
Create Sheets – View Frame Group and Layouts

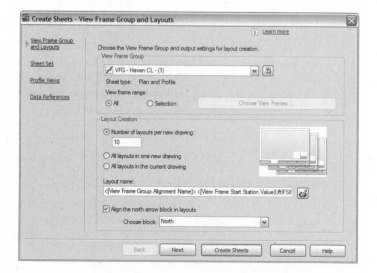

FIGURE 20.12
Select View Frames using standard Windows techniques

Layout Creation   In this section, you define where and how the new layouts for each sheet are created as well as the name format for these sheets, and you specify information about the alignment of the north arrow block.

There are three options for creating layout sheets: You can have all of the layout tabs created in the current drawing (the drawing you are in while executing the Create Sheets wizard); all the new layouts can be created in a new drawing file; or you can have the layouts created in multiple new drawing files, limiting the maximum number of layout sheets created in each file.

Number Of Layouts Per New Drawing   This option creates layouts in new drawing files and limits the maximum number of layouts per drawing file to the value you enter in the text box. For best performance, Autodesk recommends that a drawing file contains no more than 10 layouts. On the last page of this wizard you are given the option to select for what objects data references will be made. These data references are then created in the new drawings.

All Layouts In One New Drawing   As the name implies, this option will create all layouts for each view frame in a single new drawing. Use this option if you have fewer than 10 view frames to ensure best performance. If you have more than 10 view frames, use the previous option. On the last page of this wizard you are given the option to select for what objects data references will be made. These data references are then created in the new drawings.

All Layouts In The Current Drawing   Choosing this option results in all layouts being created in the current drawing. There are two different scenarios you need to be aware of when working with this option. As we'll explain later, a view frame group can be shared via Vault and referenced into other drawings as a data reference.

◆   When creating sheets, it is possible that your drawing has referenced the view frame group from another drawing or Vault (rather than having the original view frame group in your current drawing). If this is the situation, you are given the option to select for what additional objects' data references will be made (such as alignments, profiles, pipes, etc.). These data references are then created in the current drawing. You select these objects on the last page of the wizard.

◆   If you are working in a drawing in which the view frames were created (and therefore you are in the drawing in which the view frame group exists), the last page of this wizard is disabled. This is because in order to create view frames (and view frame groups), the alignment (and possibly the profile) must either exist in the current drawing or be referenced as a data reference (recall the prerequisites for creating view frames mentioned earlier.)

Layout Name   Use this text box to enter a name for each new layout. As with other named objects in Civil 3D, you can use the Name template to create a name format that includes information about the object being named.

Align The North Arrow Block In Layouts   If the template file you've selected contains a north arrow block, it can be aligned so that it points north on each layout sheet. The block must exist in the template. If there are multiple blocks, select the one you want to use from the drop-down menu.

WHERE AM I?

We highly recommend that you set up the Name template for the layouts so that it includes the alignment name and the station range. This conforms to the way many organizations create sheets, helps automate the creation of a sheet index, and in general makes it easier to navigate a DWG file with several layout tabs.

CREATE SHEETS PAGE

The second page of the wizard (Figure 20.13) is used to determine whether a new or existing sheet set (`.dst`) is used and the location of the DST file. Sheet name and storage location are also defined here. Additionally, on this page you decide whether or not to add the sheet set file (`.dst`) and the sheet files (`.dwg`) to the project Vault.

Vault   The first item on this page is the check box Add File To Vault. This option is available only if you are logged into vault. If you are not logged in, click the Log Into Vault button and log in. Once you are logged in, the box is selected and the drawing sheet set (`.dst`) and drawing sheets (`.dwg`) created by this wizard will be added to the project.

Sheet Set   In this section of the page, you select whether to create a new DST file or to add the sheets created by this wizard to an existing DST file.

New Sheet Set   By selecting this option, you create a new sheet set. You must enter a name for the DST file and a storage location. By default, the sheet set is created in the same folder as the current drawing. You can change this by clicking the ellipsis and selecting a new location.

Add To Existing Sheet Set   Selecting this option lets you select an existing sheet set file to which the new sheets created by this wizard will be added. Click the ellipsis to browse to the existing DST file location.

Sheets   The last section of the page is used to set the name and storage location for any new DWG files created by this wizard. On the previous page of the wizard, you had the choice of creating new files or creating the sheet layout in the current drawing. If you chose the latter option, the Sheets section on this page of the wizard is inactive. If you chose the former, here you enter the sheet file (DWG) name and the storage location.

WHAT IS A SHEET?

This page can be a little confusing due to the way the word *sheets* is used. In some places, *sheets* refers to layout tabs within a given drawing (`.dwg`) file. On this page, though, the word *sheets* is used in the context of Sheet Set Manager and refers to the DWG file itself.

FIGURE 20.13
Create Sheets –
Sheet Set

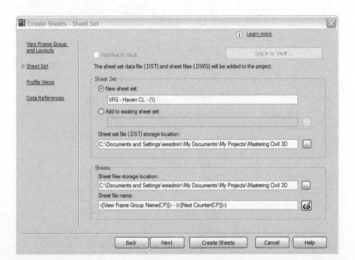

PROFILE VIEWS PAGE

The next page of the wizard (Figure 20.14) lists the profile view style and the band set selected in the Create View Frames wizard. You cannot change these selections here. You can, however, make adjustments to other profile settings.

The Other Profile View Options section lets you modify certain profile view options either by running the Profile View wizard or by using an existing profile view in your drawing as an example. Regardless of what option you choose, the "other options" that can be changed are limited to:

◆ Split profile view options from the Profile View height page of the Profile View wizard

◆ All options on the Profile Display page

◆ Most of the Data Band Page settings

◆ All settings on the Multiple Plot Options page

See Chapter 8 for details on each of these settings.

FIGURE 20.14

Create Sheets – Profile Views

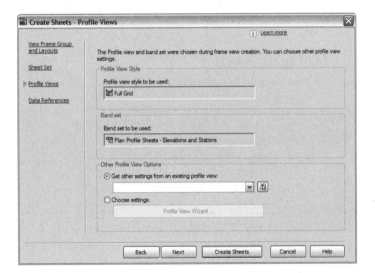

DATA REFERENCES PAGE

The final page of the Create Sheets wizard (Figure 20.15) is used to create data references in the drawing files that contain your layout sheets. Based on the view frame group used to create the sheets and the type of sheets (plan, profile, plan and profile), certain objects are selected by default. You have the option to select additional objects for which references will be made. You can either pick them from the list or click the Pick From Drawing button 🔳 and select the objects from the drawing.

Creating references to pipe networks that are to be shown in plan and or profile views is common. If you choose to create references for pipe network objects, you can also copy the labels for those network objects into the sheet's drawing file. This is convenient in that you won't need to relabel your networks.

FIGURE 20.15
Select Create Sheets –
Data References

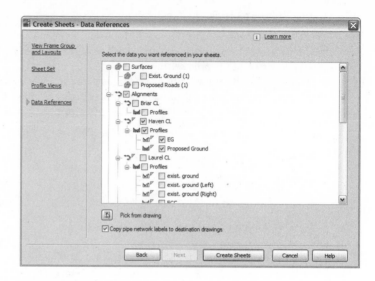

Managing Sheets

After you've completed all pages of the wizard, you create the sheets by clicking the Create Sheets button. Doing so completes the wizard and starts the creation process. If you are creating sheets with profile views, you are prompted to select a profile view origin. Civil 3D then displays several dialog boxes, indicating the process status for the various tasks such as creating the new sheet drawings and creating the DST file.

If the Sheet Set Manager (SSM) is not currently open, it opens with the newly created DST file loaded. The sheets are listed and the details of the drawing files for each sheet appear in the Details area (Figure 20.16).

FIGURE 20.16
New sheets in Sheet
Set Manager

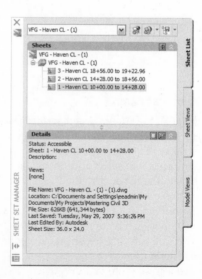

If you double-click to open the new drawing file that contains the newly created sheets, you'll see layout sheet tabs created for each of the view frames. The sheets are named using the Name template as defined in the Create Sheets wizard. Figure 20.17 shows the names that result from the following template:

```
<[View Frame Group Alignment Name]> <[View Frame Start Station Value]>
to <[View Frame End Station Value]>
```

FIGURE 20.17
The template results in the "Haven CL" tab names shown here

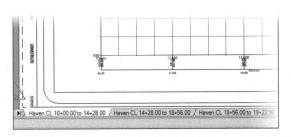

To create the final sheets in this new drawing, Civil 3D externally references (XRefs) the drawing containing the view frames; creates data references (DRefs) for the alignments, profiles, and any additional objects you selected in the Create Sheets wizard; and, if profile sheet types were selected in the wizard, creates profile views in the final sheet drawing.

Finally, if you selected the Vault option, the drawing file containing the sheets as well as the DST file have been checked into your project.

Let's look at an exercise to pull all these concepts together:

1. Open Sheets_Wizard.dwg from the CD. This drawing contains the view frame group, alignment, and profile for Haven Road. Note the drawing does not have profile views.

2. Select General ➤ Plan Production Tools ➤ Create Sheets. This launches the Create Sheets wizard.

3. On the View Frame Group And Layouts page, confirm View Frame Range is set to All; Number Of Layouts Per Drawings is set to 10; and Align The North Block In Layouts is checked. Click Next.

4. On the Sheet Set page, select the New Sheet Set option and for both the Sheet Set File Storage Location and Sheet Files Storage Location, use the ellipsis to browse to C:\Mastering Civil 3D 2008\CH 20\Final Sheets and click OK. Click Next.

5. On the Profile Views page, for Other Profile View Options, select Choose Settings and then click the Profile View Wizard button. The Create Multiple Profile Views dialog opens.

6. On the left side of the Create Multiple Profile Views dialog, select the Profile Display Options to jump to that page.

   For the Proposed Ground profile, scroll to the right and modify the Labels setting, changing it from Standard to Complete Label Set, as shown in Figure 20.18. After selecting the label set, click OK and then click Next to advance to the Data Bands page.

7. On the Data Bands page, change Profile2 to Proposed Ground, as shown in Figure 20.19. Click Finish to return to the Create Sheets wizard. Click Next to advance to the Data References page.

FIGURE 20.18
Change the labels for the Proposed Ground profile.

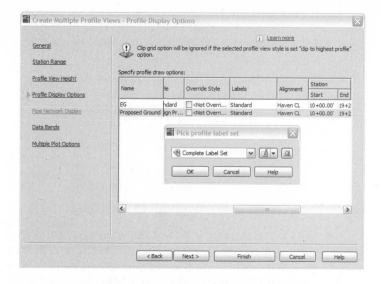

FIGURE 20.19
Set Profile2 to Proposed Ground.

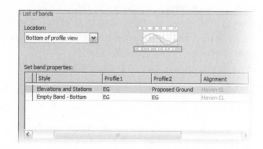

8. On the Data References page, confirm that Haven CL and both of its profiles are checked. Click Create Sheets to complete the wizard.

9. Before actually creating the sheets, Civil 3D must save your current drawing. Click OK when prompted. The drawing is saved and you are prompted for an insertion point for the profile view. The location you pick will be the lower-left corner of the profile view grid. Select an open area in the drawing, above the left side of the site plan. Civil 3D then displays a progress dialog; then the Panorama with information about the results of the sheet creation process is displayed. Close the Panorama window.

INVISIBLE PROFILE VIEWS

Note that the profile views are only created in the current drawing if you selected the option to create all layouts in the current drawing. Since that was not what we did in this exercise, the profile views are not created in the current drawing. Rather, they are created in the sheet drawing files in model space in a location relative to the point you selected in this step.

---

10. After the sheet creation process is complete, notice the Sheet Set Manager window is now open (Figure 20.20). Click the sheet number 1 named Haven CL 10+00.00 to 14+28.00. Notice the name conforms to the Name template and includes the alignment name and the station range for the sheet. Review the details listed for the sheet. In particular, note the filename and storage location.

11. Double-click this sheet to open the new sheets drawing and display the layout tab for Haven CL 10+00.00 to 14+28.00. Review the multiple tabs created in this drawing file. The template used also takes advantage of AutoCAD fields, some of which do not have values assigned.

FIGURE 20.20

Sheet Set Manager

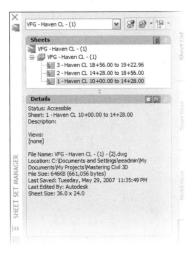

Supporting Components

At the beginning of this chapter, we mentioned that there are several prerequisites to using the plan production tools in Civil 3D. The list includes drawing templates (DWT) set up to work with the Plan Production feature and styles for the object generated by this feature. In this section of the chapter, we'll look at preparing these items for use in creating your finished sheets.

Templates

Civil 3D ships with several predefined template files set up for various types of sheets that Plan Production can create. By default, these templates are installed in a subfolder called Plan Production, which is located in the standard Template folder. You can see the Template folder location by opening the Files tab of the Options dialog as shown in Figure 20.21.

Figure 20.22 shows the default contents of the Plan Production subfolder. Notice there are templates for Plan, Profile, and Plan and Profile sheet types. There are metric and imperial versions of each of these.

Each template contains layout tabs with pages set to various sheet sizes and plan scales. For example, the `Civil 3D (Imperial) Plan and Profile.dwt` template has layouts created at various ANSI and ARCH sheets sizes and scales, as shown in Figure 20.23.

FIGURE 20.21
Template files
location

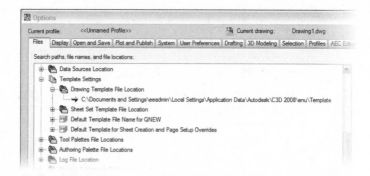

FIGURE 20.22
Plan Production
DWT files

FIGURE 20.23
Various predefined
layouts in
standard DWT

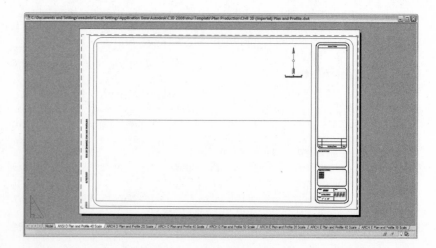

The viewports in these templates must be rectangular in shape and must have Viewport Type set to either Plan or Profile, depending on the intended use. Viewport Type is set on the Design tab of the Properties dialog, as shown in Figure 20.24.

FIGURE 20.24
Viewport
Properties –
Viewport Type

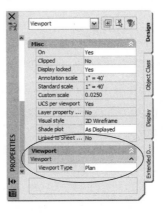

IRREGULAR VIEWPORT SHAPES

Just because the viewports must start out rectangular doesn't mean they have to stay that way. Experiment with creating viewports from rectangular polylines having vertices at the midpoint of each side of the viewport (and not just at the corners). After you've created your sheets using the Plan Production tool, you can stretch your viewport into irregular shapes.

Styles and Settings

If you've used previous versions of Civil 3D, you know it ships with several general template files that contain styles for all Civil 3D objects. These templates include object and label styles for the components used in plan production. They also include default feature and command settings for plan production. There are two main objects used in plan production: view frames and match lines. Match lines are associated with view frames, which are collected in view frame groups. Let's look at the object and label styles for each component in more detail:

View Frames   The styles for view frame objects and labels are very straightforward. The object style has only a single component: View Frame Border. View frame label styles are similar to other label styles used elsewhere in Civil 3D. The Label Style Composer is used to add Text, Line Block, and Reference Text components. Referenced Text can be used to include object information from an Alignment, Cogo Point, Parcel, Profile, or Surface in your view frame label.

Match Lines   Like view frames, match line styles are pretty basic. The object style has two components: the Lines and a component called the Match Line Mask. This second component controls the masking hatch that is displayed in the overlap area beyond the match line and warrants further explanation. Figures 20.25 and 20.26 show the Component hatch display settings for a match line style and the resulting sheet.

The match line style is defined in the drawing containing the view frames. Any changes to the style must be made in the view frames drawing; the drawing must then be saved and the XRef updated in the sheets drawings. If the layout sheets were created in the drawing in which the view frames exist, the match line style updates are automatically displayed on the layout sheets.

View Frame Groups The View Frame Group object has no styles, only feature and command settings (similar to subassemblies). The feature settings for this group are important because they are used to control the default settings for view frames and match lines. These default settings can be overridden by the command settings.

FIGURE 20.25
The display of the indicated area, beyond the match line, is controlled by the Component Hatch Line settings of the match line object style.

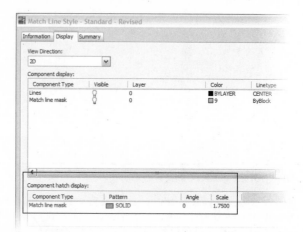

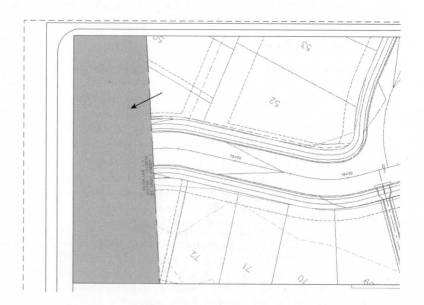

FIGURE 20.26

Notice the hatching pattern has been updated to reflect the changes to the Component Hatch Line settings of the match line object style.

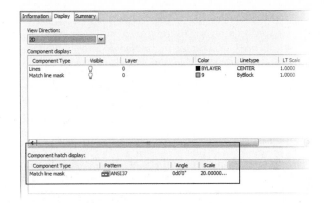

The Bottom Line

Create view frames. When you create view frames, you must select the template file that contains the layout tabs that will be used as the basis for your sheets. This template must contain predefined viewports. You can define these viewports with extra vertices so you change their shape after the sheets have been created.

Master It Open the Mastering Plan Production 1 drawing. Run the Create View Frames wizard to create sheets in the current drawing. (Accept defaults for all other values.)

Create sheets and use Sheet Set Manager. Sheets can be created in new drawing files or in the current drawing. Use the option to create sheets in the current drawing when a) you've referenced in the view frame group, or b) you have a small project. Additionally, the resulting sheets are based on the template you chose when you created the view frames. If the template contains customized viewports, you can modify the shape of the viewport to better fit your sheet needs.

Master It Open the Mastering Plan Production 2 drawing. Run the Create Sheets wizard to create plan and profile sheets for Haven CL using the template `Mastering (Imperial) Plan and Profile.dwt`. This template has a custom-made viewport with extra vertices. (Accept defaults for all other values.)

Edit sheet templates and styles associated with plan production. The Create View Frames command uses predefined styles for view frames and match lines. These styles must exist in the drawing in which you create the view frame group. You can create match line styles to meet your specific needs.

Master It Open the Mastering Plan Production 3 drawing and modify the match line component hatch display style setting to make the linework beyond the match line appear screened.

Chapter 21

Playing Nice with Others: LDT and LandXML

As much as we'd love to see the whole world move to a Civil 3D model with real coordinates so we could all just share data without pause, it's simply not going to happen this year. In land development, we work with a large number of team partners on most projects. This can include architects, contractors, other civil engineers, planners, and landscape architects on a small job. On a large job, the number of people on this list could double or triple. An important part of being a good team member is sharing data cleanly. In this chapter, we'll look at importing Land Desktop and LandXML data and exporting data in drawing and LandXML formats.

In this chapter, you'll learn to:

◆ Discern the design elements in a LandXML data file

◆ Import a Land Desktop project

◆ Import a LandXML file to create a surface, alignments, and profiles

◆ Create an AutoCAD drawing that can be read without special enablers

What Is LandXML?

For years, there was the humble text file. These files were the lingua franca of written documents and data input. We still use text files for many tasks, in spite of the evolution of Microsoft Word DOC files, PDFs, and other common written formats. The problems occur when you try to send your Word document to someone running OpenOffice or WordPerfect. Formatting falls apart, font information is lost, and paragraphs don't justify like they should. Bring in the simple text file and stylize again! The idea is that by having a base-level format of the truly important part of the document in question, almost anyone can read and deal with the data as they wish.

LandXML is the text file of the land-development world. Created in January 2000 by an international consortium, LandXML is a nonproprietary data format that allows the exchange of land-development-design elements between varying products. Members of the LandXML.org consortium include Autodesk Inc., Trimble Navigation, Bentley Systems Inc., and the U.S. Army Corps of Engineers. By working together to define a common language and then including LandXML tools in their own programs, these member groups have created a better translation mechanism for the land-development community at large. Each version of this common language is known as a *schema* and contains important information about the format of the data that is included.

HANDY-DANDY NOTEPAD

As we look at XML files in this chapter, we'll be using XML Notepad from Microsoft. It's free and small, and it makes reading the XML files much easier. We highly recommend you install it before beginning these exercises! Although you can view or edit XML files with standard Windows Notepad, it's not something you really want to do.

An XML file is simply a specially formatted text file, similar to HTML or any of the modern web-based formats. Using an XML reader, these files can actually be read and even edited. In this exercise, we'll look at a sample XML file and the sections it contains:

1. Open the `Niblo.xml` file.

2. Expand the LandXML portion as shown in Figure 21.1. This version is the LandXML schema that was used to create the file.

3. Expand the Project folder to view the name of the drawing the XML file was created from.

4. Expand the Application folder to view the name of the program that created the file, the version of that program, and the creation timestamp on the XML file.

5. Expand the Alignments folder to explore the information associated with an alignment, as shown in Figure 21.2.

6. When you're done poking around, close the file without saving changes.

The schema defines how much information can be associated and defined in the XML file. In the case of alignments, Figure 21.2 shows both a ProfSurf and ProfAlign folder under the Profile folder. These folders refer to a sampled surface profile and a layout profile, respectively. By learning and understanding the names used in the XML file, you can actually discern the contained information before you import it to your Civil 3D model. We'll look at that step in the next section.

FIGURE 21.1

Niblo.xml file in XML Notepad for reviewing

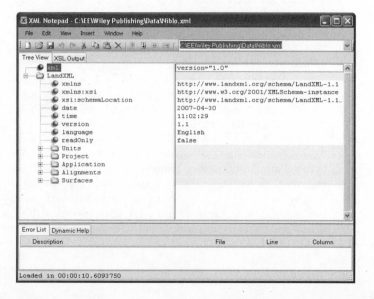

FIGURE 21.2

Niblo.xml file with the Carson's Way alignment section expanded

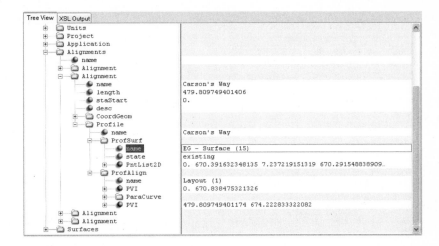

Handling Inbound Data

The data conversion process takes place throughout the project. In the beginning of the job, bringing data into the Civil 3D object model is a crucial step. This data can be from existing LDT projects in the office, LDT data you've acquired from other consultants, or LandXML files from other packages. In this section, we'll look at how we can use both LDT and LandXML data to create a Civil 3D object model ready for design. We'll import Land Desktop Project data and then some other data as a LandXML file.

Importing Land Desktop Data

Most of the firms moving to Civil 3D are coming from a Land Desktop (LDT) background. In this environment, they had surfaces, alignments, profiles—the full gamut of project-design elements. By converting existing LDT data into a Civil 3D model, you ensure that these resources can continue to be used and pay dividends into the future. In this exercise, we'll import the LDT project that has provided much of the data in previous chapters:

1. Create a new Civil 3D drawing using the `AutoCAD Civil 3D (Imperial) NCS Extended` template file.

2. Choose File ➤ Import ➤ Import Data From Land Desktop.

3. Click the Browse button circled in the upper right of Figure 21.3.

4. In the Browse For Folder dialog, expand the LDT Import folder, as shown in Figure 21.4, and click OK.

5. Click OK to dismiss the warning about pipes that appears. This warning is simply a reminder to indicate that you need a pipe part in the parts list to match the sizes described in the LDT project.

FIGURE 21.3
The Import Data From
Autodesk Land Desk-
top Project dialog

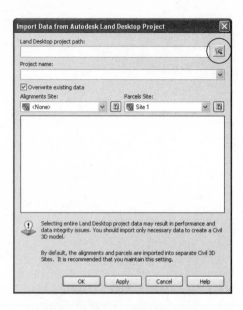

FIGURE 21.4
Selecting an LDT
project path

6. Select Conklin, and click OK. The Import Data From Autodesk Land Desktop Project dialog opens.

7. Uncheck the Pipe Runs portion of the data.

8. Uncheck the Alignments heading, then check the PROP RD alignment, as shown in Figure 21.5. Note that some branches have been collapsed for clarity.

9. Verify the Alignments Site is set to None.

10. Click OK to import the LDT data.

11. Click OK to dismiss the Import Data From Autodesk Land Desktop Project dialog.

12. Perform a Zoom Extents to view the imported data, as shown in Figure 21.6.

13. Close the drawing without saving changes.

FIGURE 21.5
LDT project selected
and ready for import

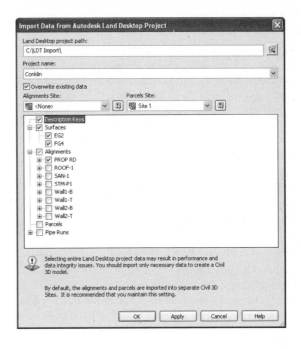

FIGURE 21.6
LDT import complete

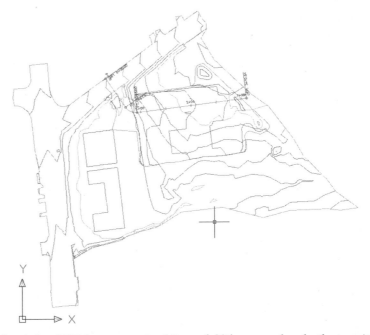

By working with existing LDT data, you extend its useful lifespan and make the transition to Civil 3D less of a traumatic change. Many firms have long histories of working with LDT data, and this ability continues to bring value to that history. In the next section, we'll look at importing LandXML, a methodology used frequently to communicate across firm boundaries.

WHAT ABOUT THE PARCELS?

You'll notice that in the example used, we didn't even attempt to use the Parcels import functions. The importing of parcels in any format takes place as importing a series of closed objects. This means that adjacent parcels often have duplicate lines. As you saw in Chapter 6, duplicate linework is one of the biggest causes of broken Civil 3D drawings. It's unfortunate, but we generally recommend reworking parcels to ensure a clean network topology.

Importing LandXML Data

There are two major sources for LandXML data. The first source is land-development packages, such as Civil 3D, InRoads, or PowerCivil. The other is the fleet of design and analysis tools, such as StormCAD or IntelliSolve. We will look first at a LandXML file created by Civil 3D, then at a LandXML file created by IntelliSolve.

LandXML from a Design Package

LandXML data is more commonly sent from outside the organization but is sometimes used when trying to capture a snapshot between the LDT and Civil 3D data. The creation of the XML file takes a picture at an instant in time, so that the source information in the XML file is always available for review. The LDT project, however, could be in flux even after the import to Civil 3D takes place, so tracing the data back could be difficult.

In this exercise, we'll look at the LandXML importing process:

1. Create a new Civil 3D drawing using the `AutoCAD Civil 3D (Imperial) NCS Extended` template file.

2. Choose File ➢ Import ➢ Import ➢ Import LandXML.

3. Navigate to the data directory and select `Niblo.xml` to display the Import LandXML dialog, shown in Figure 21.7.

4. Expand the Alignments Name and Surfaces branches, as shown in Figure 21.7, to review the data prior to importing the file.

FIGURE 21.7
The LandXML file
open for review

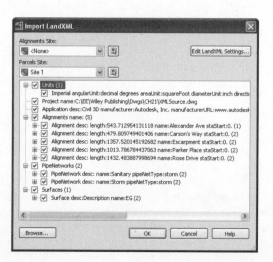

5. Expand the Surfaces (1) ≻ Surface Desc branches to reveal the details in the XML file, as shown in Figure 21.8.

6. Uncheck the Source Data box (see Figure 21.8), so the contours from which the surface was created are *not* imported.

7. Click OK to import the data. Civil 3D will import the objects and zoom to the extents, as shown in Figure 21.9.

FIGURE 21.8

Expand the Surfaces branch in the Import LandXML dialog.

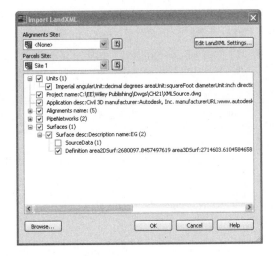

FIGURE 21.9

LandXML import completed

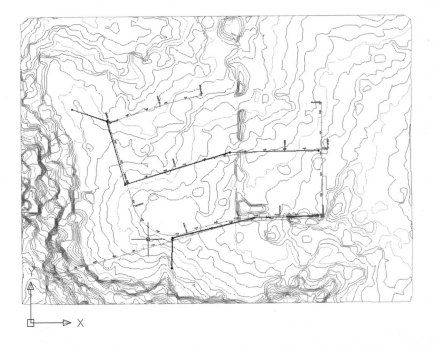

This data is ready for use, but let's look at some interesting things that come about during the LandXML process. The surface, alignments, and pipes are three major things to be concerned with:

◆ Surfaces are created with a default style of Contours 2′ And 10′ (Background). The Surface Properties dialog in Figure 21.10 shows a more interesting option. Notice how the surface was built on the basis of the import of the XML file, but then a snapshot was automatically generated. Snapshots allow us to rebuild the surface from that point forward. What does this mean for you as a user? It means that we could hypothetically send the drawing without the XML file and the surface would still build. This method works well when you want to add a basic level of protection to your surface information. It's not perfect, but it can be interesting.

◆ Alignments move to the siteless collection, as shown in Figure 21.11. Many Civil 3D users like working this way instead of the prior requirement of working within a site. Importing into the siteless Alignments collection also means that random parcels are not created upon the XML import. Profiles are imported with alignments, but profile views are not created. Review Chapter 9 for information on creating and manipulating profile views. Also, because LandXML schemas define alignments and other objects as hard-coded objects, the relationships are not preserved. Each component of an alignment becomes a fixed entity, with no understanding of the component on either end of itself.

◆ Pipes must have a matching part size in both the target drawing and source XML file. Your pipe network will not import if there is no valid pipe size in the current parts family as is called out in the XML file. See Chapter 14 for information about part lists and part families.

By using XML data from other sources, you eliminate the human error of importing by redrawing objects or the computational errors that come from importing points without breaklines in surfaces. LandXML allows for the easy sharing of the critical data without the burden of the full drawing information. Now that we've made some data, let's share it back out in the next section.

By using LandXML as the translation system, even programs that have no direct hook into Civil 3D can be used as auxiliary design tools. Now that we've imported a number of different files and formats, let's look at the best way to get our Civil 3D model out to team members.

FIGURE 21.10
Surface Properties after LandXML import

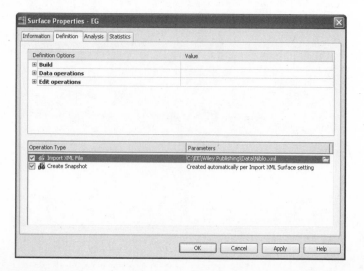

FIGURE 21.11
Imported alignments
assigned with no site

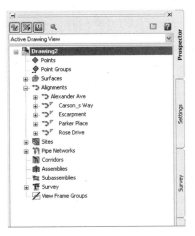

 Real World Scenario

LANDXML FROM AN ANALYSIS PACKAGE

Most civil engineering firms have at least one or two specialized analysis packages in the office. These can include tools for airport design, flow analysis, or soil mapping. Many of these packages are starting to include LandXML as an output format. In this exercise, we'll review an XML file created by the IntelliSolve program and import it into a blank Civil 3D drawing to see how the objects are converted:

1. Create a new Civil 3D drawing using the AutoCAD Civil 3D (Imperial) NCS Extended template file.

2. Choose File Import ➢ Import ➢ Import LandXML.

3. Navigate to the Data directory and select Intellisolve.xml. The Import LandXML dialog appears.

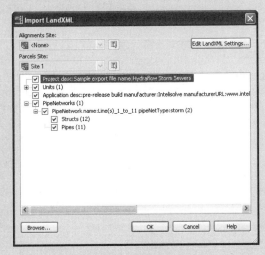

4. Click OK to finish the import. The drawing will zoom extents as in the other exercise and should look like this:

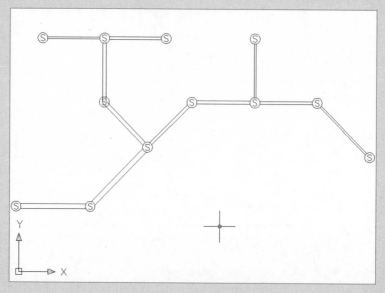

If you'd like to see some more samples of LandXML from other design packages, check out www.landxml.org and click Samples. Sample files are available from many of the major consortium partners. Additionally, these files can be freely used as long as they are not modified.

Sharing the Model

Once you've created an active Civil 3D model, you inevitably have to share it. In many cases, this means simply printing plans. But your better team members will recognize the value in your design information and want something at a higher information level. In this section, we'll look at creating XML files from Civil 3D and creating AutoCAD drawing files that can be shared.

Creating LandXML files

Creating a LandXML file is very simple—about three clicks total. The only hard part is dealing with the options and the schema involved on the other end. Because LandXML.org occasionally revises the schema to include new object information, going backward with LandXML isn't any easier than going backward with Civil 3D objects. In these exercises, we'll have to use the schema built into Civil 3D, but remember that your recipient might not have the latest schema. A little homework will go a long way in easing the frustrations.

In this exercise, we'll create a few XML files with various options, and then analyze them in XML Notepad:

1. Open the XMLSource.dwg file.

2. In Prospector, right-click the drawing name and select Export LandXML to display the dialog in Figure 21.12.

3. Click OK.

4. Navigate to the desktop (or some other suitable location), and click Save to create the XML file.

   That's it. Simple, right? Now, let's look at some of the options in the LandXML export:

5. Switch to the Settings tab in Prospector.

6. Right-click the drawing name and select Edit LandXML Settings.

7. Switch to the Export tab, as shown in Figure 21.13.

FIGURE 21.12
The Export To
LandXML dialog

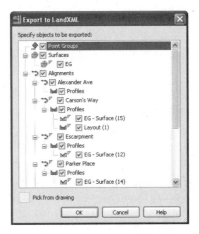

FIGURE 21.13
The Export tab
in the LandXML
Settings dialog

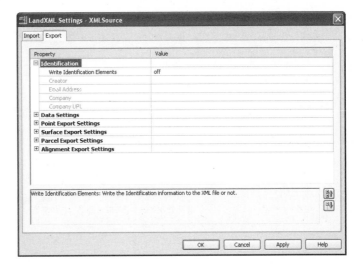

Because there are a fair number of options, we'll look at them as we have in other dialogs:

◆ **Identification** controls information written to the file to help identify the original source firm or person. This can include a name, phone number, e-mail address, or URL.

◆ **Data Settings** determine what foot standard is used, the rotation format, and the ability to create a read-only XML file. This read-only setting is applied both through the XML file itself and as a Windows read-only flag on the file.

◆ **Point Export Settings** control which point data field is used as the code (or name field), the full description, whether or not to include point references (DREFs), the tolerance for points that tie to parcel cogo information, and description keys.

◆ **Surface Export Settings** control whether the surface is exported as points and faces or simply points and whether or not watershed values are exported.

◆ **Parcel Export Settings** simply assign the direction of parcel creation: clockwise or counterclockwise.

◆ **Alignment Export Settings** determine if cross-sectional data is exported with the alignments.

Some programs may or may not use all these values, but any program built on the current schema should accept the file created with these values included. To see how these changes look in the output, complete this exercise.

8. Under the Surface Export Settings, change the Surface Data option to Points Only, as shown in Figure 21.14.

9. Click OK to dismiss the dialog.

10. Export a new LandXML file as we did in the first four steps of this exercise. *Be sure not to overwrite the first file!*

11. Open the XML file from the first exercise in XML Notepad.

12. Scroll down in the tree view shown on the left and expand the Surfaces folder, as shown in Figure 21.15.

FIGURE 21.14
Changing the Surface
Data option

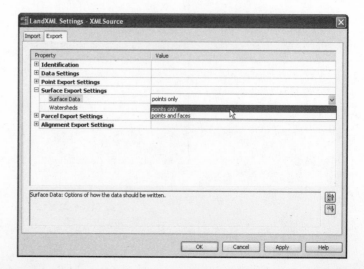

13. Choose Window ➢ New Window in XML Notepad.

14. Open the second XML file created.

15. Expand the tree view as we did for the first file. Place the windows near each other to create a view similar to Figure 21.16.

FIGURE 21.15
LandXML file with Surface set to Points And Faces

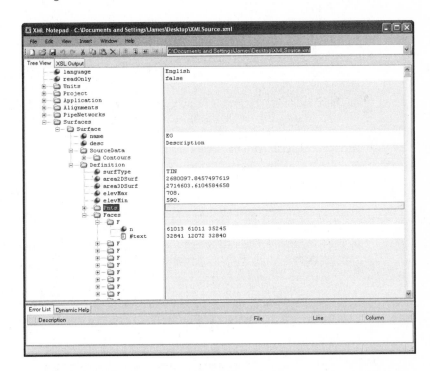

FIGURE 21.16
Comparing LandXML files with XML Notepad

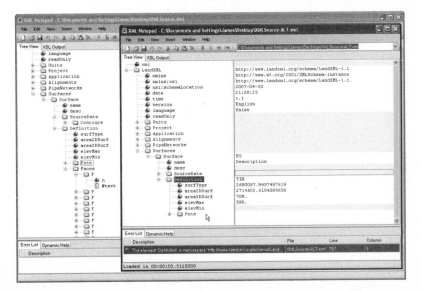

Notice that the Surface definition in the second file (named XMLSource-ALT in the figure) lacks the Faces branch. By changing the settings, we changed the structure of the file created. In this case, we've created a lesser file, in that a surface created from the second LandXML file will not necessarily triangulate in the same way as the source file. Creating a LandXML file is pretty straightforward, as you've seen, and unless you have a good reason, changing the settings generally isn't suggested.

Creating an AutoCAD Drawing

The unfortunate reality is that many of the partners in a land-development project team don't want your design data—they just want the linework. Because Civil 3D objects are so complex, this isn't simple to achieve. In this section, we'll look at a couple of options for creating drawing files that might be suitable. The first is using proxy graphics or object enablers. The second is to "dumb down" our drawing to make it more palatable to other users.

OBJECT ENABLERS AND PROXY GRAPHICS

For years, the main methods of dealing with custom objects (objects that don't exist in the core AutoCAD product) were to use proxy graphics or object enablers. Neither is an ideal situation, but if you can convince the recipient of your data to deal with one of these methods, it's better than the explosion of objects we will look at in the next section.

Proxy graphics work by creating a simple linework version of the Civil 3D objects being drawn in your design file. These graphics are just that: graphics. They cannot be used in any meaningful way for design, but will display properly on the recipient's computer, assuming the drawing version is correct. The main problem with this approach is visible in Figure 21.17.

As you can see here, the file with proxy graphics is approximately 10 percent larger. This is for a very simple Civil 3D file with a single surface, four alignments, and very few labels. Since every label, profile view, alignment, contour, and so on in a drawing must be represented by a proxy graphic, this difference gets larger as the drawing gets more complex.

FIGURE 21.17
File Properties for a drawing with and without proxy graphics

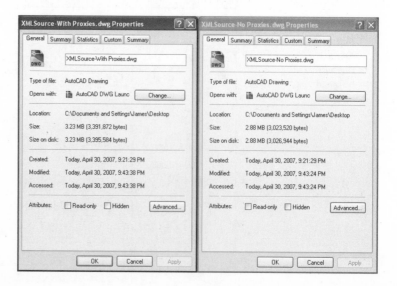

PROXY GRAPHICS AND YOU

On the basis of feedback during the beta program for Civil 3D 2008, proxy graphics have actually been turned off by default in the shipping templates. You'll have to turn them back on if you use these templates. To do this, type **proxygraphics** at the command line and enter **1**.

The better answer (especially from your viewpoint!) is to use an object enabler on the recipient's end. These applications, written by Autodesk, provide the ability to draw Civil 3D objects without proxy graphics embedded in the file. They do require an installation on the recipient's computer, but it is a onetime operation. Unfortunately, since these files have to be located, downloaded, and installed, many users simply won't do it. Object enablers can be located by searching the Autodesk site under the Utilities And Drivers page for the recipient's product.

Both options require that the recipient be on the same core version as the Civil 3D user. Since this isn't always the case, we'll look at creating other usable formats in the next section.

STRIPPING CUSTOM OBJECTS

The most drastic option for sharing data with non-Civil 3D users is to destroy the model and strip out the custom Civil 3D objects. This is a one-way trip, and the resulting file is made up simply of lines, arcs, polylines, and other native AutoCAD objects. In this exercise, we'll export a file with a variety of Civil 3D objects and then go look at the resulting file:

1. Open the XMLSource.dwg file.

2. Choose File ➤ Export ➤ Export To AutoCAD ➤ 2007 Format.

3. Navigate to the desktop or some convenient location and click Save. The file is saved, but your original file is left untouched!

4. Open your exported file.

5. Zoom in on one of the "alignments," and pick any piece, as shown in Figure 21.18.

FIGURE 21.18
Alignment arc after
Export To AutoCAD

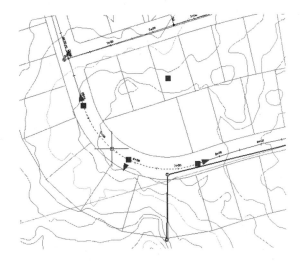

This file is considerably smaller than the original Civil 3D drawing but contains none of the original's intelligence. Re-creating the data would be possible, but since every piece is independent, it would be tedious.

WHAT VIEW DID YOU WANT?

One of the interesting facets of the Export To AutoCAD functionality is that it gives you exactly what you see on screen. Export a surface with a contour style in plan view, and you'll get flat polylines with no elevation. Turn to an isometric view before exporting, and you'll get the 3D representation of that surface. If your surface shows contours in the 3D view, you'll get polylines at elevation. A 3D TIN view will generate a whole host of 3D faces. It's all view dependent.

The Bottom Line

Discern the design elements in a LandXML data file. LandXML.org is an international consortium of software firms, equipment manufacturers, consultants, and other land-development professionals. By creating a lingua franca for the industry, they've made sharing design data between design and analysis packages a simple import/export operation.

> **Master It** Download the `Campground.xml` file from the `LandXML.org` website and list the creating program, along with the alignments and the surfaces it contains.

Import a Land Desktop project. Many Civil 3D firms have a huge repository of LDT projects. By using the import LDT project data functionality of Civil 3D, this data's lifespan can be extended, and the value of the information it contains can continue to grow.

> **Master It** Import the STM-P3 Pipe Run from the Conklin LDT Project data source and count the number of pipes and structures that successfully import.

Import a LandXML file to create a surface, alignments, and profiles. As more and more firms use Civil 3D, they'll want to share the design data without giving up their full drawing files. Using LandXML to share import data allows the accurate transmission of data in a standardized format and gives the end recipient the ability to manipulate the entities as needed.

> **Master It** Complete the import of the `Campground.xml` file into a new Civil 3D drawing.

Create an AutoCAD drawing that can be read without special enablers. Since many members of your design team will not be working with Civil 3D, it's important to deliver information to them in a manner they can use. Using the built-in tools to create drawings consisting of purely native AutoCAD objects strips these drawings of their design intelligence but provides a workable route to data sharing with almost any CAD user.

> **Master It** Convert the drawing you just made from `Campground.xml` to an R2004 AutoCAD drawing.

Chapter 22

Get The Picture: Visualization

Since Civil 3D is built on AutoCAD, all the functionality of AutoCAD is available and adaptable to Civil 3D objects. Before the 2007 release, building 3D objects, 3D navigation, and rendering in the AutoCAD environment was possible but not very intuitive. In 2007, substantial changes were made to these tools in AutoCAD, which makes creating rendered scenes simple. Also, several Civil 3D objects have tools built in to make rendering straightforward.

This chapter is meant to be an introduction to visualization. For more information, see the AutoCAD Users Guide, which is built into the Help menu. Also, there are many robust AutoCAD rendering texts and learning resources.

In this chapter, you'll learn to:

◆ Apply render materials to a corridor using a code set style

◆ Apply a Realistic visual style to a corridor model

◆ Create a 3D DWF from a corridor model

AutoCAD 3D Modeling Workspace

Civil 3D 2008 comes with several default workspaces. In previous chapters, we discussed the standard workspaces for Civil 3D–related tasks. Two workspaces are particularly suited for rendering work. The first is the Visualization And Rendering Workspace, as shown in Figure 22.1, which contains the Civil 3D Toolspace, as well as menus, toolbars, and palettes that are useful when doing visualization tasks. The second is the AutoCAD 3D Modeling workspace, which contains more AutoCAD-focused tools and menus in addition to the Dashboard.

The Dashboard

The Dashboard is an AutoCAD palette that came about in AutoCAD 2007. It originally included only tools to assist with 3D modeling tools. While the Dashboard, as shown in Figure 22.2, is still geared toward 3D modeling and visualization, you can customize its content much as you would a regular tool palette by right-clicking on the spine of the palette and choosing your desired content.

FIGURE 22.1

The Visualization and
Rendering Workspace

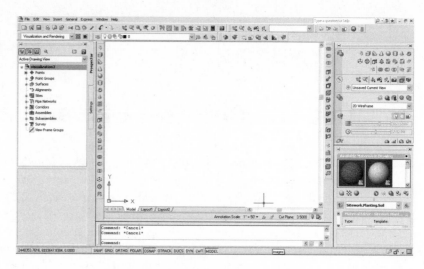

FIGURE 22.2

The Dashboard

By default, the Dashboard contains several panels that will be frequently used during visualization that we will investigate here. Most Dashboard panels can be expanded by clicking on the arrows that appear when you click each dashboard icon located on the left side of each panel. See Figure 22.3.

The Visual Styles Control Panel   The Visual Styles control panel (Figure 22.4) allows you to toggle through different visual styles (which we will discuss in the next section), as well as edit visual styles and adjust things like edge jitter, overhang, and silhouette.

The Lights Control Panel   The Lights control panel (Figure 22.5) contains tools and settings for adjusting and adding lighting, including establishing the sun's date, time, and geographic location.

The Materials Control Panel The Materials control panel (Figure 22.6) provides tools for mapping, assigning, and editing render materials.

The 3D Navigate Control Panel The 3D Navigate control panel (Figure 22.7) provides tools for panning, zooming, setting cameras, and creating walkthroughs. It also has a dropdown option for toggling between different named views.

The Render Control Panel The Render control panel (Figure 22.7) is used to create still renderings and adjust the settings for renderings.

FIGURE 22.3
Expanding Dashboard
control panels

FIGURE 22.4
The Visual Styles
control panel

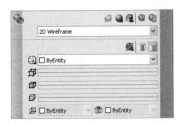

FIGURE 22.5
The Lights
control panel

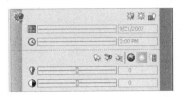

FIGURE 22.6
The Materials
control panel

FIGURE 22.7
The 3D Navigate and
Render control panels

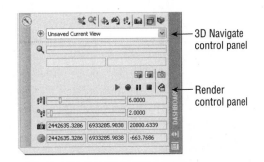

Adding Control Panels to the Dashboard

Control panels can be added to the Dashboard by right-clicking the spine of the palette, as shown in Figure 22.8. They can also be docked or anchored like any other dockable window in the AutoCAD environment.

FIGURE 22.8
Adding control panels
to the Dashboard

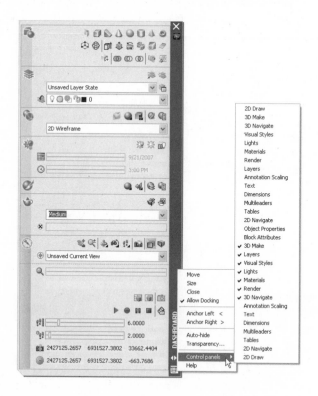

Applying Different Visual Styles

A visual style is a group of settings that stores your preferences for the display of faces, edges, shading, and texture. There are five default visual styles, and you can create your own custom visual styles as desired. The Visual Styles toolbar (Figure 22.9) is an AutoCAD toolbar that you can add to any workspace.

2D Wireframe   When the visual style is set to 2D Wireframe, objects are shown as lines and curves. Most likely, you now do most of your work in 2D Wireframe. Raster Images, OLE objects, linetypes, and lineweights are shown in this visual style. Figure 22.10 shows a corridor in 2D Wireframe.

3D Wireframe   Applying the 3D Wireframe visual style in plan view will look almost identical to 2D Wireframe. Objects are represented using lines and curves. A corridor shown in 3D Wireframe can be seen in Figure 22.11.

> **SWITCHING TO 3D VIEWS**
>
> While working in the AutoCAD environment, you can navigate your model by using tools found on the 3D Navigation toolbar, the Dashboard, or the View menu. You can change from top view to an isometric view, use a constrained or unconstrained 3D orbit, or use any combination of these tools to see your model from a different perspective.

FIGURE 22.9
The Visual
Styles toolbar

FIGURE 22.10
A corridor shown in
top view with 2D
Wireframe visual style
applied

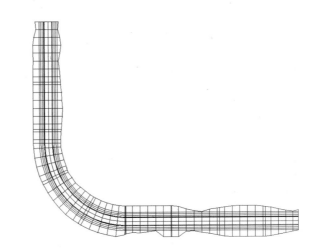

FIGURE 22.11
A corridor shown in
isometric view with
3D Wireframe visual
style applied. Note
that the 3D faces of the
corridor are visible.

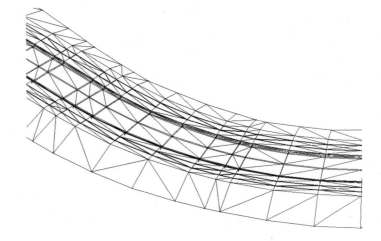

3D Hidden The 3D Hidden visual style is similar to the 3D Wireframe visual style, as shown in Figure 22.12. The only difference is that any back faces are hidden.

Conceptual The Conceptual visual style was created to make your 3D objects appear smoother and perhaps easier to see without looking "real." It is similar to the 3D hidden visual style with some warm and cool colors applied, as Figure 22.13 shows. This visual style is useful for giving your models a little more contrast without having to assign a render material.

Realistic The Realistic visual style is similar to the 3D wireframe visual style, as Figure 22.14 shows. In addition to showing the 3D faces of your model, this visual style smoothes the edges and shows any render materials you have assigned.

FIGURE 22.12
A corridor shown in isometric view with 3D Hidden visual style applied. Note that the 3D faces of the corridor are not visible.

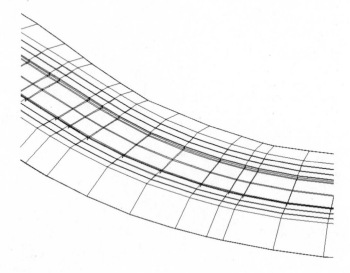

FIGURE 22.13
A corridor shown in isometric view with Conceptual visual style applied. Note that the 3D faces are not visible.

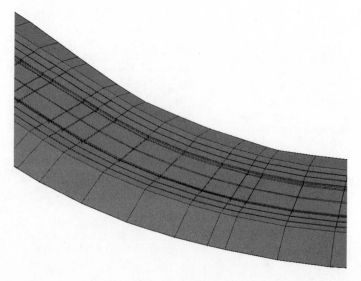

The Visual Styles Manager   The Visual Styles Manager provides an opportunity to customize the default visual styles and create new visual styles. Access the Visual Styles Manager by clicking the Manage Visual Styles button on the Visual Styles toolbar (Figure 22.15).

In the Visual Styles Manager (Figure 22.16), you can copy an existing visual style as a foundation for modification. All of the settings in the Visual Styles Manager are covered in detail in the AutoCAD Users Guide.

FIGURE 22.14

A corridor (with render materials applied) shown in isometric view with Realistic visual style applied. Note that 3D faces are visible.

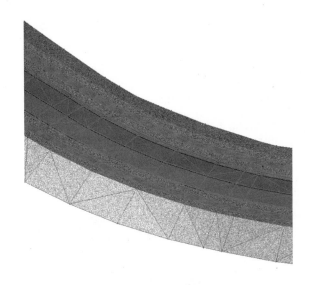

FIGURE 22.15

Accessing the Visual Styles Manager

FIGURE 22.16

The Visual Styles Manager

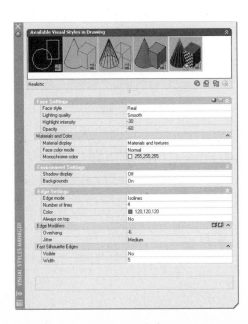

Render Materials

Render materials provide realistic colors, patterns, and textures to your drawing and Civil 3D objects. For example, you can assign a grass render material to an existing ground surface or a concrete render material to piping and sidewalks.

When you install Civil 3D, a materials library of approximately 100 render materials is installed by default. You will be given the choice of installing the full materials library during install that includes some 200 additional materials. If you neglect to toggle the button for this at install, you can always add the full materials library later by modifying your Civil 3D install under Add/Remove Programs.

In addition to the 300 materials that are provided by the materials library, you can create your own custom render materials from images, or edit those that are provided.

By default, many render materials have been built into the sample tool palettes, and additional material tool palettes can be created. Render materials can be dragged directly from the tool palette onto many objects. Figure 22.17 shows a simple box where an exposed concrete render material has been applied using the render material on the tool palette.

Civil 3D objects can be assigned render materials as part of their object properties, or in the case of corridors, their code set. We will look into that in more detail in the next section.

FIGURE 22.17
A simple box with a concrete render material applied from the tool palette

Visualizing Civil 3D Objects

Several Civil 3D objects have rendering options built into their properties. When working on visualization of Civil 3D objects, it is probably best to create a new drawing for the purposes of visualization. One approach would be to create a new drawing and create data references of your desired objects in the visualization drawing, then apply render materials and custom code sets. This will allow you to keep a dynamic model but prevent your main modeling drawings from getting bogged down with heavy materials and visual style applications.

Applying a Visual Style

If you'd like to view your model in the AutoCAD environment to get an idea of what a true rendering would look like, you can simply apply a Realistic visual style to your drawing and switch to an isometric view.

DON'T SAVE "REALISTIC"

Do not save your drawing with the Realistic view applied. Before saving, switch to a wireframe visual style. There have been occasions where saving the drawing with a Realistic visual style applied has caused drawing corruption problems.

The default Realistic visual style shows isolines. Since with Civil 3D objects isolines include TIN lines and 3D faces, they often cloud your model with lots of gray triangles. Also by default, textures are applied. Sometimes removing the texture application makes your model easier to comprehend in the AutoCAD environment.

To create a customized visual style, simply copy the default Realistic visual style by right-clicking on it in the Visual Styles Manager, then right-click to paste the copy (Figure 22.18).

FIGURE 22.18
Make a copy of the default Realistic visual style.

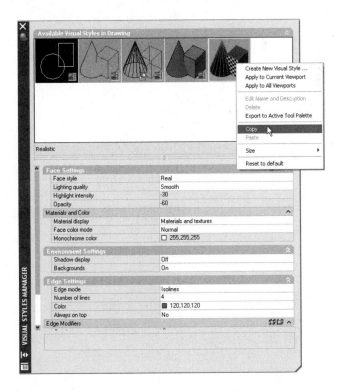

In your new visual style, change the Material Display toggle from Materials and Textures to Materials, and change the Edge Mode toggle from Isolines to none. You can rename your new visual style by right-clicking on the style and choosing Edit Name And Description. Apply this customized visual style by right-clicking it and choosing Apply To Current Viewports. An example of this visual style appears in Figure 22.19.

FIGURE 22.19
A corridor model and multiview blocks with a customized Realistic visual style applied

Visualizing a Surface

The first Civil 3D object that is meaningful to render is a surface. Every surface created in Civil 3D has a render material assigned upon creation (Figure 22.20).

In order for a render material to be visible when the Realistic visual style is applied, your current surface style must have triangles set to visible (Figure 22.21). This applies to both rendering in 2D and 3D.

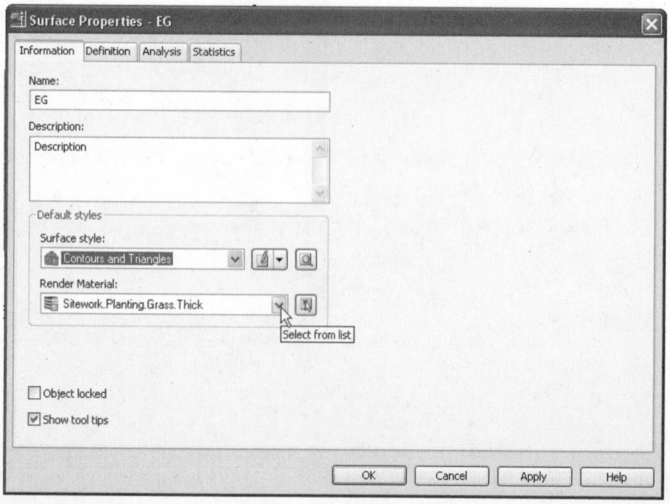

FIGURE 22.20
The Surface Properties box and Render Materials dropdown

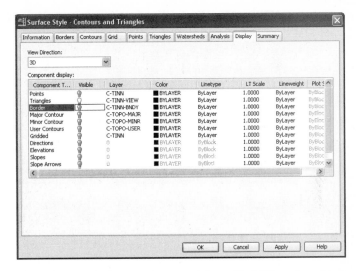

FIGURE 22.21
Triangles must be visible in 3D in order to see the render material applied.

In this exercise, you will learn how to apply a render material to a Civil 3D surface object, apply different visual styles, and customize a Realistic visual style:

1. Open the drawing file Visualization-1.dwg. Note that there is an existing ground surface shown in isometric view.

2. Switch your workspace to the Visualization And Rendering workspace.

3. Select the surface. Right-click and choose Surface Properties.

4. From the Render Material dropdown, choose Sitework.Planting.Grass.Short. Click OK.

5. Locate the Visual Styles dropdown on the Visual Styles control panel of the Dashboard. See Figure 22.4 to help identify this control panel. Change the visual style from 2D Wireframe to Realistic.

6. Zoom in on the surface and note that the grass render material has been applied but that there are also still gray isolines visible from the TIN.

7. Change the visual style to Conceptual to see its effect. Note that warm and cool colors are applied to show a more "conceptual" effect on the surface.

8. Change the visual style to 3D Wireframe for ease of navigation.

9. Access the Visual Styles Manager by clicking the Visual Styles Manager button in the Visual Styles control panel.

10. Make a copy of the Realistic visual style by choosing it, right-clicking, and choosing Copy from the shortcut menu (Figure 22.18). Then, right-click in the white space and click Paste. A new visual style should appear.

11. Select your visual style and right-click. Choose Edit Name And Description.

12. Change the name of the visual style to **Realistic-Civil 3D**. Delete the description and leave it blank. Click OK.

13. In the lower part of the Visual Styles Manager window, change the Edge mode from Isolines to None.

14. Right-click on your new visual style icon in the top part of the Visual Styles Manager window and choose Apply To Current Viewport. Close the Visual Styles Manager window.

15. Zoom in on your surface and notice that the gray isolines are gone.

16. Return to the Visual Styles Manager window. Select your Realistic Civil 3D visual style. In the bottom part of the Visual Styles Manager window, change the Material display from Materials and Textures to Materials.

17. Minimize or move your Visual Styles Manager out of the way so that you can see the effect of removing the textures from your visual style. Your surface should appear smooth and green.

18. A drawing called `Visualization-1 Finished.dwg` has been provided for your review. Note that the drawing has been saved with the 3D Wireframe visual style applied. Simply switch to the Realistic Civil 3D visual style to see the finished product.

Visualizing a Corridor

In previous releases, rendering corridors was a bit of an arduous process that involved some difficult boundary creation. The process has been made much simpler in Civil 3D 2008.

In Chapter 12, we explored the idea of links within the corridor object. For rendering, we can assign a certain render material based on the link code in a code set style. For example, the Paving code can be assigned an asphalt render material, while the Sidewalk code can be assigned a concrete render material. Additionally, you can assign preset styles to your corridor feature lines in the code set style.

Every time a code set style that was created for rendering is applied to a corridor, those links will automatically be assigned the correct render materials.

CREATING CODE SET STYLES

Code set styles are located on the Settings tab of the Toolspace under the General ➢ Multipurpose Styles ➢ Code Set Styles.

The default template includes a code set (Figure 22.22) that already has render materials assigned. You can also make your own custom code set by copying one of the existing sets.

The Code Set Style dialog does not resize, so scroll over to the right to locate the Render Material column. If it makes it easier, you can drag the Render Material column closer to the Link Name column (Figure 22.23).

In each link row, you can assign an appropriate render material.

Once this code set is assigned in the Corridor Properties, you can see your rendering by changing from 2D Wireframe to a Realistic visual style (Figure 22.24).

In addition to adding render materials to your code set style, you may want to adjust the visibility of the links, points, shapes, and feature lines themselves.

> **CORRIDOR FEATURE LINES AND CODE SET STYLES**
>
> When you build your corridor, the default code set style in your Command settings is applied to links, points, shapes, render materials, material area fill styles, label styles, and feature lines. Once the corridor is built, changes to the code set style will update all of these items except the feature lines. Changes to feature lines once the corridor is built must be made in Corridor Properties.

FIGURE 22.22
The Code Set Style dialog. Note the list of link code names on the left side.

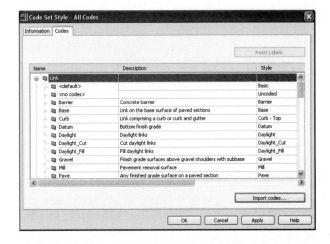

FIGURE 22.23
Move the render material column closer to the Link Name column.

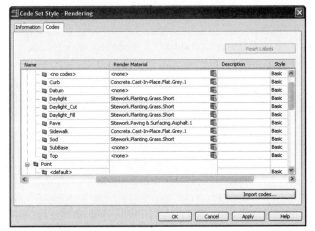

FIGURE 22.24
A corridor with render materials assigned through the code set style

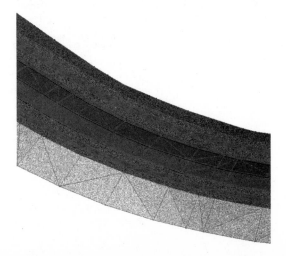

The following exercise leads you through applying a code set style to a corridor model and applying a Realistic visual style:

1. Open the drawing file `Visualization-2.dwg`. Note that a corridor is shown. Change your workspace to Visualization And Rendering if it is not already current.

2. Select the corridor. Right-click and choose Corridor Properties. Switch to the Codes tab.

3. Note that the Basic code set style is currently applied. In the Code Set Style dropdown, choose All Codes With Render Materials. Note that there are render materials listed in the Render Material column for this code set style. Click OK.

4. Switch the visual style from 2D Wireframe to Realistic. Note that materials and textures are applied.

5. Switch the visual style from Realistic to Realistic Civil 3D (the same visual style created in the last exercise.) Note that materials are applied, but isolines and textures are turned off.

6. Use the Views dropdown in the 3D Navigate control panel (Figure 22.7) to switch to the 3D Corridor View. Toggle between the different visual styles to see their effect in 3D.

7. Switch back to the Corridor Top view using the Views dropdown in the 3D Navigate control panel. If you would like to save your drawing, be sure to refresh the 2D Wireframe visual style before saving.

8. Note that `Visualization-2 Finished.dwg` has been provided on the CD for your review. Note that the drawing has been saved with the 2D Wireframe visual style applied. Simply switch to the Realistic Civil 3D visual style to see the finished product.

Visualizing a Pipe Network

Civil 3D pipes and structures can be assigned appropriate render materials. There are items in the Standard materials library that mimic the look of ductile iron, concrete, plastic, or many others.

Pipes and structures can be assigned render materials using the individual pipe and structure properties once the pipe is in the drawing. A better method is to assign the render materials in your parts list (Figure 22.25) before you begin designing your pipe network. This will ensure that every pipe created from this parts list already has the proper render material assigned.

FIGURE 22.25
Assigning render materials for pipes in the parts list

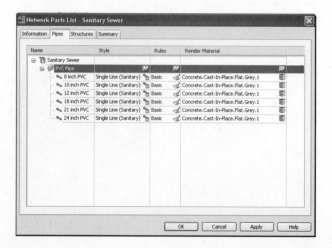

The following exercise leads you through adding render materials to a drawing and applying them to two pipe networks:

1. Open the drawing file `Visualization-3.dwg`. Note that there are two pipe networks in the drawing: a concrete storm drainage network and a PVC sanitary sewer network. Change your workspace to Visualization And Rendering if it is not already current.

2. Bring in your tool palette by pressing Ctrl+3 or by clicking the tool palette icon.

3. Right-click on the spine of the tool palette and choose Materials Library (Figure 22.26). This tool palette group should be present by default if you installed the Materials Library when installing Civil 3D.

4. Locate the Concrete - Materials Library tool palette. Select the Concrete.Cast-In-Place.Flat .Polished.Grey entry and hold down your left mouse button. Move your mouse over into the drawing area, then release the left mouse button. This will "drag" the render material into the drawing and make it available to assign to objects.

5. Switch to the Wood and Plastics – Materials Library tool palette. Select the Woods-Plastics. Plastics.PVC.White entry and drag it into the drawing, as in step 4.

6. Dismiss the tool palette.

7. Select pipe SD-1. Right-click and choose Pipe Properties.

8. In the Render Material dropdown, choose Concrete.Cast-In-Place.Flat.Polished.Grey. Click OK.

FIGURE 22.26
Switch to the
Materials Library
tool palette group.

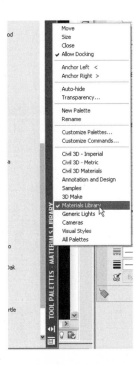

9. Select STM MH 1. Right-click and choose Structure Properties.

10. In the Render Material dropdown, choose Concrete.Cast-In-Place.Flat.Polished.Grey. Click OK.

11. Locate the Sanitary Sewer Network under the Pipe Networks tree of the Prospector. Select the Pipes entry.

12. In the preview pane that shows the list of pipes, use your Shift key to select all pipes. Right-click on the Render Material column and choose Edit.

13. In the Select Render Material dialog, choose Woods-Plastics.Plastics.PVC.White. Click OK. Your Prospector should look like Figure 22.27.

14. Select the Sanitary Sewer Network Structures tree. Using the same technique as step 13, assign the Concrete.Cast-In-Place.Flat.Grey.1 render material to all of the sanitary structures.

15. Use the Views dropdown on the 3D Navigate control panel (Figure 22.7) to switch to Southwest Isometric.

16. Switch to the Realistic visual style. Your pipes and structures should take on the appearance of concrete and PVC (Figure 22.28).

17. If desired, follow the steps from earlier exercises to create a Realistic visual style that turns off isolines and/or textures.

18. Note that Visualization-3 Finished.dwg has been provided on the companion CD for your review. Note that the drawing has been saved with the 2D Wireframe visual style applied. Simply switch to the Realistic Civil 3D visual style to see the finished product.

FIGURE 22.27

Assign a render material to a batch of pipes in Prospector.

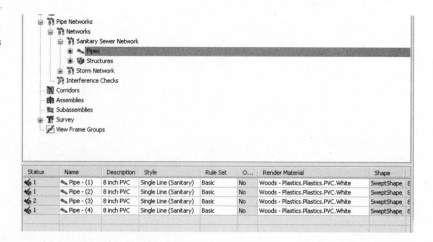

FIGURE 22.28
A close-up look at
Structure-3 with the
Realistic visual style
applied

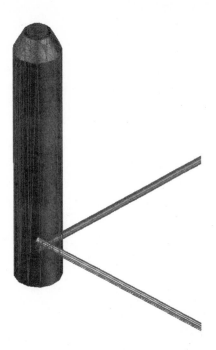

Visualizing AutoCAD Objects

Beyond applying rendering materials to Civil 3D objects, you can also use native AutoCAD objects
to flesh out your visuals.

SOLIDS

You may find AutoCAD solids to be useful as conceptual buildings or fixtures in your drawing.
Explore these tools (shown in Figure 22.29) and see the AutoCAD User's Guide located in the Help
menu for more information about these useful objects.

BLOCKS

There are many sources for 3D blocks that represent trees, benches, light posts, and other site development fixtures. Some free samples can be obtained through the DesignCenter Online. Design-
Center Online is accessed by opening the DesignCenter and selecting the DC Online tab as shown
in Figure 22.30. You can also draw your own, or buy an inexpensive CD of 3D blocks from many
sources. There are many ways these blocks can be constructed, but typically they have a component
suitable for plan view on one layer and a 3D component on another layer.

FIGURE 22.29
The solid creation
tools on the AutoCAD
modeling toolbar

FIGURE 22.30
DesignCenter Online.

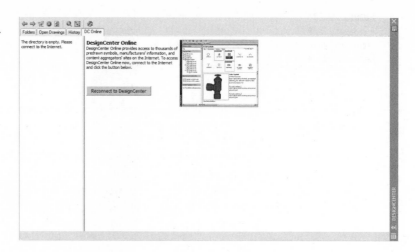

MULTIVIEW BLOCKS

Multiview blocks have been drawn to look a certain way in plan (Figure 22.31), profile, section, and 3D model views (Figure 22.32).

FIGURE 22.31
A tree multiview block in plan view

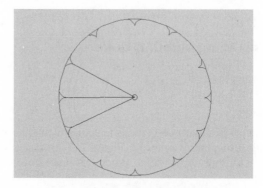

FIGURE 22.32
The same tree multiview block in 3D view

This eliminates the redundancy problem from typical 3D blocks. There is a collection of sample multiview blocks that install with Civil 3D. Blocks in this collection include trees, light standards, houses, buildings, and more. By default, the Multiview Block library can be found at

```
C:\Program Files\AutoCAD Civil 3D 2008\Data\Symbols\Myblocks
```

If you customize your installation, or you are using Windows Vista, you may have your Multiview Block library in a different location.

Multiview blocks can be inserted as traditional blocks, or can be used as part of a marker style or point style.

MOVING OBJECTS TO SURFACE AND EXTRACTING OBJECTS FROM SURFACES

In order to use items such as 3D blocks or multiview blocks, you need to move those blocks up to the appropriate elevation. In that case, you could use the Move Blocks To Surface command.

There may also be cases where you would like to extract a feature from a surface, such as a single contour line. The Extract Objects From Surface command is useful in that situation.

These tools, and more, can be found under Surfaces ➤ Utilities (Figure 22.33).

You can also build 3D or multiview blocks into surface labels or point styles to achieve a similar effect. Trees, light standards, power poles, and similar blocks would be good choices for building into point styles.

FIGURE 22.33

Civil 3D surface utilities

The following exercise will lead you through moving multiview tree blocks from elevation zero to surface elevation:

1. Open the drawing file Visualization-4.dwg. Note that there is a surface in the drawing, along with as many multiview tree blocks inserted at elevation zero.

2. Switch to the Civil 3D Complete workspace, or any workspace containing the Surfaces menu.

3. Choose Surfaces ➤ Utilities ➤ Move Blocks To Surface.

4. In the Move Blocks To Surface dialog, choose both Apple and Colorado Blue Spruce blocks. Click OK.

5. Switch your workspace to Visualization And Rendering.

6. Using the 3D Navigate control panel, switch the view to Southwest Isometric.

7. Zoom in on some trees. Your results should be similar to Figure 22.34.

8. Switch to the Conceptual visual style to note its effects.

9. Note that `Visualization-4 Finished.dwg` has been provided on the CD for your review. Note that the drawing has been saved with the 3D Wireframe visual style applied. Simply switch to the Conceptual visual style to see the finished product.

FIGURE 22.34
Multiview tree blocks moved to surface

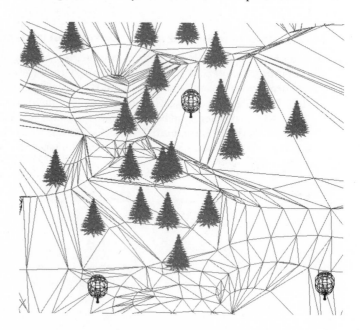

Creating a 3D DWF from a Corridor Model

Another simple way to visualize your model is through a 3D DWF. You may be familiar with standard DWF for plan sheet transmittal, plotting, and archiving. DWFs can be shared with non-CAD users through DWF Design Review, a free application that can be downloaded from the Autodesk website. DWFs can also be embedded into web pages or Microsoft PowerPoint presentations, and used in many other ways. A 3D DWF is the same idea, except it includes the model aspects of your drawing, including render materials, and allows for orbiting and other navigation tools.

To create a 3D DWF, you can use the File ➤ Publish tool, or simply type **3DDWFPUBLISH** at the command line. Civil 3D will prompt you for a filename and location for your new DWF file; then it will ask if you would like to open the resulting file. The 3D DWF will open in Autodesk Design Review (Figure 22.35).

The navigation tools in the Design Review environment are identical to those in an AutoCAD based interface, such as 3D orbit, pan, and zoom.

FIGURE 22.35
The Autodesk Design Review interface for viewing a 3D DWF

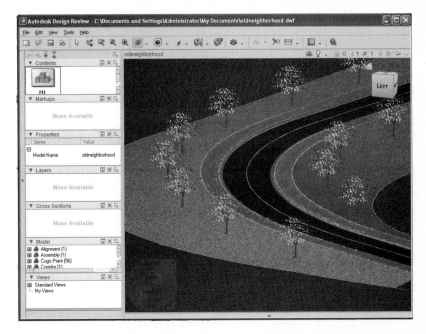

The following exercise will lead you through creating a 3D DWF from a corridor model:

1. Open the drawing file `Visualization-5.dwg`. Note that there is a corridor in this drawing.

2. Switch to the Visualization And Rendering workspace if it is not already current.

3. Apply the Realistic Civil 3D visual style.

4. Type **3DDWFPUBLISH** at the command line. In the resulting dialog, name your DWF and choose a location to save the resulting file. Click OK.

5. A dialog will appear asking you if you would like to view the DWF. Click Yes.

6. Autodesk Design Review should automatically open and appear similar to Figure 22.35. Explore your 3DDWF.

7. A completed DWF, called `Visualization-5.dwf`, has been provided on the CD.

Creating a Quick Rendering from a Corridor Model

A true rendering applies the render materials, lighting settings, shadows, and other advanced settings to an image or video clip. In this section, we'll prepare a more detailed image of a designed corridor.

A QUICK RENDERING

You can make a simple rendering with little preparation by simply navigating your model until your viewport/screen shows what you'd like to see rendered. Execute the Render command from the Dashboard or View menu, or by typing **-render** at the command line. The resulting image will look similar to Figure 22.36. If choosing from the Dashboard, View menu, or other location, the Render button looks like a little green teapot.

FIGURE 22.36
A quickly rendered
scene at medium
quality with no
shadows, lighting,
or other advanced
settings

ADJUSTING LIGHTING

If you would like a more realistic-looking rendering, you can adjust the lighting settings to provide sunlight and shadow effect. One effect that improves the realism of your rendering is to change the geographic location of your drawing (Figure 22.37).

You can further adjust the sun by clicking the Edit the Sun button (Figure 22.38).

In Sun Properties (Figure 22.39), it is possible to refine the time of day, intensity, and more.

FIGURE 22.37
Change the
geographic
location

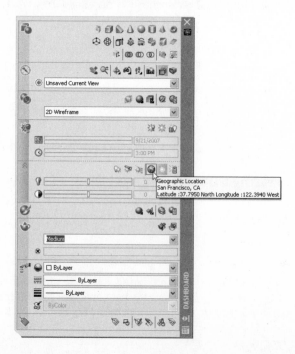

FIGURE 22.38
The Edit the Sun button on the Dashboard

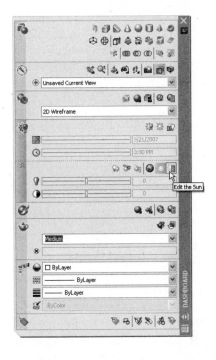

FIGURE 22.39
Adjust the sun settings.

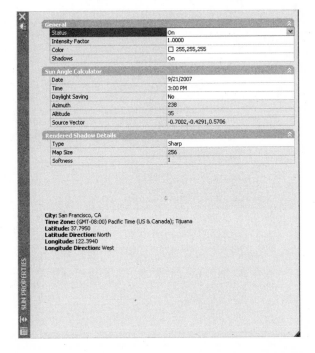

ADVANCED SETTINGS

If you would like to further customize your scene, you can add custom lights, sky, and more. Explore the "Creating Realistic Images and Graphics" portion of the AutoCAD Users Guide.

The following exercise will lead you through creating a simple rendered image from a corridor model:

1. Open the drawing file `Visualization-6.dwg`. Note that there is a corridor in this drawing.

2. Switch to the Visualization And Rendering workspace if it is not already current.

3. Locate the Render button in the Render control panel. The Render button appears as a little green teapot with a lightning bolt next to it. Click the render button.

4. A rendering window should appear and draw a quick rendered image of the scene. You can save this image if desired.

 Real World Scenario

RENDERING A CORRIDOR AND BOULEVARD TREES

This exercise will lead you through adding multiview blocks as points to a road design; then you will create a custom visual style, create a simple rendering, and create a fly-through AVI.

1. Open the drawing `Visualization Corridor and Trees.dwg`.

2. Note that there is already a corridor in the drawing with the appropriate code style set applied, as well as a road surface built with a contour style applied. There is an existing ground surface in this drawing. If you go into Surface Properties, you will see that there is a grass render material applied. Also note that there is an empty point group called Tree with a Tree point style applied

3. Set some tree points. Choose Points ➤ Create Points ➤ Surface ➤ Polyline/Contour Vertices to set points on the road surface every 60′ along the polylines. When you create them, give them the description **tree** so that they are collected into the Tree point group.

4. If your points do not immediately look like the Tree point style, right-click the point group and choose Update. Your trees should appear as small trees along the polylines.

5. Erase or freeze the polylines.

6. Switch the drawing to isometric view.

7. Choose the corridor surface and change it to the _No Display style so that the triangles from the road surface do not get in the way of the corridor model.

8. Open the Visual Styles toolbar, or switch your workspace to the Visualization And Rendering workspace so that you can access the Visual Styles Editor. Bring up the Visual Styles Editor.

9. Copy the Realistic visual style and create and apply a visual style that turns Edgemode to None and Material display to Materials Only. Use the Custom Realistic visual style that is already in the drawing as an example if needed.

10. Once you have applied your Custom Realistic visual style, you should see a black road, gray sidewalks, green daylight, and dark green existing ground. Toggle between other visual styles to observe their effect.

11. Switch to the Visualization And Rendering workspace if you haven't already.

12. Execute the Render command by clicking the Teapot icon in the Render section of the Dashboard. A temporary render window will appear with a preview of your image. You can save this image, or go back to the drawing and change the view on your screen to be more zoomed in, a different angle, or something similar, and redo the rendering.

13. Type **3DDWFPUBLISH** at the command line. Name the DWF file and choose a location to save it. Once the file has been created, open the file and explore the Autodesk Design Review interface and the 3D model.

14. Change the visual style in the drawing to a wireframe style to make navigation faster.

15. Change back to top view and the Civil 3D Complete Workspace.

Now we will create a motion path animation. You'll take a polyline from the road elevation and move it 15´ into the air to serve as the motion path.

16. Use Corridors ➢ Utilities ➢ Create Polyline From Corridor to extract the crown feature line from the corridor.

17. Move this polyline 15´ in the positive Z direction. The easiest way is to use the AutoCAD Move command from 0,0,0 to 0,0,15.

18. Access the Motion Path Animation window by selecting View ➢ Motion Path Animation.

19. In the Motion Path Animation dialog, choose the following options to make a simple wireframe drive-through:

Camera: Choose Path, then use the Select button to go into the drawing and choose your polyline. This is the path that the camera will follow.

Target: Leave defaults

Animation Settings:

Frame Rate: 15 fps

Number Of Frames: 300

Duration: 20 seconds

Visual Style: 3D Wireframe

Format: AVI

Resolution: 640×480

Corner Deceleration: Checked

When Previewing Show Camera Preview: Checked

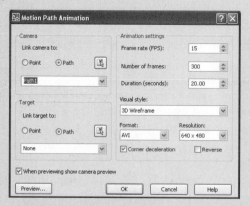

20. Click OK to send the AVI to be created. Depending on your computer specifications, this could take a few minutes or longer.

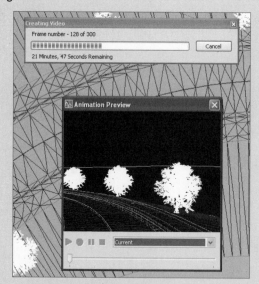

21. Once the preview window closes, locate the AVI file on your computer and play the video in your favorite media player.

22. Repeat the process using a different resolution or visual style. For a fully rendered drive-through, choose the Rendered option from the Visual Styles dropdown. This may take several hours depending on your frame rate, resolution, and processor speed, but the results can be quite spectacular for a public hearing or similar event.

23. A completed visualization drawing, DWF, wireframe AVI, and rendered AVI are included on the CD for your exploration.

The Bottom Line

Apply render materials to a corridor using a code set style.   Visualizing corridors is useful for creating complete site models for your own better understanding of the design, and for sharing with your clients and regulating agencies. The first step in visualizing a corridor is to apply a code set style that will automatically assign render materials to certain codes.

> **Master It**   Open the drawing file `Mastering Visualization.dwg`. Apply the All Codes code set style.

Apply a Realistic visual style to a corridor model.   Once the appropriate code set style has been assigned, the corridor can be seen with its render materials with a Realistic visual style applied.

> **Master It**   Continue working in the file `Mastering Visualization.dwg`. Apply the Realistic visual style to the drawing.

Create a 3D DWF from a corridor model.   One way you can share your visualized corridor is through 3D DWF. Autodesk Design Review is a free application that you can direct your clients to download from Autodesk.com. 3D DWFs can be opened, navigated, and analyzed using Design Review.

> **Master It**   Continue working in the file `Mastering Visualization.dwg`. Create a 3D DWF from the drawing and open it in Autodesk Design Review.

Appendix A

The Bottom Line

Each "The Bottom Line" section in the chapters suggests exercises to deepen skills and understanding. Sometimes there is only one possible solution, but often you are encouraged to use your skills and creativity to create something that builds on what you know and lets you explore one of many possible solutions.

Chapter 1: Getting Dirty: The Basics of Civil 3D

Find any Civil 3D object with just a few clicks.   By using Prospector to view object data collections, you can minimize the panning and zooming that are part of working in a CAD program. When common subdivisions can have hundreds of parcels or a complex corridor can have dozens of alignments, jumping to the desired one nearly instantly shaves time off everyday tasks.

Master It   Open SampleSite.dwg from the sample data set and find the parcel Property : 9 without using any AutoCAD commands.

Solution

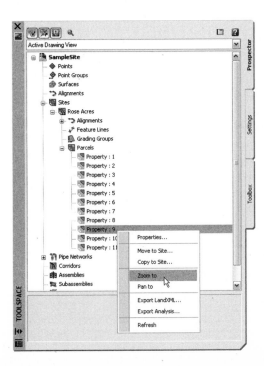

Modify the drawing scale and default object layers. Civil 3D understands the end goal of most drawings is to create hard-copy construction documents. By setting a drawing scale and then setting many sizes in terms of plotted inches or millimeters, Civil 3D removes much of the mental gymnastics that other programs require when sizing text and symbology. By setting object layers at a drawing scale, Civil 3D makes uniformity of drawing files easier than ever to accomplish.

Master It Change `SampleSite.dwg` from a 40-scale drawing to a 200-scale drawing.

Solution

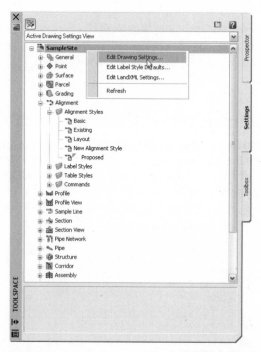

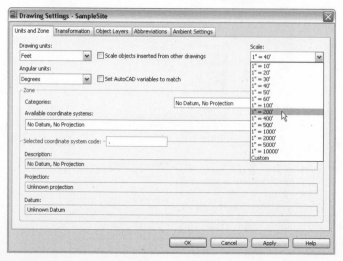

Modify the display of Civil 3D tooltips. The interactive display of object tooltips makes it easy to keep your focus on the drawing instead of an inquiry or report tools. When too many objects fill up a drawing however, it can be information overload, so Civil 3D gives you granular control over the heads-up display tooltips.

Master It Within the same Sample Site drawing, turn off the tooltips for the Carson's Way alignment.

Solution Right-click on the alignment in the drawing window or in Prospector and bring up the Alignment Properties dialog. Then deselect the checkbox on the lower left of the Information tab.

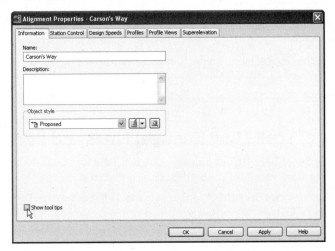

Add a new tool to the Toolbox. The Toolbox provides a convenient way to access macros and reports. Many third-party developers are exploiting this convenient interface as an easier way to add functionality without disturbing users' workspaces.

Master It Add the Import From Excel macro from `C:\Program Files\Autocad Civil 3D 2008\Sample\Civil 3D API\VBA\Pipe\` and select `Pipe Sample Application.dvb`.

Solution Follow the same procedure as in the exercise, but use `Pipe.Samples .ImportFromExcel` for the Macro Name field.

Create a basic label style. Label styles determine the appearance of Civil 3D annotation. The creation of label styles will constitute a major part of the effort in making the transition to Civil 3D as a primary platform for plan production. Your skills will grow with the job requirements if you start with basic labels and then make more complicated labels as needed.

Master It Create a copy of the Elevation Only Point label style, name it **Elevation With Border**, and add a border to the text component.

Solution

1. Switch to the Settings tab in Toolspace, expand the Point branch, and then expand the Label Styles branch.

2. Right-click on the Elevation Only label style, and select Copy.

3. Change the name to **Elevation With Border** on the Information tab.

4. On the Layout tab, set Border Visibility to True, and click OK.

Create a new object style. Object styles in Civil 3D allow the user to quit managing the display through layer modification and move to a more streamlined style-based control. Creating enough object styles to meet the demands of plan production work will be the other major task in preparing to move to Civil 3D.

Master It Create a new Surface style named **Contours_Grid** and set it to show contours in plan views but a grid display in any 3D view.

Solution

1. In the Settings tab, expand the Surface branch and right-click on the Surface Styles folder. Select New from the pop-up menu.

2. Rename the New Surface Style to **Contours_Grid** in the Name text box on the Information tab.

3. On the Display tab, with the View Direction set to 2D, turn off Border, and turn on Major Contours and Minor Contours.

4. Change the View Direction to 3D, turn off Triangles, and turn on Gridded.

Chapter 2: Took Long Enough: Lines and Curves

Create a series of lines by bearing and distance. By far the most commonly used command when re-creating a deed is Line By Bearing and Distance.

Master It Open the Mastering Lines and Curves.dwg file. Start from the Civil 3D point labeled START and use any appropriate tool to create lines with the following bearings and distances (note that the Direction input format for this drawing has been set to DD.MMSSSS):

N 57°06′56.75″ E; 135.441′

S 41°57′03.67″ E; 118.754′

S 27°44′41.63″ W; 112.426′

N 50°55′57.00″ W; 181.333′

Solution

1. Select Lines/Curves ➤ Create Lines ➤ Line By Bearing.

2. Use the Point Object transparent command to select the point labeled START.

3. In the command line, specify quadrant 1↵ **57.065675**↵ **135.441**↵.

4. Specify quadrant 2↵ **41.570367**↵ **118.754**↵.

5. Specify quadrant 3↵ **27.444163**↵ **112.426**↵.

6. Specify quadrant 4↵ **50.555700**↵ **181.333**↵.

7. Press ↵ again to leave the command.

Use the Inquiry commands to confirm that lines are drawn correctly.

Master It Continue working in your drawing. Use any appropriate Inquiry command to confirm that each line has been drawn correctly.

Solution

1. Click the Line and Arc Information button on the Inquiry Commands toolbar.

2. Select each line drawn earlier and compare to the list at the beginning of the exercise.

Create a curve tangent to the end of a line. It is rare that a property stands alone. Often, there are adjacent properties, easements, or alignments that must be created from their legal descriptions.

Master It Create a curve tangent to the end of the first line drawn in the first exercise that meets the following specifications:

Radius: 200.00´; Arc Length: 66.580´

Solution

1. Select Lines/Curves ➢ Create Curves ➢ Curve From End Of Object.

2. Select the first line drawn (N 57° 06´56.75″ E; 135.441´)

3. On the command line, press ↵ to confirm the radius.

4. On the command line, enter **200.00**↵.

5. Enter **L**↵ to specify length.

6. Enter **66.580**↵.

Create a best-fit line for a series of Civil 3D points. Surveyed point data is rarely perfect. When creating drawing linework, it is often necessary to create a best-fit line to make up for irregular shots.

Master It Locate the Edge of Pavement (EOP) points in the drawing. Use the Line By Best Fit command to create a line using these points.

Solution

1. Select Lines/Curves ➢ Create Best Fit Entities ➢ Curve Create Line.

2. In the dialog, choose From Civil 3D Points and click OK.

3. Pick the EOP point objects and press ↵.

4. A Panorama window appears. Review the results, then dismiss the window by clicking the green check mark. A best-fit line is drawn.

Label lines and curves. Though converting linework to parcels or alignments offers you the most robust labeling and analysis options, basic line and curve labeling tools are available when conversion is not appropriate.

Master It Add line and curve labels to each entity created in the exercises. Choose a label that will specify the bearing and distance for your lines and length, radius, and delta of your curve.

Solution

1. Select Lines/Curves ➤ Add Line/Curve Labels ➤ Multiple Segment.

2. Choose each line and curve. The default label should be acceptable. If not, select a label, right-click, and choose Label Properties. In the resulting AutoCAD Properties box, you can select an alternative label.

Chapter 3: Lay of the Land: Survey

Properly collect field data and import it into AutoCAD Civil 3D 2008.   You learned best practices for collecting data, how the data is translated into a useable format for the survey database, and how to import that data into a survey database. You learned what commands draw linework in a raw data file, and how to include those commands into your data collection techniques so that the linework is created correctly when the fieldbook is imported into the program.

Master It   In this exercise, you will create a new drawing and a new survey database and import the Shopping_Center.fbk file into the drawing.

Solution

1. Create a new drawing using a template of your choice.

2. On the Survey Tab, create a new survey database.

3. Create a new network in the newly created survey database.

4. Import the Shopping_Center.fbk file and edit the options to insert both the figures and the points.

Set up styles that will correctly display your linework.   You learned how to set up styles for figures. You also learned that figures can be set as breaklines for surface creation and lot lines and that they can go on their own layer and be displayed in many different ways.

Master It   In this exercise, you will use the Mastering1.dwg file and survey database from the previous exercise and create figure styles and a figure prefix database for the various figures in the database.

Solution

1. Open the drawing file.

2. Open the survey database created in the previous exercise if it's not already open.

3. Expand the Figures branch of the survey database.

4. Create and apply styles to the various figures in the database to display the information as you'd like.

Create and edit fieldbook files.   You learned how to create fieldbook files using various data collection techniques and how to modify the various data in the files to achieve a very accurate survey database.

Master It   In this exercise, you will create a new drawing and survey database. Import the traverse.fbk file and rotate the entire network so that a line running from point number 3 to point number 4 is running due east. Then, export that FBK file to a new file and import the new file into a new network to verify the changes.

Solution

1. Create a new drawing and survey database and import the `traverse.fbk` file into a network.

2. Create construction lines to determine your reference angle.

3. Using the Translate Survey Network command, rotate the network.

4. Export a new FBK file.

5. Create another new drawing and survey database and import the new FBK file. Your drawing should look like `mastering2.dwg`.

Manipulate your survey data. You learned how to use the traverse analysis and adjustments to create data with a higher precision.

Master It In this exercise, you will use the survey database and network from the previous exercises in this chapter. You will analyze and adjust the traverse using the following criteria:

- Use the Compass Rule for Horizontal Adjustment.
- Use the Length Weighted Distribution Method for Vertical Adjustment.
- Use a Horizontal Closure Limit of 1:25,000.
- Use a Vertical Closure Limit of 1:25,000.

Solution

1. Open a new drawing and create a new survey database and network, and import the `traverse.fbk` fieldbook.

2. Create a new traverse from the four points.

3. Perform a traverse analysis on the newly created traverse, and apply the changes to the survey database.

4. The results from the traverse analysis can be found in the following files:

5. `batrav.trv.txt`

6. `fvtrav.trv.txt`

7. `antrav.trv.txt`

8. `trav.lso.txt`

Chapter 4: X Marks the Spot: Points

Import points from a text file using description key matching. Most engineering offices receive text files containing point data at some point during a project. Description keys provide a way to automatically assign the appropriate styles, layers, and labels to newly imported points.

Master It Create a new drawing from _AutoCAD Civil 3D (Imperial) NCS Extended .dwt. Revise the Civil 3D description key set to use the following parameters:

Code	Point Style	Point Label Style	Format	Layer
GS	Standard	Elevation Only	Ground Shot	V-NODE
GUY	Guy Pole	Elevation and Description	Guy Pole	V-NODE
HYD	Hydrant (existing)	Elevation and Description	Existing Hydrant	V-NODE-WATR
TOP	Standard	Point#-Elevation-Description	Top of Curb	V-NODE
TREE	Tree	Elevation and Description	Existing Tree	V-NODE-TREE

Import the MasteringPointsPNEZDspace.txt file from the data location and confirm that the description keys made the appropriate matches by looking at a handful of points of each type. Do the trees look like trees? Do the hydrants look like hydrants?

Solution

1. Select File ➢ New, and create a drawing from _AutoCAD Civil 3D (Imperial) NCS Extended.dwt.

2. Switch to the Settings tab of Toolspace and locate the description key set called Civil 3D. Right-click and choose Edit Keys.

3. Delete any two keys by right-clicking on each one and choosing Delete.

4. Revise the remaining key to match the GS specifications listed under the Master It instructions for this exercise.

5. Right-click on the GS key and choose New. Create the four additional keys listed in the instructions. Exit the dialog.

6. Select Points ➢ Import/Export Points ➢ Import Points. Select PNEZD Space Delimited from the dropdown menu in the Format selection box, and navigate out to the MasteringPointsPNEZDspace.txt file. Click OK.

7. Zoom in to see the points. Note that each description key parameter (style, label, format, and layer) has been respected. Your hydrants should appear as hydrants on the correct layer, your trees should appear as trees on the correct layer, and so on.

Create a point group. Building a surface using a point group is a very common task. Among other criteria, you may want to filter out any points with zero or negative elevations from your Topo point group.

Master It Create a new point group called Topo that includes all points *except* those with elevations of zero or less.

Solution

1. In Prospector, right-click on Point Groups and choose New.

2. On the Information tab, enter **Topo** as the name of the point group.

3. Switch to the Exclude tab.

4. Check the With Elevations Matching box and type **<=0** in the field.

5. Click OK and confirm in Prospector that there are no points with an elevation zero or less in the point group.

Export points to LandXML and ASCII format.   It is often necessary to export a LandXML or an ASCII file of points for stakeout or data-sharing purposes. Unless you want to export every point from your drawing, it is best to create a point group that isolates the desired point collection.

Master It   Create a new point group that includes all of the points with a raw description of TOP. Export this point group via LandXML and to a PNEZD Comma Delimited text file.

Solution

1. In Prospector, right-click on Point Groups and choose New.

2. On the Information tab, enter **Top Of Curb** as the name of the new point group.

3. Switch to the Include tab.

4. Check the With Raw Descriptions Matching box and type **TOP** in the field.

5. Click OK and confirm in Prospector that all the points have the description of TOP.

6. Right-click on the Top Of Curb point group and choose Export To LandXML

7. Click OK.

8. Choose a location to save your LandXML file, then click Save.

9. Navigate out to the LandXML file to confirm it was created.

10. Right-click on the Top Of Curb point group and choose Export Points.

11. Choose the PNEZD Comma Delimited Format and a destination file, and confirm that the Limit To Points In Point Group box is checked. Click OK.

12. Navigate out to the ASCII file to confirm it was created.

Create a point table.   Point tables provide an opportunity to list and study point properties. In addition to basic point tables that list number, elevation, description, and similar options, point table formats can be customized to include user-defined property fields.

Master It   Create a point table for the Topo point group using the PNEZD format table style.

Solution

1. Select Points ➢ Add Tables.

2. Choose the PNEZD format for the table style.

3. Click Point Groups and choose the Topo point group.

4. Click OK.

5. The command line will prompt you to choose a location for the upper-left corner of the point table. Choose a location on your screen somewhere to the right of the project.

6. Zoom in and confirm your point table.

Chapter 5: The Ground Up: Surfaces in Civil 3D

Create a preliminary surface using freely available data. Almost every land development project involves a surface at some point. During the planning stages, freely available data can give you a good feel for the lay of the land, allowing design exploration before money is spent on fieldwork or aerial topography. Imprecise at best, this free data should never be used as a replacement for final design topography, but it's a great starting point.

Master It Create a new drawing from the Civil 3D Extended template and bring in a Google Earth surface for your home or office location. Be sure to set a proper coordinate system to get this surface in the right place.

Solution

1. On the main menu, choose File ➤ New.

2. Select the NCS Extended.dwt file, and click Open.

3. Change to the Settings tab, and right-click the drawing name to open the Drawing Settings dialog. Select an appropriate coordinate system.

4. In Google Earth, locate your home or office using the search engine.

5. On the main menu, choose File ➤ Import ➤ Import Image And Surface From Google Earth.

Modify and update a TIN surface. TIN surface creation is mathematically precise, but sometimes the assumptions behind the equations leave something to be desired. By using the editing tools built into Civil 3D, you can create a more realistic surface model.

Master It Modify your Google Earth surface to only show an area immediately around your home or office. Create an irregular shaped boundary and apply it to the Google Earth surface.

Solution

1. Draw a polyline that includes the desired area.

2. Expand the Google Earth Surface branch in Prospector.

3. Expand the Definition branch.

4. Right-click Boundaries and select the Add option.

5. Select the newly created polyline and click Add to complete.

Prepare a slope analysis. Surface analysis tools allow users to view more than contours and triangles in Civil 3D. Engineers working with nontechnical team members can create strong, meaningful analysis displays to convey important site information using the built-in analysis methods in Civil 3D.

Master It Create an Elevation Banding analysis of your home or office surface and insert a legend to help clarify the image.

Solution

1. Right-click the surface and bring up the Surface Properties dialog.

2. Change the Surface Style field to Elevation Banding (2D).

3. Change to the Elevation tab and run an Elevation analysis.

4. Click OK to close the dialog, then from the main menu, choose Surfaces ➢ Add Legend Table and enter **E** at the command line to create a legend.

Label surface contours and spot elevations. Showing a stack of contours is useless without context. Using the automated labeling tools in Civil 3D, you can create dynamic labels that update and reflect changes to your surface as your design evolves.

Master It Label the contours on your Google Earth surface at a 1′ and a 5′ interval.

Solution

1. Change the Surface Style to Contours 1′ and 5′ (Design).

2. From the main menu, choose Surfaces ➢ Add Surface Labels ➢ Contour Multiple.

3. Pick a point on one side of the site, and draw a contour label line across the entire site. Repeat if needed.

Chapter 6: Don't Fence Me In: Parcels

Create a boundary parcel from objects. The first step to any parceling project is to create an outer boundary for the site.

Master It Open the `Mastering Parcels.dwg` file. Convert the polyline in the drawing to a parcel.

Solution

1. Choose Parcels ➢ Create Parcel From Objects.

2. At the `Select lines, arcs, or polylines to convert into parcels or [Xref]:` prompt, pick the polyline that represents the site boundary. Press ↵.

3. The Create Parcels – From Objects dialog appears. Select Subdivision Lots, Property, and Name, Square Foot And Acres from the dropdown menu in the Site, Parcel Style, and Area Label Style selection boxes, respectively. Keep the default values for the remaining options. Click OK to dismiss the dialog.

4. The boundary polyline will form parcel segments that react with the alignment. Area labels are placed at the newly created parcel centroids.

Create a right-of-way parcel using the right-of-way tool. For many projects, the ROW parcel will serve as frontage for subdivision parcels. For straightforward sites, the automatic Create ROW tool provides a quick way to create this parcel.

Master It Continue working in the Mastering Parcels.dwg file. Create a ROW parcel that is offset by 25′ on either side of the road centerline with 25′ fillets at the parcel boundary.

Solution

1. Choose Parcels ➢ Create ROW.

2. At the Select parcels: prompt, pick your newly created parcels on screen. Press ↵ to stop picking parcels. The Create Right of Way dialog appears.

3. Expand the Create Parcel Right Of Way parameter, and enter 25′ in the Offset From Alignment text box.

4. Expand the Cleanup At Parcel Boundaries parameter. Enter 25′ in the Fillet Radius At Parcel Boundary Intersections text box. Select Fillet from the dropdown menu in the Cleanup Method selection box.

5. Click OK to dismiss the dialog and create the ROW parcels.

Create subdivision lots automatically by layout. The biggest challenge when creating a subdivision plan is optimizing the number of lots. The precise sizing parcel tools provide a means to automate this process.

Master It Continue working in the Mastering Parcels.dwg file. Create a series of lots with a minimum of 10,000 square feet and 100′ frontage.

Solution

1. Choose Parcels ➢ Create Parcel By Layout.

2. Expand the Parcel Layout Tools toolbar.

3. Change the value of the following parameters by clicking in the Value column and typing in the new values:

   Default Area: **10000 Sq. Ft.**

   Minimum Frontage: **100′**

4. Change the following parameters by clicking in the Value column and selecting the appropriate option from the dropdown menu.

   Automatic Mode: On

   Remainder Distribution: Redistribute Remainder

5. Click the Slide Angle – Create tool. The Create Parcels – Layout dialog appears.

6. Select Subdivision Lots, Single Family, and Name Square Foot & Acres from the dropdown menu in the Site, Parcel Style, and Area Label Style selection box, respectively. Keep the default values for the rest of the options. Click OK to dismiss the dialog.

7. At the Pick a point within the parcel to be subdivided: prompt, pick any point inside one of your property parcels.

8. At the `Select start point on frontage:` prompt, use your Endpoint osnap to pick the point of curvature along the ROW parcel segment.

9. The parcel jig will appear. Move your mouse slowly along the ROW parcel segment and notice that the parcel jig follows the segment. At the `Select end point on frontage:` prompt, use your Endpoint osnap to pick the point of curvature along the ROW parcel segment.

10. At the `Specify angle at frontage:` prompt, type **90**. Press ↵.

11. At the `Specify area <10000 Sq. Ft.>:` prompt, press ↵ to accept the default value of 10,000 square feet. Press ↵.

12. Repeat steps 4 through 10 for the other property parcels, if desired.

Add multiple parcel segment labels. Every subdivision plat must be appropriately labeled. Parcels can be quickly labeled with their bearings, distances, direction, and more using the segment labeling tools.

Master It Continue working in the `Mastering Parcels.dwg` file. Place Bearing Over Distance labels on every parcel line segment and Delta Over Length And Radius labels on every parcel curve segment using the Multiple Segment Labeling tool.

Solution

1. Choose Parcels ➤ Add Parcel Labels ➤ Add Parcel Labels.

2. In the Add Labels dialog, select Multiple Segment, Bearing Over Distance, and Delta Over Length And Radius from the dropdown list in the Label Type, Line Label Style, and Curve Label Style selection boxes, respectively.

3. Click Add.

4. At the `Select parcel to be labeled by clicking on area label or [CLockwise/COunterclockwise]<CLockwise>:` prompt, pick the area label for each of your single-family parcels.

5. Press ↵ to exit the command.

Chapter 7: Laying a Path: Alignments

Create an alignment from a polyline. Creating alignments based on polylines is a traditional method of building up engineering models. With Civil 3D's built-in tools for conversion, correction, and alignment reversal, it's easy to use the linework prepared by others to start your design model. These alignments lack the intelligence of crafted alignments, however, and should be used sparingly.

Master It Open the `Mastering Alignments.dwg` file and create alignments from the linework found there.

Solution

1. Use Create Alignments From Polyline on three of the four objects.

2. The fourth object has to be converted to a pline, then converted to an alignment.

Create a reverse curve that never loses tangency.   Using the alignment layout tools, we can build intelligence into the objects we design. One of the most common errors introduced to engineering designs is curves and lines that are not tangent, requiring expensive revisions and resubmittals. The free, floating, and fixed components can make smart alignments in a large number of combinations available to solve almost any design problem.

Master It   Open the `Mastering Alignments.dwg` file and create an alignment from the linework on the right. Create a reverse curve with both radii equal to 200, and with a pass-through point in the center of the displayed circle.

Solution

1. Trace both lines with Fixed Segments.

2. Float a curve segment from the north end with a pass-through point in the center of the circle.

3. Fillet the floating curve and the last fixed segment with a 200′ radius.

Replace a component of an alignment with another component type.   One of the goals in using a dynamic modeling solution is to find better solutions, not just a solution. In the layout of alignments, this can mean changing components out along the design path, or changing the way they are defined. Civil 3D's ability to modify alignments' geometric construction without destroying the object or forcing a new definition allows the designer to experiment without destroying the data already based on an alignment.

Master It   Convert the arc indicated in the `Mastering Alignments.dwg` file to a free arc that is a function of the two adjoining segments. The curve radius is 150′.

Solution

1. Select the indicated alignment, right-click, and select Edit Alignment Geometry. The Alignment Layout Tools toolbar opens.

2. Delete the indicated arc segment using the Delete Sub-Entity tool.

3. Select the Free Curve Fillet (Between Two Entities, Radius) tool.

4. Pick the two segments and set the radius at the command line.

Create a new label set.   Label sets allow us to determine the appearance of an alignment's labels and quickly standardize that appearance across all the objects of the same nature. By creating sets that reflect their intended use, we can make it easy for a designer to quickly label alignments according to specifications with little understanding of the requirement itself.

Master It   Within the `Mastering Alignments.dwg` file, create a new label set containing only major station labels, and apply it to all of the alignments in that drawing.

Solution

1. On the Settings tab, expand the Alignment ➢ Label Styles ➢ Label Sets branch.

2. Right-click on Major & Minor and select Copy to open the Alignment Label Set dialog.

3. On the Information tab, change the Name field to Major Only. Switch to the Labels tab.

4. In the Type field, delete the Minor Stations label.

5. Right-click on each alignment, and select Edit Alignment Labels.

6. Import the Major Only label set.

7. Repeat for each label.

Solutions may vary!

Override individual labels with other styles. In spite of our desire to have uniform labeling styles and appearances between alignments within a single drawing, project, or firm, there are always exceptions. Using the AutoCAD Ctrl-click element selection methods, we can access commands that modify individual labels and let us modify our labels or even change their style completely.

Master It Create a copy of the Perpendicular With Tick Major Station style called Major With Marker. Change the Tick Block Name to Marker Pnt. Replace some of your major station labels with this new style, but not all.

Solution

1. On the Settings tab, expand the Alignment ➤ Label Styles ➤ Station ➤ Major Station branch.

2. Right-click on Perpendicular With Tick and select Copy.

3. Change Name to Major Delta.

4. Change to the Layout tab.

5. Change to the Tick Component.

6. Change the Block Name Value field from AeccTickLine to Market Pnt in the Select A Block dialog.

7. Click OK to close.

8. Open the AutoCAD OPM palette.

9. Ctrl-click to select a major station label.

10. On the AutoCAD OPM palette, set the Major Station Label to Major With Marker.

Chapter 8: Cut to the Chase: Profiles

Sample a surface profile with offset samples. Working with surface data to create dynamic sampled profiles is an important advantage in working with a three-dimensional model. Quick viewing of various surface slices with grip editing of alignments makes for a very effective preliminary planning tool. Combined with offset data to meet review agency requirements, profiles are robust design tools in Civil 3D 2008.

Master It Open the Mastering Profile.dwg file and sample the ground surface along Alignment - (2), along with offset values at 15´ left and 25´ right of the alignment.

Solution

1. Select Profile Sample From Surface.

2. Set values as shown.

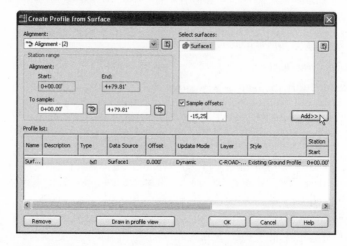

Lay out a design profile on the basis of a table of data. Many programs and designers work by creating pairs of station and elevation data. The tools built into Civil 3D allow the user to input this data precisely and quickly.

Master It In the Mastering Profiles.dwg file, create a layout profile on Alignment (4) with the following information:

Station	PVI Elevation	Curve Length
0+00	694	
2+90	696.50	250´
5+43.16	688	

Solution

1. Pick the Alignment - (4) profile.

2. Set the L-value of the Curve settings to 250´.

3. Use the Transparent Commands toolbar to enter station elevation data.

Alternately, a text file could be used and imported.

Add and modify individual components in a design profile. The ability to delete, modify, and edit the individual components of the design profile while maintaining the relationships is an important concept in the 3D modeling world. The ability to tweak the design allows you to pursue a better solution, not just a working solution.

Master It In the Mastering Profile.dwg file, move the third PVI (currently at 9+65, 687) to (9+50, 690). Then add a 175´ parabolic vertical curve at this point.

Solution

1. Grid-edit the PVI to the desired point or use Panorama to set the value.

2. Use the Free Vertical Parabola (PVI based) tool and enter an L setting of 175.

Apply a standard label set. Standardization of appearance is one of the major benefits of using Civil 3D styles in labeling. By applying label sets, you can quickly create plot-ready profile views that have the required information for review.

Master It In the `Mastering Profile.dwg` file, apply the Road Profiles label set to all layout profiles.

Solution

1. Pick the layout profile, right-click, and select the Edit Labels option.

2. Click Import Label Set and select the Road Profile Labels set.

3. Repeat for all layout profiles.

Chapter 9: Slice and Dice: Profile Views in Civil 3D

Create a simple view as part of the sampling process. It's not very often that you want to sample a surface without creating a view of that data. By combing the steps into one quick process, you save time and effort as profile views are generated.

Master It Open the `Mastering Profile Views.dwg` file and create a view using the Full Grid profile view style for the Alexander Ave alignment. Display only the layout profile, with the EG and offsets at 15′ left and 25′ right.

Solution From the main menu, select Profiles ➢ Create Profile View and change Style to Full Grid. Then click Create Profile View and modify the profile view properties as shown.

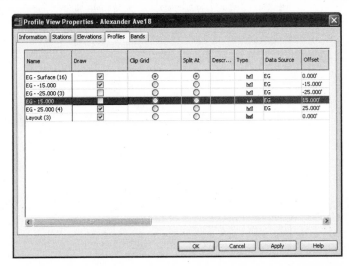

Change profile views and band sets as needed. Using profile view styles and band sets allows for the quick customization and standardization of profile data. Since it's easy to change the styles and bands, many users find that they design using one style, and then change the style as required for submission.

Master It Change the Alexander Ave profile view to the Mastering style and assign the EG+FG And Offsets band set. Assign appropriate profiles to the bands.

Solution Change the profile view style to Mastering, then switch to the Bands tab. Click the Import Band Set button, and make the choices shown. Return to the Bands tab and set the remaining options.

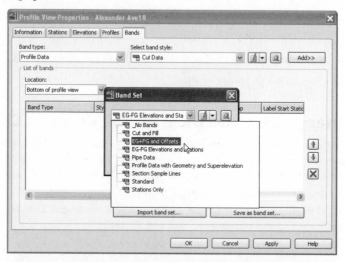

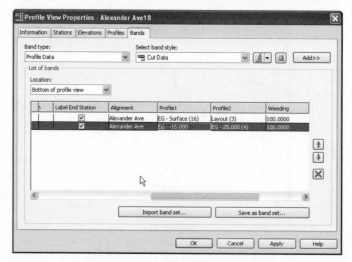

Split profile views into smaller views. Designing in one continuous profile view makes the designer's job easier, but plotting typically requires multiple views. Using the wizard or individual profile view properties makes it easy to split apart profile view information for presentation or submittal purposes.

Master It Create a new pair of profile views for the Parker Place alignment, each 600´ long. Assign the Mastering profile view style but no bands.

Solution Choose Profiles ➤ Create Multiple Profile Views and set options as shown. Note: The profile views may need the elevations reassigned to Automatic to have a decent grid buffer.

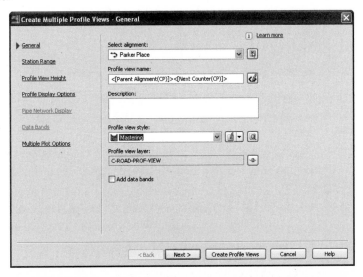

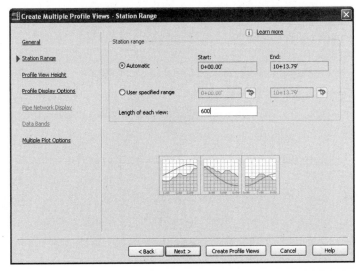

Chapter 10: Templates Plus: Assemblies and Subassemblies

Create a typical road assembly with lanes, curb, gutter, and sidewalk. Most corridors are built to model roads. The most common assembly used in these road corridors is some variation of a typical road section consisting of lanes, curb, gutter, and sidewalk.

Master It Create a new drawing from the _AutoCAD Civil 3D (Imperial) NCS Extended.dwt template. Build a symmetrical assembly using BasicLane, BasicCurbandGutter, and BasicSidewalk. Use widths and slopes of your choosing.

Solution

1. Create a new drawing from the _AutoCAD Civil 3D (Imperial) NCS Extended.dwt template.

2. Choose Corridors ➤ Create Assembly.

3. Name your assembly and set styles as appropriate.

4. Pick a location in your drawing for the assembly.

5. Choose Corridors ➤ Subassembly Tool Palettes and locate the Imperial-Basic tool palette.

6. Click the BasicLane button on the tool palette. Use the AutoCAD Properties palette and follow the command-line prompts to set the BasicLane on the left and right sides of your assembly.

7. Repeat the process with the BasicCurbandGutter and BasicSidewalk. Refer to the first section of this chapter for additional information.

8. Save the drawing for use in the next Master It exercise.

Edit an assembly. Once an assembly has been created, it can be easily edited to reflect a design change. Often, at the beginning of a project, you won't know the final lane width. You can build your assembly and corridor model with one lane width, then later change the width and rebuild the model immediately.

Master It Working in the same drawing, edit the width of each BasicLane to 14′, and change the cross slope of each BasicLane to -3.08%.

Solution

1. Pick your assembly and right-click. Select the Assembly Properties option.

2. Switch to the Construction tab.

3. On the left side of the dialog, select the first BasicLane. On the right side, change the slope to -3.08% and the width to 14′.

4. Repeat the process for the second BasicLane.

5. Click OK, and view the results. Your lane should have adjusted size and slope.

6. Save the drawing for use in the next Master It exercise.

Add daylighting to a typical road assembly.   Often the most difficult part of a designer's job is figuring out how to grade the area between the last hard engineered point in the cross section (such as the back of a sidewalk) and existing ground. There is an extensive catalog of daylighting subassemblies to assist with this task.

Master It   Working in the same drawing, add the DaylightMinWidth to both sides of your typical road assembly. Establish a minimum width of 10′.

Solution

1. Choose Corridors ➢ Subassembly Tool Palettes and locate the Imperial-Daylight tool palette.

2. Click the DaylightMinWidth button on the tool palette. Use the AutoCAD Properties box and follow the command-line prompts to set the DaylightMinWidth on the left and right sides of your assembly.

3. You should now have daylighting subassemblies visible on both sides of your assembly.

Chapter 11: Easy Does It: Basic Corridors

Build a single baseline corridor from an alignment, profile, and assembly.   Corridors are created from the combination of alignments, profiles, and assemblies. While corridors can be used to model many things, most corridors are used for road design.

Master It   Open the `Mastering Corridors.dwg` file. Build a corridor on the basis of the Project Road alignment, the Project Road Finished Ground profile, and the Project Typical Road Assembly.

Solution

1. Choose Corridors ➢ Create Simple Corridor.

2. Pick the Project Road alignment, the Project Road Finished Ground profile, and the Project Typical Road Assembly. Target the Existing Ground surface.

Create a corridor surface.   The corridor model can be used to build a surface. This corridor surface can then be analyzed and annotated to produce finished road plans.

Master It   Continue working in the `Mastering Corridors.dwg` file. Create a corridor surface from Top links.

Solution

1. Open the Corridor Properties dialog and switch to the Surfaces tab.

2. Click Create Surface, then the plus (+) sign to add Top links.

3. Click OK to dismiss the dialog. The corridor and surface will build.

Add an automatic boundary to a corridor surface.   Surfaces can be improved with the addition of a boundary. Single baseline corridors can take advantage of automatic boundary creation.

Master It   Continue working in the `Mastering Corridors.dwg` file. Use the Automatic Boundary Creation tool to add a boundary using the Daylight code.

Solution

1. Open the Corridor Properties dialog and switch to the Boundaries tab.

2. Right-click on the surface entry and click Add Automatically ➤ Daylight.

3. Click OK to dismiss the dialog. The corridor and surface will build.

Chapter 12: The Road Ahead: Advanced Corridors

Add a baseline to a corridor model for a cul-de-sac. Though for simple corridors you may think of a baseline as a road centerline, other elements of a road design can be used as a baseline. In the case of a cul-de-sac, the EOP, top of curb, or any other appropriate feature can be converted to an alignment and profile and used as a baseline.

Master It Open the `Mastering Advanced Corridors.dwg` file. Add the cul-de-sac alignment and profile to the corridor as a baseline. Create a region under this baseline that applies the Typical Intersection assembly.

Solution

1. Pick the corridor, right-click, and select Corridor Properties. Switch to the Parameters tab on the dialog.

2. Click Add Baseline. In the Pick A Horizontal Alignment dialog, select Cul-de-sac EOP. Click OK.

3. Click in the Profile column and select the Cul-de-sac EOP FG in the Select A Profile dialog. Click OK.

4. Right-click on the new baseline and select Add Region. In the Select An Assembly dialog, select Intersection Typical Assembly. Click OK.

5. Click OK to dismiss the dialog and build the corridor.

Add alignment and profile targets to a region for a cul-de-sac. Adding a baseline isn't always enough. Some corridor models require the use of targets. In the case of a cul-de-sac, the lane elevations are often driven by the cul-de-sac centerline alignment and profile.

Master It Continue working in the `Mastering Advanced Corridors.dwg` file. Add the Second Road alignment and Second Road FG profile as targets to the cul-de-sac region. Adjust the Assembly Application Frequency to 5′ and make sure the corridor samples at profile PVIs.

Solution

1. Open the Corridor Properties dialog and switch to the Parameters tab.

2. Click the Target Mapping button in the appropriate region.

3. In the Target Mapping dialog, select Second Road alignment as the Transition Alignment and Second Road FG profile as the Transition Profile. Click OK.

4. Click the Frequency button in the appropriate region. In the Frequency To Apply To Assemblies dialog, change the Frequency Along Curves to 5′ and the At Profile High/ Low Point value to Yes. Click OK.

5. Click OK again and build the corridor.

Use the interactive boundary tool to add a boundary to the corridor surface. Every good surface needs a boundary to prevent bad triangulation. Bad triangulation creates inaccurate and unsightly contours. Civil 3D provides several tools for creating corridor surface boundaries, including an Interactive Boundary tool.

Master It Continue working in the `Mastering Advanced Corridors.dwg` file. Create an interactive corridor surface boundary for the entire corridor model.

Solution

1. Open the Corridor Properties dialog and switch to the Boundaries tab.

2. Pick the corridor surface. Right-click and select Add Interactively.

3. Follow the command-line prompts to add a feature line–based boundary around the entire corridor.

4. Enter **C**↵.

5. Click OK to dismiss the dialog and rebuild the corridor.

6. An example of the finished exercise can be found in the `Mastering Advanced Corridors Finished.dwg` file.

Chapter 13: Stacking Up: Cross Sections

Create sample lines. Before any section views can be displayed, sections must be created from sample lines.

Master It Open `sections1.dwg` and create sample lines along the alignment every 50′.

Solution Using the Old Settlers Way alignment, sample all data except the datum surface. Create sample lines by station range and set your sample line distance to 50′.

Create section views. Just as profiles can only be shown in profile views, sections require section views to display. Section views can be plotted individually or all at once. You can even set them up to be broken up into sheets.

Master It In the previous drawing, you created sample lines. In that same drawing, create section views for all the sample lines.

Solution Using the Create Multiple Sections command, create section views for all sample lines. You will use the Plot All option and add no labels to the views.

Define materials. Materials are required to be defined before any quantities can be displayed. You learned that materials can be defined from surfaces or from corridor shapes. Corridors must exist for shape selection and surfaces must already be created for comparison in material lists.

Master It Using `sections4.dwg`, create a materials list that compares Surface2 with Old Settlers Way Top Road Surface.

Solution To create this materials list, you will need to use Cut and Fill criteria. The EG surface will be Surface2, and the Datum will be Old Settlers Way Top Road Surface.

Generate volume reports. Volume reports give you numbers that can be used for cost estimating on any given project. Typically, construction companies calculate their own quantities, but developers often want to know approximate volumes for budgeting purposes.

Master It   Continue using `sections4.dwg`. Use the materials list created earlier to generate a volume report. Create an XML report and a table that can be displayed on the drawing.

Solution   You will use the Cut and Fill table style to display the volume calculations on the drawing. It should be set to dynamically update in the event that the quantities change (if the profile is adjusted or the alignment is moved).

Chapter 14: The Tool Chest: Parts Lists and Part Builder

Add pipe and structure families to a new parts list.   Before you can begin to design your pipe network, you must ensure you have the appropriate pipes and structures at your disposal.

Master It   Create a new drawing from the `_AutoCAD Civil 3D (Imperial) NCS Extended.dwt`. Create a new parts list called Typical Storm Drainage. (There is already a Storm Sewer parts list in this template. Ignore it or delete it, but do not use it. Create your own for this exercise.)

Add 12″, 15″, 18″, 24″, 36″, and 48″ Concrete Circular Pipe to the parts list.

Add a Rectangular Structure Slab Top Rectangular Frame with an inner structure width and length of 15″, and a Rectangular Structure Slab Top Rectangular Frame with an inner structure width of 15″ and a length of 18″, and a Concentric Cylindrical Structure with an inner diameter of 48″ to the parts list.

Solution

1. Choose File ➢ New, and create a drawing from `_AutoCAD Civil 3D (Imperial) NCS Extended.dwt`.

2. Locate the Parts Lists entry on the Settings tab of Toolspace under Pipe Network. Right-click and choose Create New Parts List.

3. On the Information tab, enter **Typical Storm Drainage** in the Name text box.

4. Switch to the Pipes tab, right-click on the Parts List entry, and choose Add Part Family.

5. In the Part Catalog dialog, check the box next to Concrete Pipe and click OK.

6. Expand the entries on the Pipes tab to find Concrete Pipe.

7. Right-click on the Concrete Pipe entry and choose Add Part Size.

8. Either add each size of pipe individually from the dropdown list in the Inner Pipe Diameter selection box, click OK, then return to the Part Size Creator dialog and repeat the process, or check the Add All Sizes box and delete any extra back on the Pipes tab.

9. Switch to the Structures tab.

10. Right-click on the Parts List entry and choose Add Part Family.

11. In the Part Catalog dialog, check the boxes next to Concentric Cylindrical Structure and Rectangular Structure Slab Top Rectangular Frame. Click OK.

12. Right-click on the Concentric Cylindrical Structure entry and choose Add Part Size.

13. In the Part Size Creator dialog, choose 48″ Inner Structure Diameter. Click OK.

14. Right-click on the Structure Slab Top Rectangular Frame entry and choose Add Part Size.

15. In the Part Size Creator dialog, change the Inner Structure Length parameter to 15″. Click OK. Repeat the process for an Inner Structure Length of 18″.

16. Click OK. Save your drawing.

Create rule sets that apply to pipes and structures in a parts list. Municipal standards and engineering judgment determine how pipes will behave in design situations. Considerations include minimum and maximum slope, cover requirements, and length guidelines. For structures, there are regulations regarding sump depth and pipe drop. These considerations can be applied to pipe network parts through the creation of rule sets.

Master It Create a new structure rule set called Storm Drain Structure Rules. Add the following rules:

Pipe Drop Across Structure

Drop Reference Location: Invert

Drop Value: 0.01′

Maximum Drop Value: 2′

Set Sump Depth

Sump Depth: 0.5′

Create a new pipe rule set called Storm Drain Pipe Rules, and add the following rules:

Cover and Slope:

Max Cover 15′

Max Slope 5%

Min Cover 4′

Min Slope 0.05%

Length Check:

Max Length 300′

Min Length 8′

Apply these rules to all pipes and structures in your Typical Storm Drainage parts list.

Solution

1. Right-click the Structure Rule Set and choose New.

2. On the Information tab, enter **Structure Rule Set Storm Drain Structure Rules** in the Name text box.

3. Switch to the Rules tab. Click Add Rule.

4. In the Add Rule dialog, choose Pipe Drop Across Structure in the Rule Name dropdown list. Click OK. (You cannot change the parameters.)

5. Change the parameters to match the directions above in the Structure Rule Set dialog.

6. Click Add Rule.

7. In the Add Rule dialog, choose Set Sump Depth in the Rule Name dropdown list. Click OK. (You cannot change the parameters in this box.)

8. Change the Sump Depth parameter in the Structure Rule Set dialog to match the directions above, and click OK.

9. Right-click the Pipe Rule Sets on the Settings tab of Toolspace under the Pipe tree, and choose New.

10. On the Information tab, enter **Pipe Rule Set Storm Drain Pipe Rules** in the Name text box.

11. Switch to the Rules tab and click Add Rule.

12. In the Add Rule dialog, choose Cover And Slope from the Rule Name dropdown list. Click OK. (You cannot change the parameters.)

13. Modify the parameters to match the parameters listed in the directions above, and click OK.

14. You should now have one structure rule set and one pipe rule set.

15. Select your Typical Storm Drainage parts list on the Settings tab. Right-click and choose Edit.

16. On the Pipes tab, click the very first button under the Rules column. Choose your Storm Drain Pipe rule set from the dropdown list. Your rule set should be applied to all of the concrete pipe.

17. Switch to the Structures tab. Use the same technique to apply your Storm Drain Structure rule set to each structure family.

18. Click OK. Save your drawing.

Apply styles to pipes and structures in a parts list. The final drafted appearance of pipes and structures in a drawing is controlled by municipal standards and company CAD standards. Civil 3D object styles allow you to control and automate the symbology used to represent pipes and structures in plan, profile, and section views.

Master It Apply the following styles to your parts list:

1. Single Line (Storm) to the 12″, 15″, 18″ Concrete Circular Pipe

2. Double Line (Storm) to the 24″, 36″, 48″ Concrete Circular Pipe

3. Storm Sewer Manhole to the Concentric Cylindrical Structure with an inner diameter of 48″

4. Catch Basin to both sizes of the Rectangular Structure Slab Top Rectangular Frame

Solution

1. Right-click on your Typical Storm Drainage parts list on the Settings tab and choose Edit.

2. On the Pipes tab, use the Style column to select the appropriate style for each size pipe.

3. On the Structures tab, use the Style column to select the appropriate style for each size of structure.

4. Click OK. Save your drawing.

Chapter 15: Running Downhill: Pipe Networks

Create a pipe network by layout.   After you have created a parts list for your pipe network, the first step toward finalizing the design is to create a Pipe Network By Layout.

Master It   Open the `Mastering Pipes.dwg` file. Choose the Pipes ➢ Create Pipe Network By Layout menu option to create a sanitary sewer pipe network.

Use the Finished Ground surface, and name only structure and pipe label styles. Do not choose an alignment at this time. Create 8″ PVC pipes and concentric manholes.

There are blocks in the drawing to assist you in placing manholes. Begin at the "START HERE" marker and place a manhole at each marker location. You can erase the markers when you have finished.

Solution

1. Choose Pipes ➢ Create Pipe Network By Layout.

2. In the Create Pipe Network dialog, set the following parameters:

   ◆ Network Name: Sanitary Sewer

   ◆ Network Parts List: Sanitary Sewer

   ◆ Surface Name: Finished Ground

   ◆ Alignment Name: None

   ◆ Structure Label Style: Name Only (Sanitary)

   ◆ Pipe Label Style: Name Only

3. Click OK. The Pipe Layout Tools toolbar appears.

4. Set the structure to Concentric Manhole and the pipe to 8 Inch PVC. Click Draw Pipes And Structures and use your Insertion osnap to place a structure at each marker location.

5. Press ↵ to exit the command.

6. Pick a marker, right-click, and choose Select Similar. Click Delete.

Create an alignment from network parts and draw parts in profile view.   Once your pipe network has been created in plan view, you would typically either add the parts to a profile view on the basis of either the road centerline or the pipe centerline.

Master It   Continue working in the `Mastering Pipes.dwg` file. Create an alignment from your pipes so that station zero is located at the START HERE structure. Create a profile view from this alignment and draw the pipes on the profile view.

Solution

1. Select Pipes ➢Utilities ➢ Create An Alignment From Network Parts.

2. Pick the START HERE structure and the last structure in the pipe run. Press ↵ to accept the selection.

3. In the Create Alignment dialog, make sure the Create Alignment And Profile View box is checked. Otherwise, accept the defaults and click OK.

4. In the Create Profile dialog, sample both the Existing Ground and Finished Ground surfaces for the profile. Click Draw In Profile View.

5. In the Create Profile View dialog, click Create Profile View and choose a location in the drawing for the profile view. A profile view showing your pipes appears.

Label a pipe network in plan and profile. Designing your pipe network is only half of the process. Engineering plans must be properly annotated.

Master It Continue working in the `Mastering Pipes.dwg` file. Add the Length Material And Slope style to profile pipes and the Data With Connected Pipes (Sanitary) style to profile structures.

Solution

1. Choose Pipes ➢ Add Pipe Network Labels ➢ Add Pipe Network Labels

2. In the Add Labels dialog, choose Entire Network Profile. For pipe labels, choose Length Material And Slope; for structure labels choose Data With Connected Pipes (Sanitary). Click Add and choose any pipe or structure in your profile.

3. Drag or adjust any profile labels as desired.

Create a dynamic pipe table. It is very common for municipalities and contractors to request a pipe or structure table for cost estimates or simply to make it easier to understand a busy plan.

Master It Continue working in the `Mastering Pipes.dwg` file. Create a pipe table for all pipes in your network.

Solution

1. Choose Pipes ➢ Add Tables ➢ Add Pipe.

2. In the Pipe Table Creation dialog, make sure your pipe network is selected. Then, accept the defaults and click OK.

Place the table in your drawing.

Chapter 16: Working the Land: Grading

Convert existing linework into feature lines. Many site features are drawn initially as simple linework for the 2D plan. By converting this linework to feature line information, you avoid a large amount of rework. Additionally, the conversion process offers the ability to drape feature lines along a surface, making further grading use easier.

Master It Open the `Mastering Grading.dwg` file from the data location. Convert the polyline describing a proposed temporary drain into a feature line and drape it across the EG surface to set elevations.

Solution

1. Select Grading ➢ Create Feature Lines From Objects.

2. Pick the polyline.

3. Toggle the Assign Elevations checkbox.

4. Click OK.

Model a simple linear grading with a feature line.   Feature lines define linear slope connections. This can be the flow of a drainage channel, the outline of a building pad, or the back of a street curb. These linear relationships can help define grading in a model, or simply allow for better understanding of design intent.

> **Master It**   Add 200′ radius fillets on the feature line just created. Set the grade from the top of the hill to the circled point to 5%, the remainder to a constant slope to be determined in the drawing. Draw a temporary profile view to verify the channel is below grade for most of its length.

> **Solution**

> 1. Choose Grading ➤ Edit Feature Lines ➤ Fillet.

> 2. Pick the feature line.

> 3. Enter **R**↵ to change the radius.

> 4. Enter **200**↵ for the radius.

> 5. Enter **A**↵ to fillet all the points.

> 6. Choose Grading ➤ Edit Feature Lines ➤ Insert Elevation Point.

> 7. Use the Center osnap to pick the center of the circle. Press ↵ to accept the elevation.

> 8. Choose Grading ➤ Edit Feature Lines ➤ Set Grade Between Points.

> 9. Pick the feature line. Pick the PI near the top of the hill.

> 10. Press ↵ to accept the elevation. Pick the elevation point at the circle's center.

> 11. Enter -5↵ to set the grade.

> 12. Pick the feature line again.

> 13. Pick the elevation point in the circle. Press ↵ to accept the elevation.

> 14. Pick the PI at the downstream end of the channel. Press ↵ to accept the elevation.

> 15. Press ↵ to exit the command.

> 16. Pick the feature line. Right-click and select Quick Profile.

> 17. Select Layout from the dropdown list in the 3D Entity Profile Style selection box.

> 18. Click OK and pick a point on the screen to draw a profile view.

Create custom grading criteria.   Using grading criteria to limit the amount of user input can help cut down on input errors and design mistakes. Defining a set to work with for a given design makes creating gradings a straightforward process.

> **Master It**   Continuing with the `Mastering Grading.dwg` file, create two new grading criteria: the first to be named Bottom, with the criteria of 5′ at 2% grade, the second to be named Sides, with criteria of daylight to a surface at a 6:1 slope in cut areas only, in fill; do not grade.

Solution

1. On the Settings tab of Toolspace, expand the Grading ➢ Grading Criteria Sets branches.

2. Right-click on Basic Set and select New.

3. Enter **Bottom** in the Name text box.

4. Switch to the Criteria tab and set as shown here:

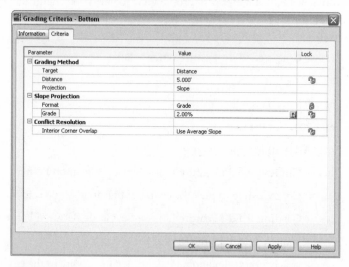

5. Click OK.

6. Right-click on Basic Set and select New.

7. Enter **Sides** in the Name text box.

8. Switch to the Criteria tab and set as shown here:

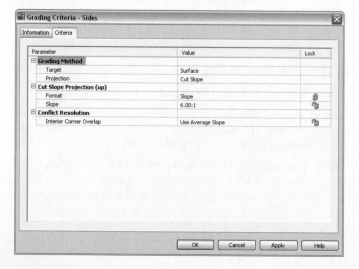

9. Click OK.

Model planar site features with grading groups. Once a feature line defines a linear feature, gradings collected in grading groups model the lateral projections from that line to other points in space. These projections combine to model a site much like a TIN surface, resulting in a dynamic design tool that works in the Civil 3D environment.

Master It Use the two grading criteria just used to define the pilot channel, with grading on both sides of the sketched centerline. Calculate the difference in volume between using 6:1 side slopes and 4:1 side slopes.

Solution

1. Choose Grading ➤ Create Grading to activate the Grading Creation Tools toolbar.

2. Click the Set The Grading Group tool.

3. Check the Automatic Surface Creation option.

4. Check the Volume Base Surface option, and click OK.

5. Click OK to accept the surface creation options.

6. Change the Grading Criteria to Bottom.

7. Click the Create Grading tool and pick the feature line.

8. Pick the left or right side. Press ↵ to model the full length.

9. Press ↵ to accept 5′ width.

10. Press ↵ to accept 2% grade.

11. Pick the main feature line again and grade the other side.

12. Change to the Sides Criteria and grade both left and right sides, accepting the default values.

13. Right-click to complete the gradings. The complete channel should look like the following:

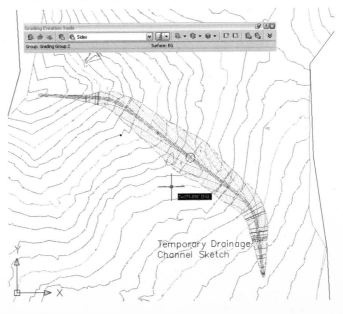

14. Pick one of the diamonds in the grading. Right-click and select Grading Group Properties.

15. Switch to the Properties tab and note the volume (approximately 17,800 Cu. Yd. Cut Net). Click OK.

16. Right-click on the diamond representing the Sides grading.

17. Click the Grading Editor tool.

18. Change the Slope to 4:1. Click OK.

19. Repeat for the other side of the channel.

20. Pick the diamond again and select Grading Group Properties.

21. The new net volume is approximately 12,500 Cu.Yd. The difference is approximately 5,300 Cu.Yd.

Chapter 17: Sharing the Model: Data Shortcuts

List the project elements available for sharing through data shortcuts and those that are not. The ability to load design information into a project environment is an important part of creating an efficient team. The main design elements of the project are available to the data shortcut mechanism, but some still are not.

Master It List the top-level branches in Prospector that cannot be shared through data shortcuts.

Solution Points, point groups, sites, corridors, assemblies, subassemblies, and survey

Create a data shortcut file from Civil 3D objects. Just creating a Civil 3D object isn't enough to share it using data shortcuts. You still have to go through the process of creating a shortcut file and exporting the linking information to allow other users to reference and analyze your data.

Master It Open the `Creating Shortcuts.dwg` file and create a `Utility.xml` shortcut file for both of the pipe networks contained in that drawing.

Solution

1. Select General ➤ Data Shortcuts ➤ Edit Data Shortcuts to display the Data Shortcuts palette in Panorama.

2. Delete any shortcuts.

3. Click Create Data Shortcuts By to pick the two pipe networks.

4. Click Export Data Shortcuts To File to create a reference file on the desktop.

Import a data shortcut and create references. Once a shortcut to a design element has been created, references can be made and managed. Team members should be communicating that these files have been created and cognizant of not overwriting them with bad information. Creating and managing references is the most critical part of keeping project team members in sync with one another.

Master It Create a new drawing, and create references to both the EG surface and a pipe network.

Solution

1. Create a new drawing from the Imperial template.

2. Select General ➤ Data Shortcuts ➤ Edit Data Shortcuts to display the Data Shortcuts palette in Panorama.

3. Import `Surface.xml` from the chapter exercise.

4. Import `Utility.xml` from the preceding Master It exercise.

5. Create references to all three objects. The drawing should look like the example shown.

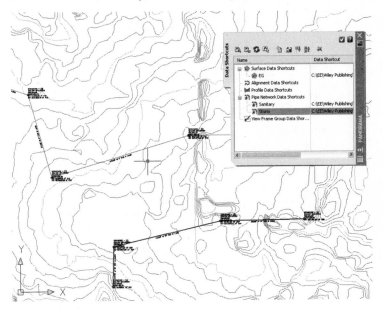

Chapter 18: Behind the Scenes: Autodesk Data Management Server

Recommend a basic ADMS and SQL installation methodology.   The complexity of corporate networks makes selecting the right combination of ADMS and Microsoft SQL software part of the challenge. Understanding the various flavors of SQL Server 2005 at a basic level, along with some limitations of the ADMS, will aid in selecting the right combination for your own needs.

Master It   For each of the following descriptions, make some general recommendations for a general setup for their ADMS and SQL needs—for example, a 30-person engineering firm with two offices that rarely share project data. The solution might be a pair of SQL Express machines, one for each office, running a flavor of Windows Server to get around any limits on concurrent connections.

1. A 100-person engineering firm with one office.

2. A 15-person firm with three offices equally split. They share data constantly.

3. A 5-person engineering firm with one office.

Solution

1. A single Windows Server machine with a full version of SQL (not Express).

2. Because they want to share project data, they should consider Replicator, which requires full versions of SQL and Windows Servers. ADMS can be run over a WAN, but performance will be up for debate. This one's the gray area of ADMS!

3. A single XP box running SQL Express will suffice if there's enough storage on the XP computer.

Create multiple vaults, users, and user groups. The enterprise nature of ADMS means it can handle multiple sets of data and user inputs at once. By creating multiple vaults to help manage data, you can make life easier on end users. Creating logins to the ADMS for each user allows the tracking of file transactions, and creating groups makes security easier to handle.

Master It Create a new vault titled EE; add Mark, James, Dana, and Marc as users to this new vault. Additionally, make Marc a vault consumer, Mark and Dana vault editors, and James an administrator. Add an architecture group. Marc is the only architect; add the other new users to the engineering group.

Solution

1. Within ADMS Console, click the Vaults folder in the left pane, right-click, and select the Create option.

2. Name the vault **EE** and click OK.

3. Select Tools Administration and click Users. Click New User and assign roles, vaults, and groups as described for these users. As a Card view, it would look like this:

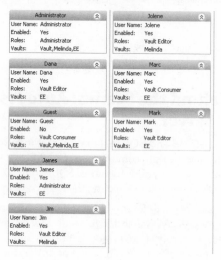

4. Close the Users dialog.

5. Click Groups. Click New and change the Name to **Architects**. Then click Add, select Marc, and close all dialogs.

Manage working folders. The working folder acts as your local desktop version of the file. Drawings are saved and edited within the working folder until checked back into the Vault. Enforcing the working folder will create a constant path for XRef information and make support easier.

Master It Set the working folder for the new EE vault to `C:\EE Projects\`. *Be sure to set this back to* `C:\Mastering Projects` *before beginning Chapter 19.*

Solution

1. Log out of Vault Explorer and log into the EE Vault.

2. Select Tools ➤ Administration. On the Files tab, click Define in the Working Folder area and change the radio button to Enforce Consistent Working Folder For All Clients.

3. Type in the desired path and click OK.

4. Log out and log in to verify the change.

Chapter 19: Teamwork: Vault Client and Civil 3D

Describe the differences between using Vault and data shortcuts. The two mechanisms in Civil 3D for sharing data are quite similar. Every firm has their nuances, and it's important to evaluate both methods of sharing data to see which one would be a better fit for the team's workflow. Recognizing the differences will allow you to make these recommendations with confidence.

Master It Describe at least three major differences between the two data-sharing methods.

Solution There are others, but these are some of the big ones:

◆ Vault requires ADMS, which is a bit more complicated than the XML files of shortcuts.

◆ Vault allows for user security levels on the project folders.

◆ Vault allows for easy version tracking and restoration.

◆ The Vault interface handles the data sharing; this is a manual process with shortcuts.

Insert Civil 3D data into a vault. Creating a project in Vault requires some care to make sure all the pieces go in the right place. Using the project template to create organizational structures similar to what is already in place is a good way to start. Adding individual components to the Vault as they fit into this structure makes for clean data organization and easy integration of new team members.

Master It Create a new project titled Bailey in the Melinda vault using the `Mastering` project template. Add the `Bailey's Run.dwg` file to the project in the `Engineering` folder, sharing all of the data within it.

Solution

1. Right-click Projects and log in to the Melinda vault.

2. Right-click Projects and select New.

3. Name the project **Bailey**, select the `Mastering` project template, and click OK.

4. Open the Bailey's Run drawing.

5. Right-click the drawing name in Prospector and select Add To Project.

6. Select the `Engineering` folder.

7. Share all the data.

Create data shortcuts.   Creating duplicate data is never good. By creating links to original data instead of working with copies, you maintain the integrity of the project information. Using data references instead of XRefs allows you to use the data behind the object instead of just the picture. This means styling and label changes can be part of the end file and allow team members to work on separate parts of the job at the same time.

Master It   Create a new drawing called **Mastering Vault**, add it to the Bailey project in the `Engineering` folder, and create references to the FG surface and to the Natures Way and Old Settlers Way alignments. Use a Contours 2′ And 10′ (Design) style for the surfaces.

Solution

1. Create a new drawing from the `NCS Extended template` and save it as **Mastering Vault** in C:\Mastering Projects\Bailey\Engineering.

2. Right-click the filename in Prospector and select Add To Project.

3. Keep the drawing checked out and step through the check-in process.

4. Expand Projects ➢ Bailey ➢ Surfaces and select FG.

5. Right-click and select Create Reference; click OK to make the reference.

6. Expand Projects ➢ Bailey ➢ Alignments and select Natures Way.

7. Right-click and select Create Reference; click OK to make the reference.

8. Repeat for Old Settlers Way.

Restore a previous version of a design file.   One of the major advantages of using a database-driven system is the ability to track file changes and restore them if necessary. Vault has a mechanism for moving data in and out of the file store. By using the restoration tools and checking in the proper files, it's easy to roll back to a prior version of a file.

Master It   Erase the Founders Court alignment from the Bailey's Run file and check it in. Then use the Vault tools to restore the previous version containing the Founders Court alignment. What version number of the Bailey's Run drawing is listed when this is complete?

Solution

1. Expand Projects ➢ Bailey ➢ Alignments and select Founders Court.

2. Right-click and select Check Out Source Drawing.

3. Use Prospector to delete Founder's Court.

4. Check Bailey's Run back into the Vault.

5. Expand the Bailey ➢ Alignments collections to confirm that the Founders Court alignment has been erased from the project.

6. In Vault Explorer, select the Bailey project `Engineering` folder.

7. Select Bailey's Run in the top right pane.

8. Right-click and select Get Previous Version.

9. Select Version 1 and click OK.

10. Return to Civil 3D.

11. Check out Bailey's Run from Projects ➢ Bailey ➢ Drawings ➢ Engineering. Be sure to deselect Get Latest Version.

12. Right-click Bailey's Run and check it back in.

13. Check Founders Court on the Share Data step.

14. Click Finish.

15. Switch to Vault Explorer and refresh the view of the `Engineering` folder. The Version for Bailey's Run should be 3.

Chapter 20: Out the Door: Plan Production

Create view frames.   When you create view frames, you must select the template file that contains the layout tabs that will be used as the basis for your sheets. This template must contain predefined viewports. You can define these viewports with extra vertices so you change their shape after the sheets have been created.

Master It   Open the Mastering Plan Production 1 drawing. Run the Create View Frames wizard to create sheets in the current drawing. (Accept defaults for all other values.)

Solution

1. Select General ➢ Plan Production Tools ➢ Create View Frames.

2. On the Alignment page, for Alignment select Haven CL from the dropdown menu. Click Next.

3. On the Sheet page, select the Plan And Profile option. Next, click the ellipsis button ⊡ to display the Select Layout As Sheet Template dialog. Click the next ellipsis ⊡ and browse to C:\Mastering Civil 3D 2008\CH 20\Data, select the template named Mastering (Imperial) Plan and Profile.dwt, and click Open.

4. Select the layout named ARCH D Plan and Profile 20 Scale and click OK.

5. Click Create View Frames.

Create sheets and use Sheet Set Manager. Sheets can be created in new drawing files or in the current drawing. Use the option to create sheets in the current drawing when a) you've referenced in the view frame group, or b) you have a small project. Additionally, the resulting sheets are based on the template you chose when you created the view frames. If the template contains customized viewports, you can modify the shape of the viewport to better fit your sheet needs.

Master It Open the Mastering Plan Production 2 drawing. Run the Create Sheets wizard to create plan and profile sheets for Haven CL using the template Mastering (Imperial) Plan and Profile.dwt. This template has a custom-made viewport with extra vertices. (Accept defaults for all other values.)

Solution

1. Select General➢ Plan Production Tools ➢ Create Sheets.

2. On the View Frame Group And Layouts page, under the Layout Section, select All Layouts In The Current Drawing.

3. Click Create Sheets.

4. Click OK to save the drawing.

5. Click a location as the profile origin.

6. Dismiss the events Panorama.

7. In Sheet Set Manager, double-click the sheet named 1- Haven CL 10+00.00 to 14+28.00.

8. Select the top, Plan View viewport. Notice the extra vertices.

9. Grip-edit the shape of the viewport by stretching the various vertices to new locations to make an irregularly shaped viewport.

Edit sheet templates and styles associated with plan production. The Create View Frames command uses predefined styles for view frames and match lines. These styles must exist in the drawing in which you create the view frame group. You can create match line styles to meet your specific needs.

Master It Open the Mastering Plan Production 3 drawing and modify the match line component hatch display style setting to make the linework beyond the match line appear screened.

Solution

1. On the Settings tab of the Toolspace palette, expand the Match Line Group, and then expand the Match Line Styles collection, right-click Standard - Revised, and select Edit.

2. On the Display tab, in the Component Display section, for the Match Line Mask component, click on the color to open the Select Color dialog.

3. On the True Color tab, select RGB from the Color Model dropdown menu.

4. For Red, Green, and Blue, enter **255** and click OK. This tells Civil 3D to set the color of the hatch pattern to match the background color.

5. Under the match line component hatch display section, change the hatch pattern to Dots by clicking the pattern name SOLID, changing the type to Predefined in the box that pops up, and selecting Dots in the Pattern Name box. When finished, click OK to return to the previous screen, and change the rotation angle to 22 degrees and the scale to 3.

6. Click OK and examine the linework beyond the match line. The dots of the hatch pattern obscure a portion of the linework, making it appear screened. Depending on the scale of your final plotted plans, you may need to experiment with the rotation and scale to get the screening effect you want.

Chapter 21: Playing Nice with Others: LDT and LandXML

Discern the design elements in a LandXML data file. LandXML.org is an international consortium of software firms, equipment manufacturers, consultants, and other land-development professionals. By creating a lingua franca for the industry, they've made sharing design data between design and analysis packages a simple import/export operation.

Master It Download the `Campground.xml` file from the `LandXML.org` website and list the creating program, along with the alignments and the surfaces it contains.

Solution

Program	Eagle Point Civil/Survey 2002
Alignments	Lunar Loop, Short Street, Quiet Road, Sunset Strip, Shady Lane, Sunshine Street
Surfaces	Original Ground Model, Campsite Model

Import a Land Desktop project. Many Civil 3D firms have a huge repository of LDT projects. By using the import LDT project data functionality of Civil 3D, this data's lifespan can be extended, and the value of the information it contains can continue to grow.

Master It Import the STM-P3 Pipe Run from the Conklin LDT Project data source and count the number of pipes and structures that successfully import.

Solution

1. Create a new Civil 3D drawing using the AutoCAD Civil 3D (Imperial) NCS Extended template file.

2. Choose File ➤ Import ➤ Import Data From Land Desktop.

3. Click Browse.

4. Navigate to the data directory, and select the LDT Import folder.

5. Click OK to dismiss the warning about pipes that appears.

6. The Import Directory acts similar to selecting the Project path if you're familiar with LDT. Select Conklin in that directory.

7. Uncheck all components except the STM-P3 pipe network and click OK to import.

8. Four (4) pipes import, and five (5) structures successfully import.

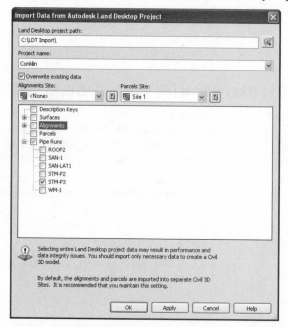

Import a LandXML file to create a surface, alignments, and profiles. As more and more firms use Civil 3D, they'll want to share the design data without giving up their full drawing files. Using LandXML to share import data allows the accurate transmission of data in a standardized format and gives the end recipient the ability to manipulate the entities as needed.

Master It Complete the import of the Campground.xml file into a new Civil 3D drawing.

Solution   Create a new drawing, and choose File ➤ Import ➤ Import LandXML. Navigate to `campground.xml` and click OK to import. The drawing should look like this:

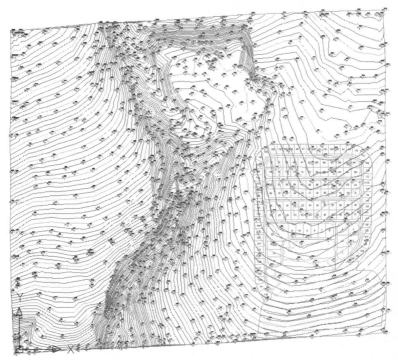

Create an AutoCAD drawing that can be read without special enablers.   Since many members of your design team will not be working with Civil 3D, it's important to deliver information to them in a manner they can use. Using the built-in tools to create drawings consisting of purely native AutoCAD objects strips these drawings of their design intelligence but provides a workable route to data sharing with almost any CAD user.

Master It   Convert the drawing you just made from `Campground.xml` to an R2004 AutoCAD drawing.

Solution   Select File ➤ Export ➤ Export To AutoCAD R2004 Format. The resulting file should display this message at the command line upon opening:

```
Opening an AutoCAD 2004/LT 2004 format file.
Regenerating model.
```

Chapter 22: Get the Picture: Visualization

Apply render materials to a corridor using a code set style.   Visualizing corridors is useful for creating complete site models for your own better understanding of the design, and for sharing with your clients and regulating agencies. The first step in visualizing a corridor is to apply a code set style that will automatically assign render materials to certain codes.

Master It Open the drawing file `Mastering Visualization.dwg`. Apply the All Codes code set style.

Solution

1. Select the corridor, right-click, and choose Corridor Properties. Switch to the Codes tab.

2. From the Code Set Style dropdown, choose All Codes.

3. Click OK.

Apply a Realistic visual style to a corridor model. Once the appropriate code set style has been assigned, the corridor can be seen with its render materials with a Realistic visual style applied.

Master It Continue working in the file `Mastering Visualization.dwg`. Apply the Realistic visual style to the drawing.

Solution

1. Continue working in `Mastering Visualization.dwg`.

2. Switch to the Visualization And Rendering workspace if it is not already current.

3. Using the Visual Styles control panel on the Dashboard, switch from the 2D Wireframe to the Realistic visual style.

Create a 3D DWF from a corridor model. One way you can share your visualized corridor is through 3D DWF. Autodesk Design Review is a free application that you can direct your clients to download from Autodesk.com. 3D DWFs can be opened, navigated, and analyzed using Design Review.

Master It Continue working in the file `Mastering Visualization.dwg`. Create a 3D DWF from the drawing and open it in Autodesk Design Review.

Solution

1. Continue working in the file `Mastering Visualization.dwg`.

2. Type **3DDWFPUBLISH** at the command line.

3. Give your DWF a name and choose a location to save it. Click OK.

4. Click Yes to open the DWF and use the navigation tools to study the resulting DWF.

Appendix B

Other Resources

In this appendix, we've listed a number of resources we have found valuable based on our years of learning and teaching Civil 3D. These links and sites are also available on the CD as a series of live links.

The nature of the Web makes it impossible to print a list that's current. We will attempt to keep a current list matching this one at `http://www.civil3d.com/index.php/resources/` as well.

Blogs

Blogs are the daily news of the Civil 3D world. They're always changing with what's hot in the discussion groups or on the author's mind, and we find these among the best. There are others out there, so don't limit yourself to just this list!

Angel's Civil 3D Thoughts (`http://acecivil3d.blogspot.com`) is run by Angel Espinoza, a former reseller application engineer turned Autodesker. One of the (if not the) first Civil 3D specific blogs, it's a great resource for getting the latest scoop on official developments in the Civil 3D world.

AutoCAD Insider (`http://heidihewett.blogs.com`) is Heidi Hewett's blog of AutoCAD tips. A popular CAD Camp and Autodesk University (AU) speaker, she does a great job of reminding us of all the great functions that we sometimes forget exist in the core product.

Avid User of Civil 3D (`http://wendyllc.blogspot.com`) is written by Wendy Lim from Malaysia. She doesn't post as often as some others, but her posts are generally eye-openers, offering new ways to look at some very common problems.

Between the Lines (`http://autodesk.blogs.com/between_the_lines`) is Shaan Hurley's constant feed of tips, links, and insight into the Autodesk world.

Daily Autocad (`http://www.dailyautocad.com`) has a tip of the day, every day. Sometimes they're simple, sometimes they're genius, but it's worth checking out.

CommTech CAD Café (`http://cadcafe.blogspot.com`) is from a relative newcomer, Brian Hailey, P.E., but is gaining a reputation as a blog not to be skipped. Brian understands the design process and consulting business better than many and offers up practical, everyday tips and tutorials to make learning Civil 3D easier. His coworker LuAnn Sims also brings some great AutoCAD tips to make it worth visiting.

civil3d.com (`http://www.civil3d.com`) is run by your authors. We offer tips, insight, and commentary on the use of Civil.

Civil 3D – Paving the Way (http://c3dpavingtheway.blogspot.com) is run by Scott McEachron. A long time AU speaker, Scott has great insight and offers tips on making C3D more effective in your office.

From the Ground Up (http://civilcommunity.autodesk.com/blogs/blog/6/) from a group of European Autodeskers offers up another view of the Civil 3D world. Posting some of the best step-by-step tutorials, it's not a blog to be missed.

The Dan and Dave Civil 3D Show (http://civilcommunity.autodesk.com/blogs/blog/4/) brings together two of the Autodesk faces of Civil 3D, Dan Philbrick and Dave Simeone, to offer insight, expertise, and tips to the Civil 3D community.

Wicked Cool Stuff (http://civilcommunity.autodesk.com/blogs/blog/5/) is a team effort from Technical Marketing Manager Dominick Gallegos and Nick Zeeben of the Autodesk QA team. They mix up a focus on the nitty-gritty and some historical insight to the product.

Websites

These sites offer up great utilities, support, and other Civil 3D tools that we find incredibly useful.

Autodesk Civil Engineering Community (http://civilcommunity.autodesk.com) is a clearinghouse for all things civil engineering related. The site offers links to blogs, discussion groups, specifications, professional societies—the works. Go join. Do it now.

Autodesk University Online (http://au.autodesk.com) lets you pick through the courses offered at Autodesk University. AU is the best bang for the buck training you can get! If you can't make it out there, at least you can read up on the great materials presented.

Civil 3D Discussion Groups (http://discussion.autodesk.com/index2.jspa?categoryID=17) is the best free support resource out there. Users, consultants, resellers, and developers all contribute to make this the first place many users look for answers to their tough questions. You'll see your authors there quite a bit!

Civil 3D product page (http://www.autodesk.com/civil3d) is the official page for the product. It features links to webcasts, demos, and updates, and you have to check in once in a while at least.

Engineered Efficiency Inc. (http://www.eng-eff.com) is the consulting firm that created the book you have in your hands. Contact us for your consulting or software needs and get training and support for professionals by professionals.

Ten Links Civil 3D List (http://www.tenlinks.com/CAD/USERS/AUTOCAD/civil3d.htm) is a constantly moving list of Civil 3D links and articles that you can subscribe to. If you can't read it all, read the daily top ten to keep yourself better educated.

Vault for Civil 3D (http://www.autodesk.com/vaultforcivil3d) is the starting page for anyone trying to comprehend how Civil 3D and Vault work together. Built specifically for the Civil 3D user, this site is host to great white papers and guides for making Vault work better for you.

Index

Note to the reader: Throughout this index boldfaced page numbers indicate primary discussions of a topic. Italicized page numbers indicate illustrations.

What's on the CD

The companion CD is home to all the demo files, samples, and bonus resources mentioned in the book. We've also included some sample applications from various resources to help make your time in Civil 3D more productive:

AutoTURN is a vehicle swept path and turn simulation CAD software used by engineers, architects, and civil drafters to help assess vehicle maneuvers for all types of roadway, highway, and site-planning projects ranging from intersections, roundabouts, loading bays, parking lots, and other vehicular facilities. Coming complete with a host of design vehicles from national standards, such as AASHTO (US), TAC (CDN), Austroads (AUS), and others, AutoTURN has been widely accepted by governing transportation agencies around the world.

Chronos for AutoCAD is a two-part system designed to log time spent working with AutoCAD. This system consists of the Chronos Log Viewer, which displays the logged data, and the DwgLog program, which generates the logs. We think it can help in measuring the gains in time you hope to achieve with Civil 3D.

Corridor EZY for Civil 3D enables you to automate the vertical design of intersections, knuckles, cul-de-sacs, and roundabouts. Using Corridor EZY, you can complete a standard T Junction or Cross Road in less than 5 minutes. Starting with the surface and alignments, Corridor EZY generates all the profiles for the roads and curbs, output of corridors that are trimmed/extended for the intersections, and creation of a single surface model of the entire road network.

EE HEC-RAS Tools use surface and alignment information in conjunction with drawn section and channel bank lines to generate an input file for direct, rectified input to the USACE HEC-RAS program. This tool cuts the typical time for this process from hours or even days to mere minutes. After analysis is complete and a HEC-RAS output file generated, all stream profiles can then be directly imported back into the original drawing, for use in floodplain mapping, Flood Insurance Study preparation, or other analysis. Using EE's toolset with the built-in Civil 3D tools, floodplain mapping can be accomplished in an afternoon.

Intersection Builder makes it easier to perform grading at roadway intersections. In Civil 3D, corridor models can be developed quite easily to model even a complex roadway cross section. The process becomes more difficult at intersections, however. Grading an intersection using a corridor model usually requires a separate alignment and profile for each curb return. Intersection Builder is a powerful tool that makes short work of this task by generating curb return alignments and profiles according to the parameters that you specify.

Q-Legal for Autodesk Civil 3D allows users to extract information from drawings by selecting blocks with attributes, text, or mtext. It works with Civil 3D parcel data as well.

Rapid Design Visualization enables any Civil 3D user to create a fully interactive visualization environment directly from their Civil 3D project. Using RDV for Civil 3D, designers can easily create drive through simulations, flyovers, and interactive simulations for proposed roads, subdivisions, underground infrastructure, interchanges, and many other complex land development projects.

The Section3D Editor and Viewer application was developed to enhance corridor modeling and cross section capabilities of Autodesk Civil 3D. Section3D can be used with any combination of alignments, profiles, and surfaces to create user-defined templates without VBA programming.